Enigma Books

Also published by Enigma Books

Hitler's Table Talk 1941–1944
Hugh Trevor-Roper, Ed.

In Stalin's Secret Service
W. G. Krivitsky

*Hitler and Mussolini: The Secret
Meetings*
Santi Corvaja

The Jews in Fascist Italy: A History
Renzo De Felice

The Man Behind the Rosenbergs
Alexander Feklisov and
Sergei Kostin

*Roosevelt and Hopkins:
An Intimate History*
Robert E. Sherwood

Diary 1937–1943
Galeazzo Ciano

*The Battle of the Casbah:
Terrorism and Counter-Terrorism in
Algeria 1955–1957*
General Paul Aussaresses

*Secret Affairs:
FDR, Cordell Hull, and Sumner
Welles*
Irwin F. Gellman

*Hitler and His Generals:
Military Conferences 1942–1945*
Helmut Heiber & David M.
Glantz, Eds.

Stalin and the Jews: The Red Book
Arno Lustiger

*The Secret Front:
Nazi Political Espionage 1938–1945*
Wilhelm Höttl

*Fighting the Nazis:
French Military Intelligence and
Counterintelligence 1935–1945*
Colonel Paul Paillole

*A Death in Washington:
Walter G. Krivitsky and the Stalin
Terror*
Gary Kern

*Hitler's Second Book:
The Unpublished Sequel
to* Mein Kampf
Gerhard L. Weinberg, ed.

*At Napoleon's Side in Russia:
The Classic Eyewitness Account*
Armand de Caulaincourt

*The Atlantic Wall
Hitler's Defenses for D-Day*
Alan F. Wilt

Jean-Baptiste Duroselle

FRANCE

and the

NAZI THREAT

The Collapse of French Diplomacy
1932-1939

Introduction by
Anthony Adamthwaite
University of California, Berkeley

Enigma Books

Enigma Books
580 Eighth Avenue, New York, NY 10018
www.enigmabooks.com

Originally published in French under the title:
La Décadence 1932-1939
3ème édition corrigée

Translated by Catherine E. Dop and Robert L. Miller

First English-language edition
ISBN 1-929631-15-4
Printed in the United States of America

Library of Congress Cataloging-in-Publication Data

Duroselle, Jean Baptiste, 1917-1994
France and the Nazi threat : the collapse of French diplomacy, 1932-1939 /
Jean-Baptiste Duroselle ; introduction by Anthony Adamthwaite ; translated by
Catherine E. Dop and Robert L. Miller.— 1st English-language ed.
    p. cm.
Translation of: La Décadence, 1932-1939.
Includes bibliographical endnotes and index.
ISBN: 1-929631-15-4
1. France—Foreign relations—1914-1940. 2. France—Politics and government—
1914-1940. I. Adamthwaite, Anthony P. II. Dop, Catherine, 1948- III. Miller,
Robert L. (Robert Lawrence), 1945- IV. Title. V. Title: France & the Nazi threat.

DC396 .D87 2004
944.081'5—dc21

FRANCE

and the

NAZI THREAT

The Collapse of French Diplomacy

1932-1939

TABLE OF CONTENTS

INTRODUCTION
by
Anthony Adamthwaite

Books that get rave reviews often quickly fade. Not so Jean-Baptiste Duroselle's *France and the Nazi Threat* (*La Décadence*). Acclaimed on publication in 1979 as a groundbreaking tour de force, it remains the classic study of France's response to the Nazi threat in the 1930s. Duroselle (1917-1994), despite doing much to foster American studies in France, is not well known in the United States. Yet he deserves to be much better known because, with his mentor Pierre Renouvin, professor of contemporary history at the Sorbonne (1933-1964), he helped pioneer a new approach to the study of international history, an approach superbly encapsulated in his investigation of France's eclipse as a great power. His reputation, however, rests on much more than one book. A substantial output addressed several major themes: American foreign relations in the first half of the twentieth century, the history of Europe, migration, the Trieste conflict, the theory and practice of international relations, the career of Georges Clemenceau, the impact of the two world wars on French society, the foreign policy of Marshal Petain's Vichy regime.[1]

Born in Paris on November 17, 1917, ten days after the Bolshevik Revolution and on the day that Clemenceau became war premier, he taught at the Paris Institut d'études politiques, thereafter at the Sorbonne. Tall, with a commanding physical presence, Duroselle was a superb teacher, offering new ideas and insights, continually pushing out the boundaries of history by engaging with other disciplines, notably sociology and psychology. Endowed with an encyclopedic memory, he wore his learning lightly, sprinkling anecdotes and personal memories, captivating audiences in the classroom and on television with warmth, wit and openness. His accessibility and empathy were a blessing for young researchers like myself seeking advice on dissertation topics. At his office in the rue Saint-Guillaume he seemed too large for a small room bursting with books .In excellent English he signposted my way and then talked enthusiastically of plans to teach for a year in Mexico. A keen sense of humor inoculated him against the occasional tediousness of academic discourse. Asked at a colloquium how he was enjoying the presentations he complained of having caught colloquitis. Long afternoon sessions can sedate rather than stimulate. Duroselle power-napped while subconsciously absorbing the text; as soon as a speaker concluded he would be on his feet firing salient questions. Gifted with exceptional energy he thought nothing of a weekly Paris-Bologna commute for a seminar at the John Hopkins Center at a time when European air and rail links were less developed than they are today. Fanaticism of any kind repelled him. A founding spirit of the new post-1968 Paris VIII Vincennes campus he envisaged it as an opportunity for renewal of the academy but shocked by the rancor and assertiveness of colleagues and some students chose to stay at the Sorbonne.

Duroselle was not one of those who from the age of seven know their vocation. The École Polytechnique, France's top-ranking school for engineers attracted him, as did a military career. Entering the École Normale Supérieure (ENS), rue d'Ulm, a nursery for the intellectual and literary elite, he hesitated until the last moment between history and philosophy. At the ENS geography fascinated him and the subject of his first scholarly article was the Gulf of Morbihan on the Breton coast. In 1940 he fought in the Battle of France, luckily without being taken prisoner. After demobilization came marriage and teaching in high school in order to support a young family. Entry to the higher levels of the teaching profession in France is by competitive examination. The most prestigious of these is the aggrégation and normally only agrégés are appointed to university posts. In the aggrégation of 1943 he took first place in history and geography. For his doctoral dissertation he chose a theme in religious history: "The beginnings of social Catholicism in France, 1822-1870." It was a natural choice, given a staunch Catholic family background and popular post-Liberation expectations of a revived Catholicism leavening a new France. These were the years of the worker-priest movement and the Abbé Pierre's rag pickers of Emmaus. Since the state and universities did not offer funding packages graduate students worked full or part time while researching. Consequently, completing a dissertation often took ten years; Duroselle finished in record time- four years. The educational system of the day with its emphasis on learning by rote might have produced closed and unimaginative minds. Fortunately, a broad historical and general culture underpinned it. As well as knowing their chosen fields apprentice historians were expected to read in all major areas. The knowledge gained enabled Duroselle to navigate confidently across the centuries.

After short spells of teaching at the universities of Saarbrücken and Lille he went to the Paris Institut d'études politiques. Then from 1958-1964 he directed the Center for the Study of International Relations at the Fondation nationale des sciences politiques. Why the switch from religious to international history? International history had fired Duroselle before he started researching social Catholicism but in the mid-1940s Renouvin, doyen of France's international historians, was reluctant to accept graduate students. Accordingly, Duroselle turned to another professor, Charles Pouthas, who proposed a topic in religious history. Nevertheless, he stayed close to Renouvin, acting as his teaching assistant from 1945-1949. Then chance took a hand. Lured by an attractive fee he contributed a chapter on the contemporary world for a collective history of the Second World War. Next came an invitation to write an international relations text. *Diplomatic History from 1919 to the Present* (*Histoire diplomatique de 1919 à nos jours*) published in 1953 launched him as an international historian. Shortly afterwards Renouvin, who had been elected dean at the Sorbonne, wished to lighten his commitments and invited Duroselle to take over responsibility for the teaching of international history at the Institut d'études politiques. Thus in 1964 he was a natural successor to Renouvin in the chair of contemporary history at Paris I Panthéon-Sorbonne (1964-1983).

International history for Duroselle signified much more than the study of France's external relations. Instead of Francocentrism came engagement with other countries and cultures, for example the vigorous promotion of North American studies. This may not now seem especially newsworthy yet in mid-twentieth century it constituted a remarkable venture.

Historians nowadays live in the "small world" described by David Lodge. They travel the globe from one conference to the next; specialists know each other and they even read each other's books when they have the time. In the 1950s they traveled rarely and knew little about one another. To be sure, specialists kept up with the scholarship of foreign colleagues but there was no great institutional intimacy. Today's extensive, ever burgeoning, networks of research institutes, conferences, colloquia, workshops, journals and fellowships did not exist. Only a minority participated in the big event of the professional calendar, the quinquennial World Congress of Historical Sciences. No regular meetings of European historians paralleled the annual London Conference of Anglo-American Historians. National history ruled the roost, leaving precious little room for anything else. Until the 1960s there was no specialist teaching of American history at the Sorbonne. Moreover, international contacts did not mobilize French historians, partly because foreign language skills were comparatively rare, partly because funding was exiguous.

Duroselle, one of the first historians to visit the United States—visiting professors from France were usually literature specialists—taught at several campuses, including Harvard and Notre Dame, Indiana. The resulting contacts with American historians and political scientists generated in 1964 the first colloquium on Franco-American history. A study of American foreign relations, *From Wilson to Roosevelt: Foreign Policy of the United States 1913-1945* (1960), quickly established itself as a standard text. It utilized public opinion polls—a brave initiative at the time since many historians dismissed them as political science tools of dubious validity. Director from 1963 of the French Fulbright Committee for the promotion of cultural and educational exchanges Duroselle persuaded the government to share funding with the United States. Thus the Fulbright became the Franco-American Committee for university and cultural exchanges. Publication in 1978 of *France and the United States: From the Beginnings to the Present*, hot on the heels of the French edition of 1976, further enhanced a lead role in North American studies. His graduate students in American history enjoyed distinguished academic careers, notably André Kaspi, Yves-Henri Nouhailhat, and Pierre Mélandri. However, Duroselle's international interests were not confined to the United States. He initiated academic rapprochements with Italy and Switzerland, institutionalized in regular conferences and the creation of a new journal, *Relations internationales*.

In the United States and Britain of the 1950s and 1960s an unreconstructed diplomatic history still ruled; in France it was dead and buried. Together Renouvin and Duroselle redefined the field, giving French historiography a strong lead over the Anglo-Saxon academy. Duroselle's study of France's descent from power in the 1930s has to be read in the context of this rethinking, which was a response to the challenge of the new history, La nouvelle histoire, chiefly represented by the work of the group associated with the review founded in 1929 and usually known as Annales. The new history in France, dominated by the trinity Lucien Febvre, Marc Bloch and Fernand Braudel, has been the most innovative of the twentieth century. Two of the leading ideas Annales advocated were a problem-centered analytical history for a conventional history of events, l'histoire évènementielle; secondly, the opening-up of the totality of human experience in place of a largely political history about kings, ministers, battles and treaties.

As a result, diplomatic and political history was in the doghouse. Conceived as the study of relations between governments and unfairly disparaged as "What one clerk said to another," diplomatic history traditionally occupied top place in Clio's hierarchy.[2] Certainly diplomatic historians had a case to answer. They assumed that the past could be cut into neat and separable slices of political, economic, social and religious history. Virtually no attempt was made to relate foreign policy to underlying societal structures: geographic conditions, demographics, economic and financial interests, ideologies and public opinion. Preoccupied with the reconstruction of bilateral and multilateral negotiations researchers followed a paper chase of official documents. This nose to the ground methodology confined consideration of wider forces and issues to assessments of national interests and aspirations defined in terms of power, prestige and security. Unsurprisingly, arguments about the future of diplomatic history, often acrimonious, rumbled through the 1930s and 1940s. Renouvin's reluctance to take on board graduate students in the mid-1940s reflected a desire for space in which to reconsider the field.

The Annales school recruited many of Duroselle's peers. Marc Bloch, one of its founders, taught him in 1938-39. Why did he stick with old-fashioned diplomatic? Annales raised two barriers: one personal; the other intellectual. In 1946 in an outburst of furor academicus Lucien Febvre, second person of the Annales trinity, attacked the work of Duroselle's dissertation director, Charles Pouthas. The vehemence and injustice of the attack, recalled Duroselle, was such that "I never wanted to write a line in Annales."[3] Although recognizing and admiring the school's positive achievements, the blanket trashing of political and diplomatic history, biography and traditional narrative angered and alienated him.

Happily, the new history did the old a good turn. In the early 1950s Renouvin rebaptised diplomatic as international relations, giving it a new remit. This was the fruit of lengthy reflection, not a hasty make over. Indeed from the early 1930s he had censured colleagues for neglecting structural forces and for assuming that the diplomatic record alone sufficed for the understanding of international relations. In 1935 he created at the Sorbonne the Institute for the Study of Contemporary International Relations. Resisting the temptation to borrow political science clothes and theoretical baggage Renouvin opted for deepening and enlarging the field as part of mainstream history. He sought to make sense of international political change by highlighting the interplay between on the one hand, global and domestic dynamics, and on the other, people, events and day-to-day decision-making.

Flagship of the new prospectus was the multi-volume *History of International Relations* (*Histoire des relations internationales, 1953-58*) a broad synopsis of international affairs from the fall of the Roman Empire in the West to the end of World War II. Renouvin directed the whole enterprise and wrote four of the eight volumes. It was a truly formidable achievement, which has not been bettered since. True, surveys spanning fifty years or more like A. J. P. Taylor's *The Struggle for Mastery in Europe, 1848-1918* (1953) and William L. Langer's *The Diplomacy of Imperialism* (1935) were plentiful but astonishingly, no one had had the courage and energy to tackle the big picture.

Building on a chronological narrative Renouvin and his team skillfully connected foreign relations and geopolitics. "Our goal," he affirmed, "is to show what are the most important transformations between peoples and to assess... the causes. These transformations have sometimes been the result of conflicts... sometimes the result of a slow evolution of deep forces, material and cultural."[4]

The History accomplished three important things. By addressing the intersection of foreign policy and long-range dynamics it rehabilitated diplomatic, restoring it to first-class citizenship in the historical profession. Secondly, while conceding Europe a central role Renouvin and associates systematically engaged with other cultures and continents. Lastly, their work analyzed not just inter-state relations but relations between

peoples. Even today after nearly half a century the eight volumes constitute a unique achievement in the literature, exemplifying the Gallic genius
for writing successful grand syntheses. Nothing comparable came from
the English-speaking world.[5] When over thirty years later Paul Kennedy's
The Rise and Fall of the Great Powers (1987) appeared it focused on the
interplay of economic change and military conflict since 1500 rather than
the general evolution of the international system. Duroselle and Renouvin
in tandem authored an *Introduction to the History of International Relations*
(*Introduction a l'Histoire des relations internationales, 1964*), defending their
choice of an historical rather than a theoretical perspective:

> We do not underestimate the value of these [theoretical] investi-
> gations, but, rather than scanning history for proof of theories elabo-
> rated beforehand, we thought it wiser to look at the past with a view
> to forming only such conclusions as the data warranted. This method,
> incidentally, may enable us to provide theorists of international rela-
> tions with new material or topics to reflect on.[6]

International relations aka diplomatic came of age in France in the
1970s with the creation of new chairs of international relations starting
with Paris X Nanterre in 1973. Energized by Duroselle the field went
from strength to strength. One key initiative was insistence on the cen-
trality of military strategy and technology. Surprisingly, Renouvin for all
his emphasis on deeper forces had rather overlooked it. His successor
successfully promoted military history in the academy as well as fostering
dialogue with the military. Increasingly research and teaching highlighted
the history of relations between peoples as well as states. Links with the
United States, Italy and Switzerland gave the French school a high international profile. In 1974 Duroselle, with Jacques Freymond of the University Institute for Advanced International Studies in Geneva, founded
the quarterly Relations Internationales, giving Francophones who previously had to publish in English-language journals their own voice. Historians, declared Duroselle in the new journal, "could no longer neglect"
insights and concepts from other social sciences.[7]

Until the 1970s French policy on the eve of World War II was a
Cinderella subject. Historians steered clear of it partly because they were
deterred by the dearth of data, partly because they assumed that there
was very little French leaders could have done to influence events.[8] Almost to a man French participants blamed Britain for leading France to

defeat. Accordingly, research focused on Britain and Germany as prime movers. France like most European states locked away its secrets for fifty years. For the prewar decade that left almost nothing in the public domain save self-serving memoirs and *The French Yellow Book*, a tendentious selection of documents printed in September 1939 as a propaganda exercise. In 1963 the foreign ministry started publishing selections from its archives in the multi -volume series *Documents diplomatiques français, 1932-1939* (Paris 1963-1986) but it was clear that readers would have a long wait before the collection reached the outbreak of war. Nor did the replacement in 1979 of the fifty-year closure period by the current thirty-year rule trigger a rush to the archives. Access remained restricted because records were being trawled for the preparation of the official series. Given this constraint the fully declassified records for the first post-World War I decade evoked most interest, provoking a new revisionist historiography of France's stance on international security, reparations, disarmament and the Ruhr occupation of 1923.

Enter Duroselle. He was the first to write with full benefit of the diplomatic record. Editorship of the official documentary series brought oversight of all files, giving him a huge advantage over competitors. Additionally, the work of graduate students in his research seminar, the most prestigious in international relations in France, enabled him to draw a much fuller and more rounded picture than would have been possible for a lone investigator. Thus *France and the Nazi Threat* was the first and for a long time the only account to be based on unrestricted access to the documents. It was not however a deeply revisionist work like Fritz Fischer's *Germany's Aims In the First World War* (1967) or Robert O. Paxton's *Vichy France: Old Guard and New Order 1940-1944* (1972) nor did it offer startling revelations about the period. Deploying captured German files Paxton effectively demolished the myth that Vichy's collaborationism shielded France from the worst of German occupation policy. But on the slide to war there was no received wisdom, only a plethora of conflicting interpretations chasing too few facts. The lasting achievement of Duroselle was to demystify the decade by establishing a persuasive explanation of diplomatic defeat based on close scrutiny of the records.

Why publish now an English translation of *La Décadence* a quarter of a century since the first French edition? For one reason, the monograph has stood the test of time, making it the classic account of France's part in the seven year run-up to the second European conflict; for another the subtle analysis and balancing of people, issues and influences brilliantly captures the distinctive perspective of France's international historians. And the theme of the book is one of the most important in twentieth century history. The fall of France was the fulcrum of the century. If French power, as many expected at the time, had withstood Hitler's onslaught the war would have had a different ending. Without victory over France Hitler would not have invaded the Soviet Union. Hostilities might have ended in a negotiated peace without becoming a world conflict, keeping France a key player in world politics. More importantly, it was the collapse of French diplomacy that led to 1940. Menaced by Hitler and Mussolini French diplomacy suffered a double defeat: failing to prevent the war of 1939; failing to ensure that if war came the nation fought in the best conditions.

The book showcases the new approach to the study of international relations devised by Renouvin and Duroselle. Analysis of issues and actions blends with sharp vignettes of personalities, the ensemble grounded in an evaluation of forces and attitudes. All in clear, taut, lively and jargon-free prose. A powerful Preface sets the scene, profiling protagonists and the political constraints with which they had to contend. Duroselle underscores the millstone of domestic politics. The ephemeral coalition governments of the 1930s responded in different ways to internal and external issues. Holding together brittle cabinets privileged caution, compromise and fudging of issues rather than decisive and timely decision-making. Important too were the roles of pressure groups and public opinion. Duroselle illuminates the activity of small decision-making groups, especially foreign minister Georges Bonnet and his allies. The core is a year-by-year narrative of how leaders perceived the pre-war international crises, what they did or did not do about them, and why they responded thus. Midway through the story four thematic chapters (VI-IX) evaluate the foreign policy making process, dissecting in turn the legacy of World War I on French opinion, the nation's self-image, economic interests, military strategy and the diplomatic machine.

How does Duroselle explain France's loss of friends and influence in the approach to war? Contrary to what some writers have alleged he does not offer decadence as a catchall interpretation. In this sense the original French title "La Décadence" was not well chosen because willy-nilly it suggests an all-pervasive moral deterioration, a rotting state and society. In fact Duroselle wrote solely about the effects of political weakness, contending that institutional insufficiencies and the prevailing political culture discouraged the reappraisal of foreign policy goals and timely initiatives. Who then were responsible—diplomats? politicians? generals? The governing elite as a whole, in Duroselle's judgment, must bear a heavy burden of "collective responsibility" for ultimate failure.[9] This is not an original insight but a restatement of the conventional explanation for the collapse of 1940 first sketched out by Marc Bloch in *Étrange défaite* (1946). But Bloch wrote without documents "in a white heat of rage" in the immediate aftermath of disaster.[10] Writing in the 1970s Duroselle pinpoints the casual, careless and slipshod style of leadership. Léon Noël, secretary general of the prime minister's office, recalled how on New Year's Day 1935 foreign minister Pierre Laval called a conference to finalize arrangements for a Rome summit. Instead of business-like discussion, participants swapped anecdotes and jokes. This was no festive exception. A month later Laval and premier Pierre-Étienne Flandin got ready for a London meeting .The two discussed travel arrangements.

Only a few, notably foreign ministers Louis Barthou and Bonnet, applied themselves seriously and single-mindedly to policy-making. During an eighteen-month tenure of the Quai d'Orsay Bonnet labored ceaselessly to stop France fighting for its ally Czechoslovakia in 1938 and for Poland in 1939. Duroselle awards diplomats higher grades than politicians or foreign ministry officials for their efforts to keep Paris well briefed on developments in leading capitals. Yet they were not always read. And even if they had been consistently heeded the war of nerves that began in 1936 called for a new kind of relationship between foreign and defense policy-making. Intergovernmental co-ordination had never been the Republic's strong suit. Ministers behaved like great feudal barons jealously guarding the independence of their departments. And liaison between the foreign ministry and war ministry was especially poor. Indeed, the whole government machine demanded drastic overhaul.

No book is perfect. *France and the Nazi Threat* has its defects. One glaring omission is the lack of a conclusion. Curiously Duroselle did not attempt in this book or its 1939-1945 sequel on the war and Vichy years any kind of general stocktaking in the light of the historiographical debate on France's downfall. The opportunity to weigh and assess diplomacy within the wider frame of society and culture was missed. The book's strength is also a weakness. The important gaps in the French record mean that Duroselle's reliance on the French papers yields little more than the bare bones of policy. Many secret documents were lost or destroyed during World War II. No official records were kept of Cabinet discussions. Thus the surviving archive largely comprises instructions from Paris, reports from French posts abroad, minutes of official meetings and, very occasionally, a think piece on policy options. Only rarely would a minister or high official make detailed annotations on incoming dispatches and telegrams. By contrast, ministers and top officials often unburdened themselves quite freely to American and British envoys. Prime Minister Édouard Daladier, for example, confided in American ambassador William C. Bullitt. If the minutes of a Franco-British conference are missing then Duroselle cites the British record. But it's an exception, not the rule. Of course, historians can easily burn their fingers using non-French sources. Policymakers rehearsed different scripts for different envoys. But the marked discrepancies between American, British and German records of conversations with foreign minister Bonnet and the minister's own account confirm his essential trickiness. Nor, despite their intrinsic importance, does Duroselle explore the Republic's foreign policy options. Did alternatives exist? Would more appeasement have satisfied Hitler and avoided conflict? This seemed to be Bonnet's working assumption in 1938-39. Were firmness and a readiness to stop Hitler by force a practical choice?

Apologists for France's eclipse have consistently pointed to perfidious Albion. Duroselle unconvincingly argues for a watered-down version in the form of the English governess, bullying and cajoling her French charges. "French statesmen," he writes, "practiced appeasement because they needed British help and were subject to constant British pressure."[11] However "the English governess" is hard to swallow. Ministers were their own worst enemies. British tutelage was deliberately fostered to shield France from the consequences of disengagement from Central and Eastern Europe. Publicly decisionmakers solicited British commitments; privately they invited a British lead. Ministers far from being reluctant recruits in a British-inspired enterprise were committed to conciliation. They cherished the illusion of economic agreements with the Fascist dictators leading to political rapprochement. Daladier, for instance, intervened personally to expedite economic talks with Germany in February 1939. Also, he toyed with the idea of inviting Göring "to make a visit to Paris."[12] Just before Hitler's occupation of Prague in mid-March he assured the Fuhrer that France was ready "to pursue and develop with the Reich the policy of collaboration affirmed in the declaration of 6 December" (Franco-German Declaration, 6 December 1938).[13]

Although on some topics like military strategy, intelligence assessment and Franco-British relations research has fleshed out Duroselle's account, the literature since the 1970s has not outdated or discredited his main findings.[14] No important new archival material has been discovered. Yet it would be quite wrong to suppose that Duroselle' story represents a scholarly consensus on France's response to the dictators. The reasons for the collapse of French diplomacy and for the subsequent debacle are as controversial and debatable as they were a quarter of a century ago; there is no agreement on what caused the eclipse. Partly this is because there are big gaps in the record, partly it's because all history is contemporary history, with each generation filtering the past through its own preoccupations and perspectives. While Bloch indicted political and military leaders collectively, other post-mortems produced different suspects: the Popular Front of 1936, a Fascist Fifth Column, perfidious Albion, and the 200 families of the Bank of France. The classic statement of this approach was Pertinax's (André Géraud) *The Gravediggers of France* (1944). In its bid for legitimacy Gaullism thickened the controversy by condemning the rottenness of both the Third Republic and Vichy. As events receded the collapse assumed an appearance of inevitability, a convergence of structural singularities: an ageing population, diseased body politic, the bloodbath of 1914-18, a Maginot mentality, deep economic depression, and social strife. 1940 administered the coup de grace to a regime on its last legs. William L. Shirer's *The Collapse of the Third Republic* (1970) encapsulated this gloom-and-doom reading.

More recently some writers, notably Robert J. Young in *France and the Origins of the Second World War* (1996), have sought to rehabilitate the governing elite, arguing that the retreats and defeats reflected not the machinations of a guilty few or a general atrophy of will but genuine doubts and uncertainties. In brief, the complexities, constraints and challenges overwhelmed well-intentioned leaders. Their recourse to ambivalence and indecision was both understandable and unavoidable. Given their plight they did the best they could: "contradiction or ambivalence is inherent in the human condition... the trick ...is to neither inculpate nor exonerate. It is to explain."[15] True, historians should not rush to judgment. Yet can explanation be separated from assessment of responsibility? Eschewing judgment leaves us with little more than a truism, namely that the French wrestled with dilemmas common to decision-makers everywhere. Demonstrably, ambiguity and uncertainty belong to the human condition. But why did the French perform so miserably in the 1930s and succeed so well after 1958? Why do some countries get their act together while others fail? Young's attempt to rehabilitate verges on determinism: things could only have happened in the way they did. Yet in everyday life our explanations of the choices people make is usually accompanied by comparative judgments about performance, effectiveness and achievement or lack of it. Why adopt different modes of discourse for the present and past? Duroselle's sympathy for the trials and tribulations of French decision-makers does not inhibit him from taking stock of character and conduct.

Understandably, the trauma of 1940 made the politics and diplomacy of the 1930s seem like a one-way street to Vichy. But in the light of what we now know about the Battle of France it makes sense to disentangle the diplomatic and military stories. 1940 was primarily a military disaster, not an inexorable outcome of a terminally sick society. Moreover, it was an Allied disaster, product of a shaky Franco-British alliance and divided counsels. Scandals, political instability and a supine foreign policy had marked other decades without leading to ruin. The post-1932 hemorrhaging of French power was not irreversible. Events were more open than Duroselle and other writers have allowed. Indeed, he errs on the side of fatalism: "Men can, at certain moments, struggle successfully against deep and blind forces. But that was not to be France's destiny. In this instance, men proved weaker than fate." France was trapped in a "mechanism, which seemed inexorable."[16]

However an alternative and arguably more cogent reading of French foreign policy would stress not the role of "deep and blind forces" but rather the chanciness and openness of events.[17] Individuals could and did make decisive differences. This was as true of France as of Germany. Ironically Bonnet's dogged fight to keep France out of war ensured not only that war came but also that France entered it in the worst circumstances. Consider the robust revival of French policy in the spring of 1939: instead of taking orders from the English governess the French demanded conscription and guarantees for Romania—and got them! More's the pity that they left it so late in the day. "The French have not been clever at taking their opportunities with us "observed Ralph Wigram, head of the Central Department of the British Foreign Office in the mid-1930s.[18] On one occasion he sent his wife to Paris, ostensibly on a shopping trip, in reality to convey privately to members of a French delegation what they should ask for in London. Shortly after the Munich Agreement of 29 September 1938 the French foreign minister's wife wrote to an English friend: "Georges has been admirable, so calm, so resolute. He never despaired. On the two final days, all the newspapers, ministers and even his assistants abandoned him... you see what a cool mind and willpower can do for the destinies of peoples."[19] If France's rulers had concentrated their minds and wills on preserving their country's great power position the history of Europe and of the world might have turned out very differently.

Anthony Adamthwaite
Berkeley, California
October 2003

FOREWORD

The purpose of this book, and the series of which it is part, is to take the vantage point of France and the French people in describing French foreign policy without diluting those very specific characteristics in the broader context of international relations. This is an ambitious project insofar as foreign policy is elaborated within a wider debate that extends beyond diplomacy. One must constantly consider the objectives set by those in key positions and the political forces at work exerting their influence and leading to the discrepancies that may appear between viewing policy objectives on one hand and considering the causes of underlying events on the other.

I have used mostly French archives and those at the Quai d'Orsay in particular. Foreign archives, namely those in Great Britain, Italy, Germany, and the United States have only been published in selective fashion and are also being studied scientifically in many cases. I have used those existing studies and materials for those specific countries. Some books and articles published in the United States and Great Britain appear to have been written using mostly British and American sources with the French archives being listed quite impressively in the bibliography but rarely appearing within the footnotes (with the exception of the excellent works by authors such as Adamthwaite, Robert Young, etc.).

I was able to use the huge body of work undertaken by the Commission for the publication of documents dealing with the origins of the war that was founded by my late teacher and friend Pierre Renouvin (who died in 1974), with the help of Maurice Baumont, historical advisor at the foreign ministry who also died in 1981. I succeeded Pierre Renouvin as president of the Commission that in 1984 became the Commission for the publication of French diplomatic documents. I am pleased to thank the various directors of the Archives: Martial de La Fournière and Guy de Commines; the head curators: Maurice Degros, Mlle. Paulette Enjaran, M. de Vienne, Georges Dethan, Mme de Nomazy and their staff. As for the team I have been leading, after the late Pierre Mandoul, François Gadrat, Colonel Chalmin, Georges Taboulet and its current members, Mr. Monicat, Degros, d'Hoop, Labaste, Marquand and Yvon Lacaze, archivist and paleographer the most knowledgeable regarding the documents of the period. I owe to all the better part of my sources of information.

I must also mention the help provided to me by my students (who for the most part are now full professors at various universities) within the framework of the Institut d'histoire des relations internationales contemporaines. Some of them (Jean-Claude Allain, Jacques Bariéty, etc.) were kind enough to reread my manuscript. Ambassadors Léon Noël, of the Institut, René Massigli, Armand Bérard, Jean Daridan continuously helped and encouraged me. I also used the written and oral remarks of Ambassador E. de Crouy-Chanel, Generals Jacques Humbert and Philippe Maurin, Colonel J. Defrasne, Yves Jann and Bernard Sinsheimer and Professor H. Batowski.

I wish to express my thanks to all. I also wish to thank the Imprimerie Nationale and its directors, Georges Bonnin and Guy Beaussang. It is very comforting for a writer to be published by this prestigious institution.

J.-B. D.

PREFACE

Aristide Briand, the "Apostle of Peace," died on March 7, 1932, just as his glory was fading. After heading the Quai d'Orsay for seven years—starting in April 1925—he had been replaced in January 1932 by the new prime minister, Pierre Laval. Briand, who was not yet seventy, had aged prematurely; he suffered from uremia, was worn out and would easily doze off. Politically, he was the victim of many factors beyond his control, as they were beyond the control of every politician of Briand's time. The most serious issue was the economic crisis engulfing the world after the Wall Street Crash (Black Thursday, October 24, 1929). For over two years France had mistakenly managed to convince itself that it was immune because of the "wisdom" of its economy based on family farming, protectionism and a mostly aging industrial base managed by small-minded businessmen, an enduring commitment to the gold standard, the containment of wages and minimal expenditures on social programs. It was basically an archaic system.

> Thanks to our well-balanced French economy and the virtues of our people—wrote *Le Temps*—France has become one of the two pillars that are now supporting the world economy.[1]

Briand, like most of his contemporaries, disdained what was referred to at the time as political economy, which, in the scale of things politicians valued, rated far below parliamentary deal-making and had become, especially after Poincaré had left the government (July 1929), a vast collection of quick fixes and sham policies. In September 1931, as "France enjoyed the final moments of prosperity,"[2] the devaluation of the British currency led to the sudden acknowledgment of a decline that had in fact begun early that same year. By the end of 1931, industrial production had dropped 23% below the 1929 average (in Germany, 42% and in the United States, 37%). The unemployment rate suddenly jumped from under 100,000 to 248,000 by January 1932.[3] The French people understood that they too were now into the crisis, and this explains in part the narrow victory of the left-wing Cartel des Gauches in the elections of May 1 and 8, 1932. As in 1924, the Radical Socialist leader Edouard Herriot became prime minister as well as foreign minister on June 3, 1932. It is at this point our narrative begins.

Still another factor, which the crisis cannot entirely explain, was the sudden surge in Germany of an ultra-nationalism that was more perverse and worrisome than that of the National Germans and the Stahlhelm of the 1920s. Prior to September 1930, there were only 14 National Socialists elected to the Reichstag. With the general elections of September 14 under a strictly proportional election system, their number climbed to 107. On July 31, 1932, just one and a half months after Herriot came to power, 230 of them returned. In the meantime in April, Adolf Hitler, who was generally thought to be something of a half-crazy stooge, not to be taken seriously, had forced the aging Marshal von Hindenburg, the standard-bearer of the old reactionary Germany, into a run-off during the presidential elections, Hitler's votes increased even more during the second round.

Besides a few small groups, no one in Germany liked France. Hitler and his NSDAP party (the German communists nicknamed them Nazis and the name became popular) hated France out of habit and because of their political doctrine. In his famous book *Mein Kampf*, that very few Frenchmen had read, he referred to France as the hereditary enemy, not a novel idea in itself (German historian Heinz-Otto Sieburg had shown how such a completely subjective thought came to be widely accepted in Germany during the crisis of 1840 and in France following the battle of Sadowa in 1866.)[4] However, as far as Hitler was concerned, those were not empty words or platonic ideas. He explained unhesitatingly and in a meandering way that elicited smiles from the professors at the École libre des sciences politiques, the need to crush France in order to fulfill his grand designs in the East, the conquest of the so-called Lebensraum in the vast expanses where the inferior and degenerate Slav race was living.

Thus, the trickle of concessions that France had made to Germany at the expense of the treaty of Versailles, culminating in the early evacuation of the Rhineland in 1930 rather than 1935, turned out to be completely useless. Germany, with its population of 65 million, appeared potentially more threatening than ever. Briand had promised that as long as he lived there would be no war. Now Briand was dead. The French people feared Germany and war. Only fourteen years had passed since "the war to end all wars" with its horrible bloodshed of 1,300,000 young men and about one hundred thousand colonial troops. France was full of crippled men. Soon the "low birth-rate classes," created by wartime conscription, of young men born between 1915 and 1918 would be of military age. What would become of France?

In the course of negotiations of the peace treaty in 1919, two issues preoccupied the French people: security and reparations—"Germany will pay!" As we will see, reparations were to be cancelled in the summer of 1932. Unrealistic even in times of relative prosperity, they would be absurd with the world economic crisis. As for security, however, it seemed to be, at least in 1932, guaranteed by the overwhelming superiority of the French army both in weapons and manpower. But would this situation last? Since February 1932 the disarmament conference was in full swing. The Treaty of Versailles presented Germany's disarmament as the first step toward world disarmament. What better opportunity for Germany either to induce France to undertake a massive reduction in its own armaments, as some well-intentioned Frenchmen and most Anglo-Saxon countries were requesting, or seize on French unwillingness to disarm to justify a massive rearmament of its own, which was the only course the German military and their natural ally, Adolf Hitler, were contemplating!

At the moment in time when we begin our study, the vast political, economic and psychological entity called France, with its enormous empire around the world, found itself in a very worrisome situation. France, like any other state, depended simultaneously on external forces—which she could deal with using dubious devices such as persuasion, bargaining, threats or the use of violence—and its internal capacity to find the indispensable answers.

In that respect France was indeed very poorly equipped. Apart from a social structure that fostered internally, more than elsewhere, those "dispersive tendencies" later identified by General de Gaulle,[5] where the class struggle was far from being the only element, France was poorly governed from a structural standpoint. Specifically, the pleasant and easygoing form of government France had opted for in 1875 and whose tradition had been set in 1877 was predicated upon the greatest distrust of power itself. Excluding the Communist far-left and a noisy but ineffectual anti-democratic far-right, the French people for the most part backed—without actually joining the parties they voted for—a few large political groups with a democratic internal structure where the rank and file played a significant role. This was the case in the SFIO Socialist, party founded on the principle of the majority openly setting its policies at party conventions. This also applied to the Radical Socialists that originated from a myriad of committees and were surrounded by a constellation of independent Radicals. The Moderate Right, heir to the former opportunists and closely wedded to economic interests rather than any ideology upheld, the same principles. It was also the case of the vast Catholic Right, which had reconciled itself with the Republic and came from committees similar to the Radicals except for the fact that they originated in the castle and the rectory or, as André Siegfried put it, often in the rectories and against the castle, rather than relying upon masonic lodges or various lay and anti-clerical organizations.

Such a built-in structure, we can state straightaway, was the most effective form of protection France possessed against fascism, which, as we shall see later, appeared to be more frightening than it was as an actual threat. But the structure worked only in a politically divided situation, mitigated by temporary alliances and unstable combinations. Haunted by the fear of a Bonapartist dictatorship and its disastrous outcome in the defeat of 1871 and the Paris Commune, the founders attributed the basic political power to Parliament. The Third Republic was actually a caricature of parliamentary government and essentially functioned as a regime dominated by an assembly. The result was an amazing inability of the French people to let themselves be governed, combined with an incredible incapacity to engage in any kind of reform, be it social, economic, fiscal or even constitutional. All this can easily be summed up in a simple statement: the structural instability of executive power in France,[6] an instability that increased naturally with the disputes tied to the economic crisis, the same crisis that brought an awesome dictatorship to power in Germany, and sparked a conservative tidal wave in Great Britain with pacifist and Gallophobic Tory governments coming to power ready to launch appeasement. This would later provoke the anger of many British historians and journalists, such as Harold Nicolson, who contrasted the "extraordinary force of personality" of a Winston Churchill to "this confused and timid gang."[7] The world crisis further accelerated the disintegration of the executive branch in France. Between June 1932 and March 1940 there were sixteen different governments, each one lasting five months and twenty-four days on average. From September 1931 to May 1940, Great Britain had only three governments lasting four, two and three years, respectively. French instability affected both left- and right-wing governments.

The worst of it was that that there appeared to be no solution. Some cabinets undoubtedly resorted to obtaining full powers and issue legal decrees that were submitted retroactively to parliamentary approval, but these were the full powers and legal decrees of unstable governments. Furthermore, any type of reform of the Constitution appeared impossible. Between 1932 and 1939 the only identifiable attempt can be attributed to the so-called National Unity government of Doumergue in September 1934. He wanted to give exclusively to the president of the republic and the president of the council (the prime minister) the right to dissolve the Chamber of Deputies, subject to the Senate's approval according to the Constitution of 1875. However, even though the executive committee of the Radical Socialist party had voted on June 13 in favor of a motion for authority of the State, the reform of the executive branch and government stability,[8] it was its president Edouard Herriot who scuttled a project he viewed as "breaking with tradition" and harboring the dark dangers of dictatorship.[9] The Socialist party also opposed it and thus everything remained unchanged as before. In a short book written in 1941 while he was a political prisoner, socialist leader Léon Blum did not clearly favor constitutional reform when he wrote: "Governmental mobility in the Third Republic was basically caused by disorder, lack of discipline and the powerlessness to make those thick and homogeneous political parties that provide the necessary basis for a representative system last."[10]

This instability had serious consequences during times of difficulties abroad. On the one hand, it didn't encourage diligence on the part of the leadership; on the other, it stifled any kind of master plan.

When one's activity is primarily focused on survival, fundamental issues are overshadowed by the need to overcome parliamentary hurdles. Furthermore, the interplay of political deal-making becomes all-important in the appointment of a cabinet minister more than the actual competence of the man. With a few exceptions (Louis Barthou, Léon Blum, Yvon Delbos, Edouard Daladier and—whether we like his politics or not—

Georges Bonnet), the men in charge of France's foreign affairs often appear to be amazingly "irresponsible." According to Jacques Bariéty's[11] definitive study, Edouard Herriot conducted the difficult 1924 negotiations without having thoroughly studied the background reports. As we shall see, this would happen once again in 1932. Armand Bérard, chief of staff and later an ambassador, wrote that his boss Joseph Paul-Boncour required no more than a three-line summary for each dispatch—which was customary—and that he annotated these in an illegible handwriting; but at least he made the effort to write his own notes. However, the author adds: "Internal politics took up most of the minister's time; as does his eloquence in which he often indulged at length and took up still more time... The support staff, his cabinet and his nephew did everything else."[12]

There were even worse cases than Herriot and Paul-Boncour. Ambassador Léon Noël, who became general secretary to the Presidency of the Council,* provides some rather scathing descriptions on the subject. Laval summoned him around New Year's Day 1935, along with the general secretary of the foreign ministry, Alexis Léger, his cabinet director Rochat and political affairs director Bargeton to prepare for his upcoming visit to Mussolini: "The meeting wasn't serious—it resembled most of the other meetings I attended at the time. The issues the two government leaders were to discuss were never mentioned. Time was spent telling anecdotes and cracking jokes."[13] One month later Laval was getting ready to travel to London with Prime Minister Pierre-Etienne Flandin. Both men had their offices at the Quai d'Orsay. "I was getting them together to prepare for the trip. It was a miserable failure. Never for one minute did they discuss what they would tell their British colleagues. They only talked about the kind of transportation they were going to use."[14] They finally traveled by ship despite the fact that Flandin was very much fond of airplanes; at Dover they found Ambassador Charles Corbin waiting to welcome them both. "I witnessed the conversation all three were having in the train to London; it was the vaguest and most general of conversations. Laval and Flandin actually came to the conference without any prior preparation of any kind. I often found the lack of seriousness in most French politicians of that time shocking and revolting."[15]

Finally, we will quote the deputy foreign minister of Poland, Count Szembek. His minister, Josef Beck, told him an anecdote he heard from

---

* The Presidency of the Council of Ministers was in effect the Prime Minister's inner cabinet. [NDT]

a foreign diplomat (the many levels of hearsay make the story sound a bit suspicious but worth relating in any case). The diplomat overheard a conversation between Pierre Laval and Marshal Pétain who had traveled to Warsaw to attend the funeral of Polish Marshal Pilsudski. "When they saw a unit of sailors one of them said: How about that, do they also have a navy? The other answered: But where do they have a port? The first one replied: It must be Danzig. Ambassador Laroche, after hearing this exchange, went up to them and explained that it was Gdynia."[16]

Sadly, such opinions dovetail with general perceptions: as Pertinax (Henri Géraud)[17] wrote of Pierre Laval, "Short on ideas and of abysmal ignorance." Léon Blum's conclusion was, "Weakness and precariousness of cabinets without a solid base nor having any time, and lacking imagination and daring."[18] There was also a lingering colossal ignorance of economic issues in the background. Alfred Sauvy attributed that weakness to the poor quality of the courses offered by law schools on the subject; these were followed by the École libre des sciences politiques where large debates on major issues were organized by the alumni association.[19] In its public finance section the École libre produced "competent senior Treasury officials," none of whom would be in charge of the nation's finances during that time.[20]

Few among the politicians included in our study were to venture beyond a kind of frightened management of public finances. "Apart from financial issues that were handled at the rue de Rivoli at the strictest arithmetical level, there were obviously issues concerning other parts of government administration but the ministry of Commerce only took care of customs tariffs and Agriculture was mostly interested in the kind of protectionism inherited from Méline."[21] Germain Martin,[22] Henry Chéron, Marcel Régnier, and Paul Marchandeau managed the rue de Rivoli for the greater part of this period; these orthodox financiers appeared to be rather colorless as they faced the monumental challenges of their time. Those who stand out were Raymond Patenôtre, a longtime undersecretary of state for the economy, the radical Georges Bonnet, and the socialist Vincent Auriol. But two men above all who played a brief role, Pierre Mendès-France as undersecretary of the Treasury in Léon Blum's second cabinet (March to April 1938) who showed an early interest in John Maynard Keynes; and the liberal economist Paul Reynaud who replaced Marchandeau as minister of Finance on November 1, 1938. Aside from Léon Blum, the other prime ministers were totally ignorant when it came to economic issues.

Considering the absence of any kind of broader plan, the picture then becomes complete. In a country where no party could command a majority on its own, no lasting partisan foreign policy was possible even though internal political quarrels did include foreign policy issues. Even better than long-term partisan policies, there could be the grand designs or what General de Gaulle referred to as great undertakings that could have overcome the internal divisions among the French people. With the exception of Barthou, who attempted in 1934 to create strong alliances for France by displaying a capacity for daring and initiative in taking necessary risks, the various French governments never engaged in any broad policies. When energies are focused on day-to-day disputes that clearly could not be resolved, the only remaining possibility is to dilute them by not taking a position and to do nothing. As we shall see in greater detail, this approach was very similar between the radical governments of 1932-1933, the moderate cabinets of Flandin and Laval in 1935 and the "transition" cabinet of Albert Sarraut in 1936, as well as those of the Popular Front and the government that Daladier formed in April 1938.

Is it possible to blame the general inability to take action and the hesitation toward any undertaking on the existing structures? Could French national character be the reason? Was it the fault of the ruling class, of the bourgeoisie?

Historians find the concept of national character rather vague. Neither cultural anthropologists of the Ruth Benedict school nor social psychologists like Inkeles or Otto Klineberg have come to a satisfying answer on this issue. The great intuitive descriptions by an André Siegfried, a Kayserling, or a Miguel de Unamuno reach some clear conclusions regarding the soul of a people. However, quite often we catch ourselves thinking that the opposite could be just as true and that the exception is almost as important as the rule. Let us examine a passage by Jules Romains, considered at the time to be the guiding light of youth,

> Our people with its propensity for ready criticism, irony, spirit of contradiction, its fear of being duped and lack of innocence as well as the inevitable disenchantments that come with being a mature nation, is perhaps, among the great peoples, the one least likely to overestimate its opportunities... It is less prone to spontaneous optimism than many others. This is good at preventing mistakes. It doesn't work as well when it stifles the gathering and galvanizing of its energies.[23]

In 1941 Léon Blum clearly asked the question, "Is this a specifically French trait or rather the characteristic of today's French bourgeoisie?"[24] With the nuances that his exceptional mind brought to such fundamental questions, Léon Blum concluded that the bourgeoisie carried a major responsibility, at least that segment of the bourgeoisie controlling business and government administration. It should be pointed out that in 1976 France produced 285,000 high school graduates,* while in 1913 there were only 8,000 and in 1935 15,000.[25] The latter number is not indicative of any social improvement from pre-World War I levels, but merely shows that young women of the bourgeoisie had also entered the fray. Obviously in 1935, as in 1913, there were graduates from lower income families, but could they avoid becoming bourgeois themselves? The country's top leaders, the politicians, businessmen, intellectuals, and administrators almost all came exclusively from the bourgeoisie, even within the Socialist Party. Only the Communist Party and the labor leadership—including the Catholic unions—were not controlled in such an exclusive manner by the bourgeois class. The gates would open wide during the Popular Front. Only after the Second World War did mass education replace that of an elite. Insofar as the main responsibility falls on the leadership class, Léon Blum was right in equating decadence with the bourgeoisie.

But then again there were various gradations; the universal right to vote was also responsible to a certain degree and implied a general outlook on the part of the popular masses and the petty bourgeois. How else can one explain the pacifist depression[26] that lasted such a long time, blinding so many people of good will to the extent and imminence of a German and Nazi threat that was both national and ideological! How can one characterize the excessive opposition to overtime, even when it became vitally important to build weapons for survival! Léon Blum honestly accepted these facts and agreed with economist Alfred Sauvy. In other words, and without seeking an explanation through the doubtful concept of national character, our conclusion is that in France in the 1930s the inability to prevent disaster came from some form of collective responsibility where the leadership class was, by definition, playing the top role.

A fundamental issue still needs to be addressed: beyond governmental instability, was there not also continuity? It cannot be denied that a solid administration did exist and would prove itself in 1940. But the administration's role is to manage and not to initiate important decisions.

---

* The number in 2003 is estimated at over 500,000. [NDT]

It becomes necessary to reach up to the higher levels to find the men who, while cabinets filed in and out, remained close to the top and could, because of their very permanence, wield exceptional authority. A careful probe leads us to conclude that three such men occupied those key positions: Marshal Philippe Pétain, the General Secretary of the Quai d'Orsay, Alexis Léger, and General Maurice Gamelin. It may appear surprising that we do not include Albert Lebrun, President of the Republic, who was elected in May 1932 and reelected on April 5, 1939. Yet there is a simple enough explanation: never before in the history of the French Republic had there been such an abysmal void. We cannot find a single initative taken by Albert Lebrun at any time, even during the most dramatic events. Rather than accumulate the quotations where those taking part in that tragedy politely describe this total absence, we offer one significant piece of evidence. In the course of the seven years and two months covered by this book, some seventeen volumes of diplomatic documents (including military documents and personal letters) covering four years and ten months have been published. The very careful choices made by Pierre Renouvin and the team mentioned in the Preface collected 8,267 documents. Lebrun is mentioned in only seven documents and always in a "passive" role; in eight volumes out of the seventeen he does not appear a single time. We must conclude that a Loubet, a Poincaré or a Millerand would have played a very different role.

Two cabinet ministers with opposite viewpoints, Jean Zay and Anatole de Monzie, kept "diaries" in 1938-1939. These include descriptions of cabinet meetings. During the period leading up to the war, Jean Zay mentions that the president spoke on three occasions in extremely vague terms. Monzie only mentions his reelection on April 5, 1939, using the occasion to give a description of the man.[27] His main shortcoming was that he was "impeccable."

> More constitutional than Mr. Raymond Poincaré, he doesn't even use his right to express an opinion on foreign policy of which he keeps diligently informed... By steadfastly cutting everyone down to size, the regime has succeeded in creating its masterpiece of innocent neutrality.

Albert Lebrun picked the presidents of the council according to the rules, he attended the funeral of King Albert I of Belgium and paid a visit to King George VI of England. That was the extent of his involvement in French foreign policy.

Marshal Philippe Pétain is too well known for us to provide a full description here. In 1932 the "Victor of Verdun" was still among the most prestigious of Frenchmen. Foch had died in 1929 and Joffre in 1931. Lyautey, who would die in 1934 and had conquered Morocco, had been minister of war but was never in command at the front in France. He disliked Pétain, who had been sent to replace him to win the "war in the Rif." Among the other Marchhals, Fayolle had died in 1928 and Franchet d'Esperey would survive until 1942 but was in poor health, soon to be confined to a wheelchair.[28] His dreamy radical right-wing ideas and close ties to the Cagoule and other military plots made him look suspicious. Loustanau-Lacau, who was appointed to Pétain's personal staff in 1935, wrote,

> Foch looked like a civil servant, Joffre like a grandfather, Lyautey like a horseman, Franchet d'Esperey like a wild boar, Fayolle like a musician but he [Pétain] who is still in shape, really does look like a Marchhal of France.[29]

Pétain therefore played a more important role than the others. As early as 1920-1921, despite Foch's opposition, he managed to get the principle of the integrity of the territory passed. He remained vice-president of the Supreme War Council until 1930 when he was nearly seventy-five, before handing over the vice presidency to Weygand. However, he continued to serve on the council where his authority invariably prevailed at key points in time. He was minister of war in the Doumergue cabinet of 1934 and was appointed ambassador to Spain in 1939 to establish relations with Franco as he approached victory. Pétain never hesitated to voice his opinions. He went from long, impressive periods of silence in public life—that can no doubt be attributed to his own "wait-and-see" attitude—to publishing newsworthy articles, such as the one in the Revue des Deux Mondes on March 1, 1935, entitled "France's security during the low birth-rate years," in which he rejected the principle of a professional army and therefore the theories of Major de Gaulle, and again in his introduction to a book by General Chauvineau, published in 1939, Is an Invasion Still Possible? Could he have harbored political ambitions? Some far-right writers would periodically refer to him as the next savior of France. "Pétain is the man we need," said Gustave Hervé, a former anti-militarist who had become an ultra-nationalist.[30] We shall see Pétain's long shadow contantly reappearing and, at times, we can measure his role in decisions that were made.

It is far more difficult to accurately judge the part played by that strange diplomat, Alexis Léger.[31] Just as strange as the poet Saint-John Perse, the 1960 Nobel prizewinner for literature. The fact that both of these identities belonged to the same person would not be so odd in a country where literature and diplomacy mixed happily together had the two faces of this Janus not been so completely separated from one another.[32] Léger was a Créole, born in 1887 on the island of Guadeloupe, the son of a lawyer who returned to his native French city of Pau in 1899. He passed the foreign ministry entrance exam in 1914, one year after Paul Morand. Like Paul Claudel, the other great poet in the diplomatic service, he had spent many years in China. He met Claudel through another poet, Francis Jammes, and Claudel then introduced him to Berthelot.[33] Like Berthelot, Léger was a regular at the Café Procope and moved in avant-garde literary circles with other writer-diplomats like Jean Giraudoux, Paul Morand, and Jean Cocteau.[34] During the war, before going to China, he had already played a role in the Delcassé cabinet where he provided press analysis to the future ambassador, Charles Corbin.[35]

As a young diplomat he enjoyed a low-key but already widespread reputation. They said that during his posting in Peking he had been deeply immersed in the study of life in China. His reports were beautifully written. Berthelot had singled him out, just like Briand, more recently during the Washington conference (1921).[36]

Paul Morand wrote:

I admire his modesty, his broad sweeping views, his elevated and active mind, his playful imagination and his mature wisdom like that of an elderly man, his selflessness, his secret life, his unfurnished apartments filled with trunks and his nomadic childhood.[37]

Jean Chauvel wrote that he would appear

[w]earing a narrow black tie, with a pasty face, a veiled look in his eyes, using elegant and refined language in a low voice.[38]

Briand picked Léger to head his cabinet, and that was the beginning of his unstoppable rise. In March 1933 he replaced Berthelot as secretary general, the highest position in the Quai d'Orsay. The "Briandist" policies would therefore continue, for a long time to come, to relentless attacks on the secretary general from the far right, specifically from the Action Française.

While Berthelot was a very hard worker with an in-depth knowledge of the issues, Léger appears to have dedicated a much smaller amount of time to diplomatic communication. Fabre-Luce wrote that he was "an easy-going poet."[39] According to Massigli[40] Léger never did any writing, which is confirmed by the files. Only Georges Bonnet mentions his "endless capacity for work."[41] He would come to the Quai at 11 a.m., leave for lunch and return around 4 p.m. staying late into the evenings, mainly to attend meetings. "He would often have long meetings with a small number of visitors, always the same ones, who came often." Among them were Elie Bois of the *Le Petit Parisien* and André de Fels, the secretary general of the Alliance Démocratique.[42] According to Chauvel, Léger paid no attention to current events even when it came to his specialty, namely the Far East and preferred discussing Chinese psychology. While he often met with the director of political affairs, he wasn't easily accessible to his subordinates of a lower rank. That at least was Chauvel's view when he was deputy director for the Far East in 1939:

> I would tell him that our public opinion wasn't prepared for the tragic events that could come... Léger would dismiss my fears. He didn't believe that there would be any tragic events in the future."[43]

Other eyewitnesses provide a much more favorable description. These were often journalists[44] like Pertinax, for instance, who received a much warmer welcome than the civil servants of the Quai:

> I went to see him regularly in the early fall of 1935 except for the many instances when I was quarreling with his minister. [He] had a deep feeling for the dignity of France, something shared by all the great servants of the State. [He was a man] of absolute moral and intellectual integrity... Contrary to the accusations that are being leveled, Alexis Léger never took the liberty of trying to impose...his own views.

Having to deal with ministers who often disliked him (Laval, Flandin, and Bonnet in particular),

> [h]e saw it as part of the functions of his position...to dispel their self-deceptions, point out their mistakes even though later on he would loyally accept their position.[45]

Pertinax summed up his policies this way:

> Of paramount importance was the understanding and collaboration with Great Britain, the need to uphold the Polish and Czechoslovak alliances, to encourage the Soviet Union to move further away from Germany, in times of danger to transform the League of Nations into a military and economic organization supportive of the western powers.[46]

Wasn't this pure Briand? The problem was to check whether Briand's wishes of the 1920s still warranted ironclad support in the 1930s.

In reading a speech he gave at New York University in 1942 regarding his great chief[47] we notice that Léger was attempting to defend a policy established in the 1920s rather than modify French diplomacy to new circumstances. Perhaps he believed too strongly in collective security, something that had become an illusion; a kind of melancholy alignment on a rather disappointing British policy. Léger never was an appeaser. He firmly believed in "pact-making," in complicated treaties that were replete with escape clauses. He was not a man ready to consider "realistic" alliances with the only powers that could help France stop Nazi Germany, namely fascist Italy and communist Russia. Just like his friend, Czech president Beneš, he remained a man of the moderate and optimistic left who refused to accept the fact that Hitler would go all the way. However, since he didn't assert himself, his role is difficult to assess. We shall attempt to do so in the course of this book. Léger probably could not, or did not wish to, play a larger personal role out of loyalty toward his superiors. As Anthony Eden, the British cabinet member who knew him well, said:

> Léger had quiet charm and gentle manners. I found him sympathetic but he had not the strength of character of his predecessor, Philippe Berthelot.[48]

The heaviest responsibility belonged to General Maurice Gamelin. Concerning this unusual character we have, in addition to various documents, a long and optimistic work—his own memoirs[49]—as well as a harsh and detailed study entitled *Le Mystère Gamelin* by Colonel Le Goyet.[50] Since the end result of his seven years as commander in chief led to the most disastrous defeat in French history, we are entitled to ask the question: was Gamelin completely mistaken? Or was it rather that, having understood where the problems were but being unable to secure what he needed, he didn't have the backbone to waive the threat of a shattering resignation? This book will offer some answers to that question.

When he became chief of the general staff in February 1931 and member of the supreme war council—the second in the French army after Weygand (on January 21, 1935), who in turn had replaced Pétain—Gamelin was still chief of staff and appeared to enjoy excellent prospects. He was born in Paris in 1872, the son and grandson of general officers of the army and attended Saint-Cyr at nineteen, graduating first in a class of 449. He was to have excellent grades and reports throughout his career. In 1889 he went to the École de Guerre and Lieutenant Colonel Lanrezac described him as:

> [s]uperior intelligence...a keen, clear, methodical and highly cultured mind; shows quick and good judgment... Has a strong, loyal, determined and fiery disposition. Strong personality. Very active having great stamina ... will be a first class officer. Must be encouraged.[51]

Gamelin was an avid reader and a disciple of Bergson; in 1906 he wrote an *Étude philosophique sur l'art de la guerre.** Once he became Joffre's aide-de-camp in 1906, Joffre didn't let him out of his sights and appointed Gamelin to join his own staff in 1914.

> Extremely jealous of his authority, he saw in Gamelin someone rather modest and self-effacing who possessed another rare gift: he could listen. He also became the confidant and close assistant of the victor of the Marne.[52]

Gamelin played a key role in the famous decision to resume the offensive on the Marne rather than on the Seine. By the end of the war he

---

* Philosophical study of the art of war. [NDT]

was among the most brilliant commanding generals in the French army. After the war he increased his awareness of the world beyond France during his missions to Brazil and the Near East. It looked as though he had everything going for him, including the support of his command-ing generals, Buat and later on Debeney, as well as that of top political leaders such as Herriot, Briand and finally Daladier. We should also add that he was extremely brave, which he proved once more in 1925-1926 during the "war of the Druses" in Syria.

But does the fact that a general who is intelligent, competent, brave, perfect at following orders, well informed as an advisor, simple and popu-lar as a person, necessarily ensure that he will also be a great commander in chief? The harsh law of history teaches us that to deserve such a title one needs, during the period leading up to combat, unbending resolve and strategic imagination. Gamelin was respectful of civilian control in the democratic sense. But shouldn't he have risen to voice his opposition on vitally important issues?

> Since he failed to understand this, Gamelin got stuck in a system
> where submissiveness no longer allowed initiatives that could rescue
> the situation. The philosopher in him overcame the man of action.[53]

* * * *

France, a country with an unstable political system, in the throes of an economic crisis it couldn't control, would manage to avoid being tempted by the efficiency of fascism. However, there exists a democratic version of efficiency, that of Lloyd George, Clemenceau, Roosevelt, and Churchill. The carnage of 1914-1918 deprived France of its moral elite, and she failed to find the men who could have altered her destiny. We shall therefore examine seven years of what appears to be a fateful mecha-nism at work. The historian may only attempt an explanation. The phi-losopher will often ask why so many opportunities were wasted. At times men struggle successfully for a purpose against the workings of deep and blind forces. But that wasn't meant to be part of France's destiny; its leaders proved to be weaker than fate itself.

Chapter I

THE RETURN OF EDOUARD HERRIOT

(June–December 1932)

Our story begins on June 3, 1932, when Edouard Herriot, president of the Radical and Radical Socialist Party, succeeded André Tardieu as prime minister. Tardieu, Clemenceau's former right-hand man, had been disowned by the "Tigre," because he had accepted a ministerial appointment to Poincaré's National Union cabinet in July 1926; he was viewed, wrongly no doubt, as the great hope of an uruly right wing. A short time before he took over, Herriot characterized him as being "irascible, passionate and aggressive."[1] His short time in office (he had only been in power since February 23) was more than eventful: Aristide Briand had died on March 7; Philippe Berthelot, secretary general of the Quay d'Orsay and a great friend of Herriot, was seriously ill; the elections of May 1 and 8 had returned a majority of the Cartel des Gauches; on May 7, Paul Doumer, President of the Republic, had been assassinated by a deranged White Russian named Gorguloff—his successor was Albert Lebrun, an engineer from the *École Polytechnique* and a longtime politician—and, most importantly abroad, Adolf Hitler had won 11.5 million votes, and then 13.5 million votes in the German presidential elections of March 13 and April 10 (with 36.7 percent), leading to the elections to the Reichstag where, on July 31, the Nazis would increase their seats from 107 to 230 (37.3 percent of the vote).

Even more threatening was the economic situation hanging over France like a black cloud, although France was probably suffering less than its neighbors in Germany, England, or the United States. Foreign capital, which had fled England after the 1931 devaluation, now flooded the French market where the Poincaré franc scrupulously maintained its parity (one-quarter and one-half of the gold franc). But those were floating funds. When the Cartel des Gauches came to power, the Stock Exchange immediately plunged at the beginning of May. What were foreign holders of French francs going to do? The budget presented by Tardieu reduced the deficit to 5 billion francs, which was still an enormous amount (out of a total budget of 41 billion).

The new Cartel des Gauches remained as orthodox as possible because the Socialists were refusing to take part in the government. Herriot wasn't sorry that they chose to do so. In his opinion, if the Socialists had been in the government, it would certainly have encouraged the flight of capital. Germain-Martin, a "classical" economist if ever there was one, became finance minister, returning to a post he had previously held. Since May 1932, there was a slight decrease in unemployment, and a slow increase in industrial production although it still reached only 90% of its September 1931 level. Alfred Sauvy correctly points out: "The economic recovery in France owes nothing to the changed political majority since it hadn't enacted a single important economic decision." And since there was no national accounting system, neither the government nor the newspapers knew that a recovery was underway.[2]

When he came to power, Herriot was very much aware of the three biggest problems France was facing and called them "so urgent, so threatening that good judgment forces us to apply all of our attention to solving them: first, the budget...then, abroad, Lausanne and Geneva."[3]

Regarding the budget, it must first be balanced once again. This matter would normally be outside the scope of the present study if one of the devices used, with the agreement of the minister of defense, Paul-Boncour, hadn't been a reduction in the defense budget. Weygand, who at the time filled the highest post in the Army, bitterly complained about this.[4]

In effect, defense spending did decrease in 1931–32. The decrease mainly affected armaments, which were broadly slashed between 1932 and 1934.[5] But Weygand also wrote that, in June 1932, he had to accept a one-twelfth reduction in the number of conscripts. This form of "spontaneous" disarmament came at the wrong time since what was being discussed at the international level by France's partners were reductions from the current level and not from previous levels of armaments.

Lausanne referred to the forthcoming international conference on German reparations. That conference held many pitfalls for France. The "Hoover moratorium" on debts between countries had suspended reparations payments for one year, ending on June 30, 1932. As early as January of that year, German Chancellor Heinrich Brüning had peremptorily announced that Germany would refuse to resume its payments. Both the United States and Britain supported him. France would certainly be isolated.

Geneva meant the disarmament conference, which had opened in February. There too, between an ultra-nationalist Germany intent on rearmament and the Anglo-Americans hostile to what they called French "militarism," France was not in a strong position.

Edouard Herriot, as he had done in 1924, decided to be his own foreign minister. He was quite a character—his jovial disposition, pipe and paunch and crumpled appearance made him instantly recognizable, yet he possessed the most refined and wide-ranging literary culture. His love for the city of Lyon, where he was mayor and his amazing ability to manipulate the Radical Socialists were well known. Was he the right man for the circumstances? Looking back, two contradictory images of Herriot emerge: on the one hand, he was an innovator[6] who truly wanted—cautiously—to bring France and Germany closer together and tried to develop France's relations with the USSR; on the other hand, he made crucial concessions several times: first when he abandoned the Ruhr in 1924, then when he gave up on reparations in 1932 and, finally, when he endorsed the principle of "equal rights" for Germany to rearm.

In *Jadis*, the book Herriot wrote after the Second World War, he discusses his government of 1932 on seventy pages, fifty-three of them dealing with foreign policy.[7] They are a strange mixture of minutiae (probably because at that time Herriot had many documents at his disposal) and "detachment." Those pages resemble a card file that Herriot reproduces, often without any attempt at a conclusion, as though the main objective were to build the author's image. When he recounts the fall of his cabinet on December 12, 1932, over the issue of payment of war debts to America, he says, "I felt no emotion. I still think today that the fall of the government brought about by my insisting on preserving the French signature was one of the finest moments of my entire public life."[8]

He preferred posturing to getting things done. François de Wendel, a powerful businessman and right-wing member of Parliament who hated Herriot, said " Very emotional, half sincere and half cunning" he created "the impression of a man without a plan, just drifting along."[9] At the opposite end of the political spectrum, Paul Faure, a socialist, thought the radicals were "mere politicos, willing to accept every compromise, every retreat."[10] And Herriot took this as a personal insult. Pierre-Olivier Lapie, who liked Herriot, but viewed him with an uncompromising eye, had some entertaining things to say about him in a chapter entitled "Preserving Glory,"[11] concerning his penchant for the grand gesture, his "honest man's vanity," an "endearing…vanity." Edouard Herriot, he wrote, is "so convinced of the correctness of his actions, he is so certain that his system is entirely justified that it becomes a defense against discouragement. Any course of action, because he has undertaken it guided by his intelligence, his careful consideration, his method and his heart, must be correct and if events go against it, then the events were wrong." Our final witness, Jules Jeanneney, who was to become president of the Senate, did not hesitate in September 1939 to attack Herriot, who at the time was president of the Chamber, as follows: "The vast illusions you have entertained towards Germany and the concessions you have made to her are enormous. This is precisely what we must now repair."[12]

1.

FRANCE AND THE END OF REPARATIONS

Our purpose here is not to examine the overall issue, but only to describe France's actions. The Lausanne conference, which had been planned prior to Herriot taking office, was scheduled to begin on June 16, 1932. On the 11th, the British Prime Minister, Ramsay Macdonald, and the head of the Foreign Office, Sir John Simon, stopped in Paris on their way to Switzerland. For the British, it was all very clear: German reparations must be canceled entirely. Herriot wrote, "I told them that I was willing to go further than the Young Moratorium but I didn't want a cancellation; … we must not let Germany strengthen her power at our

expense nor must we let her upset the economic balance in her favor…
I showed that Germany could continue her payments."[13] Therefore, the
initial French position couldn't have been clearer. But Herriot report-
edly thought the meeting had been so "cordial," so "intimate," that he
made a first concession—Germany would not be required to pay anything on July 1, on the condition that this non-payment be considered a
"suspension."

On June 13, Herriot arrived in Geneva. On the 15th, he was in
Lausanne for last minute preparations. On the 16th, the conference began. Along with the prime minister, the French delegation included
Germain-Martin, minister of finance, Julien Durand, minister of commerce, Joseph Paganon, undersecretary of state for foreign affairs and
Georges Bonnet, all of them Radicals. From the start, two factors weakened Herriot's resolve: Macdonald suggested that the discussions on war
debt (France was in debt both to England and the United States) and
those on reparations be linked. Then Herriot had a conversation with the
new German chancellor, von Papen, who appealed to his compassion by
invoking "the misery and disquiet of the German people."[14] As a result,
it was decided as early as June 17 that the reparation payments would be
suspended for the duration of the conference. Herriot was satisfied because he had a sentence inserted stipulating that the solution to the problem would be sought "within the framework of a universal settlement."

On the same day, speaking after von Papen who complained about
Germany's fate, and Neville Chamberlain who wanted a "clean slate" for
everyone, Herriot lined up the figures prepared by his team of experts,
showing that France stood to lose more than her partners would from a
suspension of payments. Sir John Simon sent a note over to him: "You
will allow me to congratulate you for putting things in such a reasonable light." Actually, Herriot had opened a new breach. He had declared
that he saw a link between improving security and restoring the world
economy. Back in Paris on Saturday, June 18, Herriot's actions received
approval of the government and of Joseph Caillaux, president of the
senate committee on finance. The "net annual balance" of reparations
was calculated (meaning the difference between the amount of reparations taken in by a country and the amount of war debt it had to pay): the
balance in Reichsmarks for France was 359.5 million, for Great Britain
66.9 million and for Italy 35.7 million. France clearly stood to lose the
most. As for Germany, as soon as the crisis ended, it would find itself in
a dominant position.

Back in Geneva on Monday, June 20th, Herriot continued the discussion with the British who were mostly worried about German recovery, for economic reasons. He thought he had the backing of several British experts, including the economist John Maynard Keynes; of Arthur Slater, director of the financial section of the League of Nations; and of the Americans, especially Senator William Borah, chairman of the senate foreign relations committee.

But the erosion of the French position took place between the 21st and the 28th. Herriot came to thinking that canceling reparations was possible on two conditions: first if America agreed to ending its war debt; and second, that Germany would pay the balance. After Herriot returned to France, Germain-Martin, Georges Bonnet and Laboulaye, a diplomat we shall discuss below, conducted the negotiations. The Germans proposed linking reparations and security; there would be military staff agreements based on "equal rights" that would serve to compensate France for its financial sacrifices. But Herriot refused "equal rights" as energetically as he refused the pure and simple cancellation of reparations. We shall see later on what happened to that vigorous attitude. As far as reparations were concerned, in any case, the range of possibilities was narrowing. The debate only concerned the final German payment. Germany offered to pay 2 billion gold marks. Herriot demanded 4 billion. Macdonald offered to mediate. Herriot agreed to come down to 3 billion. Von Papen accepted with "a heavy heart." So, by July 8, reparations had been canceled, except for a balance that Germany, in the end, would not pay.[15]

Furthermore, Herriot had made this conditional upon the cancellation of France's war debt to the United States. But the Americans seemed extremely unlikely to accept.[16] Again, an equivocation was to allow giving in on this essential question. This was the so-called "gentlemen's agreement" of July 8, a document that does not appear in the final draft of the Lausanne Conference (drawn up on July 2 and signed on the 9th). Adopted by France, Belgium, Italy and Great Britain, this unofficial agreement stipulated that "as concerns the creditor governments [creditors of reparations]…the ratification [of the Lausanne accords] would not be effected until a satisfactory solution had been found as concerned these countries and their own creditors." This meant that the cancellation of reparation payments would be ratified when and only when the United States had agreed to cancel their war debts. If that were impossible, then "the agreement with Germany will not be ratified."[17] This amounted to sheer obfuscation, even outright lying, for everyone knew that the situation was such that Germany would no longer make any payments no matter what the American attitude was. Consequently, this "gentlemen's agreement" was nothing but a screen behind which Herriot could modestly hide the broad withdrawal he had accepted from his initial position.

It is possible to see this withdrawal as inevitable in the face of pressing economic necessity. One had to be realistic. The United States would be faulted for not seeing how the turmoil caused by the world crisis made their position as pitiless creditors to insolvent debtors futile; but this criticism applies to France as well where Germany was concerned. In this sense, Herriot was right. But why begin with a completely opposite position? And, most of all, why not "trade" on the important concession granted to Germany? As we shall see, Herriot would proceed in that direction, but he would be completely unsuccessful.

England, for its part, offered France a very strange type of compensation, the "trust agreement." On July 13, the French cabinet unanimously approved, without reservations, two texts submitted by the British ambassador, Lord Tyrrell. In a memorandum dated July 12, England proposed to establish "a better system of European relations." "We should very frankly exchange views and information with one another regarding all issues that could arise of a nature similar to that which has just been so happily resolved at Lausanne and that could touch upon the European state of affairs." Such a pact was to be public and other nations would be asked to join it.[18]

Countries promising to consult each other regarding their problems is often idle talk. But Herriot was even more delighted because Macdonald, who was traveling in the French prime minister's special train carriage, had expressed "a great pleasure to work with you again." There were, of course, some "bad guys" in both countries: Churchill and Lloyd George in Great Britain, the "Blumites" in Paris. But both heads of government were kindred sprits.

The emptiness of such an agreement became clear very soon. Herriot wrote to Macdonald[19] that their "friendship was like that of two older brothers wanting to help the junior members of the family."[20] But the younger brothers were worried. The trust agreement seemed so futile that the third party countries were convinced it was hiding something more sinister. Colonel Beck of Poland thought so,[21] as did the Germans who felt, quite wrongly, that they could detect in it a secret renewal of the Entente Cordiale, one of their bad memories.[22] Germany agreed to subscribe to the agreement but wanted it restricted to the great powers, there-fore excluding Poland and Czechoslovakia, for instance.[23] Herriot wished on the contrary to extend it to all of Europe.[24] Still, Germany adhered to it on July 25.[25] The Americans feared that it would lead to a European conspiracy against the repayment of war debts.[26]

The trust agreement, interpreted narrowly, meant that the English and the French would consult each other on every matter before any negotiation. Almost immediately, the British refused to do so, particularly regarding their debts to the United States. By October and November 1932, it was only being mentioned occasionally, and it became irrelevant. Having obtained what they wanted, namely the end of reparations, the British leaders did not worry much about consulting with France. They preferred—as they did in Lausanne—to make a decision unilaterally and then bring the French progressively to accept their own views. We shall see many examples of this in the future.

2.

HERRIOT, DISARMAMENT AND "EQUAL RIGHTS"

The year 1932 had seen the tentative beginnings of an unhappy disarmament conference that had opened in Geneva on February 2 and that, apart from the members of the League of Nations, included the United States and the USSR. The conference originated with the Treaty of Versailles requiring Germany to limit its troops to 100,000 men and its armaments to light weapons, and presented this unilateral disarma-ment as a prelude to general disarmament. The Americans and the Brit-ish whose power was mainly in the navy, had established a system of disarmament to their benefit in that area (at the Washington conference of 1921–1922, and the London conference of 1930). They were both favorable to a broad disarmament of the ground forces because it would affect them very little. *For the Anglo-Saxon countries disarmament was the way to ensure security.*

In 1932 France was said to have "the strongest army in the world." For that reason, the French were constantly accused of being "militaris-tic." Every single government was equally deaf to Anglo-American think-ing. For them, security had to come before disarmament and France, with its population of 40 million, could not face a Germany of 65 million unless she was disarmed—as prescribed in the treaty of Versailles—but also prevented from rearming by a system of automatic sanctions. Herriot had been the main champion of the "Geneva protocol" of 1924, that would have made arbitration mandatory and which the British and Americans had rejected. Refusal of arbitration would be the criteria for aggression. In that event, all members of the League of Nations would automatically apply military sanctions, in other words make war on the aggressor. The pact of the League of Nations made sanctions conditional to the unanimous approval of the Council, which was unrealistic. This had happened very recently. In September 1931, when the Japanese attacked China to take over Manchuria, the Council refrained from issuing any sanctions, and the world looked on powerlessly throughout 1932, as the Japanese invasion went ahead.

Herriot's 1924 formula, "Arbitration, security, disarmament," remained the table of the law for him, his predecessors and successors. In other words, France would never agree to disarm *before* its security was guaranteed, either through a new Geneva protocol, or by means of a vast regional network of alliances. "Beginning in 1924, French diplomacy reiterated unfailingly and on every occasion the link between security, disarmament and mutual assistance."[27]

Faced with the French position,[28] Germany was rearming, and France knew it. In 1927, Briand, in a badly conceived grandiose gesture, abandoned the principle of military control. The Germans were taking advantage of this as best they could. The Army Chief of Staff's *Deuxième Bureau* (military intelligence) was providing a lot of information on the subject. The German military's obvious intention, and particularly that of General von Schleicher who had the greatest influence (he was to become chancellor on December 2, 1932), was to transform the Reichswehr from its Treaty of Versailles numbers to a force of 21 divisions. This was what Germans called the *Umbau*.[29]

Germany's clandestine, but well established rearmament, posed a terrible problem for France. She was faced not only with Germany systematically widening the breach, but also with the two powerful Anglo-Saxon countries that basically were encouraging her to disarm. In effect, the disarmament conference turned into a debate between France, wanting to keep its margin of security, and Germany, seeking to be granted "equal rights" for armament issues (*Gleichberechtigung*) as a prelude to actual equality. There were a few rare Germans who probably would have preferred to see France partially disarm rather than have Germany rearm but none in military circles, and the rise of national socialism didn't favor them. Shouldn't France have accepted "general disarmament" in order to help those Germans who were thinking along those lines?

Before the period covered by this study, there had been the "Tardieu Plan," the first French initiative in Geneva, introduced on February 5, 1932. It didn't get much discussion. It proposed that an international force be created, composed of national contingents from each country, through regional agreements for mutual assistance, within the League of Nations framework. This force would have use of bombers, heavy artillery, and some warships that would then no longer be at the disposal of national armies.

The Tardieu Plan was practically forgotten by the time Herriot came to power. Immediately, the new German chancellor, von Papen, began a sort campaign to charm Herriot. In mid-June, in Lausanne, the chancellor offered to work out all outstanding questions in a wide-ranging Franco-German negotiation.[30] He was proposing—as we have mentioned—that reparations be canceled and that, in exchange, France and Germany enter a customs union and cooperate regarding trade with Eastern Europe, where Germany was making alarming inroads. Concerning armaments, he was asking—like all the German participants in the Geneva conference—for the famous equal rights. But, in order to "satisfy the French need for security," he also proposed a military entente and contacts between military staffs. The secretary of state for foreign affairs, von Bülow, met several times in Lausanne with André de Laboulaye, the deputy director for political affairs.

These meetings took place between June 16 and July 7.[31] When, on June 18, Bülow invited Laboulaye to lunch in a restaurant in Vevey, he suggested that the four great European powers (excluding the USSR) act in concert "whenever an incident occurred that could endanger peace in Europe." This was a prefiguration of the Four Power Pact of 1933, which we shall examine in the following chapter. Laboulaye voiced an immediate objection: what would happen to the medium and small countries allied with France, and particularly Poland? Bülow felt that the "international contingent" of the Tardieu plan was unrealistic. According to him, commercial and military relations between Germany and Russia were good, but he pretended to fear bolshevism. He added that he had met with some of Hitler's emissaries and that they were beginning to favor a rapprochement with France.[32]

Although he favored Franco-German reconciliation, Herriot was suspicious. The anti-Soviet declarations that von Papen and von Bülow were making clashed with his own plan for a rapprochement with the USSR. The British, on July 5, declared they were opposed to these Franco-German special relations and offered in exchange the "Trust Agreement" mentioned above. On July 7, Herriot, together with Paul-Boncour and Laboulaye, met with von Papen and von Bülow. He firmly rejected the German proposal.[33] He refused to mix financial and military issues, "Lausanne and Geneva."

It therefore became necessary to return to a solution for disarmament that would satisfy French demands for security. When France clearly turned down the proposal for bilateral Franco-German negotiations, on September 11,[34] Germany reacted swiftly. On the 14th she declared she would not return to the disarmament conference table until the principle of "equal rights" had been established in her favor. At the same time, Herriot, who hadn't much liked the American plan for disarmament (the Hoover Plan of June 22 proposing the elimination of one-third or one-quarter of existing armaments), asked Paul-Boncour, the minister of war and the highest ranking French representative in Geneva, to prepare a draft.[35]

This plan, dated October 14,[36] was adopted by the French government on October 28 and submitted to the Geneva conference on November 14. It was called the "French constructive plan." This highly technical project stressed the fact that "in matters of disarmament and security, progress must be parallel." The *political* stipulations were aimed at ensuring quasi-automatic assistance in the case of aggression, a kind of "common action." The *military* provisions aimed at bringing the land forces of European states back to "a *general standard type—that of a national short term service army with limited forces*—unable to carry out a sudden offensive."

These national armies would not be allowed heavy weapons. But the partner nations would maintain *specialized units* equipped with powerful arms, which would be at the disposal of the League of Nations. All other heavy weaponry would be stored under international control. Apart from military sanctions, they could be used in cases of "legitimate self-defense." Weapons manufacturing would be "controlled and organized internationally." Furthermore, at least once a year, an *international inspection* would make sure that all parties to the agreement were correctly fulfilling their obligations.

The October 14 plan was submitted to the top French military authorities. The army and the navy provided highly critical comments. The main discussion took place on October 22, 1932,[37] attended by Herriot and six government ministers. Also present were Marshal Pétain, who at the time was inspector for the air defense of the territory; General Weygand, Vice-President of the *Conseil supérieur de la guerre* [Supreme War Council], and his second in command, General Gamelin, army chief of staff, together with their colleagues of the navy, Admiral Durand-Viel, the air force, and General Hergault, for the colonies. They were assisted by a diplomat, René Massigli, head of the French delegation to the League of Nations and other high-ranking officials, together with some officers acting as secretaries, among them Major de Gaulle.[38] There were to be other meetings on October 24, in the morning and in the afternoon.[39] In a final, even more formal meeting, on October 28, the Supreme Military Committee, chaired by Albert Lebrun himself, signed on to the "French constructive plan," over General Weygand's formal disapproval.[40]

These debates are quite touching and one would like to quote from them at length. On one side stood Herriot and Paul-Boncour, left-wing patriots seduced by the idea of collective security and disarmament, who saw in this plan a grand gesture from France that would force its partners' admiration and allow France and Germany to find reconciliation. On the other, the military—and particularly Weygand and Pétain—were clinging to the only tangible reality: the margin of superiority between the French forces and the Germans. Herriot and Weygand, wrote Bariéty,[41] "were both aware of what the Reichswehr was preparing; they were both equally obsessed by the threat of a war of revenge, but differed completely on the ways to prevent it." Pétain, like Weygand, based his views on "Germany's well-known bad faith." France, he argued, had already made deep cuts in its forces by reducing military service to one year. "The new guarantees we are being offered are nothing but pacts and promises. To assume that...these promises will be fulfilled...to agree to reduce France's military strength without any real compensation, means seriously jeopardizing French security and opening the possibility that the country will be thrust into war under the worst military and diplomatic conditions." Herriot stated, "The defense of a country wasn't only the matter of its soldiers and its cannons, but also the excellence of its legal position." To which Weygand replied, "A demonstration of one's legal case does not necessarily mean weakness... I would like the Council to understand how I feel. I am responsible for defending the border with troops and not with words." Paul-Boncour commented, "Lack of imagination."[42]

France was a democratic country where civilians had control over the military. The plan was therefore adopted on October 28 and published on November 14.

Disappointment and failure immediately followed. The plan, which Herriot and Boncour wanted to be striking and grandiose, was to play a very minor role in the debates during the conference. It was discussed in February 1933, long after Herriot had been forced out of power. What the British were interested in was Germany's return to the conference table, which the Germans had made conditional to the "equal rights" that Herriot rightly felt were so dangerous. Whatever the risks, the British fully supported the German position.

The period between November 15 and December 10 is the story of the crumbling of the French position. First, the German reaction to the "French constructive plan" was "clearly unfavorable."[43] Then, British delegate Sir John Simon and Arthur Henderson, the British chairman of the Geneva conference, insisted in their speeches on "equal rights" and implied that the French proposal accepted it in principle.[44] The American delegate Norman Davis, who was known to be a Francophile, said he was "shocked by how complicated the plan was."[45] Massigli, the French delegate, remarked that "The British government seems to want to persist ever more…in assuming the role of arbiter between Germany and France."[46] Strange arbiter indeed, since the British were entirely favorable to the German position!

And so Herriot floundered. On November 23 he agreed to a five-partner discussion in which Germany would participate, since Great Britain and the United States had begged him to accept.[47]

Circumvented by the clever Macdonald, who assured him that France would not be isolated, he arrived in Geneva on December 3, 1932. In the debates he intended to link his constructive plan to the principle of equal rights.[48] On the 3rd, together with Paul-Boncour, he met Macdonald and Sir John Simon in the Hotel des Bergues, headquarters of the French delegation to the League of Nations.[49] That meeting would turn out to be his "last stand." On December 6, the first five-power meeting took place in the Hotel Beau Rivage, the residence of the British delegation, known for its "painted ceilings depicting birds against a blue sky, in the style of the 1880s, when the Empress of Austria whiled away her solitude in travel."[50] Herriot summed up the French position as follows: "France agrees that the purpose of the conference is to grant Germany and the other countries that have been disarmed, according to the treaties, equal rights within a framework that would guarantee security for all nations as well as for itself."[51] Since the German response, on December 8, seemed fairly acceptable—at least to those who believed in abstractions—the agreement was signed on December 10 at 2:30 p.m. Germany obtained the *Gleichberechtigung* in exchange for two trifles; it was prepared to accept (later) conditions that included "security"; it would (immediately) return to the disarmament conference.

The Germans had won straight down the line. The British thought they had won. France had lost and Herriot didn't realize it. "Equal rights" was the lever that enabled the German army, in the space of five years, to outclass the French; it was to plunge France into the abyss and visit suffering and decline upon England.

3.

HERRIOT'S POSITIVE CONTRIBUTION: THE FRANCO-SOVIET AGREEMENT

After examining how Herriot "let go" on the issue of reparations and "equal rights," and how he obtained nothing but words in exchange, we still shouldn't be unfair to him. His initiative did yield positive results in the rapprochement with the USSR. As for the rest, the strength of the wave of public sentiment he represented must be taken into account. Herriot was in a sense the victim of both his followers and his opponents.

Among his adversaries, the communists, who were at the time using the tactic called "class against class," opposed the League of Nations as a creation of the treaties of 1919, themselves the result of the "imperialist war." The disarmament conference was therefore only a farce, while at the same time "war was raging in China."[52] Once again the purpose was, to encircle the USSR. And yet the USSR was present in Geneva. Maxim Litvinov, the People's Commissar for Foreign Affairs, went so far as to propose universal and total disarmament (though without any provisions for control). According to the daily *L'Humanité*, the Tardieu Plan, in creating an "international force," was attempting to launch "an international White Army."[53] The "French constructive plan" elicited similar criticism.[54]

The Communists, it must be said, were going through a weak period. They had obtained only 796,000 votes in the elections of 1932 out of a total of 9,579,000 votes cast (8.3 percent). They were violently fighting the Socialists of the SFIO, just like their comrades of the KPD did battle with the German Social Democrats. They were isolated and did not belong to the Cartel.

The socialist movement was much stronger and garnered 1,964,000 votes in the elections (20.5 percent). Although the SFIO was part of the Cartel des Gauches in the elections and supported the government in principle, in fact they did not agree with Herriot on the issue of France's security. Although they were divided into many factions, they can all be described as pacifists. For them—as for the British—disarmament should not "follow" security, but was conditional to it. They agreed to the "international force" of Tardieu's plan but wanted to abolish national armies. Some wanted an immediate abolition to set an example, which was "unilateral disarmament." Party leader Léon Blum did not go as far, but he did demand rapid progressive disarmament and exerted relentless daily pressure on Herriot's cabinet. The old "right wing" of the SFIO, which supported national defense above all, had left the party. The most striking example was that of Joseph Paul-Boncour. At the congress of Tours in 1931, the party, in spite of his efforts, had maintained and strengthened its traditional position, which was a blanket rejection of military funding. Was that the reason why Paul-Boncour resigned? Perhaps as was the case for Aristide Briand in 1905–1906, his ambition to be a cabinet minister or even become prime minister could have played a part. In any case, Herriot offered him the ministry of war, and Paul-Boncour was to succeed him—for just five weeks—at the head of government from December 1932 to January 1933. None of this would have been possible had Paul-Boncour been a member of the SFIO.

The Radical Socialist wing (with 1,836,000 votes, or 19.1 percent), together with various radical and independent socialists (with 1,093,000 votes or 11.4 percent), basically supported the government. However, Edouard Herriot had adversaries inside his party and Edouard Daladier, a deputy from the Vaucluse, was their leader.

Then there was the Right, totaling 3,880,000 votes, or 40 percent of the total (as opposed to 4,098,000 for the Cartel and 796,000 for the Communists). The Right had 259 seats in the new chamber of deputies (it had previously held 334). The Cartel had 348—of which 129 belonged to the SFIO. The Communists had 12 deputies.[55] The Right was generally opposed to disarmament, suspicious of Germany, had little faith in the League of Nations, and looked upon the "failed disarmament conference" with hostility and contempt: "In five and a half months of more or less fruitless discussions, everyone's uppermost feeling is that we should end this as soon as possible."[56] Although it accepted the Tardieu Plan with reservations, since Tardieu was on the right, the majority of the centrist press shot down the "French constructive plan."[57] It was, wrote Léon Daudet in *L'Action Française*, a "memorandum of disorder and illusion."[58]

In order to have a majority in Parliament and therefore survive, Herriot had to tread a narrow path between the Socialists demanding some gesture toward disarmament as a show of good will, and to set a good example, and the right, opposed to any form of disarmament, even a controlled disarmament. It is true that the right was not unanimous. The French ambassador to Berlin, François-Poncet, who had worked for the Comité des Forges and held posts in moderate governments, was not opposed to some form of concessions for "equal rights" and partial German rearmament.[59] That position had the backing of a major right-wing daily, *Le Matin*.[60]

During an October 28, 1932 foreign policy debate in the Chamber, Herriot was very clever in presenting his "constructive plan." The socialists, led by Léon Blum, supported the plan, as did a large segment of the right. The vote of confidence passed by a majority of 430 to 20 (among those voting against were the radical Franklin-Bouillon and the moderate Louis Marin).[61] Léon Blum's phrase was remarkable for the niceties of its formulation: "We don't accept that Germany's justified claim for equal rights should serve to justify that country's rearmament."

This situation explains why Herriot felt he had to seek firmer ground on which to establish his foreign policy. He found it in his negotiations with the USSR. Although he strongly opposed the French Communists, Herriot was fascinated by the Soviet experience. He traveled to Russia in the fall of 1922 and negotiated and shepherded France's recognition of the USSR in October 1924. He was now interested in actively pursuing the negotiations, which Briand had initiated but actually engaged in only half-heartedly.[62]

The initiative had come from the Soviets in September 1927. Ambassador Rakovski, who was about to leave his post, had offered Briand to negotiate a Franco-Soviet nonaggression pact. This was a normal gesture. At that time, the USSR, thinking that it was being encircled, was seeking many such pacts, with Turkey, with Germany—the famous Treaty of Berlin of April 24, 1926—with the Baltic States and more. The new ambassador, Dovgalevsky, began negotiations but they dragged on because Briand wanted to make the pact conditional to an agreement on the reimbursement of tsarist debts.

An event related to the economy gave the negotiations a new start in October 1930. The French government issued a decree restricting Soviet imports, because the USSR was accused of dumping its products. Since the only consequence of this decree was to favor German exports, French exporters complained. They had the "Franco-Russian Parliamentary Group" that had just been set up by Bergery, a radical, and Anatole de Monzie, an independent socialist, lobby Pierre Laval, who was then prime minister. The French ambassador in Moscow was instructed to meet with Litvinov and found that the Soviets were prepared to negotiate not just on commercial matters but also on eventual nonaggression pacts with France and its ally Poland.

The timing was rather good. Fear of Germany was on the rise since the Reichstag elections of September 1930, while Soviet Russia's image in France was improving. The success of the first Five Year Plan seemed impressive. Herbette, who had become rabidly anti-Soviet, left his post in Moscow in March 1931. A commercial agreement putting an end to the customs war was signed on May 1, 1931. Count François Dejean, appointed to Moscow in November, wanted to further a rapprochement. Finally, since the USSR was taking part in the preliminary work of the disarmament conference, Briand met with Litvinov in Geneva on May 21, 1931.

The negotiations resumed once again, mostly in Paris, between the secretary general of the Quai d'Orsay, Philippe Berthelot and Ambassador Dovgalevsky. A nonaggression treaty was initialed. But then the *New York Herald* of August 19, 1931, leaked information revealing the existence of the negotiations. The right-wing press reacted vehemently: "Poland," a trusted ally, "was being abandoned" (even though Weygand, Briand, and Laval did not trust Poland that much). The Germans, who enjoyed good relations with the Soviets since the Rapallo accords of April 1922, also became alarmed.

Laval, an expert schemer, hesitated between a nonaggression pact with the USSR or with Germany. Once more, everything stopped and the Tardieu government took no action to reopen the talks. Tardieu was tempted by the prospect of an economic alliance along the Danube, which aroused the USSR's suspicion. At the disarmament conference, Tardieu quarreled with Litvinov. Finally, part of the French right took a pro-Japanese position on the Manchuria issue whereas the USSR supported China in vain.

Herriot's return to power revived the negotiations once again. This time though, they would reach a conclusion. As Dejean wrote, "Since Soviet Russia is as big as a continent with a population of 170 million, it would, in my opinion, be much more of a threat if it remains isolated than if it enters international politics. Isolated it will keep to the principles underlying its constitution, meaning communism, in their purest form. If it enters into relationships with the bourgeois powers, it will eventually be forced to change and to subscribe to their methods in economic and political matters."[63] Dejean also insisted on the interest the Soviets demonstrated in the pact project.[64]

At the same time, of course, von Papen and von Bülow were offering France a Franco-German rapprochement. There was also a strange move made in Geneva on July 7 by Colonel Kobayashi, head of the Japanese military delegation, who approached René Massigli. The colonel, speaking for his superior, General Matsui, and in the name of "some military circles in Japan," was very straightforward. He offered a "close rapprochement with France" which, he said, "would give France precious military guarantees against Russia" and "would keep Indochina safe from communism." Massigli immediately responded that "whatever the ties of friendship between France and Japan may be, France could not offend other great powers," and that, since it had underwritten the covenant of the League of Nations, "it could not enter into any contracts which might be in contradiction with the principles of that pact"[65]—thereby alluding to the Japanese aggression in Manchuria. Léger, the head of political affairs at the Quai d'Orsay, reacted by saying, "Not acceptable; avoid any answer." Such was also the fate of a proposal made by General Koïso, Vice-Minister for War, who asked French Ambassador Count D. de Martel for financial aid for the development...of Manchuria![66]

The French government was therefore approached both by Germany and Japan but preferred a rapprochement with the USSR. Still, it was necessary to reassure Poland and Romania, Russia's two neighbors and France's allies—a long-standing problem that we shall follow up to 1939. In fact, on July 25, Poland, following France's strong recommendation, signed one of these "non-intervention pacts" with the USSR that the Soviets were accumulating. The difficulties with Romania were greater and finally Herriot decided to go ahead anyway.[67]

Herriot had been briefed at the end of July about the state of the Franco-Soviet talks.[68] Although commercial negotiations were virtually stopped because of the credit requirements of the USSR, the nonaggression pact was almost ready. The problem was that the good relations between the Reichswehr and the Red Army since the beginning of the 1920s were fairly well known in France.[69] Herriot decided to forge ahead regardless. He offered no explanation in his memoirs, *Jadis*.[70] On the other hand, at the Radical Party Congress that took place in Toulouse from November 3 to 6, he mentioned that it would be signed very shortly. He presented the future pact as one of the elements of his policy for peace, of which the "constructive plan" was the crowning element at the time. For the ministry of foreign affairs, the real goal was to ensure the USSR's neutrality between France and Germany. "That's the most one can expect from it. . . The Franco-Soviet treaty can only help dispel the German illusion that a revision of the Treaty of Versailles might be possible with Moscow's assistance."[71] This represented a very accurate view of an extremely important phenomenon taking place at the time. Having been excluded from the treaties of 1919, the Soviet Union viewed them as abhorrent. As Germany had done, it requested their *revision*. This revisionist camp, which occasionally included Italy, weighed heavily on European diplomacy. Now, though, the USSR was distancing itself more and more from the revisionists, perhaps because of the rise of National Socialism. This had become Stalin's new policy and Litvinov was its spokesman. It would be fully laid out in *Pravda* on May 10, 1933, in an article written by Karl Radek. From now on, wrote Radek, the USSR would no longer ask for a revision of the frontiers because it "might lead to a new world war."

This was how the pact was viewed despite its somewhat insignificant main clauses when Herriot and Ambassador Valerian Dovgalevsky signed it on November 29.[72] Article 1 was a commitment to mutual nonaggression, individual or collective. Article 2 was a promise not to help or abet an aggressor against any of the two contracting parties. Article 5 was a commitment "to refrain from interfering in any way" in the internal affairs of the other country (this was aimed at the PCF, the French Communist Party, but had no effect since the Soviet government pretended that all relations within international communism were the responsibility of the Komintern). Any conflict between the two countries would be settled by peaceful means (Art. 6).

Germany's "very strong reaction," according to Ambassador François-Poncet, confirmed that this agreement could be a prelude to closer ties.[73]

4.

The Debts, the United States, and the Fall of Herriot

Herriot was going to fall "in a big way" on December 12, 1932, by a margin of 402 votes to 196. On October 28, he had received 430 votes against 20. These numbers are a good illustration of the "life expectancy" of French governments.

The problem concerned the debts incurred by the French state from April 1917 to 1919 to the United States that had been "consolidated" after much effort by the Mellon-Bérenger agreement in April 1926, which the French Parliament had belatedly ratified in July 1929. France was to make annual payments until…1988! The French government never obtained from the United States what it called the "guarantee clause," that is, a formal link between the payment of German reparations to France and the annual payments France was to make to the United States. At the most, the 1929 Young Plan had set the same very realistic, 1988 date for the end of reparations and for the repayment of war debts. The matter generated intense commentary and created an awful climate between the French and the Americans. "We paid with our blood—1,396,000 dead on the French side and less than 50,000 Americans during the First World War. You are Shylocks," wrote the French. To which the Americans responded, "A commercial debt is a sacred debt and international morality demands that you pay it back."

What French public opinion found most irritating was actually less the American demand for repayment than its constant support of the poor Germans to be freed from the intolerable burden of reparations. Furthermore, the United States in 1930 had instituted a tremendous customs tariff, called the "Hawley-Smoot Tariff," of an average 59 percent duty on imports, which exporters found intolerable. How could one pay anything back if it wasn't possible to export massively into the creditor country since it was the only way to secure currency? And then the world economic crisis erupted.[74]

Naturally, the Germans blamed the French—who were just as protectionist—for doing exactly the same thing. "We cannot pay reparations." But what made all the difference was the psychological argument. After all, the Germans were the enemy whereas the French, the British and the Americans were brothers in arms. And now the Americans were taking Germany's side on the reparations issue, refusing to make even the smallest concession to the French on the war debt!

Forced to give up on reparations, apart from the illusory final payment at the Lausanne conference, Herriot had first made it conditional to canceling the war debts. He had fallen back on the "gentlemen's agreement" discussed previously, but the United States considered the "gentlemen's agreement" as null and void. Emmanuel Mönick, the financial attaché in Washington, became aware of this very quickly. On August 16, he met with Ogden Mills, President Hoover's Treasury Secretary. The Secretary expressed his satisfaction that the reparations had ended. "In his opinion, international commerce can only benefit from this... As for the debt problem, he took up the subject himself and told me very openly that he did not see any possibility for discussion before the American elections of November 8." The debts had become an election issue in a country mired in depression.

The next installment was due on December 15. What could be done? First, establish a common front with the British. But Great Britain, despite the "gentlemen's agreement," and the "trust agreement" notwithstanding, intended to go it alone. Sir Frederick Leith-Ross, a treasury expert, told the French financial attaché, Jacques Rueff, and the assistant manager of commercial relations of the Quai d'Orsay, "the negotiations to be entered were to remain on a strictly individual basis. The British government would keep us confidentially informed, regarding the first steps it would take right after the November 8 elections." This clearly showed the only reason for these fake agreements, which was to draw Herriot into the trap of concessions that Britain wanted made.[75] The British method, all the way up to and including 1939, would remain unchanged—to not consult with France in advance, but to make a unilateral decision and then to communicate it to the French. There would be many examples of this, some of them rather dramatic.

On November 10, Herriot asked his ambassador to Washington, the poet Paul Claudel—who was also a staunch "Briandist"—to deliver a note to the American government suggesting "a reappraisal of the debt question" preceded by an extension of the moratorium. France surely deserved as much. "The readiness showed in Lausanne…was clear proof that it is actively interested in Europe's prompt economic recovery."[76]

According to Claudel, this proposal had little chance of success. Certainly, the Eastern newspapers would favor a revision. But Congress "is unanimously opposed to the moratorium." "Some degree of leniency is being shown to England but as to France many politicians indicate that it doesn't deserve any." In any case, the newly elected president, Franklin D. Roosevelt, who was only to take office in March 1933, didn't seem very much inclined to show any generosity in the matter.[77] On November 23, the American government answered the French diplomatic note of November 10 with the utmost clarity. No moratorium or suspension of payments could be granted by the December 15 deadline. An opening was hinted at: "If the payment is made, the chances for a positive review of the entire matter would be, in my opinion, greatly enhanced."[78]

This last sentence may have appeared critical to Herriot. The banker Jean Monnet, although less well known in those days than he was to be later on, was already very friendly with an amazing number of influential American and British officials and businessmen. He advised Jacques Rueff, the financial attaché in London, to meet the deadline of December 15. "Default by France would make any collaboration between our two countries impossible for thirty years at least!"[79]

While contacts in Washington and in London were repeatedly being made—to no avail—and the legal advisors of the Quai d'Orsay issued more advice, Edouard Herriot decided on a course of action. France would meet its financial obligations—19.26 million US dollars, roughly 481 million francs, the equivalent of one twenty-fourth of the French budget—due on December 15. Public opinion was in an uproar. Everyone opposed the payment. The press, as well as the foreign affairs committee, and finance committees in Parliament and the Senate were either dubious or hostile.

The issue was debated from December 12 to 14. On the 14th, Herriot knew that Great Britain would make its payment. He delivered a moving speech on the 12th. "These commitments which France has taken were approved by the elected representatives of the French people. We must honor the law and honor our contracts…the honor of France lies in its defense of the eternal laws of political morality. I will not allow France's signature to be invalidated."[80] This flight of oratory was met with much applause on the left. But once the great principles were set aside, it was the money that mattered. On December 14, under the attacks of the right (with Louis Marin) and the socialists (with Vincent Auriol), "in a climate of feverish lassitude,"[81] Herriot fell. "You are going to isolate France. You are going to shatter our solidarity with England. You gentlemen, for 480 million, are going to destroy all that! At a time when dictatorial regimes are spreading in every direction... would you be willing to break up the alliance of liberty against dictatorship, for 480 million francs?"

The vote was 402 against, 196 in favor. The collusion between the socialists and the right (in spite of Paul Reynaud and Ybarnegaray) was a fatal blow to the payment of the war debts and to Edouard Herriot. He would later be part of the government several times, but never again as prime minister. A country is not governed by grand gestures, good intentions and approximation. This time the French parliament was expressing popular sentiment and was true to the nation's chauvinistic, tight-fisted self, ignorant of the roundabout ways of Anglo-American moralism. "Herriot is low class," wrote P.-O. Lapie.[82] But he had wanted to elevate the nation to the same qualities of honesty that he lived by. The French people, outraged by what they considered to be American injustice, refused to follow him.

There is another explanation for Herriot's downfall. Paul-Boncour hints that certain financial circles, with a lot of influence on many right-wing deputies, were only too glad to find a "nationalistic" pretext for Herriot's downfall. His projected budget, however cautious, tended to increase direct taxation. Just as in 1924, the "wall of money" resisted attempts at reform by the Cartel des Gauches.

Chapter II

THE YEAR OF PAUL-BONCOUR

(December 18, 1932–January 30, 1934)

I apologize for using an individual's name as the title of some chapters. If the official responsible for foreign policy had a strong, dominating personality, the imprint of his "style" will be felt in his country's overall diplomacy, with positive or negative results. But it is also true that individuals, however prestigious they may be, have limited room to maneuver and that some deep pressures are at work easing their task while other forces are actively countering them. Some of these men—and this is true for Joseph Paul-Boncour and Edouard Herriot—were emblematic and indeed the spokesmen for some fundamental trends operating in France, a country by then tormented by the world crisis, and ruled by a kind of compromise between powerful interests and the middle classes, which in turn controlled the outcome of any free election.

Nineteen thirty-three was one of the worse years of the prewar period regarding government instability, economic difficulty and financial scandals. From the fall of Herriot (December 14, 1932) to the "events" of February 6, 1934, there were five different cabinets that, apart from the first one (Paul-Boncour until January 1933) were all headed by radical socialists: Edouard Daladier (January 31–October 24, 1933); Albert Sarraut (October 26–November 23, 1933); Camille Chautemps (November 26, 1933–January 27, 1934); and again Daladier (January 30–February 7, 1934).

Paul-Boncour was in charge of the Quai d'Orsay under each one of those governments (except for the two final weeks of the last Daladier cabinet). Only four other politicians were to keep their positions throughout that same period—Edouard Daladier remained at the ministry of war, Camille Chautemps at the ministry of the interior, Anatole de Monzie at the ministry of education and Pierre Cot at the ministry of air.

Short, with a thick white mane and gifted with a kind of lyrical eloquence almost equal to Briand, Joseph Paul-Boncour was certainly the most loyal and striking disciple of the "Apostle of Peace." This was the reason he found himself fully agreeing with the new secretary general of the Quai d'Orsay, Alexis Léger. It had all started in 1924, during the year of the first Cartel, when Briand, escorted by Paul-Boncour, made his initial appearance at the League of Nations, which he would enthrall with his eloquent speechmaking. "Briand, Herriot and myself all practiced a similar foreign policy, each according to his temperament and to the circumstances. A policy based on the League of Nations and the establishment of peace through collective security, so that from 1924 to 1934, the same goals were being pursued; our efforts were sustained by the fact that, whatever the government in power was at the time, Briand and I were the permanent representatives of France at the League of Nations."[1] When Paul-Boncour picked his cabinet without asking Herriot to participate, that consistency became undone: "He who in the morning talked of the physical impossibility of separating our two destinies later let it be torn asunder."[2] Herriot consoled himself by becoming chairman of the foreign affairs committee in Parliament, where he succeeded Paul-Boncour on February 8, 1933. Thus, the collaboration continued and Paul-Boncour would later send Herriot on important missions to the United States and the USSR. Paul-Boncour was personally behind an important change—a wide-ranging diplomatic rotation. In the spring of 1933, Charles Corbin took over from the aging Aimé de Fleuriau in London (March 13); Paul Claudel left Washington to fill Corbin's post in the Belgian capital (March 13); Henri de Jouvenel was appointed (for six months) to Rome (January 22); and Charles Alphand was appointed to Moscow (March 13). Topping off these changes, Paul-Boncour named Alexis Léger, the number one "Briandist" and great backer of collective security, as secretary general (March 13).

The problem was that the policy of collective security now appeared like an anachronism. The Japanese military cynically demonstrated in 1931 and 1932 that it was totally ineffectual. Then, on January 30, 1933, something much more threatening took place when Hitler was summoned by the old president, Marshal von Hindenburg, and became the Reichs chancellor France was powerless to do anything about it.

1.

How Did the French
React to Hitler's Coming to Power?[3]

The French ambassador to Berlin, André François-Poncet, in office since October 1931, was an *agrégé** in German; he had been elected a deputy and served as undersecretary of state. He had spent much of his previous career as a journalist and was probably the most knowledgeable person in France regarding Hitler and national socialism. His hesitations in 1932 say much about the ability of the French to gauge the Nazis' chances of coming to power. During the summer of 1932 he had warned of the unstoppable rise to power of the Nazi movement, but by September he and his colleagues were less sanguine. Lieutenant-Colonel de La Forest-Divonne, the deputy military attaché, soon to be posted to Switzerland, had this to say on September 27: "It is obvious that Hitler didn't seize the moment, and a hard fall is bound to follow his meteoric rise."[4] Knowing that Hitler no longer wanted to seize power through a putsch as he had attempted in 1923, and that he wanted to take over legally, François-Poncet felt optimistic about the situation when the Nazis suffered a relative defeat in the general elections of November 6, 1932 (196 Nazi deputies were elected, down from 230, or 33.1 percent compared to 37.3 percent). "A clear defeat," "The spell is broken," "The force of attraction seems…to have cracked."[5] Throughout December his dispatches emphasized the internal divisions within the Nazi party and underscored the energy of the new chancellor, General von Schleicher. "The wait-and-see policy to which Hitler seems to have resigned himself can only be disastrous for his party."… "In any case, the quarrel between Hitler

---

* Roughly equivalent to a Ph.D. degree.

and Strasser should be seen as a fatal illness for the Nazi party."[6] "The disintegration of the Nazi movement is continuing at a very quick pace."[7] Only after the Nazi success in the elections in Lippe, in January 1933, does the ambassador once again believe in the possibility of Hitler's coming to power, which in fact happened two weeks later to the day.

Many French commentators shared the same conflicting impression. In the November 8 and 9, 1932, issues of *Le Populaire*, Léon Blum confidently wrote, "Hitler is now definitely cut off from power. He is even, if I may say so, cut off from the hope of coming to power." *L'Œuvre*, dated January 1, 1933, proclaimed "Hitlerism's sorry demise."[8] On the same day, Oreste Rosenfeld wrote in *Le Populaire*, "Hitler's disappearance from the political scene is likely." These were left-wing newspapers; the right was no more enlightened. Hitler "missed the boat," wrote Bernus in *Les Débats*. Delebecque, in *L'Action française*, spoke of "Hitler's twilight." "Does Hitler still exist?" asked Léon Bailby in the September 29 issue of *L'Intransigeant*. Pertinax thought that "The General Boulanger of Germany has lost his timing" (*Echo de Paris*, November 7, 1932), and he held to this idea in the *Echo de Paris* of December 16, 1932: "Hitler is on the wane… Supreme power will never come his way."[9]

Events were to invalidate these mistaken forecasts. Hitler, summoned by the elderly president von Hindenburg, was appointed chancellor legally on January 30, 1933.

After minimizing Hitler's chances, the French newspapers acknowledged that Hindenburg had given in. They clearly understood the reasons why von Papen had maneuvered behind the scenes; the Junkers were rabidly opposed to von Schleicher because he seemed to threaten their large estates in eastern Germany. Finally, Hindenburg himself had been circumvented since he too had become a landowner through national gifts. All this was very surprising. But was it all that serious? The socialists denounced the German Communist Party's policy of "class against class"; "the criminal split that Moscow wants and encourages continues to divide the working class."[10] Conversely, the communists attacked social democracy's "policy of the lesser evil," and once again, denounced the treaty of Versailles, the reparations, the drawing up of arbitrary borders, the "impossible corridor," and the belief in German guilt. Gabriel Péri declared "a battle against the Treaty of Versailles and Hitlerism, its bastard child."[11]

There were many issues facing public opinion during the first months of Hitlerism. The many open questions can be summarized as follows:

Was Hitlerism a threat to France? Could it be viewed as a "model" to be followed? What was Hitler's program?

The French public did not immediately perceive the new kinds of threats posed by Hitlerism. Without a doubt Hitler was a rousing tribune, a mass leader, but was he capable of being a statesman? *Le Temps*, a newspaper connected to the Quai d'Orsay, voiced its doubts: "The new Chancellor will probably quickly fail at this game, and his popularity will not survive the demise of his reputation as a miracle maker."[12] Hitler was "a demagogue," "a house painter," "a General Boulanger," nothing but a pawn in the hands of more powerful, and indeed more dangerous forces, such as the Reichswehr, and the old Prussian elite, both of them hereditary enemies of France. "The Reichswehr…, like a mysterious force, stands face to face with the triumphant militias of German Fascism."[13] And there were other forces, such as the socialists and even the communists. *L'Humanité*, after the burning of the Reichstag and following the elections and the infamous ceremony at the Garrison church in Potsdam, on March 21, still proudly declared that, "the organization of our party in Germany has remained intact." And then there were other parties within the government. "In a coalition government Hitler has less power than Hitler as dictator."[14]

Still, clouds were gathering. Hitler was holding out, eliminating his opponents one by one, and naming his flunkies to all the key posts. This was dictatorship; this was fascism, the bogeyman of the left. This was revanchist Germany, hated by the right. The well-known shift of the extreme antidemocratic anti-German nationalist factions over to neutralism and pacifism, based on anti-communism and anti-Semitism, was barely visible in 1933.[15] Only two journalists known for their eccentric outbursts, Gustave Hervé, in *La Victoire* and Marcel Bucard pretended to rejoice, "Oh! Happy Germany… its suffering is at long last over… It has been saved, saved by Hitler, as Italy was saved by Mussolini, after the long red wave that sought to engulf it after the war"… It was "proof that, even in the teeth of a collectivist and communist revolution, a great people can rise up and quickly overcome."[16] Other right-wing newspapers, such as *L'Echo de Paris*, saw some good in the German regime at a time when France was moving in the opposite direction. But what was good for Germany was bad for France. France must recover: "Against the Third Reich it was urgent that France erect the Fourth Republic."[17] One could quote many instances of this kind of thinking, but it is more effective to ask what the French people *knew* about Hitlerism as a system.

This can be measured by one fairly obvious criterion. In 1925 Hitler wrote *Mein Kampf*. In that shapeless, repetitious and rambling book, amid a mass of peremptory statements, Hitler did reveal his program—to correct the wrong visited by the Diktat of Versailles upon the superior race of the tall Aryan blond-haired dolichocephals, whose purest representatives could be found in Germany; to create a "Greater Germany" that would include all the Germans torn from the motherland; and to conquer a vital *Lebensraum* in the East, without pity for the degenerate race of the Slavs, in order to give Germany breathing space and to provide access to the resources she lacked. Since France (not England) was Germany's "hereditary foe," these goals could only be reached once France was crushed.

All this was clearly spelled out. Historians, and especially German historians, wonder how far Hitler considered *Mein Kampf* to be a *ne varietur* program, or whether, independently of tactics, he was largely an opportunist.[18] "Did the dictator believe in his manifesto or was he a disciple of Machiavelli?"[19]

Our goal in these pages is to understand the French attitude. Whatever the objective reality was, knowledge of *Mein Kampf* was essential. Goebbels would later say, "In 1933, a French prime minister should have said (and if I had been in his place I would have said), 'This new Reichs chancellor, he's the man who wrote *Mein Kampf*… We cannot afford to have such a man on our doorstep. He must disappear or we must declare war against him.'"[20]

The problem of *Mein Kampf* for the history of French foreign policy is twofold: first, there is the issue of whether it was read in France. Second, was it was taken seriously? After all, people in France were used to electoral programs never being implemented after the election had been won and accepted in practice that there was a difference between the demagogic utopia of dreams and the constraints of reality.

The fact is that the first edition of *Mein Kampf* in French, translated by J. Gaudefroy-Demombynes and A. Calmettes, was not published before 1934 and that few people in France could read German.

Let's take the case of a first-rate German scholar such as Ambassador François-Poncet. He had indeed read *Mein Kampf*. But did he give it the importance it deserved? He had an *agrégation* in German, was an eminent journalist and had chosen to become a career diplomat on September 23, 1931, as ambassador to Berlin, precisely in order to "insure that the government received more accurate information about what was happening on the other side of the Rhine." Immediately following Hitler's rise to power, he acquired exceptional standing in the capital.

According to François Seydoux, who worked with him, "The position he enjoyed in Germany inside the diplomatic corps was unparalleled. After Hitler, there were Göring, Goebbels, Rudolf Hess, Baldur von Schirach, and then came François-Poncet. He was saluted in the Tiergarten when he took a walk. His witticisms were famous. He was considered to be an expert on the real Germany."[21]

"His work, his profession, and the need to write filled his life." He remained "deeply influenced by his many years working as a journalist and as press chief. Just like a newspaper or even a news agency correspondent, he wanted to keep Paris informed on an on-going basis."[22]

His dedication and honesty were beyond question. In 1936, after he had just sent several dispatches where he discounted the possibility of a rapprochement between Germany and Italy,[23] one of his aides, Captain Stehlin, discovered by chance that an ultra secret mission of Italian aviators was in Berlin.[24] Stehlin warned the ambassador; François-Poncet at first accused him of having too much imagination. Then, impressed by the young man's conviction, immediately wrote a telegram where he disavowed his previous position.[25]

François-Poncet had a penetrating mind, was very well informed and clearly provided an enormous amount of information about Germany, most of it extremely relevant. Still, he harbored a relative *optimism* as to the future of relations between the two countries.

First, François-Poncet didn't appear to take *Mein Kampf* very seriously, not seeing in it the "plan," which, as subsequent events were to demonstrate, Hitler would follow to the letter. Based solely on the year 1936, for example, written documents show that he mentioned the Nazi "Bible" only five times (the mention appears even less frequently in later years). He didn't allude to it at all in the brilliant general report he sent to the department on March 9, 1936.[26]

Furthermore, when he quoted *Mein Kampf*, the ambassador hesitated between two interpretations. Sometimes he saw it as the actual source of Hitler's thinking; for example on racism, as it replaced pre-war pan-Germanism. "Some pages of *Mein Kampf* actually do shed a very troubling light on the sincerity of his intentions."[27] He felt the same way about the issue of *Lebensraum*: Hitler didn't seek it in the colonies, but in Eastern Europe (*Drang nach Osten, Boden und Raum*). François-Poncet wrote, "It would be wrong to think that because Hitler wrote these pages ten years ago, they are no longer relevant and don't inspire the Führer's current feelings. On the contrary, this program is being 'carried out systematically.'"[28] This was true also of Hitler's hope in an alliance with England,[29] and of the question of the Anschluss, of Danzig and the Corridor.[30]

More often, though, François-Poncet thought that Hitler had "changed since the time he was writing *Mein Kampf*," especially regarding the "colonial idea," to which Schacht supposedly had won him over.[31]

He reported a "curious piece of information" given him by the Romanian (ambassador) Comnène. According to Comnène, "Hitler loves this book like a first-born. He will never change a word of it. But he is preparing a second book. After three years in power and with the experience and responsibilities of government, he will unveil his new ideas, his new doctrines and this second book will put many doubts and fears to rest."[32] Often, after meeting with the Führer, François-Poncet was inclined to think "how much the Führer has progressed since the time he was writing *Mein Kampf*."[33]

Paul Reynaud would later say that French politicians had not read Hitler's book. "Every chapter of the war was there in black and white. Hitler wrote *Mein Kampf* during his years in prison, and the entire history of the Second World War is in *Mein Kampf*... The Soviets, contrary to most of the French public, had indeed read *Mein Kampf*."[34]

The same was true for the French press. In a detailed study of the press at the beginning of the Nazi regime, the German historian Kimmel also referred to that fact.[35] In the end it appears that only a handful of specialists had read the book closely and, even then, probably relatively late. Among those was Henri Jordan, director of the French Academic House in Berlin[36] and a few officers of the *Deuxième Bureau*. General Gauché, head of the *Deuxième Bureau*, wrote that his service "always considered *Mein Kampf* a document of capital importance, fundamental and absolutely relevant, which, once the hyperbole and the passionate outbursts were cleared away, held the key to Hitler's future actions."[37]

2.

A TOTAL FAILURE:
DISARMAMENT AND THE FRANCO-GERMAN RAPPROCHEMENT

Paul-Boncour was probably not among those who spent much time mulling over *Mein Kampf*.[38] But, being true to the League of Nations, and like everyone else in France who was uncertain as to what Hitler had in store, it was normal that he should try through disarmament to include the new Germany in the search for peace. In fact, contrary to what he was to do in the case of Italy, as we shall see later on, he didn't launch any great initiatives.

Before Hitler came to power, the idea of a long-term rapprochement between France and Germany had inspired a few generous souls, and some realistic businessmen in both countries.

First, some approaches were made by a small group of Catholics, whose most famous member was Marc Sangnier, the founder of the *Sillon* and of *Jeune République*. The majority of Catholics, by contrast, together with the National Catholic Federation, presided over by General de Castelnau, vigorously pursued traditional anti-German nationalism. So did Louis Marin's *Fédération Républicaine*, along with *L'Écho de Paris* and *L'Action française*. Wasn't one justified, given the rise of Nazism, to mistrust what German scholar Robert d'Harcourt, a professor at the Catholic Institute, termed the "cowardice" of the German Catholic Center?[39] Those in favor of a rapprochement were generally "left-wing" Catholics, and pacifists like Georges Bidault, Louis Terrenoire, Francisque Gay, Georges Hoog, Maurice Vaussard, the Catholic labor leader Gaston Tessier; the founder of *Esprit*, Emmanuel Mounier; writers such as François Mauriac and Count de Pange, who was originally from Lorraine; and journalists such as Vladimir d'Ormesson and Father Merklen. The newspaper *La Croix* expressed the hope that "the peace-loving elites of both countries would get to know each other."[40]

For these men, Hitler's rise to power came as a surprise and caused a sense of disillusionment. "All the promising endeavors I believed in," wrote Jean de Pange, "the Rhineland policy, the Saar policy, the Alsatian policy, and finally the rapprochement between the intellectual elites of both countries, it all failed miserably."[41]

The attempts made by the CFAID (*Comité Franco-Allemand d'information et de documentation*), created in 1926, were very different. The *Comité's* main movers were a large industrialist from Luxemburg, Emil Mayrisch and his wife, a writer, a friend of André Gide and an active member of the "*decades*" organized by Paul Desjardins in Pontigny.[42] In 1926 Mayrisch had pushed through a very important economic initiative, the international steel entente, between France, the Saar, Belgium, and Luxemburg.[43] Mayrisch died accidentally in 1928, and Pierre Viénot, who had become his son-in-law, carried on until December 1929. In 1936 Viénot would become a socialist deputy and undersecretary of state for Foreign Affairs in the Popular Front cabinet.

While doing research in the archives of the Wilhelmstrasse and the Zentralarchiv at Potsdam, Jacques Bariéty and Charles Bloch discovered an attempt at a Franco-German rapprochement in 1932 and 1933, which, even though it hadn't originated with the moribund CFAID, would still not have been possible had the Committee not done the groundwork.

It was "the private initiative of bankers and industrialists who feared the consequences of the crisis and of the confrontation between the two countries,…both governments were informed of the meetings to which they simply sent unofficial observers."[44] The first meeting took place in Luxemburg on April 29–30, 1932; the second was in Paris on January 29 and 30, 1933. On the French side, the participants were René Duchemin, president of the Kuhlmann company and head of the *Confédération nationale de la production française*; Louis Marlio, former councilor at the *Conseil d'État*, administrator of the *Chemins de fer de l'est* and other companies; Jean Parmentier, a senior treasury official and former director of the *Mouvement général des fonds*, and Vladimir d'Ormesson, an editorial writer who was very close to the diplomats and had written a widely discussed and sensational book that had been translated into several languages, *Confiance en l'Allemagne?* (1928).* As we have mentioned, he was also active in Catholic circles. On the German side, there were also some large industrialists, such as Professor Carl Bosch, director of *Badische Anilin*, who collaborated with Kuhlmann; Dr. Bücher, who had worked at the foreign ministry and headed the famous *Allgemeine Elektrizitätsgesellschaft* (AEG); and Clemens Lammers, a deputy of the Catholic Center, close to Chancellor Brüning. Also present at the meetings were Aloys Meyer, who had succeeded Mayrisch at ARBED, the Belgian banker Barbanson and Camille Gutt, who was later to become Belgian minister of finance and director of the International Monetary Fund.

---

* Should we trust Germany?

The talks in Luxemburg were very open. The French agreed to a moratorium on reparations, while the Germans accepted that payments would resume after the crisis through a system based on issuing German government bonds. The Germans asked for French loans—in 1932 France had more funds available than the other great powers—in order to replace the faltering American credit. The French wanted these loans to be guaranteed by both governments. Disarmament was also discussed, but less successfully. The Germans proposed talks between the high commands of both armies, the idea again having been put forward by von Papen in July 1932 at the Lausanne conference. In fact, von Papen had been a member of the CFAID.

Finally, they discussed the Polish Corridor. Couldn't it be returned to Germany? Poland, in exchange, would annex Lithuania. The French then stated as a condition that Germany guarantee its eastern borders, the so-called "Eastern Locarno."

The meetings resumed in Paris on January 29 and 30, 1933, with the same partners (except Marlio and Lammers). "The French delegation certainly had fewer ties with the government in Paris than it had under Tardieu, but the fact that Parmentier attended proves that they maintained contact with certain high-ranking civil servants." On the German side, von Papen, who was no longer chancellor but was orchestrating the many intrigues that would return him to power as Hitler's deputy chancellor on the same day—January 30—was kept informed.[45] The second conference concluded that the German-Polish border in the Corridor and in Upper Silesia would be modified with Poland receiving Memel at Lithuania's expense in exchange. Germany would agree to guarantee its eastern borders. A security pact, along with general staff agreements, was to be reached between France, Belgium, Germany, and Poland. Germany would be granted a colonial mandate. Economic issues were not discussed.

That meeting, as it turned out, had very little effect. Hitler wasn't told about it. The German Minister of Foreign Affairs, von Neurath, and his deputy von Bülow, expressed their disagreement on all points. Did the French government approve of the plan, as Duchemin believed? No trace of it can be found in the archives.

In any case, after the proclamation of "equal rights" and after Hitler had come to power, the question of disarmament continued to dominate the relations between the two countries. Germany had already expressed doubts as to the "French constructive plan," demanding that compulsory military service be reinstated.[46] Thus, the Geneva conference became mired, for a while, in minor details. Should plenary and public meetings be held, as France wished?[47] Or should the five member conversations be resumed, as the English suggested?[48] Massigli telegraphed Paul-Boncour, "It is hardly necessary to point out to your excellency how risky such meetings would be for us, we would find ourselves caught between the German-Italian bloc, a neutral United States and an undecided Great Britain."[49]

Was Great Britain, however, really that undecided? On March 7, the conference's political committee had practically rejected the "French constructive plan."[50] Macdonald was thinking of a new disarmament plan. He "therefore played the role of arbiter" between France and Germany, once again forgetting about the old alliance. He again forgot to consult his French partners. Massigli wrote, "Isn't it time we had a talk with Sir John Simon and told him that, without in any way wishing to curtail the British Prime Minister's freedom of initiative, the French delegate is entitled to expect, in a matter of such vital importance for France, not to be faced with some kind of summons?" What had happened to the "trust agreement."[51]

In effect, having conceded just about everything in 1932, France was back to square one in 1933. But, this time, there was Hitler and he was very busy: the Reichstag fire, the elimination of the communists and the elections of March 5, returning 288 Nazi and 52 German-nationalist deputies to the Reichstag, were all great successes, even though he didn't quite have an absolute majority. Was his silence something to be feared? Ambassador François-Poncet didn't think so. "It would be wrong...to turn the Hitler movement into a bogeyman. ... It sows the seeds of its own divisions and weakness... Germany's opportunities for rearmament remain constrained by its economic and financial situation."[52] François-Poncet attended the grandiose ceremony of March 21, when the new Reichstag met in the Garnisonkirche at Potsdam. He was inspired to write an excellent report, evoking the paradox of this half-Austrian Hitler, "placing himself, with great pomp, under the aegis of the kings of ancient Prussia... Time will soon come, then, when it is possible to ask what one may expect of German facism."[53]

That time came on April 8 when Hitler received the French ambassador for the first time. It was to be the first of a long series of meetings, since Hitler seemed prepared to grant France special treatment. As Professor Hildebrand and Professor Jacobsen have noted, in the first three years of his government, Hitler spent almost fifty percent of the time allotted to consultations in talks with the French and British representatives.[54] And François-Poncet got even more time than his British colleague.

At the April 8 meeting Hitler was as gentle as a lamb. "I repeat, my government is sincerely, deeply pacifist. We are all convinced that war, even if it were to be victorious, would cost much sacrifice and bring very little gain. What is important for Germany is to overcome unemployment and economic hardship." Hitler was "courteous and friendly, not at all self-conscious." François-Poncet had the impression that he wanted a Franco-German agreement.[55]

In fact, the plan Macdonald had been preparing was presented on March 17. It entirely omitted the idea of the mutual assistance pact that France held dear. On the other hand, it offered Germany the perfect means for launching a very profitable "leap forward." Quietly ignoring the fact that Germany had been more or less secretly involved in a substantial rearmament,[56] it proposed to reduce the armies of all the main continental powers to the level of 200,000 men. Germany would therefore be able to double the size of the army allowed by the Treaty of Versailles. All the other powers, and particularly France, were to disarm until they reached that level. Worse, as Daladier, who was prime minister at the time pointed out to Macdonald, no provisions had been made for a system of oversight. The concept of oversight was becoming increasingly central to French policy. Daladier was to announce it on March 2 in a speech to the British and American press association.[57] He mentioned "oversight" again on March 16, and made it the centerpiece of French policy on May 2 at a cabinet meeting and on May 20 in a staff meeting. The controls would include: 1) budgets; 2) technical issues—relating to armament categories; 3) arms manufacturing; and 4) troop levels. There would be a four-year trial period to gauge the effectiveness of controls. Stockpiling or destruction of surplus weapons would be carried out during a four-year period afterward.[58] That was the only condition whereby France was ready to support the Macdonald plan.

Therefore, France was abandoning the old idea of a mutual assistance pact, which would guarantee security, and replacing it with the oversight system. This change seemed to be linked to Daladier himself, who would long remain the promoter of controls. The United States, Switzerland, Norway, Finland, the Netherlands, Poland, the countries of the Little Entente and the USSR, all subscribed to this system. Its success depended, of course, on British and German response.

On June 8, 1933,[59] in a conversation held at the Quai d'Orsay between France, Great Britain and the United States, Daladier and Paul-Boncour defended their oversight plan. The British and the Americans accepted the principle, but declared that France must *first* make a gesture toward disarmament. What the Americans and the British wanted was "to ensure that the conference would succeed"—meaning "that it is agreed...that the interlocutor is in good faith." Daladier replied that, "Germany has already partially rearmed...which is why we must be particularly cautious." There had to be an observation period, since he "doubted the sincerity of Germany's intentions." Daladier added, "A dictatorial regime can set the moment when it will launch an attack in advance and therefore prepare its build-up accordingly." To which Norman Davis, the American negotiator, answered: Start disarming first, then we will accept controls. It was a dialog of the deaf.

Hitler must have been watching all this with glee. By setting the 200,000-man army as a basis for discussion, Macdonald was handing him the arguments to protest that the Reichswehr had only 100,000 men (a number it already largely exceeded). The British and the Americans, by asking France to make a "gesture" and by trying to water down the principle of an oversight system, were allowing him to look good; all he had to do was play along and pretend to be a pacifist first and foremost. While the democratic countries embarked in byzantine discussions on whether to adjourn the conference or not, Hitler gave a great "speech for peace on May 17, 1933"[60] in the Reichstag. He declared his willingness to abide by the treaty and, at the same time, asked for the arms forbidden by the Treaty of Versailles as "samples." "Hitler and his friends want peace," wrote François-Poncet, "not because they have stopped idolizing strength, but because peace is for them a requirement and, as for strength, they just don't have it."[61]

In the same way, Hitler adhered with apparent enthusiasm to the Four Power Pact that we will mention later on.[62] While he was busy eliminating political parties, he signed a concordat with the Vatican. Minister of Foreign Affairs, von Neurath, proposed "direct contacts" between France and Germany. He mentioned a possible meeting with Prime Minister Daladier, who found the idea very attractive.[63] While he was persecuting the Jews, and making incendiary speeches to the SA and even allowing the SA in Kehl to inscribe "Strasburg" on their flag, he again met with François-Poncet on September 15 to say, "with the greatest tone of sincerity, that at no time had he contemplated and would never contemplate challenging the border between France and Germany, because he knew very well that most Alsatians didn't like the Germans." Moreover he would abide by the Locarno accords. "My one ambition," he added, "is that some day in the future there will be a monument dedicated to me as the man who reconciled France and Germany."[64]

Did Hitler really want bilateral negotiations with France? In any case, he intended to rearm as quickly as possible. Throughout the summer of 1933, the French tried to convince the British and the Americans of Germany's "lapses," which were clearly obvious.[65] In spite of the evidence, Hitler had a perfect excuse to do as he pleased—Germany had been promised "equal rights" in December 1932. And now France wanted an eight-year "probation" period? That amounted to a breach of trust and, in that case, there was only one solution, one that both General Renondeau and François-Poncet had sensed in early September[66]—to walk out of the disarmament conference. On October 14, 1933, Sir John Simon announced at the conference that the French, British, Italians and the Americans agreed to the probation period.[67] Immediately, on the very same day, Hitler announced that Germany was leaving the conference. To further increase what the French chargé d'affaires Pierre Arnal called "a bomb blast," *he also announced that Germany was leaving the League of Nations.*[68]

3.

THE FOUR POWER PACT
AND THE OUTLINE OF A FRANCO-ITALIAN RAPPROCHEMENT

In the vague attempts at a rapprochement between France and Germany, Paul-Boncour's role had been practically nil. Only François-Poncet and, to some degree, Daladier, had been involved. The opposite was true of another attempt, which Paul-Boncour valued highly, a rapprochement with Italy.

Of course, he carried a millstone around his neck. Until 1932 he had been a member of the Socialist Party, which was violently hostile to

Mussolini, whose henchmen had assassinated Italian socialist Matteotti. In parliament, whenever the word Italy was uttered in a foreign policy debate, one of the socialists would interrupt the speaker with a cry of "Matteotti!" Paul-Boncour had even gone further. In a flight of eloquence, he had at one time compared the Duce to a "Mardi-Gras Caesar."[69] Mussolini had never forgiven him. And yet, Paul-Boncour wrote that "I always have been a strong supporter of friendship with Italy, because I am convinced that, apart from our being neighbors, an alliance between Mediterranean countries constitutes a useful counterweight to the German, British and American powers in the West." Of course, friendship with fascist Italy was more problematic. But the Duce's power had been consolidated. "In 1933, there was no alternative."[70] First, in January 1933, Paul-Boncour named his "old friend" Henry de Jouvenel ambassador to Rome. He had long been a member of the French delegation to the League of Nations, and, like Paul-Boncour, he believed in it "with all his heart."[71] For a while he had been High Commissioner to the mandates of Syria and Lebanon and had become a senator. He had only agreed to a six months' mission but was determined to see it through. De Jouvenel took a large file covering the pending issues between the two countries: the status of Italians in Tunisia; colonial compensations owed to Italy by France under article 15 of the treaty of London of April 26, 1915; the border question in Libya and the idea—that had already surfaced in 1932—of "France's disengagement from Ethiopia," although Ethiopia was a member of the League of Nations. Before de Jouvenel's mission, René Massigli made contacts in Geneva and in December 1932, more importantly, another senator, Henry Bérenger, president of the senate committee on foreign affairs, had traveled to Rome. The idea was spreading in Paris that "it was advisable to establish a general policy agreement reserving North Africa for France and Central Europe for Italy."[72] Bad relations between Italy and Yugoslavia, an ally of France, remained the main obstacle.

Paul-Boncour told de Jouvenel tha they must "establish, during these few months, the basis for a long-term understanding," and in particular "prevent the split that might appear between the Little Entente, friendly toward France, and the nations trying to claim Italy's support against the Little Entente."[73]

Mussolini was actually to take the initiative. Hitler's rise to power worried him. He felt nothing but contempt for Hitler's race-driven pseudo-fascism. He feared Hitler might attempt to carry out the *Anschluss* with Austria and wanted to avoid it at all costs. On his first visit, on March 3,

1933, de Jouvenel was wondering how he could induce the Duce to spell out the goals of his foreign policy, but Mussolini was immediately willing to play along. "I didn't think it would be so easy."[74] He said that "we must have a less tense relationship and we should move closer in our views regarding the organization of Europe." Halfway between an alliance and being good neighbors, why not seek a "political entente?"

What Mussolini was going to propose became clear by March 17. He had made his decision, at a meeting of the fascist Grand Council, to rebuild the pre-1914 "concert of Europe" for Europe, meaning a "directorate of four" to include Italy, England, France and Germany.[75]

From then on, everything was to revolve around the Italian project. There would be a *positive* phase lasting until June 7, when the Four Power Pact was initialed, and July 15, when it was signed. Then came a *negative* phase, when the pact and the Franco-Italian rapprochement floundered and eventually crumbled.

The vicissitudes of the Four Power Pact stemmed from the deeply contradictory goals each country had assigned it. In the first Italian draft, article 2 stated that "the four powers reaffirm the principle of revision of the peace treaties, according to the clauses of the covenant of the League of Nations, whenever situations arise that might lead to conflict between states."[76] Mussolini, who supported the "dissatisfied" central European countries—Austria, Hungary, and Bulgaria—saw this as a means to eventually grant them compensation. For France, which was allied to the "satisfied" countries, the pact's main goal was to "keep Germany in line." This was exactly what Mussolini dangled before de Jouvenel: "We either line up two by two, England and France on the one side and Italy and Germany on the other, and bloc against bloc we oppose each other, and go down the path to grievous events, or the four of us agree and collaborate, and only then will Europe and the world breathe easier." He even saw the possibility of reestablishing enough trust to promote "the resumption of economic activity."[77]

The negotiations would prove to be lengthy and complicated. Macdonald, like the French, was unhappy about article 2, which was the only significant article in Mussolini's plan. Still, it was important not to break with Italy. To quote Paul-Boncour, "It was the beginning of something truly great." Everyone in the Cartel des Gauches voiced their approval of the pact, except Herriot. Caillaux supported it; Prime Minister Daladier preferred to let the Quai d'Orsay remodel it to suit France's aims, which meant watering it down.[78] Mussolini was very hopeful and suggested that Daladier pay a visit to Rome. Everyone praised de Jouvenel. "Mr. Mussolini and Mr. Macdonald are delighted and are convinced that the collaboration they are proposing will put an end to Europe's malaise; it will bring back trust, foster economic recovery and solve the debt problem." The German ambassador to Rome, on the other hand, "did not conceal his bitterness."[79]

The first problem was to lure Germany into the Four Power Pact, and Germany certainly had no wish to be "kept in line" on the issue of rearmament, for example. Germany's acceptance wasn't negotiated by French diplomacy, but rather by Mussolini. Hitler decided to join the pact because he wanted to please Mussolini. The Wilhelmstrasse, on the contrary, thought it was fraught with danger.[80]

For France, the difficulties related to Poland and the Little Entente. Alexis Léger was a great friend and admirer of Czech President Beneš, who was also a friend of Paul-Boncour. Did Léger hinder the successful outcome of the Four Power Pact? Paul-Boncour mentions a rumor according to which Léger had a "phobia" about Italy, but he dismissed it: "Léger was quite incapable of any kind of phobia because his mind was so totally flexible."[81] But this is not entirely convincing. The League of Nations desk at the Quai d'Orsay drew up a completely innocuous counterplan, written by Dulong and Fouques-Duparc on March 22, which Massigli sent to Léger. It referred mostly to loyalty to the League of Nations. The term "revision" had disappeared.[82]

For two months there would be a sort of pendulum movement between the Italian project, which irritated France's allies, and the French project, which displeased the Italians. On the French side, Paul-Boncour's actions showed the same hesitation since he would at times follow Léger and the Quai d'Orsay, or go with de Jouvenel who was prepared to agree to every concession in order to make the Four Power Pact and the rapprochement with Italy succeed. Let us suppose that France had a stable and self-assured government at the time, one that would have realized that *perhaps it was time to revise a policy based on ineffectual alliances with weak countries, and that the only way to ensure its safety and contain Germany was by allying itself with the great powers.* De Jouvenel was very much aware of this issue and set it out most convincingly in a noteworthy telegram dated March 25.[83] We shall quote the following:

> Since France is shouldering the weight of four nations by itself, two of which had disappeared from the map of Europe for a long

time[84] while the other two have tripled in territory and in population;[85] that she can now place the existence and future of these four threatened nations under the guarantee of the four western powers, this being the condition for drawing the United States closer to Europe; is it not France's interest alone as the sole guarantor of peace between Germany and Poland and Germany and Czechoslovakia; is it not in the interest of those four endangered nations to seek such a contract even if it means making a few localized concessions to France?

But Beneš was telling Jean Paul-Boncour, the nephew and assistant of Paul-Boncour, that the project of the Four Power Pact was "utterly ridiculous" and that the Little Entente had decided to "openly resist it."[86] Both the Romanian minister Titulescu[87] and the Turkish president Mustapha Kemal[88] agreed. The Polish minister for foreign affairs, Joseph Beck, was the most negative. Furious that Poland should not be considered one of the great powers, he completely opposed any revisions. Beck threatened to pull out of the League of Nations and—something to be remembered—to seek a rapprochement with Germany.[89]

The hapless Paul-Boncour, caught in the crossfire, saw compromise as the only way out, to "continue to amend the draft with the firm intention of safeguarding its useful features while eliminating its risks."[90] His relations with de Jouvenel took on an increasingly bittersweet tone. His point of view prevailed and the result on June 7 was a text, as Sir John Simon put it, "so insipid, that here in Britain we have a hard time understanding what sudden difficulties prevented the great powers from reaching an agreement that was essentially an expression of good will intended to rekindle a feeling of trust on the eve of the economic conference."[91] Still, the authorization to initial was given only after de Jouvenel protested once more and after Léger had made one last effort to further water down an already insipid text.[92] On the same day, June 7, Mussolini, in a speech to the Senate, greatly praised France and, according to de Jouvenel, was cheered by the entire floor.[93] The Germans made a show of appearing to be very pleased.[94]

De Jouvenel, on the other hand, felt the pact was a "beginning."[95] He had initiated a rapprochement between France and Italy. It was to be followed by financial and colonial negotiations, talks on disarmament, and the drawing up of a common plan for European policy. Italy, he said, was "ready to enter into negotiations as soon as we show the slightest willingness." It might be a good idea, as Mussolini was suggesting, to "set up a small Franco-Italian committee." It would be good for Daladier to visit Rome, either before or after the signature. In short, de Jouvenel felt he had fulfilled his mission. It was now time for him to resign his post and return to his Senate seat. He left Rome on July 20, 1933, with high hopes for the future. His successor, Count Charles Pineton de Chambrun, was appointed on July 29. "I have known Chambrun for a long time," de Jouvenel wrote to Alexis Léger. "He has an open personality, which, in my opinion, can only appeal to Mr. Mussolini."[96]

4.

The Pursuit
of Rapprochement with the USSR

While relations with Germany were disconcerting from the start, and relations with Italy were full of pitfalls, the talks with Moscow were gratifying to Paul-Boncour.[97] Obviously, if the rapprochement continued to progress, it was largely due to the Soviet attitude which in turn was greatly influenced by Hitler's rise to power.[98]

The first step was to ratify the non-aggression pact of December 1932. Paul-Boncour was rather optimistic because several members of Daladier's government were ardent supporters of the USSR. Anatole de Monzie, minister of national education, for example, had made a spectacular trip to Russia, culminating in a book he wrote in 1924.[99] He had played a major role in the "recognition" of 1924 during the hopeless negotiations over the tsarist debt and, again, in 1931 had published another book favorable to the Soviets.[100] Pierre Cot, the young minister of air, and part of the newly elected radicals—the group nicknamed the "Young Turks"—shared the same opinion. The debate took place on May 16 and 18 and Herriot reminded the audience that our most Christian King, Francis I, had indeed struck an alliance with the Muslim Turks.[101]

The Chamber voted in favor of ratification 554 to one (Tardieu voted against), and 41 abstentions (among them Louis Marin, Flandin, Mandel, and Scapini, who were all right-wing deputies). The socialists were not very enthusiastic but voted to ratify. The ones who found themselves in a quandary were the communists, who were in the habit of rejecting anything the government proposed. Jacques Duclos, their spokesman, announced a vote in favor, but cautioned, "We very much fear that this pact is nothing but a sham to hide a continuing policy of aggression against the Soviet Union."[102]

After this spectacular success, further steps became possible, even more so since there were indications that the Red Army and the Reichswehr had severed their military ties. The secret German "training camps" had lost their usefulness with the announcement of "equal rights." Hitler was vigorously fighting German communism, and violently attacked international communism. Ambassador François-Poncet was closely following these developments. He carefully pointed out whatever seemed to indicate a continued special relationship: newspaper articles, the brochure written by General von Seeckt, and commercial relations (in 1932 the USSR had been "the biggest customer by far, for German industrial products.)"[103] In May 1933, Germany ratified a 1931 protocol that renewed the non-aggression treaty of 1926. Meanwhile, François-Poncet noted how Hitler was particularly friendly to the Soviet ambassador.[104]

What Paris didn't know was that the dismantling of German military installations in Moscow was going on unabated. On September 23 there was a farewell banquet just before the German officers were to leave. The atmosphere was cordial, but the break was taking place.[105]

Several factors contributed to the Franco-Soviet rapprochement. First was the development of commercial relations. The USSR had generally been a net creditor in its balance of payments with France (470 million in 1932). In the past, revenues from the "Russian bonds" made up for this deficit, which was mainly created by oil. Something had to be found to replace those revenues. The best way was to "create a purchasing program with France." But this implied granting loans, and the French state could not guarantee them until the Russian debt had been resolved. This was the reason France felt it could buy Russian oil through a barter system.[106] Ambassador Alphand (see below) backed granting credit since, in his opinion, the USSR, due to its state-controlled economy, was "virtually one of the best debtors in the world."[107]

But personal contacts played a greater role than vague commercial efforts. On March 13, Charles Alphand was appointed as the new French ambassador to Moscow. On June 14 he presented his credentials to President Kalinin who mentioned "the extremely desirable political rapprochement," which was in any case "in the nature of things."[108] Also, for the first time a French military attaché, appointed by Daladier on February 15, 1933, was sent to the USSR. He spoke Russian fluently and was extremely well received.[109] During a reception, Marshal Budienny, a hero of the civil war, had, while being somewhat inebriated, even kissed him on the mouth! It appears that the idea of sending a military attaché originated with an officer in Weygand's cabinet, Lieutenant-Colonel de Lattre de Tassigny, in October 1932. This officer happened to be a friend of Ostrovski, the president of the *Société Française du Pétrole Russe.*

Closer relations crystallized during the summer of 1933. France signed a declaration that the Soviets had produced, defining the aggressor. Alphand met with Molotov, who was a member of the Politburo.[110] But the trips to Russia were to be the most important events.

First, Herriot repeated his 1922 gesture to visit the Soviet Union "as a private citizen and a tourist." He took a trip in August 1933 and was given a warm welcome. N. Bulganin, president of the Moscow Soviet, invited 150 people to a banquet in his honor. During this banquet, Kaminski, president of the Moscow Regional Soviet, alluded to a possible Franco-Soviet alliance for the first time and described how vigorously the USSR was preparing for its defense. "And it is my hope," he stated, "that we will carry out this defense together." The entire room then burst into cries of "Vive la France!"[111]

Then Pierre Cot, the minister of air, made another important trip. He had been invited by the Soviet embassy in Paris and discussed it with Daladier on June 4, saying that the visit would give him the opportunity to create an outlet for the French aeronautics industry "in order to maintain its vital potential for national defense."[112] The trip, which took place from September 13 to 22, was particularly fruitful. Pierre Cot traveled with General Barrès, who was the inspector of the air force, and some technicians. He was able to observe the progress made by the Soviet aeronautics industry and thought it capable in a few years of becoming two to three times stronger than Germany's. Its equipment was "equal or slightly superior" to the French equipment in service at the time. He also noted that the USSR was detaching itself from Germany and was seeking closer ties to France. French language learning had become compulsory in Soviet military academies. Pierre Cot thought military exchanges had to be increased, Marshal Tukhachevsky should be invited to France, and an air force mission sent to Moscow. A contract for mutual industrial assistance in case of war should be drafted and, finally, the possibility of a mutual assistance pact was to be examined.[113]

Other visits came later, notably that of a delegation of the scientists Jean Perrin, Paul Langevin and Paul Mazon. On the Soviet side, Litvinov visited Paris in July 1933. He dined with Paul-Boncour, who mentioned the possibility of the USSR joining the League of Nations.

These overtures yielded two results during the period we are examining. First, in August 1933 a provisional commercial protocol was signed in Paris. France would ease the entry of Soviet merchandise by increasing its quotas and other measures. The USSR would sign contracts with French industry for 300 million francs and France would extend up to 22 months' credit.[114] The time had come, wrote ambassador Alphand, to take Germany's place. Germany had been selling about 20 billion francs' worth of merchandise to the USSR since the Treaty of Berlin of 1926. "We must prove that we are capable of supplying machines that are as good as the German or American ones, which they think are the only ones in the world."[115] As a matter of fact, the USSR asked for intensified technical aid for the navy[116] and the air force.[117] The commercial agreement itself was dated January 9, 1934.[118]

The second result was even more important. The Soviets officially proposed that the two countries go further and contemplate a real alliance, which Paris thought was probably compatible with the Franco-Polish alliance. Alphand, who had to weigh the meaning of this rapprochement, was troubled by this possibility.[119] But Paul-Boncour and the Quai d'Orsay found it more and more appealing and on January 2, 1934, Soviet Ambassador Dovgalevsky told Alexis Léger that the USSR was, first, prepared to become part of the League of Nations on certain conditions; and, second, that his country wanted "an agreement for mutual defense that would include only the USSR, France, Belgium, Czechoslovakia, Poland, Lithuania, Latvia, Estonia and Finland."[120]

Therefore, on the eve of Paul-Boncour's departure from the Quai d'Orsay, France and the USSR had improved their relations to such a point that *the issue of an alliance had thus been raised.*

5.

THE MOVE TOWARD ECONOMIC NATIONALISM

Neither Paul-Boncour, who was hardly qualified in financial matters, and not Herriot, nor Daladier, could direct France's external economic policy, insofar as it could be "directed" to any degree. The ministers of finance in 1933, Henri Chéron, "the treasure hoarder," and later, Georges

Bonnet, did play a role. Raymond Patenôtre, the undersecretary of state for economic affairs, also had considerable influence (except during the short Sarraut ministry)—he was the only man on the moderate left to recommend devaluation. Certainly, at the technical level, the most influential people were Wilfrid Baumgartner, the director of the *Mouvement général des fonds* at the Ministry of Finance, his assistant, and the financial attachés in London (Jacques Rueff) and in Washington (Emmanuel Mönick).

All of them wanted to develop some sort of worldwide economic cooperation. So did the key ambassadors: François-Poncet dreamt of Franco-German economic collaboration; de Jouvenel wished to privilege Franco-Italian relations; Paul Claudel wanted ties with the United States and with Belgium; Charles Corbin with England and Charles Alphand with Moscow.

And yet a kind of fateful destiny seemed to push the entire world and particularly France, into remaining isolated. The end of reparations and war debts in 1932 was just one of the signs of general disorder where every country fended for itself in seeking to apply its own methods.

A quick look at France's balance sheet will explain how this happened. First, the balance of payments, which had been positive at the end of the twenties, became broadly negative. Taking 100 as a base number for 1928, the following chart clearly shows this change:[121]

	Exports	Imports
1930	89	123
1931	76	122
1932	58	102
1933	59	107
1934	61	91
1935	55	89
1936	52	98

The deficit was 1.3 billion gold francs in 1929 and 2.5 billion in 1936 despite the decrease in foreign trade.

From 1927 to 1931, the balance of trade, which included "invisible exports," had a positive yearly balance of 3 billion gold francs. Between 1932 and 1935, this positive balance turned into an average yearly deficit of 2.7 billion. France stopped paying its debts to England and the United States, and the number of foreign workers decreased sharply while income from tourism collapsed. The revenue from "services" remained fairly stable, but the interest on funds invested in foreign countries, which had been growing until 1933, began decreasing. Also, French exports were increasingly based on foodstuffs and raw materials while manufactured goods were decreasing. French industry's position in the international markets was steadily weakening, except for some "new" industries.

Of course it was also true that all markets were shrinking. In 1931–1932, Great Britain had put an end to its long-standing free market. We have already mentioned the huge Hawley-Smoot tariff of 1930 in the United States.

More importantly, the relative international monetary unity, with currencies tied to the gold standard, came to an end. Three national "blocs" were then formed. The gold standard bloc, including France, Italy, Switzerland, Belgium, the Netherlands, and Luxemburg, kept the parity with gold and a relatively free currency market.

The second group adopted a system of "exchange controls." This was the Soviet system from inception. In 1931 it was adopted by Germany, followed by twenty-one other countries. When Dr. Hjalmar Schacht was named president of the Reichsbank on March 17, 1933, the system was reinforced under the pretext that it was necessary to prevent the Jews from exporting their capital. Within this system the currency can theoretically be linked to the gold standard but its market is not free and exporting it is forbidden. For instance, foreign exporters were obliged to spend the revenues from their sales inside Germany. The system allowed the state to manipulate its currency freely and, obviously, constituted a powerful check on foreign trade.

The third group was made up of the countries whose currency was off the gold standard and thus effectively devaluating it, their goal being to boost exports. The "gold-standard bloc" of countries, where prices were high, were consequently severely hurt. England abandoned the gold standard in September 1931, followed by the Commonwealth (except Canada), Japan, most of South America and Central Europe. The United States followed suit in April 1933 after Roosevelt's election. Canada joined in at the same time.

The measures taken by France to fight against these various systems were totally *ad hoc*. Internally, France followed a policy of deflation—in order to lower prices—which is not directly relevant to our study but whose effects would eventually influence foreign policy. Deflation was a source of discontent. Chancellor Brüning's policy of deflation in Germany in 1930 had led to the election of 107 Nazis and increased votes for the communists; similarly, deflation in France explains the crises of February 1934 and, later the rise of the Popular Front, events that were both to weigh heavily on the country's fate.

Externally, the various French governments resorted to taking a few classic measures:

1. They began by raising import tariffs in 1931, starting with farm products; then they cancelled trade agreements and established a surtax on goods originating from countries that had devalued their currency. Finally, they set up a system of quotas.

2. In order for French importers to be paid by the countries that had established exchange controls, the Paris chamber of commerce was allowed, by a decree of December 3, 1931, to create an "office of compensation" that collected the funds owed by French importers, using them to pay French exporters selling to countries with exchange controls. But, for this system to work efficiently, imports and exports to a particular country had to be matched. French importers were asked to obtain an "import permit." Lastly, "clearance agreements" were signed in 1933 and 1934 with Hungary, Austria, Bulgaria, Greece, Yugoslavia, Turkey, Romania, some Latin-American countries, and finally, with Germany. After 1935, clearance agreements would be replaced either by "private barter agreements," where a balance was maintained, or through "payment agreements." From then on the central bank collected the funds instead of the "office of compensation."

   This system held up international trade and, complicated everything, giving too much incentive to imports (in order to secure the funds necessary to pay the exporters). France would have preferred multilateral agreements. They were discussed at the council of the League of Nations, but nothing came of those discussions.

3. Beginning in July and August 1931, France first unilaterally established "quotas" on farm products in order to limit imports; then, after negotiating with its partners, it set quotas on industrial products (which is why these were called "bilateral quotas" or "friendly quotas"). The quota system lies halfway between export duties and putting a stop to all trade. It protected the producers at home, but created endless detailed negotiations. After setting a global quota for each product, it was divided among the different countries that

might export to France, in proportion to goods bought during the "normal" period! It becomes immediately obvious how rigid and arbitrary such a system was.

In 1933, the year we are examining in this chapter, any remaining hope of reorganizing international trade vanished mainly because the new president of the United States, Franklin D. Roosevelt, had decided to solve the economic crisis at the level of his own country and not at the international level. His predecessor, Herbert Hoover, had considered a multilateral solution, and offered to call a broad world economic conference in order to handle the daunting issue of debt.

The conference was prepared during the first months of 1933. It was to be held in London. France sent Jean Parmentier to the preparatory commission. Parmentier, was an honorary director of the *Mouvement general des fonds*, favored a rigid solution to the problem of war debts.[122] He felt that, through the Hoover moratorium, the United States had rescinded previous agreements, so that it became necessary to renegotiate the issue. Paul Claudel and his financial attaché Mönick, on the other hand, thought that there should be a "gesture" to coincide with Roosevelt's inauguration on March 4. Both remained optimistic since they believed Roosevelt favored a compromise solution. On January 10, 1933, Claudel met secretly with the president-elect "in a friendly house." Paul-Boncour sent him detailed instructions for the meeting, knowing full well that to ask the French parliament to go back on its December 15, 1932, vote would be a lost cause.[123] Just as Claudel and Mönick had hoped, the discussion was "entirely interesting and pleasant. Roosevelt is a man of the world but without any affectation, full of humanity—a man whom I sensed was a true friend of France." Roosevelt was a great charmer. He mentioned how the United States had only repaid their war debts of the eighteenth century under the Restoration and then without interest. "We do not consider France to have defaulted"—it has simply delayed one of its payments. But on every other subject he remained vague. He did not consider a moratorium, but a *modus vivendi*. He was enigmatic about the gold standard and trade tariffs, and asked Claudel to come and see him again. He did not commit to anything.[124] The French were somewhat disappointed, therefore, when negotiations on the debt opened between the British and the Americans. England had made a payment on December 15 and the Americans didn't know that it would be the last one. Claudel took comfort in the thought that, from the sidelines, "France was about to witness a very bitter and very close fight between the two countries."[125]

In February, before Roosevelt became president, there was a moment of hope. Paul-Boncour received the American diplomat William Bullitt, a personal friend of Roosevelt's. The president-elect had told him to ask the French government to send over a "confidential emissary."[126]

Who should go? Paul-Boncour thought of Herriot who answered that he felt honored by the choice but "the obligations of political life" kept him from leaving and he put off his trip for a few weeks. So Mönick was sent to meet with Roosevelt.[127] The meeting took place on February 18 in New York. Mönick was very surprised that Roosevelt barely mentioned the debt issue, but talked instead of a vast and very vague plan of cooperation. "The fate of western civilization will be in jeopardy, Roosevelt said, unless the United States, France, and England begin to collaborate efficiently and in the immediate future." This was the reason he wanted to meet with an eminent political figure.[128] France and England would talk with the United States as equal partners. The Quai d'Orsay thought this represented a "coup de théâtre."[129] They could see the United States and France bringing England back to the gold standard.

There was a "coup de théâtre" but it came from a completely different direction. Herriot, who had finally made himself available, was sent to Washington with stately pomp.[130] But, as he was sailing the Atlantic on the *Ile-de-France*, he suddenly learned, on April 20, that far from again linking the British pound to the gold standard, Roosevelt had decided to unlink the dollar. Herriot's disappointment was softened by the fact that Roosevelt came to greet him on the steps of the White House. He enjoyed that sort of flattery. Conversations were held in the presence of British Prime Minister Macdonald who was then in Washington. They ranged over all international matters. Roosevelt, according to Herriot, was the one who took the lead in demanding payment of the debt installment. Herriot, who had proposed this payment, was easily convinced. But, back in Paris, he could not "alter a decision that did us such harm."[131] It seems that in late April, Daladier and Paul-Boncour had thought of "proposing to parliament that the December installment be paid," on condition that there be a new agreement.[132] These conditions, however, would not be accepted and the negotiations were grinding to a halt. On June 1, André Lefèvre de Laboulaye, who had succeeded Paul Claudel as ambassador to Washington, was told by Bullitt that Roosevelt had forbidden the American delegation in London to broach the subject of the debt.[133]

The deep disappointment that was felt when the United States left the "gold bloc," deepened even further because of the American attitude at the London conference in June where sixty-four nations were participating. The European experts, who had "prepared" it under the auspices of the League of Nations, had proposed a classic internationalist program. The gold standard was to be reestablished, currency exchange controls abolished, and trade tariffs lowered. The French representative, George Bonnet, fought a losing battle. Lined up against him were the United States, England, and Germany. The failure of the conference—which Roosevelt was seeking—became clear when, on June 22, a very modest proposal for the *de facto* stabilization of currencies was swiftly rejected by the American delegation.[134] The only countries to sign on to the wish that "gold be reestablished as the international monetary standard"[135] were those of the "gold bloc."

Jacques Rueff, a great expert and one of the most insightful observers of this period, wrote soon after,[136] "The entire world economy fell into deep chaos; in every sector, in every market, in goods and services, in the capital markets and the workforce markets, any stability was destroyed; everywhere, suffering and often despair and ruin revealed the human face of the economic catastrophe that was devastating the entire world."

As for Paul-Boncour, all he could do was accept economic nationalism. "There is no need to demonstrate the danger of a view that tends to isolate countries and, by abolishing any commonality of interest between them, weakens the very basis of their peaceful relations."[137]

Chapter III

THE BARTHOU ERA

(1934)

French public opinion in 1933 was less interested in Hitler, the Four Power Pact, the London conference or Franco-Soviet relations than in the crisis and the suffering caused by deflation and the various scandals. Several arrests at the very end of December, including those of the director of the *Crédit municipal* in Bayonne and Deputy Mayor Garat, brought to light a series of irregularities masterminded by an international swindler, Alexander Stavisky, who committed suicide on January 7, 1934. Since the Cartel des Gauches was in power at the time, right-wing politicians and newspapers launched campaigns against corruption. We shall not get into the Stavisky affair but rather measure its consequences. First, the Chautemps cabinet fell on January 27, 1934—and Paul-Boncour left the Quai d'Orsay; this was followed by unrest and a series of riots. The main riot, on February 6, led to Daladier's resignation after a very short time in office. This was the end of the Cartel des Gauches and the beginning of an era of violent attacks against its leaders: Herriot, Daladier, Chautemps, and even Paul-Boncour (he had been the lawyer of Stavisky's wife, Arlette Simon, long before her marriage).

Albert Lebrun, president of the republic, thought the solution was to form a government of "national union" with a leader who would be "above all parties, and who through his prestige and authority could bring back unity and internal peace. Mr. Lebrun first thought of Louis Barthou, but everyone agreed on Gaston Doumergue."

Doumergue had been president of the republic from 1924 to 1931, and had retired to his home in Tournefeuille, near Toulouse. He was preparing to leave on a pleasure trip to Egypt. He accepted, and having been out of touch with parliament, quite naturally looked to his contemporaries and the former prime ministers whom he knew personally.[1]

The new government was in stark contrast to those that had preceded it. For one thing, it contained many elderly men. Barthou was 72, Doumergue was 71 and the minister of war, Marshal Pétain, was 78. As *Le Figaro* put it: the government "raised great hopes and brought great disappointments... It is a raft built on stormy seas and painfully at that. The navigation is—for the most part— in the hands of veterans, men who were young before the war or in 1900. Public opinion had not requested their return."[2] It didn't really create national union; the hostility of the communists and the socialists (they staged demonstrations on February 9 and 12) made that clear. It was in fact a massive return of the right. Two state ministers flanked Doumergue—Tardieu for the right and Herriot for the left. This wasn't the first time Herriot took part in a "union" government. He had done so before with Poincaré in July 1926. The business-oriented right wing with Flandin, Piétri, and Laval and the Catholic Right with Louis Marin were both strongly represented, along with seven radicals.

Still, somewhat unwittingly, Doumergue scored a coup in distributing the ministerial posts when he appointed Louis Barthou to the Quai d'Orsay.

1.

Louis Barthou and His Plans

As research progresses and more documents in the archives become available, the importance of Barthou's tenure at the Quai d'Orsay stands out. What is increasingly clear is that, for a brief period, one clearly senses an unmistakable recovery on the path toward decadence. It is even tempting and rather futile at the same time to speculate over what might have happened had Barthou not been shot on October 9, 1934. His intentions and his plans remain shrouded in mystery. What role did he play personally? What part did ministry officials or even his ministerial cabinet have remains unclear.[3]

He was not liked personally and did not attract much sympathy. He had risen from humble origins as an important local leader.[4] He was born in Oloron-Sainte-Marie near Pau, on August 25, 1862, the same year as Briand, who was from Nantes. Barthou's father owned a hardware store and his grandfather had been an elementary school teacher. His family was deeply republican. He was a very good student, became a great admirer of Victor Hugo, Michelet, and Claude Bernard and had anticlerical views. Like many men with political ambitions, he became a lawyer in Pau. "The passion for politics," he wrote, "is not linked to family tradition; it is a personal calling... Politics is the art of governing; it is the will, the passion to lead. Those who have no taste for it have difficulty acquiring it but those who love it find it even more difficult to give up."[5] At 26 he was elected to the Pau city council and in 1889, at 27, became the for the Oloron area. He remained a deputy until he was elected to the Senate in 1924 and was therefore very much a seasoned member of parliament with a career spanning 46 years! In that sense he resembled Poincaré, who had also been elected at a very young age, rather than Briand, who was first elected at 40. In 1894, when he was only 32, he was appointed to his first cabinet post (as minister of public works). He would hold cabinet appointments seven times before the First World War, and was once Prime Minister, from 1913 to 1914. He was wealthy, having married the daughter of an important merchant. His only son was killed in December 1914 at Thann, a source of endless sorrow.

After the war, he was the chairman of the committee of the Treaty of Versailles to parliament, after which he was appointed minister of national defense under Briand and Poincaré from 1921 to 1924. An influential senator during the Cartel des Gauches period; his last cabinet post had been as minister of justice under Poincaré from 1926 to 1929.

When Doumergue put together his government in February 1934, Barthou was ready to serve.[6] Why was he appointed to foreign affairs? Probably because of his long experience and his patriotism.

He remains mysterious and difficult to assess as a man. He had many enemies. *L'Action française* had singled him out for years[7] and Sennep, a caricaturist, had published a vicious little book in which Barthou was accused of sexual perversions and portrayed with a dog's tail. That kind of pamphlet discredited its author more than the victim. A more serious accusation was that of political infidelity. At the end of the nineteenth century, the radicals dubbed him "the traitor," because he had provoked the fall of the Brisson cabinet in 1898. The socialists didn't like him any better. Jaurès accused him of corruption, saying he had been paid by the *Compagnie des chemins de fer du Midi.* They fought in a duel and an "honor jury" vouched for his complete honesty. Still, the communists hated him even more. He had violently attacked the Soviets at the Genoa Conference of 1922 and, as Poincaré's minister of justice, had prosecuted several communists: Jacques Doriot, Marcel Cachin, André Marty, Jacques Duclos, and Paul Vaillant-Couturier. His allegiance to Poincaré, whose ideas he by and large shared, doesn't seem to have been unfailing.[8]

Louis Barthou was a member of the *Alliance Démocratique,* a moderate republican party, founded in 1902 and favorable to the "Bloc des Gauches" of the time. Above all, he was a liberal and a patriot[9] with little interest in social issues. He admired Paul Déroulède and was part of a generation that was deeply hostile to Germany. "We must enforce the treaty," he said on September 2, 1919. "We must do so in a spirit of fairness but also with unbending rigor." He also used the phrase, "This peace is a vigilant peace."[10] Therefore, he showed little enthusiasm for the politics of Briand. "I would have liked some changes, a slower pace and some precautions."[11]

To complete the portrait of the man we should point to his great culture. He dedicated his fortune to book collecting and spent his leisure time writing. Diderot, Lamartine, Victor Hugo, Musset, Baudelaire and the French revolution were his favorite subjects. He wrote a remarkable biography of *Danton.* But he was not an ivory tower-type scholar. He liked sports, practiced gymnastics daily and went on long hiking trips in the Alps around Bürgenstock in Switzerland, where he spent his vacations. Despite his stuffy appearance—he sported a goatee and wore spectacles—he was full of vim and vigor and worked at a furious pace. The documents he read were so thoroughly annotated that at the Quai d'Orsay his notes could be used as the basis for a response. Paul-Boncour, his predecessor at the Quai d'Orsay, was glad to see him pursue the same policies with "a vigor that age had not diminished. He charged into politics, upset the old boys, more than our people did with those who had preceded us."[12] His Belgian counterpart, Paul Hymans, spoke of his wit and "his *béarnais* verve."[13]

Barthou was essentially a very creative man of action, a doer and a realist; he was more of an opportunist rather than doctrinaire. It would be difficult to identify him with any kind of structured plan. Still, we can outline his main initiatives before moving on to a detailed description of events.

First, he viewed *Germany as the enemy.* Those who for internal political reasons preferred Germany to the USSR were totally mistaken. On March 5 he received Ribbentrop who, referring to *Mein Kampf,* said the book reflected outdated circumstances. It was passé. Barthou, who had read the book, stopped him short by asking, quite innocently, why then was it being constantly reprinted?[14]

The security of France was the main goal. "Security above all," he wrote in the margin of a document,[15] and this was his motto. However, he didn't feel it could be guaranteed by the League of Nations. His predecessor, Paul-Boncour, called this the "turning point of 1934."[16]

In the absence of collective security, it became necessary to enter into alliances, or to strengthen the existing ones. But that view was in contrast with the British who did not want to isolate Germany. So be it! Barthou was quite prepared to overcome the British obstacle. He knew that beyond the terms of the Locarno treaty, he could not count on a British alliance. All he asked was that England not prevent France from entering into alliances it deemed necessary! Indeed, England was relatively unconcerned by the alliances France struck with Poland (this alliance was much compromised when Germany and Poland signed an agreement on January 26, 1934), with Czechoslovakia, Yugoslavia, and Romania or even with the secret military convention with Belgium. Barthou went through the usual unimportant French ritual of visiting the allied capitals. A Franco-Italian alliance would have much greater value. But above all else an alliance with the USSR was something France could count on. What if the British disliked the idea? They would be ignored.

It seems quite clear that Barthou conceived of a *direct Franco-Soviet alliance,* above and beyond the Eastern pact as we shall show further ahead.[17]

And so the very same man who hounded the communists didn't hesitate regarding the most obviously realistic alliance. For a long time he had been critical of France's unrealistic policy towards Moscow. This is what he said, for example, in a speech on March 26, 1920:[18] "The way we deal with Russia will determine the path it takes with Germany." Up until then, he said, France had conducted an "unfortunate policy" towards

Russia. "We had a policy of force… It failed. Then there was a policy of metaphors (*applause and laughter on the extreme left*)…this policy was first defined by the image of the "*cordon sanitaire*," then it was further sharpened by the image of barbed wire." But other countries were trying to enter into a relationship with the USSR. "And so, my dear colleagues, we must take heed, first for the protection of our interests, but also for the preservation of our authority. Certainly, we are going to be latecomers, but I would not want us to be too late."

The Soviets did not dislike this type of pragmatic politician, fiercely anti-communist inside his country but seeking an alliance with the USSR. I personally heard old ambassador Maïsky say, that with all due proportion, he deemed Barthou another Churchill.

2.

THE NOTE OF APRIL 17, 1934

There were at least two critical issues where Barthou felt powerless. The first was France's economic isolation, something we will discuss later on.[19] The second issue was German rearmament. This was precisely what Germany was doing since leaving the disarmament conference and the League of Nations. We shall start with this issue since Barthou gave it his undivided attention and all his energy for two months.

What was the meaning of the German decision? The Quai d'Orsay and the French delegation in Geneva were trying to figure it out and a few officials had already reached a conclusion. For Captain Decoux of the navy staff, "the French government is 'playing games' in pretending to the world that the British and the Americans are behind us… Indeed they are, on condition that we disarm and become defenseless on the ground, on the sea and in the air."[20] François-Poncet, after reading an interview Hitler gave to the journalist Fernand de Brinon—someone we shall encounter later on—on November 22, 1933, in *Le Matin*, still felt that Hitler was only seeking partial rearmament and that he wished to return to the League of Nations.[21]

Things would take a new turn when Hitler, assisted by von Neurath, received François-Poncet for an hour and a half on November 24, 1933. Hitler declared that he fundamentally hoped for an "immediate and far ranging disarmament of all the great powers." But he did not believe it would take place. That was why he was asking that Germany be allowed not just a 200,000-man army, as Macdonald was proposing, but 300,000 men recruited on a short-term basis, plus a "number to be discussed" of fighter planes, 150 mm cannon, and light tanks. At the same time, the British declared that it seemed inappropriate to investigate German rearmament! Paul-Boncour expressed "extreme surprise."[22] But why should he be surprised? England expected France to disarm or Germany to rearm, wishing to see France negotiate directly with Germany on that issue.[23] This was very dangerous as Viénot, the deputy delegate to the disarmament conference, wrote to Massigli, Boncour, Léger, Chautemps, and Daladier. "Even from a defensive standpoint, the almost tragic battle that our diplomatic services are now fighting is on the verge of being lost." Since October 14, France no longer has the initiative. Direct conversations will force us to break with Germany. When that happens, and it will come soon, we will have lost."[24]

On January 6, 1934, the French section at the League of Nations provided the following comparison between French and German forces. In 1914 France had a standing army of 754,000 men stationed within its borders; it now had only 350,000 men, of which only 175,000 were battle-ready. It could mobilize 2,800,000 reservists. As for Germany, the Reichswehr was already 150,000 men strong, with another 40,000 paramilitary policemen, and 1,200,000 men in the SA and the SS.[25] The balance was tipping in its favor. On February 20, Pétain estimated the "total number of Hitler's troop capacity"[26] to be 2,500,000 men.

When Barthou took over at the Quai d'Orsay, the agenda was full. He immediately took on the key issue: the 300,000-man calculation as the total amount of troops allowed in both French and German armies had to be made along clear guidelines. Germany wanted to include French colonial troops in that number; France also wanted to include SA and SS troops. This discrepancy had to be cleared before the issue of whether France ought to sign an accord with Germany on the basis of 300,000 men could be agreed to or whether talks should be terminated. Throughout the winter, in an exchange of notes[27] and conversations conducted through diplomatic channels, France, England, Italy and Germany discussed these points in remarkable detail.

In a memorandum dated January 29, 1934, the British proposed a Franco-German compromise, since "the inability to strike a perfect agreement would be a terrible setback for all those in favor of peace."[28] They did not include controls on location, but were limited to a vague system of consultations, and trusted the German government to resolve the question of the SA and the SS. The "trial period" the French had wanted was abandoned, and finally, in Massigli's opinion, the project "seems closer to German than to French thinking." Massigli also added, "England cannot be an impartial arbiter; when something doesn't concern her directly, she either doesn't pay any attention and doesn't even mention it, or tends to pander to German interests, while at the same time demanding that France make inordinate concessions. Conversely, when the issue is of direct importance to the United Kingdom, French wishes are no longer taken into account; witness the case, for instance, of the air force."[29] We are the only ones—it is written in another note[30]—who aren't driven by the desire to sign an agreement. England wants an agreement for ideological reasons, Italy as an economic measure, and Germany "because it would absolve her, cost-free, of the hidden violation of international treaties it has conducted for the past fifteen years. Therefore, let us obtain as much as we can for our good will. Let us give in only against concessions. But if we refuse an agreement, we must take precautions to ensure that the responsibility for the failure of the British plan will not be attributed to the French government."[31]

With this in mind, the army general staff prepared a note, on March 5, weighing the pros and cons. Signing would mean limiting German rearmament, substituting a freely agreed treaty to the *Diktat* of Versailles, "making it possible, *if the system of controls is effective*, to draw up evidence of violations of the agreement, that could be used at the international level," to finally bring about a détente in Europe. But everything would depend on the effectiveness of controls. If they weren't effective, then we would end up playing Germany's game and increasing the prestige of Hitler's regime. Signing an agreement also meant, "dangerously postponing the inevitable return to the system of alliances." (Here the general staff appeared to be in step with the main point in Barthou's thinking.)[32]

Weygand, vice president of the Supreme War Council, opted for breaking with Germany.[33] He cited "the nefarious accord of December 11, 1932"—meaning the granting of "equal rights." The German threat was greater than ever. Would it be possible to count on controls to guarantee security? "What was control worth in the absence of sanctions?" "Anything is better than disarming when Germany is rearming."[34] Marshal Pétain, the minister of war, agreed with Weygand;[35] Barthou, on the other hand, insisted in many of his notes on the need for controls and "guarantees of implementation." Military sanctions must be "absolutely automatic." But Barthou, the Quai d'Orsay and France's ambassador to Germany, all favored signing an agreement. François-Poncet came to Paris on April 9, 1934. "Limited and controlled rearmament," he explained to the government ministers, "was better than the unlimited, unchecked and unrepressed rearmament of the Reich."[36]

Then there was Doumergue who called a special commission on April 14, 1934, to review the facts. Both state ministers, Herriot and Tardieu, also took part, as did the military authorities and Weygand, Gamelin and Admiral Durand-Viel. René Massigli represented the Quai d'Orsay. Weygand defended his well-established position forcefully. Massigli stated his objections and Tardieu supported Weygand: "We don't believe in controls." As for Herriot, he was for an arms agreement but did not press his position as forcefully.[37]

A decision had to emerge from this debate and the many notes, thoughts and statistics compiled for months. François-Poncet wrote a dramatic account of the last minute hesitations.[38] According to him, he was the one who sealed Barthou's decision, but Barthou told him, "You should be arguing all this upstairs, not here!" Meaning in Doumergue's office, which was on the floor just above at the Quai d'Orsay. But when he did go to see the Prime Minister, the ambassador could not get a word in edgewise; Doumergue cut him off and started on "a totally irrelevant soliloquy." This meant, according to the ambassador, that he had already made up his mind.

Still, the documents don't tell the same story, there are no traces of such forceful resistance in any of them and no sign that Barthou ever thought of resigning and refrained from doing so out of patriotic duty. As a matter of fact, two notes, dated April 16, resulted from the April 14 discussions. The first one, addressed to the minister, was from the French office at the League of Nations. It established the conditions for a disarmament agreement. A system of controls must be instituted "with perfect reciprocity," under the oversight of a permanent commission of the League of Nations; it should not be left to the countries themselves. It would be automatic and permanent and would not "search for minute violations," but would pursue a general evaluation regarding observance of the agreement. It would deal chiefly with weapons manufacturing, which would be subject to fixed quotas, and with arms budgets, which would be capped.[39] This document doesn't evince any forceful recommendations either way. Obviously, the Quai d'Orsay didn't share François-Poncet's relative optimism.

The other note was written by Doumergue himself.[40] Since the last British note, he said, "a most serious and important event has occurred." What had happened was the surprise announcement on March 22 that the German military budget was to be greatly increased, a jump of 352 million marks. Germany had made clear its intention to rearm, come what may, and it was doing so unilaterally. "By taking this action, Germany appears to have turned any discussion about guaranteeing the implementation of the disarmament agreement, moot." The only solution for France was "to see to its own security." In the margin of this note, Barthou, who, according to François-Poncet, received it directly from the prime minister, had written, "This note was handed to me by Mr. Gaston Doumergue for the purpose of laying out the main ideas of our response to Great Britain. It must be placed in the file." There is not a word showing Barthou heroically resisting a solution he supposedly abhorred.

As early as the next day, April 17, the cabinet unanimously approved a document prepared by the staff of the Quai d'Orsay, but extensively and carefully edited by Barthou.[41] The document was the communiqué that would be handed to Sir Ronald Campbell, the councilor at the British embassy. It was a ringing declaration announcing that France would no longer pursue useless negotiations with Germany. The point made was similar to the one contained in Doumergue's note. Germany "intends to increase dramatically and immediately the power not only of its army but also of its navy and air force." It was doing so "against the stipulations of the treaty, which, in the absence of any agreement, still determines the status of its armaments." And so France must "place the conditions of its own security ahead of any other consideration." Only Germany's return to the League of Nations, would permit France to consider a disarmament agreement. But there was no sign that Germany had any such intention. France had made greater sacrifices in the war than any other country. "Its commitment to peace must not be mistaken for an abdication of its defense."

France in effect still allowed, albeit in vague terms, the disarmament conference to continue its work but, *having reached the conclusion that nothing could prevent Germany from rearming, France was refusing to disarm.* Didn't France still enjoy an overwhelming superiority over her rival? The point was to avoid losing that superiority. But this concerned the future. "We shall see"—as Gamelin told François-Poncet—"how long it takes Germany to catch up with the 20 billion we have spent on armaments."[42]

The April 17 note led to much debate; it was generally approved in France where government bonds increased. Many in Britain, on the other hand, took the position that France was responsible for rearmament.

For Barthou, this felt like freedom. The debate in the cabinet, as he told Campbell, "was one of the best I have ever experienced during my long career as minister."[43] When he met Arthur Henderson on April 7, he said, "I don't in the least enjoy, even though I am an academician, writing a different diplomatic note every other week. Conversations would certainly be a more efficient method." In fact, Barthou was a realist and did not quite believe in the efficacy of controls, even at a time when that idea was gospel truth for the French political class. In any case, had controls uncovered important German infractions, would they be followed by effective sanctions? Would we close our eyes like the British government or would we complain about our fate, as the French government did?

The situation was now clear; the time had come to strengthen France. Louis Barthou was very skeptical of collective security and determined to achieve it through alliances.

In the short term, the episode led to a semi-heroic conclusion that didn't displease France's touchy chauvinism. In a sense, the French weren't wrong; they were finally granted the satisfaction of witnessing a French minister standing fast against England.

At the end of May 1934, Barthou was in Geneva for more talks about disarmament, but without believing in them. On the 30th, Sir John Simon gave a speech where he pandered to Germany and criticized France. For him, there was only one plan—the British one and he seemed to "forget that there was a French plan and an Italian plan as well as the British plan." On April 16, the German position was very close to the British position. "The unspoken conclusion was obvious: the French clearly were the obstacle to any agreement."

Barthou replied "very forcefully." His speech was, according to Massigli, "one of the most important ever made in Geneva."[44] In an aggressively sarcastic tone, Barthou referred to Sir John Simon as "my dear colleague and not quite a friend" and restated the fact that France too had a plan for disarmament, even if Sir John Simon pretended not to know about it. England might not care a fig, but for France, security was a requirement. In the end, what the British government really wanted France to do was allow Germany to rearm. He even quoted Mirabeau's words: "War is Prussia's main industry."[45]

Sir John Simon was furious, and considered leaving Geneva. Barthou saved the day by inviting all his opposite numbers to lunch on June 1. The Belgian minister Hymans has written a colorful account of those peacemaking festivities. "Barthou poured out his Mediterranean wit and all his literary erudition in seeking to charm and impress the British statesman, who listened and accepted what was being said with a smile, soon participating in the conversation showing how well versed his was in literary matters." They discussed Thucydides, the Peloponnesian war and the art of public speaking.[46] It was a day of relaxation, which, according to Massigli, "...seemed to have underlined the failure of the operation attempted two days before to place the blame for the failure of the conference squarely on France."[47]

3.

THE VISIT OF THE SMALLER ALLIES

The Four Power Pact signed in July 1933 is a necessary starting point. The content had been watered down to such an extent that it had no vigor left to it because France feared to disappoint Poland and the three countries of the Little Entente—Czechoslovakia, Romania, and Yugoslavia—while those countries did their best to eliminate whatever remained of the pact. On August 15, 1933, during a visit of the new ambassador, de Chambrun, Mussolini felt that "an atmosphere of the Four Power Pact still existed."[48] Paul-Boncour then offered an outline for discussion, aimed at "not letting opposite blocs, subject to conflicting influences, appear in Eastern and Central Europe."[49] He was actually alluding to economic links.

In any case, those economic links were being discussed to no avail since 1919. As to reconciling Hungary, which wanted part of Slovakia and part of Transylvania, with Czechoslovakia and Romania, which did not wish to be dismembered, it was like placing a circle in a square.[50] Let us proceed with caution, was Mussolini's comment to ambassador de Chambrun on September 4, 1933.[51] In February 1933 the Little Entente was in fact reinforced, but in the past tense, meaning that it remained directed against Hungary, Bulgaria and the restoration of the Hapsburgs but not at all against Nazi Germany, despite the fact that the date coincided with Hitler's rise to power. In September 1933 Czech President

Mazaryk defended his project of a "Danube Federation." But his partners didn't follow suit, especially Austria and Hungary, and Mussolini was against it.[52] Furthermore Romanian foreign minister Titulescu at the end of the fall of 1933, began a policy of rapprochement with Greece, Turkey and Yugoslavia that resulted in the signing of the Balkan Pact in Athens on February 9, 1934.[53] These events, while of interest to French diplomacy, were taking place, for the most part, without her involvement. Italy was clearly hostile. The split remained unchanged between "revisionist" and "satisfied" countries.

Mussolini himself buried the Four Power Pact after Germany left the League of Nations. Speaking to the Chamber of Fasces and Corporations on November 14, he condemned the treaties and the League of Nations. He asked for a territorial revision because, as he said, "Europe couldn't reach an understanding if great injustices were not first set right." "Lately there had been," he added, "a heavy silence regarding the Four Power Pact." Too bad, Italy would not take new initiatives on that issue.[54] And he added in a lofty article published on December 31, 1933, and ringing like a bad omen that, "Barring a revision through the Four Power Pact, the last word will belong to 'his majesty the Cannon!'"

With Poland things would go much further. Its leaders, Marshal Pilsudski and Colonel Beck, practiced a eighteenth-century brand of foreign policy full of secrecy and cynicism. That's how Jules Laroche[55] and Léon Noël,[56] the two French ambassadors at that time, assessed it. In 1933 the changes in Polish diplomacy were quite spectacular. As France's ally, Poland leaked a rumor of a joint preventive war against Hitler.[57] France would have no part of it.[58] The rumor started, no doubt, with an incident on March 13, 1933—the landing of Polish units on the Westerplatte opposite Danzig in what appeared as a "provocation of Germany."[59] The troops very quickly returned to their ships.

Following the Four Power Pact, the situation took an entirely different turn—that of a definite rapprochement between Poland and Nazi Germany. During a meeting on November 2, 1933, Jules Laroche asked Beck whether Germany had offered him a non-aggression pact. No, he answered. "Naturally should such an offer be made we would examine it seriously."[60] As he observed the various steps taken by Lipski, his Polish colleague, François-Poncet was becoming increasingly suspicious. Germany was attempting to "dismantle the stones from the wall that hemmed in its ambitions one by one."[61] In point of fact, Hitler's Germany operated "through conspiracy and dramatic coups" and "regrettably the Poles appear to like that method." A German-Polish declaration[62] was then made on November 16, announcing ongoing negotiations between the two countries. Was it a Polish or a German initiative? Was it reassuring or worrisome? French diplomacy was vigorously seeking to understand those issues until January 26, 1934, a few days before Louis Barthou took over and Lipski's explicit denials notwithstanding—the Polish tour de valse was announced officially: *the two countries were signing a non-aggression declaration.*

What could the motivations have been? The answer is outside our subject, which is to study French foreign policy and not that of Poland or Germany. It is true that ambassadors François-Poncet, Laroche, and Léon Noël (who was then in Prague) were carefully analyzing that event in many reports and cables. They concluded that while reaffirming its loyalty to the alliance with France, Poland had switched sides. "That agreement won't last ten years!" said Beneš to Léon Noël.[63] François-Poncet was particularly angry because on January 24 he met his Polish colleague Lipski who lied by omission, hiding the fact that he was about to sign the pact with Hitler's Germany. From then on there could no trust. We could no longer treat him as an ally.[64] Laroche was also just as incensed. Marshal Pilsudski and Colonel Beck received him on January 29 when he voiced his complaints. The meeting was lively. After all, said the Marshal, who had trouble expressing himself but knew how to be ironic, he acted this way because of the uncertainty of French policy and its endless concessions under pressure coming from Great Britain and now Italy. "Important cable" wrote Louis Barthou in the margin on February 11.[65]

Poland was therefore the first country to play the well-known game of signing a treaty with a potential opponent whose blatant bad faith was obvious, using the pretense of holding thunder at bay. Between the German-Polish declaration of January 26, 1934, and the German-Soviet Pact of August 23, 1939, many countries would follow an ineffectual policy of frightened egoism! And France is not to be excluded.

Barthou wanted to put an end to this incipient dislocation, first by increasing contacts. He tirelessly began a whole series of pilgrimages to the small allied states.

The first visit was to Belgium, which had signed a secret military agreement with France on September 7, 1920, and later the Locarno treaties of 1925. Since that date the interpretations by the two countries regarding the 1920 agreement were growing progressively farther apart. The French objective was to avoid another 1914 and be able to enter into

Belgium fast enough in the event of war with Germany. The Belgians were suspicious of such a broad interpretation, which ended up giving France the right to occupy their country. Some people, such as the socialist Vandervelde and many other Flemish leaders, advocated simply canceling the agreement since they viewed the Locarno treaties as being more than adequate. Belgium had to avoid above all being drawn into a conflict because of France's other allies. The most controversial article concerned Belgium's obligation to mobilize immediately "in case Germany issued a general call to arms." With an exchange of letters in February 1931 between Belgian minister Hymans and French ambassador Peretti della Rocca, it was agreed to mention the 1920 agreement but to reduce it to "military cooperation between Belgium and France in case of an unprovoked aggression by Germany."[66]

That toning down didn't go far enough for the Belgians. Would they allow French troops to enter their territory in the event—something that was forbidden by Locarno—of a violation of the Rhineland demilitarized zone? Paul Claudel, the new ambassador, was asked to inquire with Hymans on November 27, 1933. On February 8, 1934, the Belgians replied that they didn't feel obligated to call on France immediately.[67]

Marshal Pétain had very awkwardly mentioned to Baron Gaiffier, the Belgian ambassador to Paris, that in case of war with Germany, France would send its armies through Belgium. The ambassador replied, "If we allow you to do so." To which Pétain replied, "with or without your permission." "In that case," said Gaiffier, "we shall welcome you with cannon fire."[68]

One week after the Belgian note King Albert I died in a mountain climbing accident and his son Leopold III became king. Barthou's March 27 visit was mostly intended to satisfy protocol. Barthou met with the king, Prime Minister de Broqueville and, more importantly, accompanied by Paul Claudel, his Belgian counterpart Paul Hymans. The conversation focused mostly on disarmament—the note of April 17 was at hand. The Belgians favored a Franco-German understanding and the military agreement was barely mentioned. Barthou just made a point of underlining the need for general staff agreements.[69]

Since the pilgrimage to Belgium yielded few results, Barthou traveled to Poland, Warsaw, and Cracow (April 22–24), right after the April 17 note, then to Czechoslovakia (April 26–27). He had specifically prepared those trips and handed a memo[70] to Ambassador Chlapowski with the questions he wanted to ask the Polish leaders. The crowds gave him a very warm welcome and Barthou's visit to Warsaw and Cracow confirmed the deep feelings of affection that the Polish people felt toward France. Barthou was direct and spontaneous. The welcome by the political leaders was less warm. Pilsudski was friendly and reiterated Poland's commitment to the alliance with France.

Beck was "tense and uptight at first." The only tangible result was that the Poles succeeded in convincing Barthou that the Polish-German agreement contained no secret clauses and that Poland had "a free hand" towards its two larger neighbors. Barthou was therefore unable to change the new line Poland had taken nor to improve the traditionally poor relationship between the Poles and the Czechoslovaks.[71]

In Prague there were more reliable friends and a foreign policy management that was less mysterious and more democratic. "A cheering crowd that wasn't normally inclined to being demonstrative" welcomed Barthou.[72] He had broad discussions with Beneš. What were Austria's chances to remain independent? What relations did Czechoslovakia have with Austria and Hungary? The proposal often raised in France of a Habsburg restoration to give Austria an identity was something Beneš rejected out of hand.[73]

In May Barthou spent part of his time in Geneva and we have mentioned his sparring with Sir John Simon. We shall discuss him [at the League] again with Litvinov later in this chapter. His last two friendship visits were postponed until June.

Barthou left on June 19 and decided to stop in Vienna to meet with Chancellor Dollfuss, who was optimistic about Austria's independence. There was Nazi terrorism in Austria "but Mr. Dollfuss noted a reduction in the attacks." The poor man obviously couldn't foresee that on July 25 he would be one of their victims himself. There was something tragic in that meeting of the two men fated to die.[74]

On June 21 Barthou arrived in Bucharest, the Romanian capital. He met with Prime Minister Tatarescu, who was also minister of war and who urgently requested the delivery of French military supplies that Romania would pay for, even with oil.[75] France could rely on the solid friendship of Foreign Minister Titulescu and had a false friend in King Carol II. The King told Barthou that he was the strongest supporter of an alliance with France. "I can only laugh," said Titulescu to French representative André Lefèvre d'Ormesson, who found the minister's words to be those of "an impulsive, egocentric, nervous, vindictive man, despite possessing a keen intelligence." D'Ormesson thought the King was "unreliable and totally underhanded."[76] "Read with interest and approved," was Barthou's notation on the margin of the document.

Yugoslavia was the final and, in a sense, the fateful stop because at that meeting Barthou invited King Alexander to visit France where they were both to die together, shot by the same criminals. There again the purpose of the trip was to maintain a strong existing friendship. The King was pleased to see that the French minister's visit brought together the various peoples—Serbs, Slovenes and Croats. Croatian Utashis were the murderers of October 9.[77]

4.

TOWARD THE GRAND ALLIANCE

At what point and why did Barthou become interested in a Franco-Russian rapprochement? As we mentioned earlier, on January 4, 1934, in the course of a conversation with Alexis Léger, Soviet Ambassador Dovgalevsky had brought up the possibility of his country participating in the League of Nations and "of a mutual defense agreement" limited to Europe. Until the April 17 Note, Barthou didn't appear to be in a hurry to consider the issue. On March 3 he cabled Ambassador Alphand that a visit to Paris by People's Commissar for Foreign Affairs Maxim Litvinov would be premature.[78] On March 30 the political affairs section addressed a memo to Barthou entitled, "Mutual assistance in Eastern Europe." France had always wanted to add an Eastern Locarno to the Western Locarno. What was being proposed was simply a regional mutual assistance pact that would include Poland, the USSR, Czechoslovakia, the Baltic states, and Germany, without making any commitments regarding the Asian portion of Russia. It clearly stated that "only with the participation or inclusion of Germany could this system take on characteristics similar to the Locarno treaties." There was no mention of France or the kind of relationship she could have to the pact.[79]

Precisely one month later, on April 28, the same political affairs section drafted a new memorandum that was to be at the origin of the Eastern Pact. France was now to play a major part. The idea of an Eastern Locarno was kept, "whereby each signatory, after committing himself to not attack any of the other parties, would also agree to provide assistance to any *neighboring* party against an aggression coming from *any signatory.*"

Thanks to this extremely clever formula that must have greatly appealed to the Briandists and the Quai d'Orsay treaty makers—Alexis Léger first and foremost—Germany and the USSR, not being neighbors, would not be obligated to provide assistance to one another. Contrary to Dovgalevsky's proposal of January 4, France would not be directly included because its only neighbor within this combination was Germany. Therefore, France would be placed in the incredible position of providing assistance only to Germany. The "Eastern Locarno" agreement would be completed by a special agreement between France and the USSR. The two countries would promise to provide each other with help and assistance in case they became victims of an aggression due to Germany's failure to abide by one or the other of those agreements. A Franco-Soviet pact clearly aimed at Germany would thus be added to the existing Western Locarno and to the Eastern Locarno still to be agreed to.[80] Léger, after approving the document, presented it orally to Rosenberg, councilor at the Soviet embassy in Paris. Barthou had therefore approved it, and had personally met with Rosenberg.

Clearly, the French minister had changed his mind. Herriot confirmed that Barthou did not favor the Franco-Soviet non-aggression pact of December 1932, and had at first, like Doumergue, slowed down the negotiations.[81] "At some point at the end of April, Barthou decided to take on the Russian alliance," as American historian William Evans Scott writes correctly. But he no doubt was wrong in attributing part of this change to the influence of Léger.[82] Obviously, like all Briandistes, he favored the Eastern Locarno, but it seems doubtful that he would back a real bilateral alliance.

The key event was the meeting between Barthou and Litvinov in Geneva on May 18, 1934.[83] Litvinov immediately agreed to the French plan but asked for some explanations on a few points: Why was Belgium being excluded? Why wouldn't France agree to join in an Eastern Pact like the one suggested by Dovgalevsky on January 4? Could Finland also be part of it? He appeared satisfied by Bartou's explanations. As the French minister explained, it was as though a river separated France and the USSR and each side was building a bridge to connect with the other. Litvinov then asked the truly critical question: Would Germany and Poland agree to take part? He doubted this very much and when Barthou told him that, according to Beck, there was no secret Polish-German agreement he expressed deep skepticism. But the question led to a critically important answer by Barthou: "*Should Germany refuse we would then be free to enter into a pact without her.*" [Emphasis added.] The fact that Barthou was thinking about a pact with the USSR exclusively is also borne out by other documents, for example, what Ambassador Laroche told Colonel Beck on July 5.[84] "I reminded him that should our combination fail, we wouldn't want to bear the responsibility in rejecting Russia's offer of collaboration and that we would undoubtedly restructure it on a strictly Franco-Soviet basis." And also what Barthou told Sir John Simon on July 9, in recalling France's old alliance with tsarist Russia saying that "should the Eastern Locarno pact fail perhaps France would feel the need, faced with the dangers of the European situation, to consider such a solution once again."[85] Beneš[86] and King Alexander[87] of Yugoslavia were also encouraging Barthou to go in that direction.

The discussion between Barthou and Litvinov then focused on the possibility of the USSR entering the League of Nations. Paul Bargeton, the political affairs director, left for Paris in order to prepare some concrete proposals for the Eastern Pact with Léger. These were handed to Litvinov on June 2[88] and revised following his comments. He was given a more complete draft on June 8.[89]

Ambassadors François-Poncet and Laroche were instructed to invite Germany and Poland, respectively, to join the future pact. They immediately encountered a wall of skepticism and resistance, as could be anticipated. How could Germany be expected, after having consistently refused to guarantee her eastern borders, to join a pact that could legitimately be seen as directed against her? "Both from a geographic and military point of view the draft of the pact is unacceptable to us," was what von Neurath told Litvinov when he went to Berlin.[90] Von Neurath also belittled the "packtomania," tending more to complicate the situation further than to ensure security.[91]

As for Colonel Beck's Poland, it was totally taken by its diplomatic flirt with Germany. Poland wanted to preserve the "equilibrium" between Germany and the USSR but with a stronger sentimental tilt toward the former. Pilsudski believed in an imminent collapse of the USSR.[92] But Poland faced the eternal problem that would reappear more acutely than ever in 1939: What would happen if the Red Army entered into Polish territory? "What may happen," wrote Payart, the French chargé d'affaires in Moscow, "once the Russian army crosses into Poland to take part in operations is that it might forget the common objective and settle into the country of transit. The danger is magnified now by the fact that the troops engaged in a potential collective action are not simply Russian but actually Soviet. They are…not only heirs to the old Russian territorial imperialism, but also see themselves as the messengers of a new social order and as the missionaries of a universal ideology that is itself imperialist."[93]

We must also point out that the two rascals were discussing the matter and delaying their official responses. By the beginning of September, however, their refusal was a matter of course, which did not displease Barthou.

The participants in the Eastern pact were not alone. France had its interests and traditional ties to Great Britain. Since the end of the Ruhr matter, France didn't even consider a security policy that was not based, first of all, on an understanding with London. As we have seen, this had already led to many concessions. The Eastern pact couldn't be launched without the prior approval or the support of the British, even if they didn't take part in the system. After all, it did introduce the USSR into the Locarno pact and the British would have to be in on it.

From the start, British reaction was expected to be cool. Anthony Eden, the minister responsible for the League of Nations had been informed in Geneva. However, there was the April 17 Note and the vengeful answer by Barthou to Sir John Simon on May 30. Following the meeting between Barthou and Litvinov, British newspapers were thundering against the Eastern pact. It was one thing to allow the USSR into the League of Nations, but to open the door to her entry into the halls of European diplomacy or even become her ally "was not popular among some of my colleagues, especially the older ones who were less realistic than Mr. Barthou."[94] When, on June 14, Ambassador Corbin went over to see Sir John Simon and the then permanent secretary of the Foreign Office, Sir Robert Vansittart, he found them extremely reticent.[95]

Barthou therefore decided to explain his position directly to the British, even if it meant being rather blunt about it. He traveled to London on July 9 and 10.[96] On the British side Sir John Simon, Eden, Vansittart, Lord Stanhope, and Sargent were present. Barthou, Léger, Massigli, Ambassador Corbin and councilor Roland de Margerie represented the French side. Sir John Simon was very cold at first. He wanted no part of a Soviet guarantee to Locarno. Barthou and Léger explained that this was a limited guarantee by the USSR to France alone. But Simon was mostly concerned about the fate of poor Germany. "To protect yourselves from Germany?" He must have thought the idea absurd.

For the Locarno treaty he insisted on its very essence—"reciprocity." Great Britain would guarantee Germany from a French aggression and France from a German one. Would the Eastern pact work the same way? Furthermore, wouldn't this pact be a good way to reopen disarmament negotiations? On the first point Barthou felt that Germany should request such a guarantee. On the second point Barthou clearly answered that the two issues should not be linked. But, answered Sir John Simon, seconded by Eden and Vansittart, this will place us in a delicate position in the House of Commons! The point didn't trouble Barthou, who brought up French public opinion. It sounded like the famous debates between Clemenceau and Lloyd George in 1919.

Barthou, in other words, did not give an inch to the British policy of "arbitrage." What he was after was *an alliance*. Alexis Léger was not as clear-cut as his chief. He reminded them that France had rejected Soviet proposals for military accords. Barthou used the phrase, "until now the French government has rejected every Soviet proposal that tended to become a military alliance." The words "until now" need to be underscored. He insisted on "the fundamental importance France attached to its friendship with England." "She does not *want* to do anything *against* Great Britain. Better still the French government does not *wish* to get into anything *without* Great Britain." Once again we note the use of the word *want* and of the word *wish*.[97] [Emphasis added.] In short, France for once had decided to do what it wanted. During a trip to London in July, navy captain Decoux found that, "The British no longer treat us like little boys ever since we have a strong government."[98]

Sir John Simon was resigned to supporting the Eastern pact, and a press statement drafted by Vansittart and Léger pointed out the conditions of British acceptance.

What struck the French the most was that British reticence and search for balance appeared exactly ten days following the "Night of the Long Knives" of June 30, 1934. We need not recount an event that took place inside Nazi Germany, namely the bloody elimination of the SA, their leader Ernst Röhm and a few other enemies of Hitler, which he proceeded to do with the army's discreet support. François-Poncet and his councilor Arnal described those events in minute detail.[99] The only time it affected French foreign policy was "the accusation of conspiracy with foreign powers" leveled by those who carried out the coup.[100] François-Poncet quickly found out that France was the target of those insinuations, of having delivered weapons to Röhm.[101] He lodged a strong protest with von Neurath[102] because "some British publications" were repeating that false story. "The purpose," he said, "was to warn British public opinion, at the time of the French foreign minister's visit to London, about the scandalous intrigues by the French government that endangered the peace."[103] The accusation was vague, unofficial, insinuating and patently absurd—as the French documents clearly show—and was forgotten by Germany as early as July 9.[104]

The Nazi system had nevertheless shown more brutally than ever before one of its characteristics. The "Night of the Long Knives" was like a settling of scores among gangsters in more ways than one. Impervious to all this, Sir John Simon tried to maintain *equilibrium* between France and Germany and be the *referee* between a democratic and fearful ally and the racist dictator, a treaty-breaking gang leader who was also a terrorist killer.[105] According to Charles Corbin, the French ambassador to London, Sir Eric Phipps, the British ambassador to Berlin came to the following conclusion regarding the "Night of the Long Knives": "Those events, as awful as they may be, can perhaps create more opportunities toward an understanding on armaments reduction."[106]

More Nazi violence followed that coup. Austrian Nazis favoring an Anschluss murdered Austrian Chancellor Dollfuss on July 25, 1934. We shall not recount those happenings that affected our subject by promoting a Franco-Italian rapprochement, which we shall examine in the next chapter. It will suffice to mention that Italy alone reacted in any meaningful way by sending a few divisions to the Brenner Pass. Barthou felt he should excuse France's lack of action, because he was also thinking, as we already mentioned, about an alliance with Italy. "The apparent coolness that the French government has felt the need to display when faced with events in Austria…should not encourage any doubts regarding the complete solidarity of the French government with the Italian government in the present situation." He then announced the rapprochement: "The idea of an international agreement to bring about a concrete and precise commitment toward Austria could be examined."[107] This and the death of the elderly President von Hindenburg (August 2, 1934), making Hitler the German head of state, no doubt eased the way for the USSR's entrance into the League of Nations.

Despite his cautious speeches, Barthou felt that the League of Nations was not effective. The entry of the USSR was not a prelude to an Eastern Locarno, which would probably fail, but of a Franco-Soviet alliance. The British felt that the League, weakened as it was by the absence of the United States and the exit of Japan, followed by that of Germany, would thus be reinforced. Czechoslovakia and Romania, two countries of the Little Entente both favorable to the Eastern pact and the League of Nations covenant, recognized the Soviet Union *de jure* on June 9, 1934. Yugoslavia refused to do so but the three members of the Little Entente enthusiastically supported the concept of regional mutual assistance agreements at a meeting in Bucharest (June 18–20).[108]

The events in Germany and Austria converted Italy to the idea that the USSR should be admitted to the League of Nations. The USSR did not want to declare its candidacy and France didn't want to be alone in supporting it. The Vatican was very much opposed to granting such international recognition to an atheist regime, and Portugal's Catholic regime supported the views of the Holy See. The Poles were also very much against it. There was opposition to Litvinov's policies within the USSR coming from his own deputy, Krestinski, and from Defense Commissar Marshal Voroshilov. That at least was the opinion of Alexis Léger.[109] Belgium wasn't that much in favor and Switzerland was completely opposed. A two-thirds vote was required. On September 12 the delegates of thirty countries issued an invitation to Moscow. The Council then unanimously decided—minus three abstentions—to give permanent membership to the USSR. After a short debate the USSR was admitted by a vote of 38 in favor, 3 against and 7 abstentions. The Soviet delegation was immediately introduced and Litvinov took the rostrum. "The goal of the USSR," he said, "is to avoid war." "My main task is now accomplished," Barthou declared to Geneviève Tabouis at the time.[110]

Barthou could now turn to the issue of the alliance, since the idea of an Eastern pact was practically defunct by the end of September, following Germany's reticence and "Poland's exaggerated diplomatic procrastination."[111] But at the same time he wanted to work on the rapprochement with Italy and with this in mind he thought of a Mediterranean pact that would play the same role as the Eastern pact. He had to foster improved relations between Italy and Yugoslavia, traditionally hostile to one another. That was the reason behind the invitation to King Alexander of

Yugoslavia, who arrived in Marseille on the cruiser *Dubrovnik* on October 9, and was murdered by Croat Ustachi gunmen a few minutes later. Barthou was also fatally shot. In the commotion everyone worried only about the King. Barthou walked to the hospital but had lost too much blood and died as he arrived. It clearly appears that the widespread panic at the scene was the cause of his death. It was an additional tragedy during that dreadful day. Barthou's death signaled the end of an ambitious foreign policy for France, the only one that could possibly still protect her from war and aggression.

5.

FRENCH PUBLIC OPINION

It remains to be seen whether Barthou's initiatives were those of a determined but isolated realist with a long-term vision or if he was responding to pressure from a variety of groups. In order to provide a short answer to that question, we must carefully separate two issues: the Franco-Soviet *rapprochement* and the *alliance* between the two countries.

A broad segment of French public opinion was clearly in favor of a rapprochement. Not just the communists obviously, but also many socialists, part of the radicals like Pierre Cot and Herriot and even some elements of the right-wing nationalists. The USSR's admission to the League of Nations was generally viewed favorably in France.

The issue becomes much more sensitive with respect to an alliance. The very nature of the Soviet regime and the existence of a French Communist Party representing 10 percent of the voters at that time meant that the foreign affairs issue of mutual assistance would automatically have internal political repercussions. For one, it would increase the prestige of the Communist Party in France, something the majority of the voters would not like at all. On the other hand, it would also reduce the party's relentless anti-militarist propaganda and therefore strengthen the French army. This explains the complex and hesitant reactions, especially once the news of the ongoing negotiations reached the newspapers, since they had widely commented upon the Barthou-Litvinov meetings in May and June. It was in July that the press was informed about the broad strokes of the Eastern pact.

Four main tendencies may be identified within French public opinion:

1. The Communist Party
(including the CGTU labor union under its control)

This group was naturally in favor of an unconditional rapprochement with the USSR. Prior to October 1934 the thought of an alliance doesn't appear to have crossed the minds of the French communist leadership at all. The initial rumors even placed the communists in a difficult position. They hadn't stopped criticizing Barthou's foreign policy, "We have every right to show the kind of aggressive propaganda that is being spread by the Tardieu-Pétain-Marquet-Barthou government to incite the chauvinist spirit and accelerate preparations for war…It's no coincidence that Barthou, the man behind the *Three Year Law*, is now leading Foreign Affairs."[112] Furthermore, the security method via alliances against the German threat was thought to be inherently bad by *L'Humanité*. An April 16 editorial was entitled "Security, a formula for war and anti-Soviet intrigues."[113] It was, "The well known doctrine of security."[114] Persistent rumors of a mutual assistance between France and the Soviet Union led *L'Humanité* to issue a cautious denial: "Let's not believe the far-fetched news issued last night about so-called sensational projects by the people's commissar."[115] Then once the rumor appeared to be true, Gabriel Péri commented that such an alliance would encourage disarmament, the world proletarians would approve of the Soviets joining the League of Nations, "and they approve even more warmly if by helping reach a Franco-Soviet mutual assistance pact, the approval helps reduce the disastrous consequences of the French Note of April 17 by depriving the French leaders of one of their reasons to overarm themselves."[116] Suspicion toward Barthou didn't abate during the months that followed. "Mr. Barthou has reached the climax of chauvinistic agitation," wrote Gabriel Péri on June 2.[117] In Geneva, "Mr. Barthou has requested that Soviet proposals be taken into consideration and underscored their importance. We find those polite statements disturbing."[118]

The rhetoric changed only in July once the Eastern pact project was made public. Gabriel Péri presented it as a "Soviet Government initiative."[119] By July 18 the matter became clear and Gabriel Péri had to take a position. "Here is the objection: Doesn't the pact bring back the policy of alliances? Doesn't it imply a military alliance between the USSR and France? Answer: An alliance is an agreement between some powers aimed at others. The Eastern pact is aimed at no one else."[120] We notice that the Communist Party had to explain why, having condemned alliances and the encirclement of Germany for fifteen years, it was suddenly backing the idea of a pact that Litvinov himself, just like Barthou, wanted to turn into an alliance.

L'Humanité, however, did not linger on such a dangerous topic. It chose rather to "drown" the Franco-Soviet pact project into the ideas closer to the wishes of its readership: the entrance of the USSR into the League of Nations[121] and the non-aggression pacts. *L'Humanité* was virtually the only French daily in September 1934 to avoid mentioning anything regarding a possible alliance between the two countries. Gabriel Péri made a show of believing that Barthou's policy of seeking alliances was "inspired by that sinister figure, the late " and was exclusively aimed at Italy.[122] We can illustrate this uncomfortable position by quoting two articles by Gabriel Péri published after Barthou's death.

> We don't forget—he wrote on October 11[123]—that Louis Barthou had been for years the implacable enemy of the working class and that he was the one who, acting for Poincaré at the Genoa conference, gave insulting answers to Tchicherin's peaceful proposals. It is a fact that at the time of his demise, Louis Barthou—by force of circumstance—thanks to the increased power of the proletarian state had lent his name to a policy of peaceful relations with the Soviet Union.

It is noteworthy that the word alliance was not used.

On October 14[124] he once again circumvented reality. "Obviously the two policies, the French and the Soviet, were not identical; obviously they responded to different issues; one uses the old alliance system as its model while the other tried to apply the principle of non-aggression to international relations. But in the end they both reach a result that is positive for peace."

By now it was clear that both the USSR and France were trying to reach an alliance and the formula of "non-aggression" appeared to be totally inappropriate.

2. *The pacifist left that favored collective security*

While they were deeply split on internal policy, the socialists and radicals were united until the spring of 1934 on the main issues of foreign policy. Barthou's program, as it began taking shape in July, started creating some uneasiness.

In July 1934 the socialists accepted the principle of "unity of action" with the communists, which was one of the origins of the Popular Front. The radicals were still far removed from such an alliance but, strangely enough, they drew much closer to communist positions in foreign policy than to the SFIO.

As early as July 13, 1934,[125] Léon Blum published an important article in *Le Populaire* entitled "National defense against fascism." He stated that, contrary to what Maurice Thorez was saying, the Communist Party had made deep policy changes, and he attributed that about-face to "instructions coming from Moscow." This meant a bilateral understanding between France and the Soviets in foreign policy. As a firm believer in collective security, Léon Blum rejected the possibility that such a rapprochement could lead to an alliance. "Messrs. Doumergue and Barthou are obviously attempting to give the Franco-Soviet rapprochement the same shape as the pre-war Franco-Russian alliance. The Socialist Party must clearly and openly declare that it will fight on this issue as on all the other issues, against the government of the *Bloc National*. It remains opposed to closed pacts that divide Europe into antagonistic clans; it remains opposed to military alliances that accelerate the armaments race."

The socialist position was both closer to its own ideas and less realistic than that of the communists who, having attacked the *Bloc National* rather harshly, reduced their criticism on only one issue: the transformation of the Eastern pact into a bilateral mutual assistance treaty. This doesn't mean that the SFIO was not pleased by the USSR's entry into the League of Nations, nor accused the right and in particular "the newspaper of Mr. Bunau-Panama" (meaning Bunau-Varilla's *Le Matin*) of opposing it.[126] Then in September the SFIO newspaper was oddly silent regarding those issues; only a "party bulletin" by Léon Ogromski expressed satisfaction with the USSR's entry into the League of Nations because it favored non-aggression pacts. Not one word was said about a possible military alliance.

The radicals accepted the idea of a real alliance much more easily. However, they had two different approaches: that of Herriot who backed all types of rapprochement including an alliance, and he told the radicals in Lyon how pleased he was to see the USSR become a member of the League.[127] The Radical-Socialist Party even issued a proclamation expressing its satisfaction.[128] But this group very quickly viewed the alliance the same way the "right-wing realists" did, as we shall see further ahead.

We may sum up this position by quoting an editorial in *L'Homme Libre*.[129] "Rejected from the Berlin orbit by Hitler's political brutality, Russia naturally turned to Paris…We think it would be a considerable mistake to reject such advances. Because whatever we may think or do, Russia is a great power whose reach, in the event of conflict, could weigh heavily on the outcome of the fighting."

There was, however, another group centered around Paul-Boncour, the League of Nations man who would readily follow the same line as Léon Blum. In July *L'Œuvre* published articles by Paul-Boncour[130] and Pierre Cot that were rather hostile to Barthou's policies. "Mr. Barthou," wrote Pierre Cot,[131] first wants to sign regional pacts before he negotiates a general armaments reduction." Other writers in *L'Œuvre*, for example, Jacques Duboin and Henry de Jouvenel,[132] however, embraced the idea of an alliance somewhat earlier. Geneviève Tabouis, who appeared to be very well informed on that issue, wrote as early as September 4[133] that Germany and Poland in all probability would turn down the Eastern pact. She inferred that France and the USSR would be left alone facing each other. "Even though it may be too early to discuss, could not the shape of this commitment be the simple assurance of mutual assistance in case of a German attack either to the East or to the West?" She advised to take this path because there could be a danger if Russia "tires of waiting for political cooperation with Europe that she has been requesting for the past year and falls back on the system of the Treaty of Rapallo." According to her, such a strong tendency did exist among the Russian military.

Those reasons were only partly convincing to Paul-Boncour. He expressed his satisfaction that the USSR was entering the League of Nations as "the only ray of light on a pretty dark horizon." A few days later, in an article entitled "A la recherché du temps perdu," he was self-congratulatory regarding the Franco-Soviet rapprochement that he had recommended to Herriot as early as 1922. He said he was in favor of a mutual assistance pact without stating if it should be collective or bilateral.[134]

3. The realistic right

A large segment of the right, while bitterly critical of the Soviet regime, was also very much aware of the Nazi threat and therefore was ready to favor a rapprochement, even an alliance, with the USSR. Furthermore, the thought of an alliance, which was so distasteful to the left-wing parties was, on the contrary, accepted by the right, which viewed it as a return to tradition. The right had always been skeptical of, or even hostile to, the League of Nations and considered the disarmament conference to be a fraud. An editorial in *Le Figaro*, published soon after the negotiations on disarmament broke down and during Barthou's trip to Warsaw,[135] was entitled "The Return to the Alliances." "Mr. Barthou's trip to Warsaw is more than a visit by a cabinet minister, it's the reversal of one policy and its replacement with another. It's the defeat of an ideology and the vengeance of realism. As a Polish newspaper writes, France is giving up the clouds to let itself be guided by the facts. France is rebuilding its diplomacy on the basis of traditional alliances."

This position, which was very close to that of Barthou, became somewhat hesitant when the intended ally was the USSR. Which attitude would prevail, mistrust of the regime or the growing respect for the increased power of the Red Army? General Niessel, who would certainly not qualify as being pro-Russian,[136] wrote in regard to the Soviet air force mission visiting France in August 1934 that the USSR's air force had made "considerable progress."[137] In the daily *Le Petit Journal*,[138] Edouard Pleiffer went even further in his praise: "Any anti-communist Frenchman who visits the USSR returns with positive things to say regarding the already vast achievements of the Soviets; he also comes back convinced that the Russian people are emerging surprisingly quickly and shall play a growing role in European affairs."

Finally, this realistic right was very responsive to the following point: if we don't reach an agreement with the USSR, she will reach one with Germany, a thought that haunted Barthou as we have previously noted. We must also quote a prophetic article by Vladimir d'Ormesson in *Le Figaro*:[139] "It is certainly desirable in Europe's present condition to prevent the leaders of the Reichswehr looking to the USSR as a factory, a training ground, and a reserve. Without a doubt, for the Reichswehr Russia remains the master card that National Socialism has lost and that it must absolutely retrieve in order to start a war in Europe once zero hour approaches."

Le Figaro, where a Dr. A. Legendre periodically published articles that were violently hostile to the USSR,[140] did not follow that line of thought to the end. A rapprochement, yes; entrance of the USSR into the League of Nations, certainly; Eastern pact, perhaps.[141] But no alliance. On the one hand, "there is the weight of a mass of 160 million people with a well-equipped army that everyone agrees has become one of Europe's best," and the fact that "the country was recapturing in Europe the diplomatic position it had occupied in the past."[142]

But on the other hand, the system changed when Germany refused to join the Eastern pact. "Such a pact would then take on the unmistakable appearance of a Franco-Soviet alliance pure and simple and *we shall say so clearly, we want no part of a Franco-Soviet alliance.* We don't want it for one thousand reasons, the first one being that it would be immoral and scandalous, the second that it would be illusory and the third that it would be fraught with dangers to us."[143]

In the face of *Le Figaro*'s rejection, *L'Écho de Paris*, whose readership was entirely middle class, accepted, on the contrary, not just the rapprochement but also the alliance. Pertinax was the backer of the rapprochement, and he wanted it to become a real alliance.[144]

L'Écho de Paris had a very interesting position. Pertinax (who was on holiday from August 8 to September 13, 1934) seemed to be particularly well informed and was haunted by the thought of a new Rapallo.[145] He was constantly supporting a mutual assistance pact,[146] and felt that the advantages of a rapprochement outweighed the disadvantages. "We shall not deny that French diplomacy has engaged in a rather shocking enterprise. Russia's communist and dictatorial institutions, its terrorism, are as far removed as they can be from the political ideals that our people cherish. But for now Russia is extremely fearful of Hitler's Germany. The French government felt it had to take the opportunity to link Russia to our side and prevent it from placing its resources at the disposal of the Reichswehr in potential war."[147]

The team at *L'Écho de Paris* also included Henri de Kérillis, a great supporter of the rapprochement who was traveling in the USSR at the time.[148] The arrival of Russian flyers in Paris was announced on the front page of the newspaper with pictures and laudatory comments.[149]

Similar positions were taken by *L'Ordre* (Émile Buré), by *Le Petit Parisien* (Georges Bonnet) and, naturally, by *Le Temps* which, as usual, was marching in step with the Quai d'Orsay.

4. The right-wing die-hards

Some right-wing large circulation dailies that were tied to financial interests such as *Le Journal* and *Le Matin* were always very much opposed to any improvement in relations with the USSR and even to its being admitted to the League of Nations. The position of *Le Matin* was quite typical, underlining the fact that "the USSR was not just another country" and that it "couldn't be anyone's friend or ally since any conflict was viewed as an opportunity to bring about revolution and the destruction of civilization."[150] "The Soviets are flirting with us and at the same time they undermine us," wrote Philippe Barrès.[151] Short unsigned editorials in larger print were constantly attacking the USSR.[152] The idea of the "Trojan horse" was used by Edmond Laskine, a university academic.[153]

The strongest opposition came from the monarchist or pro-fascist far right, where *L'Action Française* was the most vocal. All of its star writers took part. Jacques Bainville ironically voiced the fact that France "must go to war singing *May God Save Stalin*."[154] J. Le Boucher, who filled in when Bainville went on vacation, used the same arguments as *Le Matin*—Russia was no ordinary nation.[155] Finally, the polemicist Léon Daudet stated in a series of articles[156] that he was not surprised to see Barthou, "a well-known sex maniac of record, who recovered and fell once again, therefore an unbalanced person," along with "the more than shady Saint-Léger," engaging in such a destructive policy. "An alliance that is a triple disaster that will cost us our colonies, *Indochina in particular*, just to please Karl Marx."[157] "For anyone who knows Barthou, the Soviet operation is a move tied to internal politics…his goal is to become Prime Minister…he wants to attract Herriot's leftists, a grotesquely pro-Soviet character, to the Red Front of Blum-Cachin…" "The alliance with the Soviets is, under any circumstances, an insane undertaking."[158] We should add this strange point, made by the leader of integral nationalism, that the very large Red Army lacked qualified staff officers. She wanted the alliance to bring in French instructors, possibly even a general, to play the same role as Weygand in Poland in 1920.

Pierre Gaxotte, like Daudet, was full of irony in *Je Suis Partout*, regarding the weakness of the Red Army, "The silly point is being made repeatedly that the Soviets are a force for peace. Lies! They are a powerless [force] for war." The same thinking appeared in less vivid terms in *Le Journal* and *Les Débats* (Pierre Bernus).

* * * *

Barthou, who knew French public opinion well, was aware that a vast majority approved the increasing rapprochement with the USSR. But he wasn't pushed into the alliance by public opinion or any pressure group. He came up with his plan alone, in secrecy and in close cooperation with Litvinov. It was even rather late (June 1934) when he asked for cabinet approval, but he had to consider the existing forces. Within the four groups we mentioned, Barthou knew there could be no opposition from the communists. He knew he never would gain the support of right-wing die-hards. He needed the backing of both the pacifist left and the right-wing realists and to break down their objections—that of the pacifists opposed to any alliance system, and that of the realists who opposed such a close rapprochement with the USSR. The method he used was clever—to wrap up the Franco-Soviet mutual assistance pact within the complicated machinery of the Eastern pact. Even though he harbored some illusions about Poland joining in, he could not imagine Germany considering it. The Polish and German refusal, therefore, brought down the entire fragile construction except for its solid base. The pact was reassuring to the supporters of "collective" security and, to those who were suspicious of the Soviet Union, that assemblage also appeared reassuring. The Eastern pact may be viewed as a psychological tool to effect the deep change that Barthou wanted to bring to French policy. He died too soon.

Chapter IV

The Laval Era

Barthou's death was the last straw for the Doumergue government, which was barely surviving. Flandin became prime minister on November 8, 1934. However, Pierre Laval had already taken over Barthou's position as of October 13. Laval would remain as minister of foreign affairs for fifteen months. What was the reason for such a choice? Laval had some experience of the Quai d'Orsay during his brief time as prime minister in 1932. In October 1931 he had traveled to the United States where everyone, including President Hoover and Secretary of State Stimson,[1] found him charming. Herriot, Tardieu and Piétri all wanted the job but Doumergue preferred Laval. Less flashy that the two state ministers, he was much more popular, providing better continuity, it was believed, to Barthou's policies. Flandin kept him on in November, as he later wrote,

> As far as I was concerned I was determined to pursue Mr. Barthou's foreign policy. In many ways it didn't match that of Monsieur Laval. But I didn't find it inconvenient because Monsieur Laval's policy of rapprochement between France and Germany would shield me from my ultra-pacifist pro-German Anglo Saxon critics and al-

low me to pursue not the policy of encirclement of Germany but rather that of opposition to German ambitions.[2]

But was that really the case? Flandin was writing after the experience of Vichy where Laval had obviously become the "collaborator" with the Nazis. This was not the case in 1934 when, on October 30, the new minister told the Chamber that for the most part he intended to follow the policies of his predecessor.

Let us just say that Laval had promoted himself vigorously. He had the unanimous support of all the major Parisian morning and evening newspapers. He was reassuring. As Claude Jeantet wrote in *Le Petit Journal*, "His diplomacy follows two guidelines: he is wedded to the French earth by his entire being but his ardent patriotism blends with a mystical belief in peace."[3] The chief editor of *Le Petit Journal* happened to be Alfred Mallet, who would later become Laval's secretary and biographer.[4] The paper's owner, Raymond Patenôtre, was an extremely wealthy politician, and very close to Laval. He owned four major regional dailies and many local newspapers, all of them supporting Laval.

Furthermore, the ties between Flandin, Laval and Patenôtre were not just personal. They truly represented the right-oriented business groups in power, and were driven more by the pressure of interests than by ideas. The French General Secretary of the League of Nations, Avenol, in a long report from late January 1935, described the new team as "neo-opportunist." He quoted radical-leaning writer Albert Thibaudet in calling them "post-war industrialists." Following the short-lived Doumergue period, the industrialists had regained their influence,

> In a shaky regime with a dislocated majority and a weak or accommodating government with easy access to the offices and commissions wouldn't they be able to seize power at the source and channel the national economy to serve their interests?... Laval was to carry out their foreign policy.

In seven months under Barthou a new policy had been launched, no longer consisting of empty words, but backed by action. Laval *"had to first gently cushion the Barthou experiment."*[5] [Emphasis added.]

There is little doubt that Avenol's anti-Laval insights came to him as a top official of an international organization, from the fact that Barthou had strengthened the Geneva organization. It was well known that Laval disliked the League of Nations, the followers of Briand at the Quai d'Orsay and Alexis Léger in particular.[6] Laval brought into his cabinet Léon Noël, the minister to Prague and a former staff member from 1931, who would make only brief appearances at the Quai d'Orsay.[7]

Laval was very intelligent but he was also more cunning than competent. He wasn't a man of clear-cut decisions but rather "everybody's friend." To one "good old alliance" like Barthou wanted, he opted for half a dozen *almost-but-not-quite* alliances. He preferred imprecision. There was a total contrast with Barthou and we shall have no problem in proving it.

It is clearly impossible to interpret all of French history during the 1930s through the murder of Barthou. Doesn't the fact that France went from a policy of firmness to one lacking any substance demonstrate that the country was uniquely predisposed to easy solutions? Laval was extremely popular in France in the fall of 1934 and would become extremely unpopular in 1935 as the man of government by decree. Abroad he was constantly accommodating everybody.

1.

A SMALL STEP TOWARDS GERMANY

Fifteen years after the Treaty of Versailles was implemented, a plebiscite was to take place in the Saar—on January 13, 1935. The population of the Saar was offered three choices: to be incorporated into Germany; into France or to retain its international status. Even though Tardieu in his 1919 report had mentioned 50,000 residents of the Saar who felt they belonged with France, it was very clear that the population of the Saar was German. The option of becoming part of France was in effect not even considered. On the other hand, since Germany had become Nazi, the National Socialist Party had brutally eliminated all other political parties. It was a reasonable possibility that the Saar, being 72% Catholic with many socialists and a large number of refugees, could opt in favor of the international solution, versus incorporation into Germany, as a temporary measure.

The League of Nations had been careful to take every precaution to guarantee freedom of choice for the people of the Saar, despite the awesome propaganda and pressure by the Nazis at every level. Since France had never accepted giving back the territory ahead of time and without a plebiscite, the outcome of the vote had to be clear. The Council of the League of Nations had set up a three-member commission headed by an Italian diplomat, Baron Pompeo Aloisi, to oversee the entire operation. He was the head of Mussolini's cabinet and "the vivid image of a Venetian Doge of the golden age."[8] France was, therefore, not directly involved and had also signed an agreement with Germany on June 2, 1934, whereby the two countries pledged not to influence the voters directly or indirectly.

On August 31, 1934, Barthou had sent a memorandum to the League, listing the guarantees France required should the Saar vote to return to Germany. The main point concerned the coalmines that were under a French consortium since the Treaty of Versailles. There would also have to be a number of assurances, since the Saar was within the demilitarized zone, that regular German army units would not be brought in, that the police forces would be limited, that no military forts nor airports would be built and even that the large number of "loading docks," dating back to Kaiser Wilhelm II, would be destroyed, on the railway network.

It was reasonable to assume—and this was Barthou's policy—a financial effort backing those in favor of the status quo to pressure Hitler and secure meaningful compensation. The majority of the French public was indifferent to the matter.[9] A few right-wing newspapers—*Le Figaro*, *L'Action Française*—were campaigning against incorporation into Germany for nationalistic reasons. A large part of the left-wing press, being against Hitler, reacted the same way. A few Catholic circles, as well as Count Jean de Pange,[10] originally from the Lorraine, was also particularly active with the support of the Vatican envoy, Monsignor Panico. There was also a French Association of the Saar, and some important industrial interests— mainly de Wendel and Peyerimhoff—were also involved. Peyerimhoff was pessimistic. "National passions will blow away all the road blocks," he told de Pange.[11] François de Wendel was still very hopeful. In discussing the issue on July 12 and October 15 the *Comité des Forges* was not as firm and would be ready to accept "an agreement allowing a franchise in France for some Saar residents."[12]

What could Laval do? At first he may have been attracted to the de Pange project to offer the people of Saar, if they voted for the status quo, ownership of all or part of the mines run by the consortium. However, he quickly went much further. He didn't know much about the Saar, which was of no interest to him. Why not do the gentlemanly thing and simply bow out? In the course of two meetings on November 16 and 24, 1934, de Wendel unsuccessfully attempted to get him to take a firm attitude. On November 7 Laval met with German Ambassador Köster, stating that, in his opinion, the Saar was 100 percent German and should return to Germany "as fast as possible."[13] It was a policy of abandonment. Wendel viewed it as the result of the poisonous influence of blatantly pro-German elements such as François de Brinon and Jean Goy.[14]

The situation, however, became clear only at the beginning of December. The Germans still feared the many French gendarmes stationed in Lorraine, and an effort was underway in the newspapers accusing France of seeking to grab the territory by force of arms.[15]

On November 15 Laval secured the approval of his policies from the Cabinet and the Parliamentary Commission on Foreign Affairs, stating that he intended "to remain faithful to Mr. Barthou's policies."[16] A Franco-British proposal was accepted by the Council of the League of Nations in December for the police at the plebiscite to be handled by an international force controlled by the Committee of Three. This eased tension considerably as François-Poncet was to note.[17]

France's passive attitude contributed to enlarge Hitler's spectacular success. On January 13, out of 528,053 voters, 2,124 chose becoming part of France; 46,613 chose to keep the status quo and 477,119, or 90% percent, voted to return to Germany. It was a "huge triumph" for the Führer, wrote François-Poncet.[18] As of January 17 the Council of the League of Nations decided to set the date for the reintroduction of German administration at March 1, 1935.

But was this the Franco-German rapprochement Laval hoped for with so little effort? In the short term, the answer was yes. During a speech on January 13, Hitler stated that he no longer had any territorial demands toward France. Laval, in a statement on January 17, "duly noted" those words and, as far as he was concerned, "the people of the Saar have freely chosen their future." Out of humanitarian concern, France welcomed as political refugees those persons escaping from Nazi domination in the Saar. However, he wanted a rapprochement with Germany and proposed to reopen negotiations to include her in the Eastern pact. Hitler was said to have answered in January, "If France and Russia want a military alliance let them go ahead! But I don't see why we need to play the role of fig leaf."[19]

The requests made by Barthou were all negotiated without too many problems in the short term, except for the tearing down of the "loading docks." The most noteworthy of those negotiations concerned Germany's repurchase of the mines of the Saar. The responsibility fell to the Committee of Three, which began in November by calling in French and German experts to Basel, then to Rome and finally to Naples. The French and the Germans chose November 22 to discuss matters directly.[20] The French delegation was chaired by Jacques Rueff, the deputy director of the *Mouvement général des fonds*, along with senior treasury official Robert Lacour-Gayet representing the Bank of France and Jacques Fouques-Duparc representing the Quai d'Orsay. One of Jacques Rueff's young deputies was treasury official Maurice Couve de Murville.[21]

The German experts offered a one-time price of 900 million francs. Since the French franc was being used in the Saar, once reannexation took place those denominations in francs were to be exchanged for Reich marks. Germany would pay back 95% of the 900 million with the francs they took in.[22] The French, who were justifiably skeptical about securing such an amount in French banknotes (it finally came to 175 million francs!), requested and obtained that the balance be paid either in certain rights on the mines in the Warndt—a portion of the southern Saar territory—and in additional coal deliveries.[23] Agreements in principle were signed in Rome on December 3, 1934, and Rueff commented that these were "followed by Germany and fulfilled quite precisely." After the plebiscite, the negotiation continued regarding its practical implementation, ending in an agreement signed in Naples on February 18, 1935.[24]

Even though Franco-German relations in the short term appeared to be taking a positive turn,[25] the main issues remained unresolved. It was a well-known fact that Germany was rearming to the maximum. By the end of November the Quai d'Orsay estimated that its army had reached 300,000 men. Germany was building airstrips, training pilots and pulling ahead of France in commercial aviation. Military expenditures were increasing.[26] On January 31 François-Poncet estimated that Germany had increased its demands and was taking a harder line regarding the armaments issue. In particular, it was refusing to let France retain a "margin of security." The Reich, he added, "was going beyond the limits it had assigned itself that were justified by honor and security. I hope the British government knows what to expect and harbors no illusions on that issue."[27] "The Reich can rely on the understanding, conciliatory and mediating attitude of Great Britain."[28] And he feared that Hitler could succeed in splitting the fragile front of France and England.

On February 4 Hitler's hardened stance became obvious. François-Poncet and British Ambassador Phipps presented him with a document regarding disarmament and, in particular, the draft of an air force agreement that had been prepared during a Franco-British meeting in London from February 1 to 3.[29] Hitler was "well disposed" to receive the document but then went into a long disquisition, complaining that he was always being accused of having ulterior motives, that France was wrong in failing to appreciate the "scope" and "merit" of his concession on Alsace-Lorraine, that he wasn't reexamining the issue of the demilitarized zone but that, should Germany be provoked, she would have no problem in deciding one day to free herself from it."[30]

François-Poncet worried even more on February 6, 1935 when a "reliable" source provided him with the minutes of a meeting between Hitler and a former deputy of Ludendoff on January 9, where he was reported to have said:

> We Germans are a people who need space to maneuver...Russia is our new space and we shall therefore perform a great service for the entire world by freeing it from the menace of a particularly Jewish form of Bolshevism. It is in accomplishing that task that I shall truly become immortal.

He also counted on the collaboration of Japan and Hungary and perhaps Romania. He felt very antagonistic towards Poland and thought that Czechoslovakia was an "abscess in Central Europe."[31]

It was in such a worrisome atmosphere that Great Britain published a *White Book* on March 5, announcing a substantial rearmament. At the same time the French government introduced a bill reestablishing conscription for two years in order to make up for the shortfalls of the "low birth-rate classes." It was the excuse that Hitler needed. The press began a violent campaign against the "enormous armaments" of countries other than Germany.[32] Göring openly stated that the "air force pact" that the British were proposing was the opportunity for him to create a specifically military air force.[33]

Then there was an announcement that the Führer wasn't feeling well. The French Parliament had voted on the two-year rule on March 15. Hitler returned from Berchtesgaden on the 16th, summoned François-Poncet and told him that he had just approved a law reestablishing compulsory conscription, increasing German forces to 36 divisions. It was all at once a unilateral violation of the Versailles treaty, the official announcement of an intense rearmament that had been going on for several years, which everyone could see, and the threatening promise of continued German military efforts way beyond what was inferred by the desire for peace and equilibrium. François-Poncet issued a strong protest and would have preferred to be recalled to Paris. Laval didn't dare go that far and the British, always seeking to be accommodating, decided to confirm a trip to Berlin that had been planned for several weeks by Sir John Simon and Anthony Eden (March 25). In truth, both British politicians had been in Paris on the 23rd, where they met with Laval and Italian undersecretary of state Fulvio Suvich and had agreed in principle to a French-British-Italian meeting at Stresa.

Clearly, Laval's policy of seeking good relations with Germany by leaving the Saar had failed.

There was clearly only one way to divert Hitler's attention from his idea of France as the "hereditary enemy" and that was to give him a free hand in the east. He attempted to secure that concession between 1933 and 1935 and again in December 1938, but did not succeed.[34]

2.

A SMALL STEP TOWARDS ITALY

Laval certainly felt much more sympathy towards Italy than Germany. After all, he and Mussolini were "men of the people." The son of a small artisan from Predappio in Romagna and the son of a little innkeeper from Châteldon in the Auvergne, each one being the owner of a few plots of land, both belonged to precisely the same social class that was almost part of the peasantry. Both liked and claimed to know farming and cattle breeding. What's more, they both had been extremist socialists who had converted to the right wing. If Mussolini's right had taken the shape of fascism and Laval remained outwardly democratic, then this could be attributed to circumstance rather than their personal disposition. Laval, as we know, did not shy away from absolute power, while he obviously did not possess the Italian's eloquence. But there were—said Léon Noël—between them

> many common characteristics—starting with, it must be stated, a certain kind of vulgarity that didn't draw either one toward things that were distinguished, elegant or refined. I don't doubt that it tended

to foster in both men a distaste for the country of Lords, social prejudice, gentlemen and traditional British monarchy.[35]

Since 1931 they had both been thinking of a Franco-Italian rapprochement. As of October 1934 Laval had inherited one of Barthou's projects to travel to Rome with the intent to go beyond friendship and perhaps enter into an alliance. The Laval trip to Rome was discussed in the fall of 1934, along with the kind of agreement that could be reached.[36] Barthou wanted to go around November. His death, together with the King of Yugoslavia, was the work of Croat Ustashis. It quickly became clear that Italy would refuse to extradite them, especially their leaders, Ante Pavelic and Kvaternik.[37] This didn't help speed things up.

Laval let it be known that he would go to Rome on condition he could reach a general agreement whereby Italy would declare its intention to establish good relations with Yugoslavia and that the Yugoslav government would accept.[38]

At the end of 1934 everything confirmed that. "The Italian government is interested in one thing alone, to reach an agreement with France going beyond an understanding on specific points and that would have the value of a real alliance."[39] Italy offered to agree with France in case Germany "declared its freedom of action where armaments were concerned."[40] Preliminary negotiations were moving ahead quickly and on December 1, undersecretary of state for foreign affairs Fulvio Suvich proposed December 20 for Laval's trip.[41]

Beyond those "external" conditions, Ambassador de Chambrun negotiated with Mussolini and Suvich in Rome what was at the core of the issue. Since the Treaty of London of 1915, France had not kept its promise to give Italy some colonial territories. Now she was ready to hand over 113,000 square kilometers in southern Libya and 800 square kilometers near Djibuti. Mussolini felt this rather thin. France wanted to end the constraints created by the 1898 agreement on the special status of the Italians in Tunisia. Mussolini was already thinking about the conquest of Ethiopia and wanted, at the very least, to secure France's economic disinterest in that country.

France dropped the idea of seeking an Italian guarantee for its Yugoslav ally, which immediately worried Belgrade,[42] and agreed to not include the Little Entente in the agreement. Mussolini made concessions on the colonial territories since he wanted to reach an agreement. French Ambassador de Chambrun was in a hurry to conclude and kept on pres-

suring the more reticent Quai d'Orsay to be more flexible. The agreement and the decision to set the dates of the trip to Rome was generated
by France's anti-Ethiopian stance following the recommendation of
Bodard, the minister to Ethiopia, after the incident at Ual-Ual (December 5, 1934) where some Italian soldiers were killed.[43]

Laval went to Rome on January 4. His conversations with Mussolini
took place on January 5 and 6. It was a lavish welcome. Besides the Duce,
Laval also met with King Victor Emmanuel III and Pope Pius XI. The
substance of those discussions is in part included in the eight agreements
signed on January 7 and in the mystery surrounding the private conversation that took place between Laval and Mussolini.[44]

The main agreements concerned:

1. French territorial concessions: 800 square kilometers of the French
Somalia; 114,000 square kilometers in southern Libya near the Tibesti
mountains;

2. France's *economic* retreat from Ethiopia in regions beyond the hin-
terland of French Somalia and the French railroad from Djibuti to Addis
Ababa. Private French interests beyond those areas were to remain and
the Italians would obtain seats on the board of directors of the railway;

3. Concerning the status of Italians in Tunisia, a detailed agreement
was to be based on the principle of the progressive end to their special
status over a thirty-year period;

4. Regarding the independence of Austria, a declaration would launch
the idea of a collective non-aggression pact among the countries on its
borders; and

5. Concerning the issue of making German rearmament official, the
two countries pledged mutual consultations should this come to pass.

There was to be a complete secrecy regarding the protocol on French
economic interests in Ethiopia.[45]

The issue of the Laval-Mussolini conversations is particularly important. At the end of 1935, in the midst of the Ethiopian war, Mussolini
stated that in Rome Laval had given him a free hand to conquer Ethiopia
politically. Laval protested and wrote him a letter, saying that he agreed to
French *economic* disinterest except for the areas mentioned above. Mussolini
answered by reiterating his point of view.[46]

Since neither of the two men was completely trustworthy and their
talks took place without any witnesses, it is very difficult to come to a
satisfactory conclusion. There are no other clues. Nothing within the

Quai d'Orsay's files mentions that Pierre Laval hinted that he would accept the Italian conquest of Ethiopia. If he did, he failed to share it confidentially with anyone else.[47] It is possible that a misunderstanding did take place. Mussolini knew the French language well for having taught it, but he could have been misled by some ambiguous expression or even a gesture. The "external" examination, meaning what we know about the way Laval conducted himself, seems to warrant that he was not given to such clear-cut and broad statements and that Mussolini was the originator of the myth.

Whatever the interpretations of the Laval-Mussolini conversations could be, it was clear that, following the Rome meetings the Duce forged ahead toward closer relations with France. Decisive proof may be found in the correspondence of the military attaché in Rome, General Parisot. On the evening of January 11, 1935 he received a phone call from Marshal Badoglio, requesting that he come to his office the following morning. Badoglio said that he was "worried by the thought that the general staffs of both countries could be caught unprepared for the possible fulfillment of the political agreements that had just been signed regarding Austria." The agreement stated that, in the event of a threat to the independence and integrity of Austria, the two countries would consult each other. In other words Badoglio wished to begin military conversations. "It seems to me that the answer to that question belongs to the government," was Parisot's answer. He requested, in the event of a positive French answer, to be in contact with the General Staff.[48] We should remember that it was at that precise moment that Gamelin took over from Weygand as the head of the French army.

The Quai d'Orsay answered on January 26[49] that "it wasn't at all opposed to military conversations." But it wished to find out beforehand about Italy's attitude towards appeasing Yugoslavia and including Czechoslovakia in the planned consultations. In other words, the French were in less of a hurry than the Italians. During a meeting with Parisot on January 29, Badoglio told him that he'd met with Mussolini the day before: "Did Parisot give you an answer?—No, but I'm expecting one any day.—When you see him, you must ask him the general question; we must be prepared with High Command agreements, as to what we want to do in case of *German mobilization.*" Parisot explained the French position and said that he would go to Paris. Badoglio went beyond what he said on January 12 and spoke of the case of German aggression against France, which implied Italian intervention. He also discussed the possibility of German mobilization and of riots within Austria, with or without German intervention. The discussions "are clearly starting," said Badoglio and added, "Nothing could be more pleasant to him as the crowning of his career than to be able to seal an agreement that he had always vigorously supported."[50]

Laval explained his policies on February 20 to the High Military Committee.[51] During a meeting on January 23 he had stated that: "at this time Italy is offering more than its neutrality." On February 20 he would be much more precise: "It's important not to answer Rome's advances too quickly. We must keep the conversations going and Marshal Badoglio hoping that they will reach a conclusion...our position with Italy is excellent, she's ready for every military, naval and economic agreement; but we must be cautious with Belgrade."

It must be pointed out that General Maurin, the Minister of War, felt that such conversations were useful and were coming at the right time.

Returning from Paris, Parisot met with Badoglio on February 21 and mentioned "the urgency felt in Paris to consider military discussions" but also that "such decisions couldn't be taken as quickly in France as in Italy due to the differences in our institutions."[52] General Roatta, head of intelligence, told Parisot that he had "demobilized" Italian intelligence operations targeting France. For the time being, a French intelligence officer was sent to Rome.[53] Parisot was complaining that everything was now "stalled."

On March 12 the French government took the initiative and agreed to a preliminary discussion in Nice at the end of March or the beginning of April.[54] By March 29 the discussions between Parisot and the Italians had made considerable progress. Five Italian officers were to be sent to French military schools. Both sides agreed to reduce their troops on the front in the Alps. The Italians preferred that Yugoslavia not intervene in Austria should the situation arise; however, they didn't make it a requirement. They wished to go further and reach a "coalition plan." France was once again slowing down the momentum.[55]

At that point there was a bolt from the blue—Germany announced it was reinstating conscription. The issue would play a role in politics for some time.

On March 22 there was a meeting of the High Military Committee in Paris,[56] preceded by a memorandum regarding comparative military strength of France and Germany,[57] which was not known with any accuracy. It was "total darkness," with "few tangible pieces of information," wrote the author. The conclusion was that, at the start of a potential conflict, Germany would have an advantage that would then fade "because of our trained reserves"; but in the case of an extended war Germany would tend to take the lead because of its greater manpower and stronger industrial base.

Italy wasn't viewed as an effective help. "The immediate assistance of Great Britain must be sought and organized."

During the meeting of the High Military Committee, Laval brought up a phone call to Mussolini a few days before. "What Marshal Badoglio wants is to get a military commitment from us regarding Austria." Laval didn't like to consider such commitments. "Let's be cautious," he said.

So France was once more basing its entire strategy on Great Britain while ignoring the pressing calls of the Italians for what could be referred to as an alliance. At another meeting of the High Military Committee on April 5 there were fewer political discussions and the focus was on strategic matters. Pétain and Gamelin felt that France could not engage in a ground offensive without a long delay and, therefore, could only rely on naval or air operations unable to produce decisive results.[58]

It was against this background that the Stresa conference got under way on April 11–14, 1935, in the magnificent palace of the Isola Bella, the largest of the Borromee Islands. Léon Noël, who took part as secretary general of the French government provided the best available account on the French side. He took very detailed notes and devoted the central chapter of his book, *Les Illusions de Stresa*,[59] to the conference. Flandin, Laval, Léger and Noël were involved in the negotiations. The British side included Prime Minister Ramsay Macdonald, Foreign Secretary Sir John Simon and the "Permanent Undersecretary," Sir Robert Vansittart. Eden was not present. Mussolini had Suvich and Baron Aloisi along with him. Léon Noël considered Mussolini to be a "vulgar" man but with amazingly insightful views. He was "simple, natural and in a good mood" with the French and formal, "stiff, with the attitude of a conquering and domineering *imperator*," toward the British. "What drew Laval and Mussolini toward one another at the time…was their shared antipathy towards England and I must add their misunderstanding of the British." Macdonald was "tall, distinguished looking, self-assured and vain…"[60] "His mental faculties were beginning to fail him," said

Churchill.[61] Sir John Simon "between the two was clearly breaking every record for hypocrisy and underhandedness." For the most part the French received a warm welcome from the Italian crowds.

The French proposed to submit a complaint to the Council of the League of Nations against the violation of the Treaty of Versailles by Germany with sanctions in case of a second violation. Mussolini agreed mindful of the Anschluss. The British refused. "Pacifist utopias" was Léon Noël's comment... There was no real front at Stresa because of that issue, despite what was claimed. As military documents we cited were to demonstrate, Mussolini was "smoldering with rage...at Germany,"[62] and would have wanted that kind of front. Mussolini spoke in favor of defending Austria and mentioned the development of the German air force.

Sir John Simon and Macdonald stated that they had promised the House of Commons to make no commitments.[63] They would only be associated "from a moral point of view." Flandin and Laval would have agreed to go much further but "for the sake of unanimity that makes almost everyone of those conferences pointless they wound up adopting the British viewpoint."[64]

The final statement was therefore vague and very disappointing to Mussolini.

Ethiopia was not mentioned once during the seven meetings of the conference nor even in private conversation, according to Kirkpatrick.[65] There was only a short private talk between Flandin and Mussolini and none between the Duce and Laval. It is possible that Mussolini felt he had been tacitly given a free hand for his Ethiopian ambitions when, coming to the final draft of the closing resolution, he spoke of "keeping the peace" and proposed adding "in Europe." Later on he would paraphrase the anecdote, saying that Flandin made some comments on the wording in that he understood Mussolini's decision "to make no commitments regarding Africa." Flandin mentioned it later on in his memoirs.[66] According to Noël, the adding of "in Europe" was agreed to without any discussion, possibly because the French and British didn't think the Italians intended to go so far as to conquer Ethiopia.

The sense that war was possible came when, on May 19, Mussolini told the British ambassador that he had decided to solve the Ethiopian problem by force of arms if necessary.[67] Actually, this progression of the Ethiopian issue did not prevent France from concluding the military discussions with the Gamelin-Badoglio meeting of June 27 in Rome. We should note that the Flandin government had been toppled in the interim and Laval had replaced him as prime minister while remaining foreign minister as well. Was there a pro-Italian tilt in his policies? We should not forget that on August 20, Pierre Laval's only daughter, Marie-José, married Count René de Chambrun, son of the general and nephew of the ambassador to Rome. Perhaps Fabry, the new minister of war, played a private role as well. Perhaps a strong anti-British mood appeared because of the naval agreement Britain signed with Germany on June 16 without consulting France.

In any case, after meeting with the military leaders of the Little Entente Gamelin traveled to Rome with lieutenant colonel Petitbon, who headed his cabinet (General Parisot was naturally also present at those meetings). He received a very warm welcome since he had met Badoglio previously in Brazil. The talks were "cordial and even affectionate," involving only ground troops with no mention of the Anschluss and the demilitarized zone of the Rhineland. "The decision to march in agreement with France had been irrevocably taken" by Mussolini. In the event of German aggression in Belgium or on the Rhine, Italy would send in nine divisions and some air force units. In case Germany attacked Italy, France would commit an army corps with two divisions. Then Gamelin, with Petitbon and Parisot, met with Mussolini, who clearly stated his intention of "solving the problem between myself and the Negus," which—he added—would not prevent Italy from remaining strong on the Brenner Pass.[68]

Gamelin and Badoglio met one last time. The former suggested that Italy remain in the League of Nations, while the latter stated that Laval had given his country a free hand in Ethiopia. No truly final agreement was signed, only a record of the conversation.[69]

One may say that this was the high point of the Franco-Italian rapprochement. Even though no agreement was signed, it was at least clear that Mussolini favored a real alliance. Laval, however, for a multitude of reasons, did not want to go the rest of the way. The signs of the coming Ethiopian conflict were to darken the budding romance during the course of the summer. Yet Gamelin was to welcome Badoglio in September at French army maneuvers. The Italian Marshal expressed his "admiration for our defensive organization in the East as well as the strong showing of our troops."[70]

3.

A Small Step Towards the USSR

Laval's secretary, Alfred Mallet, felt that "Laval, the former revolutionary, wasn't displeased to sign an agreement with a "proletarian" democracy. The word doesn't scare him at all."[71]

Yet the revolutionary was a man of the right and the treaty he was drafting was to be signed only after being stripped of everything Barthou wanted it to contain. One may legitimately wonder about the role played by internal politics in his decisions. The pact was dated May 2; Laval's trip to Moscow took place from May 13 to 15; the Flandin government fell on May 30. Laval wanted to be his successor and would succeed in doing so. As of November 10, during a "useful and friendly" meeting,[72] Laval assured Litvinov that the French government was committed to the policy, implying "the mutual assistance of France and Russia."[73] On November 23 radical socialist deputy Archimbaud, the chairman of the war budget committee, referred to the Franco-Soviet agreement as practically sealed in a speech at the Chamber of Deputies.[74] Wasn't it a military alliance after all?[75] The French government issued a denial that displeased Litvinov. As long as the negotiations were ongoing, Litvinov wanted some guarantees.

On December 5, 1934, Laval and Litvinov met in Geneva and signed a protocol that was satisfactory to Litvinov. They agreed to avoid entering into any political pact that could risk compromising the Eastern agreements and to keep each other informed. This was intended to "contribute in general to reinforcing the spirit of mutual trust in government relations between the two countries."[76]

Negotiations proceeded very slowly. Minister of Commerce Marchandeau went to Moscow at the end of November 1934 to revise the temporary commercial agreement of January 11, 1934. This failed because the USSR demanded a loan of 2 billion francs that France did not want to extend. The 1934 agreement was therefore cancelled.

Among all the government ministers, Edouard Herriot was the most interested and favorable to negotiations with the USSR. In his memoirs, *Jadis*, he conveniently provides some brief glimpses of cabinet discussions at the time. Herriot believed in the power of the Red Army and followed with interest Deputy People's Commissar for Defense Tukhachevsky's speech on January 30. "An agreement with the Soviet

Union is our best, our strongest guarantee," but opposition remained very strong. "It makes me angry to see that the French press and public opinion are refusing to abide by this tremendous event. Every time I mention the Red Army in a speech I hear insults."[77]

From the end of February to the beginning of April 1935 Franco-Soviet negotiations made no progress. The German rearmament coup was monopolizing everyone's attention. But, as Scott points out, it forced Laval to speed up negotiations with the Soviets. The issue came up at the beginning of April. At a cabinet meeting on April 6, just before the Stresa conference, Laval—who was probably thinking that the Eastern Pact was now dead—spoke of "a multilateral non-aggression and consultation pact with bilateral mutual assistance pacts" and he read the text of a draft of a bilateral pact that he had offered to Ambassador Potemkin. The pact mentioned the League of Nations very frequently in order to avoid excessive *automatism* within the alliance.[78] Potemkin was not very satisfied. During the April 9 cabinet meeting Laval was more specific: "Whatever happens at Stresa we will sign a bilateral mutual assistance pact with the USSR."[79] The government agreed and Laval would first have to consult with England and Poland.

Laval met with the British at Stresa, where the development of security in Eastern Europe was discussed. The British were even hopeful of getting Germany to join some kind of Eastern Pact. Laval, however, went to Geneva right after Stresa, where he made a statement to the Council on April 16 that was opposed to the German position. France, Great Britain and Italy passed a resolution condemning Germany's "unilateral action." And so the Eastern Pact faded, as Barthou had already foreseen, in favor of a Franco-Soviet pact. But in contrast to Barthou—and the difference was considerable in itself—Laval was attempting to weaken the pact by requesting that mutual assistance be subjected to a decision of the Council of the League of Nations. Litvinov was not too favorable to that statement but accepted it grudgingly. On April 19, at another cabinet meeting, Laval read his draft text. Herriot was more or less satisfied and "pleased to see Laval happily changing in the right direction."

The cabinet approved, despite some misgivings coming from President Lebrun, who pointed out the absence of common borders between Germany and the USSR and had doubts about the value of the Red Army. Minister of War General Maurin shared this opinion. It is worth noting that Louis Marin, even though he was a right-wing politician supported the pact and the military agreements.[80]

The issue that everyone worried about concerned the internal repercussions such a treaty would have. Wouldn't it encourage communist propaganda, especially in the army? On the other hand, was it not a way of pressuring the French Communist Party into toning down its permanent and violently anti-militarist campaign? The Cabinet approved and authorized Laval to sign, but a last minute problem cropped up and delayed the signing by two full weeks. The Quai d'Orsay (most probably influenced by Léger) thought the wording was much too automatic and added another clause stating that to come to the help of the other party, it would be required to wait for the recommendations of the League of Nations. On April 30 Herriot intervened between Laval and Potemkin, saying, "The Russians want to take us further than we wish to go." Like Barthou earlier, they wanted a real alliance with a military agreement, something much too precise for Laval, who preferred things to be kept vague. In convoluted language that is not easy for the layman to understand, the two countries promised:

1. To consult one another in the event of the threat of war or danger of aggression;

2. To come to one another's immediate aid and assistance in case of unprovoked aggression "according to the conditions described in article 15 paragraph 7 of the Covenant of the League of Nations"; and

3. To come to one another's immediate aid and assistance acting under article 16 of the Covenant of the League of Nations.

Furthermore, article 4 stated that nothing would prevent the fulfillment of the mission of the League of Nations, and an additional protocol interpreted article 3 as allowing help and assistance, even if the council hadn't made any recommendations.

The treaty would in no way contradict already existing commitments toward third-party states. The possibility of entering into an Eastern Pact was also mentioned.

On May 2 Laval and Potemkin signed this masterpiece of confusion in Paris. Any international law expert can find under any pretense twenty potential escape clauses. "Pactomania" had never reached such heights of hair splitting niceties.

On May 7 Laval provided the Cabinet with some explanations and decided to travel to Moscow on May 13, 14, and 15. Léger and Rochat, as well as Ambassador Alphand, of course, went with him. He met with Stalin, Molotov and Litvinov. They were given a friendly and elaborate welcome. Stalin was jovial and his French counterpart liked him. The final communiqué approved of the treaty, but at Laval's request, a sentence was added: "Mr. Stalin understands and fully approves of the national defense policy France is pursuing so that her armed forces are at the level of strength her security requires." Those words, said Herriot, were to cause "strong reactions within extreme left groups." But the communists immediately halted their attacks on the army, which was the desired outcome.

Laval traveled from Moscow to Warsaw to attend the funeral of Marshal Pilsudski, where he joined Marshal Pétain the official representative of the French government. He also met with Göring with whom he had a long talk, witnessed by Léger and Rochat. Göring came right out saying that Germany was opposed to the Franco-Soviet pact. Hitler would say so publicly in a long speech on May 21. It signaled the beginning of a long dispute. We shall examine its consequences in the next chapter. Scott correctly contrasts the "bold policies" of Barthou to the "subtle policies" of Laval.

4.

A SMALL STEP TOWARDS ENGLAND

The British had watched Barthou's bold moves with considerable amazement. He was determined, in spite of their negative reaction, to pursue his goal of a Franco-Soviet rapprochement that would include an alliance. Laval, on the other hand, reverted to the old ways, which meant that in spite of having rather different objectives, he followed the tradition of Franco-British entente. The British persevered with their plans for European reconciliation, which meant bringing Germany back to Geneva and reopening disarmament negotiations. That was the "great task of 1935" and it implied that France would have to "swallow a bitter pill" with the cancellation of part V of the treaty of Versailles concerning German disarmament.[81]

The French stood by the memo of April 17, 1934; such negotiations appeared superfluous to them. They were irritated to see that London held them responsible for German rearmament. A "negative" responsibility seemed insignificant compared to the obvious "positive" intentions of Hitler to arm himself to the teeth. They disliked seeing England so determined to play mediator between their country and Nazi Germany.

What they wanted was to get the British to back Democracy vs. Dictatorship, which appeared to be a distant, but strong desire.

French attempts at a rapprochement with Germany and Italy were viewed by London as good marks for France. But there were bad marks as well, for example, when the French openly rejoiced at Japan's decision to withdraw from the 1922 naval disarmament agreement signed in Washington.

There was a strange clash during this episode between the French navy, supported by minister of the navy, F. Piétri, and Pierre Laval. Laval said: let's wait until Japan actually pulls out of the treaty. If the Japanese do nothing by December 31, 1934, we can state that the Washington agreement is not satisfactory to us.[82] The naval officers replied that this was a cowardly attitude. Captain Decoux told the naval attaché in London, "I strongly feel that it's shameful for a great power (which I assume we still are) to hide behind Japan in as crucial an issue as the Washington agreement for our naval policy."[83] In the end, France let Japan take the initiative, but the British were to complain about it.

The Ethiopian affair progressively overshadowed this background. Until May 1935 it didn't yet appear to be "virulent." The British were still going after their perpetually unfinished grand design, namely, the attempt to restart disarmament talks. At this time the key moment was Prime Minister Flandin's trip to London with Laval on February 1 to 3, 1935. Léon Noël, General Secretary of the Government, René Massigli, Ambassador Charles Corbin and his councilor Roland de Margerie, also accompanied them. Léon Noël has written a vivid and revealing account of that meeting.[84] According to him, Flandin and Laval were not very well prepared for a discussion. Noël was flabbergasted to hear the British propose a debate on the final communiqué: "The negative effect of such an approach was obvious. It would force the participants to focus much more on the effect the statement was to have rather than on the issues themselves." And the issues were important enough: German rearmament and the threat to Austria.

Noël noticed the extremely friendly attitude toward France on the part of Baldwin and even of Eden. Baldwin would soon become prime minister. He could also see that the British were "shocked" by Laval's bad manners.

The main issue being debated was the British proposal for an "Air Force Pact" that was intended to acknowledge but limit German rearmament as well. The French experts had come with impressive files regarding German rearmament. The British preferred reaching an agreement to just filing a complaint. We must recognize that either method was useless with Hitler.

Once Hitler made his massive rearmament "official" on March 16, Sir John Simon became momentarily discouraged. However, he shrugged it off and—as we have seen previously—the French had the unpleasant surprise of finding out that he was nevertheless going to take his planned trip to Berlin. This all goes to show the vast misunderstanding that permeated Franco-British relations.

The Ethiopian issue would complicate everything. We shall recall that it really began when, after several border incidents, a more serious one took place on December 5, 1934, at Ual Ual.[85] It was an Ethiopian attack on a unit of Italian colonial troops in the Ogaden, an Ethiopian territory that Mussolini's army had been occupying for several years. The importance was not in the incident itself but Mussolini's determination to find an excuse for a vast colonial conquest.

Bodard, the French minister at Addis Ababa, sent many interesting cables on the Ual Ual matter and its consequences. "If Ethiopia doesn't bend the conflict could get bigger."[86] But during the Franco-Italian romance and whatever Laval may have told Mussolini during the Rome meetings, the main point for France was to get Ethiopia to give in with apologies, payments for damages, etc., and, above all, once Ethiopia tried to file its complaint with the League of Nations to "avoid getting the League of Nations, council involved."[87] And do as little as possible about anything else. Once the British offered to act as mediators, they asked the French to join them. Laval politely turned down the offer that, as Léger explained, "was meaningless following the Rome agreements" where we had reaffirmed our respect of Ethiopia's independence.[88] Just as when the Ethiopian minister to Paris requested France's support, he was told, "It looks as if the main role is to be played by the British delegation."[89]

Parker has aptly characterized this policy: "The easiest solution was to let the Italians, the League of Nations, the British and the Ethiopians handle the Ethiopian problem while expressing support to everyone involved. Unfortunately Mussolini and the British government made such a solution impossible."[90]

The conflict kept on growing without the French government—anxious to keep its "special relationship" with Italy—making any serious contribution. At the beginning of November, Italian troops garrisoned in Eritrea and Somalia were estimated at 8,500.[91] By February 15 the

French consuls and the deputy military attaché, Catoire, signaled the mobilization of the class of 1911 and the creation of two divisions.[92] On the 16th Suvich stated that those divisions were meant to be sent to Eritrea, while Marshal Graziani was appointed commander in chief in Africa.[93] From then on every week would bring troop transports and warships through the Suez Canal—which the British couldn't close because of the 1888 agreement.

Yet it was still possible not to believe the worst would happen and the Stresa conference in April took place without Ethiopia being mentioned even once.

As we have seen, it was on May 19 that Mussolini told the British ambassador that he intended to have it out with the Negus. From then on the British could no longer keep the issue "in brackets" as they had done at Stresa. We shall not describe in detail the momentous events in Great Britain in June:

1. The change of government: Baldwin replaced Macdonald as prime minister, Sir Samuel Hoare took over at the Foreign Office from Sir John Simon; Anthony Eden became minister for League of Nations affairs;

2. A huge newspaper poll called the "Peace Ballot" brought some 12 million responses in favor of strong action by the League of Nations against the aggressors but short of war (the results were published on June 27); and

3. The British-German naval agreement of June 18, 1935, whereby the British unilaterally allowed Germany, the Treaty of Versailles notwithstanding, the right to build a fleet equal to 35 percent of their own. They had informed the French but didn't ask for their views. A strong complaint was therefore issued.[94]

What policies were being considered to counter the threat? In absolute terms two possible positions emerge: *resistance* and *appeasement*. Resistance meant starting the collective security process in the event Italy were to attack Ethiopia. Aggression would be acknowledged and the League of Nations would decide on sanctions—military if there was the will, but in any case economic and financial. Appeasement, by contrast, meant an effort to avoid war or put an end to it once it had started by offering enough to satisfy Italy while preserving Ethiopian independence. There were many possible solutions but they were divided into two groups: either the concession to be made to Italy of a more or less large portion of Ethiopia; or the establishment over all of Ethiopia of a sort of League of Nations mandate that would be given to Italy. It was a device to accept Italy's protectorate over a country that Mussolini was coveting.

In examining French and British policies on this matter it clearly appears before and after October 2, 1935, when Mussolini ordered the attack on Ethiopia, that both policies were very much focused on attempting to combine various degrees of resistance and appeasement.

The objective for France was to keep its "privileged relationship" with Italy while, at the same time, appearing to agree with the League of Nations. France had few interests directly affected by the crisis besides the security of Djibuti and the railway linking it to Addis Ababa. The Rome agreements provided guarantees on those two issues. Ideally the best approach would be to take part in the sanctions only very mildly, simply to appear to be respectful of collective security which was the stated basis of French policy.

Great Britain had much larger stakes in the matter. Egypt and the Anglo-Egyptian Sudan were squeezed between Italian Libya and Ethiopia. It was a matter of survival, not simply a strategic issue. Should the waters of the Blue Nile and Lake Tana, its natural Ethiopian reservoir, be used for irrigation upstream it would create a disaster downstream, which was Britain's responsibility. Its interests, therefore, went hand in hand with the "Peace Ballot," which also, unfortunately, showed a determination not to go to war. This meant that no available means, even appeasement, would be overlooked to avoid war. On June 24 Eden had attempted a bilateral negotiation with Mussolini. He traveled to Rome after stopping in Paris and offered Mussolini a solution with vast territorial concessions in the Ogaden in exchange for compensation by Great Britain to Ethiopia in the form of an opening to the ocean in British Somaliland. Mussolini had rejected this indignantly and France had issued a protest, proof enough that the British actually didn't only pursue a policy of resistance.

British doubts about France's attitude were seen in dramatic tones. Could Laval be trusted? Whose side would France choose to be on, Italy or England?

During the entire period preceding October 2, the British didn't know what the French attitude would be but were pleased to see her drawing closer to them. On June 19 Hoare still thought that France would be on Italy's side. On August 21, however, he found that there was an "Anglo-French front." From August 16 to 18, Laval, Eden, and Baron Aloisi held talks in Paris. The British were ready to accept the French concept of a veiled protectorate by Italy under the auspices of the League of Nations.[95] But once again Mussolini was to reject that concession repeatedly, then and in September, when a Committee of Five appointed by the League of Nations reached a similar conclusion.[96]

It was in September that the situation became serious. As Corbin wrote on September 1, "One of the main worries of the British public right now is to know what the position of the French government will be when the Italo-Ethiopian conflict is discussed in Geneva."[97] In Rome Ambassador de Chambrun was instructed to encourage Mussolini to be cautious and met with him on September 3. Mussolini was "worried" but "always cordial" as he was attempting to avoid a situation that would force him to withdraw from the League of Nations.[98] The Italians were very displeased with the statements made by French Professor Gaston Jèze, the legal advisor to Ethiopia. The Italian press, for the most part, and Virginio Gayda, in particular, in the *Giornale d'Italia* attempted to keep France out of any action decided by the League of Nations and wrote glowing words about "the new Franco-Italian friendship that had been forged for the most part by the personal initiative of Mr. Laval."[99]

During that same month of September Italian reinforcements poured into Eritrea and Somalia. On the other hand, following a British cabinet decision on August 22, part of the "Home Fleet" was dispatched to the Mediterranean during the second half of September in the hope that this naval concentration would deter Italy.[100] Mussolini declared himself "humiliated."[101] However, at the same time France and Britain kept on discussing potential appeasement through territorial concessions to Italy. This was the focus of an important meeting in Geneva at the Hotel des Bergues on September 10 and 11 between Laval, Léger, and Massigli on one side and Hoare, Eden and Strang on the other.[102]

While the French government was trying to prevent war by attempting to satisfy Italy, it was also considering the issue of sanctions. Among the many memos written on the issue we shall extract the following comment that clearly stated the later position France took: "What could be recommended are gradual sanctions that take Italy's specific economic condition into account."[103]

On October 2 Mussolini issued the order to his army to invade Ethiopia. Even though this action was quite predictable, it still captured the imagination because of its suddenness. The Council of the League of Nations met on October 5. It first listened to the representatives of Italy and Ethiopia.[104] The Assembly was called to meet on the 9th, and on the 10th Baron Aloisi skillfully made the case for his government's position. The other speakers, including Laval, supported the basic principles that involved economic sanctions.[105] We shall not get into the complicated details of the proceedings but will focus on the main actions taken by France.

First, France did everything it possibly could to *delay* the vote in favor of sanctions while the British were in a hurry.[106] The chosen method was to have the Committee of Eighteen in charge of sanctions study the issue.[107] Laval then undertook many conciliatory moves toward Mussolini.[108] Finally, Laval tried successfully to weaken the sanctions.[109] Sanctions were decided upon between October 11 and November 18 and remained exclusively limited to the economic and financial areas. They did not include a number of products that were necessary to conduct military operations—iron, steel, copper, lead, zinc, cotton, wool, and most of all oil.

In spite of the very strong reaction of Italian public opinion against the "sanctionists," Mussolini—whom Chambrun met on November 12— said that "we must not blame France" and he gave instructions to the press to follow that line.[110] He realized how soft France's support for the League of Nations actually was. Yet France did make another important concession to Great Britain when, on September 24, she asked France to provide naval support in case of war between Britain and Italy. The minimum would be opening French ports to British ships. The first French answer on October 5 was very vague but on October 18 Laval agreed to this naval support. Deputy Navy Chief of Staff Admiral Decoux went to London on October 30 to meet with Admiral Chatfield, First Lord of the Admiralty, to set up the details of the potential collaboration. When Decoux voiced his opinion doubting that Italy might attack England, Admiral Chatfield answered, "With the dictators you never can tell. No one can say for sure that Mr. Mussolini will not take some serious decisions someday." Other military and air force discussions took place in November and December.[111] Laval had thus succeeded in carrying out a remarkable maneuver in reaching military agreements with both potential adversaries, Italy and Great Britain. These were not in fact actual agreements since they were negotiated in his particular style, but oral statements and written communiqués. Pierre Laval's golden rule appears to have been to never quite go all the way on anything.

During the course of conversations regarding sanctions and military issues, the war was taking a positive course for Italy, followed by more difficult circumstances. The possibility, already outlined in August and September, of making territorial concessions to Italy that could be satisfactory and to stop the war, then resurfaced. Mussolini was thinking about an annexation of the borderlands of Ethiopia and collective domination of the central part of the country. This was what Laval communicated to the British government on October 24.[112] At a meeting at Geneva's Hotel des Bergues on November 1 (Laval, Massigli, de Saint-Quentin—Hoare, Eden), the idea was offered once more by Hoare. Rather than a form of mandate, he preferred territorial concessions on the condition Italy would offer Ethiopia an opening to the ocean. Laval had "no preference" one way or the other either for a concession or a mandate. This was the origin of the "Hoare-Laval Plan."[113]

Nothing much happened in November. Baldwin had dissolved the British Parliament on October 25 and general elections took place on November 15, returning to the House of Commons a weakened but very substantial conservative majority.

Those Conservatives, starting with their leaders Baldwin and Hoare, had not been very energetic towards the Italian aggressors. To reach an agreement even at Ethiopia's expense had already been discussed on numerous occasions. The more the Italians penetrated deeper into Ethiopia the greater the concessions Ethiopia would be forced to make. Hoare had openly backed that view on November 1. It also allowed him to delay a potentially dangerous debate concerning oil sanctions that were being vocally demanded by anti-fascists around the world. Laval, Baldwin and possibly Mussolini all shared the need to reestablish peace by finding a solution to the problem. Without any regard for the Ethiopians,[114] Mussolini called them barbarians. The leaders of the world's two largest colonial empires were not saying as much but were not far from thinking that way. The British feared Mussolini might launch a desperate attack in the event of oil sanctions. The British army was weak and if the fleet was much stronger than its Italian opponent it was also vulnerable to air attack. British military circles also suspected that France would not participate in any action.

All this explains how not just Hoare but even permanent Undersecretary Vansittart, a vigorous defender of collective security, both ended up approving a negotiation on the basis of what is described above. At the end of November Laval pressed the issue, and Léger proposed a meeting between Laval and Hoare. Since the latter was to go on holiday in Switzerland, he decided to stop in Paris. Vansittart went with him.

Conversations took place in Paris on December 7 and 8.[115] Taking advantage of British concerns and mixing half-hearted promises of military help with the proposals regarding Ethiopia, Laval was able to get his plan approved which then became the "Hoare-Laval plan" intended to remain secret. Italy would get two-thirds of Ethiopia in exchange for a small outlet to the ocean that it was prepared to give to that country. Italy would in effect have a protectorate over the rest.

What was to follow is well known. On December 13 a leak to the French press in *L'Œuvre* (Geneviève Tabouis) and *L'Echo de Paris* (Pertinax) told the world that the great champions of collective security offered an enormous payoff to the aggressors. Hoare was convinced that the leak originated in the Quai d'Orsay, "Was it intentional or due to negligence?"[116] Did it come from Alexis Léger, who opposed the proposal and tried to scuttle it by making it public? Or was it Pierre Comert, head of the press office?[117] There is no conclusive proof. The plan failed because of the violent protest by public opinion, especially among the British. It ended up forcing Hoare to resign—he was replaced by Anthony Eden on December 22. Laval lasted a few more weeks in power. By causing the indignation of the radicals, followed by their resignation from his cabinet, the Hoare-Laval plan ended Laval's active political career on January 22, 1936, for a period of five years.

Laval had therefore made an empty gesture to the Germans and reached an important agreement with Italy without wanting to get into an alliance, he signed a mutual assistance pact with the USSR, which he emptied of any effectiveness; and he backed British policy for sanctions and made sure they would not work. As Roland de Margerie told a German diplomat, "The whole legacy of Barthou didn't sit well with Laval."[118]

Chapter V

THE RHINELAND TRAGEDY

(January–June 1936)

A t the beginning of 1936 three main foreign policy issues were, or rather should have been, on the French people's mind: the sanctions problem in the Italian-Ethiopian war; the ratification of the Franco-Soviet mutual assistance pact; and, finally, a possible Hitlerian coup in the Rhineland demilitarized zone—the left bank of the Rhine and a 50-kilometer strip on the right bank.

The Sarraut government, which replaced the Laval cabinet on January 24, 1936—it was to be the last of the National Union governments—presented itself to the country and to Parliament as a "transition" cabinet.

We have seen that the fall of Laval on January 22, 1936, was due to a decision by the Radical Socialist Party to join the Front that the socialists and communists had started back in June and July 1934, which, once enlarged, became the "Popular Front." Laval was under attack on three issues: his very accommodating attitude toward Italian aggression in Ethiopia characterized by the willful ineffectiveness of the sanctions and the Hoare-Laval plan; his tolerant attitude toward the "leagues," meaning the threat of fascist subversion in France which was in effect more potential than real; and his deflationary economic policy, which irritated everyone. The rivalry between Daladier and Herriot within the Radical Party was to settle the matter. Daladier—who in any case hated the communists much more than his rival—was eager to seek revenge against the National Union for having instigated his downfall on February 7, 1934. There was no other way but to join the Popular Front. Herriot had been forced to resign as president of his party on December 18, 1935. For over one month he succeeded in holding together enough radicals to allow for the survival of Laval's cabinet. But on January 22 the radical ministers resigned and the rest of the Laval government withdrew.

Albert Sarraut, who was the quintessential Radical-Socialist and brother of Maurice Sarraut, the all-powerful publisher of *La Dépêche de Toulouse*, was called upon. Albert was outwardly full of energy but rather hesitant deep down. He put together a strange cabinet that included the right (Flandin at Foreign Affairs, Piétri at Marine, Mandel at the PTT, etc.), but where the radical socialists and independent socialists were by far the dominant element. Paul-Boncour was minister of state and permanent representative to the League of Nations. Georges Bonnet was minister of commerce and industry. Marcel Déat, a university professor and dissident socialist, became, due to his great experience no doubt, minister of air. Only General Louis Maurin among the military ministers had real experience. He was returning to the ministry of war once again, a position he had held after Marshal Pétain in the Flandin cabinet. He was a great artilleryman and had served under Joffre. We shall attempt to explain his role, which was different from Gamelin's. Maurin and Gamelin were classmates at the École de Guerre (1899) and had both been among Joffre's "special envoys" in 1914.

Such a government was paralyzed in every possible direction. Both those in favor and those opposed to the Popular Front could only reach a few compromise decisions that everyone could agree to. Since it knew beyond a doubt that it could not last, it had to delay the big decisions and take as little action as possible.

1.

Internal and Foreign Policy
up to March 7, 1936

The potential for a Popular Front victory—which, contrary to the Cartel des Gauches, included the communists—caused some rather acrimonious friction. For some it represented an enthusiastic hope, while in others it brought out strong hostility that could sometimes turn violent. The event that startled the imagination of the French people the most before March 7 was the attack by the "camelots du roi," who were returning from the funeral of Jacques Bainville, the Action Française historian, against socialist leader Léon Blum on February 13. Wounded in the head, he had to cease all political activity for several weeks. The attack prompted the Sarraut cabinet to dissolve the Ligue d'Action Française and its satellite organizations, a sure sign of the increasing tensions among the French people.

The war in Ethiopia fit squarely into this picture. The Popular Front was naturally anti-fascist and the right wing was generally pro-Italian, for ideological reasons among the small fascist groups, and out of colonial sympathy among most of the moderate right. The public followed military operations with great interest, the problems the Italians encountered in Ethiopia,[1] renewed optimism surfaced in Rome at the beginning of February[2] and that month actually saw some key military successes.

But the problem was different as far as France was concerned. The issue was to assess whether the basically ineffective economic sanctions decided by the League of Nations in October 1935 could be reinforced by an oil embargo. Obviously there was a good chance for it to also not be decisive. Since the United States[3] and Germany[4] were not members of the League of Nations, they would not be compelled to observe it despite the "moral embargo" that had been proclaimed—uselessly—by U.S. Secretary of State Cordell Hull. Mussolini's Italy, however, would certainly be very much affected. Once he found out about the new Sarraut government coming to power in France, Mussolini told French Ambassador de Chambrun that such an embargo "would have overwhelming consequences on Franco-Italian friendship" and he suggested that Sarraut take a reassuring position during his government's policy statement.[5] Sarraut's statement was completely vague and insignificant at best. He merely touched on "the respect for international commitments and the development of collective security according to the principles of the League of Nations."[6]

The matter, like all those requiring a decision from an undecided group, was going to drag on. The Committee of Eighteen at the League of Nations, which was tracking how the sanctions were applied was basically favorable—but only in theory—to an oil embargo. The committee asked a "sub-committee on oil" to study the issue during its meeting on February 3, 1936. At the Quai d'Orsay the feeling was that it would probably not reach "positive conclusions."[7] Flandin was kept well informed about the disintegrating Ethiopian army by Bodard, the French minister at Addis Ababa—"an excellent agent," he wrote[8]—and preferred to seek an "honorable solution" with an "appeal for conciliation addressed to the belligerent parties,"[9] meaning that he was ready to abandon Ethiopia to its sad fate. When Anthony Eden, as head of the Foreign Office, pressed him in Geneva to enact the oil embargo, he answered in a memorandum where he stated, "If the oil embargo were to be declared, Italy would leave the League of Nations. She will naturally seek a closer relationship with Germany...But there is a serious risk: Germany may be tempted to take advantage of the situation in the demilitarized zone." The memorandum was dated March 3, four days before the German move. It is easy to see how strong that kind of argumentation was![10] As for Paul-Boncour, he didn't even mention that important issue in his memoirs, even though he was the minister of state in charge of the League of Nations.

The issue of ratification of the Franco-Soviet pact was being handled in much the same way. Following a long delay, which worried the USSR,[11] the government presented the draft of the ratification bill following the usual procedure; most of the right-wing newspapers rejected the pact because, at the same time as the Popular Front, it helped reintroduce the Communist Party by creating space for it in French politics. Hatred of the USSR found its expression in some newspapers like *L'Action Française:* "a bad pact" wrote J. Delbecque.[12] By voting to ratify it "the Chamber voted for revolution and war."[13] Similar thoughts were published in Léon Bailby's *Le Jour.*[14] More often there was mostly a lot of suspicion about it. The left was mostly favorable; this became clear in the program of "demands of the popular groupings" that included the Communist Party, the SFIO, the Radical-Socialists and the *Union Socialiste et Républicaine*, the main labor union leadership, the CGT and CGTU, that were just about to merge, the League for Human Rights, the Vigilance Committee of Anti-fascists Intellectuals, etc. The section entitled "Defense of Peace" was very abstract, and yet paragraph 7 stated: "Extend to the countries of Eastern and Central Europe the system of pacts open to everyone, especially the principles of the Franco-Soviet Pact."[15]

Yet there were some exceptions on the right where Paul Reynaud, for instance, defended the treaty and on the left where some pacifists were not too favorable, such as the socialist Paul Faure ("We have decided to vote in favor of the Franco-Soviet Pact but are determined to avoid being drawn into a system of military alliances") and Marceau Pivert most of all, who was critical of the "alliance fever."[16]

Following a debate that need not be analyzed here, the Chamber of Deputies voted to ratify by a vote of 353 vs. 164 on February 27. The 93 Socialists, 10 Communists, and 141 out of 146 Radical-Socialists all voted in favor. To these 244 votes were added those of the other backers of the Popular Front, such as Marcel Déat's *Union Socialiste et Républicaine (USR)*, some eighty moderate "realist" deputies who followed Paul Reynaud and Minister Flandin and approved the pact. On March 5 the foreign affairs commission in the Senate proposed ratification and the Senate voted to ratify on March 12—after Hitler's coup—by 231 votes in favor to 52 against.

2.

THE FORECASTS
ABOUT THE DEMILITARIZED ZONE

We have set aside one of the major points made by those opposed to the Franco-Soviet Pact, namely the threat coming from Hitler. The threat was a fact since his major speech of May 21, 1935, a few days after the Pact was signed; a June 1, 1935, memorandum by the Wilhelmstrasse was more specific regarding those points.[17] The Treaty of Versailles in articles 42 and 43 had forbidden Germany from keeping military units or building fortifications on the left bank of the Rhine and an area 50 kilometers wide on the right bank. With the 1925 Locarno Treaty, Germany on one side and France and Belgium on the other, agreed under a guarantee by Great Britain and Italy to respect each other's borders and confirmed a clause which Germany agreed that the entrance of the Reichswehr into the demilitarized zone would be considered an act of aggression as serious as the crossing of a border. Versailles was a *Diktat* but Locarno had been entered into freely.

As early as September 1933 War Minister Daladier had informed the Quai d'Orsay that if Germany reoccupied the demilitarized zone, "the foundations of our national defense would be deeply altered."[18]

On May 21, 1935, Hitler had again reiterated that he would abide by the Locarno agreements. It is true that at Locarno it had been stated that should Germany attack one of its neighbors that were France's allies—Poland or Czechoslovakia—France would send its troops across the Franco-German border. The logic the Germans used was that, through the alliance with the USSR against Germany—according to Hitler this was the logic of an "encirclement alliance"—France was unilaterally adding a third instance that would allow her to cross the German border, that of German attack on the USSR (that didn't have common borders.) *Therefore she would be in breach of the Locarno agreement.* "In this manner he [Hitler] keeps a door open and a way to claim, when he feels it would be appropriate, that other signatories meaning France, having breached the treaty, it would then become null and void."[19]

During the entire period from May 21, 1935 to January 1936, Hitler, von Neurath, Ribbentrop, and German diplomats never stopped attacking the Franco-Soviet Pact while they upheld Germany's support for Locarno. At times they alluded to the fact that the ratification of the Franco-Soviet Pact would constitute a "breach of Locarno." However, even though the French government had been warned, and was well aware that Hitler wanted to reoccupy the Rhineland for both military and psychological reasons, it could still legitimately wonder whether he would dare make the move.

The issue of information in the months of January, February, and the beginning of March 1936 thus became of paramount importance. When would Hitler make his move? Would it be sooner or at a later date? Would he proceed by using policemen in disguise or a brutal entry by the Reichswehr?

Since we know the outcome after March 7, 1936, we shall refrain from criticizing the ambassador for his many changing views. And yet these were expressed. It will suffice to carefully read the *Documents Diplomatiques Français*. We shall limit ourselves to a few examples.

Both Hitler on November 21, 1935,[20] and Bülow on January 10, 1936,[21] offered assurances regarding Germany's intention to abide by the Locarno Treaty while denouncing the Franco-Soviet Pact as a violation of Locarno. The ambassador responded: "You behave as if you were seeking legal excuses early on to justify some future action that is already on your mind and could be, for example, to suddenly occupy the demilitarized zone." By January there was deep concern. The remilitarization was to take place in 1937 at the latest (according to General Renondeau, military attaché in Berlin), perhaps in June 1936 when the Reichstag was scheduled to meet.[22] Charles Corbin, the ambassador to London, predicted in 1936.[23] On January 24 François-Poncet came to the conclusion that "Germany doesn't intend to withdraw from the Locarno Treaty or to cancel it by placing us brutally in front of a *fait accompli* similar to that of March 16, 1935. That is not her intention *for now*. But the future remains uncertain."[24]

Only the French consuls general in Cologne (Dobler)[25] and mostly in Düsseldorf (Noël Henry), seeing many "technical" preparations being made locally, concluded that Germany would "without a doubt" respond to the ratification of the Franco-Soviet Pact.[26]

Despite these warnings, François-Poncet became more optimistic by February. "It is…probable that for the moment we will not be facing a *fait accompli*."[27] The occupation of the Rhineland "will not in all likelihood happen in the weeks to come."[28] "Nervousness and unease" in Germany, he wrote on February 27. But "she will *probably* avoid the irreparable step… She will not proceed with a sudden military occupation of the Rhineland area."[29] And on March 6 he still reports information coming from a British informer who "doesn't think we should infer…that Mr. Hitler could be preparing the sudden occupation of the Rhineland at a very early date."[30] It is true that the ambassador always prefaced his reports by saying that Hitler was all-powerful, and that he was absolutely capable of making instantaneous decisions. "What will Hitler do?" he cabled on March 6 at 9:45 p.m. "We still don't know which side will prevail in the last few days, between those in favor of moderation or violence."[31]

Dobler, the former consul general in Cologne, testifying to the committee of inquiry after the war accused François-Poncet of not taking his information seriously enough and even of telling him, "You shouldn't send such cables they get people worried."[32] Dobler also stated that at the Quai, starting with Alexis Léger, there was a "screen put up by those sedentary officials opposed to distributing information in France coming from agents overseas."[33] Flandin told the same committee, "I was one of the rare foreign ministers who read every cable"—an unproven statement in view of the very few comments penciled in by the minister on the documents themselves—and said he had read some of Dobler's cables.[34] One may wonder if, in this case, Dobler was not settling a personal grievance against the powerful man who was in charge of the embassy.

Besides François-Poncet and his team of diplomats, other information was provided by the military attachés.

In Berlin the naval attaché was Captain Tracou. General Renondeau was the military attaché since 1930 and Léon Poincaré, an aeronautics engineer and the son of the renowned mathematician, was the air force attaché. Renondeau had long been stationed in Tokyo, knew Japanese, was a graduate of the École Polytechnique, and a highly cultured man. "He always showed great intellectual curiosity, was calm and collected and always very courteous."[35] Stehlin gave the following description of Léon Poincaré:

"I have rarely met a man with such a keen gift for observation. In his memory he could photograph anything of interest. His reports were extensive, complete, and full of drawings and graphs. No one made more of a contribution than he did in effectively describing the German air force."[36]

Were the military attachés better informed than the ambassadors? There is evidence that they did not pass along all the information they obtained to their ambassador. For example, Jules-François Blondel, the chargé d'affaires in Rome from 1936 to 1938, recollected, "There was such a team spirit in every section of that embassy that I felt I could ask our five special attachés to hand me a report on their observations in their specialty every six months ...It was an unusual request that could cause friction due to the various administrative autonomies. But I did succeed."[37]

This goes to show that daily communications left much to be desired. However, it does appear that the relationship among General Renondeau, Léon Poincaré, and Ambassador François-Poncet was good. They consulted daily about predictions regarding the demilitarized zone (François-Poncet met with his entire staff every day).

If we examine, for example, the information relating to the probable remilitarization of the Rhineland, we find that General Renondeau was slightly more pessimistic than his ambassador. As early as June 19, 1935, he wrote to Minister of War Fabry that the German government—which was setting up recruitment offices inside the demilitarized zone—was *currently* committed to respecting the demilitarization clauses. But he added,

"There is no doubt that the issue of their cancellation will come up some day." The problem was to find out whether it would be a matter of "several months or several years."[38] On December 10[39] he reported that Hitler, according to Generals Reichenau and von Stulpnagel, confirmed the zone would not be tampered with. "I am very skeptical," he added. It was possible that Hitler would act by surprise, and 1937 appeared to be the outer limit. On January 15 a rumor was circulating that the reoccupation would take place on January 30. "There are no clues," he writes, to confirm this information. "There is no doubt in my mind that the demilitarized zone will be reoccupied by Germany; only the date remains unknown. We must accept the fact that it may take place rather soon"[40] On March 4, using a report from Dobler, about which the embassy had consulted with him, and listing many clues, he concluded that the reoccupation was imminent but didn't reach a firm conclusion.[41]

Colonel de La Forest-Divonne, the military attaché in Switzerland, was much more explicit but in the opposite direction. Basing his conclusion on the fact that barracks in the Rhineland were not completely repaired, according to information provided by the consul general in Basel, he stated on February 27 that he did not believe in "an early occupation of the Rhineland area."[42]

In conclusion, according to *available* information (which was not necessarily *read*), the French government could reasonably conclude that Hitler would soon reoccupy the zone but that, until the evening of March 6, it did not know the date nor the circumstances.

The newspapers were mentioning this possibility less than they discussed the war in Ethiopia or the Franco-Soviet Pact. Part of the left-wing press didn't even mention the issue fearing that it might work against the ratification of the treaty. The communist daily *L'Humanité* was basically silent about it except for two rather vague articles by Gabriel Péri[43] and Paul Nizan.[44] The socialist *Le Populaire* was *completely* silent. The only mention appeared on March 7 as German units were on the march. It was an unsigned news item dated "Berlin, March 6," stating that Hitler was about to invoke "the right" to occupy the Rhineland area. "However, it doesn't mean that Adolf Hitler wants to turn this unilateral rejection of the Treaties of Versailles and Locarno into an ultimatum or a *fait accompli.*"

The newspaper *L'Œuvre*, which was closer to the radicals, had a much better informed writer in Geneviève Tabouis. She did write about the issue from time to time but reached different conclusions. On January 14 the news "concerning the demilitarized zone was increasingly alarming." Great Britain "already hinted that she wouldn't take any action if such an event took place."[45] Then, after François-Poncet took an initiative with von Bülow, there was a wave of optimism: "It is believed in international circles in the capital of the Reich that Hitler's government was surprised by the strong attitude Paris was showing on this occasion."[46] When Flandin traveled to London, Tabouis again addressed the German threat: "A joint declaration could possibly influence the decisions Germany will make."[47] But "London feels that the French are exaggerating about the seriousness of the situation."[48] London also believes that Hitler will not move before the Berlin Olympics, scheduled for August 1936.[49] *Cassandra's* optimism increased in February: "It is generally thought that the Germans will not occupy the demilitarized zone but that they are keeping the possibility in abeyance should it become necessary."[50] It all ended on March 6 with a prophecy of the same vintage as *Le Populaire*: "News from Berlin has it that the Germans will proceed by slow infiltration to get around if not breach articles 42 and 43 of the Treaty of Versailles."[51]

Even though the subject only came up occasionally, the right-wing newspapers were much more eager than the left to mention the remilitarization of the Rhineland since this was an argument against the Franco-Soviet Pact.

As an example there was no dearth of articles on the subject in *L'Action Française* and *Le Jour*. Would they provide Hitler's government an excuse? IS A SHOWDOWN ABOUT TO HAPPEN?,[52] TOWARDS A COUP,[53] HITLER, MASTER OF THE HOUR, are the headlines usually found in the monarchist daily. On February 26 J. Delbecque[54] accurately described what he expected would happen. Will Germany "use the Franco-Soviet Pact ratification as an excuse to break the Locarno Treaty and reoccupy the demilitarized zone?" What would France's attitude then be? "Without making any prophecies we may surmise that we will lodge an energetic protest to Berlin, that we will agree with Great Britain and Belgium (let's no longer even mention Italy, alas!) and take some protective measures on the border. Then what?"

In *Le Jour* Léon Bailby asked what part Britain would agree to play. "Will she make commitments on the Rhine?"[55] "Was the Rhineland issue discussed in London?" (during the Eden-Flandin meeting). "The minister of foreign affairs said yesterday that France will not allow the remilitarization of the Rhineland area. Will you remain as firm all the way?"[56]

When, on February 29, *Paris-Midi* published an interview with Hitler by Bertrand de Jouvenel, everyone drew a sigh of relief. Hitler sounded unfocused and sentimental. He made a point of "his wish to leave no stone unturned to improve Franco-German relations."[57] What a charming man who bore no grudges just two days after the Franco-Soviet Pact was ratified! But just a minute! The interview took place on February 21 and was set up by the German embassy in Paris. Hitler "wanted to impress French public opinion while the debate on the Franco-Soviet Pact was taking place." He noticed, however, that his interview was published only after ratification took place. Was that some manipulation by François-Poncet? Or the Quai d'Orsay? On the morning of March 2 an important meeting took place at the Reich Chancellery with the military leaders and ministers in attendance. Once the decision was made, Hitler received François-Poncet at 11:30 p.m. "I could see the nervousness, the worry and embarrassment displayed by the chancellor," wrote the ambassador. The *Paris-Midi* interview was already "an old story" to him.[58]

The entrance of the German army units on March 7 into the Rhineland demilitarized zone was like a bolt from the blue. While public opinion had always known about some vague threat, it had never taken it seriously. The tragedy took place without the French being prepared for it.

3.

Was a Countermove Planned?

Despite obvious gaps in available information, the Quai d'Orsay and the military ministries were well aware that a German operation into the demilitarized zone was not to be excluded. Responsibility for a countermove rested with the cabinet alone. Was such a counter-move considered?[59]

At several times from January to March 7, 1936, the Quai d'Orsay drew the attention of the Ministry of War to the idea of a counter-move. A memo from Foreign Affairs dated February brought up the problem very effectively: "It is appropriate to see which precautions or responses should be prepared in the very short term, should Germany take any initiative to unilaterally breach the status of the demilitarized zone. It is up to the Ministry of War to make recommendations."[60] The commercial relations department of the Quai d'Orsay was considering economic sanctions. Since François-Poncet's reports described Germany's economic condition in rather dark colors, the diplomats felt optimistic about the effectiveness of those sanctions that could, if applied, "have fateful consequences for the Reich that could endanger the regime itself."[61] However, Flandin and at least his closest deputy, René Massigli, felt it was necessary to go further and consider a military response. On February 7 a meeting took place at the Ministry of War with four ministers—Flandin, General Maurin, Piétri and Déat—assisted by the chiefs of staff of the three branches of the military: Gamelin, Admiral Durand-Viel and General Pujo. Flandin clearly brought up the issue of "countermeasures." According to the minutes,[62] the military offered no response. The answer came in a dispatch from the Army High Command signed by Maurin, dated February 12, and addressed to Flandin that didn't mention anything about a *countermove* but only precautions: "I am considering reducing the number of measures now planned to a minimum in the event of a threat of sudden attack in order to avoid offering any real excuse for a conflict."[63]

The existing plan of concentration, called plan D *bis*, in effect since April 15, 1935, before general mobilization, called for three series of "precautionary" measures allowing the deployment of the "covering units" in 23 days. These were:

a. "Simple Alert" level: regular army units go to their areas including the Maginot Line;

b. "Reinforced Alert" level where border reservists are called up;

c. The "Security" level, allowing the call-up of many regulars and reservists to set up a "solid defensive front." Including 21 infantry divisions of which 7 are motorized and 5 cavalry divisions including the DLM [Light Motorized Division];[64]

d. The "Simple or reinforced" cover with three available classes and many reservists.

[a. Implied no "call-up"; b. A call-up of about 35,000 men; c. 120,000; d. 1 million men.[65]]

Precautionary measures had nothing to do with a response. Flandin immediately informed General Maurin of this.[66] He agreed with him that the government alone could make a decision on the substance of the issue but it could also consider the appropriate actions to be taken if they had been prepared. "It actually means for us not just to respond to a possible initiative on Germany's part but, if possible, to discourage the Reich from going down that path." To this, General Maurin responded on February 17 by listing once more the precautionary measures. As for the rest: "It could be contrary to French interests to use our right to occupy the demilitarized zone… We would actually risk being considered the aggressor and thus find ourselves alone facing Germany. Such an operation couldn't be considered without the full support of the British government."[67]

The Quai d'Orsay could only take note of the general staff's refusal. In a document probably written by Massigli, one reads that General Maurin's letter "says nothing regarding initiatives France could take to intimidate or force the opponent to retreat." It only discusses moves that are intended as "guarantees in order to protect us from a further development of the German initiative."[68] The Quai d'Orsay and the cabinet both resigned themselves at the meeting of February 27. Despite the possibility offered by the Locarno agreements to act alone without waiting for a decision of the Council of the League of Nations in the event of a "blatant and unquestionable breach" of Locarno, "the French government will take no isolated action. It will only act in agreement with the signatories of Locarno." It only reserves the right to take "preparatory" actions. Belgian Ambassador de Kerchove was informed as of February 27 and Eden a few days later in Geneva.[69]

The French government, therefore, decided in advance to side with the general staff but this still requires an explanation: Was Gamelin thinking that the reoccupation of the demilitarized zone would be insignificant? Not at all. At a meeting of the chiefs of staff on February 19, where no ministers were in attendance, he made the surprising statement: "We must do everything we can to keep the clauses of the treaty of Versailles regarding the demilitarized zone at least up to the moment when the impact of the low birth rate classes is no longer felt in our manpower meaning until 1940 or 1942."

Do everything? Except acting alone militarily. And what if, as it appears very probable, Great Britain and Belgium refused to cooperate?[70] Why not attempt to take action with just French troops since France has the right to do so in case of a "blatant breach?"

There is a general answer to this. The French army was based on a *defensive* doctrine. There were no plans to engage "a potential expeditionary corps" quickly beyond the Maginot Line (an expression used by Gamelin himself.)[71] As Michalon and Vernet write,[72] "Therefore following the military triumph of the army of 1918, the regular French army, designed to include three million men at mobilization, had become within fifteen years and in spite of its 400,000 men a cumbersome mass incapable of having immediate operational capabilities."

But there was also another, more compelling, motivation. *Gamelin believed that the German armed forces were already stronger than the French forces.*

The idea was making the rounds in political circles. On January 30, during the debate regarding the Sarraut government's policy statement, the ultra-nationalist Radical Franklin-Bouillon declared, "Today Germany has an army twice the size of ours and two times better equipped." And he quoted the War Budget Committee Chairman Léon Archimbaud (Radical): "I said so because it's the truth!" he cried out.[73]

Gamelin, it was assumed, was much better informed than the members of Parliament. However, his estimates don't match what we know today. Starting in April 1935, Gamelin spoke in terms of a German army "of 32 infantry divisions, doubling possibly even by the end of 1935 and 50 divisions of Grenzschutz (border protection units) reaching the planned 120 divisions."[74] Facing them, what could the French army do, since it had only 350,000 men (20 infantry divisions, 3 North African divisions, 2 light mechanized divisions and 8 fortress brigades)?[75] Furthermore, Gamelin thought that in a long war—and he didn't conceive of any other—German manpower would overwhelm the French.

One could conclude that Gamelin's mistake originated in faulty evaluations by the *Deuxième Bureau* of the Army General Staff, which was in charge of intelligence gathering. However, *Deuxième Bureau* was well informed. As Colonel Defrasne wrote, its assessments "for the most part corroborate recent works by German authors, both in their manpower or location."[76] In March 1936 the *Deuxième Bureau* estimated that Germany had an army of 480,000 men coming from a very mixed recruitment: 90,000 from the old Reichswehr; 90,000 that joined in 1934; 90,000 that joined in 1935; 50,000 policemen incorporated into the army and 160,000 conscripts from the class of 1934. On paper this was a far cry from the 32 divisions that could be doubled as described by Gamelin. But this army had a fundamental weakness prior to 1937 that could not be overcome: the lack of officers. These numbered 4,300 in 1933 when 30,000 were required. Despite the hasty training of younger officers, the recall of many retired officers, and the promotions of NCOs, there would still be only 13,000 by the end of 1935.[77] To these one must add the huge paramilitary formations: 1,000,000 SA; 30,000 SS; 350,000 NSKK—Nazi transport services—and 400,000 Labor Front members. The *Deuxième Bureau*, however, considered their military worth as practically nil. These militias, even armed with rifles, cannot be compared to trained reservists, and then how could they be mobilized since there were no officers?

There had to be someone else who, using these reassuring numbers, would then extrapolate them. This was, in fact, the key to the problem.

By estimating the manpower of the units present in the Rhineland on March 11 at 60,000 men—seven divisions—Gamelin, *despite the Deuxième Bureau*, added another 235,000 auxiliary troops but, above all, *rather than describing them as 235,000 disorganized men, transformed that evaluation into fifteen divisions, that is, into combat-ready units.* Therefore, the French were already facing twenty-two German divisions![78]

To whom and to what can such a high wire exercise be attributed? Was Gamelin attempting, through excessively cautious precautions, to overestimate the enemy's troop strength in order not to be in a weaker position? Was he the victim of the fears of some of his subordinates? According to eyewitnesses, the *Troisième Bureau* was not at fault. Since we know today that Generals von Fritsch and von Blomberg, frightened by Hitler's bold move, were recommending the cancellation of the March 7 operation; and we know of the calculated risk he was willing to take: the French are stronger than we are but will not dare respond! With our knowledge that Hitler was ready to sound the retreat immediately, should the French army cross the border,[79] then the sheer enormity of that responsibility becomes apparent. General Maurin and the government, not having direct access to *Deuxième Bureau* intelligence, could not know that they were being misled regarding the size of the German forces. Strangely enough, Gamelin would write later on in his memoirs that in 1936 France let the "last opportunity" go by to beat Hitler's Germany.[80] This statement sounds rather naïve.

4.

The Decision
To Not React and Getting Bogged Down

François-Poncet's first dispatch of March 7 reached the Quai d'Orsay at 9:30 a.m.[81] The ambassador announced that the Reichstag was being summoned to a noon session. He was received by von Neurath at 10:30 a.m. immediately following the Italian ambassador. The German minister handed him a nine-page memorandum breaking the Locarno Pact and offering a negotiation that would create a demilitarized zone on both sides of the border. The ambassador protested "in the most vigorous and solemn manner" against this unilateral breach of the Locarno Pact which Germany had signed of her own free will. He asked von Neurath whether Germany would send troops into the demilitarized zone. A few symbolic units, answered the minister. The cable reached the Quai d'Orsay at 11:30 a.m.[82] Another cable phoned in at 3:40 p.m. stated that 19 battalions and 13 artillery groups were taking part in the operation.[83]

The coup took place early on a Saturday morning. All the French morning papers were already published, unaware that the irreparable move was taking place, and some dailies—mainly *Le Populaire*—had awkwardly published optimistic articles. Saturday turned out to be a good day. Members of Parliament and cabinet ministers, almost to a man, were off in their electoral districts far away from Paris. Public opinion found out on the radio—there were still few listeners in those days—and from the evening papers. The government was unable to meet on March 7. In the afternoon Albert Sarraut met with the three defense ministers, State Minister Paul-Boncour and Georges Mandel, minister of the PTT. The latter two supported a firm attitude, while the others hesitated. Decisions were delayed until the following day since they necessarily belonged to the full cabinet. On the military side General Maurin had issued the order in advance to enact the "simple alert." Corps commanders recalled soldiers who were on leave; troops were dispatched to the Maginot Line. Then they waited to see whether the reservists would be called up once more. According to the calculations by Michalon and Vernet,[84] in two days some 55,000 men were sent to the border to face some 30,000 German soldiers.

The big decision was scheduled for the cabinet meetings of Sunday, March 8, and Monday, March 9. It had actually been prepared by the meeting of February 27, where it was agreed that France would take no isolated action. The problem was to see whether, faced by a brutal event, there wouldn't be a stronger reaction.

It becomes necessary before examining the government's role to take into account the mood of public opinion and its reaction. The public was not prepared and it was amazed and frightened, displaying a rare unanimous reaction: "Above all, no war!" The newspapers published on Sunday, March 8, all firmly opposed any strong reaction. War was something the political opposition wanted. In other words, the March 7 events, so threatening to France, were reduced to an internal political dispute. The Communists issued a statement:

"Men, women, young people: unite to prevent the curse of war from descending upon us once again… Let us bring about the unity of the French nation against those who would lead us to carnage." And they were "the Laval clique," the right—Taittinger, Philippe Henriot, Kérillis— the businessmen de Wendel and Schneider, the "traitor" Doriot and war veteran Jean Goy.[85] The Socialists gave Paul Faure a column (Léon Blum was still at Muret at the home of Vincent Auriol, convalescing after being wounded on February 13). This is what Paul Faure wrote: "The view we reject is that war could be the end result of the diplomatic conflict created by Berlin's *coup de théâtre*."[86] Furthermore, Oreste Rosenfeld and Marceau Pivert were vigorously objecting to the "provocative" attitude of the French government that had dared send troops to man…the Maginot Line! The CGT, reunited once more, voted a resolution on March 11, demanding "that the country not lose the necessary calm."[87] The Socialist members of Parliament stated that any action outside the League of Nations would effectively "reduce the current serious clash to a simple problem involving pride and prestige."

The radical *L'Œuvre* entitled its editorial of March 8, "Serious? Yes. The end of everything? We shall see." On the same day Geneviève Tabouis was asking "whether France would enforce respect for international law." How? "France will not mobilize, she will not even call up some classes but will prepare security measures, for example, by occupying the fortifications in the Rhineland and enforcing economic, financial, and even military sanctions by most countries at the League of Nations." The "even military" takes on a comic and tragic significance under the circumstances. In any case, there would be negotiations with Germany.[88]

The left was up in arms against the right-wing warmongers and demanded peace. But the right was incensed at the left-wing warmongers and also demanded peace, under threat by the Bolsheviks and their supporters. The headline of *Le Matin* on March 8 read: "Adolf Hitler has forcefully indicated the communist threat."[89] Leon Bailby announced in *Le Jour*, "We are already involved in a Russo-German war."[90] He pretended to complain that there had been no retaliation but added that "in order for it to happen it cannot only be French, it must be Anglo-French above all."[91] Colonel de La Rocque the leader of the *Croix de Feu*, thought there could be only one solution: to have "a government that is representative of the vital, social and energetic part of the "reconciled" nation.[92] Marcel Bucard's "Francist" movement felt that "the threat could only be eliminated by a direct and loyal agreement between France, Italy and Germany."[93]

As usual, the most violent position was that of *L'Action Française*. A banner headline on March 8 read: "The Republic has assassinated the peace." On March 9 a second banner headline screamed, "SARRAUT AND FLANDIN GET OUT!", followed by "GET OUT YOU BUNCH OF CUCKOLDS!" on March 10. Maurras provided the following commentary: "And first of all no war. We don't want war... We are ready to offer the last drop of blood for our country's independence... We will not shed any...for words that are meaningless."[94]

Among the veterans' associations the CNAC was pleased "in seeing how the nation once again showed its cool self control" and declared its support for the government. The UFAC suggested "forbidding any kind of action that could cause anxiety in the country" and voiced its trust in the League of Nations. The main association, UNC, berated the League of Nations, declaring that the country was in danger, and proposed the formation of "a government of French reconciliation and national defense" and the postponement of the elections. It would agree, "if necessary," to the recall of the latest classes of conscripts that had been discharged—a very bold move indeed.[95] This would earn them a sarcastic comment by the communists: "The UNC wants to mobilize several classes. We understand the type of interests that move them in any case."[96]

We have not chosen to quote some of these texts at length for their intellectual value but rather to show that a weak government was in some way swept up in a pacifist tornado. A few isolated men did wish that France take immediate military action. However, all organizations, groups, newspapers, political parties, and trade unions stood up against the odious prospect of a war just seventeen and one half years following the previous slaughter.

Without the benefit of the minutes of the cabinet meetings held on Sunday, March 8, and Monday, March 9, we do not have reliable information as to what actually took place, and the Parliamentary Commission of Inquiry did not provide a clear chronological description. Following his March 8 speech, Albert Sarraut spoke on radio in strong terms that included the words: "We will not allow that Strasbourg be exposed to German cannon fire." According to René Massigli, who had written the speech, he had added that sentence and underlined it so that Sarraut could decide whether to keep it or not since it could suggest a forceful reaction.[97] Sarraut did not think it sounded negative and kept it, which resulted in a drop in the stock market on Monday, March 9. However, the cabinet took the big decision that day that France would appeal to the countries that had signed the Locarno agreement and to the League of Nations. In other words, it did not see Hitler's brutal move as a "flagrant" breach of Locarno.

In any case, France had consulted its allies. Belgium had picked the date of March 6 to permanently end the secret military agreement of September 1920,[98] choosing a narrow interpretation of Locarno. England was merely "lukewarm," as Ambassador Corbin had noted, toward a French policy that was too conciliatory towards Italy. Anthony Eden, the new head of the Foreign Office since January 2, did not appear to back a firm attitude at all. No British historian ever considered Prime Minister Stanley Baldwin as the embodiment of a firm policy. "The position of Downing Street," wrote Corbin, "seems to be as follows: take no initiatives, create no obstacles."[99] It will come as no surprise that Eden's main initiative on March 7 consisted in preventing the French from doing anything at all. He made some calls to Flandin that we were unable to trace in the archives. He also met with Corbin in the late morning of March 7. The German action was, he said, "deplorable," but "he feels that due to the seriousness of the circumstances it would be desirable that no action that could irreparably influence the future be taken before the governments affected, and mainly those of France and Great Britain had the opportunity to consult with one another."[100] What did General Maurin say at the cabinet meeting?

In his opinion a partial and temporary military demonstration would not force Hitler to turn back. He therefore wanted the government to consider going to war. This meant British support, if possible, and in any case *French general mobilization*. "That request elicited loud protests from the cabinet," wrote Flandin. "A general mobilization six weeks before elections was insane."[101] According to Flandin who was writing long after those events, the only ones "in favor of immediate military action" (limited in scope, no doubt) were himself, Sarraut, Paul-Boncour, and Mandel (the one closest to Maurin). But in the midst of the usual commotion Mandel said nothing. Paul-Boncour spoke with Maurin[102] about calling up available men. Finally, everything led to the decision to do nothing at all.

The only promise of external support came from Poland and the USSR. Beck summoned Ambassador Léon Noël at 5 p.m. on March 7 and brought up the "alliance" between France and Poland, suggesting they stay in very close contact.[103] On March 10 in London Soviet Ambassador Maisky had a meeting with Corbin and told him that "the government of the USSR was willing to participate in any action against Germany that was taken by the League of Nations."[104] But Polish enthusiasm was short-lived and Léon Noël remained skeptical. During the night of March 7 to 8 the Polish press agency *Iskra* issued a communiqué that was favorable to Germany.[105] The Soviets were convinced, as Maisky said, "that any German aggression can only be prevented with strong opposition and not by agreeing to the offers made by the Reich." The French government, however, did not appear to want the pact it had just ratified to come into play.

The Paris *Bourse* was back up on Tuesday, March 10. In Berlin, following two nervous days, "an almost unfettered optimism prevails."[106]

The negotiations that were to take place beginning March 12, while France was in the thick of its election campaign, are well known. Anthony Eden probably provides the best account on the subject.[107] French documents confirm that Eden clearly understood several points: first, "neither before nor during the dispute were the French ministers firmly agreed upon a settled course of action. Theirs was the agony of an essentially pacific, democratic country believing that, in this instance, pacifism was not enough and searching for stronger action that might be carried through with the support of their own people but without the risk of war."[108] The main negotiator Flandin, on the other hand, was deeply troubled. In private conversations with British negotiators he generally approved their realistic approach. However, during the conferences he backed much more demanding positions that were impossible to sustain and could only be implemented through the use of force.[109] In a speech at the House of Commons on March 9, Eden had clearly explained Britain's hesitation at getting into a policy of retaliation.

The first phase lasted from March 10 to 19. It included a series of meetings of the countries that had signed Locarno, except Germany (and Italy being represented only by its ambassador) then by the Council of the League of Nations. The meetings took place on March 10 in Paris and later in London. On March 11 Flandin left for the British capital feeling confident.[110] He thought he could "take guarantees" without "too much trouble." He asked the Navy—which was flabbergasted—for a blockade plan. Alexis Léger told Admiral Durand-Veil that "we can seriously…reduce, even by an honorable compromise, Germany's strength and prestige."[111]

Let us digress to examine the inclinations for "taking guarantees" that the military leaders discussed for a few days. The Navy felt that the operations Flandin was suggesting to occupy Heligoland, blockade Bremen or Hamburg, and seize German ships in the high seas were, despite the fact that it was clearly superior to the German navy, "as adventurous as they were unproductive."[112] Security measures would first be necessary. In any case British cooperation was necessary—its fleet was concentrated in the Eastern Mediterranean since September 1935 —as well as Italy's, which was totally absorbed by the war in Ethiopia.

Air Force Chief of Staff General Pujo, whose authority was too weak compared to the army's, did not want to undertake bombing raids without the full mobilization of his units, including those of *Défense aérienne du territoire*, because Paris was vulnerable to an attack. The French air force was still relatively stronger than Germany's.[113]

Then there was the army. In October 1932, when Germany only had about 100,000 soldiers, plan D called for the complete occupation of the Saar. The plan included 3 infantry divisions, 1 cavalry division and a Senegalese brigade. Plan D *bis* of April 1935 included "taking guarantees in the Saar" without listing the units. In his book *Servir*,[114] Gamelin states that he gave an order in February 1936 to prepare for a possible operation limited to the left bank of the Saar. According to le Goyet, who conducted a thorough investigation, there is no trace of any such order in army archives.[115] Only on March 11 did the Superior War Council propose—within the framework of the League of Nations—either the occupation of the left bank of the Saar or the occupation of Luxembourg.[116] But this required going to the "reinforced security" stage of 1,200,000 men. There was very little enthusiasm to go around. The operation would take eight days to get going. We would quickly be up against the bulk of the German army, and all this would cost at least 20 million francs a day. For the left bank of the Saar alone, 10 infantry divisions, 1 cavalry and five army corps organic units or three times more troops than were planned for the entire Saar in 1932.[117]

With these ambitious drafts and a memo from Massigli to remind him correctly that "the question at hand is to find out whether Europe was to become German or not,"[118] Flandin presented the French position: to agree with the Locarno powers to ask the Council of the League of Nations for economic and later military sanctions and to refuse negotiations with Hitler based upon his March 7 proposals.

He immediately encountered the polite but firm opposition of Anthony Eden. Sanctions against Germany? That was out of the question. France had rejected oil sanctions against Italy. British public opinion did not feel concerned by the reoccupation of what was, after all, German territory. The French alliances in Central Europe were of no interest; the British did not want any military sanctions and were strongly opposed to economic ones. The French were mistaken in any case if they thought they would get a general consensus among other members of the League of Nations for sanctions. Neither the Scandinavians nor the Latin Americans would accept them. Eden did agree that one of Hitler's proposals— for a demilitarized zone straddling both borders of France and Belgium— was absurd because it would include the length of the Maginot Line. On the other hand, it was necessary to consider his non-aggression pact offers and, since he brought up the issue, to encourage him to rejoin the League of Nations.[119] Flandin, in conversation with a few British leaders, became indignant and threatened to leave the League of Nations. Massigli didn't hide his thinking from Harold Nicolson: "He's very bitter and feels that we're traitors."[120]

Flandin then fell back on a new position: he would only negotiate with the Germans if they evacuated the demilitarized zone or at least if they sent no further troops into the Rhineland area and pledged not to build any fortifications![121] Eden then invited Germany to send an observer to the meeting of the Council of the League of Nations. Hitler picked the Nazi Joachim von Ribbentrop (he was to be appointed ambassador to England on August 11). For now "confused discussions were taking place."[122]

March 19 turned out to be a key date. First, Ribbentrop was allowed into the Council—and he naturally rejected all the French proposals. Other offers were made: keep a 20-kilometer demilitarized area under the control of international troops, and bring the problem of the zone to the court of The Hague. On March 24 Hitler vigorously rejected those "dishonorable" proposals. In other words, the forcible takeover had been accepted by attrition and the British views of an actual negotiation with Hitler. He had therefore won.[123]

France, however, was not losing everything. England obviously had a major stake in preventing a German invasion of Belgium or France. Locarno, with its system of guarantees, fulfilled that task. Whatever was left of Locarno had to be preserved. On that same March 19, 1936, England extended its guarantee to France and Belgium in the event of a German invasion. In his memoirs Flandin brags about it as a great personal achievement and refers to it as "the Franco-British alliance."[124] This was written with the benefit of hindsight. More accurately, this agreement should be called the natural extension of British policy. The main guarantee of Locarno was upheld without Germany, which had unilaterally breached the treaty. The stipulations regarding the demilitarized zone, which the British never thought much of, and which no longer actually existed, were cut. The only new point was to start military talks among the British, French, and Belgians. Eden was able to gain acceptance for these points in the House of Commons. Ambassador Corbin, who wasn't completely reassured by the speech, felt there was good reason "to declare oneself satisfied" with the agreement of March 19.[125]

The negotiations then bogged down amid widespread indifference on the part of the French, by now totally focused on the elections. In a speech on April 1, Hitler offered a new plan[126] that included twenty-five-year non-aggression pacts and Germany's possible return to the League of Nations, with many new stipulations for humanizing warfare. This proposal was obviously aimed at British public opinion.[127] On April 3, Sarraut, Flandin and Paul-Boncour took stock of the situation with Ambassadors François-Poncet, Corbin, de Chambrun, and Laroche, as well as Alexis Léger and Charles Rochat, Flandin's cabinet director. François-Poncet gave a long presentation on the events that took place, suggesting a discussion of the new German plan. "Through discussions, we can pressure Mr. Hitler into being more precise about his aims and block his traps with some counter-traps." Corbin pointed out "the willful illusions and optimism" of British public opinion and the absence of "definite ideas" in the government in London. The decision was reached to answer Germany but remain vigilant. François-Poncet concluded: "We must make some concessions to the public's naïveté but we must also be armed."

The French counterproposals were rejected by Germany and the negotiations ended there.[128]

Regarding military discussions—which Italy refused to attend—these turned out to be completely useless.[129] General Schweisguth Deputy Chief of Staff of the Army, was representing France. Gamelin had told him, "We need no help to defend the Franco-German border," and General Maurin said, "To make them understand that we can hold out alone if need be." However, British soldiers would be necessary to help the Belgians. They settled on a plan to ferry over two British divisions. The British refused to provide any kind of details regarding their deployment. They were "kept closely in check by the Foreign Office…"

As for the Belgians, they played "a rather secondary role." The outcome of these discussions, said Schweisguth, allowed for the creation of "cordial and very pleasant personal contacts." But as to the heart of the matter "the results appeared to be quite meager."[130]

France just lost more than a buffer zone and the opportunity to defend its allies in the East. Its prestige had plummeted. Scores of cables and dispatches from French representatives all over the world attested to this drastic drop. The government in Vienna was the most affected of all: Who would now prevent the Anschluss?[131] The Czechoslovaks were frightened at the thought of becoming a German satellite. Beneš was "discouraged."[132] The same was true for Yugoslavia[133] and Romania.[134] In Poland Colonel Beck felt strengthened in his bid for rapprochement with Germany. As early as May, Italy began to drift away from France and look to Hitler with greater interest. François-Poncet concluded that the incredibly passive German masses "allowed themselves to be molded like soft putty."[135] "Their criteria is based on success. Hitler is a great man because he's bold and events prove that he is right."[136]

We shall end the account of this awful event with three quotations from the period. It is too easy today to reconstruct history and hand out a series of bad marks to the protagonists, as Charles Serre did in the report he culled from the Parliamentary Commission of Inquiry.[137] We have shown that the French people wanted no part whatsoever of any brutal action, and was therefore the main culprit. This cannot be held against it since it is very hard for a democracy, which had been bled dry on top of it, to consider a preventive war even though it may be justified.

Those countries that were friendly toward France, as Greek Minister Politis said, were "worried about a type of thinking that appears to be pervasive in France itself. Their representatives in France, in contact with different segments of the population in the various regions were struck by the kind of *pacifist depression*[138] surfacing in many circles. They appear to want to keep the peace at any cost, barricaded behind what was called "the Maginot wall," letting events on the outside unfold as they may, without seeing that a people engaged in such policy…could no longer lay claim to being called a great power."[139]

To this farsighted opinion we may add that of the Minister of Marine, François Piétri. At a meeting of the military ministers and the chiefs of staff on April 4, 1936, Prime Minister Sarraut pompously opened the discussion: "France cannot accept that Germany build fortifications in the former demilitarized zone. We would be prevented from providing useful assistance to our Eastern allies." This was correct and accurately described the worst consequence of Hitler's brutal move. But what could be done? Two and a half hours of debate on the absence of an attack unit, about the theories of Major de Gaulle—that Gamelin rejected—on the naval blockade, came to no conclusion. Upon returning to the Ministry of Marine with Admiral Abrial, François Piétri made the following comment, which we find essential to underscore: *"Some people persist in refusing to accept the fact that in facing a strong country the only type of coercion is war."*[140]

Finally, Pope Pius XI provides us with the third quote. On March 16 he received French Ambassador Charles-Roux and told him straight away, "Had you ordered the immediate advance of 200,000 men into the zone the Germans had reoccupied you would have done everyone a very great favor."[141]

Chapter VI

THE ATMOSPHERE

The preceding exposition is part of a larger picture. We shall call "atmosphere" the components that make up the psychological environment. Without extensive definitive works[1] we can examine only a number of key problems. We will not focus on the changing moods of public opinion, which we have observed and shall keep on monitoring at significant moments, but will rather examine the deeper trends.

1.

THE STATUS OF FRENCH PATRIOTISM

Rather than being triumphant and victorious, France in the 1930s was a nation wounded in its flesh, its land and its spirit. The wound ran deep enough to require more than one generation to heal. France was the country of Europe that had lost the greatest number of human lives with respect to its population, the death of young people that destabilized the nation and deprived it forever of material and creative forces. The biggest battles in the war took place on the French front. It was there that the people's works, the fruits of their labor, their houses, factories, culti-vated land, roads, bridges, canals, and mines had been ravaged by shelling or systematic destruction by the enemy. All human works are destined to ruin; war, however, caused that ruin to take place several decades, if not several centuries, before its time.

Following the great consensus of the *Union sacrée* and the wave of enthusiasm of November 11, France came out of the war more lacerated than ever before. The working class wanted its reward for the sacrifices it made. If that reward was delayed too long, the proletariat would become more than ever an "alien body" within the nation. National values, praised by some people, were fading among large groups of the population and replaced by other values such as pacifism, internationalism or, more of-ten, by a selfish demand for immediate enjoyment at any cost. The "good bourgeoisie" that had been savaged in its flesh was now facing a new and transient world of "war profiteers" and "nouveaux riches."

France was also more isolated in the world than many people real-ized. It was fashionable to admire the victors of the Marne and Verdun, to invite French military missions and successful cultural missions that were temporarily able to mask the inexorable progress of English as the universal language. But jealousy, hatred or even loathing towards a France that "had died in the field of honor" were dominant. The Germans hated the French, whom they felt were behind the harshness of the Treaty. The British, as Lloyd George was said to have told Clemenceau, now consid-ered the strongest military power on the continent to be an enemy. The Laborites condemned its militarism; the Conservatives, in the wake of the *Times* (owned by Lord and Lady Astor and edited by Geoffrey Dawson), remembered the colonial rivalries more vividly than the Entente Cordiale. The Italians complained that their war effort was not appreciated and their colonial demands had been forgotten. For the Soviets, France was the champion of the interventionists, bent upon destroying the young proletarian state. The Americans, whose only contact in France had been with merchants and fast women, returned home disappointed and spread-ing the legend that the French in their harshness had "rented the trenches" to the Sammies* who had come like brothers to the rescue.

France appeared, sadly, as a country in ruins, ravaged by hatred and social unrest, a tired and suffering nation. The survivors were shouldering the heavy burden of the First World War. All the men born before 1900,

---

* French word for "doughboys."

Edouard Herriot, a key political figure of France's
Third Republic.

General Maurice Gamelin, commander in chief of the French army during the 1930s.

left
General Maxime Weygand.

below
Admiral Jean-François Darlan.

above
Colonel Charles De Gaulle.

below
Alexis Léger, secretary general of the Quai d'Orsay.

André François-Poncet, French ambassador to Berlin (1931–1938) and Rome (1938–1940).

left
Robert Coulondre, ambassador to Moscow
(1936–1938) and to Berlin (1938–1939).

below
René Massigli, a key director at the Quai d'Orsay
and ambassador to Turkey.

The Disarmament Conference in Geneva, with Joseph Paul-Boncour presiding at the head of the table *(far end)*.

Hitler and Franz von Papen as deputy chancellor at the formal opening of the
Reichstag at Potsdam's Garnisonkirche in 1933.

above
Herriot signs the Franco-Soviet Pact on
November 29, 1932.

right
Joseph Paul-Boncour returns from Geneva
with his daughter.

Students in Paris demonstrate against payments of war debts to the United States in 1932.

left
(Left to right) Louis Barthou, Edvard
Beneš and Ambassador Léon Noël.

below
The signing of the Four Power Pact
in July 1933 in Rome. (*Left to right*)
von Hassel, the German ambassador;
Mussolini; Sir John Simon, the British
ambassador; and de Jouvenel, the
French ambassador.

The murder of King Alexander I of Yugoslavia in Marseille also took the life of Louis Barthou, French foreign minister, on October 9, 1934.

Pierre Laval *(center)* and German ambassador Köster sign an agreement on the Saar in December 1934.

The Franco-Italian Pact was signed in Rome on January 7, 1935: Mussolini *(seated)* with French ambassador de Chambrun behind him, and Pierre Laval in conversation with Baron Pompeo Aloisi.

The French delegation arriving at Stresa: Pierre-Etienne Flandin and Pierre Laval.

above
The Stresa Conference of April 11 and 14,
1935: *(Left to right)* Pierre Laval, Mussolini,
Ramsay Macdonald (British prime minister),
and Pierre-Etienne Flandin.

right
Léon Blum leaves the Elysée Palace followed
by Pierre Cot *(left)* and Vincent Auriol on
August 13, 1936.

with the exception of those deferred, the ones needed for special tasks and the draft dodgers, took part in the war. Young boys played games consisting of digging trenches and gloriously attacking those of the enemy. Nobody wanted to play the part of the "Boche," an easy one because fathers and uncles brought back the hated pointed helmets as trophies. The smaller kids were often forced to wear them, knowing the part they were expected to play by howling and playing dead under the blows of the invincible ones. At the end of the school day they would play with rusty old cannon that almost every little town displayed. There were monuments to the war dead, commemorative ceremonies and parades of war veterans almost everywhere. Adult women remembered their anxieties and sorrows. Women outnumbered men in France. Since the 1920s young women and some war widows were competing for the men who had survived.[2] Other widows, dressed in black, were to remain faithful to their memories. According to their disposition the heroes either talked about their experiences or remained stubbornly silent. Some who had become pacifists wouldn't allow their children to play those horrible games.

Reactions differed, however, starting with the statement "Better Hitler than war!" all the way to the enthusiasm of a new graduate of Saint-Cyr Military Academy or, in a totally different environment, the resolve of the convinced anti-fascist. Everyone sensed that new alignments were taking place. Before 1914 patriotism had its symbols: the flag, the *Marseillaise*, military parades with marching bands, the draped statue of Strasbourg. It all still existed but the statue of Strasbourg was no longer draped; France was "satisfied" and even, to use Bismarck's words, "saturated." Patriotism had become defensive and was consequently less exciting. The importance of the old symbols declined without them disappearing.

In the mid-1930s the tricolor banner had a strange fate: on the one hand, it was held up in opposition to the red flag. In the early summer of 1936, in those neighborhoods that voted for moderate candidates, its presence at the windows was a sign of opposition to the Popular Front. Young men were "brawling" a lot (it was the expression used at the time.) Some wore a tricolor on their lapels, others a red ribbon or a flower. That was the way the two "sides" singled themselves out.

At the same time, the left, including the communists, engaged in a sweeping effort to demonstrate that patriotism was not a right-wing monopoly expressed, for example, in the famous statement read on July 14, 1935, by Jean Perrin at the Buffalo cyclodrome in Montrouge:

> "They robbed you of Joan of Arc, a daughter of the people whom the king had abandoned when the popular sweep gave him victory…They tried to grab the flag of 89, that noble tricolor flag of republican victories… They also attempted to take the heroic *Marseillaise* away from us, that fierce revolutionary song that forced every throne in Europe to tremble."[3]

In her excellent study of the July 14 holidays,[4] Miss Rosamonde Sanson described the reverse movements coming together at the same time: on the one hand, a "fading away" following the triumphant July 14, 1919; on the other, a "recuperation" by an originally hostile left that first showed indifference and then approval of the "resurrection of the myth." July 14 once again became a "people's holiday."

The left that had invented the May 1st holiday now also adopted the anniversary of the storming of the Bastille. It added the red flag to the tricolor and the *Marseillaise* to the *Internationale*. All this was enough to frighten many moderates but also the pacifist left that now felt nostalgic for the good old days. This can best explain the fading of the old symbols rather than a real decline in nationalism, even though the latter changed its myths, shedding the chauvinist and bellicose attitude, increasingly drawn towards those great assemblies of people such as international sports events. We shall discuss the Olympic games of August 1936 in Chapter X. The too few historical studies of the Tour de France[5] and the World Soccer Cup indicate a giant wave of passion that cannot be understood without referring to the strong vibrant presence of national feeling. Perhaps there was somewhat less cheering when the troops were on parade but the Tour de France drew the most burning passions. The racers were grouped in national teams. Between 1930 and 1939 the Tour ended in victory six times for the French (André Leducq in 1930 and 1932, Antonin Magne in 1931 and 1934, Georges Speicher in 1933, Roger Lapébie in 1937), three times for the Belgians (1935, 1936, and 1939), and once by the Italian Gino Bartali in 1938. The French victory in 1937 almost created a diplomatic incident. Lapébie, who was from Bordeaux, was second in the general classification, and some of his supporters threw rocks at the Belgian Sylvère Maés, who was leading. The entire Belgian team left the Tour in protest. Needless to say, André Leducq or Antonin Magne were much better known and more "popular" than any ambassador, general or most cabinet ministers.

In any event, national solidarity is opposed to class solidarity. Once the left co-opted the feelings and symbols of the homeland as its own, it had to accept a new kind of cohesion. The "Union Sacrée" formula did not sit well with the left because it was considered a scam—this did not prevent, on a few short-lived occasions, a wave of unity from sweeping the country, for example on September 2, 1939, in a different form than that of 1914 before the slaughter.

2.

THE FRENCH
TRAVELED VERY LITTLE OVERSEAS

There is a startling contrast between the French people in 1936 and those today. While they share very little interest in permanent emigration, travel abroad, which is so common today, was practically unknown. Everything conspired to give the Frenchman of 1936 the reputation of being a "homebody." The average income level, which was much lower than today, made such expenses impossible. The tradition of being rooted to the land was very strong. But the peasants never took vacations; workers and employees had no paid vacations prior to 1936, except for a handful of pioneering businesses. Only the bourgeois, professionals, professors, school teachers and government employees went on vacation. Without going into too much detail, we estimate that over 80 percent of the French people had no opportunity for leisure travel. As for the bourgeois, many owned a castle, a country house or a family home often located close to the city where they lived and where they generally would spend the summer. If ordinary people were able to cross the borders, it was because of exceptional circumstances or a specific professional need.

Specific needs? War. The soldiers of the Army of the Orient, those sent to Italy as reinforcements, the prisoners in Germany, those who were part of the occupying armies, the sailors sent to the Russian ports of the Black Sea—all of them experienced the great change of scenery. In some rare cases military service could take place in "mobile forces" (70,000 in July 1932 out of a total 358,000 in metropolitan France). These "mobile forces" may occasionally be deployed in "colonial" operations such as Syria and Morocco in 1926–1927. The army in North Africa and the colonial troops themselves included, besides career officers and non-commissioned officers,[6] small numbers of volunteers from France but no draftees.

Exceptional professions? Of course, a few tens of thousands of sailors engaged in long distance fishing, commerce or the navy travel to foreign lands, stopping at a few rare ports of call. There were also a few thousand civil servants or agents of the various colonies or protectorates. There was a larger group of officers and non-commissioned officers of the colonial and North African troops. The career of an officer serving outside France meant being stationed during two- and three-year assignments to AOF, AEF, Madagascar, and Indochina. These colonial postings were also interspersed with trips back to France.

The missionaries made up another more stable category. At the beginning of the twentieth century, half the Catholic missionaries in the world were French. In 1930, out of 8,993 missionary priests, there were 3,000 French nationals, or 33 percent. If the same proportion is applied to the nuns and friars, there were some 1,000 friars out of 2,886 and 9,500 French nuns out of a total of 28,099,[7] or some 14,500 French nationals scattered around the world but mostly within the Empire.

France, on the other hand, was at the time a country little versed in export activity, with only a very small number of commercial agents abroad. Few French engineers were ready to leave for extended periods even though they could be found in those countries with large French investments: Poland, Czechoslovakia, Romania, Spain. However, when the USSR was recruiting foreign specialists for its capital projects, it turned mostly to Americans and Germans. According to the chemist Jules Cotte, who spent part of his life in the USSR, out of some 10,000 foreign technicians and engineers working there during the mid-1930s, there were only about 50 French nationals, a tiny number compared to the pre-war period.[8] As Cotte wrote in 1938, "only close technical collaboration can make the Franco-Soviet Pact fully effective."[9] He concludes, "Alas in the USSR we were represented by our past glories"; since 1917 some 3000 French titles had been translated into Russian representing 50 million copies.[10]

Among French citizens working overseas there were the professors and schoolteachers at the high schools or schools managed by the *Service des Œuvres* of the Quai d'Orsay or the French Lay Mission. There were several hundred *Alliance Française* in the world, especially in Central Europe and South America. But contrary to the vast numbers of "cooperation" teachers today, there were few persons apart from members of religious congregations involved in a career outside France.

Today's "exchanges" of professors and students were practically nonexistent. It was by chance that high-level French intellectuals were called to teach at American universities, for example. People such as historian Gilbert Chinard at Johns Hopkins and literary historian Henri Peyre at Yale were to have an enormous influence but their numbers were very small. An example from the official records: in 1932–1933 only four professors, most of them in literature, were officially invited for short periods by American universities. In 1928 there were 117 French students in the United States (out of a total 8,932 foreigners) and 528 Americans in France (out of 14,368 foreigners.)[11] A few very high level students were admitted at the French school in Athens, in Rome, at the Casa Velasquez in Madrid,[12] or for artists to the Villa Medici in Rome. These were for the most part archeologists and medievalists and their exposure to contemporary situations remained superficial.

The Havas agency and a few rare newspapers had foreign correspondents. Marcel Dunan for *Le Temps* in Vienna and Camille Lemercier in Berlin were highly knowledgeable of the local scene. There was only one correspondent, Fransalès, from *Paris-Midi* in New York in 1938.

Beyond these few strokes there was occasional tourism that was, as we indicated, the exclusive domain of the bourgeoisie. It could start with the stay of the future high school graduate in an English family, very rarely in Germany or Austria, sometimes in Italy or Spain. The economic crisis, the inhospitable nature of the fascist regime, the mounting unrest in Spain after 1931 and the coming to power of National Socialism did not encourage tourism either by students or adults.[13] The tradition of the honeymoon at the great Italian lakes faded with the decline of the bourgeoisie. The "nouveaux riches" did not share those genteel ways. There were associations of university professors, such as the Guillaume-Budé association, that organized low-cost travel to Greece or Italy. There no longer were any "massive" pilgrimages to Rome and those to the Holy Land stopped in 1936 with the civil war in Palestine.

We therefore find that: 1) The number of French citizens traveling outside France was significantly less than today and even more so for French women. Except for North Africa, permanent emigration was minimal; 2) Deep knowledge of foreign countries was limited only to a tiny elite of diplomats, officers, government officials, intellectuals and missionaries, which was totally inadequate to have any broad influence in those societies; 3) Most people leaving France did not go to foreign countries but to visit the Empire that could satisfy those in search of the exotic; 4) Therefore, there was very little knowledge of other countries, allowing for slogans and stereotypes to be readily accepted; 5) But the worst part was the "lack of curiosity" about foreign countries, "a kind of withdrawal unto ourselves and our past."[14]

3.

FOREIGN TOURISTS IN FRANCE

Apart from a small number of very specialized professionals during the 1930s, the French people were, for the most part, entrenched homebodies. They knew close to nothing about foreign countries and how those countries viewed the French.

Foreign tourists didn't provide much information. Besides the language barrier, contacts were rare except with hotel professionals. The French didn't have a reputation for being particularly welcoming in their homes. In 1929 France was the first country for foreign tourists in the world with two million visitors. The economic crisis had a large impact, especially on French prices, which remained very high until 1935 because of the "gold-block." By 1938 France had only one million visitors and was in fifth place behind Italy, Germany, Switzerland, and Austria.[15]

Among the motivations of foreign tourists during the 1930s we can point to the tours by veterans visiting the battlefields and visits to spas[16] — citizens from fifty countries visited Vichy in 1938. Conventions were very often held in France, as well as a few exceptional events such as the *Exposition Coloniale* of 1931 and the *Exposition Universelle* of 1937. Pilgrimages, to Lourdes in particular, also played an important part. But one must not forget the existence of the *old tourism* of the great hotels developed by the Swiss César Ritz, to whom André Siegfried dedicated one of his most brilliant essays.[17] A great number of the British aristocracy, which provided the leadership of the Conservative Party and governed England from 1931 to 1940, preferred to vacation in France at Deauville, La Baule and the Riviera. But this did not mean that those men—which included Churchill, Halifax, Eden, Duff Cooper, Spears, Nicolson, and hundreds of others—met with the "locals." They often kept to themselves or visited other English speakers, such as Somerset Maugham.

4.

IMMIGRATION:

A DILUTED FORM OF FOREIGN INFLUENCE

Did immigration play a significant part as a factor in French foreign policy? Immigration appears to be a spontaneous phenomenon, or, less frequently, a kind of slow organized movement that may at some point tragically change public attitudes. Immigration is inevitable in an under-populated country (but what does "underpopulated" mean?) and has not been studied from the point of view of international relations. We shall limit ourselves to a temporary set of conclusions based on the figures provided by the works of Jean-Charles Bonnet and Ralph Schor.[18]

The number of foreigners recorded in France during the 1911 census was 1,150,000. In 1921 it was 1,631,000 and in 1932, 2,890,000, a figure that clearly did not reflect the true situation due to the high number of illegal persons present. In other words, 7 percent of the population in France included foreigners versus 2.8 percent in 1911.[19] The increase was constant and rapid up until 1931. The demographic needs of France, which had been bled dry, the manpower requirements for reconstruction and increasingly for the hard labor the French no longer wished to perform, encouraged the government and most of all private companies to hire foreign workers. These were 1.6 million in 1931 out of a total of 3 million in the active population.[20] The economic crisis brought higher unemployment (and encouraged many to leave voluntarily), fewer arrivals and, at least up to 1936, tighter controls, denials of entry and expulsions. At that time the type of immigration changed: the mainly "economic" type was replaced, in part at least, by "political" immigrants in the form of often massive arrivals of refugees.

Between 1921 and 1939 about 1 million foreigners were naturalized.[21]

At its highest point the breakdown by nationality was as follows: 800,000 Italians, 508,000 Poles, 352,000 Spaniards, 254,000 Belgians, 98,000 Swiss; Russians, Germans and Africans were slightly below

100,000. Even though there were fewer women than men (except for the Germans), they came in large numbers. Only the African workers were almost exclusively male.

About half of the immigrant workers are employed in the processing industries. Many Poles were working in the mining industry—these were half of all the miners in France—and in agriculture, the Italians in agriculture and trade, the Spaniards in agriculture, etc.[22]

Immigrants caused many problems for the social and internal policies of the country, which worried the ministers of the Interior and Labor—from January to March 1938 the Chautemps cabinet even created an undersecretary for immigration under a young Catholic attorney, Philippe Serre, who was part of the *Jeune République* movement. Serre was elected to Parliament as a deputy from Briey in 1933 in the department of Meurthe-et-Moselle, following in the footsteps of the great ironworks industrialist François de Wendel whom he failed to defeat in 1932 and became a senator.[23] As head of his cabinet, Serre had appointed one of his friends, Professor Edouard Dolléans, who specialized in social issues.

These internal issues go beyond our subject but we must attempt to gauge the "weight" of immigration in its entirety and according to the nationalities concerned.

A rejectionist movement, similar to "nativism" in the United States in the 1920s, developed in France during the 1930s in the wake of the economic crisis and unemployment. "Undesirable competitors," "bothersome guests," wrote Jean-Charles Bonnet in describing these reactions. Leading a movement with some clearly racist attitudes, we find the right-wing nationalists who had always been anti-Semitic. Few were the days when the "foreigners" and the "odd balls" were not being insulted by *L'Action Française* or *L'Ami du Peuple*. Every political party, with many noticeable differences in approach, was concerned with the issue (79 members of Parliament out of 610 mentioned the issue in their electoral programs of 1932). Only the PCF took a stand as "the party of immigrant and colonial workers."[24] The issue of "national work" had always been popular because it completely omitted the fact that French excluded themselves from certain kinds of jobs. On the other hand, the presence of foreigners within the professions (doctors) or in business caused some very loud protest. However, the communists were not alone in refusing arbitrary limitations. Oddly, they found themselves, and for completely different reasons, within the same "internationalist" camp as top management circles: chambers of commerce, committee for coal mines, committee for ironworks and its newspaper, *Le Temps*, were opposed to "filtering" or to "sending back."[25] This was also the case of Paul Reynaud, proving his very broad outlook.

Xenophobia coincides with the "defense of national work." We shall quote, along with J.C. Bonnet,[26] a few noteworthy statements: "a swarming mob of outlaws" (Colonel de la Rocque); "France to the Frenchmen" (rallying cry of February 6, 1934); "First we must clean the home front" (Pierre Gaxotte); "useless mouths," "parasites," "vermin" (*Le Jour, Le Matin, Gringoire*).

The murder of the president of the Republic, Paul Doumer by the Russian Gorguloff (May 6, 1932) and that of Louis Barthou by the Croatian Ustashi under Mussolini's protection (October 9, 1934) only helped sharpen that tendency. A statement by Joseph Denais, a moderate right-wing member of Parliament, sums it up: "France can well ensure the well-being of all its sons only if it isn't forced to be the world's innkeeper where the undesirables from the entire world seek refuge."[27]

Only a few more generous minorities, aware of the overwhelming human tragedy implied by any kind of immigration, clearly opted for a welcoming attitude. The *Ligue des droits de l'homme* [League for Human Rights], some Catholic circles (Monsignor Chaptal, the deputy Bishop of Paris) the *Ligue internationale contre l'antisémitisme* [International League Against Anti-Semitism] the *Secours rouge international* [Red Aid, a communist organization], the reunited CGT and many committees strenuously came to the defense of the dignity and status of foreigners. That was also the role played only too briefly by Undersecretary of State Philippe Serre, a precursor of the Christian Democrats.

In examining the groups of foreigners one after the other some specific issues emerge.

The political refugees of the First World War did not cause major problems. The 67,000 White Russians included in the 1926 census certainly did not cause any pro-Soviet feelings. The policy of suspicion toward the USSR could be explained by other, more important, reasons. The 26,000 Armenians in France, according to the count, did not stop France from seeking the friendship and later, after 1936, an alliance with Turkey, their mortal enemy. The same was true for the Hungarians who had fled the Horthy regime and the first Italian anti-fascists.[28]

Among the larger groups the Belgians and the Poles were the ones causing the least problems. The Polish government, however, was not in favor of emigration. It made an effort to preserve the nationality of its citizens by creating schools, newspapers and sending priests. Perhaps this issue prompted Colonel Beck's demand for colonies for Poland, especially after 1936. In any case no significant diplomatic incidents can be seen.

The huge Italian contingent was the oldest and that become more easily assimilated, blending slowly into the French population, especially when it purchased abandoned farms in southwestern France and went into farming. It nevertheless played a particular role because of fascist activity. Mussolini hated emigration, which he considered a loss of Italian life forces. He therefore tried to maintain among Italians overseas the nationalist faith and the fascist spirit when possible. He pulled out all the stops through schools, action by the consuls, the organization of children's vacation camps in Italy, and conscription for military service. It is worth mentioning that "very often the sons of foreigners born in France refused to be naturalized to avoid being subjected to the same military obligations as the French."[29]

Did the Duce succeed in his efforts? Everything indicates on the contrary that the bulk of Italian workers backed anti-fascism. Some of them joined the International Brigades during the Spanish Civil War and the dialog on the front at Guadalajara from one line to the other is well known: "Noi siamo Italiani" (We are Italians), cried out Mussolini's "volunteers." "E noi siamo gli Italiani di Garibaldi" (And we are Garibald's Italians), was the Republican answer.

Most of the time, contrary to what took place at the end of the nineteenth century, relations between French and foreign workers were generally good. The labor unions were making sure this was the case, even though they noticed the way immigrant workers were "under-unionized."

For the Spaniards the issue was mostly a passive one. With the fall of Barcelona (January 26, 1939), huge columns of refugees—over 400,000—marched north toward France through the hills and the mountains, egged on by misery and fear.[30] A negotiation took place in January 1939 between the Spanish Republican government and France that we shall examine further ahead.

Events, however, moved faster than the talks. There was a debate in the Chamber of Deputies on March 10, 14, and 16, 1939, regarding the welcome that couldn't be denied to these poor people. The deputy from the Basses-Pyrénées, Ybarnegaray, and right-hand man to Colonel de

La Rocque, refused that "crushing burden." The minister of the interior, Albert Sarraut, defended his improvised welcome of the refugees. An organization was created and camps were set up with 170,000 refugees divided into 77 departments. A few very large camps held loyalist soldiers and militiamen. This tidal wave amounted to an estimated total of 450,000 people. The French government in agreement with the Franco government, only wished to keep those who were compromised; only 200,000 agreed to return to Spain. Mexico and some Latin American countries welcomed a few tens of thousands.[31]

German refugees were far fewer than the Spaniards and entered France gradually. There were communists, socialists, Catholics, and, most of all, Jews—all of whom were completely destitute. Following the Anschluss on March 28, 1938, President Roosevelt tried to organize a "non-political" system to rescue these unfortunate people. France agreed for a committee to meet at Evian, assembling thirty-two countries that began its work on July 6 under the honorary chairmanship of Henry Bérenger, president of the Foreign Affairs Commission of the Senate. Germany and the USSR had not been invited nor had Poland, a country of emigration. By that time 150,000 out of 600,000 German Jews had emigrated, and France had welcomed 10,000. Except for the Dominican Republic, every country found excuses to avoid making any promises in providing shelter. On October 4, after Munich, the French, American and British ambassadors took an initiative towards Ribbentrop for the Jews to be allowed to take their possessions with them. He simply replied that Germany's goal was to be rid of the Jews.[32]

American Undersecretary of State Sumner Welles discussed the issue with Bonnet and Daladier, as well as the possibility of sending some Jews to selected French colonies.[33] At a meeting between Chamberlain, Halifax, Daladier, and Bonnet in Paris on November 24, French and British colonies were discussed once again.[34] Bonnet said there were 40,000 German Jews in France and that "our country is saturated with foreigners." In the end, only short-term solutions were considered. Many of these unfortunate people were to become victims of one of the worst clauses in the June 1940 armistice, which allowed them to be handed over to Nazi Germany.

5

FOREIGN COUNTRIES AS SEEN IN LITERATURE

For most Frenchmen the outside world appeared only through movies and books. Films certainly had a considerable impact but they magnified only existing stereotypes. The supremacy of American films showed the French an artificial society created by Hollywood or the monotony of the "westerns." What can one say about Flanders as they appear in *La Kermesse Héroïque*? Articles and books had some influence on very different levels.

The French have a strong tradition of long distance exploration and reading travel stories is something they enjoy. Since "unexplored lands" were dwindling, the adventurer's travels replaced exploration (Henri de Monfried in the Red Sea) or the sportsman (Alain Gerbault in his solo crossing of the Atlantic) or those of anthropologists, geologists or geographers. In the 1930s, a large series in twenty volumes called *La géographie universelle*, edited by Paul Vidal de La Blache and Lucien Gallois, and later by Emmanuel de Martonne and Albert Demangeon, was published. The prestigious geographers who were Vidal de La Blache's disciples (de Martonne was his son-in-law), such as Henri Baulig, Jules Sion, Max Sorre, Augustin Bernard, and other eminent specialists, worked on this giant undertaking. The French school of geography was at its best sending young researchers to Japan (Francis Ruellan), Brazil (Pierre Monbeig), Southeast Asia (Pierre Gourou), North Africa (Jean Dresh), and many other locations. André Siegfried, who was more of a "sociologist" and a "humanist," published books about the United States and Canada with a wide readership like those by Demangeon on the British Empire. The young ethnologist Jacques Soustelle was among the pioneers of pre-Colombian studies in Mexico. Raoul Blanchard for the Alpine areas and Daniel Faucher for the Mediterranean regions and the Pyrenees were also part of this prestigious group.

These were scientific works aimed at a small elite. The audience for travel stories by great journalists and writers was much wider. As Albert Thibaudet wrote, "From the war to the economic crisis, if a writer didn't spend part of the year traveling the world on a mission, giving lectures or being a reporter, he would stand out."[35] There were many books about the French Empire,[36] the United States (Georges Duhamel, Jules Romains), the USSR (André Gide, Edouard Herriot); India and Ceylon (André

Chevrillon, Francis de Goisset), China and Tibet (the "Croisière Jaune" sponsored by Citroën, André Malraux), England (Paul Morand) and books resulting from long reporting pieces by Albert Londres, Henri Béraud, etc.

Fiction, even more than travel literature, indulged in the exotic. Thibaudet finds "the adventure novels" by Pierre MacOrlan and Pierre Benoit different from the "planetary novel," that is, more literary. There were even "Quai d'Orsay" writers encouraged by the mandarin Philippe Berthelot,[37] Paul Claudel,[38] Paul Morand, and Jean Giraudoux.[39]

Translations of works of fiction were once more on the increase. The "Feux Croisés" series, created by Plon in 1927, was edited by Charles Du Bos and Gabriel Marcel; the "Du monde entier" series issued by Gallimard in 1931 gave Anglo-Saxon titles a dominant position, D.H. Lawrence, Aldous Huxley, Rosamond Lehman, Charles Morgan, and Elizabeth Goudge were at the top of the list, followed by the enormous success of *Gone With the Wind* by Margaret Mitchell. In 1935 11 percent of the books published in France were translations (compared to 2 percent in Germany and in England). The chart below shows[40] the primacy of the English language, although the statistics do not break out the American part.

Without presuming to provide a complete description of such an enormous issue, we shall attempt, using as an example, France's main partners to draw the picture created by traveling writers for the benefit of the armchair travelers.

	1929	1931	1933	1935
English	148	232	234	402
German	78	125	153	178
Russian	62	31	31	54
Italian	27	52	40	33
Spanish	22	20	17	19

Germany was first among France's worries. Since few people traveled there, very little was known about the country and few Germans came to France; besides feelings, foreign exchange controls set up in 1932 made any kind of foreign travel virtually impossible. Germany was also the target of lingering passions and stereotypes based on hatred.

Few French writers knew contemporary Germany[41] except for a few German specialists like Edmond Vermeil and Robert d'Harcourt, and some rare historians like Pierre Benaërts or Maurice Baumont. Jean Giraudoux played an important role among the writers, and the image he created was that of an idyllic Germany until 1937. At that time he was still referring to the Hitler regime as a "public safety regime."[42] The writer who stood out was Romain Rolland.[43] Few Frenchmen had as many German friends as he did before the war. While completely separated from nationalism, the author of *Au dessus de la mêlée* was one of those rare writers who had not forgotten the importance of the enemy's culture. He turned to the USSR at the beginning of the 1930s, but never became a card-carrying communist. He returned to France after an extended exile and from 1937 on lived in Vezelay. His new intellectual position led him to shed "non-violence" and condemn Nazi Germany. Anti-fascism now became more important and in 1933 he solemnly refused the "Goethe medal."

Since 1930 the fear of war had reappeared. Ladislas Mysyrowicz showed how French literature stopped producing flamboyant war novels after 1930. With the economic crisis and the rise of Nazism the German ghost reappeared. As Giono admitted in *Europe* in 1934, "I can't forget the war. I would like to. At times I go for two or three days without thinking about it then suddenly I see it, I feel and hear it...and I'm afraid."[44] And Jean Guéhenno in *Journal d'un homme de quarante ans*: "War is on the rise and I can feel the same fear, the same crushing fatigue. We weren't born for this."[45]

Rolland, Giono, and Guéhenno were men of the left with pacifist tendencies. A "period piece," *La guerre de Troie n'aura pas lieu*, a play by Jean Giraudoux, opened in 1935 and belonged to the same school of thought. However, it was impossible not to notice a right-wing pacifism displaying an identical weariness.[46] While the former was deep seated, modified and affected by hatred of fascism, the latter—at least among the extremists—originated in a virulent form of nationalism that was chauvinist and "fundamentalist" as well as attracted to fascist "order," the only one capable of stopping the Bolshevik threat. Among these right-wing pacifists attracted to Germany we can cite Louis-Ferdinand Céline in *Voyage au bout de la nuit* (1932) and *Bagatelles pour un massacre* (1937), a virtual "justification of desertion and cowardice,"[47] and also *La Comédie de Charleroi* (1934) by Drieu La Rochelle. Céline and Drieu both had one thing in common with Hitler: anti-Semitism.

Another very important "cliché" should also be noted with respect to Germany and fascist Italy, which compares France as an "old" country to the "young" countries.

France was in effect a country with low birth rates: the excess of births over deaths disappeared in the 1930s and a small increase in deaths over births was recorded. But was this a *French* characteristic or a western one? Actually, the French birth rate was higher than that of England in 1936. Hitler's natalist policies gave Germany a slight edge, while Mussolini was unable to counter a steady decline in Italy that had been higher to begin with. During the years 1926–1930 France's net reproduction rate was higher than that of England, Germany, and Sweden. It is true that France, due no doubt to the backward conditions of family farming and the awful accommodations available to the working class, had a higher mortality rate than neighboring countries.[48]

It mattered little that Western countries were in roughly the same situation and that France wasn't worse off. A kind of orchestrated or unconscious thinking placed it among the "old" and therefore decadent countries. She was being compared to "young" and "dynamic" countries such as pre-Hitler Germany, and even more with Hitler in power, and to Mussolini's Italy.

The worst book on the subject was certainly the one by Friedrich Sieburg, *Dieu est-il Français?** The first French translation was published in 1940, the first German edition in 1929. We say "the worst" because Sieburg, who was the Paris correspondent of the *Frankfurter Zeitung* since 1923, enjoyed showing an emotional affection toward France. The future Nazi that he was forgave nothing as he wrote long segments on the easy life one could live there.

"France hanging on to the coattails of humanity is slowing down a race that can either lead the world toward the stars or into the abyss." "An island in a changing universe, the rationalistic France with the blood of civilization flowing through its veins is beginning to fear progress while a romantic Germany with its faith in destiny has turned progress into its…religion."[49] Every intellectual group attempting to promote Franco-German understanding prior to Hitler's rise to power got bogged down by this false issue. For example, a conference of Catholic professors in July 1931 at Cologne and in December of the same year at Juvisy centered its debate on the issue of France's "old age." The book published as a result was entitled *Dynamisme et statisme.*[50] Reverend Delos, a Dominican, saw in German dynamism "the mystique of race." Oddly, his German counterpart, Professor Hermann Platz of Bonn University, advised caution in

---

* *Is God French?*

accepting such a "technical" opposition and instead praised the "boiling over" of French dynamism, and rather wisely concluded that great defeats aroused nations more than victories.

On the other hand, Pierre Viénot, who would be part of the Léon Blum government, also extolled German dynamism, using very reasonable words after spending six years in Berlin and the Rhineland. "It's the forward movement encouraged by anxiety." Was it because many young people joined the National Socialist Party that energy was equated with youth? "Strange youth…especially when compared to France's apparent aging. Where does it come from? Why and how does Germany get to be younger than France? The empire of Charlemagne had both countries as one."[51]

We should also quote the young Raymond Aron who was a lecturer at the University of Cologne after graduating from the École Normale. From December 1930 to June 1931 the group *L'Union pour la vérité*, founded by Paul Desjardins, organized "free discussions" on "Franco-German problems after the war."[52] Among those participating were well-known historians such as Camille Bloch and Jules Isaac; the writers André Chamson, Ramon Fernandez, Jean Guéhenno, Vladimir d'Ormesson, and Jean de Pange; German scholars and philosophers also took part. While agreeing that there was "a truly admirable energy within the German people," Raymond Aron offered a clear explanation: "Dynamism-Stagnation"—"Let's understand the circumstances first…During the Boulanger affair we were thought to be the agitated, unstable nation always searching while the Germans were sure of themselves and of their destiny. Let us not forget the inevitable conservatism of the victor and the inevitable revolutionary bent of the vanquished."

The insidious confusion of the desire for peace and the wish to keep the status quo with old age, and the desire for change and bellicose spirit with youth, was a favorite myth of the dictators. To go and get oneself killed for the salvation and glory of the homeland requires both enthusiasm and obedience. Then it's not just peace that looks "old" but democracy as well. Rather than seeing in those internal tensions a rich source of change, the fascist regimes take them as a negative scattering of energies. To accept France's "old age" is in some ways, even though one may be against it, equivalent to justifying the so-called will to "be young." Italy, which at times felt unjustly despised by French arrogance, was whipped up to a frenzy that sought to justify the paramilitary organization of its youth. "Youth and war are two concepts joined by a tradition that is recognizable and now verified by experience."[53]

Jules Romains wrote, "A people may become intoxicated by the idea of old age. It is a morbid idea... Old age for a people is first of all a state of mind...that is to say something tied to the spirit and the will."[54]

While Germany remained the hereditary enemy, England was the country of the "Entente cordiale." But what a disappointment! Almost every Frenchman felt it to be an unreliable ally and in some parts of the world, such as the Middle East, or in the colonies it would turn into an implacable adversary, and an underhanded enemy, the "Perfidious Albion." There were some hated symbols of the unfriendly attitude, such as Lloyd George, who sabotaged the Versailles Treaty, and most of all T.E. Lawrence, the author of *The Seven Pillars of Wisdom*, who with the help of the Syrian Bedouins fought the Turks and occupied Damascus. In an excellent thesis Michel Larès proved that Lawrence was favorable to France on the one hand, and that on the other after 1921 he had ceased all political activity and joined the Royal Air Force as a private leading the life of a recluse.[55] It made no difference; the French were convinced that Lawrence, up until his death in a motorcycle accident in 1935, was an agent of the intelligence service and had not stopped getting the Arabs in the Near East riled up against the French.

The degree of misunderstanding we have seen in the two countries at almost every page of our first five chapters was actually reciprocated. The Frenchmen able to understand the "gentleman" were very few— Abel Hermant, André Maurois, Francis de Croisset, Paul Morand.[56] The conservative majority leadership of Great Britain from 1931 to 1940 was deeply "Gallophobic." Lord and Lady Astor—the latter was an American while he was a member of Parliament in the House of Commons owned the *Times* of London—and the editor Geoffrey Dawson were engaged in a daily anti-French offensive that was favorable to Germany even though it was Nazi. The Astors eagerly invited Nazi politicians to their estate at Cliveden first and foremost Joachim von Ribbentrop. Part of British aristocracy followed their lead. Three prime ministers in a row—Macdonald, the repentant Laborite, Stanley Baldwin and Neville Chamberlain, were influenced by this Gallophobic atmosphere, as were even the heads of the Foreign Office—Sir John Simon, Sir Samuel Hoare, and Lord Halifax, the only exception being Anthony Eden who was forced to resign on February 27, 1938. The same would happen to the permanent secretary of the Foreign Office, Vansittart, who had been deprived of any real power in 1937 by being "promoted" to diplomatic councilor to the government. As for France's other friends,

Winston Churchill, Leo Amery, and Harold Nicolson, they had all been carefully removed from power.[57]

Apparently the reason for this fundamental misunderstanding was the absence of personal ties of friendship between French and British political leaders after 1931. A careful reading of the memoirs and biographies on both sides will be convincing enough. While a Clemenceau had enjoyed warm and enduring friendships in England and later Jean Monnet would base his influence on his connections to many British and American leaders, in the 1931–1940 period there seems to be a large void. When the British—Eden, Duff Cooper, and Nicholson—go to the Riviera on vacation, it was to meet other British friends. A "professional" Francophile like Major-General Sir Edward Spears, former liaison officer, conservative MP, and president of the Franco-British parliamentary committee was proud of his many friendships in France. In reading his recollections of his meetings in 1939 with the owners of châteaux in Dordogne, the Lot, or Normandy, one gathers the impression that he picked the "gens du monde"—he uses the French expression—that were influenced by the defeatism of *L'Action Française* and who were a poor sampling of France's elected officials.[58]

Conversely, we find no trace of any deep friendships of French political leaders with the British. Daladier had an English brother-in-law but didn't go much further in his personal relations with the British. These relations were certainly courteous but not at all personal. Perhaps this absence of closeness may be explained by social differences. The conservative leadership, as Harold Nicolson points out,[59] comes from the aristocracy, the gentry, people of a different era, "asleep in their hereditary comforts" as Ambassador Corbin says.[60] The French leaders—Herriot, Laval, and Daladier—came from the petty bourgeoisie that felt out of place with the Tories. Nicolson, recalling Daladier at a dinner at the French embassy, admits that he was "not greatly impressed." "…[C]ompared to our own ministers, who were resplendent in stars and ribbons, he looked like some Iberian merchant visiting the Roman Senate."[61]

There were relationships, for example between Lord Halifax and the philosopher from Grenoble, Jacques Chevalier, who later was to become a minister in the Vichy government, or between the member of parliament Jacques Bardoux, a highly respected specialist of England, and his former Oxford classmates Sir John Simon—the Appeaser—and Leo Amery—the Francophile. But Bardoux wasn't playing a star role.[62]

It should also be pointed out that among high-level French officials, many had never traveled to England. Léon Noël, after switching from being head of the Sûreté to the diplomatic service, went there for the first time at age 48;[63] General Giraud was over 65 in 1943.[64]

"Perfidious or cordial Albion?" in the eyes of French writers. The great "comparatist" Marius-François Guyard answered the question by saying that it was an uneven struggle. England's friends were liberals and moderates, while its opponents were violent and extremist types who made much more noise than the others.[65] But this remained limited to narrow circles. The masses were probably indifferent.

6.

THE INFLUENCE
OF FOREIGN PROPAGANDA ON PUBLIC OPINION

"The manipulated, incoherent and fanatical press was most certainly a very imperfect reflection of the country's image," wrote Georges Bidault in 1938.[66] Actually, everything seems to indicate that beyond the support coming from business circles, a large number of French newspapers received financial contributions from foreign countries.[67] A few top newsmen said as much, for instance Pierre Lazareff in his 1943 book *Dernière Édition* or, better still, Pertinax (Henri Géraud) in *Les fossoyeurs* which he wrote in New York. According to Daladier's testimony to the commission of inquiry looking into the Stavisky case on April 18, 1934, fourfifths of the newspapers were being financed by contributions.[68]

For the period 1932–1939 a few facts are known among a mass of others that remained hidden because that type of relationship necessarily took place covertly. One should also be cautious because it is easy to engage in calumny and because the amounts of money a government hands over to one of its agents to purchase the friendship of a newspaper or a journalist don't always reach the intended beneficiary.

In studying the archives of the Italian Ministry of Popular Culture ("Minculpop"), Max Gallo used the letters of the Commendatore Amedeo Landini, an Italian consular agent of the in Paris handling contacts with the press between 1922 and 1940.[69] There are even letters from Mussolini himself that are quite contemptuous of the French newspapers. Landini and his deputy Pettinati financed the pro-fascist newspapers *Le Franciste* of Marcel Bucard (900,000 francs from May 1934 to September 1935) and *L'Emancipation Nationale* of Jacques Doriot's Parti Populaire Français. They had complete control of the *Revue Hebdomadaire* and bought, or attempted to buy, *L'Ami du Peuple*, the former newspaper belonging to François Coty in 1935 that was failing miserably in any case. They owned the Agence Transalpine and financed several others. According to Gallo, they even managed to tone down in this manner the anti-Italian senti-ments of radical newspapers. *La Dépêche de Toulouse*, owned by Maurice Sarraut, was awarded "advertising contracts" and then it attacked the sanc-tions policy against Italy. The radical deputy Léon Archambaud was said to have received 3 million francs in 1935 to put pressure on his friends and for his newspaper *L'Éclaireur de Nice*.[70]

For Germany we have more information on the period prior to 1932, thanks to the work by Jacques Bariéty.[71] German involvement after Hitler's rise to power is not as well known. We do know, for example, that *La Presse* received German funds in 1934-1935, that the daily *Notre Temps* was receiving financial support from the German embassy starting in 1936—it would buy 4,000 yearly subscriptions—and that it purchased the weekly *Le Cri des Peuples* in 1938. Landini's correspondence quoted by Max Gallo indicates that the pacifist newsman Victor Margueritte, who was very vocal in defending the absence of German guilt in the outbreak of the First World War, also wrote in German-supported newspapers after Hitler's rise to power. It seems that this did produce results since he could write on October 27, 1933: "One has no right to doubt Mr. Hitler's good faith," and wrote to Landini on March 26, 1936: "Mussolini is the only man of genius in the world today." The *Prima Agency* headed since 1934 by Paul Ferdonnet, who was to become the "traitor from Stuttgart," was a Nazi agency. The funds did not come from Dr. Schmoll, the Ger-man press attaché in Paris, but rather from chemical or pharmaceutical companies that overpaid exorbitant fees for their advertising. In fact, in July 1939 the news editor of *Le Temps* and the head of advertising at *Le Figaro* were both arrested.[72]

There are also indications of funding coming from Americans, Greeks, Bulgarians, Spaniards, and Hungarians. It appears that the British had rather close ties to Elie Bois, the editor of *Le Petit Parisien*, while *L'Action Française* accused *Le Temps*, at least up until 1929, of receiving funds from just about everyone, even from the USSR.

Regarding the USSR, the specialists at the Renseignements Généraux tried to establish the funding of *L'Humanité* at least through all of 1934.[73]

But the Soviets also financed in 1938 and until May 1939 *La Liberté* run by Jacques Doriot, possibly, according to Alfred Kupferman to establish the existence of a pro-Nazi newspaper in Paris.[74]

With all these indications one could think, as did the American *Time* magazine in 1938, that the French press was the most corrupt in the world. Ageron offers an explanation: a newspaper was sold for 0.25 centimes, or four times less than a British or German paper and half the price of a Swiss daily.[75]

There is no indication that such awful habits had much of an influence on public opinion. Foreign "philanthropists" must have had big hopes in this area. In a democracy the variety of opinions displayed by the dailies—far more numerous than they are today—is a guarantee because the reader is always searching for the paper he prefers and can always switch. Furthermore, did foreign policy articles have many readers?

Other propaganda methods were required. We shall concentrate on Germany because they are the most pertinent to our subject. An effective peacetime propaganda may encourage some very honest and democratic-leaning citizens to think that Germany was, after all, less dangerous than it appeared and that an agreement could be possible.

The Nazi government was segmented into a number of rival "fiefdoms." Ambassador Köster and his press attaché Dr. Schmoll were handling the purchase of newspapers. Propaganda Minister Goebbels also showed an interest. He had made the first attempt at a pseudo-rapprochement by trying to take over the *Comité France-Allemagne*. The German branch of this committee, the *Deutsche-Französische Gesellschaft*, or DFG, had emigrated to Paris when Hitler came to power because it was anti-Nazi. Goebbels assigned an official of I.G. Farben Industrie named Ilgner to get things under his control. The operation failed and the president of the DFG, the anti-Nazi Grautoff, preferred to shut down the association in July 1934. At that point Ribbentrop made his move.[76]

Joachim von Ribbentrop was a recently hatched Nazi and had been Hitler's private foreign policy advisor since 1930. He had a low intellect but a gift for flattery that brought him to increasingly important positions. He was sent on missions to England—where high society opened its doors to him—and to France. He hated Foreign Minister von Neurath and in April 1934 created a small party office for foreign policy soon referred to as the *"Ribbentrop-Dienststelle."* Hitler took a keen interest in the initiative, not for espionage operations but rather to set up contacts between Germans and foreigners.

In France Ribbentrop mostly relied on two men. The first was French journalist Fernand de Brinon, born in 1885, a staunch backer of Franco-German understanding, whose reputation was made by having published the first interview of Hitler granted to a French journalist.[77] In 1934 he also published with Bernard Grasset, a publisher who believed in an understanding with Hitler's Germany, a small book entitled *France Allemagne 1918–1934* where he offered a "one-sided" account of Franco-German relations after the First World War. Naturally he felt that the attempts to bring France and Germany closer together prior to 1933 were good only if pursued after Hitler's rise to power. Because Pierre Viénot, whom we have mentioned, took a stand against Hitler he was attacked by Brinon. He also refused "to accept any lessons from the émigrés."[78]

Fernand de Brinon knew how to get along with people. He became friendly with François de Wendel as a journalist at the *Débats* and had a falling out later on.[79] In December 1933 he managed to have Ribbentrop meet Louis Barthou at his home.[80] For a short time he had the ear of Daladier who, as a brave veteran, was at times fascinated by a sentimental rapprochement that could avoid a war.[81] What a beautiful thing a meeting between Daladier and Hitler would be on the bridge at Kehl with the two old and loyal opponents shaking hands!

The other, no doubt more naïve, protagonist was the German Otto Abetz. Abetz was an art teacher from Baden, a reader of Romain Rolland, in love with French culture and involved in the youth movements of the 1920s centering mostly on the meetings of young French and Germans in the summer of 1930 in the Black Forest at the top of the Sohlberg. It is worth noting that the main French speaker was Jean Luchaire, the founder of the daily *Notre Temps*. A *Cercle du Sohlberg (Sohlbergkreis)* was created for the movement to continue. With Hitler in power the German side of the Sohlbergkreis was taken over by the Hitler Youth. A meeting took place in Berlin in January 1934 where Drieu La Rochelle underlined the importance of Germanic blood in French blood. Ribbentrop summoned Abetz in July 1934 and told him his mission was to organize youth meetings and meetings between German and French veterans. Abetz thus became part of the *Ribbentrop-Dienststelle*.

Abetz was successful from the very beginning. In August 1934 he set up a veteran's meeting in Baden-Baden. On November 2, All Souls Day, a new delegation led by Jean Goy, a member of Parliament and vice president of the UNC, was received by Hitler. An interview with Hitler by Jean Goy was published by *Paris-Midi*. The UNC president, Georges

Lebecq, repudiated Goy but at the association's convention the latter was elected as president. The UFAC, the second large association closer to the radicals and its president, Henri Pichot, followed suit. Pichot traveled to Germany three times in 1934–1935. Scapini, who had been blinded in the war and was also a member of Parliament from Paris, followed with a meeting with Hitler in March 1935 at Godesburg. Hitler had been temporarily blinded by exposure to gassing in 1918. The meeting took on sentimental overtones. In February 1935, 4,000 veterans from the two countries marched in the streets of Besançon and finally, in 1936, an impressive reunion took place at Douaumont.

None of this went too far even though some people became concerned (Franklin-Bouillon and Jean Goy fought in a duel; Kérillis made no bones of his hatred of Abetz). Yet a strange atmosphere was being created. Books in favor of an understanding were published in 1934. Besides the one by de Brinon, we should quote Louis Bertrand's *Hitler* and *Le couple France-Allemagne* by Jules Romains.

This brought about the reestablishment in October 1935 of the *Comité France-Allemagne* and the DFG. François-Poncet was present at the inauguration of the two new committees at the castle of Montbijou near Berlin. There were two German professors as presidents: Achim von Arnim and Friedrich Grimm, who published a book in 1938, *Hitler et la France*, with interviews Hitler had given to French newspapers. On the French side was Fernand de Brinon, along with Professor Fourneau of the Institut Pasteur played the leading role. Jules Romains whose plays were staged in Germany, received such a triumphant welcome that he joined the *Comité*. In any case, up to 1939, when Jules Romains broke with the group,[82] every French government, including those of the Popular Front, was regularly funding it. Its mouthpiece was Jean Luchaire's *Notre Temps*. From the 1936 Olympic games to the Franco-German declaration of December 6, 1938, after the Paris *Exposition Universelle* of 1937 there were to be many events taking place. There was a certain ambiguity to it all. Wasn't it a moving and enriching experience to reconcile two great peoples? And, at the same time, was such reconciliation possible with Hitler as one of the partners? It did help his plans, and a few honest and patriotic Frenchmen became the pawns of this subtle propaganda for several years.

The "exchanges" went on as well. Whether they were film makers stunned by the reception they were given, the choir of *Les Petits Chanteurs à la croix de bois*, lecturers (for example on November 26, 1938, Benoist-Méchin in Stuttgart spoke about "The French soldier and the German soldier"[83]), every opportunity was put to good use. We should also point out the visit by the horsemen of the Saumur *Cadre Noir* to their German comrades. At first the school's commander, General Bridoux, did not attend. He would do so in January 1939 when he met the Nazi leaders and was to speak highly of the "open comradeship" that was created. Later on General Bridoux was to become a fanatical pro-German in the Vichy government.[84]

Starting in 1936, the feeling that German propaganda was combined with espionage became a real "myth." The Civil War in Spain gave rise to the expression "fifth column" with the most extreme elements of the right and left accusing each other of being just that.[85] The ambassador to Berlin, Coulondre, sent a cable about the German propaganda budget which he termed "extraordinarily powerful." The budget of Goebbels' ministry was 30 million marks—or 640 million French francs at the "tourist-mark" rate, to which we must add 200 million marks (4,250 billion francs) in taxes on radio, press resources, secret foreign ministry funds, the party treasury and its annexes—for example, the 17 million members of the "Workers Front" were being taxed automatically.

Germany was collectively dedicated to propaganda.[86] One shouldn't forget the Organization of Germans Overseas headed by Dr. Bohle that was funding the Alsatian separatists.[87] Coulondre estimated that the Nazi Reich was spending several billion marks on propaganda. Obviously, France was not the only country to "benefit" from this.

Is it possible to evaluate its effectiveness? It may be less important than the fact itself. As Coulondre wrote, "Fortunately its own excesses sometimes hamper its effectiveness." Propaganda did not create left-wing anti-fascist pacifism nor right-wing anti-Soviet pacifism. It did not cause excited reactions in certain groups by itself. *L'Action Française* was a good example, as were the right-wing weeklies *Candide* and *Je suis partout* that were not German publications. As American historian Eugen Weber correctly points out, "The disciples of Maurras took very different positions...Some, like Jean Héritier, Georges Blond and Bernard Faÿ, backed Fernand de Brinon to reach an understanding with Germany, others like Dumoulin de La Barthète withdrew from pro-German organizations as soon as they understood the situation."[88] He could also have added activist monarchists such as Jacques Renouvin or Guillain de Bénouville.

In the end the public responds to propaganda when it coincides to its deeper tendencies. One may conclude that Goebbels, Ribbentrop and Abetz didn't have the magic touch where the French public was concerned.

Chapter VII

FRANCE'S
WORLDWIDE ECONOMIC INTERESTS

Even in a system where the middle class controls practically every power center, clearly the objectives of the governments—that were the direct result of male universal suffrage—and those of business interests overlapped but did not exactly match. There appeared to be two "power centers" trying to use each other. For larger initiatives governmental power is required. Political power attempts to use, especially overseas, the influence wielded by the capitalists. But to be in power one must be elected by large groups of voters and therefore the concessions made to vast interests had to be limited, even more so because they were, contrary to myth—of "the two hundred families," "the merchants of cannon," "the great capitalists"—violently antagonistic among themselves and did not possess a single center.

The First World War, by using a large portion of French capital, made the display of economic imperialism abroad even less effective. France had lost a large portion of its credit and foreign investments. She was in a new world where tangible pre-war realities were shattered. This was true for every economic instrument: the currency, the budget, and foreign investments.

The franc, which had been taken off the gold standard in 1914, had only been de facto stabilized in 1926 and legally in the spring of 1928. The coming of the world crisis gave the monetary issue an entirely new and hitherto unknown dimension. The positive balanced budgets prior to 1914 covered a huge permanent deficit in the trade balance. Without having solved the export issue the revenues were being whittled away. About two-thirds of all investments and placements had been lost, encouraging a very cautious public to remain extremely fearful. The one hope was the Empire, which was under political and military control. A rather considerable source of disillusionment!

Yet foreign affairs had never been so pressured by economic matters. With war debt, reparations and all types of intercountry debt, there was a need for new staff that would be capable of holding the most technical kinds of discussions. Relations between the Quai d'Orsay and the ministries of finance and commerce were bound to increase. Young treasury officials and a few other specialists were promoted to prestigious positions and part of the country's fate would be in their hands if the politicians, tied to tradition and an all-powerful Parliament that was not well informed, did not constantly act to hold them back.

This was the great revamping of the diplomatic service that was just beginning. After the war, with the economic crisis it would cause a lot of confusion and a terrible incoherence.

1.

THE "GOLD-BLOC"

Currency, one of the state's main attributes, can be used as a powerful weapon by the government in its foreign relations. The French were accustomed, since Controller General Orry in 1735 and even more since the establishment of the franc-germinal, to the great stability of their national currency that had lasted up to 1914, and felt that the franc should be tied to the gold standard; they had failed to understand its weakness resulting from the war. Just like Poincaré, they were looking for a return to normalcy after the war. As Sauvy wrote, "The era of the gold standard" looked more like a "golden age."[1] Churchill had been successful in England where the sterling had been restored in 1923 to its parity with gold, as it was prior to 1914. When the Poincaré franc returned to the gold standard in 1928 at only one-quarter and one-half of its traditional value it was felt to be the equivalent of bankruptcy, which may have been inevitable, but was painful and seen as a form of theft. The French loved gold; they hoarded it in private and considered the gold reserves of the Bank of France to be extremely important. We should add that Keynes was the author of a much more relativist theory, and was known to the French only because of his small book published in 1919, *The Economic Consequences of the Peace*, which that they viewed as a Gallophobic pamphlet and the expression of the worst aspects of "perfidious Albion." Very few specialists showed any interest in his broader economic theories. Even at the political level the French view of monetary issues was extremely rudimentary.

England's decision to devaluate in September 1931, allowing the sterling to float, was viewed with amazement. With Roosevelt's election there was the hope of compelling the British into a stabilization when the new American devaluation had distressed the French people. The failure of the London conference proved that parity with gold could not be reinstated for all world currencies. Those who had neither devalued nor imposed exchange controls should at least stick together. Faced with monetary chaos, France, Belgium, the Netherlands, Switzerland, and Italy called themselves gold-bloc countries followed with interest by Poland. Georges Bonnet, who was finance minister from January 31, 1933 to January 21, 1934, considered himself its originator.[2]

As France enjoyed increased production from mid-1932 until June 1933 (the industrial production index at 100 in 1929 had fallen to 77 in June 1932 and was back up to 91 by June 1933) and a decrease in unemployment—the indicator most sensitive in the eyes of public opinion—the establishment of the gold-bloc was apparently ushering a return to prosperity.

However, starting in the summer of 1933, the trend was reversed in all gold-bloc countries while British industrial production rose by 10%. The reasons for the relapse appeared to be coming from abroad and not from within.[3] By January 1934 the industrial production index was at 79.5 and unemployment was on the rise. The French governments, those of 1933 as well as the Doumergue government in 1934, were well aware that French prices were too high but they only considered internal methods to bring them down. This was the "deflationary" action, consisting of multiple measures to reduce the cost of goods. This affected salaries, pensions, taxes on prices, and even discouraged manufacturers from buying new machinery. The government unanimously rejected the external cure consisting in a devaluation to lower French costs to the same levels as the British and seriously stimulate lagging exports.

Yet in 1934 and 1935 there would be a lively dispute having direct bearing on certain issues that interest us directly.[4] Paul Reynaud was the main supporter of devaluation in France. He wrote in his memoirs that the idea came to him at the beginning of 1933.[5] If this is the case he didn't show it because for part of 1934 he preached deflation and budgetary restraints along with most of the right.[6] Not only in 1933 but in his first speech of 1934 on February 20, he simply explained the deflation-devaluation dilemma without taking a position for the latter. He felt that devaluation, "the fashionable solution," would mean yet another amputation of national wealth.[7]

He became a convert during his second speech on June 28. It probably happened once he took stock of the then unfavorable economic situation. It took a lot of courage on his part. Germain-Martin, the finance minister in the Doumergue government, had made an impression by condemning this Anglo-Saxon and therefore suspicious method. The entire right-wing press approved that line of thinking. On the left the communists and the radicals were against devaluation. The socialists—Léon Blum, Vincent Auriol—were less adamant. According to them, the crisis was a product of the capitalist system: "Devaluation is a capitalist illness." But should it be definitively excluded?[8] As for the great economists of the day—Charles Rist, Roger Nathan, Jean Meynial, Robert Wolf, René Courtin, Gaëtan Pirou—they were all silent on the issue of the discrepancy between French and foreign prices.[9]

On June 28, 1934, Paul Reynaud acknowledged that the crisis was worsening for the gold-bloc countries, while economic improvement was taking place in the thirty-five countries that had devalued. French prices, "dragged down" inside the country, were too high in gold-francs overseas compared to world prices. The result was a contradictory government effort to attempt to get prices to rise internally while lowering them abroad. This absurd situation could one day bring about a French devaluation "not by choice but rather forced upon us, an operation that wouldn't take place gradually but under duress."

The speech came unexpectedly and provoked all kinds of attacks by the right-wing press. *L'Action Française*, which had always hated Paul Reynaud, was happy to have a new reason to hurl insults at him. The "devaluator" was generally described as a false prophet. Some showed "indignant surprise." "He has," wrote Lucien Romier in *Le Figaro*, "seriously damaged the Doumergue cabinet's financial policy and undermined or at least negatively affected France's monetary position."[10] *Le Temps* wrote that it was "a call for an easy artificial monetary policy."[11] "The devaluators must be viewed as defeatists."[12] It was equivalent to treason for a man of the right to make such statements. Devaluation "would end up ruining our middle class."[13] Mr. Paul Reynaud "appears to have bought into the theories of Mr. Keynes and Mr. Roosevelt's brain trust."[14]

This condemnation, backed by most business leaders (C.J. Gignoux, Duchemin, Fougère, Citroën, Lambert-Ribot, Peyerimhoff) and Joseph Caillaux, Doumergue, Germain-Martin, Pierre-Etienne Flandin, the press and its experts, the chambers of commerce, the council of regents of the Bank of France with the "duumvirate Wendel-Rothschild"[15] and Governor Jean Tannery—basically all of France's experts and semi-experts and "interests"—is somewhat surprising since it always discussed France but never brought up the gold-bloc.[16]

Interestingly enough, there was a rather weak attempt to strengthen the solidarity among countries committed to the gold bloc. Perhaps international solidarity could provide solutions to the consequences of an excessively rigid policy. In April 1934 the French chamber of commerce in Lausanne informed the ministry of foreign affairs of the creation of a "committee for the economic strengthening of the gold-bloc."[17] The Marseille chamber of commerce joined it on July 12, followed by many other organizations. The committee was followed on October 15 by a "grouping of economic organizations favoring an understanding among gold-bloc countries" led by Eugène Fougère who had long been president of the National Association for Economic Expansion and was a republican deputy elected in the Loire department. There were three Belgian organizations that also joined as well as two Italians, two Dutch, two Swiss and seven French that were the most important ones.[18]

This was an opportunity to exert enormous pressure on the government and, in fact, the minister of commerce and industry, Lamoureux, agreed with the Belgians on September 24 and 25 to invite a commission of experts to meet in Brussels. The six gold-bloc countries and their colonies did, after all, represent 24% of world trade, with 36% of gold reserves, and 250 million consumers. Wouldn't it be possible to transform this "monetary bloc" into an "economic bloc"?[19]

A meeting of the delegates of the gold-bloc countries was held in Switzerland on September 24 and 25, where it was decided to set up a "permanent commission."[20] On the French side on September 29, Bonnefous-Craponne, head of commercial agreements at the ministry of commerce; de la Baume, deputy director of commercial relations at the Quai d'Orsay; Devinat, head of the office of compensation, and several top officials from finance, agriculture and mining prepared the meeting of the permanent commission. It was necessary, through multilateral agreements, to increase trade among the six countries. A decision was made for the French delegation to be headed by Lamoureux, along with Bonnefous-Craponne, Robert Coulondre, deputy director of commercial affairs at the Quai d'Orsay; Jacques Rueff, deputy director of the *Mouvement Général des Fonds*; Billet, deputy director at the ministry of agriculture; and Lynman, inspector general of the highway department.[21]

There were high expectations in France. *"The creation of this common commercial entity is a new and essential event in the history of Europe's economic organization."*[22] [Emphasis added.]

The commission met in Brussels on October 19 and 20. It set up subcommittees for commercial propaganda, tourism and transportation that met in November.

The results were extremely disappointing. Besides a few agreements on tourism and customs, the only decision was to offer a ten percent increase in trade among member countries.[23] But this remained wishful thinking. No one wanted to increase the import quotas awarded to the other participants. On January 29, 1935, Marchandeau, the new minister of commerce and industry, wrote to Laval, the minister of foreign affairs, that he did not favor preferential tariffs to the other bloc countries.[24] The permanent commission was indeed created and was supposed to meet again in March 1935 but no one believed in it. "It doesn't appear," wrote the deputy director of political and commercial affairs, "that this diplomatic activity has yielded any substantial results."

French ambassadors and ministers overseas sent in their impressions regarding this issue. Only the British were pleased: "Great Britain is very much interested to see the gold-bloc continue, since British exporters and industry now have an advantage over their French, Belgian, and Dutch competitors."[25]

The Americans were worried. Was this not "a challenge to the Anglo-Saxon countries" a way of "forcing Great Britain back to the gold standard"? That, at least, was the reaction of the press because official circles "do not seem to take the matter very seriously."[26] Canada reacted the same way.[27]

No one among the members shared the optimism of the French. Initially the Italians would have preferred that the meeting not be held,[28] and they had to be solicited to send a single, very unofficial, delegate. But the Belgian reaction was the most serious. Belgium had been reticent from the start, even though the meeting was to take place in Brussels. There was a strong movement in the country against the backers of the gold-bloc and in favor of devaluation. "Stubborn pride of the smaller nations," wrote the commercial councilor Bouchet, adding, "In spite of the efforts of a few supporters, a unanimous Belgian feeling accused France of the worst misdeeds in commercial relations... It is no secret here that the active elements in the country favor devaluation." Belgium was still hesitating between the gold-bloc and the sterling-bloc.[29] The Brussels conference, rather than quieting its worries, once again made it feel France's overbearing influence.[30]

How and why a new Belgian government led by Paul Van Zeeland was formed in March 1935 and the reasons behind its devaluation of the Belgian franc are beyond the confines of this subject. Undoubtedly the Belgian decision put France in an uncomfortable position. The main point was that in the course of one year, between February 1935 and February 1936, the index of industrial manufacturing increased by 23 percent in Belgium and 11 percent in France; unemployment was reduced by 24 percent in Belgium and 3 percent in France. Why did the Flandin government—which fell on May 30 after a large depletion in gold (5 billion between May 24 and 31)—and the Laval government that followed both persist in keeping and even increasing deflation?

When the new Laval government requested full powers it passed a bill on June 8, 1935, that read as follows in its single paragraph:

"In order to avoid a devaluation of the currency, the Senate and the Chamber of Deputies authorize the government..., etc." On June 7 Pierre Laval set up a commission, consisting of Jacques Rueff, C.J. Gignoux, and Raoul Dautry, to propose actions to "avoid the devaluation of the currency."[31]

There was a very stubborn attitude on the right. The crisis at the end of May wound up focusing on a violent campaign against a government where Paul Reynaud would be in charge of finance and decide a devaluation. He spoke again very bravely on May 30. The problem, he said, was both "technical" and "political." On the technical level it was not the time to devaluate: "I want no part of a devaluation enacted in a moment of panic." But the political aspect was filled with strong feelings: "Those who portray devaluation to the good people of this country as a scarecrow are acting badly against the national interest."[32]

Paul Reynaud now had some followers: Raymond Patenôtre, Marcel Déat and, in some ways, Léon Blum. Among the top officials, Wilfrid Baumgartner, head of the *Mouvement général des fonds*, shared most of Paul Reynaud's ideas.[33] Emmanuel Mönick, the financial attaché in London, was credited with converting Léon Blum.[34] Jacques Rueff, who had studied British unemployment and had been involved in the 1928 stabilization, was also convinced that the policy of deflation was absurd and, due to the high parity of the currency, it was necessary to devaluate. He did what he could to attract Laval's attention but was unable to convince him. In his autobiography he writes about the "tragedy of the gold-bloc."[35]

It would take the Popular Front to enact what was unavoidable, and until then the disputes about other issues were concentrated on devaluation. Yet in April 1935 French prices were 21 percent higher than the British (they had been 22 percent lower in 1929).[36] Paul Reynaud published a pamphlet entitled *Jeunesse, quelle France veux-tu?** in June 1936. He did not expect to be reelected in 1936 and this was his political "last will and testament." Actually, despite the opposition of part of the right, he was voted in with a 27-vote lead over the communist candidate.

The monetary issue was very significant with respect to French behavior in foreign policy. What is striking to the historian is to see the small contribution by the top officials—neither Barthou nor Laval prior to May 1935, nor Léger—at the Quai d'Orsay in the matter. The initiative to strengthen the gold-bloc came from Lucien Lamoureux, the minister of commerce and industry. Two men at foreign affairs were following the issue very closely: Robert Coulondre, one of the two deputy directors at political and commercial affairs (the other, René Massigli, was too busy with problems of disarmament, the League of Nations and Ethiopia), and the deputy director of commercial affairs, Renon de La Baume.

It was a "normal" situation at a time when the mind-set that was later termed "technocratic" did not exist at all. Of the two main leaders in favor of devaluation, only Paul Reynaud could fit a description that remained anachronistic. The other leader, Raymond Putenôtre, was essentially a businessman.[37] In studying the period that immediately followed at

---

* *Youth, What Kind of France Do You Want?* [NDT]

the beginning of the Popular Front,[38] René Girault correctly states that "the usual divisions between economic history, foreign affairs, internal political history actually succeeded in separating the analysis of facts that were closely related to one another."[39] But this is not only the fault of the historians. It also originates with the politicians; the division also exists within the activities of those responsible and the documents prove it. Only a few unusually gifted men, such as Paul Reynaud, Léon Blum, and perhaps also Georges Bonnet, were aware that no effective foreign policy was possible if one was economically the prisoner of the crisis and, therefore, economic and foreign policy were intimately connected. Other politicians and the general public, *even more so*, felt that monetary issues were a matter of internal politics between 1933 and 1936, unrelated to foreign issues. The economic incompetence of the French leaders drew them to this differentiation and a desire to solve monetary issues "emotionally." Paul Reynaud, who saw this as a technical issue, did not have the human touch; his raspy, high-pitched voice was not exciting. People did not like him that much even though he was right.

2.

OVERVIEW OF FRENCH FOREIGN TRADE

It was a French tradition for foreign trade to show a large deficit. This was directly traceable to the atmosphere generally influenced by Malthusianism that turned into protectionism—especially in agriculture— by the pittance earnings kind of thinking that encouraged companies to invest as little as possible, to use outdated machinery to the very end and save money on sending commercial agents abroad. Such a mentality can only be turned around when things get desperate. But that was not the case for France prior to 1914 because the huge trade deficit was more than covered by invisible exports and, in particular, by the revenues of capital invested overseas.

In the 1920s something odd took place that neither the leadership nor public opinion quite understood. In 1924, 1925, 1926, and 1927 exports had been higher than imports. This took place because of the low exchange rate of the franc and not due to the budgetary discipline of Poincaré. The linking of the franc to the gold standard, on the contrary, brought back the trade deficit slowly at first, then more severely.

In the 1930s the deficit grew to gigantic proportions. A simple chart will show this[40] (values are in millions of Poincaré francs):

GENERAL TRADE (INCLUDING EXPORTS)

	Imports	Exports	Total	Deficit
1931	42,601	30,878	73,479	11,725
1932	30,235	20,035	50,270	10,200
1933	28,794	18,776	47,570	10,018
1934	23,397	18,126	41,523	5,271
1935	21,075	15,732	36,807	5,343
1936	25,788	15,745	41,533	10,043
1937	43,961	24,490	68,451	19,471
1938	46,336	31,210	77,546	15,126
1939 (first 9 months)	32,539	23,832	56,371	8,707

There was monetary stability up to September 1936. One can see a steady decrease in global trade and a still high but decreasing deficit. After 1936 the consequences of various devaluations were felt but price increases and problems of production affected imports even more and they grew slightly in volume. Exports returned in 1937 to their 1930 levels, then fell in the 1938 recession.[41]

This would not be that serious if the invisible revenues had remained positive. But it was only marginally the case that was translated into the following revenues[42] (in millions of Poincaré francs):

1931—3,012	1935—700
1932—4,815	1936—2,803
1933—2,950	1937—3,995
1934—1,250	1938—120

Our aim, following this general overview of the situation, is not a detailed analysis but to see how these events affected foreign policy.

Obviously, a detailed study should be undertaken based upon the reports of the commercial attachés, consuls, ministries of commerce and finance, etc. As long as that kind of research is missing, we must limit ourselves to making assumptions. We shall offer the following.

1. Foreign trade, the main component of the country's "international life," appears to be a secondary feature in foreign affairs during the 1930s.

The entire tradition made it such. Before 1914 trade was a private activity. It took four years of war to set up "interventionism," completely unknown until then. After the armistice the French government, influenced by Clémentel and Jean Monnet, wanted to keep the international bureaus created during the war. The Americans moved quickly to set things right. The almost total freedom imposed by the world's number one economic power had certainly played a role in the crisis. Since 1931 and, most of all, after the failure of the London conference in 1933, the failure of any currency and trade cooperation among countries led to isolated actions at the national level by increasing customs duties, setting up prohibitions, quotas, sometimes even exchange controls, and what it forced others to do: compensations, clearing, and barter.

The French state, which floundered amid unstable governments and Malthusian economists, was trying as best it could to adjust to the new circumstances.

But foreign affairs did not feel concerned. Traditionally the diplomats provided a lot of information on foreign economies—Corbin, François-Poncet, Coulondre, and Léon Noël sent in many reports on these issues. The commercial attachés who reported to the ministry of commerce with copies to the Quai d'Orsay were negotiating piecemeal, on a daily basis, modifications and even entire commercial agreements. They helped French exporters but didn't take the initiative.

This role belonged to private organizations such as the chambers of commerce. The state continued to play a minor role.

2. The division between monetary issues—as we have seen—and "higher policy" also existed in commercial matters. Obviously, when a minister of foreign affairs traveled abroad, he took a few experts along and did not forget in the course of long discussions to bring up some issues regarding exchange and trade; but beyond trading in arms and munitions it only represented a smaller part of the conversations.

In other words, the idea that a close connection existed between prosperous foreign trade and power was rarely expressed or even felt. An increase in exports was considered as one device, among many others, to solve the crisis by giving a bit more work to the French people, not as part of a broader strategy. The Empire was therefore expected to make up for the failings of foreign countries.

3. The tradition of *financial* action—loans, capital investments (which we will examine in the next paragraph)—and *commercial* initiatives more or less independent from one another had been reduced somewhat from

the pre-war period. Yet in those countries where France had a top-ranking position economically, others—Germany, England, the United States—were overtaking it from the commercial point of view. This was true of Czechoslovakia (France was the second largest investor), Romania (France was second with only 6.1 percent of Romanian imports and 8 percent of exports, way behind Germany and England in 1937) and even with Poland (France was the first investor easily overtaken in trade by Germany, the United States, and England.) Those three countries where France still had large investments were not on the list of its ten largest suppliers; only Czechoslovakia was in tenth place in the list of its first ten clients. France was selling ten times less there than in Belgium.

4. It was only in 1938 and mostly after Munich that France appears to discover the links between power and trade. Was it because of Georges Bonnet, who had been finance minister before going to the Quai d'Orsay? Or was it the progress of German policy in Central Europe that dovetailed with its increasing commercial influence? In any case there were some attempts to take action.[43] But it was very late. The minister to Prague, Lacroix, paraphrased a Czech daily on December 28, 1938, when he wrote the revealing statement: "The collapse of the French system didn't start with the events in September. It originates with the fact that *France has greatly neglected the economic side of the struggle for influence.*"[44] [Emphasis added.]

3.

LINGERING ECONOMIC IMPERIALISM

The period we are examining still does not have detailed works similar to those for the years that preceded 1914.[45] However, every indication is that the power of French finance abroad had sharply declined after the First World War. In 1905 Prime Minister Rouvier, a banker was thinking of replacing the traditional policy of conquests and alliances with a more discreet economic hegemony that would bear greater fruits and be more exacting. It was the time when Russia in its immensity was "France's Far West" and when there existed bastions of French investment capital in Eastern Europe, the Ottoman Empire, and Latin America. In 1914 it was estimated at 45 billion gold francs, of which 41 were invested abroad and far behind (only 4 billion) in the colonies.[46]

The war destroyed that kind of power, second only to Great Britain. In various ways she used up part of the capital invested overseas and greatly increased France's foreign debt. Pre-war loans to defeated countries, namely the Ottoman Empire and Austria-Hungary, were not repaid or only partially. The massive loan of 13 to 15 billion made to Russia or invested into Russian companies was wiped out by the Bolshevik refusal to honor the tsarist debt and the nationalization of the Soviet economy.

For the banks the 1914 moratorium, the prohibition stated in the law of April 3, 1918, extended for ten more years to finance loans to foreign states, greatly reduced the playing field. Until 1925 they were hampered by some large industries, such as Schneider of Le Creusot, which created their own banking instruments. The instability of foreign exchange, up to the introduction of the Poincaré franc in 1928, encouraged floating capital speculation not external investments. According to the historical accounts by the technicians of the time, Alfred Pose and Achille Dauphin-Meunier,[47] they again were very prosperous from 1925 to 1929. Then after that, the crisis and the collapse of stock market values and the shrinking of the economy placed them in a difficult situation.

Naturally, in the 1920s, in particular, serious efforts were made to rebuild, especially among the allied countries in Eastern Europe. But as Georges Soutou, the author of one of the best studies on these attempts wrote, which it was only a "poor man's imperialism."[48]

We may add that statistical models allowing for comparisons are difficult to set. To transform "current francs" into "constant francs" (gold-franc or the Poincaré franc equal one-quarter and one-half of the gold franc) is a thankless task.

We may say at the outset that the few calculations of French government investments and loans outside metropolitan France (foreign countries + the Empire) differed widely.

Based on a study by the *Royal Institute of International Affairs* published in 1937 in the *Statistical Yearbook of the League of Nations* and a very detailed study of Eastern Europe by Czechoslovak historian Alice Teichova,[49] the total reaches 72 billion Poincaré francs or *16 billion gold francs of 1930* and 60 billion Poincaré francs or *13.3 billion gold francs in 1933* because of repatriation and falling stock values due to the world economic crisis. She estimates foreign investments to be 60 percent overseas and 40 percent in the Empire or, very roughly, 9.6 billion gold francs abroad and 6.4 billion in the Empire in 1930.

Chronologically speaking, out of the 72 billion (or 16 billion gold francs), 35 billion (or 7.9 billion gold-francs) were residuals of the pre-war investments;[50] 5 (about 1 billion gold francs) were made up of colonial borrowing and, in the second place, foreign borrowing that took place between 1919 and 1928; 10 (about 2 billion gold francs) came from long-term foreign investments between 1919 and 1928; 22 billion (or 5 billion gold francs) included long-term investments in the Empire or overseas between 1928 and 1933.

Jacques Marseille[51] used a 1943 Vichy report to reach much higher numbers through a series of extrapolations (but were the Vichy figures correct? Wasn't it expedient at the time to increase them?). The investigation centered on Indochina, Madagascar, AOF, AEF, and the smaller colonies. It didn't include North Africa. In 1914 there was an investment of 1.176 billion francs in those territories. The Vichy report estimated at 120 billion of 1940 francs all public and private investments in the same territories equal to 8.7 billion gold francs. A first extrapolation that would add in North Africa reached 17.5 billion gold francs. Then Marseille estimated the Empire's portion at 45 percent to reach a total investment of foreign plus Empire of 37 billion gold francs in 1940 almost as much as in 1914. Furthermore, Marseille also used the book by Varga and Mendelssohn, *Données complémentaires a l'impérialisme de Lénine*, based on the works of the Americans Moulton and Lewis estimating French investments in 1924 at 27 billion gold francs and in 1940 at 40 billion gold francs.

Finally, the OECE in its 1950 report estimated at 18.5 billion gold francs the 1939 French foreign investments but noted that this amount "generally did not" include the investments made by the home country into its overseas territories.

Here are, therefore, two extreme numbers—*16 billion in 1930, according to Mrs. Teichova, and 38 billion in 1940, according to Marseille*—that indicate the need for a much more comprehensive study of the issue. Mrs. Teichova writes of a loss of 2.7 billion between 1930 and 1933.

Clearly, after 1930 France made an effort in public investments overseas. Manuela Semidei has pointed out that from 1931 to 1934 four laws appropriated colonial loans of up to 5.7 billion Poincaré francs (about 1.2 billion gold francs). From 1929 to 1940 the total of these loans came to 15 billion or 3.2 billion gold francs. Private investments came no doubt on top of that number.

Nevertheless, if Mrs. Teichova's estimates (which were certainly correct for Central and Eastern Europe) are undoubtedly below their real levels, they are still closer to reality than Marseille's numbers, which are too optimistic. I will make the following assumptions:

1. The numbers offered by Moulton and Paslovsky, American experts who wanted France to repay its wartime debts, may have been artificially increased (just by adding in a number of French receivables that would actually never be paid or, at least, only by a small fraction).

2. In 1940 in the Empire, where no major industries existed except for mining, the increase in investments from 4 billion in 1914 to 17.5 billion in 1940 appears possible but very high.

3. I am more inclined to agree with the conclusions offered by J.-C. Debeir.[52] For the period 1919–1930, "except for the two years immediately following the war where the liabilities resulting from the conflict were being reduced, foreign investment reached the levels comparable to the Belle Époque," but two important and lasting changes that were closely connected appeared:

Short-term capital, which represented a small portion of exported capital, was now the largest;

The direction toward the least developed countries (Russia, Ottoman Empire…) changed after the war toward the great world financial centers (London, New York…) Therefore, long-term investments—the only ones of interest to us—were relatively small. After that they were mostly directed toward the Empire.

As a non-specialist I do not seek to pass judgment but to clearly show how little we know and hope for the works of future economic historians to fill the gap.

* * *

What were the motivations behind those investments? The profit motive was obviously the leading one. Significantly, France practically did not create any industries in the Empire—except for mining—and there was no attempt to benefit from low industrial wages overseas in underdeveloped countries. The Empire provided France with mining and tropical agricultural products; a kind of "autarchic" mindset prevailed throughout the crisis years, meaning that certain French needs were being satisfied within the Empire. The best examples were the rubber plantations in Indochina which provided all of France's rubber needs in 1939.

The political motivation appears to have been much stronger. It was a time-honored French tradition. Had not the old Franco-Russian alliance been purchased with multiple loans? Mrs. Teichova forces the issue a bit when she writes:[53]

It's an historical fact that the Quai d'Orsay had close ties to French high finance and that overseas capital investment was strongly influenced…not only motivated by profit but also by colonial interests and French political power policy. French capital investments acting in unison were directed toward Europe and above all Poland and the states of the Little Entente. Later in the 1930s new French investments were almost entirely aimed at the colonies.

Were the ties between the Quai d'Orsay and high finance as tight as Mrs. Teichova claims? Considerable research would certainly be required to clarify that issue. Clearly Paléologue, who was secretary general in 1920, was connected to Le Creusot; and Philippe Berthelot, who was his successor, had been compromised in 1921 because of his ties, through his brother, to the Banque Industrielle de Chine; and François-Poncet had worked for the Comité des Forges. It is also well known that once ambassadors retired, they tried to improve their positions by joining one or more boards of directors.[54] However, the steps taken by financiers at the Quai d'Orsay, especially under Léger, seemed few and far between and the matters they discussed were often in the national interest.[55]

We should point out that in the highly contentious books about business circles published by Henry Coston or Albert Aymé-Martin and in the work by Emmanuel Beau de Loménie, *Les responsabilités des dynasties bourgeoises*,[56] and even the doctoral dissertation by Jean-Noël Jeanneney, *François de Wendel*, the names of French diplomats Coulondre, Noël, Jules and Charles-Arsène Henry, Corbin, Thierry, Dampierre, Pila, Fleuriau, Herbette, Laroche, Charvériat, Bargeton, Rochat, Happenot, Naggiar, Massigli, Roger Cambon, and Margerie *never appeared a single time* if not in the context of their diplomatic duties. The name of Léger appeared in Jeanneney's book because de Wendel hated that "heir to Briand," that "red" at the Quai d'Orsay.[57]

The connections indeed existed socially, at times financially, in any case within the same social class. They were not very tight.

We will not make a detailed analysis of every investment. When it is only a sprinkling then clearly the part played by French capital in foreign policy had to be nil.[58] We will only examine the Eastern European "bastion." France, contrary to the United States, had few in Germany (where some steel works owned a number of mines prior to 1914), nor in the defeated countries of Bulgaria and Hungary.[59] Out of 5.6 billion reichmarks owed by German banks to foreign creditors as of March 31, 1931, the United States' portion was 37.1 percent and that of England, 20.4 percent. France came after Switzerland and Holland with 6.5 percent.[60] On the other hand, it had a strong position in Poland, Czechoslovakia, Romania, and Yugoslavia, and large interests in Austria.

In Poland, quite remarkably, many investments took place while it was still part of tsarist Russia. It was, in fact, the only kind of investment of that kind where France remained in first place ahead of the United States and Germany. In 1938 the estimated amount of French investments was 15 billion francs in banking (about equal to England) and most of all in industry. French companies were producing 6.5 million tons of coal, 400,000 tons of steel, 75,000 tons of zinc, 300,000 tons of basic oils, and 225,000 tons of refined oils. Two billion kilometric tons were also shipped on French lines.

The older French industries had appeared as early as 1878: in mining and steelworks, the *Société des Forges* and Huta-Bankowa, the *Société des Charbonnages*, and the mines at Sosnowiec; in the textile industry, the *Union Textile* had been set up by Motte from Roubaix, the *Czestochorienne*, the *Société pour l'industrie textile*, the *Société Zyrardew* that was owned by Marcel Boussac.

Most of these industries had been destroyed by the war and started with French capital once again. New investors came after the war, in the mines in Upper Silesia, in the oil regions in Boryslav and Polanka, in electricity, the chemical industry (branches of Air Liquide and Kuhlmann.) French capital partnered with the Polish state to create the *Société des mines fiscales* of the Polish state, the consortium of the port of Gdynia, and the Polish railroad company.[61]

They were all members of the French *Groupement des industriels français* in Poland.

Poland was also granted French state loans. During the period we are examining, one particularly large loan came with the Rambouillet agreement (signed on September 6, 1936), and that was confirmed as permanent through an exchange of letters on September 17. The French government, by the Rambouillet agreement, placed 2 billion francs at Poland's disposal in installments of 500 million for four years. It was understood that this entire amount would be used for military supplies except for 400 million earmarked for the Silesia-Baltic railroad. The military supplies would come from orders placed in France or purchases made in Poland "toward the creation and development of the Polish war industry." Noël complained bitterly about Boussac's intrigues who, according to him, benefited from the French funding at the expense of Poland's defense. Charvériat, assistant director of political affairs, wrote on October 5, 1938, that, despite Poland's attitude during the Munich crisis, "this vast development of our industry in Poland" encouraged to "maintain economic and financial cooperation." However, Léger's disciple then added, "What appears to be subject to revision are the political and military agreements that tie us to Poland. In this way we would give our collaboration *a purely economic and financial* character, which is much more effective and less dangerous that what we have followed so far."[62] We shall see further ahead what happened to that wish.[63]

Foreign debt in Yugoslavia was gigantic, representing 85 percent of total debt. In December 1937, 65 percent of the funding of corporations was foreign. France came ahead of Great Britain and the United States. French capital was mostly invested in mining (the mines at Bor). Even when Germany annexed Austria and part of Czechoslovakia—each one being very active in Yugoslav banking, the wood industry, sugar and textiles—it remained behind France.

Most of industry and banking in *Romania* belonged to French, American and British investments. France was just behind Great Britain and ahead of the United States and Belgium. The following chart (in millions of lei) is from an excellent book by Swiss historian Philippe Marguerat:[64]

	Capital Stock Total 1937	Great Britain	France
Banking	8,800	586	410
Industry	33,800	4,939	2,699
Trade and Insurance	4,000	29	57
Other	—	50	100
Total	46,600	5,604	3,266

France was in a very good position in the banking industry through the Banque de Paris et des Pays-Bas, which had large interests in two large Romanian banks, and the Banque de l'Union Parisienne, which held a majority of the Banca Commerciala Romana. In steelworks the CEPI (*Compagnie Européenne de participation financière*), an international holding company with Romanian, British, and French capital—through the Banque des pays de l'Europe Centrale—controlled a large company, Resita, which was the largest in Eastern Europe after Skoda. All of Romanian steel production was controlled by CEPI. Other French capital (namely the *Société française d'études et d'entreprises*) had interests in railroad equipment, armaments, etc.

In textiles a few companies from Tourcoing (Caulliez-Coisne) and Mulhouse (Dollfuss-Mieg) owned large interests that were on the increase between 1935 and 1937.

Finally, 45 percent of the oil business was controlled by British, French, Belgian, and Dutch investments. Five out of seven large companies "obey French or British decisions." One of them, Columbia, had almost entirely French stock ownership (the Omnium français des pétroles and the Desmarais group).

The Romanian government had a large foreign debt. France lent it on April 1, 1939, some 18.7 billion lei, or 27 percent.

In 1918 Czechoslovakia was already largely industrialized (50 percent of the population was involved in secondary or tertiary activities). It represented 70 percent of Austro-Hungarian industry (for 26 percent of the population), exporting and importing capital at the same time. Between the wars Czechoslovakia used foreign capital as a matter of course, particularly coming from France, to replace the Germans and Austrians. There was, once again, a connection between politics and the economy. Later on,[65] we shall look at France's financial role in Czechoslovakia in greater detail. We may say at the outset that France came behind Great Britain but had a doubly strong position because of banking (44.5 percent of foreign investments) and the machine tool industry. The French company Schneider et Cie. actually controlled the powerful Skoda factories through the Banque européenne industrielle et financière.

For France the "Czechoslovak bastion" was actually a Schneider—Le Creusot position. The company had taken over the Banque de l'Union parisienne—a cornerstone of Protestant banking—and was very powerful within the Credit Lyonnais. It also created the Union européene industrielle et financière, which financed operations in Czechoslovakia and Austria (*Société d'escompte de Basse-Autriche, Osterreichische Berg-und Hüttenwerke*) and in Poland.

The regulatory role for most of these countries was played by the *Banque des pays de l'Europe centrale*, headquartered in Paris, with a branch in Vienna (*Zentraleuropaische Lander Bank Niederlassung Wien*) handling investments in Czechoslovakia (where it controlled the *Banque du commerce et de l'industrie*), in Poland, Yugoslavia and Romania. The famous economist Charles Rist was a long-time president of the Prague branch. Following the Anschluss (March 1938), the Banque des pays de l'Europe centrale had to divest its Viennese branch to the *Dresdner Bank* of Germany, but kept up its interests in Czechoslovakia as long as possible and in the other countries where it had investments.

We should also point out that France had slid from second place for capital investments abroad behind Great Britain and Germany in 1914 to third place after Great Britain and the United States; the latter two had foreign investments in 1930 six times larger than in 1913. Great Britain had granted few foreign loans before 1914 and had opted for industrial investments and consequently suffered far fewer losses because of the war than France did.

4.

THE EMPIRE

The unofficial name "Empire" was being used more and more by the French as globally meaning their colonies, protectorates, and mandates. Yet the colonies were administered by the ministry of the colonies (except for Algeria which was divided into departments). The real protectorates (Morocco and Tunisia) were part of the ministry of foreign affairs that supervised the residents general. The protectorates in Indochina (Annam, Tonkin, Principalities in Laos, Cambodia) were like the colony of Cochinchina under the control of the ministry of the colonies, and the entire area was under a single governor general. French West Africa (AOF), French Equatorial Africa (AEF), Madagascar and its smaller islands (Comores, la Réunion) and the French Coast of the Somalis and Djibuti were all colonies; Togo and Cameroon were category B mandates (lands considered unprepared for independence for a longer period), under special administration and the mandated power was to report to the League of Nations. However, the ministry of the colonies was actually in charge, as well as of the colonies in America (the tiny islands of Saint-Pierre-et-Miquelon, the Antilles—Martinique, Guadeloupe, and their islands—and French Guyana), plus the five cities in India, the islands of the Pacific, French Polynesia and New Caledonia. Finally, the ministry of foreign affairs administered the category A mandates in the "Levant"—Syria and Lebanon—headed by a high commissioner. A few small deserted islands in the South Seas (Kerguelen, Amsterdam, Saint-Paul) and Adélie on the continent of Antarctica made up this impressive list.

In all it represented about 12 million square kilometers and a population of about 60 million (20 million were located in Indochina.) Such spaces—including the 5 million square kilometers of the Sahara—were a vast assemblage of identical colors on the map but actually translated into huge differences at the demographic, economic and strategic levels. For example, a certain "base"-oriented strategy that favored this scattering (insufficient at the time of the coal-driven navy, it became acceptable with oil powered furnaces and the piston engine.) The very remote territories, Indochina included, could not be defended, however, while the vast components of North Africa and Black Africa appeared to be a kind of rear base for metropolitan France and actually did play that role.

France's relations with the different parts of its Empire do not enter into our investigation since it is part of a common foreign policy decided by the home country. There could be an exception regarding the mandates in Syria and Lebanon where there was a strong desire for independence and the nationalists tried to replace the submissive relationship with state-to-state type relations. This, however, is a different subject and part of the vast decolonization movement. In 1939 France was firmly in charge of its mandates as the incident of the sandjak of Alexandretta was to prove.[66]

The Empire only comes into play here as an "object" and implied a number of issues of prestige, economics, strategy and defense where France was concerned. It was to French power a "backup," a "reinforcement" and an "area to fall back to." Large interests were concentrated there. It provoked jealousies and even demands, and held a more or less modest place in French foreign policy during the 1930s.

The war had, no doubt, reduced the general indifference of the French population. Some 569,000 soldiers and 200,000 workers had come to help the mother country, and 71,000 had "died for France," including 35,900 North Africans, a rather low number considering the 1,300,000 Frenchmen killed and, at the same time, huge if one remembers that those men often behaved heroically being French "subjects" and not full-fledged French citizens.[67]

With prosperity at the end of the 1920s, the wave of public opinion favoring "an even greater France" got underway. In 1929 there were some "38 committees or private colonial leagues, 12 agencies and more or less official councils" located in Paris. In 1930 there were 71 colonial newspapers in Paris and 5 in the provinces. The best known writers went on the African or Asian pilgrimage: André Gide, Paul Morand, Louis Gillet, Roland Dorgelès, Maurice Dekobra, Jean d'Esme, André DeMayson, Albert Londres, Henri de Monfried, etc.[68] Major newspapers increased their reporting and sections on colonial issues, focusing attention on the difficulties of colonization; the Rif war, the Druse war, and the Tonkin insurrection (the Yen Bay incident in February 1930) helped glorify great military victories, condemn foreign incursions and fuel anti-communist propaganda. The Colonial Exhibition from May to November 1931 at Vincennes was intended, according to the minister of the colonies Paul Reynaud, "to make the French people aware of their Empire" and received 7 million visitors.[69]

Was it a passing fancy? Ageron notes that the number of colonial titles tended to decrease. Out of about 14,500 yearly titles legally recorded, 439 colonial titles were registered in 1929; 361 in 1930; 395 in 1931; 194 in 1933 and 196 in 1934. Lectures were attracting fewer attendees, and colonial films brought in reduced box office sales. Gabriel Hanotaux, who had authored, in collaboration with Martineau, the *Histoire des colonies françaises* between 1926 and 1930, said in 1935 that "public opinion fell asleep after the success of the Colonial exhibition."[70]

Actually, the main motivation was not anti-colonialism but rather indifference. A tiny number of candidates in the 1932 elections discussed colonial matters in their platforms. The Colonial Party—a group of deputies and senators of different political tendencies favoring colonization—disappeared after the 1932 elections.[71] The Communist Party was anti-colonialist in its doctrine and some of its rank and file even played an active part in supporting the Druses and the Rif insurgents. Later on, faced with the colonial demands by fascist countries, it would modify its position. The Socialist Party actively denounced colonization's brutalities, terror, repression, and exploitation; since 1931 it published a monthly supplement to *Le Populaire* entitled *Colonisation et Socialisme.* However, only a minority condemned colonialism as such (22.6 percent of the votes at the 1938 convention, according to Ageron). The *Ligue des droits de l'homme*, a 150,000-member organization voted in favor of the anti-colonialist motion introduced by Felicien Challaye by 1,523 votes to 634 (70.7 percent to 29.9 percent). The early rumblings of nascent nationalisms in the colonies led to the publication of anti-colonialist books, the most famous being *Indochine SOS* (1935) by André Viollis. These were rather isolated initiatives, as were the articles by colonial nationalists published in *La Flèche*, edited by Gaston Bergery. There were no "outspoken anti-colonialists" among the radicals; at the most we can mention Joseph Caillaux, who called for an association of European states, including Germany and Italy, to develop the colonies, a kind of "Eurafrica" before its time. There were some Catholics with attitudes critical to the abuses of colonization (*Semaines sociales, Annales de la jeunesse coloniale française*) but, for the most part, the right was very much in favor of colonization.

The economic crisis, followed by the international crisis, gave rise to another reaction that Tardieu discussed in 1931, namely "the Empire as salvation." In an unpublished and important study, J. Marseille[72] shows that "a deeper change took place in the *function* assigned to the Empire... Up to 1935–1936 the Empire was basically a *market* for the French consumer manufacturing industry but during the closing years of the 1930s it became a *resource center* while basic industries began penetrating the colonial market."

We mentioned earlier that we were still unsure of the total amount of investments in the Empire.[73]

Public investments took place for the most part through loans taken by the colonies on the French market. Between 1931 and 1934 four laws authorized colonial borrowing up to 5.7 billion, about half of these as credits for purchases destined to the colonies. The state was merely extending a guarantee. From 1929 to 1940 these loans were to total 15 billion and were part of the budgets of the colonies or the protectorates (the debt service was 40 percent of the AEF budget and 35 percent for Morocco). The colonies also complained about the fact that they were expected to participate in France's military budget and requested higher subsidies.

In December 1934, following an idea that Daladier had launched in 1933 a Franco-colonial economic conference was called together. In a world full of high protectionist tariffs, the idea was to take stock of the opportunities the Empire could offer. The conference recommended creating a Colonial Equipment Fund, but the result was disappointing and the actions taken were rather timid. The government failed to create the fund, and there was sharp rivalry between French and overseas producers (wine, sugar cane, Brazilian coffees or from AOF, etc.).

The result was that colonial trade, amounting to 13.1 percent of total French trade in 1927, reached 25 percent in 1932; 27.6 percent in 1934 and 30.3 percent in 1936, but it must be said that trade overall was strongly decreasing and this, therefore, did not represent progress. The numbers seem to indicate that the Empire was benefiting more from this "autarchy" than France itself. French exports to the colonies in 1938 were 35 percent lower than in 1929, or in constant franc values, 9.7 billion Poincaré francs in 1929, 4.7 billion in 1936, 3.6 billion in 1938. Only manufactured products remained constant. Conversely, colonial exports to France increased by 30 percent during the same period from 1929 to 1938. The trade deficit with the colonies did not stop growing.[74]

Clearly: "salvation through the Empire" was a myth. The French people couldn't fail noticing that buying from the colonies was to buy goods that were twice as expensive"[75]

Yet even if the Empire was a commercial burden, it appeared to be a source of strength with some justification in providing soldiers, bases, space and opportunities for youth. Hitler's long-standing colonial demands—but pressing too hard for them—and those Mussolini unleashed at the end of 1938[76] drew the attention of many circles. The issue in the end came down to whether we should agree to fight for the Empire's integrity. Shouldn't we concede some territory to appease Germany? This was the position of radical deputy Jean Piot, who wrote in the radical daily L'Œuvre. However, a poll of its readers showed that 102,671, or 57 percent, rejected that concession while 79,884 accepted it. Among those who were ready to "renounce" were well-known politicians such as Anatole de Monzie, Pierre-Etienne Flandin, and Adrien Marquet. In Barrages a small pacifist magazine, Ageron wrote this priceless line: "I refuse to believe that there could be a Parliament criminal enough to start a world war engulfing Europe to keep a few hundred budget eaters alive on a sandy earth full of crocodiles." New polling techniques and the creation of IFOP indicated a stiffening of French public opinion.

Answers to the question: "Do you believe Germany should be given colonies?"

	Yes	No	Don't Know
October 1938	59	33	8

If the question was narrowed to *giving back* the old German colonies under French mandate, the answer at the end of December 1938 (following the November 30 Italian demands and the wave of indignation they brought with them) was completely different:

	Yes	No	Don't know
December 1938	22	70	8

And in February 1939:

	Yes	No	Don't know
February 1939	28	67	2

The response to Italian demands as well was:

	Yes	No	Don't know
February 1939	6	89	5

It must be pointed out that attachment to the Empire was stronger among youth under age 30 and older people over 60; 53 percent of the French people at the same date felt that the colonial Empire was France—which indicated considerable progress since 1930, according to Ageron. But regarding the fateful question, "Are you ready to fight rather than give up any one of our colonial possessions?", the answer was:

Yes	No	Don't know
40	44	16

The issue took the shape of a vast "Eurafrica," a dream from the 1920s. Ageron[77] indicates the book *Réforme de la France* published by the group called "of July 9" (1934) that included Jules Romains, Alfred Fabre-Luce, Paul Marion, Louis Vallon, and Pierre-Olivier Lapie. The idea was to distract the Europeans away from their border disputes to offer them "economic fusion" with North and West Africa.

But these generous ideas couldn't stop the rise of fascism. The "renouncers" used them in their schemes to appease Germany, thinking that Hitler would renounce the conquests of *Lebensraum* if he were offered free access to colonial raw materials. This plan was not coming exclusively from President Roosevelt, who turned it into one of the main ingredients of his policy between 1937 and 1939. Some men on the moderate left in France, such as Albert Sarraut, Charles Spinasse, André Philip (a socialist member of Parliament), Paul Rivet (president of the *Comité des intellectuels anti-fascistes*), René Belin (deputy secretary general of the CGT), Gaston Bergery (founder of the frontist movement), Anatole de Monzie, some right-wing pacifists attracted to Dr. Schacht, and men such as Robert Delavignette, the director of the *École Coloniale*,[78] continued to hatch plans for Eurafrica as Nazi officials would periodically bring up, without seeing any kind of urgency, the idea that Germany had a "right" to have colonies. On March 3, 1939, the French government offered to create "Franco-German consortiums" in Morocco, Guinea, and Cameroon.

All such projects were meaningless. Hitler did want Europe and even Africa but not that way.

Chapter VIII

ELUSIVE SECURITY

E veryone in France wanted security. The tragedy was that a victorious France of the early 1920s created *two contradictory security systems*. The first was the brainchild of diplomats, with the help of Foch, who spent most of his time at inter-allied organizations and was thus separated from the French army. The vigorous impetus of Philippe Berthelot and a few others instituted, beyond collective security, a system of Eastern alliances and an alliance with Belgium, which was the only area where armies could maneuver since the border between France and Germany wasn't suited for lightning attacks because of the Rhine and the hills of Lorraine.

The second system belonged to the military headed by Pétain. "To that skeptical and pedestrian mind, the entire pre-1914 thinking was wrong; no more panache, swagger, or enthusiasm for vast abstract concepts. We must remain focused on recent experience and practical problems. Everything must be based on technique and be tied to tactics... Experience taught him that continuous and fortified fronts are essential... Therefore the defensive posture will be the queen of war."[1]

On one hand there was a vast all-encompassing vision, the necessary *maneuvering* to help the allies in seeking to engage a large number of enemy forces. On the other hand, there was a *defensive* posture preparing a vast mobilization behind a fortified barrier.

Furthermore, defensive security is not completely consistent. Rather than planning for the total fortification of dangerous borders—*including the Belgian frontier*—the choice went to a compromise solution, planning to use Belgium for some type of maneuver. This continued despite the fact that after March 1936 Belgium declared that it no longer wanted that arrangement.[2] The supporters of the defensive school of thought, therefore, did not follow its logical conclusions.

How could such a chasm be allowed between two incompatible views of security? Because of the French army's crushing superiority during the 1920s over the Reichswehr, the issue remained at a distant theoretical level. The 1930s would see the tragic consequences when choices, or at least coordination, was required. Was it because of the laziness of public opinion? Or was it because of the inefficient cooperation between the competent government ministries? Was it due to the weakness and instability of the executive branch? All of these elements certainly played a role at the same time. In this chapter we shall examine the military aspects of the problem.

Tragedies lead to the search for those responsible and the nation's determination to seek revenge. Two of our sources, the Riom trial under Vichy and the parliamentary commission of inquiry after the Liberation, were the results of that unavoidable search. Both efforts show that, besides a few clear-cut cases, responsibility gets diluted and the causes are to be found in greater depth. As early as 1940 the great historian Marc Bloch had discovered as much. "In a nation no professional group can be held solely responsible for its actions…The military staff worked with the instruments the country had provided. They lived in a psychological climate that was not entirely of their making. They were the products of the human circles they came from and what the French community allowed them to become. Therefore, having shown according to his experience, what he thought were the faults of our military command and the part they played in our defeat, a fair-minded person can't stop there without creating an impression of treason."[3]

A key book by General Tournoux, *Défense des frontières*, would unravel later on the mechanism between the military command, the executive branch and Parliament, and between Parliament and the entire nation.

1.

THE DOCTRINE

In addressing the *Société d'histoire moderne*, General Beaufre characterized French military doctrine, which had remained unchanged between
the two wars, as a "non-strategy." What he meant was that strategic thinking was a constant evaluation of what was in the balance, the means
available and the risks involved. The absence of a goal—France was a
"satisfied" country—and the elimination of risk led French military plan-
ners to focus exclusively on the means; to accumulate the means to a
single end, to achieve security through a defensive strategy.

As early as August 1914 hundreds of thousands of soldiers wearing
red pants had experienced in their flesh what one of them, Lieutenant de
Gaulle, wrote about in his notebook: "nothing can oppose all-powerful
fire-power."[4] Trench warfare seemed to be the ultimate form of combat,
leading to the study and testing of the "method," meaning the conditions
required for a breakthrough in the density of artillery shells, deployment
of units, etc. The great originator of the "method" was General Pétain,
commander in chief of French troops from May 1917. He provided a
vivid demonstration in October 1917 during the limited offensive of the
Malmaison, inflicting greater losses on the enemy with reduced French
losses and taking a small portion of the Chemin des Dames, a long pla-
teau located south of Laon in a west to east direction. Of course, it could
also be argued that by replacing the "method" with "surprise," General
Ludendorff had successfully broken through the Italian lines at Caporetto.
Furthermore, by using the same tactics on May 27, 1918, his troops had
wiped out the entire Chemin des Dames in two hours. The importance
the young American army gave to *open warfare*—a war of movement—
and the little regard it showed for its French instructors who were teaching *trench warfare* should have also been noticed. The example of Foch
and his "butting blows," resembling those of his opponent Ludendorff,
should have been examined.

Yet, immediately following the war, the French were obsessed by the
trenches. To replace those open trenches that were dirty, muddy and dangerous with comfortable fortifications, built of thick slabs of concrete
covering one's head, was something everyone wanted. The "French wall"
and the "continuous front" became part of the national vocabulary starting in 1920, as well as the "inviolability of the territory," implying a string

of fortifications along the border. Those were the ideas of Marshall Pétain, who as vice president of the Supreme War Council was head of the French army until 1931. They were shared by General Buat, the chief of staff.

Neither Marshal Foch, who wanted France's line of defense to be on the Rhine, nor Marshal Joffre, who wanted a defense in depth, could get their views adopted. However, General Guillaumat, in command of French occupation troops in Germany, did his best to fight the Pétain system. "The French wall is a dream, financially speaking, and is perhaps dangerous from the military point of view. It could lead to subordinating any war plan…to the existing or planned fortification. It's better to build a strong army that can take the offensive. What money is left over, if any, would then be used to organize fortifications as a home base."[5]

Debeney replaced Buat (who died in 1923) until 1929 and was close to Guillaumat's views but focused on reductions in military service, damaging to his main idea of the "nation at arms."[6]

A sort of compromise was worked out between the two positions by the Commission for Border Defense, created on December 31, 1925; the northeastern border with Germany was to be fortified. For the Belgian border the secret military agreement of September 1920 appeared to be fundamental because it allowed taking action into Belgian territory. A number of "mobile fortification parks" would back up that move in the non-fortified zone. The Ardennes, located between the non-fortified and the fortified zones, were considered impenetrable and were intended as the "destruction zone."

Paul Painlevé, who was minister of war, almost uninterruptedly from November 1925 to November 1929, and a strong backer of Pétain, whom he had appointed in 1917. He liked the defensive approach and fortifications. It was on his initiative that studies of fortifications for the northeastern areas were ordered. His successor, André Maginot—a war veteran—however, introduced the law to build a wall that was then called the "Maginot Line" passed on January 14, 1930.[7] It should be pointed out that the legislation was obviously connected to the decision made in the summer of 1929 to evacuate most of the Rhineland early on. Even though facing the future line was the entire thick expanse of the Rhineland demilitarized zone, there were no longer any French soldiers on the other side of the border. Taking advance precautions was a good idea since construction would be expensive and slow.

The French worked on the Maginot Line uninterruptedly from 1930 to 1939.[8] The initial funds of 2,900 million francs voted by Parliament were quickly used up. A law of July 6, 1934, authorized 1,275 million francs for 1934 and 1935. The workforce was made up in part by North African regiments. As of January 1, 1936, the system was sufficiently advanced for the Commission for the Defense of the Borders, now called "Commission for the Organization of Fortified Areas," to be disbanded.[9] It was high time; two months later German troops were to arrive on that same border to dig in and begin building fortifications on their side.

The creation of a fortified line does not imply that a country's strategy should be *defensive*. It can be viewed as a base from which a powerful and rapid army group could attack the enemy. But at a time of tightened budgets[10] and soon of less numerous classes of conscripts, how could France pay for concrete and mechanized weapons? That was Guillaumat's forecast. The Maginot Line also required permanent troops or "fortress units," thereby reducing the number of soldiers available for mobile forces. But there was above everything else the "deployment doctrine." This originated in a fundamental document, the IGU—the temporary instruction on the engagement of large units—dated October 6, 1921, and by and large Pétain's inspiration.[11]

The IGU begins with ever increasing firepower. Therefore defensive units must also be increased. The war will actually require the mobilization of huge masses prepared through universal conscription. Regular army units with reduced manpower—"the cover"—were to protect the massive call-up or prevent that of the enemy. A progressively more solid defensive front was set up and that was the location from where the counteroffensive would begin later on. The offensive was therefore postponed until that time. Something not considered during peacetime planning, as Michalon and Vernet noted,[12] "The idea of a rapid movement beyond the borders with a small number of units but armed with modern weapons, didn't seem to appear...*within official military thinking.*"

On August 12, 1936, the temporary IGU was replaced with new instructions, repeating the same ideas stating that fifteen years later "the body of doctrine set by eminent leaders following the victory must remain the charter for the deployment of large units." Technical progress, the revolution of the combustion engine that some unofficial theorists demonstrated effectively were viewed by established authorities as "not changing the basic existing rules from a tactical stand point."[13]

In a noteworthy study published in 1976, General Vial[14] compared the IGU to the equivalent document of the German military, also dated 1921, the *Führung und Gefecht der verbundenen Waffen* (FuG). It also concluded—

who wouldn't have?—that superior firepower was essential and wanted to use it for movement and battlefield action. As Vial states, the IGU's "cautionary approach" became a "vigorous approach" in the German document. To the French "grinding strategy," the Germans opposed an "annihilation strategy." In 1921 they could be bold in their theories since their forces had been greatly reduced by the treaty and couldn't stop the French army. But be it national character or the influence of the authors, they immediately decided to go beyond the First World War. Pétain did not want to do that. His successors, Weygand then Gamelin, felt that there was no need to do so either; Weygand because he was saddled with financial and manpower shortages; and Gamelin no doubt out of respect for authority and a propensity toward compromise. French doctrine would remain unchanged in 1939–1940. All France had to do was hold out until…1941.

After the doctrine we may now examine the *plans*. At this point it was *plan D bis* that was operational since April 15, 1935. Those expecting to find grand strategic and tactical views as in the German "Schlieffen plan" of 1906 or "Overlord," the Anglo-American plan of 1943–1944, will be disappointed. It is only a simple "concentration plan" that puts into application the sacred principles of the IGU.[15]

We shall examine the composition of the army later on—both regular army and reservists—and we have seen the different measures that had been planned in March 1936: alert, reinforced alert and security. We shall only mention the plan's conclusions:

"1. Cover the vital centers near the border;

2. Cover mobilization and concentration operations;

3. Give units being assembled sufficient time to acquire necessary cohesion. Only then *and according to the march of events may we think about improving the situation along the initial defensive front to begin the counter-offensive at the right moment.*"[16]

What was the strategic doctrine of the French air force and navy at the time? Both branches of the service, because of their mobility and rather rapid changes in strength compared to potential adversaries, had specific problems from the strategic standpoint.

The key issue for the air force was its relationship to the ground forces that were all-powerful in the 1920s.[17] The army saw the air force as an extension of its strategy, which meant ensuring the protection of mobilization behind the fortified line that the air force was expected to protect. Marshal Pétain, who had been appointed inspector general of air force defense of the territory in 1931, felt that the Maginot Line was not enough. He concluded that a *defensive* air force was required but readily accepted that it would be independent and under the command of an air force general. Weygand had much more conventional views, and felt that much closer collaboration was required and that, with the exception of a reduced general reserve, the air force should be under the army's command. The army needed a strong air arm for intelligence and reconnaissance, a fighter unit within every army corps and a bomber unit that would closely cooperate in the battle on the ground. The air force was therefore expected to be a *cooperative air force*.

The air force had a grand and much bolder vision of its role. In order to disrupt an enemy air attack, it would need to engage in an air battle "that may require the deployment of all of its available units."[18] This was not intended to be an all-out offensive. The air force did not adopt the famous doctrine of Italian General Douhet who thought victory could be achieved by using only the air force, that bombing the civilian population would break enemy morale. "That manner of waging war cannot be used by us and we refuse to attack the civilian population if only as reprisals. We therefore refuse in advance to seek the decisive outcome through the air force alone." The Spanish Civil War would confirm those views: "The material and moral results of air force bombing either of cities or fortifications have in general been very much inferior to the capabilities used," wrote Captain de Colbert, the military attaché in Lisbon.[19]

The air force chief of staff wanted to convince the Army High Command of the "fundamental nature of the "air battle." If it's lost and the enemy dominates the skies, then he may freely support his ground troops and win the battle. "The ground army troop command must do its utmost to help the air force during that initial battle."[20] The air force therefore stops being an auxiliary arm of the army.

At the time the air force was attempting to secure its independence,[21] but it would succeed only in part. Budget cuts meant cost reductions, so the army and air force agreed to spare the fighter units. But the army was ready to reduce the bomber units (in case of war, civilian aircraft were to be requisitioned as transport planes!). The air force, on the contrary, proposed to reduce reconnaissance units, something the army wanted no part of.

The end result was the worst imaginable compromise: the BCR or air force cruiser, a multiseater plane used as a bomber on combat missions and reconnaissance, that could be engaged either as part of the "general reserve" under the control of the air force or as part of the "cooperative air force" that the army wanted. From a technical point of view, the solution was awful;[22] the aircraft was rated under more specialized planes for each one of its three missions. It should be pointed out that plan 1[23] of air force rearmament calling for building 1,023 planes was limited to prototypes of the years 1928-1930. It planned for 480 fighter planes, 471 bombers (310 of which were BCRs) and 411 reconnaissance planes. It was a victory of sorts for the air force, while the army general staff was very displeased and wanted to create its own air force. In 1937 the ministries of war and the navy requested that air force units be "permanently attributed" to their branch of the military.

Oddly enough, the Navy's doctrine in 1936 was much more "defensive." As Philippe Masson wrote, "At the time of the remilitarization of the Rhineland, the navy's position, even though in a coordinated reaction it enjoyed in principle, the overwhelming superiority of the combined naval forces of France, England and Italy, it was not...any different from that of the army."[24]

The navy's doctrine came from the naval statute of 1924 based on a potential conflict with secondary European navies—namely with Italy as an ally of Germany. It must "ensure the protection of the coast lines, the security of naval communications overseas and with the Empire regarding commercial activity representing two thirds of the trade and amounting to some 32 million tons. The navy was also to protect communications between France and North Africa that in case of war could provide 300,000 troops and as many workers."[25] It was therefore not surprising that Admiral Durand-Viel, navy chief of staff, refused any offensive action in March 1936 such as the blockade of Bremen or Hamburg, the occupation of Heligoland or the capture of German ships. He would rather defend the North Sea and the Channel since the bulk of the British navy was located in the Eastern Mediterranean at the time. This situation, as we shall see, would change greatly in later years.

2.

THE CONDITIONS
OF FRANCE'S ARMED FORCES IN 1936

Regarding ground forces, Plan *D bis* provides an accurate picture of their conditions.[26] The regular army in France included twenty infantry divisions and five cavalry divisions with the fortress troops (equivalent to nine or ten divisions) plus one white colonial division, one North African division stationed in France, and four North African divisions stationed in North Africa.

General mobilization in France, besides the reinforcement of the regular army, would provide "units in formation": seventeen category A divisions; ten category B divisions of "battle worthy class"; eight category B divisions for "secondary missions." The mobile force would produce two white colonial divisions; four North African divisions; and four Senegalese divisions for a total of seventy infantry divisions, five cavalry divisions and the fortress troops. These numbers should be compared to those on November 11, 1918: 109 infantry divisions and eight cavalry divisions. These fortress troops actually absorbed a good portion of troops that could have been maneuvering in the field.

Facing such numbers, according to the *Deuxième Bureau*, Germany at the beginning of 1935 had twenty-one infantry divisions and three cavalry divisions. But since reestablishing conscription on March 16, 1935, it practically reached thirty-six regular army divisions. The kind of troop strength that could be added to the regular army by the paramilitary units used as reservists was not known.

What were the main characteristics of the French army? First of all, it enjoyed unblemished prestige and an unchanged attitude. "New ideas not subjected to the test of fire found only a limited audience."[27] In 1935 the French infantry was still the *queen of battles*, the main weapon that other specialties were meant to support."[28] The main difference with 1914 was the extreme care found in every military school curriculum to spare human lives. Everything seemed to encourage slowness in the infantry. Regulations called for cautious advances, approaching marches, engagement, attack, organization of captured territory, setting up forward positions, resistance positions, secondary positions; nothing had changed since 1918.

"The doctrine requires that we not be seduced by the mirage of generalized motorization." Besides very few motorized units, infantry regiments had no trucks of their own. That was considered "wasteful." They were to be convoyed by regular troop transport units or by requisitioned civilian vehicles. The best option was to proceed on foot, getting everywhere without needing fuel. They were less vulnerable while columns of trucks were so cumbersome. France had many horses and fodder to spare.[29]

The tanks were a natural subdivision of the infantry and there were many light FT-type tanks from...1918, slow and practically blind. The regular tanks being built were the midsize DI model (under 20 tons) that traveled at eight kilometers per hour. Tanks were not part of divisions and were kept as general reserves, given to the divisions as required. It should be pointed out that radios were beginning to be used but they were still heavy and cumbersome in 1940; the infantry preferred the telephone and dispatch riders.

Artillery was strong and very technical. The 75 mm cannon had not yet been replaced by the 105 mm. General Maurin, the great artillery man, had invented a new method to set the range no longer at the battery level but by entire groups called the "central firing position" (later adopted by NATO). It was more reliable, faster and easier to use. But the artillery was still slow with few motorized units, relying mostly on horses to get everywhere. Horses did the job but at a speed of four kilometers per hour.

Thanks to General Weygand who was a cavalryman at heart, there were still 5 cavalry divisions. In 1932 these included one motorized brigade and two brigades on horseback. The first light mechanized division, the D.I.M., was formed in 1935 and motorization increased after that.

This mass of men—some 400,000 in peacetime, 3 million at mobilization—was very precisely organized. It was still meant to handle "the integrity of the territory." It was slow. General Beaufre compared "the young German army" to the "French military machine." The former had felt "the stimulating effects of defeats," while the other suffered from the "extreme stiffness of the state." The Germans were "free from any ties to the past." "Our system of making war was heavy, with large concentrations, seeking the security of a continuous front did not seem attractive to them despite our prestige." They didn't suffer the disadvantages of "our intellectual security."[30]

France still had an advantage of sorts with the *air force*. The estimate by General Christienne and by Buffotot[31] provides the following numbers at the beginning of 1936:

	French air force	Luftwaffe
Fighter planes	350 (217 up to date)	108
Bombers	234 (197 up to date)	612
Reconnaissance	514 (193 up to date)	144
Total	1098 (607 up to date)	864

Fighter plane performance was about the same with the faster French Dewoitine 500-501 going at 360 k. per hour against the Heinkel 51 at 330 k. per hour. But while the best French bomber had a top speed of 310 k. per hour and a range of 1200 k. the new Junkers 86 went 360 k. per hour with a range of 2,000 kilometers. The balance was therefore about to shift.

France's slight superiority was going to disappear but, unfortunately, the persistent blind faith in that advantage would linger until 1937.[32] Specialized publications were disseminating the myth. "Today France has an excellent front line air force despite the contrary opinion of some incompetent and negative critics," wrote *L'Aérophile* in March 1936. In April 1936 *L'Aérophile* felt that the Luftwaffe was clearly inferior (lack of mid-level personnel, quality of the equipment, etc.). In December 1936 the same magazine declared that by the spring of 1938 France would have "the most powerful air force in Europe." For the time being, "it's reassuring to have a magnificent front line air force that was unparalleled in Europe." "Our technology isn't at all behind, far from it," wrote General X in *L'Air*'s December 1, 1937, issue. Pierre Cot said that *L'Aéronautique*, edited by Henri Bouché, was "the only scientific aircraft magazine in France," and that Bouché was the best French specialist in the field of aviation."[33] In 1937 Bouché was critical of "alarmism" regarding our "purported weakness."

Yet on August 20 and 21, 1937, an unfortunate event worried public opinion: the French had been defeated in the Istres-Damascus-Paris race. The worst was that the Savoia 79 bombers of the Italian army were as fast as the French fighter planes.

This didn't stop Pierre Dignac, a member of Parliament who was thought of as a respected specialist, to declare in a speech on December 12, 1937: "The French air force is the best in the world after Russia...the aircraft equipment is worthy of its personnel."[34] What was more serious was that the air ministers fed the illusion. This was understandable coming from Marcel Déat in March 1936.[35] It's much more surprising with Pierre Cot at the December 11, 1937, session of the Chamber[36] (and in his book published in 1939), where one reads statements such as, "according to every expert the French air force has the best crews and military leadership. What's more, the French air force is the only one to have trained and well-instructed reserves."

We shall conclude with Friedenson and Lecuit[37]: "This thinking by the bulk of public opinion until the end of 1937 can be attributed to the chauvinism typical of French nationalism, the memory of France's military air force superiority from 1914 to 1930, the pressure from the aircraft manufacturing industry "lobby," the part played by propaganda to brainwash people's thinking drummed up by a segment of the newspapers since 1914 and the very deep pacifism that encouraged French experts and leaders to reassure public opinion."

No further illusions were possible by 1938. General Armengaud sounded the alarm in a May article in the publication *La Revue militaire générale*.[38] Yet the dispute between the army and the air force continued.

Finally, concerning the *navy*, the French remained far superior to Germany while the Italian navy was just about as large. In early 1936 the French navy included three older refurbished battleships with the *Dunkerque*, whose budget was approved in 1931 and was completed in 1937, and the *Strasbourg*, which was completed in 1939. It had no real aircraft carriers (the *Béarn* was "an experimental ship.") The French 2,500-ton destroyers outclassed the Italian models but were inferior to the German (*Nürnberg* class) and Italian (*Condottiere* class) in light cruisers. The French battleships of the *Lorraine* class were better armed than the three German "pocket battleships" of the *Deutschland* class (14,000 tons) but slower.

The following chart from the article by Philippe Masson[39] illustrates the number of forces in 1936:

	France	Germany	Italy
Line Battleships	3 (plus *Dunkerque* being completed)	3	4
Aircraft carriers	1	—	—
Heavy cruisers	7	—	7
Light cruisers	4	6	10
Destroyer hunters	25	—	10
Destroyers	19	15	20
Submarines	50	19	56

3.

The High Command

The French military machine, while steeped in tradition and extremely stiff,[40] remained very large and ready to play an important part if properly used. From top to bottom those who were in charge—the officers—had a responsibility in the exercise of foreign policy. The army's prestige and the actual or implicit threat it represented in the use of force were permanent factors that took on particular significance at times of danger.

The most important man was the vice-president of the Superior War Council: Pétain up to 1931, then Weygand starting on January 21, 1935, followed by Gamelin. Weygand was chief of the general staff under Pétain and Gamelin had the same position under Weygand. In taking over the top job, Gamelin also remained chief of the general staff. On January 21, 1938, Gamelin was appointed chief of staff of national defense, meaning that he now accumulated authority over the three branches of the military while retaining direct command of the ground forces. Until then he was equal to the other chiefs of staff, the navy (Admiral Durand-Viel was replaced by Admiral Darlan in 1937 who was part of Superior Council of the Marine and had been head of the cabinet of the Minister of Marine at the beginning of the Popular Front), and that of the air force.

The air force, as we have noted, was trying hard to secure its independence from the army. The first move came in 1928 with the creation of the air ministry—over the objections of the army general staff. The first minister, Laurent Eynac, prepared the proposed laws to create an independent "military air force." In August 1931 a Superior Air Council was created—over the objections of General Weygand. Thanks to Pierre Cot (air minister in 1933), the ministry was given more authority. Pierre Cot was the first to use the term "air force," making it official. With the law of July 2, 1934, General Denain, a flyer and Air Minister at the time, organized the "air forces" into four peacetime air regions. There remained, however, a serious constraint. In time of war only the "reserved" forces came under the command of an air force general. The others, the "forces of cooperation" were part of the army and, while they were under the command of a general officer of the air force, he reported to an army general in charge of a specific theater of operations. In other words, at the time of mobilization part of the air force was shifted to the "ground" troops, causing "a complete disorganization of the air force lasting several days."[41]

It must also be pointed out that the DAT (défense aérienne du territoire) reported to the army until 1938. The air force chiefs of staff at this time were General Denain (air minister from February 1934 to January 1936) and General Vuillemin. The newly found autonomy and creation of the Air Ministry as a third cabinet ministry alongside War and Marine, dating back to the Ancien Régime, was followed at the same time by the grouping of all three branches of the armed forces under the single authority of National Defense.

At the government level the first short-lived attempt to create a Ministry of National Defense took place on February 20, 1932, in the Tardieu cabinet which lasted until June. The idea originated with André Maginot in 1931, and became necessary during periods of weak budgets,

> "A whole book would be required—said General de Gugnac—to tell the story of the counterproductive efforts of our ministries that were side by side and didn't know each other. It should be pointed out that the statistical charts of the War ministry had no knowledge of the ones at the Marine ministry; that the calibers used by one branch were never used by the other... As night flights increased, the Air Force studied navigation using the compass and the sextant. Years went by before they thought of asking the Navy about its methods and procedures."[42]

The elections of 1932 brought in Herriot to replace Tardieu and the ministry was eliminated. It did reappear for ten days at the beginning of 1934 in the Daladier cabinet. The Popular Front brought it back to stay in June 1936 with Daladier at the head (his duties were "Minister of National Defense and War," proving that the army was actually superior to the other two branches of the military). Daladier was to hold that position until May 1940.

The Ministry of National Defense in 1932 created two important agencies: the General Secretariat of National Defense and the key High Military Committee. There were also permanent offices to ensure coordination.

The High Military Committee[43] was created in March 1932 and changed its name after the June elections to High Committee in Charge of National Defense Requirements; its chairman was Air Minister Painlevé. In February 1934 the government placed it under the nominal leadership of Prime Minister Doumergue but it actually was under Pétain as Minister of War. The name High Military Committee reappeared on December 11, 1934. Some very powerful leaders were part of the committee: the primem, the ministers of the three branches of the military, the vice presidents of the superior councils of War, Marine and Air, along with the three chiefs of the general staff and the inspector general of the DAT—Pétain at that time. "The High Military Committee examines and coordinates issues that are pertinent to the general organization of the ground troops, the navy and air forces and how these are used, the general armaments programs and the apportionment of funds that are attributed to that particular organization and the relevant programs."

What did it do? At first there was little activity: four meetings from May to July 1932 (with only one that included the uniformed services); two in March 1933; one in October 1933 (only of the uniformed services); one on March 8, 1934. Except for the March 8, 1934, meeting that examined the conditions for disarmament, the issues discussed were generally related to command in wartime, but rivalries between the three branches of the service prevented reaching any decisions.

The decree of December 11, 1934 widened its role and there was at least one meeting per month. Flandin as prime minister consulted with the committee regarding the military implications of diplomatic issues, which meant inviting Foreign Minister Laval, Secretary General Alexis Léger and other top Quai d'Orsay officials. We had noted earlier[44] how the committee examined German rearmament, the issue of an alliance with Italy, the Anschluss and Ethiopia.

The High Military Committee did not meet in an official capacity from September 1935 to April 1936. However, François Piétri, its founder in 1932 and now Minister of Marine made sure it met unofficially every fortnight from September to November 1935 (without Prime Minister Laval.) The consequences of the war in Ethiopia, the stocking of fuel oil, etc., were all examined. The 1936 meetings were also unofficial and focused on the reoccupation of the Rhineland. There were seven meetings from March 8 to April 30. "The various possibilities were examined without ever reaching definite decisions thus remaining undecided and ambivalent reflecting the troubled views of the country's political and military leaders."[45]

As soon as the Popular Front came to power, a decree of June 6, 1936, replaced the High Military Committee with the Permanent Committee of National Defense with a slightly wider membership that included the minister of foreign affairs and the secretary general of the Ministry of Foreign Affairs, Alexis Léger, as well as the secretary general of national defense, Robert Jacomet.

The Permanent Committee met four times in 1936 (the first meeting was on June 26), six times in 1937, twice in 1938 (on March 15 and December 5) and once in 1939 (on February 24). Daladier became prime minister in April 1938 and held only two meetings until the outbreak of the war. Since Daladier was both prime minister and minister of national defense and war, working closely with Gamelin, recently appointed chief of staff of national defense as well as of the army, it may explain why he felt that there was enough coordination around him. Military meetings, especially at the chiefs of staff level, became more frequent.

In 1936 Léon Blum created at a much lower level a "weekly liaison committee" that met at the ministry of foreign affairs, bringing together the director of political affairs and his deputy, with the representatives of the three military staffs and a representative of General Bührer, the colonial chief of staff. The purpose of that meeting was purely informational.

The military machine was coordinating and organizing itself. The results, however, cannot be termed very satisfactory. On one end the system was heavy. If France's military defense coordination required the presence of the prime minister and four other ministers, then this will explain the small number of meetings that took place. Furthermore, the title of Chief of the General Staff of National Defense was only symbolic for Gamelin. The ministers of Marine and Air considered themselves responsible only toward Parliament and tended to "by-pass" Gamelin, much to the satisfaction of their superior officers. More importantly, there was the personality of Daladier—conscientious, hardworking, honest but often hesitant to make a decision,[46] and the character of Gamelin whose other traits need to be examined.

In taking over from Weygand on January 21, 1935, he listened to the many ongoing technical problems and said, "You know I am a strategist."[47] "He wanted to be at the conceptual rather than the practical level... He didn't want to get involved and stoop down to the technicalities of getting things done; he wanted to be seen as an intellectual, who did not condescend to handling details," as Pierre Le Goyet commented.[48]

He had worked with Joffre in the past and wanted to imitate him, not realizing that Joffre's dominant trait was a very strong domineering personal authority, coupled with a clever way of never tolerating potential rivals. But what did Gamelin actually do? He in fact would have liked to be the only commander; but with the kind of "ostentatious humility" of someone "falsely modest,"[49] he never requested the position. He also surrounded himself with men who were almost his equals like General Colson, Major General of the Armies, and General Georges, Deputy Chief of the General Staff (since July 2, 1939). Within the organization of the wartime high command, Gamelin set up four theaters of operations: the Northeast (Georges); the Southeast (Billotte); North Africa (Noguès); and the Middle East (Huntziger and later Weygand). The Northeast included three-fourths of the forces. Gamelin and Georges shared the same GHQ. Which one of the two was in charge? With Joffre it would have taken less than one hour to find out. "Joffre would concentrate, Gamelin scatters and dilutes." Gamelin "felt comfortable when matters were unsettled, vague, in a double command; he relied on his intelligence and flexibility to slip out of the most intractable situations…He sets up the chessboard but lets others take the initiative."[50] This worked well in peacetime, but war reveals weaknesses, demonstrating that decisions cannot be made by committees but by individuals and that, contrary to the thinking of most third raters, men are not interchangeable. The most efficient structures are powerless without true character.

What was the quality of the French officer corps under those top commanders? If we may be allowed to generalize, the commanders were of high quality but uneven; the commanding officers, with a few notable exceptions, were overwhelmed by their task, while the middle ranks were absolutely first class.

To give examples of the first and second points is rather difficult. The men who were leading the armies in 1939–1940—Giraud, Blanchard, Corap,[51] Huntziger, Frère,[52] Billotte, etc.,…were competent and dedicated officers but much too steeped in military doctrine to bypass it. Giraud, the hero of prison escapes, and a leader of men, would play a key role in North Africa; Frère was to become the head of the ORA, the Organization of Resistance of the Army. As a former commandant of the Special Military School at Saint-Cyr, he was also a great leader and later died in a concentration camp. Billotte died in an accident in June 1940 before he could show his talent. Huntziger, who signed the Armistice, became a cabinet minister during the early Vichy period.

Among the colonels of 1937–1939 we must not forget that there were Charles de Gaulle, Alphonse Juin, Jean de Lattre de Tassigny and many other less well-known officers who were also heroic and effective leaders. Yet the accounts of the defeat (of 1940) are replete with embarrassing anecdotes about officers retreating much too fast or even ahead of their men. It was at that level that such incidents occurred. The top officer ranks in 1939 should have included thousands of regular army officers who had been killed as lieutenants between 1914 and 1918.

We do have for both those categories some actual facts provided mostly by General Weygand.

First, since 1911 there existed a "school for Marshals," the nickname of the Center for Higher Military Studies. Every year some forty colonels or generals who were brigade commanders, most of them certified for staff work, were appointed to take a number of theoretical courses and practical exercises. Weygand was commanding the center at the end of the 1920s. He attempted, he said "to fight against conformity, to stimulate the imagination and the willingness to take initiatives, encouraging the development of the personality and character."[53] But he also could see how some participants felt that their stay at the Center was a necessary chore to secure promotion to a higher rank. Since the lowest rank was colonel and that the officer had to have completed his time as a commander, the average age was ten years higher than what it was prior to 1914.

This aging process was also obvious with the generals. Contrary to popular belief, "political" appointments were rare. The vice president of the Superior War Council established an "aptitude list." In three cases during the years Weygand was in charge (1931–1935), the minister appointed officers who were not on the list. Weygand felt that "Marshal Pétain was strangely reluctant to promoting elite officers to the higher ranks."[54] The struggle to bring younger men to the ranks of the army failed. In 1940 French colonels who were closer to 60 were facing German colonels of 40.

There is far more evidence in favor of the third part of my statement regarding the excellence of the younger officers. Many were the sons of middle-class families choosing a military career and being virtually the only ones to graduate from high school through the baccalauréat exam that opened the doors to higher education. The father's example, a patriotic spirit, the deeper influence of the boy scouts, coupled with the economic crisis that plunged many families into a precarious life, encouraged several thousand youths to take the competitive exams for military school and a career that could not provide wealth but did offer financial security and the magnet of adventure—the vast French Empire provided the attraction of the exotic. While the number of openings was reduced from 1,930 to 1,935, they increased sharply right after that date. For the army alone 1,093 new second lieutenants or equivalent rank were recruited in 1932 through competitive entrance exams (including the quartermaster and medical corps, etc.) and only 173 from the ranks. Even the École Polytechnique was basically a reservoir of officers. Out of 250 graduates per year on average, except for the "boot" that provided the engineers required by the state, all the others were sent to the artillery, the engineer corps and even the navy or the air force. Few of them were to choose civilian careers.

The competitive entry examinations were hard. The Écoles admitted one candidate out of five or six (Saint-Cyr) and one out of ten or twelve (Polytechnique, École Navale, École de l'Air created in 1935). The "spirit" of the École was already present in the preparatory schools known as "taupes" (or special math classes) for Polytechnique, and the "corniches" for Saint-Cyr. Public high schools were providing the greater number of candidates by far over the old Jesuit-run École des Postes (which became Sainte-Geneviève in Versailles) that still retained its top rank and prestige.

Most of those young officers undoubtedly belonged to the "right-wing" bourgeoisie but most of them subscribed to the principle that the army did not vote, being "the silent corps."* They felt an emotional hostility to the Popular Front, but the army, after all, was no longer used to breaking up striking workers.

The French army could possible have become "political" enough to support the right wing, but France's captains and lieutenants of the 1930s did not resemble the conspirational and warmongering Japanese officers of the same period. A career officer, Loustanau-Lacau, basically failed in 1938 when he tried to create anti-communist recruitment "cells" in the army called the "Corvignolles network." According to the statements made by that strange character (who stood apart from the CSAR—also known as the "Cagoule," the creation of an engineer Eugène Deloncle, because he refused to view the USSR as an enemy on the same level as Germany), the recruits were mostly reserve officers from his own age group (majors and colonels).

---

* "La grande muette" referred to an army that did not take sides in internal politics. [NDT]

The valor of those young officers became apparent in 1940 and during the campaigns in Tunisia, Italy, southern France, and Alsace, or as leaders of many secret army "maquis" (later known as the ORA). Many of them were to die later in Indochina.

4.

The Heretics

The benefit of hindsight makes it easy to criticize today French military doctrine in the 1930s. Those who were part of that tight pre-war hierarchy required visionary spirit and much courage to voice any kind of criticism, whether it be intellectually by rejecting the "authority principle" and taking a position against some very prestigious leaders, or, more practically, by rejecting the doctrine of the high-ranking officers they reported to. It was hard for any heretics to further their careers inside a Church that upheld infallibility.

While the mission of the famous *École supérieure de guerre*, the traditional institution founded in 1876, was not to elaborate military doctrine, but in very practical terms to train well-rounded staff officers, military thinking only tended to exist within and around it.[55] Many officers wrote about the school in their memoirs, from the odd account by Loustanau-Lacau,[56] who was admitted in 1922 in the 44th class, the same one as Captain de Gaulle,[57] to Colonel Schneider's study, *L'École de guerre des années 30*,[58] and General Renauld's work on the 60th class graduating in 1938.[59] The conclusion offered by the latter was, "despite the dedication and conscientiousness of the school as an institution…[it] had no influence over the evolution—which did not happen in any case—of French military thinking. On the contrary it was dominated by conformity and the influence of the teachings of 1914–1918." General Beaufre, who was admitted to Saint-Cyr in 1921 and entered the *École de guerre* in 1930, also felt that "it was a good secondary staff school occasionally with a few outstanding courses…The emptiness of the school was due to the fact that a very narrow doctrine was taught where tactics…became something akin to an engineer's blueprint…it was technical and comfortable, even reassuring, but fundamentally wrong."[60]

Yet, despite the prestige of the top commander, many officers like Charles de Gaulle or Beaufre benefited from their dissatisfaction. When he joined the army's general staff, Beaufre reported to Captain Zeller, later to become a great resistance fighter and a governor of Paris, who told him, "There is something you must be aware of, my dear friend. Do you know General Gamelin?... Well, General Gamelin is an idiot."[61] And Beaufre found out that "[t]he thing that our commanders were most worried about was the presentation of the paperwork." Depressed and exhausted by useless clashes with the finance ministry, the army high command "had...basically created a form of wisdom out of skepticism and determination... The only force left was inertia."[62]

A few semi-heretics and some greater heretics faced up to that inertia. In the first category we shall place General Estienne, "the father of the tanks," who described in 1921 the "huge strategic and tactical advantage represented by 100,000 men having the capability of covering eighty kilometers in one night fully loaded with weapons and supplies over the heavy armies of the past... They needed 8,000 tanks and 4,000 tracked tanks."[63] According to Ruhlmann,[64] we can also quote General Hering, the sponsor of "the great spaces strategy," and General Flavigny, "father of light mechanized divisions." There was also Captain Mérat, who in 1920 produced a report entitled *Extrapolations*, that Mysyrowicz showed so admirably to be way ahead of its time as to the use of air forces and tanks.[65]

But let us now turn to the two greatest heretics: Charles de Gaulle and Admiral Castex.

De Gaulle had long been Pétain's protégé—Admiral de Gaulle (his son) was named Philippe after the Marshal—but this did not prevent him from having a clear and creative mind. What the two men did have in common was a vast culture, a sense of style and even of majesty. But de Gaulle had read, among others, the British military writer Liddell-Hart and his concept of a "gold medal army" (a small, very powerful and mobile army replacing the large masses of infantry), Colonel Fuller and General Estienne. Pétain had objected to the poor graduating rank of Captain de Gaulle at the *École de Guerre* because of his unconventional ideas and perhaps also due to his arrogant personality. Pétain had compelled the *École de Guerre* to take de Gaulle as a lecturer (resulting in the book de Gaulle published in 1932, entitled *Le Fil de l'épée*).[66] In 1932 Pétain had de Gaulle appointed as secretary of the High Military Committee. For two years de Gaulle sat in on the discussions of the top military leaders—Pétain, Weygand, and Gamelin. During that time he wrote *Vers l'armée de métier*, published in 1934.[67]

It was the era of low military budgets and one-year conscription, when there was uncertainty about the "cover" and France was vulnerable. While the Maginot Line was a big help, it failed to cover the areas where the Germans were thinking of an attack on France: Belgium and the northern French plains where their armies "could easily pick the time and place." Belgium could not be expected to sacrifice itself for France, which must defend herself. Using a defensive strategy? "The passive defender will be surprised, pinned down and turned." If the defender is mobile and prepares for a war based on speed, as the Germans were clearly doing, "he can reach the necessary locations to forestall the unexpected and take the initiative…it is by maneuvering that France will be covered."[68]

An elite unit was required for trhe complicated maneuvering and handling of rapid, powerful equipment; one-year conscription was not enough for training such units. A professional army was therefore required, which was a more reliable system than the massive mobilization of men with very little training. Such an army would number about 100,000, broken down into seven divisions (six heavy and one light) "entirely motorized, tracked and only partially armored." It was therefore possible 1) to act alone in a limited operation consisting of taking territory as a guarantee; and 2) to have a spearhead for the national army that could then occupy the conquered territory. Tanks would open the path for the motorized infantry and mechanized artillery.

The book—which made no mention of the air force—was not intended to be technical. What de Gaulle wanted to provide was "a summation for an action program." was a major in 1927, lieutenant colonel in 1932 and a full colonel in 1938; at the time he was probably not planning to engage in a political career. If he failed to prevail with the military, he could try getting his ideas adopted by the politicians. Most of them backed the Maginot Line and some, like Léon Blum and the majority of the left, viewed the title of the book as a threat to democracy. The fear of fascism increased after February 6, 1934, and political debate was very much involved with the issue of the "Leagues." Was de Gaulle trying to provide a "praetorian guard" to the right-wing agitators?[69] The national union government of Doumergue included Marshal Pétain as minister of war, by now extremely irritated at his former protégé. General Maurin admired and followed Pétain's course as did Fabry, the minister of win the Laval cabinet. When they even had any clue regarding de Gaulle's thinking, the moderates governing France were, for various reasons, just as hostile to the heretic as the left. The openness to his ideas was therefore extremely narrow.

As secretary of the Military High Committee, de Gaulle met Paul-Boncour and had some involvement in the French build-up plan of 1932. Paul-Boncour held him in high esteem but supported collective security and greatly admired the Maginot Line. In the end, de Gaulle decided to approach Paul Reynaud, who had a political future and was himself a heretic since he opposed the politics of deflation and favored devaluation in 1934. He was no doubt a very intelligent man, troubled by the contradiction between diplomacy and strategic doctrine. Doctor Auburtin, a friend of both men, introduced de Gaulle to Reynaud in December 1934.[70] It was the time when the debate regarding the reestablishment of two-year conscription was getting underway. Paul Reynaud, in a speech on March 15, 1935, was critical of the defensive strategy. This led Prime Minister Flandin to call him an "idiot"[71] and elicited a vigorous answer from General Maurin, who also favored a defensive policy but pointed out—it was Weygand's position as well—that circumstances did not favor an overhaul of France's military system.

Paul Reynaud went much further. On March 28, 1935, he introduced a bill "for which General [sic] de Gaulle deserves all the credit," he said,[72] in an attempt to create "an armored corps." He returned to the idea of the 6 armored divisions de Gaulle had planned, including 500 tanks each added to the light mechanized division that was already operational. Pétain, Weygand and Debeney were extremely critical even before the debate got underway. Debeney was in favor of the offensive but with powerful waves of infantry and felt the tanks were too vulnerable. The Chamber rejected the project after a lively debate on December 26, 1935. Paul Reynaud continued to fight, publishing a book entitled *Le problème militaire français* where he spelled out Colonel de Gaulle's ideas.

It was all to be a useless exercise. In 1937 de Gaulle was sent to Metz to take over the command of a tank regiment. His books had been moderately successful. The backers of the defensive strategy, as well as those who favored the classic type of offensive, were against him. Weygand was undoubtedly the closest to his views. On March 1, 1935, Pétain published a widely discussed article in the *Revue des deux mondes* entitled "France's security in the low birth-rate years."[73] "Our national defense must be based on the principle of the nation at arms." The system should not be changed and, in any case, it would be impossible to bring about without enough volunteers to create a professional army. Later on the rift between Pétain and de Gaulle became irreparable. In 1938 de Gaulle published a book that Pétain had asked him to ghost-write in 1922 to be published under his name, entitled *La France et son armée*. dedicated the book to the aging Marshal, who was deeply irritated, and attempted to pressure the publisher, Plon not to sell it.[74]

did not succeed among the journalists either. Rémy Roure who wrote in *Le Temps* under the pseudonym of Pierre Fervacque, was one of his admirers. He met Raymond Cartier at *L'Écho de Paris*. Only *L'Époque*, a newspaper that continued *L'Écho de Paris*, edited by André Pironneau and Henry de Kérillis with Raymond, gave him full support and occasionally published his articles. *L'Action Française*, influenced by Weygand, criticized him politely while it waged an extremely violent campaign against Paul Reynaud.[75] Pertinax introduced de Gaulle to Colonel de Lattre de Tassigny who disapproved of him, and the conversation between the two turned violent.[76]

In the end Gamelin was the main opponent to the ideas of Charles de Gaulle, who had the support of Lieutenant Colonel Perré, head of the tank section, and of infantry headquarters. Because of Gamelin, Daladier was convinced that de Gaulle's ideas were bad and the new "Instruction on the deployment of large units," issued in August 1936, made no mention of the creation of armored divisions in the future or as in the terminology used at the time—"armor-plated."[77]

Admiral Castex failed to reach the pinnacle of history like de Gaulle. Born in 1878, he was twelve years older than the colonel. He was a remarkable strategic philosopher and a prolific writer at a young age, believing that ideas were "ageless, had no rank…and even fewer stars."[78]

For a long time Admiral Castex was part of the navy's historical service and a professor; in 1939 he was in command of one of the most important French naval areas ("Admiral Nord" in Dunkirk). But the navy, which had allowed him to publish what others viewed as pure abominations,[79] transferred him into the reserves in October 1939.

We will simply give a short overview of what he proposed. Castex was convinced that there was necessarily "one" strategy. Therefore, all divisions among the various branches of the service and between the military and the political were absurd. He had no confidence in the French security system. He later wrote, "The French government's war plans before 1940 looked like a long water snake, meaning that many people referred to it but few had ever actually seen it and no one was quite sure that it did, in fact, exist." Admiral Castex's pre-war ideas regarding the preparation of the war of 1939 have been brilliantly summarized in a chapter of *Mélanges Stratégiques*.[80] They clashed head on with the views of the High Command, as well as those of General de Gaulle. Castex felt that the only possible strategy for France and Great Britain against Italy and Germany was a *totally defensive* one. The enemy was, and would remain, stronger; therefore, a long war that could break his will was required. Just like Wellington at Torre Vedras, a powerful "western redoubt" prolonging the Maginot Line to the sea, extending it in depth, had to be created using naval superiority, as well as the vast African expanses, to the maximum. He wanted the same six armored divisions with heavy tanks not for the offensive but only for a defensive strategy and to "take and hold on to territory."

Since only what is defensible can be defended, France would only keep the vast African lands of its Empire. To everyone's amazement, Admiral Castex, at the time of the colonial exhibition in 1931, quietly wrote that Indochina would have to be abandoned: "Who will take Indochina off our hands?" he asked. "It is total wishful thinking to believe we can defend Indochina against the Japanese." France should also, "as soon as possible," get out of Syria and Lebanon by granting them the independence they demanded. "I can already hear the loud outcry berating the solutions I described about our centuries-old interests and our prestige, etc. Actually our interest and prestige are based on the strength of our geo-strategic position and our armed forces. By focusing on the Europe-Africa axis we shall improve both to everyone's benefit."

Chapter IX

THE DIPLOMATIC MACHINE

1.

THE QUAI D'ORSAY

During the 1930s the Ministry of Foreign Affairs[1] was gloriously located at the Quai d'Orsay, near the Seine, one of the focal points of France's prestige. The minister worked at the desk said to have belonged to Vergennes, but other eminent shadows were present as well, those of Théophile Delcassé and, most of all, of Aristide Briand. Not only was there a sculpture at the honor gate commemorating the "Apostle of Peace," but many of his disciples and admirers were in key positions, with the Secretary General, Alexis Léger, overseeing everyone.

And yet this was a thin agency with a small budget that was of little interest to the members of Parliament.

Total personnel in 1935, excluding lower echelon employees and the "chancellery clerks," was 686 for the most part in the two "careers," the prestigious diplomatic career and the lesser consular service. Known as *The Career* par excellence, the diplomatic service shined in a kind of halo. It included only 191 persons, while the consular service reached 398. To these must be added a kind of hybrid group of thirty-three interpreter secretaries for the Middle East and thirty-six for the Far East, six code clerks and one archivist. About 120 out of the 686 employees worked "in the Department," meaning in Paris—according to rather poorly organized rotations. However, the department also used high level specialists who did not belong to either career: finance inspectors, attorneys from the *Conseil d'État*, jurists increasing the number of Paris-based employees—excluding lower level personnel—to about 230 persons. Diplomats were recruited through examinations since 1868 ("the consul students"). During the period we are examining, the "big exam" allowed only a small number of applicants: 12 in 1930, 11 in 1931, 6 in 1932, 5 in 1934, 4 in 1935, 2 in 1936, 7 in 1937, 7 in 1938, 8 in 1939. The numbers for the "little exam" for the consulates were slightly higher.

Examinations were prepared at the *École libre des sciences politiques* in so-called "stables" supervised by young diplomats. History, international law, both public and private, and economic geography played the most important role once the barrier of the language requirements (two foreign languages) was fulfilled. Political economy was virtually nonexistent. In practical terms, but nowhere written into the regulations, the career was in fact reserved for the families of the "notables" of the aristocracy or the high bourgeoisie with a slight advantage to the brothers, sons or nephews of diplomats. An "internship grade," issued by a commission of four high-ranking diplomats grading the manners and appearance of the candidates, weighed greatly on the examination. Such a system could create intolerable favoritism. But that rarely happened. It obviously did favor a "class" recruitment but the exam was very difficult and those who passed had to be highly cultured and with a superior level of knowledge. They were, therefore, at the top of their social class. Because of the exam and the small number of officers, the career was very homogeneous with everyone knowing each other.[2]

It should be said that it included only one woman prior to 1939.

Did such a social selection lead to a narrow policy based exclusively on relationships, avoiding the vital forces and the popular leaders in foreign countries? In many cases, actually, the diplomatic corps of those days became the stuff of caricature. Roger Peyrefitte, who had not yet been expelled from the career during the 1930s, collected a number of anecdotes, that were more or less authentic, in his novel *Les Ambassades*, in a mixture of scandal and ridicule. More critical but with an acid pen, Jacques Baeyens wrote *Au bout du Quai, souvenirs irrespectueux d'un diplomate* (1975). Paul Allard's 1938 book, *Le Quai d'Orsay, son personnel ses rouages, ses dessous*, is very superficial.

The politicians didn't always like the diplomats. Jean Zay was no doubt the harshest critic. While meeting the French minister to Belgrade, de

Dampierre, and hearing him say "there is no public opinion in Yugoslavia," he reached a general conclusion: "What did most of our diplomatic agents abroad know? What was their insight during the fateful years? With a few exceptions these aristocratic individuals, brilliant graduates of the *École des sciences politiques*, were the prisoners of their personal opinions, their prejudices, their secret desires. They avoided any contacts with the people." And he went on to accuse them of being biased, because they disapproved of the republic and even of preferring the local fascists.[3]

What Jean Zay claimed was commonplace, actually appears to have been the exception. After reading thousands of documents, dispatches and telegrams, I am convinced, on the contrary, that French diplomats in those days made a huge effort to be informed about the real situation, including popular and labor reactions to events. In any case, as minister of national education, Jean Zay had few contacts with them. The Popular Front found it unnecessary to either purge anyone or even proceed with "diplomatic rotations" of any consequence. The only two known changes during the period we are covering were that of Paul-Boncour in March 1933 and of Georges Bonnet in October 1938. Both took place for either technical or personal reasons. There was never any trace of conspiracy and French diplomats even silently supporting *L'Action Française* must have been extremely rare.[4] French diplomats are seen working as hard as possible to forge a real alliance between France and the USSR, as well as with fascist Italy.

Those were not the characteristics of a limited and reactionary attitude. Many diplomats would refuse to serve Vichy, at least after November 1942. Many, like René Massigli, Stanislas Ostrorog, Louis de Guiringaud, Armand Bérard, and Jean Chauvel, went to London or Algiers. Many took part in the Resistance. In 1945–1947 few purges would become permanent.[5]

The department's organization chart was rather simple. Around the minister and his cabinet (which always included many diplomats) the secretary general was in charge and handled most matters. Only the *information and press service*, headed by an academic, Pierre Comert until October 1938, and the office of mail and pouches both reported directly to the minister. If we concentrate on the main functions the key department was the Directorate of Political and Commercial Affairs, divided into ten offices or divisions. Beyond the personnel office, headed for a long time by Louis de Robien and whose most famous member was Jean Giraudoux, the inspector general of diplomatic posts; the archives service; the protocol service headed since 1920 by Pierre Becq de Fouquières, a permanent fixture; the office of chancelleries and legal affairs, the office of administrative affairs and international unions; the office of property and private interests.

The division of political and commercial affairs was by far the most interesting. It was divided into four geographic subdivisions: Europe; Asia and Oceania (Pacific); Africa-Levant (including Tunisia, Morocco, Syria, and Lebanon); and America. There were also two functional subdivisions: commercial affairs and the League of Nations, the office of French works overseas that was headed during the entire period by Jean Marx, in effect the original office of cultural relations. Finally, there were the code office, the legal section, headed by Jules Basdevant, a prominent professor of law, and the office of control of foreigners.

The European subdivision was the inner sanctum, handling general affairs and compiling all incoming information, including the incoming reports of the military attachés. There was, therefore, a pyramid of sorts

> Secretary General
> Director of Political and Economic Affairs
> Adjunct Director
> Deputy Director for Europe,

and we found an amazing continuity. Since we have already discussed Léger, we shall concentrate on the other officials.

Paul Bargeton was born in 1882, began his career in the Near East, fought in the war at Salonika and became one of the most important officials at the Quai d'Orsay. He was a Protestant and at the center of a "Protestant clan" of sorts with Massigli, Coulondre, Albert Kamerer, Victor de Lacroix, and, earlier, Jacques Seydoux de Clausonne, whose son François passed the big exam first in his class in 1928. Bargeton would replace Claudel as ambassador to Brussels in 1937.

René Massigli, who later became Commissioner for Foreign Affairs under General de Gaulle, was one of the stronger personalities in the Quai d'Orsay. For many years he held both positions as adjunct director and deputy director for the League of Nations. He was constantly traveling from Paris to Geneva. His memoirs and papers stored at the Quai d'Orsay show his ceaseless activity and a perfect knowledge of the files. Massigli was the main advocate of active resistance to Hitler, and we have seen the initiatives he took in 1936. He was also loyal to the League of

Nations and agreed with Léger on that issue. However, he also disagreed on many other points; he was, for example, less hostile than the secretary general to a rapprochement with Italy. Their disagreement was complete at Munich, leading Bonnet to appoint Massigli as ambassador to Ankara.

There was not only a group of Protestants around Massigli. The backers of the League, especially André de Laboulaye, gave him complete support.

	Secretary General	Director of Political and Economic Affairs	Adjunct Director	Director Deputy for Europe	Deputy
1932	Berthelot	Léger	Lefebvre de Laboulaye	Bargeton	
1933	Berthelot Léger (Feb. 28)	Léger Bargeton (Mar. 24)	Lefebvre de Laboulaye Massigli (Mar. 24) Coulondre (Mar. 24)	Charvériat (Mar. 24)	Rochat
1934	Léger	Bargeton	Massigli Coulondre	Charvériat	Rochat
1935	Léger	Bargeton	Massigli Coulondre	Charvériat	Rochat
1936	Léger	Bargeton	Massigli Coulondre (Jan.-Oct.)	Charvériat	Rochat
1937	Léger	Bargeton Massigli	Massigli Charvériat (Oct.)	Charvériat Rochat (Oct.)	Rochat
1938	Léger	Massigli Charvériat (Oct.)	Charvériat Rochat (Oct.)	Rochat	
1939	Léger	Charvériat	Rochat	Hoppenot	

Emile Charvériat, born in 1880, was one of the rare examples of an official who had practically never left the Department. He was Léger's most loyal follower and not at all close to Massigli. "A conscientious functionary, reliable and loyal to his friends. He adopted all of Léger's views on the issues and even imitated his phraseology."[6] He had "a white face, was completely aloof, saying so little as to remain almost silent," in the end proving to be rather passive.[7]

Charles Rochat, born in 1892, had a much stronger personality. He was also a disciple of Léger and would become his indirect successor as secretary general under Vichy. Armand Bérard penned an excellent portrait of Rochat when Yvon Delbos was minister. "A solid man from Savoy, a bit on the heavy side... Charles Rochat had already been cabinet director of the previous minister and had specialized in that position. He had a perfect knowledge of the files that he kept in impeccable order so that the minister would have the right document instantly in hand, committing the previous ones to memory. He prepared the diplomatic meetings and was on top of his work...(he) had the minister's full confidence as well as that of the secretary general, Alexis Léger. He knew everything, watched over every detail, always moving from his office to the adjoining office of the minister who called him incessantly. He was a born administrator. It was in any case the whole life of that childless man."[8]

Charvériat and Rochat both represented the most solid core of the "Léger team." They were not too favorable to Massigli, friendly to Beneš, opposed Colonel Beck, were anti-Italian and said to be connected to the Freemasons. Henri Hoppenot and Etienne de Croy were its standard-bearers, along with André Ganem, a high official of the League of Nations in the cabinet of Yvon Delbos.

Without an extremely detailed study of the notations on the documents, it is difficult to assess the role played at the various levels between the secretary general and the deputy director for Europe.[9] No doubt Alexis Léger, who did not communicate enough with his deputy directors,[10] was in constant contact with Charvériat and Rochat, whatever position they were holding—their importance was increasing steadily within the hierarchy. Since Rochat had been the cabinet director of men as different as Laval and Delbos while maintaining his regular duties—in 1936–1937 he was also deputy director for Asia—this enhanced the harmony between the administrative services regarding most important matters. Were other issues being neglected? Among Léger's papers we found an eloquent personal letter from Albert Bodard, minister to Ethiopia, dated August 8, 1935—a time when that country was at the center of world attention: "I have been in Ethiopia for the past ten months where I am working heartily. I have still not received a single word of appreciation or encouragement from the Department."[11]

As we have already noted, the Department doesn't at all appear to have been "creative." Its officials understood the world system as set up by the League of Nations perfectly. They appeared overwhelmed by the deep changes Hitler brought to their ways. Only Massigli and his group seemed to be truly aware of the unfolding tragedy.

2.

THE AMBASSADORS

Besides the Vatican Nuncio, there were twelve embassies, forty-six legations and four consulates general in Paris handling diplomatic relations with France. Overseas, France had fourteen embassies and thirteen legations, plus eight consulates general having diplomatic status (as in Bolivia, Ecuador, Saudi Arabia, Yemen, Liberia, Panama, Iraq, Palestine, and Transjordan). A single legation handled all of Central America.

Only those legations located in Austria, Czechoslovakia, Yugoslavia, and Romania really played a key role. The important work was done by the embassies, which were divided into various categories. In Rome the Vatican was a unique case occupied by François Charles-Roux throughout our period. Two embassies were created for the small neighboring countries of Belgium and Switzerland. Two countries in Latin America— Brazil and Argentina—also had embassies. The former Ottoman Empire, now Turkey, kept its traditional embassy, as did Spain. The other embassies were reserved exclusively for the great powers: the United Kingdom, Germany, Italy, the USSR, the United States, Japan, and Poland that was added later.

French ambassadors were prestigious officials. The *Annuaire diplomatique* gave them the title of "excellency." At official ceremonies they wore a sumptuous embroidered uniform and since they represented the president of the Republic himself to foreign countries, protocol gave them theoretical rights of precedence over their own minister. About thirty men occupied these posts from 1932 to 1939. A few, like Alexis Léger, who had the title of ambassador even though he had not left the Department since 1921, and Paul Claudel were among France's literary giants. Ambassadors rarely career diplomats but actually politicians like Henry de Jouvenel, ambassador to Rome in 1933, and Georges Bonnet, ambassador to Washington from 1936 to 1937. No one remained at the same location as long as Camille Barrère (in Rome from 1898 to 1925), Jules Jusserand (in the United States from 1902 to 1924) or Paul Cambon (in Great Britain from 1898 to 1920). The longest stay during our period was André François-Poncet (in Berlin from October 1931 to October 1938). Faster rotations were introduced with the result that Paul Claudel was ambassador to Tokyo (five years), to Washington (seven years) and to Brussels (three years.) Charles Corbin was in Madrid (two years), Brussels (two years) and London (seven years). Jean Herbette was in Moscow for seven years, then in Madrid for five years.

Some of these men played a key role. Besides François-Poncet whom we have already discussed, others also deserve our attention, like Charles Corbin, Léon Noël, Emile Naggiar and Robert Coulondre. While not attempting to draw their "portrait," we can nevertheless show what they had in common and what their individual contribution amounted to.

André François-Poncet, Jean Herbette, and Léon Noël had all entered the diplomatic service rather late in life, having skipped the lower echelons. Herbette was the son of an ambassador and worked as a laboratory technician at the Paris Science University, then as a news reporter. He was picked to go to Moscow in 1924 because of his connections to certain Soviet circles.

Léon Noël was an attorney at the *Conseil d'état* before becoming prefect of the department of Haut-Rhin and later director of the Sûreté générale (the police). He was the director of the cabinet of André Tardieu at the time the latter was both prime minister and minister of foreign affairs in February 1932; the same year he had entered the diplomatic service as minister plenipotentiary heading the French Legation in Prague. He was appointed ambassador to Warsaw on February 15, 1935.

All five belonged to the same generation: Corbin was born in 1881; Naggiar in 1883; Coulondre in 1885; François-Poncet in 1887; and Léon Noël in 1888. They were all, therefore, about fifty years of age—younger than the generals leading the army. Without mentioning Pétain (born in 1856) and Weygand (born in 1867), Gamelin, born in 1872, was nine years older than Corbin and sixteen years older than Léon Noël.

They were all first-class observers of the countries they covered, being particularly interested in getting to know the society of their posting as well as the character of the top leaders. Corbin, a former director of political affairs and "one of our most distinguished and subtle diplomats as well as the best informed...always smartly attired, discreet and not very talkative,"[12] was passionately expecting, with a kind of sad realism, the slow signs of Britain's change toward an attitude of firmness. He carefully analyzed the debates in the House of Commons, the newspapers, at trade-union conventions and even, starting in 1938, the public opinion polls. His distinguished appearance and elegance made him a favorite of the aristocracy, the class of many conservatives in the government.[13] He clearly favored Churchill, Eden, Leo Amery, Duff Cooper, Harold Nicolson, and, above all, Vansittart—all Francophiles. His telegrams contained courteous but stern opinions of the "big four"—Neville Chamberlain, Sir John Simon, Sir Samuel Hoare, and Lord Halifax—who favored *appeasement.* His love of precision led him to dislike the constantly evasive explanations offered by the British. He was very friendly with Vansittart and would get him to discuss confidential matters,[14] speaking with him very openly and not hesitating to be strongly critical of British policy.[15] "Corbin's diplomacy was tenacious beneath a bland surface," as Eden wrote.[16] Franco-British negotiations, as a result, took place mostly in London rather than in Paris. Corbin opposed Munich and the fact that he was not present at the airport when Chamberlain returned was widely noticed.

Corbin's dispatches were not literary pieces such as those from François-Poncet, and while he was a good writer he preferred precision to colorful images. His minister, Councilor Roger Cambon, who was the same age, and the first secretary, Roland de Margerie, who was posted there almost during the entire period we are covering, seconded him very well in London. Corbin was also on good terms with Alexis Léger, even though his personal correspondence was strictly confined to business. He was too discreet to criticize Léger for not being firm enough. The relations between Corbin and Léger could be described the same way Naggiar spoke of his relations with the secretary general: "loyal and critically affectionate."[17]

Before becoming ambassador to the Soviet Union, Emile Naggiar had been consul, then consul general, in the Far East and in Montréal, deputy director for Asia-Pacific, minister plenipotentiary to Belgrade and ambassador to Chiang Kai-Shek. He certainly did not possess the stature of the others, yet his telegrams and reports show a deep understanding of the politics of the Far East and the Soviet Union. He did not attempt to describe Russian society and, in any case, it was virtually impossible for him to travel within a country where France had no consulates. Yet he was very aware of a possible rapprochement between Germany and the USSR.

The younger diplomats didn't think as highly of Robert Coulondre as of François-Poncet, Corbin or Léon Noël. Neither Chauvel[18] nor Armand Bérard[19] in their memoirs seems to have liked him very much. When Chauvel went seeking "advice from experienced colleagues"[20] under Vichy, he turned to Léon Noël, Corbin, Charles-Roux and Ponsot. The strength of Coulondre rested in his ability to predict certain events a long time in advance, for example, the annihilation of Czechoslovakia and the fourth partition of Poland. The mistakes he made—just like anyone else—in his assessments originated mostly from General Didelet, his military attaché in Berlin.[21] The description given by Captain Stehlin, the air attaché, seems closest to the truth: "Robert Coulondre was different from his predecessor in physical appearance and seemed friendlier when you first met him. He looked shy with pleasant smiling eyes in a square face and a high, willful forehead. His moral, intellectual qualities and his compassion were of the same stuff as his predecessor."[22] While François-Poncet wrote broad descriptions where he examined every possible scenario, Coulondre in much less flamboyant prose would limit himself only to one possibility.

As a great servant of the state, he attempted in the USSR to give meaning to the Franco-Soviet alliance and, upon leaving, was well aware that he had failed.[23] In accordance with government policy he at first attempted a rapprochement with Germany. But "very quickly [he] became convinced that matters wouldn't remain frozen in the situation created by the Munich agreements for very long."[24] Coulondre was above all a man who possessed a lot of common sense and a healthy understanding of his German counterparts, who couldn't help being doubtful when Gamelin told him that the French army was very powerful or when Daladier said that Gamelin and Georges were "admirable leaders." Having been deputy political director of economic affairs (Massigli was in charge of the political side), he was a good observer of the German economy. Like Léon Noël, he tried to keep informed regarding France's power and was also disappointed by the weakness or even the mythical character of the information he was given.[25] As Léon Noël wrote, "At that time—and the other French representatives around the world were in the same situation—I was far from knowing…the true extent of disarray within our army, navy and air force... Our High Command and the government itself had worked at keeping up the illusions that permeated French public opinion... Under the pretense of providing overseas propaganda we were being misled as well regarding the true situation of our armaments."[26]

After serving as minister to Prague, where he had excellent relations with Eduard Beneš, Léon Noël was appointed to a difficult position at a delicate moment in 1935. The low esteem Corbin showed for Sir John Simon or Samuel Hoare reflected only on their policies and was not at all personal. In Warsaw, however, Noël had to deal with the strange and tortuous Colonel Beck who took an instant dislike to him.[27] Naturally, he worked incessantly toward improving Franco-Polish relations. He quickly understood the abyss existing between Polish public opinion, largely pro-French, and the pro-German policies of the leadership, which he thought were insane. After Munich he suggested something of a weakening of the alliance, seeking to remove its "automatic" character.[28] He did not believe in a real alliance with the Soviets. Léon Noël, said de Monzie, was "a paragon of diplomatic virtue... He observes to a maximum and recommends a minimum. He doesn't get mixed up in the debates of the restless city."[29]

Léon Noël had tolerable relations with Laval and Flandin[30] whom he did not find very dedicated; they were good with Léon Blum and acceptable with Yvon Delbos.[31] They deteriorated with Georges Bonnet in 1938–1939. As for Léger "and his clan,"[32] he thoroughly disapproved of their policies. The worst would be that at a crucial moment in the spring of 1939, he was kept in the dark about negotiations in Paris between Bonnet and the Polish ambassador and between Gamelin and Polish military leaders. He did not hesitate to complain loudly in his telegrams about those happenings.

The impression one gathers in closing this quick survey is that the Quai d'Orsay produced some excellent ambassadors, eager to accumulate a wealth of information, having a mind of their own who would not depart from their assignments that involved recommending solutions and who kept their personal views strictly in tune with the policies of their state, while being expert at handling their local teams of diplomats and attachés.

However, one may legitimately ask whether the Quai d'Orsay and the minister of foreign affairs in particular always knew how best to use them. This was in part related to the minister's relations with his envoys. We have seen in several cases, for example, with Naggiar, Coulondre and Léon Noël that there was a serious lack of communication regarding negotiations taking place in Paris. François-Poncet would complain from Rome of being "by-passed" by a mission that Georges Bonnet entrusted to Paul Baudoin. He repeated his criticism—Coulondre would complain about it as well—regarding the contacts of pro-German journalist Fernand de Brinon and the Nazi leadership.

Whether it was Laval, whose world view was rather superficial; Delbos, who was hypnotized by a limited number of issues; or Bonnet, whose vision was much broader but who liked to use complicated and secretive methods, the proposals and plans offered by the ambassadors do not appear to have been followed. As for relations with the Quai d'Orsay, these would seem to have been better when Massigli acted as a counterweight to Léger, in a manner of speaking. Once the latter succeeded in removing his "rival" and in replacing him with the men of his "clan"—Charvériat and Rochat—relations became more difficult with the exception of Corbin, whose style was less confrontational than that of Naggiar or Léon Noël, and less authoritarian than François-Poncet. Massigli, a graduate of the École Normale Supérieure, was on a first-name basis with his fellow graduate François-Poncet. Léon Noël had nothing but praise for Massigli who was "always candid and insightful."[33]

3.

THE SPECIALIZED ATTACHÉS

French embassies and legations overseas also had a number of attachés, along with the ambassadors or the ministers and their specifically diplomatic staff. In 1935 there were thirty-four commercial attachés, twenty-six military attachés, ten naval attachés, eleven air force attachés and three or four financial attachés. The distribution was not the same everywhere. Sometimes one military attaché covered several countries, which was also the case of the commercial attachés.

We shall not go into the detail of the work of the commercial attachés, which was mostly of a technical nature. During the period we are examining financial attachés were posted only in New York (Emmanuel Mönick from 1930 to 1934), London (Jacques Rueff from 1930 to 1936, then Emmanuel Mönick), Berlin and Rome (Roumillac).

They reported to the director of the *Mouvement général des fonds* at the Ministry of Finance (Wilfrid Baumgartner from 1935 to 1937; Jacques Rueff was appointed director general in April 1937).

Jacques Rueff wrote a very lively memoir of his experience as a financial attaché in London,[34] where he was living when the world economic crisis began and of necessity became extremely active. He was at the same time "the representative of the French treasury to the British treasury" and an observer of economic and financial matters "in a financial market that still was then—like Washington today—the first in the world." He administered the sterling accounts of the French treasury, maintaining excellent relations with London bankers and managed to have a "trusting collaboration" with the controller of the treasury Sir Frederick Leith-Ross, and his deputy, Sir David Waley, "his fraternal friends," as he called them. He gave many lectures on economic subjects, was friendly with Keynes, led many missions to other foreign countries and prepared the big conferences, especially those of Lausanne in 1932 and London in 1933. Rueff shuttled constantly between London and Paris in an old Air France two-engine plane with an aluminum fuselage. Because of his expertise—this was also the case of Emmanuel Mönick—the financial attaché to London had a decisive influence over France's general policies.

Mönick, Rueff and Baumgartner were younger men playing a more important role than their minister in monetary and international financial matters. We have described some facets of their work and shall examine them once more later on.

The mission of the attachés of the three branches of the military[35] was basically to gather so-called "open" information about the countries they were responsible for. At times they also had officers of the intelligence service as "adjunct" attachés.

In 1935 there were twenty-six military attachés. Beyond their mission as representatives, they were also supposed to provide information while they were forbidden from engaging in any espionage. They were always supposed to submit their reports to the ambassador. The army, navy and air force attachés (these were created in 1920 and called *air attachés* starting in 1932) worked independently from one another but were supposed to share their information. Adjunct attachés could not gather confidential information about the countries they were accredited to but worked on neighboring countries. The only well-known example was that of Captain Stehlin in Berlin, showing how easily that rule could be ignored with the connivance of the country itself. They were only supposed to inform the military attaché of the "general content" of information they gathered and sent back to the general staff in sealed envelopes in the diplomatic pouch. One of these attachés was Major Fustier, who was ordered out of Belgium in 1939.

The attachés themselves are of greater interest for our purposes. Their correspondence was addressed to the minister of their branch of the military. A copy was very often sent, however, to the Quai d'Orsay. While specifically focused on military forces, they often widened their observations to politics, social issues, and local economics, and it is very useful to compare their cables and reports to those of the ambassador who, in any case, was aware of their content. They generally had excellent relations with the ambassador and had an ongoing and even daily working relationship.

How were they recruited? Except in the smaller countries, they were generally at the lieutenant colonel rank and all of them had seen action in the First World War. As staff officers they had attended the *École Supérieure de Guerre* and sometimes for the very high positions were graduates of the Center for High Military Studies. They were theoretically expected to have excellent language fluency and experience of foreign countries. This could be acquired through inter-allied commission work or as liaison officers with foreign armies. For example, General Parisot, military attaché to Italy from 1933 to 1937, had been sent to the Piave front in 1917. He had learned the language and been on the staff of the Duke of Aosta. General Lelong, military attaché in London from 1936 to 1939, had spent time with Gamelin in Brazil. An odd case was that of General Renondeau, military attaché in Tokyo until 1928 after having served in a Japanese regiment for one year and becoming a distinguished Japan specialist. He was posted in Berlin (from 1935 to 1938), where he quickly mastered German. Major de La Forest-Divonne (adjunct attaché in Germany in 1935 and later attaché in Switzerland) had an Austrian mother. Captain Stehlin, originally from Alsace, was completely bilingual.

These officers would often rotate from one assignment to the next and once they had put in time as colonels in a command, they ended their military careers in these very special postings. Others went on to distinguished military careers after starting out as young adjunct attachés (Generals Bethouart, Mast, Ganeval, and Stehlin).

Appointments to secondary posts didn't seem to follow any strict rules. There were more graduates of Saint-Cyr than of Polytechnique. Sophistication, appearance, and social relations could play a major role. Appointments were carefully examined both for the most important allied or neighboring countries (Great Britain, Belgium, Switzerland) the doubtful countries (USSR) or potential enemies (Germany, and Italy since 1936).

A few examples: Lieutenant-Colonel de La Forest-Divonne[36] provided some very specific information regarding the Swiss army. He had an excellent relationship with corps commander Colonel Borel, head of the infantry and a dedicated Francophile (he had studied at the École Supérieure de Guerre), La Forest-Divonne feared that a pro-German officer, Colonel Wille, would be appointed to head the Swiss army. Actually it would be Colonel Guisan. From his observation post in Bern he was in the right spot to gather information about Germany.[37] He also obtained intelligence on the Spanish Civil War, the Communist political movements and even the USSR. He was also concerned with a possible Nazi attack on France through Switzerland and was able[38] to carry out unofficial negotiations with the Swiss general staff from 1936 to 1939.

From London General Lelong kept Paris informed in detail of the progress made by the British army. His relations with his British counterparts, Generals Lord Ismay, Ironside, and Gort, were excellent.[39] He often discussed with them the conscription issue, which would only be implemented in April 1939, and he played a decisive role, starting in February 1939, in preparing for the smooth functioning of the French-English military conversations where he successfully created a positive atmosphere of comradeship and trust.[40]

In Italy General Parisot "didn't confine himself to the simple role of observer and representative. He tried to play a key part in Franco-Italian relations, taking advantage of his "vague" instructions."[41] During the time of rapprochement in 1934–1935, he took advantage of his good relations with Marshal Badoglio whom he had met when he was on the staff of General Diaz in 1917. He thought of him as being "an outstanding man who consistently behaved in an extremely correct manner towards me."[42] Parisot, as a practicing Catholic, organized veteran pilgrimages to Rome. He attended maneuvers and took part in military meetings in 1935. He predicted the Ethiopian expedition as early as October 1934 and explained to the government the contradiction between the rapprochement policy and this new threat.

For three years (1934–1937) his assistant, Captain Catoire, kept a very important diary that described in detail the different "impressions" emanating from military circles in Rome. He was opposed to the Duce's "militaristic and warrior spirit" and little by little witnessed the deteriorating relationship. On April 2, 1936, while the French embassy still believed it could keep Italy in the anti-Hitler camp, he noted "[t]heir common interests at this time will draw Italy and German fatefully closer to one another." He could also see that Ambassador de Chambrun "had been kept unbelievably in the dark about the situation since March 7."

At the same time Captain Stehlin met a group of Italian officers in Berlin by accident in a bar and found out some key information allowing him to convince François-Poncet that the two dictators were drawing closer together. We have already mentioned that incident.[43] Therefore military informers did precede diplomatic reporting on occasion.

The Berlin team was quite outstanding, at least up to the fall of 1938. General Renondeau, the aeronautical engineer Léon Poincaré and, starting in 1937, Air Force Colonel de Geffrier were excellent specialists, progressively following the build-up of the Wehrmacht and the Luftwaffe. And then there was Stehlin, who had the advantage of speaking the language and of having been very well trained as an intelligence officer. His personal charm with women also led him to having several affairs and to forming friendships with his counterparts; Ambassador François-Poncet was "like a father" to him after a difficult beginning; as were German Air Force Generals Bodenschatz, Udet and Marshal Göring. A strange affair took place between Stehlin and one of Göring's sisters, Olga Riegle. He became a friend of the family and as much as we may surmise—at least this was Stehlin's own impression[44]—Göring was pleased to pass on a number of real intelligence items that actually made a considerable impression and contributed to demoralize the French even more. The high point was reached during General Vuillemin's visit to Germany in August 1938. Meanwhile, Stehlin was flying in German military planes and was on very friendly terms with many officers as he sent a lot of intelligence back to Paris—which was duly ignored—about the revolutionary air and ground tactics adopted by the Germans. "It was our duty to inform as completely, precisely and objectively as we could. We never once tried to alarm the French High Command."[45]

They may have tried to avoid alarming them, but not to minimize the acquired German strength. Once General Didelet, replaced Renondeau in December 1938 the opposite was to happen. Didelet who didn't understand German well enough, offered the idea of a "German bluff" for a long time and the fact that it would be impossible for Hitler to wage war in the west before 1942. Didelet was a deeply honest man but also stubborn and self-assured, managing at times to convince his ambassador, Gamelin and the government that his views were correct. In this sense the mistaken analysis—which the *Deuxième Bureau* attempted to correct as best it could—may have influenced the course of events.[46]

The best information about countries far removed often originated with the military attaché. Colonel Lombard in the United States was carefully following the issues of aircraft purchases[47] and the revisions to the Neutrality Act.[48] He felt that "public opinion in general supported the sale of arms and ordnance to the democratic countries."[49] In Argentina, Uruguay, Brazil, and Peru, military attachés were closely following German political, cultural, ideological and economic penetration.[50] Faced with Axis propaganda, a naval officer requested some strong action: "Don't just always send us Cécile Sorel."[51]

The adjunct military attaché Lieutenant Guillermaz, a future Chinese specialist, provided very precise information from China. He offered the best explanation about the interruption in Japanese offensive operations in 1938, the failure of Japanese negotiations with Chiang Kai-Shek, the Kuomintang's terrorism, the beginnings of the attempt to form a pro-Japanese government by Wang Chin-Wei, and the importance of the Burma Road, opened in December 1938.[52]

We shall also mention the effectiveness and reliability of the information provided by men like Colonel Mendras, and even more by General Palasse[53] in Moscow or like General d'Arbonneau and his successor General Musse in Poland, on who was in constant contact with General Stashiewicz, the chief of staff, and often with General Smigly-Rydz; Musse would play an important role with Léon Noël in August 1939.[54] He was very much opposed to the Soviets and felt that "for many Poles the Russian threat was greater than the one from Germany." "In the USSR today there is no energy...anyone with any authority who stands out is eliminated."[55] The air force attaché in Moscow, Luguet, felt on the contrary that the regime was "entirely solid," the army "very strong" and that the economic potential was "very great." But he said, "The USSR will probably attempt to avoid a land war."[56] General Palasse was pessimistic about the Red Army in April 1938[57] and on June 13, 1939, sent an important report analyzing Russia's war potential where he confirmed his conclusions but felt that the weakness due to the purge was only temporary. His impression was that of "a well led army, disciplined and well trained... I therefore think that the USSR can play a key role in the balance of peaceful forces we are trying to put together in Europe."[58]

* * * *

In attempting a rapid assessment of the work done by the "diplomatic machine" we reach the following conclusions:

1. There is no real evidence of serious "human errors" as such. The personnel of the department and the embassies did not attempt to alter what they felt was the truth to please anyone. Not only were there no serious mistakes but French observers, whether diplomats or attachés, were mostly well informed and objective. If they made mistakes they were willing to admit to them;

2. The behavior of the diplomatic corps, staffed mostly with high society "notables," did enjoy a relatively luxurious social life, but this did not prevent them from attributing a lot of importance to the reactions of other social classes and groups in the population at large. Even though most of them were "on the right" or moderate radicals, the diplomats did not alter either their reporting methods or their assessments when the government was "left-wing." They acted as servants of the state and applied the policies of the government in power;

3. Yet the system often broke down. Communications between the department and overseas posts, and the ceaseless flow of dispatches and cables was often poorly managed. Who was reading the various documents? Who was responsible when an ambassador in a foreign country was not informed about negotiations that concerned him? Since there wasn't a single service at the Quai d'Orsay similar to the *Deuxième Bureau* of the Army General Staff to classify incoming information and reach a conclusion, wasn't there a sense of drift? One gathers the impression that communication among some offices and the minister's cabinet was far from perfect;

4. In the end, however, the biggest shortcoming of the system was the lack of liaison between diplomacy and the army. We have already seen as did Paul Reynaud or General Beaufre, that there was a discrepancy between the alliance system and defensive strategy. Why wasn't this discussed more? Why didn't the matter receive greater attention

when ambassadors and military men expressed their concern? Actually, besides occasional meetings, liaison took place either at too high a level—within the cabinet—or too low—since the summer of 1936 during the weekly meeting at the Quai d'Orsay or too rarely—at the High Military Committee and later the Permanent Committee of National Defense.

Establishing better coordination was a government matter related to parliamentary oversight. But, after all, the French people had the government and parliament they had chosen.

Chapter X

THE POPULAR FRONT

1936-1937

The elections of April 26 and May 3, 1936, returned a strong majority of the alliance of the Communists (72 deputies), the SFIO Socialists (146 deputies) and the Radical-Socialists (115 deputies), with a few additional smaller groups—USR, Jeune République—and a smaller minority of independent Radicals (45 deputies.) There were therefore 378 deputies belonging to the Front versus 236 from the moderate opposition.[1]

The major unrest taking place at election time, with strikes and workers occupying the factories from the elections until June 12, 1936, along with expectations of deep social reforms, contributed to driving France inward and overshadowed foreign policy for a time. The situation was serious, however: the Rhineland was now under German control, Italy was victorious in Ethiopia, and both events had undermined France's prestige. "The landscape was littered with ruins," as Pierre Renouvin was to write.[2]

Events—such as the civil war in Spain—were to quickly awaken the attention of a public opinion that was, for the time being, completely absorbed with its own affairs.

The June 23 foreign policy debate would not give way to a reappraisal. "Commitment to peace," "collective security," "limitation of armaments," "there is nothing in this program that is any different from the usual ideas."[3]

Yet the new man in charge, Léon Blum, was anything but an ordinary politician. He was 64 years old, like Édouard Herriot, highly cultured and similarly moved by strong passions. The resemblance, however, stops there. Herriot liked to appear as a crumpled bon vivant, something that Léon Blum, who dressed with quiet elegance and had a touch of the artist about him—Lavallière tie and large brimmed hats—found distasteful. Herriot was always a crowd pleaser who spoke from the heart. Léon Blum was no less deeply passionate but kept his feelings under tighter control. His low voice prevented him from being an orator like Briand. But the audience listened intently and everything he said sounded impressive. His written speeches are far better than those of the more "eloquent" orators.

Only right-wing extremists and—depending upon the tactical moment—the Communists denied that he was intelligent, generous and honest.

Above all, he was simultaneously competent and a visionary. As André Blumel, his cabinet chief, said, "Léon Blum was not just a politician, he was also a writer, a novelist, a journalist, a short story writer, a literary critic and a civil law jurist."[4] We should also add that he had a great awareness of economic issues compared to his contemporaries. His economic policy was not, as Jean Marcel Jeanneney wrote, "the result of improvisations nor due to circumstance but rather the application of a doctrine that had been thought through over a long period of time."[5] He would change his views "while the left in 1936 knew very little about crisis therapy."[6] During the second Blum cabinet, March–April 1938, thanks to Georges Boris, he had become acquainted with the thinking of John Maynard Keynes.[7]

Like Doumergue in 1934, Léon Blum was prime minister without holding any other additional ministry. "He was a man," wrote Blumel, "who was used to working alone very quickly and he would seek out many opinions and ask for a lot of advice but then reached his own decisions."[8] André Blumel, Jules Moch, the secretary general in the prime minister's office (later replaced by Yves Chataigneau), the historian Jean Maurain, Oreste Rosenfeld, the editor-in-chief of *Le Populaire*, the historian Charles-André Julien, and a few others helped "spare him a number of unnecessary meetings."[9]

This made it possible for him to focus on the issues. Ch.-A. Julien said, "He was very authoritative," possessing great "enthusiasm" and the "need to act...to create...to work," but he was also "full of scruples." "He would never have done anything he felt was contrary to the law and to rectitude."[10]

These memoirs of his close aides, appropriately collected in the volume *Léon Blum chef de gouvernement*,[11] makes our search for other more distant and doubtful testimony unnecessary.

Yet in many areas, but especially in foreign policy, the Popular Front experience produced rather meager results. No doubt terrible events will defeat the best of men but the historian must examine all the facets of the issue, including personal circumstances.

There was a weakness in Léon Blum. The visionary doesn't appear to have displayed sound judgment. We have already quoted several writings concerning Hitler's probable rise to power, the need for unilateral disarmament, the illusion that Germany could be given "equal rights" and thus prevent it—without the use of force—from actually reaching parity in armaments, and others that make it doubtful he could overcome his own illusions. The "dreamer" was much more attractive than the cynic but he did make some dangerous mistakes.

Blum undoubtedly wished to put Herriot in charge of the Quai d'Orsay. He met with him on May 19 but Herriot turned down the offer, preferring his position as President of the Chamber of Deputies; in any case, Herriot was not enthusiastic about the Popular Front. Paul-Boncour, as a dissident of the Socialist Party, could not be considered— nor Daladier, Chautemps or Georges Bonnet (who was to be appointed ambassador to Washington in January 1937) were to Blum's liking. The balancing of the cabinet required a Radical. Blum finally decided on Yvon Delbos, a less experienced man but with strong opinions, one of his friends and a neighbor (they both lived in the same building on the Île Saint-Louis), a man whose docility he could predict, elected to Parliament from the Dordogne, and a graduate of the École Normale Superieure with an advanced degree in literature.[12] Pierre Viénot, a former leader of Franco-German rapprochement became Under Secretary of State for Foreign Affairs, particularly in charge of the protectorates and the Middle East mandates.

Delbos was a hard working loyalist, certainly no imaginative visionary. In examining his dedication or the limits of his imagination, two contradictory and converging conclusions may be reached—that of

Armand Bérard, who was on Pierre Viénot's staff, and that of Delbos himself: "diligent worker, devoid of any prejudice, dispassionate, except when it came to republican principles, he was nevertheless capable of great obstinacy..." "A loyal partner, Léon Blum seeking to control French policy and our initiatives overseas found in him a loyal collaborator, and an associate who would not undertake anything important without consulting him."[13]

This is what Léon Noël had to say: "A mediocre personality, a good man but without character and lacking authority who remained at Foreign Affairs for two years. An old-fashioned Radical, somewhat a sectarian ideologue, who furthermore acquiesced with docility to the recommendations of Alexis Léger..."[14]

We shall allow events themselves to draw the conclusions to these descriptions.

1.

A TIMID BEGINNING

Public opinion understood during the first few weeks of the new government that it should not expect any spectacular changes.

With a socialist at the helm, a member of the party that was more resolutely opposed to Mussolini, one could have expected that France's position toward Italy would have stiffened. Italy had just completed its conquest of Ethiopia, at least in principle, and the king of Italy was proclaimed emperor of Ethiopia on May 9. Clearly "annexation didn't automatically resolve all of Italy's problems. She had to station several hundreds of thousands of men in Ethiopia and its financial and economic problems were just beginning."[15] But the coincidence of that "dizzying" success and the victory of the Popular Front in France prompted the coming together of Italy and Germany, resulting in October in the formation of the Rome-Berlin Axis. The air force attaché in Berlin, Captain Stehlin, was the first to discover this rapprochement when by chance he met an Italian general, who was head of operations of the air force, wearing civilian clothes in the lobby of the Eden Hotel in the company of several officers and Major von Donat, head of the French section of the Luftwaffe intelligence branch. We have already mentioned that incident,[16] indicating how sincere and objective Ambassador

François-Poncet was in his analysis. Stehlin places that meeting at the end of April. It actually took place on May 28,[17] just a few days before the announced formation of the Léon Blum government. François-Poncet wrote on May 16: "The collaboration of those two fascisms is more likely now than their opposition to one another." He felt the chance event of May 28 to be "troubling." According to the political section as of May 11 and 12, Mussolini was still telling Count Coudenhove-Kalergi of "his preference for a policy of open and frank collaboration with France."[18] Everything changed in the middle of May. Ambassador de Chambrun, in Rome, noted on June 5 "the possibility of a German-Italian combination was becoming likely." Journalist Bertrand de Jouvenel also met with Mussolini on June 3 and, while the Duce praised the merits of a Franco-Italian understanding he no longer believed that it could be achieved. "The head of the Italian government feels that the new French government is made up of men who are his adversaries. On the other hand under the present circumstances he doubts French power. The recent factory occupations in particular had made a strong impression on him." In other words, de Jouvenel was "pessimistic."[19]

Italy was threatening to leave the League of Nations if sanctions were not lifted, and appeared less eager to oppose the Anschluss (as indicated by its support of a German-Austrian agreement signed on July 11). Two issues, therefore, faced the new minister Yvon Delbos: Should sanctions be lifted? Should France recognize the conquest of Ethiopia?

Regarding the first issue, being debated in Geneva and with the British since the end of April, France could only follow England. The latter indicated "it resigned itself to accepting the existing situation."[20] Delbos felt that France could not take the initiative but was "ready to approve any suggestion coming from the British government." British leaders Eden and Vansittart wished to announce as of June 27 that they had the approval of the French government. Corbin felt "there was an advantage to affirming Franco-British cooperation so that it would progressively come to be accepted by that country."[21]

Italy was to obtain what it wanted. Mussolini handed the Ministry of Foreign Affairs, which he was running himself, to his son-in-law, Count Ciano, who was known to be pro-German. Countess Edda Ciano, visiting Germany, received a very warm welcome by Hitler and Goebbels. Ambassador Attolico "appeared to be completely dedicated to Italo-German rapprochement."[22] The League of Nations assembly decided to suspend sanctions against Italy on July 4. This was no reason for celebration for Léon Blum and Yvon Delbos. On June 23, Blum at the Senate and Delbos at the Chamber of Deputies read the government's foreign policy declaration affirming the principle of collective security and their faith in the League of Nations.

There was no immediate requirement for France to recognize the conquest of Ethiopia if not for the problem of the embassy in Rome. Léger disliked Charles de Chambrun and succeeded in getting Delbos to retire him as of October 31, 1936.[23] His successor would have to be accredited to "the King of Italy and Emperor of Ethiopia." The Popular Front government, using the pretense that this implied an indirect recognition, refused to send the designated successor, Count de Saint-Quentin, who was Deputy Director of Africa and Levant at the Quai d'Orsay. France would maintain this position for two years as it was represented by its chargé d'affaires at the embassy, Councilor Jules Blondel.

Relations with Germany did not fare any better. It was decided not to attempt to correct any of the negative consequences of the remilitarization of the Rhineland.

The military drew some conclusions. In a memorandum written by Gamelin after consulting the members of the Superior War Council, as well as Marshals Pétain and Franchet d'Esperey, Gamelin[24] proved—which was easy enough—that "Germany's military power had continued to increase." But he added, "this increased power has not yet given the German army clear cut superiority." Gamelin assumed that in case of a German aggression, British, Czechoslovak, and Belgian forces would certainly participate. On May 15 Franco-Belgian military talks were held in Gamelin's office.[25] It would all depend on the Belgians' "call." "The Belgians will have to call us as soon as possible. The French vanguard will immediately respond and other forces will follow. We will fight together on the Albert Canal; its defense is a common Franco-Belgian safeguard." The issue is therefore to find out what the Belgians would do. In his June report Gamelin showed that beyond England, Czechoslovakia, and Belgium, France's "fundamental interest" of *"from the single perspective of the equilibrium of the land forces"* implied *"keeping our military agreements with Italy and consolidating the Franco-Polish alliance."* A few days later, on June 26 the new organization Blum had created (by a decree of June 6, 1936) known as Permanent Committee of National Defense met under the chairmanship of Edouard Daladier. Blum was present at the meeting.[26] "The general plans of national defense," said Daladier, "are a governmental matter." The "main point" was that "France had a defensive policy." All issues were discussed, especially that of the considerable effort required to increase the air force.

Daladier appeared before the army commission of the Chamber on July 1 to speak very candidly about "the precise inventory of the situation." He pointed out that Germany had an army of 500,000, men soon to become 650,000, and was making a huge effort to add new equipment. He said, "Germany was building its army on the idea of a war of movement." France had 20 divisions. "Since we have a fortified barrier we have deployed our mechanized elements in the form of general reserves." Daladier very judiciously deplored that linear form of defense. He would have preferred a scaled defense and far more armaments at every level, especially mechanized cannon. "I know that the French army is very much attached to tradition. It has nevertheless made a considerable effort at motorization." If Italy remained neutral, Daladier felt confident: "We have the capability of preventing the invasion of the territory."[27]

This was all rather optimistic. However, a note written on June 30 by the director of political affairs, Bargeton, was not. It showed that France did not really have an alliance with Yugoslavia and Romania; that the treaties with Poland and Czechoslovakia were "unlimited as to providing assistance but limited on the contrary as to the countries against whom the assistance would be directed," and that the treaty with the USSR was still unclear. There was a lack of coordination among those treaties. "Among the five countries having a treaty of "alliance" with France, few consider each other as allies. Weakness is not the only result of the current situation; it also concentrates any action taken against peace on France."[28]

How could France get out of that bad situation? By detecting the signs of a German attack in Austria, Danzig, and elsewhere. That was the focus of the activity of François-Poncet, Léon Noël and Puaux, in particular.

Wouldn't it be possible to take further steps and try for a "western agreement" with Germany? François-Poncet felt that the Germans would agree to it.[29] The best way to make a favorable impression was to begin with fair play and take part in the Berlin Olympics scheduled for August.[30]

A law passed in June 1934 had appropriated just over 4 million francs in four installments to prepare for the games. Various anti-fascist movements, including the Communist Party, were against France's participation in what appeared to be a coming glorification of Nazism. But sports leaders and Count de Baillet-Latour, the president of the International Olympic Committee, which had secured the participation of non-Aryans, supported sending French athletes. France had taken part in the Winter Games at Garmisch-Partenkirchen but the coup of March 7, 1936, took place immediately after. What would the Popular Front do?

It solved the problem on July 6, 1936, by approving funding for the Games of the General Sports Federation of Workers, scheduled to take place in Barcelona but interrupted by the Spanish civil war.

François-Poncet finally did attend the "grandiose" opening ceremony of the Games on August 1. It was to be a huge German propaganda success. In front of 120,000 spectators in the world's largest stadium built for the occasion, the Führer "really looked like a victor at the peak of his glory." The only saving grace was that the German audience warmly cheered the French team,[31] a rather meager consolation. The Germans won the most medals, even ahead of the Americans, 38 to 24...and 7 for France. Pierre Gaxotte wrote: "The Berlin Olympics end in a triumph. But where are the French? Without bicycle racing and weight lifting no one would hear about us... We look very poor in international competitions."[32] And L'Humanité concluded: "Sports were used in Berlin but they were not well served."[33]

The issue of the Olympics seemed unimportant only on the surface. In fact, they touched a much wider audience than the broadest and most visible diplomatic initiatives. Nevertheless, in its relations with Germany, the government had to explore every opportunity to reach an agreement. The first possibility was a renewal of Locarno with German participation. Despite initial misgivings, Anthony Eden accepted a meeting of the three western Locarno powers—France, Belgium, and Great Britain, but without Italy—on July 23 in London. This meeting came after that of March 19[34] and the conversations were based on the British communiqués of July 17 and 20,[35] outlining the task "to find the best way to ensure peace in Europe through a general agreement." The goal was to negotiate a new agreement replacing Locarno. Italy and Germany would be asked to participate, once the scope of the discussions could be broadened.

Léon Blum took advantage of those discussions to voice his worries to Baldwin, Eden, and Halifax, representing the British cabinet, and to the Belgian ministers Van Zeeland and Spaak. "The deep conviction on the part of the Prime Minister was that a Franco-German agreement, even though it might be guaranteed by Great Britain and Italy, would not be sufficient to avert any danger of war in Europe." He therefore was hoping for "a general peace agreement."[36] The London meeting was useless. Despite many efforts, Germany rejected any such negotiations.[37]

Therefore, direct Franco-German negotiations would be attempted. The go-between was the famous economics minister and governor of the Reichsbank, Dr. Hjalmar Schacht. Much more than Hitler, Schacht showed an interest in German colonial demands. He was hoping in any case for Germany to return somehow to the free market, an issue about which he would be consistently disappointed. It was not certain that Schacht was in fact being a faithful interpreter of Hitler himself. On August 3 Schacht hosted a luncheon in honor of Emile Labeyrie, the governor of the Bank of France, and on August 25 he traveled to Paris.[38] Was it a polite gesture or "the starting point of a long-term political initiative?" He wanted to meet with Blum, Delbos, Auriol, Chautemps, Daladier, and Bastid. François-Poncet recommended that talk with him "in depth and very openly."[39] In the meantime, on August 24 Germany decided to lengthen conscription, bringing the German army from 500,000 to 700,000 men.[40] "The day will come," commented François-Poncet, "when Germany will have to choose between war and bankruptcy." This was a source of worry for Schacht.

The meeting between Blum and Schacht took place on the morning of August 28.[41] Schacht had met with Hitler before leaving. "He approves of the general thrust of my statements...you should understand that Chancellor Hitler is a man of genius." Blum explained his views to his guest regarding a "general agreement" and why he preferred naming it so rather than bilateral agreements (such as the German-Polish or German-Austrian agreements). Blum admitted that an anti-fascist ideology did exist in France: "I am not just French, I am a Marxist and I am Jewish." He pointed out that the Germans were anti-Communist and opposed to the League of Nations. Why not get rid of ideologies? The Franco-Soviet alliance was tied to German rearmament, just as the Franco-Russian alliance of 1893. In order to reach an agreement, Blum did not reject out of hand a discussion about the colonies. Why not have an immediate three-way negotiation between Germany, France and Great Britain? Schacht agreed but said "I must report our conversation and be sure that the Chancellor approves..." Blum replied, "I ardently hope we can succeed."[42]

There was not to be any such success. During a discussion between Blum and Eden in Paris on September 20, 1936, the French prime minister described his conversation with Schacht to the British.[43] Hitler's position, clearly favoring autarchy as stated at the Nuremberg party rally in September,[44] appeared to exclude Schacht's attempts to reach a measure of economic liberalization.[45] François-Poncet met with Schacht on October 3 and found him "disappointed and worried." His personal credibility, wrote the ambassador, was undergoing "a new period of crisis."[46] Jean Aris, the financial attaché, also shared this view and reported that Hitler scolded Schacht about "the vanity of his Franco-German conversations." He had not even predicted the devaluation of the French franc. Göring had just been granted powers as "economic dictator"[47] by a decree dated October 18.[48] Any idea of direct Franco-German negotiations vanished. At that time as well, the king of the Belgians announced that Belgium from now on would ensure its own defense—and France therefore should not expect it to open up its territory unless it were attacked. There was also the Rome-Berlin agreement, which Mussolini described as being not a diaphragm but an axis. François-Poncet concluded on November 10[49] that it was best not to pursue the Locarno-type discussion.

2.

THE BEGINNING OF NON-INTERVENTION IN SPAIN

Léon Blum was unlucky. On July 17, six weeks after forming the Popular Front government, Spain was rocked by a military coup. The friendly regime of the "Frente Popular," resulting from the February elections, was under attack from Morocco and inside Spain by a military revolt that, customarily, was seeking a rapid seizure of power. For many reasons that we shall not detail here, the coup led by Generals Sanjurjo and Franco became a long civil war lasting almost three years.

Logically, the French Popular Front was inclined to help its Spanish counterpart,[50] based on political sympathies, many personal friendships and quite simply international law, which did not forbid delivering arms to a legitimate government. That was Léon Blum's initial reaction. As early as July 20, following a request from the Spanish government, Léon Blum promised Spain's chargé d'affaires, that airplanes, guns and ammunition would be delivered. A Franco-Spanish agreement of December 1935 had set aside 20 million francs for such an occurrence. On the 21st

Blum informed Delbos, Daladier and Air Minister Pierre Cot. Fernando de Los Rios, a special envoy of the Spanish government, was responsible for drawing up the list of goods to be purchased.

As early as July 22 a few right-wing newspapers discussed French intervention in the war but then limited their comments to arms shipments. They objected, arguing that it would further weaken national defense. Furthermore, would this not encourage Hitler into sending arms to the "nationalists"?

Blum and Delbos, as we know, were in London on July 23 and returned on the evening of the 24th. In London Blum told Pertinax, a journalist at *L'Écho de Paris*, that he wanted to ship arms to Spain and told Eden as well.

Everything changed on the 24th and 25th. Spanish envoy Fernando de Los Rios took part in a meeting of several ministers at Blum's private residence. Pierre Cot was in favor of making the shipments. Delbos was against it. He did not want the 25 Potez airplanes promised to Spain to be delivered by French pilots. The council of ministers met on the afternoon of July 25. What decisions did it take?[51] François-Poncet reported that in Berlin "it was being implied that should France back Moscow's side in Spain it would be taking a serious step."[52] The political affairs section of the Quai d'Orsay feared that the fascist countries might be driven into recognizing the rebel government.[53] On July 23 Delbos informed Auriol that French customs had to stop war supplies from being shipped into Spain. He informed Herbette,[54] the French ambassador to Madrid, of this decision taken at "a cabinet meeting on July 25." Only civilian airplanes supplied by private industry to the Spanish government would be authorized. On July 30 Blum and Delbos declared to the foreign affairs committee of the Senate that no armaments were being supplied to Spain. Delbos did so again at the Chamber on July 31. They were both congratulated.

Yet the matter came up again on August 1. There was news of Italian planes on their way to Spanish Morocco. Two of them were forced to land on July 30 in French Morocco[55] (it was thought for a long time that they had orders to fly before July 17, which would have been proof of Italian collusion. We now know that this was not the case). Therefore, following a meeting of the council of ministers on the evening of August 1, the French government decided to resume its deliveries but the ambassadors in London and Rome were asked to propose to the two governments a common non-intervention policy to avoid the creation of any "power blocs." Seventeen Dewoitine airplanes were actually shipped between August 5 and August 8. The objective was to exert pressure on Italy and Germany soon after.[56]

The British agreed as early as August 4 but on condition that the Germans, Italians and Portuguese do the same.[57] Delbos doggedly pursued the issue from then on. The German response appeared to be positive but only if the USSR took part in the planned agreement.[58] On August 5 Admiral Darlan went to London for a meeting with Admiral Chatfield. Darlan feared Italian plans for the Balearic Islands and German plans regarding the Canary Islands. The British admiral was worried. Why had Darlan taken such a trip rather than go through diplomatic channels? It would seem that Darlan had acted mostly on his own initiative. He would do so on various occasions later on.[59]

The USSR agreed to the principle of non-intervention on August 6.[60] Ciano replied that he also agreed, with some reservations, on the same day.[61]

France then changed its position for the third time. Following a council of ministers meeting during the night of August 8 to 9, France returned to a tougher version of its July 27 position whereby even the exportation of civilian aircraft was prohibited. This position was to be firm, except if the non-intervention agreement was signed quickly.[62]

On August 15 the French proposal became a Franco-British plan and on September 8 the International Control Commission held its first meeting in London. Germany, Italy, the USSR, France, Great Britain—twenty-five countries in all—agreed to the principle of non-intervention, which was detrimental to the legitimate government of Spain. Three more countries, including Portugal, joined later on.

By mid-October since the non-intervention agreement failed to prevent the totalitarian countries—Italy and Germany to Franco and the USSR to the loyalists—from shipping weapons and "volunteers" (for the USSR the Comintern set up the International Brigades), France then began a form of "relaxed non-intervention."[63] By delivering spare parts and some weapons through Mexico, France was able to reduce the disadvantages of the system for the beleaguered loyalists. However, the alibi of the "security curtain" had been created.

We shall examine the effects of this policy on public opinion further ahead. It remains to be explained how Léon Blum, "torn and anguished" as his son described him,[64] ended up accepting a policy that was contrary to his feelings. Pierre Renouvin's previously mentioned study examines the issue very thoroughly.

First of all there was the resistance of the right—which was against Blum on almost every issue—but also from parts of his own majority. The top representative of the radicals was the minister of foreign affairs, Yvon Delbos. Within the cabinet Chautemps, Paul Bastid and Daladier were also opposed. Outside the government important public figures such as Jules Jeanneney, the president of the Senate, and Edouard Herriot the president of the Chamber, were also opposed. Among the socialists Spinasse, Paul Faure, Jardiller, Rivière, and Bedouce favored non-intervention. Backing the shipment of arms to Spain within the cabinet were the socialists Vincent Auriol, minister of finance; Roger Salengro, minister of the interior; Marius Moutet, minister of colonies; Georges Monnet and Lebas; among the radicals Pierre Cot, Jean Zay, Gaston Violette and Gasnier-Duparc.[65] The non-interventionists were the most vocal. To pursue the delivery of weapons would most probably lead to the break-up of the first Popular Front government after just two months in office and in the midst of deep social change. A torn Léon Blum thought of resigning but then decided against it.

The second factor had to do with British influence. The first non-intervention decision was taken after a trip to London. In official discussions with the British on July 23, Spain was never even mentioned. On the other hand, there were private conversations on the issue. Blum and his entire staff sensed the lack of enthusiasm displayed by the British Tories in power towards the Spanish Frente Popular. Léon Blum sought and maintained excellent relations with the British. It was difficult to "take the lead" without British support in helping the Republicans in Madrid. The idea of non-intervention, therefore, seems to have originated *from the French side*, but quickly gained the wholehearted support of the British.

During his deposition to the Parliamentary Commission of Inquiry in 1945,[66] Léon Blum underscored the dangers of a general conflict which the opposing parties could have started by intervening on opposite sides in Spain. From war by proxy through the Spaniards to a direct war there seemed to be a very short step indeed. That at least was what Léon Blum seriously believed. The excitement in France during the summer of 1936, the March 7 incident and the recent end of the war in Ethiopia should all be kept in mind.

A final explanation, weaker in a sense than the others may be possible. Did Blum fear a possible civil war in France in the event he openly took sides in foreign policy? But even in times of great stress the French could not be compared to the Spaniards. Since December 2, 1851, the military *coup d'état* was not part of France's heritage. The possibility cannot be entirely dismissed even though it has been rarely considered in this context.

3.

THE GREAT DEVALUATION AND THE LESSER ONES[67]

During its first weeks in office the Popular Front made its mark through great social reforms—the forty-hour law, paid vacations, the Matignon agreements with a significant increase in salaries, collective bargaining laws etc. Even though purchasing power had increased, industrial production decreased (using 1929 as an index of 100, it reached 87 in May and 81 in September). Unemployment was also increasing. By September 1936 there were 34,000 more unemployed than in September 1935. Retail prices increased by 5.5 percent from May to September (1936), while the balance of payments improved slightly because of the slowdown in industrial imports. Gold on hand at the Bank of France went from 62.8 billion in April to 52.6 billion in September. The difference between French and foreign prices continued to increase.[68]

All this obviously had an impact on foreign affairs. As Paul Reynaud stated as early as June 1934, there was only one possible cure: devaluation. Opposition to the idea had been weakening since 1935. Emmanuel Mönick found that financial experts in New York and in London were advising France to devalue, as was Horace Finaly, the director general of the Banque de Paris et des Pays-Bas.[69] Emmanuel Mönick, the financial attaché in London, "should be credited with having persuaded the Prime Minister of the need for a devaluation of the franc."[70] Blum met with Mönick following Herriot's recommendation. He made the case for two possible solutions: to either hold the level of the franc like Germany, but then isolating it on the open market through autarchy and foreign exchange controls ("In the race with Germany it would be inevitably defeated") or "enter the fray in agreement and with the support of the other two western democracies, Great Britain and the United States... France could then tap into all the international resources required for its activity and rearmament. However, the unavoidable condition would be the alignment of the franc on the dollar and the pound sterling."[71]

Blum answered, "I'm told that a devaluation of the franc will automatically bring about countermeasures from England and the United States." Mönick replied, "I am absolutely convinced that the opposite is true." Blum then asked him to sound out the British, since he was the financial attaché in London. However, Mönick thoroughly understood how things worked between London and Washington, where he had also served as financial attaché. The British would first consult the Americans. "We would be wasting time by starting with Great Britain. We also lose an opportunity to make our case in the best possible light with President Roosevelt. I know the President of the United States well enough to believe that he will say "yes"; and once President Roosevelt has said "yes" the British government cannot say "no.""[72]

After thinking it over for a week, Blum, who in the meantime had formed his cabinet, decided to send Mönick to Washington. To keep it completely secret, it was rumored that he was "going on vacation near his old posting."[73] In the United States he met with Roosevelt and Treasury Secretary Henry Morgenthau, Jr., and by mid-June he had secured their agreement in principle. Back in London he met with Neville Chamberlain, chancellor of the exchequer, who also agreed. The discussion continued when Blum traveled to England on July 23. Blum was still hesitating. But Mönick knew that he could bring some pressure to bear on the prime minister. His reports were decrypted directly by Wilfrid Baumgartner, director of the *Mouvement general des fonds*.[74] Later on Jacques Rueff, who was deputy director since 1934, would also become aware of those reports. Rueff replaced Baumgartner in April 1937 when the latter became director of the treasury. The president of the Republic, Albert Lebrun, had a copy of those cables. Jules Moch, the secretary general of the cabinet, was informed, but not his closest staff.[75]

The delay in Léon Blum's decision was due to that summer's activity, the social legislation being passed and the Spanish civil war. On the other hand, a law was enacted on August 11 allowing for the nationalization of war-related industries (it would be applied in part to the aeronautics factories). A four-year plan for national defense was adopted on September 7, increasing the funding allocated immediately from 9 to 14 billion francs. With these escalating expenditures the financial situation remained critical. The "wall of money" once again was opposing a left-wing government. Finance Minister Vincent Auriol appealed to those who controlled floating capital funds on June 23, asking them to buy treasury bonds. However, the capitalists, anticipating a devaluation, pre-ferred to invest in foreign currency. On August 10 Emile Labeyrie, the new governor of the Bank of France who favored a government-con-trolled economy and foreign exchange controls, requested that Vincent Auriol scrutinize the gold funds that had been withdrawn.[76] In a speech at Muret on August 22, Auriol denounced the "cheaters" and gave them until September 4 to repatriate their capital funds. He announced publicly that he would not accept the alignment of the franc on the pound sterling.

The decision was made on September 8 following the flight of gold at a meeting in Vincent Auriol's office, which included Baumgartner, Rueff, Mönick and the American financial attaché Cochran. A note was drafted, requesting "a real economic and monetary peace" from London and Washington. The value of the franc was to be set at a new level reflecting world pricing. "The final objective of the contracting parties was the re-turn to the international gold-standard."[77] While the Anglo-Saxons ap-proved of the devaluation of the franc they were not ready to reestablish a vast "gold-bloc" around the new franc. On September 10 Morgenthau made a proposal to Auriol for a simple "declaration" showing British and American commitment to helping the franc. He didn't want a more in-volved statement nor a fixed exchange rate. These were the same posi-tions at the failed London conference of 1933. Chamberlain responded only on September 14 and also rejected limiting his freedom of action to a formal agreement.

Blum, Auriol and their staff were disappointed. On September 16 they at least considered that the "statement" be a joint one signed by Roosevelt and Morgenthau, Baldwin and Chamberlain, Blum and Auriol. They encountered a British-American refusal to mention a potential par-ity with gold. The Americans would only go so far as to accept a de facto stabilization of the three currencies. On September 19 Roosevelt agreed to the joint statement on that basis. Chamberlain also agreed after a call from Blum at midnight of the 23rd.[78] It was made public on the 25th at 8 p.m. It took two days to set up the technical requirements: a French devaluation between 24 and 32 percent and a British-American commit-ment of an exchange rate of 5 dollars to one pound sterling. Measures were to be established to defend the exchange rates. "It's not an exag-geration to say that the September 25 statement was the first step toward European economic reconstruction...wasn't the inclusion of the United States in an inter-European debate the guarantee of a return to the mid-1930s coordination between the United States and Europe?"[79]

The currency law of October 1, 1936, put an end to the Poincaré franc. The franc was no longer measured as being 65.6 milligrams of gold but was now between 43 and 49 milligrams. Private negotiations on gold transactions were forbidden unless specifically authorized by the Bank of France. This meant the end of convertibility. Any private citizen owning more than 200 grams of gold had to declare them to the Bank. Finally, a stabilization fund of 10 billion francs for foreign exchange was created (partly from the excess created by the reevaluation of the gold entries held by the Bank of France).[80] Public opinion, used to viewing devaluation as bankruptcy, was extremely critical of that law.

Devaluation came very late and followed a whole series of statements by Vincent Auriol asserting it would not take place. It paved the way for "extraordinary business activity."[81] The index of industrial production climbed from 81 in September to 91 in December—12 percent in just three months. In December 1936 the real unemployment rate was the lowest since 1934 but, as Sauvy noted, there were seasonal adjustments correcting that number. "In point of fact not a single cabinet member, nor any decision maker was aware of that crucial index." The fact that unemployment was being reduced was not publicized. What impressed the public were the uncorrected raw numbers and the gold losses of 449 tons or 7 billion in September, 2 billion in October, 17 billion in November, and 144 billion again in December. Price increases—12 percent from September to December—were also troubling to the public. What was not being measured was the fact that French prices, for the first time since 1931, were dropping below British prices, leading Sauvy to conclude: "Some excellent prospects were opening up for the French economy now that it had jumped over the gold fence holding it down… The only negative aspect was that no one knew what was going on; the ship had a rudder but no lookout." Léon Blum was about to reap an extraordinary "political victory."[82]

The absence of a "national accountancy" and the brutal introduction of the forty-hour law were to quickly tear the situation asunder. Industrial production reached 94 in March 1937, reversing its course after that. By June the index was back at 89. Some of these facts led Léon Blum to announce in a radio broadcast speech on February 13, 1937, that a "pause" was required.

Some top officials, Jacques Rueff in particular, were not as optimistic in retrospect as Alfred Sauvy. Rueff felt that neither exchange controls nor another devaluation could solve the recurring crisis. He met with Léon Blum at his private residence at the Quai de Bourbon on February 6 at the request of Vincent Auriol himself. According to Rueff, capital flight was the most worrisome of all the issues that could threaten the new franc. Blum talked about the "wall of money" and was thinking about a "national union" government similar to that of Poincaré in July 1926 in order to reestablish "trust," even though this clashed with his social beliefs. Jacques Rueff offered a much simpler explanation: the "roots of our problems are due to the huge treasury deficit."[83] The "pause" meant a return to a savings policy.

Several measures were taken to instill confidence in those holding capital funds. A statement was issued regarding the "pause" on March 5 following consultations among Léon Blum, Vincent Auriol, and Economics Minister Charles Spinasse announcing more flexible measures and savings. Regulations of private trading in gold were no longer being enforced. On March 12 a large bond for national defense was issued with a guaranteed redemption. Finally, on March 8 a management commission, "including not only competent officials but those whose prior duties and positions would be reassuring,"[84] for the stabilization fund of foreign exchange was set up. Its members included the economist Charles Rist, very much a part of the business world, Paul Baudoin, the director of the Banque d'Indochine, and a top official, Jacques Rueff himself. The commission would meet every morning at the Bank of France to stem the flight of gold as best it could, stopping it temporarily at the beginning of March. But the three "commissioners" pointed out that "some easy habits of largesse going back several years had to be shed further." On June 7 the commissioners noted that "a new and deeper depreciation of the currency" was about to take place. Rist and Baudoin resigned on June 14 and Rueff, who was a civil servant, stated that he shared his colleagues' views. He was ready to leave the *Mouvement général des fonds* because a major disagreement with Vincent Auriol left no room for a close working relationship.[85] Instead, the government fell during the night of June 20–21, 1937, when the Senate refused to vote in favor of the full financial powers it had requested to fight the crisis.

This serious episode would be discussed for a long time to come. As far as Léon Jouhaux, the secretary general of the CGT was concerned, it was "part of the criminal attempts by the underground forces of big capitalism."[86]

Jacques Rueff felt this was all due to the fundamental weakness of the treasury stemming from the failure to "clean up." On June 28 he made a proposal to the new finance minister Georges Bonnet (who returned from Washington only on the 28th where he had been ambassador) to reduce the borrowing requirements of the treasury. "In order to reach this goal there were two requirements: a truly balanced budget and the elimination from the treasury of all expenses not related to national defense."[87] Alfred Sauvy felt that the problem related entirely to production, which, while evenly spread, was being strangled by the forty-hour law. "Underground orchestra conductor," "economic production," "financial cleaning-up"—each one played a role. The result was the dramatic end of a great experiment.

The new cabinet headed by Chautemps was not the one to lead France out of the crisis. Georges Bonnet was a good technician but realized that the 10 billion in the foreign currency stabilization fund had evaporated and that the Bank could count on 40 billion Poincaré francs in June 1936. One of his first decisions in July 1937 was to unilaterally let the franc float on the market. This was yet another devaluation. The pound sterling went from 110.8 francs at the beginning of 1937 to 147.20 by December. Contrary to the previous devaluation, the reason it took place was not because French prices were too high. "It's no longer the specific reviving cure but the shot in the arm giving artificial vigor for a limited time."[88] In 1937 the economy did pick up when production went from an index of 89 in June to 91.7 in December. Foreign trade provided the stimulus, but was not to be a lasting one.

The franc was devalued a third time by a decree of May 4, 1938, at the beginning of the Daladier government. As in July 1937 the French government announced "this measure in no way changes the determination of the French government to abide by the tripartite agreement." The pound sterling reached 175 francs. "The French government assures that its policy is intended to take the franc to a level commensurate with the economic situation and not to secure any commercial advantages. The current depreciation of the French currency would be the final one." The chancellor of the exchequer replied: "Following the agreement with the American government, the British government has concluded that France's initiative is not incompatible with the Tripartite Agreement. That agreement therefore is valid and in force and effect."[89] One may wonder how this could be.

4.

A Western Grand Design?

René Girault felt he could conclude the important article we have cited as follows:

> An organic plan appears to have been set up by Anglo-American strategists in the fall of 1936; its main points were to be that the western powers were still rich and dynamic enough to "buy off the peace" from the fascist countries by offering them credits or advance payments in exchange for political and economic commitments… Was Popular Front France ready to join in? The September 1936 Tripartite Agreement was the first commitment… Once again the top financial and diplomatic officials in the bureaucracy would channel ministerial decision-making."[90]

My feeling is that the real story was rather modest, shabby and far more scattered. Emmanuel Mönick may certainly have thought up such a grand design. The key position he held in London and his closeness to Washington, which he knew well, led him to conclude that it was possible for Europe to draw closer to a completely isolationist United States politically (the second Neutrality Act was passed on August 31, 1936, and the one regarding the Spanish civil war would be passed in January 1937) and economically because the huge tariffs of the Hawley-Smoot Act of 1930 and the 1934 Johnson Act denied any credit to debtors in default. A plan that would include the possible reimbursement of war debts likely to meet with American approval was an idea Mönick had consistently supported since 1932.

At first he took action unofficially and gave U.S. Ambassador William Bullitt a memo entitled "President Roosevelt and War Debts" that came to the following conclusion:

> The need to take the initiative very soon in the area of the economy and finance in order to save the peace—The need for tight Anglo-Franco-American cooperation for initiative to succeed…— The need to think through the economic and financial action…that in any case must lead to negotiations and results.

Mönick informed the French government of the move and the initial reactions it prompted on December 22.[91] He annotated the document, adding, "The government is well aware of the personal friendship between myself and Mr. W.C. Bullitt."

What he did not know was that on November 24 Bullitt had sent Roosevelt a report of his conversation with some very unpleasant comments. He found there existed in Paris "a violent, nervous desire to get us involved in the next war." This included Blum, the British ambassador, Herriot, Claudel, Geneviève Tabouis, and the French cabinet ministers. All of them "play the same phonograph record on the tune: war is unavoidable and Europe is doomed to destruction if President Roosevelt doesn't get involved." And Bullitt's recommendation was to reject any "proposal based on principle." Mönick wanted to pay Roosevelt a visit while he was at the Inter-American Conference in Buenos Aires but Bullitt discouraged him from doing so.[92]

On December 20 Bullitt wrote another letter to Roosevelt. He wrote that he took it upon himself to tell Delbos, Bonnet and Mönick that Roosevelt would never agree to make commitments in Europe. The only solution for peace was Franco-German reconciliation—Bullitt's great idea since he came to France. But "for different reasons the British, Italians and Russians are all against a Franco-German rapprochement." Enclosed with the letter was Mönick's memorandum on the issue of debt resolution. Bullitt's recommendation to Roosevelt was to view it with the greatest caution.[93]

Mönick was very optimistic in his note to the French government: "Bullitt answered me right away that he agreed with me as to the need and probability of some action for peace by President Roosevelt." Bullitt told him that a "European peace plan implied a preliminary discussion between France and Germany." On December 18 Bullitt stated that "Roosevelt will not address…European issues during his inaugural speech to Congress on January 2" and that "the issue of war debts was not the most important one right now."[94]

To speak of a grand western plan originating with the Anglo-Saxon countries, therefore, appears to be very tenuous. Besides, the men in charge of American foreign policy, like Cordell Hull, did not even mention it. Hull believed that a "crusade for economic health"[95] was required, meaning a series of multilateral agreements lowering trade barriers. Roosevelt's great idea, which took shape in 1937 when he appointed Sumner Welles undersecretary of state, was to draw the fascists away from aggression by offering them access to raw materials. However, the British were to reject that plan—the French were not consulted—as early as January 1938. Roosevelt himself was not too favorable to Cordell Hull's plan.

On the British side there is no trace of a Western plan of sorts in the memoirs of Eden, Halifax, Nicolson, Duff Cooper, Oliver Harvey, Vansittart, Strang, etc. Nor does it appear in the *Documents on British Foreign Policy*. The British hoped, in vain, for a treaty replacing Locarno and a rapprochement with Italy prompting the "gentleman's agreement" of January 2, 1937, that Delbos had approved of in advance.

Then there was France. For a time its relations with England were good. There was obvious sympathy on the part of Blum and Delbos toward Baldwin and Eden, which was reciprocated.[96] Things were to change completely in June 1937 once Chamberlain took over from Baldwin and Chautemps replaced Blum. Ties of this kind did not exist with the United States. When Georges Bonnet was appointed ambassador to Washington (January 16, 1937), Bullitt wrote to Roosevelt: "I don't think you'll like him. He is extremely intelligent and competent on economic and financial matters but he's not a man of character. You may remember that he led the French delegation to the London economic conference where he led the attacks against you."[97]

Had the French government accepted the Mönick plan? Neither the meeting Delbos had with German Ambassador Welczeck on December 23,[98] nor that of François-Poncet with Schacht on December 31[99] appeared to go beyond some vague economic projects. The Spanish civil war was the main topic of discussion. The meetings between Sir Frederick Leith-Ross and Schacht on February 2, 1937, involved the colonies and not economic plans.[100] Due to Eden's visit to Paris on January 20, where he was to have dinner at Léon Blum's home with Delbos, Massigli prepared a note entitled *Elements for a discussion with Mr. Eden*. Most of it deals with events in Spain and the impossible Locarno negotiation. On December 19 Eden had publicly stated that Great Britain would support France and Belgium in the event of aggression and Delbos had immediately asserted that the reverse was also true. The most interesting part of Massigli's text was entitled *Germany and Europe*. The key sentence read, "A political solution cannot be separated from an economic solution." Germany, however, had to provide some reassurance as to the goals it was pursuing.[101] There were rumors that the two men discussed large international financial companies but Eden fails to mention anything of the sort in his memoirs.

5.

1937: A COLORLESS YEAR

It turned out to be one of the most inactive years in the history of French diplomacy. Yvon Delbos made every possible effort to ensure success of the non-intervention policy, practically a dead issue since October 1936. It was not just a huge effort amounting to nothing but also an endless and useless attempt to prevent others from taking action.

Public opinion was also affected. Following the hot summer of 1936, the great hopes and disputes as well as a few achievements in internal politics, the crisis began once again. The men were exhausted and the Popular Front lost its luster; faith was slipping away. Diplomats were watching events intently and a description of what the government knew could be made, if that were our purpose. But no action whatsoever was taken.

French public opinion was ardently moved by the civil war in Spain, further exacerbating the divisions that existed among the French people. While enjoying the comforts of peace daily for three years that seemed guaranteed by the shield of non-intervention, the French public followed that horrible contest blow by blow.[102]

It should first be noted that besides the communists, a minority of socialists and a very small group of radical "young turks," including Pierre Cot, Pierre Mendès-France, and Jean Zay, a very large majority of French opinion was obviously pleased with non-intervention. The "interventionists" consequently took a very visible position. Paul Langevin, Jean-Richard Bloch and André Chamson assembled a number of intellectuals in the Franco-Spanish Committee. The Communist Party was the only major organization opposing the blockade. *L'Humanité* condemned the "so-called neutrality" that "caused the massacre of our Spanish brothers"[103] on a daily basis. When the Comintern set up a fund managed by Thorez and Togliatti, then created the International Brigades and appointed French communist André Marty as their leader—an assignment he would fulfill with extreme brutality[104]—the breach between socialists and communists widened even further. Léon Blum defended his policies in an important speech on September 6 at the Luna Park. Maurice Thorez gave a rebuttal causing relations between the two parties to become strained while Franco-Soviet relations suffered even further. France disapproved of the flap by the Soviet delegate at the London Committee on October 24 and worried about the letter where Stalin promised help to "Spanish revolutionary masses." Robert Coulondre, the new French ambassador, expressed his concern regarding the "ideological push" that would draw France into "internal divisions and isolation abroad."[105] According to Jacques Fauvet, 10,000 Frenchmen were to fight in the International Brigades almost all of them communists; 3,000 of them were killed.[106]

While a majority of the French public accepted the comfortable "neutrality," they were divided into pro-Franco and pro-Republican factions.[107] It may be stated that with very rare exceptions the socialists and radical socialists were in theory favorable to a loyalist victory. Their attitude was similar to the British Labourites who overwhelmingly supported non-intervention but were favorable to the republicans.

The position of the French right wing was less clear. German and Italian support to Franco with funds, weapons and "volunteers" (which Mussolini admitted, while Hitler provided fewer of them skillfully camouflaged—the famous air force Condor Legion), should have led all French nationalists to fear: 1) the establishment of an enemy on France's southern border; 2) the creation of German and Italian bases threatening communications to French North Africa; 3) the development of resources in Spain, principally iron ore mining by the "Axis," created in October and then named by Mussolini on November 1.

Ideology, however, got the upper hand. Anti-communism, exacerbated by the success of the Popular Front, turned to an anti-Soviet attitude. The right was taking a stand against "the Reds." Franco was viewed as a defender of society. Jacques Bardoux, president of the Republican Federation of the Massif Central and also a member of the Institut, was heading the most virulent campaign. In several pamphlets—*Les Soviets contre la France* (1936), *Le chaos espagnol, Eviterons-nous la contagion?* (1937), *Staline contre l'Europe: les preuves du complot communiste* (1937)—and many articles the same author accused a sort of "underground orchestrator" who was, among other things, setting up a communist insurrection in Morocco.[108]

The entire traditional right wing then followed suit. This was the case of every large newspaper in Paris and in the provinces, the large circulation weeklies and *Candide* and *Gringoire* in particular; the major cultural journals like *La Revue des Deux Mondes* or *La Revue de Paris*; and the Academy. The business dailies were complaining about the anti-Franco stance of the Popular Front, which could wipe out all French interests. The Catholic right was frightened by the anti-clerical attitude of the Republicans and the fact that the church in Spain supported Franco. He was viewed as leading a real crusade against atheism, the killing of priests, and the ransacking of the churches. Paul Claudel was Franco's greatest advocate.

The far right went to even greater extremes, especially *L'Action Française* and Jacques Doriot's PPF. Nationalist Spain viewed Charles Maurras as a great man. Colonel de la Rocque's *Parti Social Français*, which reached the height of its influence at the end of 1936, was much more discreet. It aimed at a rapprochement with the Franco forces to turn them into "our friends of tomorrow."[109] At the PSF, as in the daily *Le Temps*, one could detect "an under estimation of the threat the dictatorships represented."[110]

The Catholic right was to give rise to the two minorities refusing to view Franco as a savior. The massacres carried out on August 14, 1936, by the Franco forces when they took Badajoz showed that cruelty existed on both sides. The most famous Catholic novelist François Mauriac wrote a vengeful article in *Le Figaro* on August 18, calling it "a soiled victory." Other Catholics of various tendencies like Jacques Maritain, a scholar of Saint Thomas Aquinas; the Dominican weekly *Sept*; Emmanuel Mounier, founder of *Esprit*; novelist Georges Bernanos and above all some Christian-Democrats—Georges Bidault in the daily *L'Aube* was the first one to take this line—attempted to separate the Church from Franco. Others were against the rebels while some supported the Basques, a Catholic population loyal to the Republic that was promising them autonomy.

Another right-wing group that did not support Nationalist Spain included all those who feared the German threat. They felt that a much stronger policy towards Franco was required. "Frenchmen Beware! The Germans are at the gates of the Pyrénées" headlined *Le Petit Démocrate*, the official daily of the Popular Democratic Party. Some top newswriters like Pertinax and Émile Buré followed that position as well as Georges Mandel, himself on very friendly terms with Buré who, since buying *L'Ami du Peuple* in October 1936, was orchestrating a campaign to resist German influence.[111] Henri de Kérillis joined them as well. But *L'Ami du Peuple* lasted for only three months. Buré's paper *L'Ordre* had a readership of 10,000 while *L'Aube* had 12,000. *Sept* (which was ordered to shut down by the Catholic Church in August 1937) had 55,000 readers.[112] This was trifling compared to the "anti-red" and pro-Franco right wing.

Léon Blum's dilemma then became quite clear. Had he followed his inclinations and opened the border, dissent among the French people would rise up. By keeping the border closed, he drew on the advantage of satisfying a majority of French opinion still deeply affected by the "pacifist depression." But he knew that the latter course favored Franco and in the long run was not a good outcome for France; he also knew that it would widen the breach between socialists and communists that had been so difficult to mend and consequently had weakened the Popular Front. He naturally tended to choose the easiest course of action, which was non-intervention. Blum would unsuccessfully attempt to reduce the advantages of this course for Franco and would at times take the rather underhanded device of closing his eyes to some clandestine passage of arms and ordnance through the Pyrénées-Orientales. Delbos followed the same policy but with a kind of happy determination. He felt comfortable with "non-intervention." Vincent Auriol, Pierre Cot and Jules Moch were in charge of a very modest undertaking that could be called "official smuggling."[113]

It would serve no purpose in this book to recount the debates in and around the London Committee. As early as October everyone could sense that its usefulness was rather minimal. It is more useful to examine the various attempts to reach some kind of result.

By the close of 1936 French policy was attempting to mediate between the two sides. As Delbos told Corbin on November 26, France could no longer take "only a wait-and-see and non-intervention position." His suggestion was a diplomatic initiative by both the French and British governments toward Berlin, Rome, and Lisbon on one side and Moscow on the other. The objective would be to get them involved in a collective mediation to reach an armistice followed by "a free national consultation" in Spain.[114]

Eden agreed to the idea with some misgivings.[115] The Franco-British initiative took place at the beginning of December and yielded no results.[116] Von Neurath was "skeptical"[117] as were the U.S. Department of State,[118] Portugal,[119] and Italy.[120] The British constitutional crisis, ending in the abdication of Edward VIII and the accession of George VI to the throne, distracted British policy from any significant foreign policy initiative for some time.

During the month of December 1936 another issue became a cause for worry, that of the volunteers. They came from Italy in military units. In October 1937 Mussolini admitted sending some 40,000 Italians.[121] Facing those well-armed troops on the other side were the International Brigades, not amounting to much. However, they did worry Delbos and Eden because they provided a justification for Italy and Germany. "The declaration of non-intervention was only an excuse."[122]

The idea then took hold that proclaiming non-intervention was useless if there were no "control." This turned out to be impossible within Spanish territory. Why not establish it within the neighboring countries, in a few ports and at sea? Delbos launched the idea in mid-December and the discussions would follow for months on end[123] regarding controls and volunteers. The USSR, Germany and Italy immediately stated that they would only take action on the volunteers once controls were in place.[124] This was a clever position allowing for the acceleration of reinforcements that could easily be extended during the entire time it took to negotiate the controls. France and Britain, on the contrary, felt that "the most pressing and important problem concerned the volunteers."[125] Delbos therefore imparted new and unrelenting instructions to the French diplomats involved but always to no avail.

The initial agreed upon principle was to have Great Britain control the nationalist coasts (the Atlantic except Galicia and the Canary Islands) and France (Galicia, Spanish Morocco, and the Island of Majorca); the republican coasts by Germany (between Malaga and Cartagena) and by Italy (from Cartagena to Port-Bou and the Island of Minorca). Both the French navy and the British admiralty were extremely reluctant because it would involve a large number of ships.[126] If the exercise was limited to controlling the ports, twenty-five ships would be enough: twelve British, five French, six Italian, and three German.

Finally on February 16, 1937, the Non-Intervention Committee adopted the French proposal for land and sea controls. The agreement on the volunteers was to be enacted on February 20 (the general non-intervention agreement would cover them as well) and the controls were to be in place by March 6.[127] François-Poncet noted that there appeared a feeling of lowered tension at that time.[128]

Actually there were several delays. The naval patrols began on a "limited basis" only as of April 20, meaning with a smaller number of "observers" than originally planned.[129] The London Committee meetings before and after that date were mired in useless discussions. It was a well-known fact that Italian "volunteers" were coming in—these were actually fully equipped military units. The Italians denied it or were evasive and the naval patrols would, furthermore, not last. On May 29 two Spanish republican aircraft attacked the German pocket battleship *Deutschland* and twenty-three German sailors were killed. On the same day a German ship bombarded Almeria and Germany announced that it was ending its participation in the controls.[130] The work of the Non-Intervention Committee was suspended. French and British efforts to have it resume its work and "internationalize" naval controls succeeded only in part. The Germans and Italians demanded that Franco be recognized as having "rights as a belligerent." In the meantime during the course of the summer, Franco occupied the Basque region. It was their condition in principal for a hypothetical withdrawal of the volunteers.

Once Germany returned to the Committee on June 16, a new incident took place on the 19th, a torpedo attack on the German cruiser *Leipzig*. Delbos suggested opening an inquiry.[131] But the matter was to be resolved differently. Germany and Italy withdrew from the Non-intervention Committee. Delbos then summoned the German and Italian ambassadors, von Welczeck and Cerruti, announcing that France and Great Britain would continue the controls on their own. The initiative yielded no results.[132]

At that point there were several attacks by unidentified submarines in the Mediterranean. The Spanish republican government claimed that they were Italian. Naturally, Italy denied it. France and England were well aware that these were acts carried out by Italy and had to pretend not to know. Both agreed to propose a conference to address "piracy in the Mediterranean."[133] France even proposed to return to an older project[134] intended to reach a "Mediterranean Pact" that would include Spain, Greece, Great Britain, France, Italy, Yugoslavia and Turkey, and possibly even the countries on the Black Sea, including the USSR. England had rejected it in 1936, opting for a direct agreement with Italy on January 2, 1937;[135] Delbos seized upon that lifevest and discussed the possibility at a council of ministers meeting on August 29.[136] This time Eden gave a polite and evasive answer; what he really wanted was a meeting of the Mediterranean powers.[137] Delbos, along with many countries, agreed but was surprised to see Germany being invited since she was not a Mediterranean country. Germany and Italy refused to go along.

The conference was held at Nyon between Geneva and Lausanne, from September 10 to 17.[138] It was very much dedicated to technical issues. It gave Delbos the opportunity to voice all his worries to Eden regarding Italy's growing influence in Spain. A few naval patrol decisions were reached and since Italy agreed to take part in those patrols, "piracy" ended as if by magic. There was another reprieve and more evidence that French policy, which remained strictly defensive, was successful in more or less avoiding incidents but could not really help the republicans nor seriously slow down Franco.

The policies of Delbos, especially once he no longer had Blum's energy backing him, no doubt avoided violent catastrophes because Hitler took no brutal initiatives in 1937. However, there were a series of near failures. We have seen it in Spain. Many other initiatives also failed, such as the attempt to reinforce the Little Entente—the alliance of three pro-French countries directed against Hungary. Why not have a French alliance with the Little Entente but this time directed against Germany? The idea was discussed throughout the end of 1936. The Czechoslovaks were favorable;[139] the Romanians somewhat less so. The Yugoslavs under Prince Paul's authoritarian regime, as regent with Prime Minister Stoyadinovich, refused to go along and were attracted to a rapprochement with Bulgaria.[140]

It was also possible to combine the alliance documents of the three countries and France along the same lines as the Franco-Polish treaty. It was a proposal coming from Victor Antonescu, the Romanian foreign minister who had replaced the pro-French Titulescu on August 29. The directorate of political affairs opposed the idea because it "would not bring about any progress."[141]

Was it wise in general to forge new ties with those Eastern allies? The directorate of political affairs remained unconvinced and once again successfully persuaded Delbos.[142] Furthermore, the British were not too keen on the idea that France would be extending its obligations.[143] The project was shelved in March 1937.

The project to bring Czechoslovakia and Poland closer together, both being allied to France, looked better. But it was like fitting a square peg in a round hole. Colonel Beck's Poland kept on "flirting" with Germany, and the Rambouillet agreements of September 1936 were an important milestone, promising Poland 2 billion francs over four years for military purchases.

The origins of the agreement are worth noting. When Delbos summoned Ambassador Léon Noël at the beginning of June, he also met with Blum and Daladier. All three ministers were in favor of maintaining the Polish alliance. Contrary to Colonel Beck, who was hated by the entire French left, it was known that General Rydz-Smigly was a Francophile. A decision was reached to confirm an invitation to the general to visit France and discuss the funding issue. Léon Noël succeeded in convincing Delbos to set the elimination of Colonel Beck as a precondition. Delbos wanted to orchestrate the move himself. The plot failed because of a trip Gamelin took to Poland from August 12 to 16, much to the ambassador's regret. Gamelin appeared to be taking the first step, when the Poles were actually the ones seeking help. Beck became suspicious and replaced Chlapowski, who was pro-French, with one of his personal friends, Julius Lukasziewicz. The negotiation took place without Noël and Delbos did not dare ask that Beck be replaced.[144] Was it because of clumsiness or had some ministers changed their minds? The matter remains unresolved.

The USSR disliked the Rambouillet agreement. It wished to complete the Franco-Soviet Pact to include a military agreement. However, the initiatives of Ambassador Potemkin and the military contacts and meetings between Delbos and Litvinov failed to produce any results. Violent anti-communism in France and the fear of losing the smaller allies in the East proved stronger. Franco-Soviet relations deteriorated. The purge of the army and the execution of Marshal Tukhachevsky (May–June 1937) put an end to any serious negotiations.[145]

By the end of 1937 Delbos, who much preferred his trips to Périgord to any long distance travel, nevertheless decided to follow in Barthou's footsteps and visit the allies. His friend André Ganem, a top official at the League of Nations, gave him the idea.[146] It was to be his swan song. The decision was reached in November. Chautemps and Delbos traveled to London, then Delbos left on December 2 on a three-week "friendship tour."[147] He passed through Berlin where von Neurath came to pay his respects on board his train. Warsaw was the first stop where he met with Rydz-Smigly and Beck. Contrary to Léon Noël's recommendations, he avoided discussing the hot topic of Polish-Czechoslovak relations.[148] From Warsaw he went to Bucharest on December 8 where he met with King Carol, Prime Minister Tatarescu and Foreign Minister Antonescu. Belgrade was the next stop on December 12 where the crowd cheered him. Warm words of little consequence were exchanged but no conclusion was reached. The trip ended with a visit to the "true friends," the Czechoslovaks (December 14). Delbos mentioned the German-speaking population of the Sudetenland and advised making some concessions. "The visit was a complete success," said Beneš. Delbos returned to Paris on December 19 but it was impossible to assess whether his trip had truly been productive or not.

In 1936–1937 France also signed treaties giving independence to Syria and Lebanon. However, those agreements were not ratified by Parliament. They were part of what were "unequal" politics rather than foreign affairs. One consequence of those decisions was that Turkey made demands over the Sandjak of Alexandretta in the Hatay region of northern Syria. The area was given a new status on January 27, 1937; we shall revisit the ramifications of those events further ahead.[149]

It was on July 26, 1937 that Japan—which had signed the Anti-Comintern Pact with Germany in November 1936—began its war against China while France, whose interests were at great risk, was unable to take any kind of action.

Chapter XI

THE YEAR OF MUNICH

1.

THE MARCH 1938 CRISIS

The months preceding the Anschluss of March 11–12, 1938, may be viewed as one of the most passive moments in French foreign policy. The diplomats saw what was happening and were carefully describing every event with very few details escaping their analysis. However, the government leaders were powerless to control events.

Some decisions were obviously kept secret. On November 5, 1937, when Hitler announced to his closest staff and his generals that it was his intention to quickly settle accounts with Austria and Czechoslovakia,[1] François-Poncet was informed of that meeting. He sent a telegram on November 6, commenting, "it is difficult to find out what the topics of that meeting were." Perhaps issues relating to raw materials? "But it still is surprising that so many high-ranking officers were summoned to the chancellery to discuss only that."[2]

On November 6 Ribbentrop was in Rome for the ceremony of Italy's joining the Anti-Comintern Pact. Blondel,[3] the French chargé d'affaires in Rome, François-Poncet,[4] and Charles Corbin,[5] the ambassador to London, all commented on the event. They did not know the key comment Mussolini made to the Nazi leader regarding Austria. Hitler was able to infer that Mussolini no longer had an interest in Austria and immediately concluded that the Anschluss could now have priority.

French diplomacy, on the other hand, had been worried about a possible Anschluss since 1934 and saw the unstoppable start of the chain of events leading to it. The minister to Vienna, Gabriel Puaux, noted as early as January 25, 1937, that he was getting "alarming information indicating that Austro-German relations have cooled considerably in last few weeks." Which method would they use? A Nazi uprising? An instigated incident? Would the Austro-German agreement of July 11, 1936, be cancelled? An ultimatum?[6] Something, in any case, was in the works and François-Poncet felt the same way.[7]

The next step took place when Austrian Chancellor Schuschnigg was summoned to Berchtesgaden on February 12, 1938. French diplomats knew of that move in advance.[8] The result was that the Nazi Arthur Seyss-Inquart became the minister of the interior in the Austrian cabinet. Questions were intensely being asked about what had been discussed, and about the meaning of the initiative that was the cause of renewed anxiety. The meeting had been "more adversarial than it was previously thought" with Hitler making ominous threats of military intervention.[9]

The only French attempt to stop the unfolding crisis took place at that time. The second Chautemps cabinet now in power was weak and lacking any kind of prestige. Yvon Delbos was in his final weeks at the Quai d'Orsay and looked "wiped out" after a year and a half of non-intervention in Spain. He was also undergoing extremely violent attacks by the communists.[10] "How can we get involved in a dispute between a country of 70 million and one of 7 million when all the cannons are on the other side?" was his purported comment to newsmen.[11]

Yet on February 17 Delbos made a proposal to the British for a joint initiative in Berlin that was to be stronger than the vague steps taken by François-Poncet and British Ambassador Nevile Henderson to Ribbentrop.[12] In a conversation with Sir Eric Phipps and in a telegram to Corbin, Delbos noted that "the Führer is counting on our passivity." He proposed, as Schuschnigg had requested, a "preferably joint and in any case coordinated" initiative, whereby both democracies would reaffirm "that in general any action tending to redraw the territorial status quo in central Europe would be resolutely opposed by the western powers." A financial and economic rapprochement of the countries along the Danube would be examined with Vienna and Prague as well.[13]

A first blow came as early as February 20, when Anthony Eden re-signed from the Foreign Office. Corbin was aware of the fact that the disagreement stemmed from Chamberlain's desire to negotiate a "gentleman's agreement" with Italy.[14]

Eden was much more concerned than Chamberlain about events in Austria and, furthermore, had an excellent relationship with Delbos, who was disheartened by his British colleague's departure and was thinking of resigning himself.[15] Lord Halifax, the new head of the Foreign Office, was one of the big four of *appeasement* along with Chamberlain, Sir John Simon and Sir Samuel Hoare.[16] Even without Halifax at foreign affairs it was easy to predict that the French proposal would not succeed in London, where working in concert with France was strongly disliked and unilateral initiatives were preferred. This was in fact the meaning of the British reply of February 25: How could Germany be threatened with "just words" that weren't followed by any action? Should Schuschnigg find out he "would have increased hope for French and British military help that will not take place." His Majesty's government wanted to pursue broad negotiations with the German government regarding central Europe...as well as disarmament. These would naturally be unilateral initiatives.[17]

One could only accept the situation with resignation. A foreign policy debate took place in the Chamber the next day. Delbos, according to British journalist Werth,[18] "tired and disappointed," again expressed his apprehension about Austria and France's commitment to the alliance with Czechoslovakia. The government won by a vote of 438 in favor to 2 opposed and 163 abstentions.

Two weeks later a very weakened Chautemps government, which had requested full powers, resigned on its own.[19] It was March 10, 1938.

In fact, independently from any French involvement, Schuschnigg announced on March 9 that a plebiscite would take place in Austria to confirm the country's desire to remain independent. It is also a matter of record that during the dramatic day of March 11 a series of German ultimatums forced Schusschnigg to cancel the plebiscite. There was no French reaction since, as chance would have it, the country was without a government, President Miklas appointed Seyss-Inquart as chancellor and then proceeded with an appeal to the Germans who entered Vienna on March 12. It was the Anschluss.

By the hour Puaux kept Delbos informed of those happenings. It was only as of 9:15 p.m. by phone and at 10:25 p.m. by telegram that Delbos issued instructions to François-Poncet along the same lines "in concert with your British colleague join the initiative he has been ordered to take."[20] The initiative in question was naturally taken unilaterally. The idea was "to protest in the strongest terms against such coercive methods based on the use of force." Such action could "have the most serious consequences." Halifax added, "I am informing the French government of this protest in case it wishes to do the same."[21]

François-Poncet therefore undertook a "parallel" initiative rather than a concerted effort by a letter to the Wilhelmstrasse dated March 12 at 11 a.m. He simply restated the language of the British note. As for British Ambassador Nevile Henderson, that night at 11 p.m. he was attending a party hosted by Göring.[22] Mrs. Dollfuss, the former chancellor's widow, was able to leave Austria on March 12 with the help of French Minister Puaux. Schuschnigg, on the other hand, became a prisoner.[23]

On the evening of March 12 Delbos sent a telegram to all the major diplomatic representations explaining the background of his actions, not forgetting to mention Britain's refusal of any concerted efforts. "The situation we must face from now on is no doubt serious; but it doesn't mean anyone should panic." No obligations toward Austria existed. However, "the situation would be entirely different the day German expansion were to attack the independence or the very existence of countries having special agreements with us." In the final analysis "the first task of the next government will be to persuade England—whom we hope has learned from these events—to lend its support to our efforts without the reservations it has displayed until now."[24]

That was to be Delbos' testament. He was not wrong. But the British call that "wishful thinking."*

2.

THE FINAL REACTION OF THE POPULAR FRONT

Since January 1938 the idea took hold to create a "National Union" government. But what kind of union? A total one "from Thorez to Louis Marin?" A partial one "from Blum to Reynaud?" The right wanted no part of it. Léon Blum, designated by President Lebrun to form a government, plus the majority of the Socialist Party and many radicals,

---

* In English in the original. [NDT]

supported that possibility. In the end Blum decided to form a Popular Front cabinet with the support of the communists but not their participation. A growing number of radicals like Georges Bonnet and Marchandeau were increasingly distancing themselves from the Popular Front. The cabinet—as it was quickly known—was destined to be fragile. Yvon Delbos, now totally discouraged, refused to join it. Blum offered the Quai d'Orsay to Paul-Boncour. Daladier was remaining at National Defense.

Blum historians have all remarked on the originality of this government. With Georges Boris and Pierre Mendès-France, Blum was very much determined to go firmly in the direction of a controlled and "left-leaning" economy. He was planning to tax capital and perhaps to impose exchange controls.[25] He was to fail in the Senate on precisely that program.

As Paul-Boncour said, there existed without a doubt a strong spirit of "resistance" in France in the foreign policy area examined in this book. Despite the fact that the Blum cabinet was short-lived, we shall devote a few words to its policy since it differed from that of Delbos and soon with Georges Bonnet's.

Following the disaster represented by the Anschluss that Hitler accomplished so easily, France had to take stock and prepare for the future. Paul-Boncour called for[26] a meeting as early as March 15 of the Permanent Committee of National Defense, chaired by Daladier as minister of national defense and war along with the ministers of the two other branches of the armed forces, the chiefs of the general staff and their deputies, Pétain, and Controller General Jacomet with Léon Blum, Paul-Boncour, and Alexis Léger as guests.[27]

Few illusions were possible. The superiority of the German army—with the additional Austrian divisions—was obvious.[28] 900,000 men versus 400,000, according to Gamelin. The confident optimism of Pierre Cot in December 1937 regarding the air force was replaced by dire pessimism. A legitimate reason for the British to reject a very firm position was their estimation of the weakness of the French air force.[29] Gamelin was so acutely aware of the fact that he annotated in his own hand a document of March 16, "Regarding the current weakness of our air force I feel there is no reason to admit as much to England."[30] The deep changes that took place on February 4 within the German high command—the "sacking" of Generals von Blomberg and von Fritsch, making Hitler commander in chief and the Armed Forces High Command (Oberkommando der Wehrmacht—OKW) now being headed by pro-Nazi General Keitel—

all consolidated the German command structure. That same day the Nazi Joachim von Ribbentrop replaced Konstantin von Neurath at foreign affairs as previously mentioned.

On March 14 and 15 Gamelin had himself written notes regarding the general conduct of the land war. It was now obvious that since the Belgians refused to open their territory, an offensive toward Germany was no longer possible.[31] "France alone, if she can still hope to effectively defend its metropolitan territory and her African empire, can only engage in a victorious war through *alliances*. More than ever it becomes absolutely necessary to have England and Poland on our side; then the Little Entente reinforced by the Balkan Entente." The total incompatibility between a *diplomacy* of smaller alliances and a defensive *strategy* had still not dawned on General Gamelin. Lord Halifax, whom most observers fail to credit with any earth-shaking vision, appears much more realistic. "Of course," wrote Corbin, "he is stubbornly convinced that shows of strength can only accelerate the conflict rather than dampen it."[32] He prefers "to spare no effort to help erase the causes for friction."[33] He felt that the smaller allies were a burden more than a help and in the impeccably courteous manner of the Foreign Office asks by which method the French would act to help Czechoslovakia: "It is...an issue His Majesty's government has thought about and cannot deny that the conclusions it has reached are far from being encouraging."[34]

All these and other issues were examined at the March 15 meeting. Daladier concluded that no direct help could be given to Czechoslovakia. Léon Blum felt that Russia would step in. However, Gamelin and Vuillemin, who displayed nothing but contempt for the Red Army, were also asking about an issue that would reappear over and over again in 1938 and 1939: Where would Soviet troops transit since neither Poland nor Romania—which had a defective and hardly usable railway system—wanted any such transit?

The situation therefore was that: 1) France had promised to help its ally Czechoslovakia—as Paul-Boncour clearly told Czech minister Osusky on March 14;[35] 2) France could do almost nothing militarily by itself; 3) England was clearly refusing to commit itself to helping France in a war it would enter in order to help Czechoslovakia; and 4) The role played by the USSR remained unclear in such a venture. The latter did propose a coalition of countries opposed to aggression but it was an indirect proposal made by Litvinov in a statement released to the press on March 17. Given the thinking in the west, it did not stand a chance.[36]

During the short month he spent at the Quai d'Orsay, Paul-Boncour was actively engaged in every effort. The best-known event was the conference he held on April 5 with the ambassadors and French ministers posted in the USSR, Poland, Czechoslovakia, and Romania.[37] The conclusions were disappointing, especially regarding Poland. Léon Noël was convinced Poland would not help Czechoslovakia—which it hated—in the event of a German attack.

Two entangled issues were still open. Blum had reluctantly backed non-intervention in Spain. Paul-Boncour had always opposed it and felt that the Quai d'Orsay had failed to give enough credit to loyalist Spain.[38] This was due to Delbos and the "ridiculous committee" in London. Could this be reversed? On March 15 at the Permanent Committee of National Defense, Blum and Paul-Boncour posed the question of an ultimatum to Franco or an operation on Spanish Morocco or the Balearic Islands. These were only questions. Gamelin and Admiral Darlan protested that this was impossible. Alexis Léger said it would be a *casus belli* for Germany and Italy. The discussion ended then and there.

But there was a leak, about which Paul-Boncour would file a complaint. Some newspapers printed a story announcing that France was about to intervene. News reporters rushed to the border on the Pyrenees to watch the invasion; Minister of the Interior Marx Dormoy was nervous. The German and Italian newspapers were incensed; British ambassador Sir Eric Phipps was upset. It became very difficult to prove that nothing was going on.[39] In any case on March 10 the nationalists undertook a victorious offensive in Aragon. It took all the energy of Spanish Prime Minister Juan Negrin, who shuffled his cabinet and got rid of the "defeatists," to stop the disintegration. The Spanish republican territories were cut in two.

The Anglo-Italian negotiations were the other issue. Paul-Boncour wanted a similar rapprochement with Italy. Could she possibly be separated from Germany? Every dispatch from Blondel, the chargé d'affaires in Rome, showed that Italian public opinion was furious about the Anschluss and that Mussolini was the only one making a show of agreeing to it. The British also wished that a Franco-Italian agreement follow the Anglo-Italian one. In their own way the British preferred to have direct negotiations and did not want France to be involved—for other reasons Ciano didn't want it either. But they were careful to keep the Quai d'Orsay well informed. Everything was linked to recognizing the conquest of Ethiopia. Paul-Boncour wanted to begin negotiations as soon as the British had finished.[40] Massigli also agreed.[41] But then the Blum government fell on April 10.

Edouard Daladier, the leader of the radical-socialists, appeared as best suited because of his centrist position to form a government that would expand further to the right without the communists—whom he hated. The socialists refused to take part; the communists supported him at first. He simply added to a radical majority a few representatives of the moderate right, namely Paul Reynaud and Georges Mandel. This was not quite the official end of the Popular Front, but it was very close at hand. National defense overshadowed every other issue. Daladier was defense minister since June 1936 and no one was complaining about his performance. He had an excellent reputation for being dedicated and energetic.

Paul-Boncour was hoping to keep foreign affairs. He recorded his meeting with Daladier on April 10 in dramatic terms. "Your position towards Czechoslovakia has people worried," said Daladier. Paul-Boncour explained his position, saying that they must be firm. Daladier, who as a man was "in good faith," hesitated, then answered, "I've thought it over: the policies you have outlined are fine, worthy of France, but I don't think we can carry them out. I shall take Georges Bonnet." If this anecdote recounted by the former minister many years later is correct, it means that Daladier had decided in advance to seek a compromise because, as Paul-Boncour added, that Georges Bonnet, whom he thought of as "keenly intelligent, who kept his cool…had tactfully and discreetly opposed the policy of resistance that I had pursued."[42]

3.

THE FALSE CRISIS OF MAY 1938

In the midst of the postwar atmosphere when the hunt was on for those "responsible" and "guilty," it was natural to target the Daladier-Georges Bonnet team that took over on April 12, 1938. It is not our purpose here either to accuse or defend them. Anyone can make mistakes and while this can affect the political effectiveness of a leader, it does not impinge upon his moral integrity. The latter does become an issue and is under harsh attack once treason, bad faith, lack of dedication and character all come into play. We shall reject the accusation of treason, which would be stupid to consider.

Daladier and Bonnet were serious, hard-working and competent men. It was often said of Daladier that, for all his insight and great energy, he would become paralyzed when faced with a crucial decision. His integrity, however, has never been questioned. Everything about Georges Bonnet proves that he knew what he wanted and was not one to back off. In 1938 he did not want to commit France without England. Toward the end of the year for a time, he wanted to disengage France from its alliances in the east. In the spring of 1939 he wanted to enter into the "grand alliance" of France, Great Britain, and the USSR as quickly as possible. Following the coup of August 23, 1939, he wanted to avoid a war with France and Great Britain standing alone against Germany.

On the one hand, Georges Bonnet was not that concerned with issues of international morality and the respect of commitments. He believed in "sacred egoism." On the other, he gave others enough ammunition to castigate him by publishing his insincere memoirs, using truncated documents and offering a different set of explanations from one volume to the next. He was used to acting in secrecy, creating the impression on several occasions that he was doing so without the knowledge of Daladier, his superior, or of Léger, the man who reported to him.

Above all there was a surprising ambiguity between promises and intentions. Paul-Boncour seems to have found the right words in this case: "The mistake of Mr. Georges Bonnet and Mr. Daladier was to not say that the policy would change and even to reassure Mr. Beneš that nothing had changed… Beneš mistakenly believed it in April 1938, or he rather pretended to believe it despite the warning by his minister in Paris, Mr. Osusky, who told him that my leaving implied negative consequences for his country's future." And he added, "The French government's excuse for not telling Czechoslovakia earlier that it should not count on us was that it was itself unsure. It was divided on that critical point."[43]

We shall revisit these divisions later on. We may say right away that Daladier hoped he was being sincere when on several occasions he publicly announced that France would stand by its commitments, while Bonnet waited at first to be sure of what the British attitude would be and then worked with every ounce of energy, veiled by an obvious flexibility, in order to disengage France. The fundamental document appears to be the note he drafted on July 20 following his conversation with Czech Minister Osusky.[44] The document is part of the Daladier papers rather than those of Bonnet. Furthermore, it bears annotations in Daladier's handwriting, as we shall see. "The objective," wrote Bonnet, "was to clearly indicate to Mr. Osusky once again what the *French position* was… The Czechoslovak government must be made clearly aware of our position: France would not go to war over the Sudeten issue. Publicly we will certainly reiterate our solidarity as the Czechoslovak government wishes— but that statement of solidarity should enable the Czechoslovak government to seek an honorable and peaceful solution. *Under no circumstances* should the Czechoslovak government think that if a war breaks out we shall be at its side, all the more since on this issue our diplomatic isolation is virtually complete." Osusky answered that he had already explained at length to Beneš what Bonnet's point of view was and spoke to him about it extensively during a trip to Prague.[45] This had probably taken place just a few days before because earlier documents are not as clear.[46] Osusky requested that this revelation remain secret. Bonnet concluded by again insisting, "The Czechoslovak government *must be convinced that France, like England, would not go to war.*"

As far as Beneš was concerned, this was actually quite new. On July 21, once he received Osusky's telegram describing the conversation, he summoned Lacroix. He was "extremely emotional" and discussed the matter with him for three hours.[47] But Daladier's three handwritten annotations are just as interesting.

1. On top of the document, where Bonnet mentioned "the French position," Daladier wrote, "It was made by the Council and not by the decision of one minister." Meaning that Bonnet went too far because the Council had not yet taken a position;

2. Next to the words "France will not go to war on the Sudeten issue," Daladier wrote, "F. would go to war if aggression?"

3. Next to the words "in no case," Daladier wrote, "what about the Council of Ministers?"

* * * *

We beg forgiveness for dedicating so much space to this crucially important document. We must now examine how things reached that point from April 12 to July 20. We shall only highlight the main events.

The first concerned the Franco-British discussions in London on April 28 and 29. Chamberlain, Halifax, Vansittart, Cadogan, Sir Orme Sargent, Strang and Roberts represented the British side; Daladier, Bonnet, Corbin, Léger, Rochat, and de Margerie the French.[48] Chamberlain was extremely clear. He kept to the points of a speech he gave on March

24 in the House of Commons. England had obligations toward France, but would not extend them should France go to war to help her ally Czechoslovakia. Neither public opinion nor the Dominions would allow it. Furthermore, the military risks of such an operation would be enormous. France and England together must obtain the necessary concessions from Beneš that would be satisfactory to Germany. Chamberlain did not think that Germany wished to annex three million German speakers in the Sudetenland, even though these were individually hoping for such an annexation. At a congress of the German Sudeten Party led by Konrad Henlein in Carlsbad, he limited his demands to the transformation of Czechoslovakia from a minority to a national state. Reluctance on the part of Beneš must be overcome to ensure peace in Europe.

Daladier had a very different viewpoint; he felt that pressure should be brought upon Beneš, who was a very wise man, in order for him to go very far by way of making concessions. "But if renewed pressure must be brought to bear on Prague, France and Great Britain have to at least be determined, if no agreement can be reached following that initiative, to support Czechoslovakia and prevent its dismemberment or disappearance." Because Hitler will not stop there. "The action Germany is pursuing aims at eliminating the last vestiges of European equilibrium, imposing a domination of the continent that would dwarf the ambitions of Napoleon." France felt that its alliance with Czechoslovakia "is of vital importance" and "it is determined to enforce its obligations."

A spirited discussion took place on these two concepts. Chamberlain was to admit "his blood boils when he sees Germany extending its domination over Europe." But can we speculate with human lives? "It is doubtful that both countries would be strong enough to impose their will on Germany even at the cost of terrible suffering and losses." Daladier stated that he fought in the infantry for four years, that "he had but one thought: to prevent the return of such atrocities." But for that we must stand firm. Chamberlain declared we couldn't "bluff" (he reminded everyone that this was an American word). Wasn't Hitler the one who was bluffing? answered Daladier. Bonnet said he didn't think Hitler could be satisfied with the autonomy of the Sudetenland. He wants "to wipe Czechoslovakia off the map of Europe." Bonnet added, "France must live up to its word and its signature. Great Britain, which teaches the importance of that duty to its schoolchildren, would be the first to not be surprised about it." Neither side changed its position.

In the course of the three weeks that followed, France carefully monitored the situation. Bonnet even dispatched the ambassador to Poland, Léon Noël, his former colleague at the *Conseil d'État* and also a former minister to Prague, to Czechoslovakia on a fact-finding mission.[49] "Hitler could act boldly once again and quickly place... Czechoslovakia in front of the dilemma, to either surrender or go to war." On the other hand, instructions were sent to Lacroix asking, at the same time as his British colleague, how Beneš planned to respond to the Sudeten demands.[50]

Suddenly around noon on May 20, Czech Minister of Foreign Affairs Krofta informed Lacroix that there were German troop concentrations in Saxony.[51] The news reached the Quai d'Orsay at 1:40 p.m. Then a telegram from General Renondeau, military attaché in Berlin, arrived bearing the same information as his Czechoslovakian colleague. Other informers were telling him of convoys to Silesia and Austria.[52] Ambassador François-Poncet was aware of the news but remained skeptical.[53] Then he was informed by the consul general in Dresden that troops garrisoned there had apparently left their barracks.[54] The Germans denied the news, but the *Deuxième Bureau*—using Czech intelligence—confirmed it.[55]

The Czechoslovak government immediately decided to mobilize one military class and technicians as of May 20, a total of 170,000 without France being involved in any way. François-Poncet recommended no mobilization, saying "It would be a mistake."[56] The Germans were lodging strong protests because of incidents in some border areas (two Sudeten residents had been killed). Georges Bonnet's only reaction was to recommend caution.[57]

The part played by France in the whole matter, both as far as information and action were concerned, was virtually nil. This was rather fortunate since *there had been no troop movements*. It was far better to see for oneself than to rely on contradictory news coming from the Czechs or the Germans. General Renondeau sent his deputy Colonel Réa to the relevant areas. The result was very clear.[58]

While unimportant in practical terms, these events had a very important psychological effect. England was actually the only country to react. Its ambassador, Nevile Henderson, took several steps at the Wilhelmstrasse seeking moderation. François-Poncet did not receive similar instructions.[59] England was not changing its position at all as shown in a memorandum that Sir Eric Phipps delivered to the Quai d'Orsay on May 22.[60] However, the press magnified and naturally distorted those events. Germany had backed off! She had retreated because of Czechoslovakia's determination and a stand by Great Britain close to French positions, as Geneviève Tabouis wrote: "The masterful way whereby Great Britain enacted the promises it had made to France during the last conversations in London—promises that were renewed relating to Czechoslovakia—allows us new hope for keeping the peace."[61] A more fundamental misreading of the facts would be difficult to imagine. England would be at France's side; she was committed to it. Vladimir d'Ormesson in *Le Figaro* and *Le Temps* were saying the same thing. "Prague's resistance along with the resistance of London and Paris" had prevailed, declared Henri de Kérillis.

These triumphant statements must have infuriated Hitler who was well aware of not having backed off since he never advanced in the first place. It is very unlikely that this played any role when he signed the general order to the Wehrmacht on May 30 to be ready to invade the Sudetenland by October 1. However, it had exacerbated his hatred of the Czechs and his determination to put an end to the issue.

Georges Bonnet kept cool throughout the incident. Undoubtedly he was more affected by the British note of May 22 than by the "crisis." The document in question was extremely to the point and its language was even authoritarian: "The British government has given Berlin the most serious warnings... But it would be very dangerous if the French government were to exaggerate the scope of those warnings." England would not intervene. France should be cautious. "The British government... absolutely expects that before taking any action making the situation more critical or that could result in exposing France to a German attack, the French government undertakes to consult with the British government. The measures that the French government must consult with the British before undertaking them include partial or general mobilization."[62]

Bonnet also knew that he could not count on Poland,[63] that the backing of the USSR was doubtful and probably ineffectual, that Russo-German collusion was possible,[64] and that, finally, any hope of closer relations with Italy had vanished. Regarding the last point as soon as the Italian-British agreements of April 16, 1938, also known as the Easter Accords, were signed, Bonnet had initiated negotiations. The Quai d'Orsay instructed Blondel, the chargé d'affaires, to request a meeting with Ciano and tell him that the French government "would be in favor of beginning Franco-Italian negotiations on short order either in Paris or in Rome."[65] The next day Blondel saw Ciano, who indicated his preference for the talks to be held in Rome "as a sign of sincere belief that they would be successful."[66] The discussions began on April 22.[67] They "are coming along well," Ciano told a French diplomat on April 28. "There is no major disagreement between France and Italy."[68] Ciano was still "very satisfied" on May 1.[69]

At this point Hitler came to Rome to pay a state visit to Mussolini from May 5 to 9. As early as May 14, Mussolini gave a speech in Genoa using a "particularly harsh tone" meant to cut off the conversations with France: "I don't know if they will reach a conclusion because in a very contemporary event such as the war in Spain we are on opposite sides of the fence." And Stresa in any case was "dead and buried."[70]

France was therefore quite isolated. It was best, in the French minister's view, to avoid taking any strong initiatives and let the British forge ahead. Did London want a French initiative in Prague? France would certainly proceed.[71] Did the British wish to send observers to the Sudetenland? Fine, France would then abstain from doing so.

On the same July 20 when Bonnet told Osusky rather roughly that France would *in no way* help Czechoslovakia, he and Daladier met Lord Halifax. "Confidentially, Lord Halifax announced that he had just sent Beneš a note asking the Czechoslovak government to accept the good offices of Lord Runciman." We underscore: Lord Halifax "announces" an initiative. He was not asking the French whether or not they agreed to it. *England was running the whole show,* with France following rather far behind. Was it in the hope that the British would get caught in a trap of their own making?[72]

4.

PRELIMINARIES TO THE GREAT CRISIS

France continued to play a passive role until Hitler's Nuremberg speech on September 12, 1938. The statement by Deputy Director of Political Affairs Charvériat at a weekly liaison meeting on August 3, describes it like this: "We must wait for the results of the Runciman mission."[73] In fact, through the vigilant activity of the diplomats at their posts, above all Lacroix and François-Poncet, the Quai d'Orsay was able to form a broad opinion regarding the situation. There are no instructions from Paris to be found if only to encourage the Czechoslovaks to caution and to make rapid concessions.[74] As usual the British were late in providing the French with precise information regarding the recommendations coming from their envoy. The first official note was dated August 30.[75] Whatever Paris knew came from meetings between Runciman and Lacroix;[76] the confidential conversations with Beneš[77] or Prime Minister Hodza.[78]

There were to be no initiatives taken by Prime Minister Daladier during the month of August. On July 12 at the Provencaux' banquet in Paris he had mentioned the May crisis and its resolution, "thanks to the good will and peaceful determination of Great Britain, of France, and also of Germany." He had taken the opportunity to reiterate that France would remain faithful to its commitments.[79] He gave another speech on radio on August 21 addressing public opinion. He justified the exceptions to the 40-hour work law in the face of German armaments. Otherwise, he was waiting.

French ambassador to Berlin François-Poncet and his military attaché, General Renondeau, were both fervently scrutinizing all the signs whereby they could detect German intentions. While greatly exaggerating the moral victory of the western countries during the pseudo-crisis of May 21 and predicting, as he had been constantly since 1935, the worst kind of economic collapse for Germany if it went to war, the ambassador, using his inside knowledge of the Nazi milieu, proved that with the armaments at his disposal Hitler could take violent action at any moment. In that sense he did not share any of the illusions of his British colleague Nevile Henderson who felt that through negotiations Hitler's attack could be delayed for one year. Beginning on June 22 (Göring's decree instituting civilian conscription) he warned Paris that Germany was mobilizing without announcing it, calling up reservists, filling out regular army units, requisitioning workers, vehicles, and horses, and stockpiling supplies. The system consisting of individual summons made the basis of any evaluation difficult.[80] François-Poncet did not believe the Runciman mission would succeed in any case. He felt the Nazi leaders would reject any accommodation and feared that, even with British support, France would be unable to stop Hitler. He was anxiously expecting the Nazi party rally at Nuremberg and Hitler's speech, no doubt proclaiming, "his determination to no longer allow that his 'blood brothers' be subjected to Czech 'oppression.'"[81]

The trip Air Force Chief of Staff General Vuillemin took to Germany (from August 16 to 21) played an exceptionally important role. As

French Premier Léon Blum *(left)* in conversation with
William C. Bullitt, U.S. ambassador to France in 1936.

Sir Samuel Hoare *(left)* arriving at Downing Street.

The Daladier cabinet of April 10, 1938. (*Front row, left to right*) Rucart, Queuille, Georges Bonnet, Camille Chautemps, E. Daladier, Albert Sarraut, L.O. Frossard, Jean Zay, Guy La Chambre. (*Back row, left to right*) Patenôtre, Campinchi, Paul Reynaud, Georges Mandel, Jules Julien, Gentin and Champetier de Ribes.

above
(Left to right) Edouard Daladier, Ambassador Charles Corbin, and Georges Bonnet arrive in London on September 18, 1938.

left
(Left to right) Georges Bonnet, Neville Chamberlain, and Edouard Daladier.

Back in London on September 25, 1938. *(Front, left to right)* Georges Bonnet, Daladier, and General Gamelin. *(Back, left to right)* Alexis Léger and Corbin.

left
Neville Chamberlain in 1938 during the Czech crisis.

below
The president of Czechoslovakia, Edvard Beneš.

Daladier *(front right)* inspects the SS Honor Guard after landing at Munich. Von Ribbentrop is on the far left and Alexis Léger is behind Daladier.

September 29, 1938, at the Munich Conference. *(Front, left to right)* Neville Chamberlain, Daladier, Hitler, Mussolini, and Galeazzo Ciano. *(Back, left to right)* Sir Horace Wilson, von Ribbentrop, von Weiszäcker, and Alexis Léger.

above
Meeting at the Quai d'Orsay on November 29–30, 1938. (*Left to right*) Chamberlain, Daladier, Bonnet, and Lord Halifax.

below
A peace demonstration in Paris in 1938.

above
The signing in Paris of the Franco-German Agreement of December 6, 1938: von Ribbentrop *(reading)* Georges Bonnet *(seated)*, with Alexis Léger at the right. Interpreter Paul Schmidt is on the left behind Ribbentrop.

below
Von Ribbentrop and Daladier at a reception at the German embassy on December 6, 1938.

left
Herriot addresses a Franco-Italian friendship event in Lyon on July 30, 1939.

below
France recognizes the Franco regime in Spain; Georges Bonnet signed the agreement in Paris on February 28, 1939.

VOILA CE QUI NOUS ATTEND, SI
LE GOUVERNEMENT N'EST PAS CAPABLE
DE SORTIR L'AVIATION FRANÇAISE DE LA
SITUATION DRAMATIQUE OÙ L'A PLACÉE
LE FRONT POPULAIRE!

A poster condemning the policies of the Popular Front and the
Daladier government.

Daladier and General Gamelin *(left)* visit the Maginot Line.

above
Defensive positions on the Maginot Line.

right
Colonel Josef Beck, the Polish foreign minister, on a visit to England in 1939.

The Anglo-French military delegation traveling to the USSR for talks in August 1939.
Admiral Drax of Great Britain *(far left)* talking to General Doumenc of the French air force.

left
The Nazi-Soviet Non-Aggression
Pact of August 25, 1939:
Josef Stalin shakes hands
with von Ribbentrop. Marshal
Shaposhnikov, Soviet chief of
staff, smiles at the camera.

below
French Army reservists jam the
Gare de l'Est on September 2,
1939, as mobilization begins.

a fellow officer he received an excellent welcome.[82] He met with Hitler and Göring. who was full of praise for Daladier, "whom we view as a firm and strong man."[83] The Germans cunningly put on a Luftwaffe display "of truly impressive power," and of industrial production, the quality of the aircraft and their weaponry, the enthusiasm and "moral strength" of the crews.[84] How could the unfortunate French air force, which Vuillemin knew only too well, stand up to that huge and forbidding machine? Captain Stehlin could see how "troubled" he appeared. As he was leaving Berlin "he told the ambassador he feared seeing our air force melt down in two weeks if faced with intensive operations against the Luftwaffe… He would repeat it to Daladier about one month later just before the Prime Minister left for Munich."[85] Making a show of one's superior strength is not such a bad device. This explains why the Germans allowed General de Geffrier, the air force attaché and his deputy Stehlin, to fly over German territory.

Victor de Lacroix, the minister to Prague, would also spend the month of August in anguish. He had the unfortunate assignment to badger Beneš, Hodza, and Krofta, and pressure them to reach agreements, insisting that they must make further concessions.[86] He undertook that task as a dutiful government official would, but did so unhappily, allowing himself at times to make suggestions and reporting back all the reasons provided by his Czechoslovak counterparts. He feared British policy more than anything, sensing it was ready in order to keep the peace to sacrifice "the integrity and the actual independence of Czechoslovakia." Great Britain, as always, was constantly providing suggestions that would weaken the Czech position, a plebiscite in the Sudetenland for instance, which Beneš was strenuously rejecting.[87] "I am perhaps too impressed by this British pressure of which Your Excellency showed me proof, it must be known to Germany and would appear to encourage German intransigence and consequently that of the Sudeten population… I know that my thoughts are going beyond the limits of the political area that is my responsibility. The confidence Your Excellency places in me…makes me duty-bound in any case to volunteer my opinions."[88]

As for the issue that was obviously haunting everyone, would Hitler be satisfied with Sudeten autonomy within a Czechoslovak federal state or would he want to annex the Sudetenland? Lacroix was among the first to ask the question and always remained skeptical of the "goodwill mission."[89] He did not hesitate repeating that Beneš was wary of Lord

Runciman. Beneš presented his concession plan to Lacroix on September 6 so that France would be informed before England; the Czechoslovak president, alluding to the British mediator, said sadly, "They always wants me to feel pessimistic and then they deceive me."[90]

* * * *

We already have seen that British initiatives were practically identical to the general views of Georges Bonnet. However, he was not the only one in charge. During a speech he gave on September 4 at the Pointe de Grave he stated that France "will remain committed to the pacts it has entered into." This seems to contradict every step he took. But one must remember that in any case the Czechs demanded the appearance of taking a firm stand. Georges Bonnet attended the inauguration of a monument commemorating the United States' entry into the war. American Ambassador William Bullitt told him something ambiguous: "Should war break out once again in Europe no one can tell whether or not the United States would be drawn into such a war." Part of the French press saw this as the sign of a move by the Americans toward intervention; Roosevelt, however, quickly denied that interpretation. In any event, as of September 4 it appeared that a firm attitude prevailed.[91] According to Bullitt, "Bonnet thinks that Germany will not risk a war with France and England during the month of September, but many other cabinet ministers believe that Hitler has already decided to strike in September."[92] That opinion was shared by Georges Scapini, a moderate deputy from Paris, blinded during the war, who had met with Ribbentrop on September 3 and reached the conclusion that for Hitler "the negotiations between the Sudeten Germans and the Czechs presided by Runciman were only…a device to gain some more time."[93] François-Poncet was also convinced that on the German side there was no longer "the slightest desire to seek a conciliation." Germany would soon have the reserve division mobilized. "There is every indication that the middle or the end of September, meaning following the Nuremberg Rally, will be the time of the fateful *X Tag* or *Day X* when Hitler will mount the attack he has been contemplating."

Bonnet had also met with German Ambassador von Welczeck on September 2, and told him "that France was definitely determined to actually stand by its commitments."[94] According to the German ambassador,[95] he also said that once the autonomy of the Sudetenland was achieved, its return to Germany—"the only satisfactory solution," in von Welczeck's words—"would happen as matter of course." The ambassador added that Bonnet's aim, once the Sudeten issue was satisfactorily resolved, was to invite us to general negotiations where our wishes not just in the economic, financial but also the colonial field would be considered in a spirit of fairness.[96] Georges Bonnet disputed that document later on.[97] In any case, he felt certain that England persisted with its intention to not intervene.

On September 7 Henlein and the Sudeten German Party decided to break off their negotiations with the Czech government. Bonnet immediately phoned Halifax.[98] The conversations between Lord Halifax and French Ambassador Corbin on September 9 caused a curious incident that is indicative of how consistent Bonnet's attitude was. Sir Eric Phipps read the British summary of that conversation[99] to Alexis Léger on September 11,[100] and transmitted the text to Bonnet on the 13th. Corbin was requesting that Halifax take a strong position, at least openly. Léger complained on the 11th that the British government was refusing to do so. On the 12th Chamberlain met the British parliamentary and political correspondents, according to Corbin, telling them "that England had no commitments in Central Europe or toward Czechoslovakia but that she would not be indifferent to a general European conflict."[101] Even though those listening provided several versions, the basic thrust was in that direction. Publicly, England was going further than she ever had toward intervention.

Georges Bonnet was furious about that statement. He was going by the British note of May 22 and now "public opinion was being told that England readily accepted the idea of going to war on the Czechoslovak issue." Bonnet felt this was going much too far. He feared that "public opinion in our two countries, mistakenly convinced of the superiority of our weaponry, would blindly pressure the governments to engage in a war that could turn out to be a disaster."[102]

Bonnet's angry display against the apparently excessive energy England showed may probably be explained by Daladier's involvement. Daladier had met the German chargé d'affaires on September 2 and the British ambassador on the 8th.[103] He felt optimistic about the strength of the Maginot Line, the weakness of the Siegfried Line and France's good internal situation. He was hopeful of Soviet help and basically felt certain that France would intervene which didn't sit well at all with Bonnet who wanted exactly the opposite. And now the British seemed to be encouraging Daladier!

5.

France Abandons Czechoslovakia

On September 12 Hitler gave his big speech in Nuremberg, and the Sudeten Germans began a series of demonstrations that the Czechoslovak police suppressed rather easily. Daladier then retook the initiative. On September 13 he sent Chamberlain a message proposing "a meeting of the heads of government of England, Germany and France," in order to "safeguard every opportunity toward an amicable resolution."[104]

But Chamberlain did not like to see France becoming directly involved in the Anglo-German negotiations. He answered immediately (at 3:20 a.m.) that "tonight he was examining another opportunity to exert direct action on Berlin."[105] Early that morning Sir Eric Phipps informed the Quai d'Orsay that Chamberlain would meet Hitler at Berchtesgaden. A communiqué was immediately issued to the press. Daladier had not been consulted about this crucially important initiative which Hitler had immediately accepted.[106]

For three days there was nothing to do but wait. Bonnet was certainly very satisfied.[107] The Germans even more so.[108] Beneš issued a "supreme call" to France through Lacroix who could only support his point of view.[109] An unhappy Beneš was even proposing to hand over some territory along with 800,000 to 900,000 Germans.[110] To this end he even secretly sent his minister of health, the Social-Democrat Jaromir Neczas, a friend of Léon Blum, to meet with Daladier.[111] Bonnet strongly insisted that Czechoslovakia not mobilize its troops.[112]

As of the evening of the 17th France still had no information.[113]

Chamberlain summoned Daladier and Bonnet to London on September 18. Léger, Corbin, Rochat, Jules Henry (who headed Bonnet's cabinet), and Roland de Margerie were present. Besides the usual top officials, Chamberlain also had with him the other great *appeasers*, Halifax, Hoare and Simon.[114]

The British position was already decided. Chamberlain gave a detailed account of his conversations with Hitler, who said he wanted the Sudetenland and had no further territorial demands in Europe. "The racial unity of the Germans is his only goal." His reasoning followed the people's right to choose their own destiny. Chamberlain obviously did not object. Runciman, who had been called to London, felt that this was, after all, readily justifiable.

Daladier's initial reaction was unequivocal: the idea that the Sudetenland was to be annexed was very new and he could not take an immediate position.

Chamberlain then underscored Beneš' mistake in engaging "delaying tactics." According to Runciman, "no mediation attempt between the Czechs and the Germans had any chance of succeeding." What was required was *self-determination*. What was France's position? At first Daladier thought, "it is always difficult to ask a friend to cut off one or both of his legs." He also felt that Czechoslovakia would not survive and that some day it would be the corridor's turn. In any case, no plebiscite was possible.

Daladier added, "France's treaty obligations are clear and inevitable... There wasn't a single one of his fellow citizens who would readily betray." Halifax then proposed a way to avoid perpetrating a betrayal. All that was required was that Hitler not attack, meaning that they had to negotiate and Hitler had promised not to use force during negotiations.

Following a discussion within the French delegation, Daladier made his first concession. In losing the Sudetenland, Czechoslovakia was also losing its fortifications, and only an *international guarantee* could replace them. This was the birth of the idea of a transfer followed by guarantees. Georges Bonnet underscored that point: "The objective is above all to give Czechoslovakia moral support in exchange for the sacrifices required with the guarantee of France and Great Britain."

The British didn't like the proposal but ended up agreeing to it. During the last phase of the meeting, on the evening of September 18, the French gave in completely. A Franco-British note was drafted[115] to be sent to Prague if the French government, which Daladier wanted to consult as soon as he returned to Paris on the morning of September 19, agreed. And it would be Daladier himself, cleverly manipulated by Chamberlain, who came to the conclusion that *"The two governments must exert very strong pressure on Prague for Czechoslovakia to accept the solution proposed by two friendly powers."* [Emphasis added.]

The following step was the meeting of the Council of Ministers on Monday morning, September 19. It was the first discussion among the ministers regarding the Czechoslovak problem. Some ministers had in fact taken a position on an individual basis.[116] Georges Bonnet had at times quickly mentioned the issue, but—as we have noted regarding the July 20 document—he was pursuing his own policies. It was rather dangerous to present the problem to the Council of Ministers, known to be divided. The risk of a break-up and cabinet crisis was looming in the midst of a European tragedy—similar to what happened during the Anschluss. When British journalist Alexander Werth, an excellent observer, described a debate on Czechoslovakia at the meeting of the Council of Ministers on September 15,[117] he was no doubt confusing some points of discussion with a binding decision. The *Carnets Secrets de Jean Zay* begin as of September 19. De Monzie, who joined the Council of Ministers at the end of August and who was a sworn enemy of Beneš, makes no mention of this as of the 15th.[118] However, on September 4 he wrote, "The Council has not yet discussed the issue."[119]

If we follow de Monzie, those supporting resistance were: Paul Reynaud, Mandel and Champetier de Ribes; the pacifists were Bonnet, Marchandeau, Guy La Chambre (the air minister who was in turn influenced by General Vuillemin), Pomaret and de Monzie himself. Chautemps "was discreetly encouraging Bonnet." He also influenced Daladier whom he impressed with his "reputation of being clever." The radicals Queuille, Rucart, and Jean Zay followed the same line. Actually we now know that Jean Zay was a firm believer in resistance. Sarraut and Campinchi "were waiting."

The debate was relatively short since the meeting began at 10:30 a.m. and Bonnet came out at 12:30.[120] Daladier summarized the London discussions by saying that he had defended the French position "with all his energy but to no avail."[121] He repeated the proposals made by Beneš to give up part of the Sudetenland. "Daladier said that the Cabinet was free to deliberate, but that it was his duty to be the first one to offer his opinion. He feels we must accept." In any case, "it would be impossible for us to help the Czechs." "Short discussion," said Jean Zay. Mandel asks clarification that the Czechs must agree to the plan. "Bonnet said that should the Czechs refuse, he would ask us to "interpret" our pact with them." Campinchi then disagreed. But the conclusion was that "it is premature to have this discussion this morning." Bonnet added, "We would never be in a worse case diplomatically," and that "he never had a meeting with Osusky without warning him confidentially that in any case we would not intervene without England." But some ministers said that was not the policy of the government. Bonnet, lowering his voice, told Campinchi that he agreed with Daladier on that point. This was totally false, as we have seen, regarding the note of July 20.

The other speakers as recorded by Jean Zay were Chautemps, de Monzie, Marchandeau, and Bonnet, who pointed out "the exaggerations of Czech propaganda." Chautemps stated that should Beneš refuse he must be warned that he could not count on us, which prompted some objections. But the issue was set aside.

De Monzie recorded a statement by Guy La Chambre who brought up a recent report by General Vuillemin that was no cause for optimism. Russia's support was also mentioned. "Bonnet proved that even though Russia could take a position she didn't want to do so." The Franco-British plan was finally approved and on a motion by Anatole de Monzie it was clear that the approval was unanimous.

The remaining task was to convince the Czechs. An unpleasant business if ever there was one, and quite sordid an operation, actually, that would take less than two days.

At 12:30, right after the meeting of the Council of Ministers, Bonnet met with the unfortunate Czech Minister Osusky. He told him about the discussions in London and indicated "the extreme difficulty we encountered in securing a British guarantee for Czechoslovakia." He underlined "the serious nature of his government's response... The British government has in fact told us that should Prague refuse it could do nothing but end its involvement in the dispute." In such a case the French government would "take stock of the *current* situation... The assistance France would be able to provide to Czechoslovakia would be totally ineffective if it did not have the assurance of British support." This was actually the position taken on July 20.[122]

At 2:15 p.m. in Prague, Lacroix and Newton, following instructions informed Beneš. The president said he needed to consult with the government and with Parliament. The two diplomats insisted "on the urgent nature of the answer" because Chamberlain had to meet with Hitler on Wednesday the 21st. They also attempted to "convince the President not to take desperate measures that included the use of force." It was a short but "extremely unpleasant" meeting.[123]

It must be noted that Bonnet had not consulted with the offices of the Quai d'Orsay. In an important note political director Massigli wrote on the same day, "not being aware of the debates that had taken place yesterday," showed the difficult problems posed by the idea of guarantees and examined "the consequences for France of *the weakening of Czechoslovakia.*" Those consequences were to be disastrous from every point of view: military, economic, intellectual and moral. "Far from getting Germany to return to a policy of cooperation, the success of its methods can only encourage it to continue. The enormous sacrifice made by the western powers will not be matched: we would be reduced once again to an act of faith in the peaceful change of the new pan-Germanism."[124]

During the entire afternoon of the 19th and the morning of September 20, there was no news coming out of the Czechoslovak deliberations. On the 20th at 1:30 p.m. Lacroix phoned that Prague was hesitating between two solutions: to accept the Franco-British plan with a few reservations, or arbitrage.[125] Bonnet immediately instructed Lacroix to say that to ask for arbitrage would be "an irreparable mistake."[126] Then by sending cables every hour Lacroix reported that the Czechs were leaning toward rejection and choosing arbitrage. It became official early in the evening.[127] The Czechoslovak government was rejecting the Franco-British note. Public opinion was supporting the government and condemning the offers coming from Paris and London.

Another initiative was in the works, however. Czech Prime Minister Hodza was "softer" than some of his ministers. He summoned Lacroix and told him, "If I went tonight and told Mr. Beneš that in case of war between Germany and Czechoslovakia about the Sudeten Germans, France, because of its commitments toward England, would not go to war, the President of the Republic would take such a declaration into consideration; the Prime Minister would immediately summon the Cabinet where all the participants are now in agreement with the President of the Republic and they would agree to it. *The Czech leaders need that cover in order to accept the Franco-British proposal.*"[128] [Emphasis added.]

Two versions exist regarding the events that took place between September 20 at 9:45 p.m., the time the message was received, and 12:30 a.m. on September 21 when Bonnet phoned in the wording of the warning message requested by Hodza to Lacroix. According to Georges Bonnet, he summoned Daladier to the Quai d'Orsay. The phoned instructions to Lacroix were drafted following a discussion with Léger and Jules Henry, who headed Bonnet's cabinet. Daladier felt that it would be impossible or useless to call a meeting of the Council of Ministers since President Lebrun (reached by phone) was at Rambouillet.[129]

According to Pierre Comert, head of the Quai d'Orsay's press office, Bonnet never once called Léger, who was waiting to be summoned during the entire evening. Everything would have taken place between Bonnet and his "brain trust." During the morning of the 21st Comert expressed his indignation to Jules Henry and criticized the fact that the minister phoned on an open line (knowing that German intelligence was listening in) rather than sending an encrypted telegram.[130] Since Léger did not provide his side of the story, it is impossible to know what really happened. Bonnet, in any case, used the opening provided by Hodza. His determination was confirmed by a phone call that same night of the 20th to the 21st by Sir Eric Phipps to Jules Henry.[131]

In the face of such a final position the Czech government was still hesitating. Mandel called Beneš several times to encourage him to resist: "Neither Paris nor London should dictate your conduct." Prague was beginning to think that the French government could fall.[132] That afternoon both the French and British were worried about Beneš' silence. Bonnet spoke to Léger and Daladier about it.

But at 5 p.m., after a final call by Beneš,[133] Czechoslovak Foreign Minister Krofta handed Lacroix a resigned and "painful" acceptance, "forced by circumstances and the many pressing requests coming from the French and British governments."[134]

6.

THE GREAT CRISIS AND MUNICH
(September 23–30)

Once again for two days France could do nothing but wait. Chamberlain went alone to meet with Hitler at Godesberg on September 22 and 23 bringing him "an acceptance intended to avoid any use of force." Corbin was instructed to tell Halifax that the French government had "full confidence" in the prime minister.[135]

Hodza resigned, along with his entire cabinet, and was replaced with General Syrovy while Chamberlain was meeting with Hitler. As early as the evening of the 22nd he phoned Halifax, and Corbin learned that "the afternoon meeting had not been satisfactory. Mr. Hitler feels that the Franco-British plan is unacceptable."[136] Everything remained confused until the evening of the 23rd as Chamberlain spent the night at Godesberg in order to decide on the morning of the 24th "whether or not the discussions should go on."[137] Significantly enough, France and England informed Czechoslovakia on the evening of the 23rd that they no longer opposed the general Czechoslovak mobilization, which was then ordered at 10:30 p.m. on the 23rd.[138] Chamberlain returned to London without having reached an agreement with Hitler and with a German memorandum—transmitted to the French—stating that Germany intended to immediately occupy all the areas it was demanding. A plebiscite would then be organized by November 25 at the latest. This was too much to take, even for Chamberlain. As early as September 24 France decided on the call-up "of some categories of reservists": 753,000 men (287,000 regular army and 266,000 from the reserves) were sent to the northeastern border.[139]

On the 25th at 3 p.m. the French Council of Ministers met once more to reach a decision. There was, noted de Monzie, a "steep rise in temperature." A communiqué released by the British Foreign Office—without consulting Bonnet, added de Monzie—announced that should Czechoslovakia be subjected to German attack, "France would be compelled to provide help and that Great Britain and Russia would certainly be at France's side."[140] There was a lot of restlessness just before the meeting of the Council of Ministers. As of the 22nd Mandel, Reynaud and Champetier de Ribes were considering handing in their resignations. Herriot and Churchill, who was visiting in Paris, talked them out of it to avoid "a crisis in the midst of a storm."[141]

As early as the 21st Bonnet, Pomaret, Mistler, Bergery and socialist deputy René Brunet, back from Prague where he had been sent by Bonnet, all agreed, against those backing "resistance," to avoid war at any price.[142] They had the support of the elderly Joseph Caillaux,[143] as well as that of Flandin who wrote to Daladier on September 24 requesting a foreign policy debate in both chambers.[144]

At the meeting of the Council of Ministers on the 25th, those pacifists previously mentioned had the backing of Guy La Chambre, Chautemps, Queuille, and Marchandeau. Those in favor of resistance were opposed to the German plan. Reynaud stated, "The Godesberg project spells the end of Czechoslovakia." Mandel and Reynaud were convinced that England would take action; Bonnet answered that "he had no information on the issue." Daladier then joined the "resisters" by saying that he viewed the London agreement as an outer limit. "He does not want to accept the immediate entry of thirty German divisions into the Sudetenland because it would mean war."[145]

Then came the pilgrimage to London. On the evening of September 25 Daladier and Bonnet, with the usual entourage, met the same British partners as on the 18th. Chamberlain again gave an account of his conversations with Hitler. Daladier stated once more that the French government had not had the time to thoroughly study the Führer's proposals.

As far as Daladier was concerned, it appeared that if Hitler did not abide by the Franco-British proposal of September 17 one had to "do one's duty"—meaning go to war. Chamberlain agreed that "it was necessary to face the serious realities of the present."

Sir John Simon then inquired whether the French forces were contemplating the invasion of Germany. Daladier optimistically hinted that this was possible. To hand over—as it had been done—3 million Sudeten citizens to Germany was "quite a difficult decision, if not a dishonorable one." Hitler would not be satisfied, meaning that he intended to destroy Czechoslovakia. "France will never accept those kinds of concessions, those who wish to do so can follow us." Chamberlain was more inclined to do so than Sir John Simon and Samuel Hoare but he "must say in all candor that there had been disturbing news in London regarding the readiness of the French air force." The French press was "not belligerent at all." "It would be a futile consolation to want to fulfill your obligations toward your friends and help them, only to discover later on that you are in no condition to do so but are actually caving in." The British were therefore not prepared to commit to war.[146] At the short meeting on the morning of the 26th it was decided that Sir Horace Wilson would carry a message to Hitler requesting to "substitute a method of negotiations to violent military action."[147]

The crisis lasted three days. Many military precautions were taken, the "black-out" started, train windows were painted blue, signs showing the names of train stops were removed and, most of all, the reservists made their way to the borders. Gamelin traveled to London on the 26th and met with the members of the Imperial Defense Committee. He was relatively optimistic but requested "the order of magnitude to send significant British military units to France."[148] Admiral Darlan shared that relative optimism,[149] but not General Vuillemin, who noted a "very pronounced...disproportion of forces." French aircraft performance (250 fighters, 320 bombers and no reserves) was clearly inferior.[150]

Yet a sizeable mystery remained. Would the Soviets step in to help Czechoslovakia? Yes, they kept on saying, on condition that France step in according to the stipulations of the Soviet-Czechoslovak pact of May 1935. But since the USSR had no common borders with either Germany or Czechoslovakia, how could she possibly intervene? Passage had to be secured through Poland or Romania at the very least. But it was a well-known fact that those countries steadfastly refused to grant passage; Litvinov then said that the League of Nations could order them to do so. Everyone, however, knew that was impossible.[151]

There would be no progress during the whole month of September. Georges Bonnet met with Litvinov on the 11th in Geneva and Litvinov did not change his position.[152] Bonnet was barely able to obtain from Romanian Minister Comnène for his country to tolerate overflights by Soviet airplanes: "When the planes flew over they could draw some shelling that would miss the target."[153] Beneš had secured the assurance from the USSR that airplanes would be sent.[154] However, the general in command of the Czechoslovak air force went to Moscow and was given only delaying answers.[155] The Soviets only sent some light reinforcements, as Colonel Palasse, the French military attaché found out, to their side of the Polish border.[156] On September 23 they announced that if Poland attacked Czechoslovakia, the USSR would cancel the Soviet-Polish Non-Aggression Pact of July 25, 1932, without notice. However, Ambassador Coulondre was unable to find out whether they would then enter Polish territory.[157] At the height of the crisis the Soviet position was clear regarding the principle involved and totally unclear as to how it would help the Czechs.[158]

The crisis reached its climax with Hitler's violent speech on the evening of the 26th. It was a clever speech where, as François-Poncet stated, he "excelled at playing the innocent."[159] Would this lead to war?

Once just about every possible concession had been made on principle, it became difficult to unleash the catastrophe on formal details. This was Bonnet's opinion. He told the Council of Ministers on the morning of September 27 that "the diplomatic situation has never been worse and we have no air force…It is impossible to go to war. I am against a general mobilization. An accommodation must be secured at any price. I face the strongest opposition of most of my colleagues. The matter of my resignation has undoubtedly come up." He saw Daladier that afternoon and "begged" him to continue his efforts toward peace. "He seems shaken. He is thinking of sending François-Poncet a telegram for a final initiative."[160] He is, said American Ambassador Bullitt, "tortuous and weak" while Daladier is "sure of himself and strong."[161] Bullitt did meet with Daladier on the 27th to convey a message from Roosevelt who "will do whatever you suggest in the pursuit of peace."[162]

Yet, despite a telegram from Bonnet to François-Poncet during the night of the 27th to the 28th proposing a guarantee to be offered to the

Germans,[163] the "saving" initiative once again originated with the British. Chamberlain easily convinced Mussolini to suggest to Hitler a four-power conference in Germany. Corbin telegraphed the news to Bonnet on September 28, 1938.[164] François-Poncet was meeting with Hitler and had to interrupt the conversation because Mussolini was calling the Führer on the telephone. He asked him to delay the mobilization and the attack for twenty-four hours.[165] Hitler agreed and decided that the conference of the four powers would take place the following day in Munich.

As he was leaving, Daladier—accompanied by Léger and Rochat but not Bonnet—received a final telegram from Beneš asking him "not to forget the twenty years of political collaboration I have had with France." We shall not recount the Munich conference in detail.[166] Daladier, like Chamberlain, gave in on practically everything. They were only able to have the occupation of the Sudetenland take place between the 1st and the 10th rather than on the 1st. They discussed guaranteeing the new borders of Czechoslovakia. Only France and Great Britain agreed to do so, while Germany and Italy stated that first the issue of Czechoslovakia's borders with Poland and Hungary had to be resolved.

7.

French Public Opinion and Munich

Much has been written on this subject.[167] Munich was a greater factor in revealing the changes at work in French thinking, even more than March 1936, more than the Popular Front.

We can turn to two public opinion polls taken by the very new *Institut français d'opinion publique* founded by a young sociologist, Jean Stoetzel, who would later be the author of a very remarkable doctoral dissertation on public opinion.[168] The Gallup method, perfected in the United States in 1935 and become popular in 1936, was now reaching France.[169] The first poll asked the question, "Do you approve of the Munich agreements?" Answer: 57% yes, 37% no. The second poll taken shortly after asked the question, "Do you think that France and England must now oppose any new demand made by Hitler?" Answer: 70% yes, 17% no. "Such a high percentage," as Ageron correctly writes,[170] "indicates clearly that some Frenchmen only accepted Munich very grudgingly."

To try to understand what appears to be a contradiction between the two polls, one must not forget that a shocked public opinion remained in a state of flux.

Initially there was the reaction of a country convinced that war was about to begin, feeling naturally relieved at the idea that it was avoided *at the last minute*. This explains why Daladier, returning from the Munich conference on September 30, was surprised to be welcomed by a huge and enthusiastic crowd. Georges Bonnet, Guy La Chambre, and Chautemps were waiting for him at Le Bourget airport. The latter was said to have told Gamelin, "So, General, not getting your share after all?"—which Gamelin, quite rightly, did not like at all.[171] And Gamelin then telling Daladier, "Mr. Prime Minister, you are about to get too warm a welcome." Several hundred thousand people did take the time to line the streets along the way and at the evening ceremony at the Arc de Triomphe.[172] It is a well established fact that Daladier felt that Munich was "an immense defeat for France and England."[173]

The daily *Paris-Soir* began a funding drive—that would eventually fail—to give Chamberlain a "house of peace" near Biarritz as a gift (he loved trout fishing). *Le Petit Parisien* opened a "golden book" where one million people were said to have signed their approval. Paris deputy Pierre Taittinger immediately wanted two streets of the French capital to be named after Chamberlain and Daladier. Pierre-Étienne Flandin sent cables congratulating the four who signed on October 1 (and therefore to Hitler and Mussolini). Masses offering thanks to God were being celebrated everywhere.

The initial reaction continued in the Chamber of Deputies on October 2. Daladier was given a long ovation. "A real victory for peace," he said. He mentioned the guarantees of the Czechoslovak borders and the need to fight for peace. The foreign policy statement was approved by a vote of 515 to 75, among them the 73 communist deputies, socialist Jean Bouhey and moderate Henri de Kérillis. As Gabriel Péri was to say, "The Communist Party refuses to be associated with the highway robbery Munich represents." Louis Marin, another moderate (who abstained), expressed his disagreement in a striking statement: "A weakened, disarmed France was sacrificing Czechoslovakia in order to avoid a war that she felt she could not fight and win, had just confessed her downfall to the entire world. It was no longer the France of Foch and Clemenceau, of the Marne and of Verdun." Kérillis said, prophetically, "Germany is insatiable and pitiless toward the weak, and you have just shown yourselves to be weak. Germany only respects the strong. *You may think she will become quiet and peaceful and I tell you she will become demanding and terrible.*[174] [Emphasis added.]

The first impression was one of enthusiasm at saving the peace, which was quickly replaced, even among those who favored Munich, by the feeling that they must live with the inevitable and that Munich was a disaster. Emmanuel Mounier in *Esprit* accused "a disoriented bourgeoisie that finds the energy only to defend itself from its fears...the lower classes confused by alcohol worrying only about their savings." In his book *L'Equinoxe de Septembre*, Montherlant wrote an oft-quoted line, "France is back to playing cards and to Tino Rossi."[175] The lingering enthusiasm was limited to extremist groups like Doriot's PPF, the newswriter Gustave Hervé, the daily *Le Matin* and the right-wing weeklies. "It's not a triumph. It's peace," wrote Léon Bailby in *Le Jour*.[176] And very quickly most Frenchmen concluded that it was a surrender.

Was that course of action right or wrong? The issue was to divide France into two groups, *pro-* and *anti-*Munich, that no longer followed the political parties. Four positions appeared very quickly.

1.   The traditional left-wing pacifists

This was a trend we have often encountered. It included a few rare intellectuals such as Roussy, a university president, Professor Rivet of the Museum,* Montel of the *Faculté des sciences*, historians Jules Isaac—even though he was a Jew—and L'Héritier, and the philosopher Gustave Monod.[177] This viewpoint was strong among independent socialists such as Marcel Déat and Adrien Marquet, the mayor of Bordeaux, and in some radical circles. Besides Georges Bonnet, one of its most vocal supporters was the minister of public works, Anatole de Monzie, who hated Beneš and Czechoslovakia; as well as Pomaret, the minister of labor, Mistler,[178] Gaston Bergery,[179] the leader of the small "frontist" group that opposed Franco, was at first favorable to Czechoslovakia and then switched to a staunch pro-Munich position; Chautemps, Queuille, and Marchandeau, all of the radical-socialists.[180] Bertrand de Jouvenel even set up a meeting on September 29 between de Monzie and Otto Abetz, "a friend of Mr. Ribbentrop."[181] However, Bertrand de Jouvenel did not belong to that group. On October 16 he wrote in the London *Times*, "The Führer will

---

Le Muséum d'histoire naturelle (Museum of Natural History). [NDT]

only be impressed if the British and French nations recover from their current lax attitude... The only logical consequence to Munich is a 52-hour week in France and establishing conscription in Great Britain. Then and only then can we speak as great nations."[182]

The socialist SFIO Party was hesitating between pacifism and active anti-fascism. The party's drift increased during the months following Munich. At the national council meeting of November 6 and 7, a moderate resolution introduced by Léon Blum was approved by 6,755 votes against 1,241 in favor of a violently anti-Munich resolution introduced by Jean Zyromski.[183] This was not significant, however. On December 24 a special national congress opened in Montrouge. The resolution introduced by Léon Blum stated that the party favored peace but was ready to participate in national defense "totally and without reservations." Paul Faure, who had just won a special election in the Saône-et-Loire, opposed him and was introducing a resolution against armaments and the Franco-Soviet Pact. "The victory of peace is possible only if one does not believe in the inevitability of war." Blum's resolution won with 4,322 votes. Faure's received 2,837 votes; there were 1,014 abstentions. It meant that one-third of the socialist rank and file included moderate pacifists, like Jean Allemane (who had written: "Better to have an agreement, even though unsatisfactory than war.").[184] as well as Spinasse and L'Héveder.[185]

The CGT, reunified in 1936, was also split along the same lines. The old "unitarians" of the CGTU, the communists and their organ *La Vie Ouvrière* were *anti*-Munich. The former "confederate" reformists, often opposed to the communists, had created the weekly *Syndicats*. Secretary General Léon Jouhaux hesitated between the two. At the Thirty-first Congress of the CGT held at Nantes from November 13 to 17 there were a few violent debates. The important event was the division of the "Syndicats" group. Jouhaux and a minority allied themselves with the pro-communists—Benoît-Frachon and his friends—to vote for an *anti*-Munich resolution introduced by René Belin, the future Vichy minister, Georges Dumoulin, André Delmas, and Jean Mathé, reaffirming the pacifist tradition of the workers' movement. The *anti*-Munich group (5,797 "Syndicats" plus 16,784 mainly iron workers and railroad employees) prevailed over the pacifists (2,289 "Syndicats" and 6,419 school teachers, postal workers and miners).

Significantly, the pacifist resolution was introduced by André Delmas,[186] one of the leaders of the National Teachers Union, which showed the strongest commitment to pacifist trends. Let us not forget that in 1914–1918 the bulk of the infantry's reserve officers—the group that suffered the heaviest losses—was recruited from two social groups, the "good bourgeoisie" and the school teachers. The SNI (teacher's union), influenced no doubt by the slaughter of its own membership took extreme positions. It opposed the Franco-Soviet Pact "inasmuch as it could become a smokescreen for an alliance," and supported non-intervention in Spain. Many came to feel "Better slavery than war." It doesn't appear that there were more than 15% communists in the SNI membership.[187] The majority was indignant that the Communist Party was accepting the tricolor flag and the *Marseillaise*. They were all very much against the "Union Sacrée." As Delmas wrote in *L'École Liberatrice* of March 26, 1938, "Union Sacrée, suicide of the popular forces."

2. *The new right-wing pacifism.*

This did not by any stretch include the entire right as many have thought. Due to the fear of communism, the USSR and its "helpers"— Beneš being one of them—many moderates and most right-wing extremists were slowly discovering that they tended toward pacifism, all the more noteworthy since they had been until recently the most enthusiastic chauvinists.

There were a few rare admirers of the Hitler regime. The small group around Fernand de Brinon was not a political party. There was no real pro-Nazi party in France; even the tiny Parti Franciste, led by Marcel Bucard, was more attuned to Italian fascism. French anti-Semites like *L'Action Française* and Darquier de Pellepoix admired German anti-Semitism but not Hitlerism generally.

L'Action Française, seriously waning at the time and being led by a few somewhat incoherent elderly men no longer attracting many youths, was elated by the election of Charles Maurras to the *Académie Française* on June 9, 1938.[188] Those who voted in his favor were Pétain, Weygand, Franchet d'Esperey and Léon Bérard—who was to reestablish relations with Franco—Louis Bertrand of the de Brinon group and Abel Bonnard, who would become a cabinet minister at Vichy.

L'Action Française congratulated Darquier de Pellepoix for denouncing any kind of collusion with Hitler.[189] Charles Maurras had spent his entire life castigating the Germans and was still going at it. But he had become ardently *pro*-Munich. On October 4 he withdrew his yearly candidacy for the Nobel Peace Prize in favor of Neville Chamberlain.[190]

Even though he would admit that Munich was a defeat for France, he still preferred that to a Soviet victory. His disciple, Thierry Maulnier, clearly said so: "A German defeat would mean the collapse of the totalitarian systems that provide the main barrier against communist revolution."[191] On September 27 the headline "Down with war!" filled the entire front page of the paper, clearly showing "the movement's inability to choose between its various hatreds."[192] The weekly *Je suis partout* basically followed the same line.

Colonel de La Rocque's French Social Party (PSF) was pro-Munich but not that favorable toward racism. "France disapproves of racism and its excesses," said La Rocque in a speech in November 1938.[193] La Rocque viewed the November 30 strike as a joint action by Berlin and Moscow.[194] He firmly opposed the gesture made by Flandin in sending Hitler a telegram. The army veteran's comment was "Defeatism gone AWOL."

Jacques Doriot's *Parti Populaire Français* took a more ambiguous position.[195] Doriot had not yet become the pro-Hitler man he was to be following the defeat. Before Munich he was saying that France would fight if necessary.[196] He did not believe in Soviet help and despised Czechoslovakia, "a creation of Philippe Berthelot." With his collaborators Claude Jeantet, Alfred Fabre-Luce and Drieu La Rochelle, he condemned war to such an extent that his newspaper *La Liberté* was banned on September 29. "We came close"—wrote *L'Emancipation Nationale* on September 30— "we must banish the war party from the nation."[197] The Communist Party was the "war party," "the foreign army camping on our land." The PPF viewed Munich as a defeat but applauded the Franco-German declaration of December 6, 1938.

There were many pacifists among the right-wing moderates. Ageron noted in regard to the poll indicating that 70% of the French wanted to resist any new demands coming from Hitler, that the total dropped to 50% among professionals and public service employees.[198] This showed the pacifism of the socialist voters but a right wing pacifism as well. Flandin was a good example. Paradoxically, Pierre Laval hated Daladier too much to really be pro-Munich. In any case, he remained silent,[199] closing his door to Otto Abetz and refusing to attend the reception on December 6th honoring Ribbentrop.[200]

Most Catholic circles held a negative view of the Hitler regime, although the "relief" associated with Munich did make a very brief appearance.[201] "The sky is blue again," wrote *La France Catholique* of October

10. But the thought of the humiliation, of the "slap across the face," as *France Réelle* stated on October 1, was also present. In those circles anti-communism and pacifism also went hand in hand.

3. The left-wing anti-Fascist resisters

This included all the communists. The Communist Party was the only one to avoid any split in 1938—it would change in September 1939—by strenuously opposing the Daladier government against the law decrees, and faithfully following the Soviet line on Munich, since the USSR had not been invited to the conference. The party, whose doctrine, as well as its feelings, was anti-Fascist, was a compact but isolated bloc. This was true, especially following the Radical Party congress at the end of October where the Popular Front was dissolved and at Daladier's request took an openly anti-communist stance.

As we have noted, two-thirds of the socialists with Léon Blum, Marx Dormoy, and part of the "Syndicats" group within the CGT also rejected pacifism. The struggle against fascism overshadowed the leftist traditions. The most significant case was that of the radicals. To follow Daladier was, in a way, to be pro-Munich. It didn't mean being a pacifist for all those involved. The best examples were Jean Zay and Edouard Herriot.

Jean Zay, a radical "Young Turk" was one of the rare ministers who opposed Munich.[202] His friend Cesar Campinchi, minister of marine,[203] followed him somewhat less strongly, not being too much in favor of Georges Bonnet whom he had defeated in June 1936 and becoming president of the radical group in Chamber. Herriot, on the other hand, was encouraging Jean Zay and other anti-Munich political leaders to not leave the government. After a brief moment of "relief" he once again became a strong believer in resistance. "Force is winning, the law is dead...let us be forceful."[204] Pierre Cot, another "Young Turk," was also a determined anti-Munich politician.

At the fringes of radicalism there were other anti-fascists. Paul-Boncour, who like Herriot was a promoter of collective security, refused to accept the Munich surrender and immediately set up a group called "Nation et Liberté." "It included socialists, radicals, syndicalists, Catholics from Jeune République[205] and the League for Human Rights." Among them was Léo Lagrange, a former minister in Léon Blum's cabinet, a socialist close to the communists who would be killed in battle in May 1940 and who was also a friend of Jean Zay, and Jean Zyromski.[206]

4. The right-wing nationalists

Except for the communists, like every other political group, the right was more seriously divided than was generally thought. For example, when Flandin sent his telegram to Hitler, Paul Reynaud resigned within the hour from their party, the *Alliance Démocratique*. "A deluge of resignations" from others followed,[207] at the same time as those from Paul Reynaud, Senator Taurines, James de Rothschild, Joseph Laniel, who later became a Prime Minister of the Fourth Republic, Louis Jacquinot, Louis Rollin, etc. At the party's congress Charles Reibel, a deputy from Seine-et-Oise who had resigned from the vice presidency, violently attacked Flandin, who answered, "I prefer exchanging telegrams to artillery shells."[208]

Young writers like Drieu La Rochelle and Bertrand de Jouvenel left Jacques Doriot's PPF. De Jouvenel also resigned from the *Comité France-Allemagne*. Another group followed, led by Pierre Pucheu, director of the *Comptoir Sidérurgique* (at the start of 1939), and a few other lieutenants of Doriot, Paul Marion, Arrighi, etc. Pucheu was linked to the Schneider group that controlled the Czechoslovak Skoda works, and he condemned the new German-Czech border. But a man of the far right such as he was in taking an anti-Munich position would cancel out the "economic Munich" legend that we shall discuss in the following chapter.

A majority of the popular democrats was anti-Munich, along with Francisque Gay, Georges Bidault, Ernest Pezet, Edmond Michelet, Robert Lecourt,[209] and Champetier de Ribes. The same applied to their daily newspaper *L'Aube* and *Temps Présent*, edited by Stanislas Fumet. In *Esprit* Emmanuel Mounier wrote about "the ignominious peace." The most anti-Munich writers in his group, like Jacques Madaule and Jean Lacroix offered their point of view in *Le Voltigeur Français*.[210]

We have noted the anti-Munich stance in the Catholic right with Louis Marin. *La Croix* was very much opposed to Chamberlain.[211] Jacques Bardoux,[212] who had been elected in October 1938 as senator from the Puy-de-Dôme, immediately took a militant position within the foreign affairs committee.[213] Part of the press followed them, especially *L'Époque* edited by Henri de Kérillis, Raymond , and André Pironneau.

Le Figaro was to wait until March 1939 before taking a position of resistance. *L'Ordre*, edited by Émile Buré, was the strongest among the right-wing newspapers, and Pertinax, who had been at *L'Écho de Paris*, was now pleased to be publishing his column there.

Finally, we must also mention Georges Mandel, the most noteworthy of the right-wing resisters, and a disciple of Clemenceau.

Curiously enough, there was the violent reaction of many young militants of the *Action Française* who broke with the movement once they discovered the beginnings of a right-wing pacifism that they found revolting. For example, the attorney Jacques Renouvin, who slapped Flandin at the congress of the *Alliance Démocratique* as he was laying a wreath as tradition had it at the Arc de Triomphe, his friend Guillain de Bénouville, who would become a general in the Resistance, that same Resistance that led to Renouvin's death in a concentration camp. Henri d'Astier de la Vigerie and Honoré d'Estienne d'Orves belonged to the same group.

The French were somewhere between those four positions, a sometimes vigilant or wait-and-see "mass"; but they were more and more attracted to the idea, despite the legend to the contrary, of resisting Hitler.

8.

THE COLLAPSE
OF FRANCE'S PRESTIGE ABROAD

Whether to save the peace or play for time, France lost the moral high ground at Munich and a prestige that had already been seriously damaged in March 1936 and March 1938. Foreign reactions relayed by French diplomats on the issue were significant. "The entire world was amazed at our retreat," wrote Léon Noël.[214]

In one country, Czechoslovakia, the honor of France was being questioned. Students were returning their diplomas; officers were doing the same with their decorations. Several of the *Alliance Française* shut down. In an eloquent letter addressed to Daladier on October 6, 1938,[215] General Faucher, head of the French military mission to Czechoslovakia, vigorously condemned, in the name of honor and efficiency, the policy of the government and sent in his resignation to the prime minister. He recalled "the indignation" of the Czechs on September 22 and then at Munich. "We cry about the treason of France, a country we love," many Czechs told him. "France has embraced the doctrine of the scrap of paper. "Why," wrote Faucher, "did you declare that you would fulfill your side of the agreement? If for any reason you felt you could not fulfill your obligations why didn't you say so clearly? The resentment of the Czechoslovaks is not a passing phenomenon but something that goes deeper."

Of all the dramatic reports describing the unhappiness of the Czechs, and the violent feelings they had toward France, the most vivid was the one written by Lacroix on October 5: "My greatest mistake in the eyes of History," Beneš told him, "will be that I was loyal to France."[216]

A loss of prestige is not, as it is too often thought, to simply be deprived of useless vanities. Prestige is a component of strength. Its loss creates unfathomable consequences.

For example, the USSR, beyond its displeasure at having been kept out of Munich, drew conclusions from the whole matter, which Ambassador Coulondre experienced as of October 4 and the importance of which would become clear during the months ahead. If, he said, the Soviet press was increasingly sarcastic about Chamberlain, it expressed "commiseration for France, which it viewed as diminished." Deputy Commissar of Foreign Affairs Potemkin spoke of the need now to reach an understanding with Germany. His words were revealing: "Poland is preparing its fourth partition."

"Our international prestige," Coulondre concluded, "is very seriously damaged by this crisis and our morale, already shaken, will suffer."[217]

The same applied to France's smaller allies. "I can't hide the fact that France's prestige didn't emerge unscathed from the Munich conference," said Colonel Merson, military attaché in Belgrade.[218] From Bucharest Minister Adrien Thierry wrote, "We must not hide the fact that since the Munich agreement Romanian opinion is very much divided regarding France. In private conversations those with left wing ideas say that our influence has ceased in Central Europe and they attack us violently, while extreme right wing elements proclaim that by calling for a close collaboration between Romania and the Reich they are backing a policy that reflects the country's true interests."[219] In Greece, the followers of Venizelos who were pro-French feel that "she had abandoned the democratic cause."[220]

The British themselves, even though "deeply impressed by the conditions of the partial mobilization of the French army," were insisting on the country's drift. France "enjoyed only a shaky stability" internally. Abroad it was the failure of the European system that France had built in 1919. "Most British viewed it as an inevitable change, many felt even that it was desirable, some of them feel it means a weakening of France's position in Europe and in the world." "Confusion," "dark acceptance of defeat," wrote *The Economist*. "Tragic weakness of French democracy," according to *The Manchester Guardian*.[221]

The loss in prestige was felt far beyond Europe. Much of American public opinion reacted that way. However, a Gallup poll taken during the first half of October yielded the following results to the question, "Do you feel that Britain and France acted for the best in giving in to Germany rather than going to war?" Yes, 59%—No, 41%.[222] Undersecretary of State Sumner Welles met with Bonnet, Chautemps and Daladier and he did not hide his worries. This prompted an initiative by Bonnet via Ambassador de Saint-Quentin at the end of November. He wished to justify French policy seeking—unsuccessfully in any case—American approval. "The American government cannot at the same time not give us any assurance of help in the event of a conflict and not approve our attempt at a European understanding."[223]

The same was true in Latin America. For example, in Bogotà, Colombia, Minister d'Aumale wrote, "Regarding recent events, Germany's prestige has increased noticeably." The press "is friendly toward us and pleased to see that our country has avoided war, but one senses a slightly patronizing tone that is more upsetting than an out and out attack."[224]

Finally, in the Far East the Franco-British surrender prompted Japan to withdraw on November 18 from the Nine Power Treaty of 1922 regarding China. Munich only increased the feeling of the weakness of the help provided by the Western democracies to China. Japanese extremists became increasingly convinced that "we can do anything to them," and in particular establish Japan's "Asian domination."[225] "The attitude of France and England," wrote Georges Picot, chargé d'affaires in Chungking, "was interpreted in the Far East as the desire by both powers to avoid conflict at any price by giving in to the threats and demands of the totalitarian countries." The Japanese took advantage of this and "to the Japanese the simple act of lodging a protest rather than resorting to force, as was done in the past against China, is in the eyes of every nation in the Far East an admission of powerlessness by the democratic countries and a tribute to the power of Japan."[226]

Chapter XII

After Munich:
Expectations and Uncertainties

B ecause the Munich decision came suddenly in the wake of a brief moment where war seemed inevitable, it created an extraordnary shock in France.

The government was well aware that France had abandoned an ally strategically placed in a difficult position but well armed nevertheless. In the formal sense it had not betrayed the alliance. Morally, things looked much worse, however, since France had demanded that the ally agree to its own surrender. A number of problems arise that we shall immediately examine: the weakness of the air force; the alliances in Eastern Europe; the possibility of a long-term agreement with Nazi Germany and Fascist Italy; the future role of the USSR; and the issue of Germany's economic dominance over part of the continent.

In light of these issues there could have been a major reversal of France's foreign policy: to accept decadence and a German Europe where France, only too pleased to keep its colonial empire, would have played second fiddle along with Italy. But was this compatible with the ideals and traditions of Daladier and Bonnet, both of them radical socialists, a

Chamber where the radicals were putting an end to the Popular Front, but that included 155 socialist SFIO deputies and 73 communists?

One could also imagine a great reversal of positions by basing France's security on a complete alliance with the USSR. Aside from the communists, however, no one was really considering it. This would have meant their coming to power at a time when their influence was clearly receding. The USSR itself was barely emerging from the great purges, especially the one affecting the Red Army in 1937. No one saw it as being strong enough to establish a useful counterweight.

The only remaining solution was *to strengthen the policy of solidarity with England*. While Chamberlain was triumphant following Munich, Daladier on the contrary understood the magnitude of the damage done. To prevent the disaster from becoming irreparable, Franco-British solidarity had to be maintained even at the cost of decisions thought to be out of the question until then, such as the recognition of Italy's conquest of Ethiopia and the signing of a peaceful declaration with Germany similar to the one Chamberlain had acheived on September 30.

It would therefore be mistaken to think that Daladier or even Bonnet were attracted to a "pro-German" policy or a British-style *appeasement*. The French were unhappily adopting appeasement because they needed England which was pressuring France to take the same attitude until Chamberlain opened his eyes.

The three men at the center of this debate—Daladier, Bonnet, and Léger—certainly agreed on this "English line." There were some sharp differences between them in the details of that policy.

Daladier viewed the need for British support as something obvious. "Not a single Frenchman will agree to go against Germany and Italy without at least the assurance of having immediate British help," he had stated at the dramatic meeting of the Council of Ministers of September 19, 1938.[1] While his main areas were internal and defense policy, Daladier "was unfamiliar with foreign policy issues." He "excelled at making statements of principle…but whenever practical and concrete issues arise he allows himself to be led by his British partners who were very clever at hiding their determination to reach an accommodation passed along as practicality."[2] He hated the dictators and was much less attracted to a rapprochement with Italy than Bonnet. As for Hitler, Daladier harbored a kind of sentimental dream of reconciliation "among war veterans." Had they not both fought gallantly in the war? Daladier, on the other hand, was wary of Bonnet. Just like the British, he disliked his secrecy, his intrigues and his maneuvers.[3] But he needed him inside the Radical Party and feared him more outside than within the government. This all stemmed from Bonnet's burning desire to follow Daladier as prime minister.[4]

Léger's position was no doubt close to that of Daladier. Inasmuch as we know the precise reactions of this very mysterious man, he also viewed Munich as a necessary evil but, on the other hand, he played a key role—with London's approval—in eliminating René Massigli, director of political affairs and the most outspoken backer of resistance.[5] On October 12 Massigli was appointed ambassador to Turkey. Another anti-Munich official, Pierre Comert, head of the press office, would be given the same treatment. Léger supported strong Franco-British ties in the hope that the British would come to a more realistic view of the German and Italian menace (he had always hated Italy).[6]

Georges Bonnet was the most difficult to understand. The problem can be attributed in part to the fact that he spent some thirty-five years after Munich incessantly crafting his own image. British historian Anthony Adamthwaite, some thirty years after Sir Lewis Namier, has written an excellent analysis of Bonnet's historiography.[7] Prior to 1940 it was written by authors sympathetic to him such as Alfred Fabre-Luce,[8] Louis Thomas,[9] and Pierre Dominique.[10]

Under the Vichy government Jacques Fouques-Duparc was in charge of reconstituting the documents that had been burned at the Quai d'Orsay on May 16, 1940. Georges Bonnet provided his papers, which were copies that a former minister was entitled to keep. These were copied under the supervision of an archivist working in the ministry. Some of the documents retained by Georges Bonnet were either hidden in his garden in the Gironde or held for safekeeping by the French consul in San Sebastian. Besides the synopsis written after the fact, there was reason to consider those documents as being authentic. We feel that Adamthwaite was a bit too suspicious on this issue.[11] It is reasonable to assume, however, that Georges Bonnet may not have provided every document and, therefore, the "Fouqus-Duparc reconstruction" may contain some rather large omissions. Finally, Georges Bonnet wrote a few long books in his own defense: *Défense de la Paix* (1946–1948) in two volumes and, much later, *Le Quai d'Orsay sous trois Républiques* (1961). The approximations, omissions and contradictions they contain have been pointed out quite often. In addition, the book *Vingt ans de vie politique* (1969) is very revealing of one aspect of Bonnet's life, namely his extreme opportunism in joining the Radical-Socialist Party

From all this and many other documents it becomes very clear that Georges Bonnet tended to tailor his statements to the various persons he was talking to. Anatole de Monzie, who hated Beneš and Czechoslovakia and, as we have noted, encouraged Bonnet into making concessions during the Munich conference, drew a portrait of the man dated November 6, 1938.[12] Monzie praised his "quite exceptional qualities." "He knew and gauged each one according to his importance at the moment. He certainly knew the political "black book," had his informers everywhere, and went to dinner strategically, he never made mistakes due to his temperament or to passion." He "would take on big risks" but "refused small skirmishes." Was he an intriguer? "No, his was a case of obvious agility, an excess of agility. He was too quick to jump on the bandwagon, on every bandwagon."

Bonnet was, in other words, the prototypical opportunist. Therefore, the Bonnet of October to December 1938 may—and would—have a view of French interests that would be completely different from that of the Bonnet after March 1939, who was different from the Bonnet of the end of August.

In October 1938 it appeared that his ideas came from a deep sense of weariness towards the smaller Eastern European allies. Like Daladier, he was loyal to the "British line" and went further than his prime minister in considering ridding France of its eastern alliances. On that subject we have the definite confirmation of Léon Noël, ambassador to Poland after having been minister to Prague and that is also borne out by the documents. Noël knew Bonnet very well, "one of my friends as a youth and a colleague at the *Conseil d'État*."[13] Léon Noël, having witnessed how a reliable ally such as Czechoslovakia had been betrayed by Colonel Beck's Poland, concluded that "we must revise our political relations with Poland not only for our security but even more for our own dignity." In a long dispatch dated October 25,[14] he carefully built his case. There was every indication that Poland was next in line and Hitler was treating her carefully only temporarily. The agreements of 1921 and 1925 were to provide "automatic" military aid between France and Poland as was the case between France and Czechoslovakia. Rather than being backed into a "new Munich," wouldn't it be preferable, while maintaining the privileged relationship, *to withdraw from the automatic na-*

ture of France's obligations? The military attaché in Warsaw, General Musse, agreed with his ambassador who traveled to Paris to gain support for his position. He obtained the unofficial approval of General Weygand (who had fought in Poland in 1920) and of General Gamelin. Then he went to see Georges Bonnet.

Bonnet wanted to go further. "The way he was speaking, he intended to quite simply cancel all of France's agreements without further delay, meaning the Franco-Polish agreements and the Franco-Soviet mutual assistance pact."[15] As we shall, see this did not happen. However, during his stay in Paris—he would not succeed in meeting with Daladier—Léon Noël found out that many officials agreed with Bonnet's opinion for a "pull-out from the East." Louis Aubert, an historian on the French delegation to the League of Nations, supported a similar viewpoint and it is possible that the memo he wrote on this subject was in fact read by the minister.[16] "We must pull back," he wrote. "Nothing could be more useless, for some time to come in any case, than to repeat the words and take once again those positions that were thwarted at Munich." In the final analysis the minister decided to leave as they were for the moment.[17]

The reason Bonnet, like Daladier, Léger and most of the politicians who were close to power, wanted to hold the "British line" and attempt a rapprochement with Germany and Italy was because of the different opinions about withdrawal, a sort of French neutralism in Eastern Europe. It wasn't due to an attraction to Germany. When Bonnet told German ambassador von Welczeck on November 7 that a Franco-German agreement would be "the fulfillment of a lifelong dream," we shouldn't forget his exceedingly strong capacity to adapt to the person he happened to be talking with.[18]

We should point out that Gamelin was also leaning toward the "British line." He said so clearly on October 12[19] and was rather skeptical about the Franco-German rapprochement. "Our only possibility to resist," wrote Admiral Darlan, navy chief of the general staff, "is in the close agreement that must exist between ourselves and England on the political level and for the preparation of military capabilities." Darlan had read the Gamelin memo we have just cited.[20]

1.

Munich and the Economy

While examining the issue of the part played by business interests in the foreign policy decisions of 1938–1939, René Girault concluded that these remained divided:[21] "For some the future was to be found in the colonial empire and therefore in the retreat from Eastern Europe. They viewed the appeasement policy as a rational one, even more so since it would bring France closer to the powers defending the established order. Nevertheless other businessmen favored solutions entailing resistance to Germany, either because they opposed Hitler's racism or due to nationalist feelings." He feels the first category would include the Lazard Bank, the Banque de l'Indochine and Paul Baudoin, its director general. He places François de Wendel in the second category. De Wendel was a friend of Georges Mandel and felt that Germany represented "the only real danger." He wanted France to respect her commitments and deplored the fact that the Czechs were unpopular among the moderates. He viewed Munich as a disaster and on October 5 said that Mandel was "the man who wanted war that the future would probably vindicate."[22]

France—as we have noted previously—had some very large interests in Czechoslovakia, a highly industrialized country with only 20% foreign debt (compared to 63% for Poland, 85% for Yugoslavia, and 90% for Romania). France was the number one investor in Poland and Yugoslavia, third in Romania behind the United States and England, second in Czechoslovakia behind England. Therefore, the very active French policy and the political aloofness of Great Britain toward Eastern Europe were not due to an obvious disproportion in their investments.

During the 1950s and 1960s the historians of communist Czechoslovakia offered the view of an "economic Munich that preceded the political Munich." In an excellent work published in 1974, the Czech historian Alice Teichova showed, through an enormous amount of statistics, that "if a tendency existed to avoid new long-term investments in Czechoslovakia, especially following Hitler's rise to power, the idea of a willful withdrawal of Western capital in order to leave a vacant space for German penetration to move in is unfounded."[23] As of December 31, 1937, before the Anschluss began to dislocate the country's economy, she estimated that British investments represented 30.8% of all foreign investments; France 21.4%; Austria 13.1%; Germany 8.8%; Switzerland 7.2% and Belgium 7.1%. After the Anschluss Germany's amount became as large as that of France. France was in first place in banking (44.5%), the mechanical industries (73.8%), in second place behind Belgium in the chemical industry (24.8%), in second place behind Austria in sugar refineries, very far behind Great Britain in second place in mining and steel works (15% to 61%), in third place behind Austria and Great Britain in textiles, and in third place behind Great Britain and Germany for glass works ceramics and porcelain (14.2%). France was weak in the electric industries compared to Germany, Switzerland, Belgium and Great Britain.

Since 1919 Schneider-Le Creusot et Cie. played a key role in the Skoda enterprises (73% of capital investments in 1919), along with its subsidiary the *Union européenne industrielle et financière* (headed by Aimé Lepercq), which employed many French engineers. The Schneider company, it must be noted, was forced to sell its shares in Skoda in December 1938 and would do so again following France's defeat for its shares in the *Compagnie métallurgique et minière*. Far from "laying the groundwork" for Germany, it held on to its position as long as possible.[24]

Schneider and de Wendel also owned a large part of the Austrian and Slovak magnesium mines.

"French influence in Skoda enterprises was decisive since its original investment by Schneider until December 1938, following the Munich agreement…The decisive nature of the French shareholders was not only due to the fact that they owned the majority of the shares but also to a network of personal and contractual financial relationships."[25] Apart from a recession in 1933, the Skoda Company continued to grow from 1921 to 1938. A capital increase in January 1937 reduced Schneider's shares to 46.49%—allowing it to maintain control but this was not at all a transfer to the Germans. On the contrary, the Czech state and banks, along with British banks and private Czechoslovak shareholders, owned the new shares. Since 60% of Skoda's weapons production went to the Czechoslovak army, one can see how the loss of the Sudetenland was a disaster for Czechoslovakia and Schneider-Le Creusot. The sale of December 31, 1938, signaled Skoda's entrance into Germany's sphere of influence.[26]

France was present in the chemical industry through the *Société française de dynamite*, part of international Nobel Trust. In the oil industry the *Société française des pétroles tchecoslovaques* held a position smaller than Royal Dutch and the American companies.

One of the four largest Czechoslovak banks (the Länderbank which became the *Banque pour le commerce et l'industrie*), 77.8% of which belonged to the *Banque des pays de l'Europe centrale* and headquartered in Paris with a branch in Vienna, played a key role by making long-term loans especially to the mechanics industry. Following the Anschluss the *Banque des pays de l'Europe centrale* had to sell its shares in its Vienna branch to the Dresdner Bank, but insisted on maintaining its Prague headquarters (which had long been headed by the famous economist Charles Rist).

Through Skoda, Schneider owned 10.5% of the bank shares that was just as important the Anglo-Czechoslovak and Prague Credit Bank. We must point out that during the period we are examining the French government had accepted two Czechoslovak loans with the guarantee of the French state: one for 600 million in 1932; the other renewing the first one and taking it to 700 million in 1937. Right after Munich Great Britain approved 20 million pounds sterling in help and France 600 million francs for Czechoslovakia.[27]

As for Munich there is every indication proving that politics took the lead over the economy.

Nevertheless, the economic consequences of the agreement appeared disastrous. While France succeeded until 1938 in holding on to its financial positions and let go of them only under duress, she discovered that little by little *Germany was taking over trade in Eastern Europe.* This was being discussed as early as the beginning of October,[28] and the decision was reached to send an economic mission to various Central and Eastern European countries headed by a young senior treasury official, Hervé Alphand.

Before recounting the inquiries of the Alphand mission, its conclusions and results, we may attempt to summarize the situation as the French viewed it. At the beginning of November, the Quai d'Orsay received from the London embassy an optimistic report by Baron Stackleberg, head of the foreign section of a group of financial newspapers in the City (*The Financial News*, the *Banker*). "In the final analysis," said Stackleberg, "I have reached the conclusion that until now France and Great Britain have not really suffered because of what is commonly referred to as 'the Germanic thrust' in Central and Eastern Europe."[29]

The French did not share that optimism at all. One of the last dispatches by François-Poncet[30] and one of the first by his successor Coulondre[31] carefully analyzed the issue. According to Coulondre, the Reich was creating the famous *Mitteleuropa* that had been announced so often for an entire century.[32] Because of the Anschluss, Germany could now use of 711 km of the Danube River (out of 2900 km). Its industry and railroads transported its products and it was planning a huge web of canals. One-third of the Danube fleet belonged to four large German companies. All the British positions that were important in the 1920s were lost and on November 14, 1936, Germany denounced the clauses of the Treaty of Versailles on international waterways.

Along with that huge structure Germany also possessed an "artificial" but very efficient component in its exchange controls. The countries that were selling to Germany could only use the Reich marks they obtained through that channel to buy German products. The Reich was willing to purchase agricultural or mining products at prices that were often 30 to 40% higher than the world markets. On the other hand, a very flexible credit system was being offered, allowing the repayment to be made in the form of products from the country that was borrowing, thus avoiding the purchase of foreign currency. The result was that since 1933 Germany had tripled its purchases and sales in the area representing 15% to 16% of its foreign trade, absorbing 30% of the exports of those countries and providing 30% to 40% of their imports. Its foreign trade was now larger than that of France, Great Britain and the United States put together.

François-Poncet provided the following chart (in millions of RM):

GERMAN FOREIGN TRADE

	Romania	Yugoslavia	Greece	Bulgaria
1934	110	67	84	53
1935	144	98	104	51
1936	195	152	131	106
1937	310	266	189	140
First 7 months 1937	179	137	98	67
First 7 months 1938	183	174	128	71

Coulondre reached the following conclusion: "It is very clear that the first objective of Germany's plans is the complete economic hegemony in the European countries along the Danube and in the Balkans."[33]

The financial attaché in London, Emmanuel Mönick, submitted a report on January 18, 1939, regarding "The economic positions of Germany and England in Central Europe."[34] He stated that "for a number of years the British were convinced that the Third Reich's economic system was dragging Germany into bankruptcy." They were now adopting "a more realistic view." This had become a political matter: "Is Germany's industrial and commercial development meant to increase the standard of living of the German people or rather to ensure Germanic dominance over Europe?" The British no longer harbored any illusions on the subject.

Even prior to Munich, following pressure from the countries concerned, the French and British governments began researching how they could counterbalance Germany's influence. But every French proposal seeking to organize a common effort was politely rejected by the British.[35] British banks and trading companies "would not accept the use of new methods or alliances that did not take existing positions into consideration."[36]

The idea of sending an entirely French mission appears to have originated at the Ministry of Commerce and Industry where Hervé Alphand was the director of commercial agreements. On October 25 a meeting took place with the diplomat Antoine Delenda.[37] The "information gathered by our largest banks and business leaders confirms that our initiative could be very effective for the investments of French funds in industrial and mining concerns…this is an area where we can compete with the Germans."[38]

The Quai d'Orsay reached an agreement with the minister of commerce to form a delegation headed by Alphand that would travel to Romania, Bulgaria and Yugoslavia. Representatives of industry, Paribas, and Baron Louis Dreyfus, as well as experts (François Bloch-Lainé among them), would accompany the government officials. The diplomats were to prepare the visit, and Alexis Léger sent out a number of telegrams. The ministries of agriculture (which was very dubious), nationald, marine and air were consulted along with finance, until recently headed by Paul Reynaud, who approved the proposal to restructure commercial and payments agreements, increase French purchases and invest private funds. On the other hand, he adamantly opposed another point in the mission's program "to increase our shipments to Central European governments by offering long-term credit for payments." This "would heavily penalize our public finances," he said. France had already issued 920 million in credit insurance to Romania, 565 to Bulgaria, 170 to Yugoslavia and 1,250 to Poland (the implemented portion of the Rambouillet agreements).

"Your program cannot work because it clashes on that important issue with an impossible situation... I must add that the countries we wish to help are searching for markets to sell their products. It isn't by selling them more but by buying more from them that we can help effectively."[39]

The armaments section of the EMA (Etat-Major des Armées)[40] was encouraging the mission to seek French investments in the copper, lead, zinc and antimony industries, steel and chemical plants. It pointed out that three important deals were still open: a group led by Schneider was competing with Krupp in Yugoslavia to build a weapons plant in Zenitra; Schneider was also bidding for permission to obtain a nitro-cellulose plant in Obliceno; and the "French Nobel" company wanted to build a gunpowder factory in Romania. Darlan was asking for the navy for help at the shipyards at Galatz in Romania and Split in Yugoslavia (controlled by the *Chantiers de la Loire*). He mentioned negotiations with the Romanians for the purchase of two submarines and also discussed the oil issue.[41]

Clearly the visit had been carefully prepared. The mission left Paris on November 15, 1938 and spent ten days in Bucharest. It then traveled to Sofia and Belgrade, returning to Paris by December 10. The final report was delivered to the minister of commerce, Frédéric Gentin, on December 19, 1938.[42]

The mission was able to "identify the reasons for France's economic decline in several of the countries visited; to immediately reach a number of commercial agreements meant to improve a situation that was detrimental to our exports and to the payment of our financial obligations"— because all the countries involved were indebted to France and not good at making payments. The mission "also seeks to show the countries in Eastern Europe that contrary to what some propaganda is saying France, without undue prejudice to legitimate competition, is not giving up on the defense of its economic and political interests in that part of Europe in any way."

The main hope was that, since the foreign trade of those countries with Germany did not provide them with any foreign currency, they therefore wished to do business with the western countries that had "free currencies." Furthermore, they were obviously aware of the threat represented by German economic hegemony. Unfortunately, their prices were too high with most of their products coming from agriculture and of no interest to the French market, while they could satisfy German needs. Should exchange rates be modified? Should exporters receive a discount? Should some quotas be increased?

To Romania, for example, where oil was 25% higher in price than American oil, the French government could lend up to 25 million, erasing any losses, if the Romanian government consented to sacrifices. The only agricultural product available was corn, competing with corn from Indochina. Could France act as reexporter of Romanian corn?

There was an agreement with Bulgaria on payment terms.[43] Both tobacco purchases by France and French armaments purchases by Bulgaria could be increased, along with railroad supplies, if credit insurance was developed. Yugoslavia would be satisfied with increasing its purchases of French agricultural products.

All this was rather thin. The delegation was also considering a long-term solution through French capital investment to create new products.

It was up to the government to decide. The ministry of foreign affairs was very much in favor of those proposals. In a letter to Daladier the Quai d'Orsay insisted on credit insurance. The objective was not to "roll back" Germany but to show "that both Paris and London would not stand by allowing it unlimited hegemony." Our method has remained that of "empty gestures."[44] An interministerial commission chaired by Daladier, with Bonnet and Gentin, met on January 13, 1939. The Quai d'Orsay continued to pressure Daladier; the new memo[45] insisted on the need to follow up on the recommendations in the Alphand report regarding corn, the reexportation of wheat, and customs tariff rebates for agricultural countries. Our allies were waiting. A Yugoslav delegation had been in Paris for two weeks and was surprised "that until then no substantive offer had been made." Great Britain agreed and purchased wheat from Yugoslavia and Romania. "The actions expected of us have a political importance above all. The time has come to decide if we are ready to consider rather small sacrifices...or whether by rejecting those actions or creating the impression that we cannot take them we are deliberately accepting that Romania and Yugoslavia...should permanently orient their economic and political life toward Germany."

However, at the same time the minister of agriculture, Henri Queuille, informed Daladier of his "complete opposition" to such an operation. France was in no position to reexport 4.5 million quintals at a time when world stocks for export were up to 150 million. This would anger the United States and the Dominions. "Strangely, representatives from foreign affairs don't seem to be aware of those risks." They demonstrated a lack of thoroughness by not consulting with us.[46]

The key meeting was held on January 30. It was chaired by Daladier and Bonnet; Gentin, Queuille, Paul Reynaud, the minister of finance, Patenôtre of the National Economy, and Georges Mandel of the Colonies were present. It was agreed that wheat stocks would be increased and a law would be drafted offering rebates to a number of countries. That was as far as they would go.[47]

In other words, the economic counteroffensive in Eastern Europe had basically fizzled. As for capital investments, these were taking place in the midst of dangerous times and many hesitated about long-term placements in threatened countries. The electrification projects in southeastern Poland being proposed by Alsthom and Paribas, and the creation of a tractor and tank factory in Romania proposed by Renault were approved by Daladier but did not happen in time.[48]

One last point. Was any serious consideration given, as some historians believe,[49] to an "economic appeasement" taking the shape of close Franco-German collaboration? François-Poncet had discussed it with Hitler on October 18. Hitler immediately sidestepped the issue in which he clearly showed no interest. Ribbentrop traveled to Paris with economic experts who held talks with the deputy director of political and commercial affairs, de La Baume. French farmers would have liked to increase their exports to Germany. We feel it is difficult to view those discussions as anything but normal commercial negotiations routinely taking place at all times between countries. Once Schacht had been permanently removed as the director of the Reich's economy, and with Funk and mostly Göring, two backers of autarky both at the helm, it is difficult to see how a wide-ranging agreement could be reached, especially with a liberal like Paul Reynaud in charge of France's economy.

True, there were half-hearted attempts here and there. Bonnet seems to have encouraged the creation, on February 28, 1939, of a Franco-German Economic Center headed by a lawyer, Baudoin-Buguet, with the support of C.-J. Gignoux, the president of the General Confederation of Business Leaders, and of Émile Mireaux, the editor of *Le Temps*. But it was a rather small affair. On the other hand, Daladier and Coulondre seemed interested in closer economic cooperation, especially at the beginning of March 1939[50] while commercial negotiations were in full swing.[51]

Had negotiations existed going far beyond commercial matters and reaching wider political opportunities, serious and noticeable traces would appear in the archives. Despite some vague projects we do not believe in the idea of an "economic appeasement" on the French side.[52]

2.

THE LIMITS
OF THE FRANCO-GERMAN RAPPROCHEMENT

To follow the "English line" in the fall of 1938 meant attempting a rapprochement with Germany. The limitations of that game were clear to everyone. There were some out and out "anti-German" leaders within the government, such as Mandel, Jean Zay, Champetier de Ribes and Paul Reynaud who, following Herriot's request, remained as ministers in the Daladier cabinet.[53] The majority was pro-Munich, some of them unhappily like Daladier, or satisfied like de Monzie (Italy's man) and his friends Pomaret and Marchandeau, or with some reservations like Queuille, Guy La Chambre, Chautemps, Sarraut and Campinchi or mysteriously like Georges Bonnet.[54]

Chamberlain had signed an agreement with Hitler on September 30 without consulting his colleague Daladier in any shape or form, and it was therefore appropriate to seek information regarding its content. There was no mention of "non-aggression" but of a "consultation" procedure and a statement of the German and British peoples to "never again go to war against one another."[55] Chamberlain and Hitler did not discuss the colonies during their meeting. Chamberlain brought up the issue of disarmament. Hitler, putting on a saintly air, replied by listing all his failed attempts in that area.[56]

Daladier, who often dreamt of a meeting with Hitler as "old war veterans," was not against a rapprochement. The German crowd had warmly cheered him as he was leaving Munich; François-Poncet felt "it was more than a chorus acting for a command performance." Hadn't Göring said that "with a man like Daladier one could talk politics"?[57] François-Poncet agreed with the idea as early as October 4. On October 5 a note by the political directorate analyzed the issue, concluding that such a Franco-German declaration "did not create a political problem and could have some positive psychological effect." However, it was preferable to negotiate "a new Western pact"—similar to the Four Power Pact—and it was necessary to define the "French position towards the Franco-Soviet and the Franco-Polish treaties."[58]

But Hitler, who when "meeting with foreign heads of state showed that he could be conciliatory, understanding, almost reasonable and moderate," quickly displayed—when it came to the borders—his "brutal, imperious, and impulsive temperament that showed impatience with any kind of contradiction." France, concluded François-Poncet, must "try everything to have a policy of détente with Germany and attempt to link her to as many commitments as possible... But...it would be mistaken to show confidence in Germany prematurely... Unfortunately, Mr. Hitler's word may have only a relative and passing value. Deep down, Hitler remains an adventurer."[59]

He would show it during his speech of October 9 in Sarrebrück where he actually attacked England by saying Germany did not need any "English nannies" and spoke kindly of France.[60] That kind of attitude practically cancelled the Four Power Pact project that sounded as if it came from Massigli. Georges Bonnet was fed up with that director of political affairs who had disapproved of Munich. Bonnet replaced him on October 24 with Émile Charvériat, Massigli's deputy up to that point, packing him off as ambassador to Ankara. It signaled a major diplomatic rotation: François-Poncet went from Berlin to Rome, Robert Coulondre from Moscow to Berlin, Naggiar from Peking to Moscow, Jules Henry replaced Eirik Labonne in Madrid who, in turn, was appointed Resident General in Tunisia on October 24. The former minister to Vienna, Gabriel Puaux, was appointed High Commissioner to the Levant.[61]

As he was about to leave Berlin, Ambassador François-Poncet met with Hitler on October 18 at the "Eagle's Nest" he had built for himself overlooking Berchtesgaden. He went by plane with Captain Stehlin. The ambassador would write the most famous of his innumerable dispatches,[62] describing the extraordinary residence as a fantastic castle of Burgraves. He discovered that Hitler "was disappointed by the aftermath of the Munich accords" and sharply critical of Britain's selfishness. François-Poncet asked him three questions: Could there be a mutual guarantee of the borders between France and Germany? Yes, answered Hitler, who preferred that formula to non-aggression. Could we return to arms limitations? There were obviously many objections. Germany was encircled and required greater weapons than all the countries that could potentially attack her. Finally, could economic relations between the two countries be improved? Hitler deferred "to others for the handling of that issue."

All told, "except for a few spats of violence against England, the Führer was calm, moderate and conciliatory." Hitler immediately gave Ribbentrop orders to study a consultation pact. "I can promise you on our part that the issue will get a favorable hearing and a serious study," added François-Poncet. The ambassador, having communicated to the French government all the reservations emanating from the personality of "this impressionable, changing and sick dictator," recommended that the agreement be negotiated. Germany was taking the initiative. "If we close our ears we shall provide her, to our disadvantage, with the alibi she is looking for, perhaps to cover her future initiatives."

Georges Bonnet immediately approved François-Poncet's proposal.[63] The latter also recommended discretion on the part of the press. Rumors were beginning to filter through.[64]

Just as preparations were getting under way, tragedy struck in Paris. A Polish Jew, Herschel Gryszpan, born in Hanover, fatally wounded the third secretary of the German embassy in Paris, Ernst von Rath, after firing two shots. The Wilhelmstrasse and the press did not blame France[65] nor would the Franco-German rapprochement have suffered had the event not caused an extremely violent reaction against the Jews in Nazi Germany. The sadly famous *Kristallnacht* (November 9–10)—with its looting of homes, and Jewish stores, burning of synagogues, beatings, attacks, and the compulsory contribution of 1 billion reichsmarks by the Jews— reminded world opinion of the true nature of the Nazi regime.[66]

Bonnet had invited Ribbentrop to visit Paris in early November. Was there an Italian initiative?[67] A desire to let some time pass after the *Kristallnacht*?[68] Did social unrest in France, which would peak with the general strike on November 30, play a role? Whatever the real reason, Ribbentrop's trip was delayed.[69]

The French government at the same time invited Chamberlain and Halifax to come to Paris. It was the first meeting of the two heads of government since Munich.[70] In view of the "British line" the matter was important enough. According to Corbin, the meeting was to have crucially important ramifications; but he was unable to identify which concrete decisions could be reached. Chamberlain, said the ambassador, remained wedded to the policy of "general appeasement." He had become "in the eyes of the entire world its living symbol." Obviously, the main worry was the condition of France's armaments and of the air force in particular.[71]

The Franco-British discussions took place on November 24 with meetings in the morning and afternoon. Besides the two prime ministers and ministers of foreign affairs, Alexis Léger and Alexander Cadogan took part, as did the two ambassadors, Corbin and Sir Eric Phipps, along with some top functionaries (Charvériat, Rochat, Strang, etc.).[72]

Two months after Munich, such a meeting could have been one of resurrection after the disaster. One can imagine the two countries setting up a Paris-London axis without mysteries or cracks to face the dictators, establishing common plans and pooling their energies. Nothing of the sort took place. The main interest of those conversations was not their content but rather their *tenor*—absolutely courteous, friendly yet formal and filled with innuendo. What transpired was not unity but subtle suspicion. Chamberlain was, after all, very satisfied with his latest achievements, Munich, the Anglo-German declaration, the implementation of the Anglo-Italian agreement. He also knew that Great Britain was making a serious effort with its air force. Daladier, facing him, was sickened at having been the man of Munich and having to face the enormous problems of rebuilding the French aviation industry (which we shall discuss later).

There was even greater disagreement on another issue. At Munich France and England had promised to guarantee the new Czechoslovakia. Germany and Italy had declared that they would also join once the Czechoslovak borders had been set with Germany, Hungary and Poland. Was it not the right time for a Franco-British initiative toward the two dictators to remind them of their promise? The political director of the Czechoslovak ministry of foreign affairs, Krno, had just pointed this out.[73]

On that issue Lord Halifax, remembering the September crisis, sought only to find a way of avoiding any kind of obligation. He succeeded by adding to the guarantee such conditions making it effective only when three guarantors out of four established that an unprovoked aggression had taken place. Three out of four meant that one of the Axis powers had to join France and England. That's impossible, said Daladier. "Mr. Chamberlain does not feel he needs to share that opinion. It could be possible that Italy would not adopt the same position as Germany." This is very interesting and confirms everything we know of the single-mindedness with which the prime minister was attempting to draw Italy away from Germany.[74] "Mr. Daladier noted that this being the case, it was preferable not to have promised a guarantee." No decision was reached.

The other issues were handled in cursory fashion. German Jewish refugees were discussed—there were 40,000 in France which, said Daladier, could take no more. Could they be sent to the colonies? The French were given the task to ask Ribbentrop a relaxation of the regulations forbidding them from taking their possessions. There were discussions—useless once again—about the impossible issue of withdrawing the foreign volunteers fighting in the Spanish civil war, and no conclusion was reached apart from an agreement between the two democracies to not recognize Franco's "belligerent" status. Franco-Soviet relations were discussed, as well as the potential Hitlerian threat to the Ukraine. Georges Bonnet took the opportunity to illustrate the limits of the Franco-Soviet Pact of 1935, which the British never liked. The Near East and Far East were briefly mentioned.

In the end Daladier and Bonnet read to their counterparts the draft of the Franco-German agreement and, as expected, were given a warm approval. But it should be noted that during this discussion there was no mention of a Four Power Pact, or of a broad initiative for an economic rapprochement with Germany, nor a broader plan for a rapprochement between the democracies and the dictatorships.

The most clear-cut conclusion one may draw from these discussions was one of *continuity*. Munich had not changed the way the two democracies behaved toward each other regarding a reversal of alliances, or the reinforcement of democratic solidarity. Chamberlain pursued his *appeasement* policy unperturbed and Daladier continued along the "English line" with increasing anxiety.

The groundwork for Ribbentrop's visit to Paris had been laid out. Daladier was extremely well prepared. He had a memorandum provided by Ambassador von Welczeck on November 19. The Quai d'Orsay provided him with a file concerning German intrigues in French West Africa, the treatment of German newsmen in France and German nationals subject to the French judicial system. More importantly there was a questionnaire regarding guarantees to Czechoslovakia, the Jewish issue, Italy's real position, the humanization of war. The document concluded that a "western" pact or a "Four Power Pact" would be inappropriate.[75]

Ribbentrop arrived in Paris on the morning of December 6. Since there was concern about popular reaction, he made few public appearances. Following lunch with Daladier at the Hôtel Matignon, the main discussions took place on December 6 in the afternoon at the Quai d'Orsay between Bonnet and Ribbentrop, accompanied by Léger and Welczek. In the evening there was a reception at the German embassy where, contrary to the legend, Jewish ministers Jean Zay and Georges Mandel had been invited. The president of the Chamber, Herriot, refused to attend and Gamelin was traveling. A second discussion took place on December 7 in the afternoon between Bonnet and Ribbentrop at the Hôtel Crillon. After having told the foreign affairs commission of the Senate that he had met with Ribbentrop on December 6 and 7, Bonnet later denied that a meeting had in fact taken place on the 7th.[76] There is a French summary of the meeting of the 6th by Léger[77] and a German embassy summary of the meetings in general.[78] Finally Paul Schmidt, Ribbentrop's interpreter appears to have been present at least in part of the conversations, but only part because, as he mentioned, "Ribbentrop spoke in French at times; at others I translated what he was saying in German."[79]

Those details are important but not as they relate to the agreement which was signed early on and was extremely simple. The two countries were convinced that peaceful relations between themselves "make up one of the essential elements to consolidate the situation in Europe." They "solemnly recognize the border between them as being permanent." They were committing themselves to consult with one another, within the limits of their agreements with third party countries, in the event of international difficulties.[80]

Several points stand out in the discussions. Ribbentrop declared that Germany was not directly interested in Italian demands in Tunisia but that the "unalterable basis of Germany's foreign policy is the Rome-Berlin axis." He pushed the issue of guarantees of the Czechoslovak borders into the future to assess the kind of relations that country would have with Germany. He hoped in Franco's victory. Bonnet brought up the issue of foreign volunteers. Ribbentrop condemned the Franco-Soviet Pact and declared that the colonial issue was "not current." Finally, we must note that from the start Bonnet brought up the possibility of extending the Franco-German rapprochement to the areas of culture, tourism, and the economy through increased exchanges. Ribbentrop agreed with the proposal that France develop purchases in the German market.

Now to the most important part: from that day forward the Germans would always claim that on December 6 France, through Bonnet, had stated that it had no further interest in Eastern Europe that was part of the German sphere of interest. Bonnet was clearly hoping for this in October. He possibly still did. But it was certainly not an element of French policy on December 6. But did he say so? The French text drafted by Léger makes no mention of the fact. What does the German text say? The term "Eastern Europe" does not appear, only "that part of Europe." Ribbentrop stated, "If France were to recognize once and for all this German sphere of interest, he would then be fully confident in the possibility of a final agreement in principle between France and Germany...." "Bonnet answered that since Munich the situation had changed radically from that point of view." But the next part of the sentence appears to indicate that he was thinking only of Czechoslovakia. Interpreter Paul Schmidt thought that Bonnet meant a disinterest in *all of Eastern Europe* and that he mentioned Czechoslovakia by itself only afterwards. However, he recognized that the translation of that sentence from French to German could have created some confusion. Alexis Léger replied in a letter written in 1952 to Amédée Outrey, director of the archives at the Quai d'Orsay, that he and not Schmidt was present in Bonnet's office. Schmidt could only have obtained his information later on. "My memory is clear… Never in the course of that conversation did I hear the French Minister of Foreign Affairs say or infer in any way possible that France could be expected to take the position that the German Foreign Minister stated later on." I dictated, he said, the December 7 note myself. The conversation "of a very general and superficial nature never reached the level of true negotiations."[81]

Yet the issue would resurface several times in 1939. On February 6, 1939, Ribbentrop expressed his surprise to Coulondre at a reference Bonnet made in Parliament (January 26) regarding "France's commitments in Eastern Europe," which he considered to be "off limits."[82] On March 19 Bonnet answered "the extravagant statement by Mr. von Weizsäcker," according to which on December 6 he, Bonnet, was said to have expressed his lack of interest in Czechoslovakia.[83]

At the beginning of July 1939, after Bonnet reiterated that France had never lost interest in Eastern Europe, Ribbentrop wrote to him on July 13, 1939, "Contrary to what is stated in your report which you have now underscored… a radical reversal had taken place in France's attitude since the Munich conference towards the issue of Eastern Europe."[84] It was obvious how far Ribbentrop was stretching the German text quoted above. Bonnet answered on July 21, "At no time either before or after the declaration of December 6 could it have been possible for the German government to think that France had decided to become disinterested in the East of Europe." Furthermore, hadn't the issue of guarantees to Czechoslovakia been discussed at length?[85]

Whether or not Ribbentrop believed or pretended to believe in this French abdication, Bonnet's position is strong. He ended up complicating it by providing differing and, as he was apt to do, repeatedly twisted statements. Even if he had *said* as much—and everything leads to conclude that he did not say it, including the German report—it was in any case a conversation and not a negotiation. The bulk of the French archives also confirm this.[86] To take the matter any further is to issue an indictment without providing any proof.

On the other hand the Franco-German declaration of December 6 was to remain inconsequential. Just as Hitler had violently attacked England in his speech at Sarrebrück barely ten days after the Anglo-German declaration, the breakup in this case came just as quickly. On December 20 Coulondre observed that, despite the declaration of December 6, there was strong German propaganda in Alsace, and he remarked that it was a "worrisome contradiction for the future."[87]

3.

THE IMPOSSIBLE
FRANCO-ITALIAN RAPPROCHEMENT

The rapprochement between Great Britain and Italy, evidenced by the agreement of April 16, 1938, was supposed to lead, in Chamberlain's mind, to a similar agreement between Italy and France. We have noted that Georges Bonnet was rather favorable. In May, however, Mussolini was noncommittal. Following France's request, England had withheld the implementation of the agreement, without specifically subordinating it to the signing of a Franco-Italian accord.[88]

After Munich, on October 26, and without consulting France, the British government decided to implement the agreement. When Chamberlain and Halifax came to Paris on November 26, the potential rapprochement between France and Italy was hardly mentioned, less than the planned pact with Germany. France had actually made the key move. Mussolini had told Daladier in Munich, "I hope that now you will no longer forget my address."[89] As early as October 3, Bonnet told Italian chargé d'affaires Renato Prunas that after three years France was sending an ambassador to Rome, implying recognition of the Italian conquests in Africa. He would be accredited to the "King of Italy, Emperor of Ethiopia."

There was little hesitation as to the choice of the ambassador. Léon Noël badly wanted the appointment that had been mentioned to him back in January 1935. Georges Bonnet, whom he knew well, offered it to him in the spring of 1938. But Léger, who was an inveterate anti-Italian, was against it. There were other candidates, including Mistler, the president of the foreign affairs commission at the Chamber, François Piétri, even Flandin, but most of all François-Poncet, who did not wish to see Tardieu's prophecy of 1931— "So you want to be the Benedetti of the last war"—come true. He requested the transfer to Rome. Léon Noël bowed out and refused Léger's proposal to replace François-Poncet in Berlin.[90] François-Poncet arrived in Rome on November 7 and was given a warm reception by the crowd, something that irritated Mussolini who told Ciano, "I dislike him."[91]

François-Poncet did not know Italy as well as he knew Germany. At first he thought things were going well. Mussolini gave him a good reception,[92] and Ciano even appears to have said, "There are only 'a few mosquitoes' between us except for the Spanish issue."[93]

The ambassador would soon be disappointed. The cloudburst took place as early as November 30 and did not concern the Spanish problem. On that day François-Poncet had been invited to attend a session of the Chamber of Fasces and Corporations meeting at Montecitorio. Ciano gave a rather moderate speech where he praised the Anglo-Italian agreement. But suddenly, following a sentence where he spoke about "the defense of the interests and national aspirations of his people," a demonstration broke out. The "deputies" began shouting "Tunisia! Corsica! Djibuti!" There was also a cry for "Savoy." There were throngs of fascists forming outside, screaming the same slogans and even "Savoy! Nice!" The minister of police,* Starace, prevented the demonstrators from going to the Farnese Palace where the French embassy was located. Mussolini watched the demonstration "impassively"—obviously he was not surprised! "Actually he did make signs that it should not last."[94]

Georges Bonnet was informed during the afternoon of December 1 and immediately sent two important telegrams, one to François-Poncet, instructing him to request an immediate meeting with Ciano—"Such behavior may appear rather unusual in the presence of the French ambassador and immediately following the unconditional recognition of the Italian Empire."[95] The second went to London, as Chamberlain and Halifax were supposed to travel to Rome in January, "It is essential that there be no reason given to Rome to hope in the success of maneuvers seeking to demonstrate, through a new worsening of Franco-Italian relations, a disassociation between French and British interests."[96]

---

* Achille Starace was the national secretary of the Fascist Party, with the rank of minister. [NDT]

What did Mussolini want? François-Poncet and the Quai d'Orsay pondered the question for several months. The date of November 30 coincided with the general strike, proving in his mind that France was weak in facing an Italy that was dynamic and sure of herself, reinforced by the Rome-Berlin Axis. Ciano received the ambassador on the evening of December 2. He was courteous, alleging that the Italian government was not responsible but coming to the conclusion that the 1935 agreements should be reexamined. "I am not asking that you hand Tunisia over to us," he said but "in any case he caught himself immediately." The "mosquitoes," said François-Poncet, had now turned into "elephants."[97] With a note of December 17, Ciano formally declared that the Laval-Mussolini accords were now "historically irrelevant."[98]

The key dilemma was the following: Did Italy wish to *negotiate* and, having asked a lot, agree to settle for less? Or was she really seeking *annexations*, and using the Axis to start a war with the support of Germany? Had this happened with Germany's backing? No! said the Germans, starting with Ribbentrop during the December 6 discussions in Paris. And on December 10, 1938, "a person close to the Führer" told Coulondre, "Do you believe that the Führer would be ready to risk for the Italians of Tunisia what he is refusing to risk for the Germans of Alsace?"[99] Daladier, encouraged by a virtually unanimous French public opinion, spoke at the Chamber and the Senate on December 13 and 19. "France will not give an inch of its territories to Italy even if it means an armed conflict."[100]

Daladier's trip to Corsica, Algeria, and Tunisia (January 2–6, 1939) was approved by most Frenchmen and by many of the local populations. But up to mid-January it was not the real source of worry for France. The main issue was the trip that the British were taking to Rome. Would they, as they had done so often before, distance themselves and, rather than reaffirming Franco-British solidarity, seek to play the role of "referees"? French diplomacy was intensely focused on that point, even more so since Lord Perth, the British ambassador to Rome, was the opposite of an aggressive personality. Perth was instructed to undertake an initiative with Ciano on December 3, to express his worry regarding the November 30 demonstrations. François-Poncet termed the initiative as probably "not having been very strong."[101] Lord Perth was someone he found deeply irritating, as noted by Hubert Lagardelle, who for years had been fulfilling an obscure mission at the Farnese Palace. In a personal letter dated November 30 he wrote, "Not only did

Lord Perth fail to have any kind of friendly relations with our ambassador, but we are kept totally in the dark about the discussions…that British diplomats are having with Count Ciano in Rome."[102]

Chamberlain did nothing to reassure the French. "During the debate this afternoon," states a note dated December 12, "he declared that in the event of an Italian attack against French territory or possessions there was no specific military commitment to France in any treaty, pact or Franco-British agreement."[103] And Colonel Beck, France's "great ally," did not hesitate to say "that France would be forced to cede Tunisia to Italy."[104] Bonnet wished that Chamberlain, who was scheduled to speak at the foreign press banquet would at least recall that the Anglo-Italian agreements guaranteed the status quo in the Mediterranean, and said as much to Ambassador Sir Eric Phipps. Chamberlain refused to do so for a trivial reason because the text of his speech had already been distributed![105] Chamberlain's visit to Rome was therefore "dangerous to us."[106] Corbin felt that "the entire Italian effort would be concentrated on London in order to get Chamberlain to react in Rome, at our expense this time, taking the same attitude as in Godesberg."[107]

Besides Bonnet's instructions to Corbin to go and see Chamberlain "to warn him loyally but categorically of France's unshakable resolve,"[108] much was expected of the conversation with British leaders in Paris on their way to Rome. But as Corbin said, Neville Chamberlain was purposefully avoiding revealing any personal inclinations. He seems to have turned the rapprochement with Italy "into his thing."[109] Halifax appeared to be much more understanding. There was a sense of relief on January 12 and 13. The Rome meeting was a failure. Mussolini remained aloof, did not state his demands toward France and revealed very little, as Halifax told François-Poncet.[110]

The French felt reassured from then on. Only François-Poncet kept on bringing up disasters originating in Italy. The Italian matter was once more reduced to the civil war in Spain, which we shall discuss in the next chapter. In truth the ambassador's pessimism appeared to be a reaction to the optimism of his colleague Lord Perth. According to François-Poncet, Mussolini was calling up reservists, was behind the Gallophobic violence of the Italian press, was sending reinforcements to Libya and engaging in an intensive propaganda effort in Tunisia. It all amounted to a "war psychosis."[111]

The Franco-Italian matter was to have two lesser consequences, while Mussolini's diplomacy was secretly and actively preparing an offensive and defensive alliance with Germany and Japan—the secrecy of which had been broken in any case.[112]

The first was when Bonnet and Daladier sent Paul Baudoin as an emissary to attempt to find out the true extent of Italian demands. At the beginning of January, Daladier requested during a phone call that Bonnet come to see him. Bonnet found Baudoin with Daladier. He had received a letter from the diplomat Terruzzi, stating that Italy had no territorial demands where France was concerned. Baudoin was the general director of the Banque d'Indochine and on his way to attend the board of directors meeting of a company in Italy. He had proposed to Daladier to have a meeting with Ciano. Daladier and Bonnet both approved of the idea. Baudoin arrived in Rome on February 1.[113] François-Poncet saw him briefly at his arrival at the railroad station but he did not pay a visit to the embassy.[114] On February 2 he saw Ciano who then drove with him to meet with Mussolini. According to his report, Italian demands were minimal: an Italian free trade zone in Djibuti; the purchase of the Addis Ababa railroad from the French company that owned it; several seats on the Suez board of directors; keeping the status of the Italians in Tunisia unchanged; and absolutely no Italian ambitions over Spanish territory, including the Balearic Islands. France, therefore, was not being asked to cede any territory.[115] Upon his return, Baudoin brought his report to Daladier's private residence in the rue Anatole-de-La-Forge. This unofficial diplomacy was undertaken with the agreement of the Quai d'Orsay. Yet the news was leaked and a press campaign began in *L'Humanité*, *Le Populaire*, and *L'Ordre*, edited by Émile Buré. Even though Daladier and Bonnet found those conversations "extremely interesting," all the commotion put a stop to the negotiations.[116] All this took place without the knowledge of Ambassador François-Poncet.

While Ciano was making some rather reassuring statements, on February 3 François-Poncet sent an extremely pessimistic telegram.[117] A few days later *Il Popolo d'Italia* published some news regarding Baudoin's visit. François-Poncet got angry.[118] "The fact that Mr. Baudoin avoided any contact with the ambassador during his visit was naturally very much noticed." Had he not been to see Mussolini?[119]

Georges Bonnet replied curtly, "The rumors you are telling me have no basis in fact. You are fully aware that any conversation, any Franco-Italian negotiation official or unofficial could only be handled by you, and that no direct or indirect transaction could not be considered outside your purview."[120] What was the scope of that mission? Daladier quickly ended it on March 20.[121] According to Italian historian Toscano, Mussolini did not believe in it. Ciano tried unsuccessfully to reopen the negotiation on March 19 by sending an emissary to Baudoin, who could only inform him of Daladier's decision.[122]

The other matter concerned reinforcements in Tunisia and Libya. England, with its presence in Egypt, was extremely sensitive to the issue. Who had initiated this problem? Following the demonstrations of November 30, the general staff analyzed the issue as early as December 1938, while the Radio Bari broadcasts to the Arab world were worrying the Residents General in Tunisia and Morocco.[123] The Italians were also occupying a small portion of French Somalia that had been ceded to them in January 1935—but that agreement had not been ratified. What could France do? asked Mandel, the minister of the colonies. In Djibuti there were 1,500 men and a dozen planes, while the Italians had 150,000 troops and 200 planes in East Africa.[124]

The matter resurfaced in February 1939. On the 17th Daladier informed Bonnet that there were at the beginning of 1939 some 60,000 Italian soldiers in Libya, 34,000 of them in Tripolitania. These troops were also being constantly reinforced, and had now reached roughly 100,000 men.[125] The Permanent Committee of National Defense took up the matter on February 24.[126] Due to recent reinforcements France had 42,000 men in Tunisia. The colonial chief of staff, General Bührer, estimated that he could send in another 6,000 as well as southern Algerian Goums. The British had 12,000 soldiers in Egypt and transferred a division of 8,000 men from Palestine. Finally, there were some 20,000 Egyptian soldiers. Gamelin pointed out that Italy could not concentrate more than 150,000 troops in Libya. Should Italy attack, France would initially take a defensive position. However, 441,000 men (fourteen infantry divisions) could be mobilized in North Africa. "After three weeks," said Gamelin, "we must take a clearly superior position over the Italians. In addition, we will have the Italians in Tunisia as hostages and it will no doubt be difficult for us to prevent them from being massacred by the natives."

The air force was an issue. According to General Vuillemin, there were 20 Italian planes in Libya, and 150 in Sardinia and southern Italy. The British had 145 planes, 32 of which were modern. Vuillemin thought it was possible to quickly send six groups to Tunisia.

Finally, French fortifications of the "Mareth Line" could be relied on. When Gamelin praised them, Daladier asked, "What about the planes?"

Gamelin answered with supreme assurance, "What can the plane do against men dug into trenches on the ground?" Daladier concluded by generalizing the issue: "If the summer of 1939 goes by without a war we will have no fears from the standpoint of the air force because we shall recapture whatever quality we had lost."

There was no obvious danger. But then an exasperating incident took place. Sir Eric Phipps received instructions from his government for an initiative ("strange" as Charvériat refers to it) inspired by his colleague in Rome, Lord Perth: If you increase your troops in Tunisia, Italy must increase its army in Libya. "The British," said General Dentz at a meeting in the Quai d'Orsay, "are accepting every Italian statement uncritically."[127]

This provided another opportunity for François-Poncet to make ironic remarks about Lord Perth[128] who was always ready to "switch roles." The entire matter was quickly overcome. On March 15 Hitler was about to show most graphically where the real danger was going to be.

4.

THE UKRAINE OR HOLLAND?

It may be stated unequivocally that the signing of the Franco-German declaration of December 6, 1938, did not change the underlying worries regarding Hitler's intentions. It became equally clear that, following Chamberlain's visit to Rome on January 12, the French felt reassured about a possibly imminent conflict provoked by Italy with German support. The diplomats, the military attachés, journalists and all the informers then began speculating. Would Hitler attempt a new violent coup? Where would it take place? For some time the East or West dilemma was basically centered on the *Ukraine-Netherlands* option. These, however, were not the only possible options.

The Ukraine appeared initially in François-Poncet's report on November 18, 1938. It came from a German Catholic leader through the Holy See. Among the "ideas boiling" in Hitler's "stormy head," this one did not sound that farfetched.[129] When he arrived in Berlin, his successor, the new ambassador Robert Coulondre, found Hitler "very much undecided," divided between the "hard liners"—Goebbels, Himmler, and Rudolf Hess—and the "moderates"—Göring, Funk, and Lammers. The latter group was in favor of a "return of the Reich to the international circles."[130] Nevertheless, it was legitimate to fear what was being prepared. Wasn't Germany attempting to instigate a revolt first in the Polish Ukraine and later in the Soviet Ukraine? It would be the start of the traditional *Drang nach Osten,* the push to the East, combined with the grandiose dream of *Lebensraum* as described in *Mein Kampf.* While Coulondre was in Paris for Ribbentrop's visit the chargé d'affaires, Hugues de Montbas, mentioned a plan that he said came from Hitler. It was to create a "greater Ukraine"—"to set up with the help of Poland, if possible, a kind of condominium, something like a 'European Manchukuo' more or less tightly vassalized with the elimination of Poland to follow later on." From Rome François-Poncet insistently raised the issue: "A Ukraine revived by him, which he would more or less openly protect, driving a kind of trident into the flesh of the Muscovites, the Poles and the Romanians...would be enough to excite his imagination, his craving for prestige and power."[131] But Noël does not think that Poland would take part in a German adventure in the East. Poland wanted—and would stubbornly continue to want—a policy of "equilibrium" between its two powerful neighbors.[132]

In any case, telling signs were being constantly detected: the visit to Vienna and Berlin of a delegation of the Ukraine National Union, which was in contact with Alfred Rosenberg; rumors of anti-Stalin unrest in the Soviet Ukraine—with some 730,000 square kilometers and a population of 34 million;[133] and above all the draft of a law in the Polish Diet on the autonomy of the Polish Ukraine (population of 6 million) by Mudryj, the head of the Ukrainian group. Léon Noël, while reporting this news, voiced doubts regarding both the rumors of unrest in the Soviet Ukraine and about the success of the initiative in Poland.[134] As Germany, after attaching the *Deutschtum* to the Reich, was preparing for the conquest of *Lebensraum,* it was understandable that many Nazi officials should discuss the Ukraine; Rosenberg's Center for Studies and Research, the offices under Goebbels; the Ost-Europa organization directed by former minister Curtius, etc.[135] Léon Noël was discreetly in contact with a member of the Polish Ukrainian group, who wanted the backing of France and England, but was counting more on Germany even though his movement was motivated by national principles rather than the concept of German hegemony.[136] Soviet Ambassador Suritz noted that both Mandel and Gamelin believed in the threat looming over the Ukraine.[137]

This wave of rumors of all kinds would abate after Colonel Beck's visit to Hitler on January 14, 1939. Coulondre asked Ambassador Lipski, who traveled to Berchtesgaden with the minister, about the content of the conversation. He was "reticent" on many issues but stated "there was absolutely no chance of a German intervention to create a greater Ukraine."[138] François-Poncet[139] and Coulondre[140] were to confirm this and the subject reappeared only from time to time.

Does this mean that French diplomacy took steps to channel the Germans toward the East to provoke a German-Soviet war? Several Soviet writers have supported such a view, Potemkin in particular.[141] It is not backed up by any documents at all. It is true that right-wing newspapers did voice such a hope, but the archives show no traces of any kind. During the weekly meetings between the Quai d'Orsay and the three branches of the military, the Ukraine was never mentioned. The only text is a note on the issue by Admiral Darlan, dated January 22: "Can England and France sustain a conflict against Germany and Italy?" Darlan, who prided himself as being a realist, stated that such a war should be avoided. "For twenty years we have had an ideological foreign policy that was land-based and exclusively European when it should have been realistic, naval and worldwide… We must first of all conserve our Empire. The rest is secondary. Also, if Germany does not support Italy's demands, we should allow her freedom of action in the East." But this represented only Darlan.[142] Furthermore, in a conversation on February 22, 1939, with Ambassador Naggiar, Litvinov brought up the mission of Fernand de Brinon to Rome. "The Commissar believes that this journalist was backing the well-known German plan to conquer the Ukraine that is viewed by some people in France and England as a miracle drug that will save the two countries from Italo-German threats."[143] Coming from de Brinon it was not something outlandish, but there would have to be proof of instructions from Daladier which have not been found. Otherwise, it is only a blatant accusation. Naggiar in any case protested vigorously.

Did Georges Bonnet dream all this up? Soviet Ambassador Suritz offered a rather plausible explanation: "Bonnet and those who shared his views would breathe a sigh of relief had the Germans really attacked the Ukraine."[144] But Bonnet did not discuss it. The "Bonnet Papers" include a "General study by the Minister's cabinet regarding the scope of the Franco-Soviet Pact," dated January 1939. The study must have been undertaken at his request and tied in—while watering it down—to his October 1938 position when he sought to cancel the pact. The cabinet concluded in this case that "without a specific military agreement," the "help and assistance" clauses were not automatic. The League of Nations, as Litvinov said, was dead. "If the League of Nations is dead then clearly the Franco-Soviet Pact disappears." The USSR, in any case, did not precisely abide by its commitments to not get involved in French matters. Finally, there was the Franco-British agreement of March 19, 1936. "The direct military help that France could bring to the USSR in case of German aggression would depend mainly on the way the cabinet in London viewed the situation."[145]

On the other hand, a few cabinet ministers such as Mandel, Patenôtre, and Campinchi did not hesitate to tell Soviet Ambassador Suritz that they favored a "revival of the Franco-Soviet Pact."[146] The British do not appear to have believed in a Ukrainian issue, nor did the Soviet ambassador to Great Britain, Maïsky, whom Corbin queried on the subject on December 16.[147] The British were not too favorable to the Franco-Soviet Pact.[148]

Starting in January the British were haunted by another threat, a sudden attack on the Netherlands. Lord Halifax, head of the Foreign Office, discussed the issue with Corbin on January 28. He no longer believed in a threat to the Ukraine but rather in an attack in the West, an air attack on London but mostly an action against the Dutch. There were no objective facts—he said—but only a series of clues. Great Britain would then be compelled to resort to force of arms. What would France do? I said—Corbin reported—"that our information did not match completely." And he mentioned the threat no longer on the Ukraine but against Romania. The Franco-British staff discussions that had been decided during the meeting of November 24 and that the British it seemed had let drag out now suddenly became urgent.[149]

At the same time Sir Eric Phipps handed Bonnet an aide-mémoire from Halifax. "All information confirms the fact that the dangerous period will begin toward the end of February." What was the French viewpoint on the risks incurred by the Netherlands?[150]

Charvériat, the director of political affairs, was immediately asked to study the issue. He drafted a note stating that France had "similar" information but originating from Germany's periphery and added, "It is not without interest to witness the British government seeking our assistance on its own initiative." It would be an opportunity to request its commitment in the event of a German attack through Switzerland, an Italian aggression and to pressure it to finally reestablish conscription.[151] Additional information came from Washington; Germany and Italy "were said to have signed an offensive and defensive alliance... Germany was said to have decided to turn toward the West." She would attack the Netherlands not Belgium.[152] The Directorate of Political Affairs was still skeptical and continued to view Germany's action as going East.[153] Only later, in order to support Italy's demands, could she turn to the West.

Georges Bonnet, still following the "English line," wanted to take advantage in order to develop "Franco-British solidarity in the event of a German threat toward the West." The Netherlands was not included in the Locarno stipulations that had been restated on March 19, 1936. The same was true regarding an Italian attack on France. Corbin was therefore instructed to see Halifax and ask him to view western security as a "single issue" so that "the solidarity of England and France" would be "assured in any event."[154] Corbin discussed the issue with Halifax and Cadogan on February 4.[155] The result was not long in coming and lifted many doubts and ambiguous phrases from the minds of the French. On February 6, 1939, in the House of Commons, Chamberlain made the following statement, "I find it necessary to clearly state that *the solidarity of interests that unites France and England is such that any threat directed against France's vital interests wherever it may come from must trigger Great Britain's immediate cooperation.*"[156] [Emphasis added.]

An official British note dated February 13 confirmed that solidarity, expressing the wish to see military discussions begin quickly.[157]

In the end the threat disappeared as quickly as it had appeared. It was a great comfort to French policy and secretly a relief to the Belgians. The French minister in The Hague, Vitrolles, met his Belgian counterpart Baron Herry, who did not hide "his satisfaction at being temporarily sheltered from German thunder."[158] Those rumors, Weizsäcker told Coulondre on February 28, "were not just absurd, they were also malevolent."[159]

5.

ROMANIA OR CZECHOSLOVAKIA?

More than the British, the French believed that the threat was aimed at Romania. The idea had serious merit when one considered that there was a German minority of 800,000 in that oil- and grain-producing country, which was obviously of economic interest to Germany. The situation was reversed compared to Czechoslovakia, where the German "colonists" were scattered in many towns of Transylvania and, above all, there was no common border between Romania and Germany. An alliance with Hungary was required if Germany intended to target Romania for its next coup.

Adrien Thierry, French minister to Romania, was not worried in the short term.[160] The French government, however, may have been influenced by the confidence displayed by one of its informers, Colonel, and later General, Didelet, who had replaced General Renondeau as military attaché in Berlin on October 25, 1938. Didelet was dogmatic, sure of himself, and very influential. General Gauché, head of the *Deuxième Bureau* attributes the "damaging" idea of the "German bluff" to him, meaning that a general war would have been impossible in 1939. Didelet's point, which was persistently rejected by the *Deuxième Bureau*, was that the German army would not be able to use its full potential before 1942; Hitler would therefore not make the mistake of starting a general war before that date.[161] Gauché added that Didelet having been politely warned by the army chief of staff, admitted to having been too adamant. We are not told, however, the date when this took place.

As early as December 12, 1938, in an important dispatch from Didelet to Daladier,[162] Didelet put forth his view of insufficient German preparation. He was well aware of an element that the Hitler specialists knew well: "The Führer wanted to accomplish the gigantic task he had assigned to himself while he was alive and…he was feeling pressed for time." However, "Germany does not have the artillery required for an offensive on the Western front at this time." Therefore the East-West dilemma was clear to him—Germany could only attack to the East. Didelet identified only three possible directions on November 12: Poland, Romania or the Russian Ukraine. In a letter to Daladier dated December 19, Gamelin mentioned Didelet's[163] "very remarkable report" which proved that his information was getting attention.

As a good information analyst, Didelet tried to focus on the most likely of the three potential targets. On January 10 he had identified it. The most threatened country was Romania. There were actually some signs of a German mobilization and that something might happen in March. But not in the West. "I continue to believe that Germany will not be ready either militarily, economically or from a moral point of view to risk a world war in 1939."[164]

Once Germany occupied Bohemia and Moravia as well as Memel, Didelet kept it up with supreme confidence. "Logically the German drive should point to the south of the Carpathian Mountains. If Germany attacked Poland now it would be a mistake."[165] "I find," he said, "two main reasons: 1. Mr. Hitler is not crazy; 2. He still does not have the capabilities to risk a general war."[166] Faced with such self-confidence, Ambassador Robert Coulondre, who was not as keen as his predecessor François-Poncet, displayed a lot of common sense. He was the first one early on to clearly draw attention to Czechoslovakia.[167]

A formal "guarantee" of that country's borders did exist, dating back to Munich as expressed by England and France. When Ribbentrop visited Paris, Bonnet asked him about a German guarantee. According to the German report, Ribbentrop answered that "everything will depend on relations between Germany and Czechoslovakia... Bonnet only stated that in the final analysis, France had decided to offer guarantees mostly under the pressure of events... Bonnet didn't delve deeper into the issue."[168] The French report did not go any further either.[169] France, therefore, forgot that side of the issue, preferring to note the "pro-German" orientation of the new Czechoslovak leaders, Hacha, Beran, and Chvalkowsky. What was taking place was "the forced integration of Czechoslovakia into the German economic structure."[170] When, prior to Ribbentrop's trip to Paris, Lacroix met with Minister of Foreign Affairs Chvalkowsky the latter expressed his wish "to know the shape and extent that those governments intended to give to the international guarantee of the new borders of the Czechoslovak state." The only possible answer was that those discussions were ongoing.[171]

France and England were naturally thinking of providing economic assistance to that unfortunate country. But as Lacroix noted, it "would not prevent the growing dependence of Czechoslovakia on Germany."[172] British plans included providing 12 million pounds sterling to Czechoslovakia as a British gift of 4 million and a loan jointly guaranteed by France and England of 8 million.[173] Georges Bonnet would agree to it,[174] but Paul Reynaud was not too favorable. "I can only continue to think that on a purely financial level, it would be impossible to justify since Czechoslovakia was sliding toward an ever closer economic domination by Germany, to agree to an additional effort on its behalf."[175]

On December 15, 1938, Coulondre therefore said that one of the obvious objectives of German policy was to "vassalize" Czechoslovakia.[176]

On February 8 one of his staff members found out during a conversation with "an important member of Hitler's entourage" that the "decomposition" (*Auflösung*) of the Czechoslovak state was expected to take place.[177] On February 16 "some of the Führer's advisers, feeling that dissolution was inevitable, would even go as far as recommending that the Reich would accelerate the process." Germany's influence was to be limited to Bohemia and Moravia.[178] In any event, the conditions Germany would require for a guarantee of the Czechoslovak borders would be such as to lead to its complete vassalization.[179] On February 26 Coulondre stated, always basing himself on serious sources, that Hitler "will complete…the vassalization of Czechoslovakia and would eventually erase Czechia from the map."[180] Once the unity of the German people, the Volkstum, had been achieved, the time would come to attack other peoples to acquire "living space."[181]

Hitler's conquest of Bohemia and Moravia on March 15—the details of which we shall not examine here—did not take place with the sudden brutality of the coups of March 1936 and March 1938. Only Neville Chamberlain displayed a rather unjustified optimism to the end.[182] As of March 11 the chargé d'affaires in Berlin, Montbas, announced that "the conflict between Czechs and Slovaks was suddenly taking a worrisome turn."[183] On the 12th he reported that troops were on the march toward the Czech border but he didn't yet feel that "a serious resolution was imminent."[184] On the other hand, the French consul in Leipzig was forecasting "a forceful action would be attempted by Germany against Czechoslovakia on March 15 or 16." It was to be "a lightning military action."[185] After having returned to Berlin on March 13, Coulondre sent a whole series of telegrams. "Everything looks as if a forceful operation was about to begin."[186] On March 14 at 6:30 p.m. he announced by phone the arrival in Berlin that evening of President Hacha and Minister Chvalkowski.[187] By March 14 there wasn't any further doubt. Corbin witnessed the shock effect of that move in Great Britain. For some time he had been looking for signs of a change in the country where "political opinion…is slow to react." But now there existed "the threat of total German hegemony over the European continent."[188] Chamberlain and Halifax were very upset. Yet as Corbin noted with some perfidy, Halifax "had only one consolation, that he no longer needed to worry about the Czech guarantee that troubled his conscience and remained unresolved."[189]

Chapter XIII

THE FAILURE OF THE GRAND ALLIANCE

(March–August 1939)

"Had I been told three weeks ago," wrote the ambassador to London, Charles Corbin, on April 4, "that during this time period the British government would have guaranteed the independence of Poland...that such a decision would have been cheered by a nearly unanimous Parliament and that no opposition to it would appear in the press or the public, I would have no doubt met such a forecast with an incredulous smile... The new orientation given to British foreign policy representing such a complete break with its traditional position is so important that it may be said without exaggeration as being of historical magnitude." Because it was no longer as with the Netherlands, a matter of contiguous territories and "bastions." "The objective was to oppose the establishment of German hegemony over continental Europe." It was a return to its origins. "The dissenting conservatives that Messers Eden, Churchill, and Duff Cooper usually represented immediately rallied in support of the government."[1]

The new attitude did not affect the top *appeasers* in the British diplomatic service. Lord Perth, who was leaving Rome permanently on April

24, 1939, departed "optimistic and reassured." He met with Mussolini, and Count Ciano came expressly to the railroad station to bid him farewell. He was convinced that it would all end up at a conference. François-Poncet, who always thought him to be a dangerous dreamer, did not share his optimism.[2]

Sir Nevile Henderson, always "an admirer of the National-Socialist regime, careful to protect Mr. Hitler's prestige, was convinced that Great Britain and Germany could agree to divide the world among them," became very angry on March 15, having been "wounded in his pride." The crisis passed. "Yesterday," wrote Coulondre on April 29, "I found him exactly the way I knew him in February." He played down his government's decision to reintroduce conscription. He found the German proposals made to Poland were quite acceptable. Basically "it appears that events barely touched Sir Nevile Henderson, like water over a mirror... It would seem that he forgot everything and failed to learn anything."[3]

1.

SPAIN:
MORAL FAILURE AND DIPLOMATIC SUCCESS

The Spanish civil war that had been such a passionate cause and was the main focus of the attention of the diplomats in 1936 and 1937 had become a secondary matter in 1938. After Munich the issue reappeared in a new light: it was becoming highly probable that the Franco forces were going to win. Should there be a very late attempt to reestablish the situation? Or, on the contrary, was it best to try and backtrack by seeking reconciliation with the victors and separate Franco from the Fascist camp?

To begin with on September 27, 1938, in the midst of the Sudeten crisis, Franco had expressed his firm decision to remain completely neutral should there be a conflict and had so informed the French consul general in San Sebastian. He also hinted that this deserved some gestures on France's part: to stop supplying the Republicans and to send a representative to Burgos, at least recognizing its "belligerent" status. However, during the fall of 1938, it was still believed that "a certain balance of the forces" existed that perhaps allowed a mediation.[4] The Negrin government accepted the withdrawal of the International Brigades' 10,000 to 12,000 men and Mussolini that of 10,000 Italians.[5] But this was a sham.

"The bulk of the Italian air force and all of the German air force are still present... Without Italian air power, without Italian artillery, without Italian tanks the offensive power of the nationalists is inconceivable," wrote Lieutenant Colonel Morel, the military attaché in Barcelona. He concluded, "Facing a poorly equipped republican army with all kinds of equipment purchased from all the arms dealers of Europe; organized and commanded by national leaders; fighting with desperate and admirable courage, there is the so-called nationalist army, well equipped with foreign matériel that was being constantly resupplied when it is not being increased and that is attempting to secure victory by attrition." And finally: "As for sportsmanship this is not a pretty picture."[6]

Should the borders be reopened to favor the Spanish republicans or should Franco's status as a belligerent be recognized? This was the French government's dilemma at the end of 1938.[7] The total withdrawal of volunteers would obviously help the loyalists. On August 15, however, Franco rejected that possibility.[8] As long as the front remained static it was more convenient to avoid any changes one way or another. At the end of the Franco-British conference of November 24, Chamberlain voiced his opposition to a mediation offered by Daladier. The idea of recognizing implicitly Franco's belligerent status was shelved. To the Spaniards' "resigned fatalism" the French offered a wait-and-see attitude.[9]

The nationalists resumed their offensive on December 24, 1939. On January 13 Ambassador Jules Henry met with the Republican prime minister, Juan Negrin, who complained that France was only shipping wheat. He wanted 10,000 trucks—at least 2,000 for the army in Catalonia.[10] The bombing of Barcelona forced Henry to evacuate the embassy. He rejected being sent a cruiser to take the trip and would attempt to travel over land.[11] The cruiser *Suffren* arrived in Barcelona in any event. A huge wave of 150,000 people, mainly women and children, were said to be on their way to the French border. For Lieutenant Colonel Morel, the military attaché, the republican units resembled poorly equipped "skeletons." Negrin's will was "indomitable" but "morale was awful." There was "no logical chance of turning the tide, nor stopping it. It is the disintegration of the popular forces."[12]

Barcelona fell on January 26. French policy was now forced to switch from wait-and-see to becoming actively engaged. The refugee problem required an urgent solution. The Spanish ambassador was requesting that France welcome them into metropolitain France or to North Africa. Bonnet proposed creating a neutral zone inside Spanish territory, but there were no accommodations nor supplies, and bombing was always a possibility.[13] France was forced to set up camps.[14]

In other words a political solution became necessary. As early as January 20 Bonnet had a conversation with a former Mexican president, Francisco de la Barra, who had just had a meeting with General Jordana, Franco's minister of foreign affairs, who asked that he, de la Barra, meet with Bonnet and Daladier. La Barra was visiting in San Sebastian with his daughter and was unable to meet with Franco who was at the front in Catalonia. Jordana, who held the Grand Cross of the Legion of Honor, told him that he felt a lot of friendship toward France. Relations were not so good with the Italians or the Germans, who were efficient but arrogant. Spain had financial obligations toward them but would not make any territorial concessions. "I give you my word of honor as a statesman and a Spaniard... You may transmit my assurance to Mr. Daladier and Mr. Bonnet." France should name a "general agent" in Burgos as England had done. It would be "possible for France through a dialog with Burgos, to detach the national government from the influence of the Rome-Berlin Axis and have its support for the development of French Mediterranean policy."[15]

This deserved further investigation. On February 2 Daladier and Bonnet sent Léon Bérard, an important national figure, a senator from the Basses-Pyrénées, and a member of the French Academy, who was very reassuring to the Franco side because he was a Catholic, on the right politically and acceptable to the French left because he was a Basque.[16] The right and part of the radical-socialists, particularly *L'Ère Nouvelle*, were in favor of the mission. Léon Blum and the socialists understood the need for recognition but hoped it would take place as late as possible. "What impatience, good God, to humiliate oneself in the face of success!"[17]

The mayor of Bilbao, de Lequerica, welcomed Bérard at the border on February 3 with great honors. He traveled to Burgos and remained there until the 6th. General Jordana received him very cordially and expressed his friendship for France. Bérard told him that he came to examine the conditions to establish relations and that the main French preoccupation was to make sure that Spain would be free of foreign troops. Jordana complained about the moral and tangible support France was giving the "Reds," but confirmed that Spain would rather go to war than cede any piece of its territory to foreigners. He mentioned the main issues that were still open such as confiscated property, and the gold from the Bank of Spain that the government had deposited in France. Finally, he clearly stated that the only kind of recognition that Franco's Spain would accept from France would be a *de jure* recognition, which implied that she would stop recognizing the Republican government.[18]

The Republican government was in bad shape. On February 5, as 150,000 soldiers joined the civilians on their way north, the president of the Spanish Republic, Azaña, who favored an immediate peace, crossed the border into France offering an armistice. Negrin, who wanted to continue fighting, immediately declared that Azaña was no longer qualified to speak for Spain. Negrin moved his offices to Valencia.[19] The secretary of the republican minister of foreign affairs, Alvarez del Vayo, sought shelter with the nationalists, taking the papers of his ministry with him. Bonnet made a note in the margin of Bérard's telegram relating the news: "That rumor was totally wrong but it helps Mr. Negrin who is eager to compromise the French government at the last minute making it impossible to establish relations with Burgos."[20]

During his last meeting with Jordana on February 6, Bérard insisted on a *de facto* recognition and sending "a general agent of the French Republic." Jordana did not give in and took a petulant tone. "Spanish public opinion feels that France is responsible for the continuation or the prolongation of the war."[21] During those discussions an awful human tragedy was taking place, the passing waves of Republican soldiers in rags, of women and children through the border at Cerbère, normally closed, was now overwhelmed by a crazy mob... Drowned in a fog that erased the horizon, whipped by icy gusts, the lines of Spanish refugees that were crowding the border posts were simply pitiful."[22] Large quantities of war supplies crossed the line and were immediately seized by the French.[23] The fate of those who fell into the hands of the nationalists intent on an implacable repression was even more dramatic. Hundreds of officers were shot by firing squads in Barcelona. France and England tried unsuccessfully to obtain a guarantee of no reprisals from Burgos.

On February 10 British ambassador Sir Eric Phipps was given the task of telling Georges Bonnet that his government was ready to recognize Franco unconditionally and as quickly as possible. It was viewed as a way of separating him from foreign influences.[24] While waiting for that recognition, Bonnet had a final contact with Republican Minister Alvarez del Vayo who thought that all hope was not lost.[25] Léon Bérard was sent back to Burgos with the government's approval—which was given quietly "so as to avoid reigniting a dispute that had never quite ended."[26]

The Chamber itself would be consulted. In January it had voted against intervention on the Republican side—374 to 228. After a short debate, on February 24 it voted in favor of recognizing Franco, 323 to 261.[27] It was the Chamber of the Popular Front. Daladier, who wanted it, voted yes. Herriot, the president of the Chamber who did not want recognition, was shocked and opposed to it but suggested to Jean Zay not to resign.[28] Bérard had a whole series of discussions with Jordana as early as February 18. He stated that France was ready for a *de jure* recognition if it was to have "the meaning and the scope of a strong reconciliation." The documents were prepared on Sunday, February 19, by Bérard on the French side with the assistance of Charles Saint and Baraduc; and on the Spanish side by the director of political affairs.[29] The atmosphere was more tense than during the first trip. Berard tried unsuccessfully to obtain a commitment of neutrality.[30] Bonnet cabled Bérard with new instructions on February 21. He wished that, for reasons of prestige, Bérard could meet with Franco. He was requesting that the nationalists accept the return to Spain of women and children—who were less threatened by reprisals—followed by the men, "except for those who were actually members of political movements." He announced that with Daladier he would propose recognition to the Cabinet within forty-eight hours of his return.[31] The British wanted to announce their recognition as early as the 24th but he agreed to wait for Bérard's return scheduled for the 25th[32] and the French Cabinet meeting set for February 27.[33] *Therefore, on February 28, Britain and France recognized Franco.* Rochat, the deputy director of political affairs,[34] brought French recognition to Burgos on March 1.

On March 2 it was made public that Marshal Pétain was appointed ambassador to Burgos. It was clever to send such a prestigious man, whose right-wing ideas were well known, to Spain. If Franco had not seen fit to receive Léon Bérard, he would certainly feel flattered to meet the victor of Verdun. We do not know whose idea it was to make such a choice, very well received by the right and viewed as a poor one by the left. The Spaniards appointed José-Felice de Lequerica, who had a reputation of being pro-German, to Paris.

Pétain focused on the refugees, Republican war equipment and the Spanish gold. He met with Jordana on the 23rd and presented his credentials to Franco on the 24th. "I wanted to stress that I took the mission offered to me because I firmly desired to reestablish between our two countries the relations that they used to have."[35]

As early as April 20 he felt optimistic. The information he gathered went to prove that there were no suspicious troop movements toward Tangier or on the border with French Morocco. Between 18,000 and 20,000 Italians, along with 7,000 Germans, remained in Spain. The rumors regarding new Italian landings were false. Finally, he had been told repeatedly enough that the new government was following a "policy of total independence for Spain." In any case no naval base was being used by the Axis powers.[36]

The most delicate issue was that of the refugees. The total number was estimated at 450,000.[37] Sarraut as interior minister thought that 50,000 of them would be seriously at risk if they returned to their country. The soldiers were disarmed and divided into five centers that the army had organized. The Basque deputy Ybarnegaray estimated the total—as of March 10—to be 226,000.[38] This sudden immigration prompted a violent debate in the Chamber on March 10, 14 and 16. "The issue goes beyond France," wrote *Le Temps*.[39] By March 15, 50,000 members of the militia had gone back. The total number of returnees didn't go beyond 200,000. Therefore, there was a mass of 200,000 to 250,000 persons that France had to shelter.

Pétain attempted to elicit from the Spaniards an effort that was viewed as justified and was to be rather thin. In July, for example, the authorities at Irun declared that they could welcome 50,000 militia at a pace of 2,500 per day. But it became extremely difficult to find volunteers willing to go back.[40]

On the other hand, there were neither difficulties nor serious delays to the return of the fleet (partly located in Bizerte). As for the gold of the Bank of Spain, a decision on the part of the French courts was required. The Franco government was impatiently asking for the gold, since it was heavily indebted to Germany and most of all to Italy. Bonnet could finally cable Pétain on July 21 that he had turned over the gold to the Spanish authorities that same day.[41]

The Pétain mission succeeded at the most important level. "Spain wants to be neutral—because—the country is exhausted and divided."[42] As embassy councilor Gazel wrote in a personal letter to Bonnet on August 6, "I feel we are on the right track in our policy of détente with Spain. The Marshal's personal reputation is considerable…we must proceed slowly and not be too ambitious."[43]

The probability in case of war of not being encumbered by a third front, "the Pyrenees front," and the certainty of not being threatened by

Axis bases in the Balearic Islands—all this was reassuring for France. No doubt the circumstances and the exhaustion of Spain did more to reach those results than the diplomacy of Daladier, Bonnet and Pétain. Yet it must be said that French diplomacy was cleverly engaged. Daladier would suffer morally from it. The left-wing press didn't mince words in accusing him of "dishonor," and "national humiliation." For him the end certainly did justify the means.

2.

ITALY REMAINS OUT OF REACH

Did security in the western Mediterranean warrant going further? For a long time this remained part of Chamberlain's thinking. The agreement between England and Italy (the Easter Agreement) was dated April 16, 1938. One year later, on April 8, 1939, Mussolini annexed Albania—on Good Friday! And yet Chamberlain intended to pursue his quest: In order to separate Italy from Germany the Anglo-Italian agreement needed to be completed by a Franco-Italian agreement.

On this point the French government was divided. Bonnet was in favor. François-Poncet, who had been announcing a catastrophe where Italy was concerned during the first three months of the year, changed his mind to thinking that a rapprochement was possible as of March 22.[44] Mussolini's March 26 speech, while extremely violent, seemed to him to be a maneuver "to push us toward having discussions."[45]

Daladier, with the support of Léger, felt much less in favor of a rapprochement. He told Baudoin on March 20 that there was no reason to pursue discussions. Yet he agreed for him to go and say so in Rome[46] and he did not close the door on discussions regarding an Italian free port in Djibuti. Two Cabinet meetings on March 27 and 29 had prepared his March 29 speech. Bonnet was preaching for conciliation and had the support of de Monzie, who was always pro-Italian, and of Chautemps and Marchandeau. On the opposite side was Campinchi who "displayed a Corsican's vigilant and punctilious passion against Italy."[47] Paul Reynaud, his longtime friend and a lawyer from the same graduating class, Mandel, Champetier de Ribes and Jean Zay all favored a firm approach.[48] Daladier made it clear above all that France refused to give up even an inch of territory. But London felt he was not closing the door on the Italians.[49] On March 30 François-Poncet thought that Ciano was worried about German influence and wished "to hear from France and England."[50] He thought that no doubt Mussolini was seeking "a reasonable agreement with France." The takeover of Albania on April 7 (announced by François-Poncet as early as April 2)[51] made the ambassador grow pessimistic once again. He thought that Italy would not evacuate Mallorca[52] and that she intended to "play the Spanish card."[53] The Italians were taking advantage of the gullibility of Chamberlain and Halifax.[54] Italy was threatening the Balkans.[55] François-Poncet was complaining that he had no contacts with Ciano.[56] When he finally did meet with him on April 25 to sign a commercial agreement, it was to learn that there had been a second Baudoin mission that failed. For the first time Ciano officially communicated to him the very moderate demands he had presented to Baudoin.[57]

On the same day Phipps delivered a note to the Quai d'Orsay requesting information on the status of Franco-Italian relations; Corbin met with Halifax who discussed the same issue with the latter, offering to act as go-between.[58]

French policy was still disoriented and disorganized. In a note dated April 17, Daladier wrote in pencil, "Should we not move and wait for Mussolini's response; should we begin negotiating with M.; should we let it go?"[59] According to him, Léger was "against" the second and third points. Bonnet complained about Baudoin, about Daladier who thought that Mussolini had made a bad speech and called Léger and Baudoin to say so, and he was miffed at not having been invited to a lunch at the home of Bois, the editor-in-chief of Le Petit Parisien with Daladier and Léger. He feared a maneuver without his knowledge against a rapprochement with Italy.[60]

Finally, on May 2, Bonnet noticed a change. Several telegrams from François-Poncet repeated the idea that the time was right to reopen talks with Italy. On April 26 he summoned Léger who, he said, was coming around to his point of view. A telegram drafted in part by Bonnet and by Léger was sent to François-Poncet on May 3, authorizing him to restart negotiations.[61] Some discussions then took place.[62] But on May 7 it was learned that a political and military pact between Germany and Italy was about to be signed.[63] It was the Pact of Steel of May 22, 1939.

Halifax came to Paris on May 20 and 21. Daladier wanted to discuss relations with the USSR (see below). Halifax was mostly interested "in using Italian influence over Germany to avert the final catastrophe." To reach that goal it would be good for France to offer Italy "reasonable satisfaction," something that the Duce could "show his people." We should note that the Pact of Steel was only two days away.

Daladier answered that he would agree to improved relations with Italy but only if these were reciprocated.

Italy must offer something in exchange, otherwise France would lose its prestige "in the eyes of the Muslim world." Finally, Daladier "was convinced that this would not lead to any results" because "Italy is in the hands of Germany."[64]

The Pact of Steel once again made François-Poncet feel pessimistic. "Mussolini is hesitating and trying to find his way," he said on May 21.[65] But on May 22 he thought that "the two partners will take new initiatives that will accelerate the course of events."[66] Coulondre agreed. Italy "may soon become only an instrument in the hands of its too powerful ally."[67] "It appears that since Lord Perth's departure the British embassy has returned to its original optimism,"[68] François-Poncet also wrote. On May 31 he met with Ciano who was strongly against "the Franco-British encirclement moves."[69] Mussolini was to announce that by the end of August "there would be changes in the political map of Europe."[70]

Chamberlain, meanwhile, had not yet said his final word.

On July 13, as negotiations with the Soviets were becoming increasingly complicated, Chamberlain wrote to Daladier that he kept on hoping that Mussolini would influence Hitler. The Franco-Italian negotiation "would help gain time." The same idea would recur in the British attitude toward the USSR.

As proof that the British felt this matter was much more important than the Moscow negotiations, Sir Eric Phipps, in handing the letter to Daladier on July 14, stated that *"the issue of war or peace probably depended on those negotiations."*[71] [Emphasis added.]

On July 17 Daladier ordered that an answer be drafted.[72] He thanked Chamberlain "for his friendly trust," recognizing as he did "that the situation in general was improving" thanks to "the determination shown by our two governments." He recalled the initiatives taken by François-Poncet on April 26, May 11 and recently on July 5. "I feel that I have anticipated and even gone beyond the suggestion you have been kind enough to make." But Mussolini would see a new French initiative as a "sign of weakness." Italy would need to offer "guarantees of neutrality." Daladier agreed to British participation in the negotiation.

When he actually sent the letter itself on July 24, Daladier became much more reserved. The entire section on British participation was cut. Daladier clearly refused to reopen a dialog with Italy. At the end he simply stated he would be willing to trust the "wisdom" of the British government.[73] Chamberlain would stop insisting. There was to be no Franco-Italian rapprochement and yet Italy did not go to war in September 1939.[74]

3.

TOWARD THE "GRAND ALLIANCE"— THE PRELIMINARY NEGOTIATIONS

The history of the negotiations between the USSR, the United Kingdom and France has been written many times. In the absence of Soviet documents we still do not know exactly which objectives Moscow was pursuing and, more precisely, whether the secret parallel negotiations between the USSR and Germany were viewed by the Kremlin leadership as a possible alternative or as the real goal. This, however, is not part of our subject.

Access to the French archives allows us to first of all correct a legend disseminated mainly by British historian A.J.P. Taylor.[75] In studying the time lag between British and Soviet notes he found that the British would take a longer time to respond while the Soviets were, on the contrary, very quick to reply. He deducted that "the Russians were anxious to reach a conclusion," and that "the delays came from the West." He forgets that the Soviets were always replying by saying "no" or added new demands which does not necessarily indicate a clear intention to reach an agreement. He also lumps together by using the expression "the West," a hesitant England, desperately slow and undecided, and a France that of the three seems to have been the *only one in a hurry to come to a conclusion.*

It appears for once that, in this haste, Daladier, Bonnet, and Léger were all in complete agreement and that the military shared their point of view. While agreeing to make haste they may not have agreed with the ultimate goal. Everything actually points to the fact that Daladier and the military leaders wanted *an alliance,* meaning the addition of the Soviet forces to the other allied forces in the event, which appeared increasingly likely, of a war, while Georges Bonnet, whose later attitude was to indicate that he continued to not want war but rather *deterrence.* In his view—

and he was absolutely correct on this point—a firm attitude on the part of France and Britain *alone* would not save Poland. Hitler was not bluffing; he had the "West Wall," he was aware of the weakness of the French air force and of the British army. However, if a strong triple entente were to challenge him, then he would probably not move forward. Deterrence, while impossible with two partners, could work if there were three.

Even though the thought of canceling the Franco-Soviet Pact of 1935, something that was on Bonnet's mind more than in passing in October 1938, was shelved, until March 15, 1939, the document remained dormant with the Soviets, who made no secret they no longer believed in it, as they took a "detached" attitude toward the Westerners[76] while discreetly offering airplanes to France[77] and getting closer—also rather discreetly—to Poland since November.[78] When Jules Basdevant, the Quai d'Orsay's legal expert, published an article in the journal *Politique Étrangère* in February 1939 expressing doubts about the current validity of the 1935 pact, Ambassador Naggiar informed the Soviet leadership that, based on his verbal instructions, the treaty remained valid as far as France was concerned.[79] Naggiar felt that the USSR was "at crossroads," having based its policies on collective security; Russia was ready to return to that policy. Otherwise, "we run the risk of seeing it pursue along all its western borders the organization of its own security system. Such a system could include, with Germany assisted by Poland and possibly Italy, an economic and technical collaboration which would free up the Reich from any worry on that end and…provide the raw materials and freedom of movement that are indispensable required for a final settling of accounts with the West."[80]

Like his colleague Coulondre, Naggiar was fully aware of the possibility of a German-Soviet understanding.

During the occupation of Bohemia and Moravia, followed by that of Memel, France could obviously not react. Bonnet instructed Coulondre rather late on March 17 of an initiative of "formal protest" against that "blatant violation of Munich."[81]

The sudden change in attitude by the British toward the USSR was to impress the French much more. Meeting with Lord Halifax on March 18, Corbin found out that he had "explored" Russia's availability.[82] Georges Bonnet met with Soviet Ambassador Suritz on the same day. "England and France have decided to intervene;" in the event of a new aggression, "they would be happy to know what the attitude of the Soviet government would be."[83] *It was therefore on March 17 and 18, 1939, that the negotiations began.*

It must be pointed out that the future target of the threat remained uncertain.[84] The British, just like the French, thought above all that Romania was in the greatest danger. Polish Ambassador Lukasziewicz told Bonnet on March 19 that he had no present fears even regarding Danzig. Romania, on the other hand, appeared to be in danger.[85] Couldn't the Polish-Romanian alliance of 1921 against Moscow also be targeted at Germany? That issue was discussed throughout the spring. But it was useless because the two countries were suspicious of each other. Lukasziewicz would entertain such an alliance only on condition that Hungary also take part (it had just annexed Carpatho-Ukraine or Ruthenia).[86] The Polish and Western concern would only surface on March 23.[87]

The British, as we know, began by proposing a joint four-power declaration (the United Kingdom, France, the USSR, and Poland) whereby those countries agreed to consult each other in the event of "action taken against the independence of a European State." Corbin clearly told Sir Alexander Cadogan that such a procedure—a simple consultation—would be an admission of weakness.[88] On the other hand, Soviet Ambassador Suritz proposed a conference to include representatives from the USSR, Poland, Turkey, Romania, England and France.[89] The British, who did not favor a conference, which they viewed as too spectacular, concluded that a British guarantee be given to Poland and Romania. The French government was informed on March 28.[90]

The Poles in their pride did not like the idea of being "guaranteed." But Polish ambassador to Berlin, Lipski, had just been negotiating with Ribbentrop. Ambassador Léon Noël was unable to obtain any definite information; finally on March 29 he found out that Ribbentrop had demanded the annexation of the free city of Danzig and the creation of an extra-territorial highway through the corridor—which corresponded to what actually happened.[91] The Poles refused and would hang on firmly to that position all the way to the war. France agreed with the new British stance and on March 31 Chamberlain issued his momentous declaration of a guarantee to Poland and Romania, stating that he was also speaking for France. Litvinov, the People's Commissar for Foreign Affairs, answered the initial British approaches with bitterness—the Western powers were not impressed by "the latest Soviet moves in favor of an effective collective resistance to aggression." This led to an evasive but highly significant conclusion. "After all a policy of isolation would probably best suit the USSR." Was it a joke? Payart, the French chargé d'affaires, asked himself. Or was it the sign of "alternating directions in the leadership's thinking?"[92] The Tass news agency denied information provided by *Le Temps* and *L'Œuvre*, according to which the USSR was committed to providing war materiél to Poland and to refuse to ship raw materials to Germany in case of war.[93]

Would it not be possible, asked Bonnet to Ambassador Suritz, to find a way, "in a form to be determined" for the USSR to promise its assistance to Poland and Romania?

However, the inescapable issue of the passage of Soviet troops remained as relevant as in 1938. Georges Bonnet discussed it once more with Suritz. "It was obvious that there had to be an agreement between the USSR and Romania or the USSR and Poland in order for the Franco-Soviet Pact to come usefully into play." But, Suritz answered, those two countries had until then refused any Soviet help. The French minister stated that he was convinced he could change their mind. He felt that in accordance with the consultation clause of the Franco-Soviet Pact it was appropriate to "begin immediate discussions between France and the USSR in order to precisely determine the help that the USSR could provide to Romania and Poland in the event of German aggression."[94] Chargé d'affaires Jean Payart (who was serving in that post since 1931, enjoyed a personal relationship with Litvinov and was considered by Jean Laloy to have "a keen mind")[95] discussed the issue with Deputy Commissar Potemkin who refused to make any commitments as long as Poland and Romania showed no interest. A collective defense, yes; but nothing else.[96] A conference among interested parties intending to show good will on the part of Poland and Romania, yes. But no negotiations outside the People's Commissariat for Foreign Affairs. General Palasse, the military attaché in Moscow, took an initiative in that direction. He was told that any contact with the High Command had to be preceded by "an agreement in principle that was to be reached at the diplomatic level."[97]

The general pattern of the coming negotiations with the USSR—first a political agreement followed by a military accord—was now clear.

At first it appeared that the Soviet government wanted to conduct negotiations in Paris. On April 13, 1939, Georges Bonnet and Ambassador Suritz had what the minister described as a "moving," long conversation. He offered a document whereby the USSR would provide immediate help and assistance to France "in the event [France] would be in a state of war with Germany due to assistance it provided to either Poland or Romania." Since Suritz noted that the USSR would not accept such a document if it did not mention reciprocity, Georges Bonnet added a new paragraph on April 14, whereby France promised help and assistance in the same manner. Georges Bonnet "pleaded eloquently." "The independence of those countries is of prime interest to the Soviet Union." Should Poland and Romania vanish, wouldn't it have a common border with Germany? Suritz agreed to transmit those proposals to his government, but he felt that if "it wanted the possibility to intervene in a conflict it would still not be willing to enter into an automatic commitment."[98] The USSR informed the British that it would be ready to possibly offer a guarantee to Romania[99] but preferred a solution whereby it would "issue a general declaration giving assistance to all (neighboring) countries...desiring the benefit of that assistance."[100]

Three positions therefore emerged.

The United Kingdom was offering three unilateral guarantees limited to Poland and Romania.

France was offering to the USSR a mutual assistance and help pact focused on Poland and Romania.[101]

As for the USSR its views were known as early as April 18, 1939. It wanted *a "plurilateral" assistance treaty that would include political and military mutual assistance between England, Franc and itself; an agreement of those three countries to provide assistance to the Eastern states neighboring Russia, Romania, Poland, Latvia, and Estonia); extending the Polish-Romanian alliance in the event of German aggression; the commitment of the three to not sign a separate peace.*

On the French side it was noted that the USSR, contrary to 1935, did not mention the League of Nations. It did not want to simply assist Poland and Romania but extended its interest to the Baltic States, showing no interest in countries neighboring France or Holland.[102]

Lord Halifax did not hide the fact that he was "suspicious"[103] with Corbin. The thinking at the Quai d'Orsay was why not limit matters to a commitment among the three powers to begin with, without making reference to others? It was a way to reach the French proposal of an automatic Franco-Soviet alliance by enlarging it. But the British wanted no part of it.[104] The result was the exasperating slowness of the little game where each one attempted to hold on to its own point of view.

4.

THE POLITICAL NEGOTIATIONS

Starting on April 18, the date of the Soviet proposal, the negotiations became extremely simple, despite what they appeared to be. The Soviets did not change their position. The British, under pressure by France, came closer to it very slowly but firmly in May, vigorously in June and in a frenzy in July, because the French wanted a three-party alliance and needed British acceptance. The Soviets were simply waiting and once their proposal was nearly agreed to they would add a new condition.

The Soviet proposals were dated April 18. The Foreign Office studied them and "felt that the study would take several days and will certainly consult with us once it has reached its conclusions."[105] It is interesting to note in passing that the method of consultation would take place only after reaching one's decision. On May 7 the British rejected the Soviet offers despite France, which—to mention only the basics—had as of April 24 rejected the British proposal for "a unilateral declaration of assistance by the Russians parallel to the public declarations by France and England but without any guarantee nor any obligation of direct or indirect assistance by the three powers toward each other." In other words, the French position was very close to that of the USSR since it tended toward a larger three-way alliance. The USSR added a list of third-party countries that were to receive guarantees. France was not too favorable since it feared Polish objections, but most of all it rejected the British system that promised no reciprocity to the Soviets.[106] The Soviets were waiting for the British mediations to bear fruit. The ambassador was surprised by the delay—and took advantage to slip in a key element: The political accords would have to be completed "by staff agreements without which any understanding would be deprived of any practical value."[107] "Danzig is not worth a war," wrote the *Times* on May 3.[108]

At this time Molotov replaced Litvinov as People's Commissar for Foreign Affairs. "It was a serious matter," commented Payart. "It seems attributed, in part at least, to the hesitations by the British government during the last negotiations."[109] The day before Marcel Déat had published his famous article in *L'Œuvre*, stating that the French people did not want to die for Danzig. This was absolutely true but was it only about Danzig? Three days later a communiqué announced the imminent signature of what would be referred to as the "Pact of Steel."[110] Then on May 7 the British counterproposals arrived in a leisurely manner. England remained with its initial proposal. Ambassador Sir William Seeds handed that answer to Molotov on May 8. Molotov "complained on that occasion about the slowness of the methods of British diplomacy." He was also surprised to see the difference between the French response (three party alliance) and the British proposal (unilateral guarantees to Poland and Romania). On May 10 the House of Commons also expressed concern regarding the delays.[111]

An article published by *Izvestia* on May 11 stated that "a single front of mutual assistance" should be created, that this project had not "been welcomed with sympathy by England and France," that the British proposals required immediate assistance by the Soviets to France and England if Poland or Romania were attacked but nothing about assistance to the USSR by France and England. "Within such a setup the USSR would be in a position of inequality."[112] This article, said Payart, forgets the French counterproposals and "sets up an abusive solidarity between France and England."[113] On May 13 Moscow rejected the British proposals and renewed its offer of a mutual assistance pact.[114]

From May 14 to 26 the British government would slowly give in and adopt the idea of a tripartite alliance. Bonnet insisted as early as the 15th "on the fears of the French government in seeing the Anglo-Soviet misunderstanding continue under the present circumstances."[115] A hard negotiation took place in London between Lord Halifax and Ambassador Maïsky.[116] If the British were giving in, it was because "the British government was being constantly prodded by the French government that didn't stop reminding it of the absolute need to conclude a tripartite pact." It was also due to "the fear both in Paris and in London, of a rapprochement between Berlin and Moscow."[117]

The main explanation for the British change was the key meeting in Geneva between Halifax, Daladier, and Bonnet on May 20 and 21, 1939. Chamberlain, said Halifax, was thinking of "the powers threatened by an aggression; to slide from there to a triple alliance meant going in a totally different direction with the possibility of provoking on the part of the German government, the kind of madness that it is precisely attempting to avoid." This was very much like Chamberlain who seemingly still failed to understand that it wasn't at all necessary to provoke Hitler for him to go on the attack. To which Daladier responded that Germany "will only be stopped when he will be convinced that he will face effective resistance by a bloc where there are no cracks." It should be noted that Bonnet and Léger, who took part in the discussions, backed the prime minister's point of view.[118]

On May 24 the British cabinet agreed to the principle of "a tripartite mutual guarantee accord." It would consult with the French government and, if it agreed, would then transmit the wording to Moscow.[119] The signing of the "Pact of Steel" between Germany and Italy probably had something to do with that about-face.[120] The French government naturally agreed and Bonnet, who summoned Suritz on May 26, spoke of the need for staff discussions in order "to reach a definite military plan that could save Poland."[121]

On May 28 the British ambassador, Sir William Seeds, and French chargé d'affaires, Payart, brought to Molotov, who was with Potemkin—the latter not uttering a word—the text of the British note that the French had approved. "Much to our surprise he did not hide that his first reaction was a negative one."[122] His objection came from the fact that the text mentioned the League of Nations! This was to be the first of Molotov's delaying maneuvers. "What can be the Soviet government's objective?" Payart[123] wondered why was there "this bias of suspicion mixed with malice?"[124] Did Seeds inform Molotov that England accepted the military accord? His answer was that the Anglo-French project was "unclear."[125]

Finally, on June 2 the Soviet counter-project came in a six-article document. From then on negotiations would focus on that document and be held in Moscow. For one month, until July 3, a confused negotiation took place regarding Article 1, meant to clarify general objectives of the alliance. The Soviet draft stated that the alliance would come into play: 1) In the event of aggression by a third party against one of the three contracting parties; 2) In the event of an aggression by a third party against one of the following eight countries: Finland, Estonia, Latvia, Poland, Romania, Greece, Turkey (countries that neighbored or were dose to the USSR), and Belgium; 3) In the event of assistance given by one of these three states to another European state having requested such assistance in order to resist a violation of its neutrality."[126]

Ambassador Naggiar, who was back in Moscow at the end of May, preferred that description and so did Bonnet.[127] It is worth mentioning that he did not get along too well with his deputy Payart, who left for France until the end of August. Naggiar, however, was "a methodical and serious person."[128]

An agreement could be reached although Molotov was a difficult and suspicious man.

His suspicion appeared in the form of statements so rude and hasty that they not only showed contempt for diplomatic custom. This kind of rough simplicity was so different from the ways of Mr. Litvinov that it appeared to be a tactical approach. It tended to show that Mr. Molotov, as a loyal collaborator of Stalin, was not content with the advantages of reciprocity that had been refused to the USSR during Mr. Litvinov's tenure...the new Commissar for Foreign Affairs now was seeking even greater advantages.[129]

The month wasted between June 2 and July 3 can be attributed to the British. On June 5 they rejected the Soviet draft of Article 1. The French government, ready to accept it, was becoming impatient. The June 6 Council of Ministers "unanimously recognized the extreme urgency of reaching an agreement in the Franco-Anglo-Russian negotiations." There remained, of course, one source of worry: Would the USSR use Article 1 to intervene in the Baltic States? On the other hand, Article 6 stated that the political agreement would only be enacted after a military agreement had been reached.[130] But it was necessary to reach a conclusion. On June 9 Corbin noted that the British counter draft was not yet ready. He was getting impatient.[131] The draft would be ready only on June 12. To complicate things further the British Cabinet, rather than transmitting it to Sir William Seeds, had it delivered to Moscow by a top Foreign Office functionary, Sir William Strang. This would have been understandable had he been given special powers, but he did not have any and was constantly forced to consult with the Foreign Office, something Seeds could have done just as well.

The British wished that the list of eight countries not be mentioned in the treaty itself but only in an appended document that would also include Holland and Switzerland. They were offering a new draft of the second paragraph of Article 1. It must be quoted to understand its exceptionally obscure language and how little it differed from the Soviet draft. The three contracting parties would intervene "once an aggression had taken place...against a European State having asked and received assistance from the interested contracting party or as a result of an earlier commitment in accordance with the wishes of the said contracting party or independently of any commitment."

The Quai d'Orsay had prepared language that was closer to the Soviet draft, but in order to underscore the solidarity between France and England refrained from presenting it.[132]

On June 15 Strang, Seeds and Naggiar solemnly handed the British draft to Molotov. On June 16 he rejected the draft stating that it created "a humiliating and unequal situation for the Soviet Union."[133] Naggiar was under the impression that the reason behind sending Strang was meant to stiffen rather than soften the British position.[134] Was it related to the June 8 debate in the House of Commons that had made such a dismal impression on Moscow, in which Chamberlain, Halifax, and Sir John Simon announced that England was ready to examine the German and Italian demands for living space? Naggiar wrote that in Moscow "what is singled out…is that England, despite appearances, is not yet fully committed to the policy of resisting aggression."[135]

Naggiar was irritated. The conversations were stalled on some subtle changes, which he said "appeared to be useless and even out of place in that they were encouraging the suspicion of the leaders of the USSR." There were, for example, endless discussions on whether or not to replace the Soviet formula of "immediate and effective assistance" with the proposed British language "all the assistance immediately at its disposal."[136] Molotov rejected a French compromise on June 22. Seeds agreed with Naggiar that the "aide-mémoire prepared in London only complicated the negotiations and perpetuated a dispute."[137] Why not accept the Russian proposal? Why not send a military and technical mission "without waiting for the results of the ongoing discussions?"[138] Bonnet felt that it was essential "that the political agreement not be subordinate to the military agreement," because in that case "we will once again enter a period of endless difficulties."[139]

Finally on June 23 London agreed to the Soviet draft of June 2 practically unchanged. But we should not anticipate. That decision included a draft proposal for Article 1. It was submitted to the French government on June 27, four days later. Then four days lapsed when finally the draft reached Molotov on July 1. Four more days and yet Bonnet had done his best. "I feel we must conclude as quickly as possible. I have strongly insisted with the British government."[140]

On July 1 there was more discussion with Molotov regarding the list of countries. Bonnet cabled that the objective is "the mutual solidarity of the three great powers…in those conditions the number of countries guaranteed is unimportant."[141] Molotov never gave an immediate answer.

He needed Stalin's approval. Strang, Seeds and Naggiar therefore went back to see him on July 3. From then on the delay again came from the Soviet side. Before a conclusion could be reached, Molotov said that 1. To have a perfect symmetry the USSR must sign bilateral pacts with Turkey and Poland; 2. On the other hand, he was proposing that in Article 1 to the word "aggression" be added the adjectives "direct or indirect." Bonnet protested. If point 1 was agreed to, it meant "to delay until an undetermined date the guarantee to be given by the USSR." As for point 2 it was a device for the USSR to take over the Baltic States following a series of internal coups d'état.[142]

Molotov quickly forgot the first demand, but the second once again prompted every existing British subtlety.[143] Naggiar feared "that due to the influence of the Foreign Office the negotiations might once more get bogged down in discussions about draft changes many of which, while they did affect the heart of the matter, elicited renewed Soviet counter-changes."[144] Molotov, therefore, upon meeting with his three counter-parts on July 8, offered a definition of indirect aggression. Naggiar felt that it was completely satisfactory.[145] The British began discussing it in great detail. *We may state that this discussion would never reach a conclusion.*

More importantly, beginning on July 8, Article 6 was to become the star issue: no political agreement would be signed without a military agreement.[146] Bonnet, having attempted to avoid that Soviet demand,[147] resigned himself to accepting it, fearing that it could be a breaking point.[148] He could foresee the difficulties. The acquiescence of Poland and Romania was required, which, he said, "was less than certain." Once more they were getting into uncharted territory. But on July 9 Molotov proved unmovable. "As long as the military agreement is not signed we cannot consider that we have a treaty."[149] This was all the more embarrassing since the press had started to write about the "grand alliance" as though it were already consummated. "We are reaching a critical moment," wrote Bonnet to Halifax, "where we find it necessary to do everything possible to succeed."[150] At the same time he complained to Corbin about "the hesitations of the British government on the threshold of a decisive moment in the negotiations," and of its "too formal an attitude at the eleventh hour."

There was a final hope as far as "deterrence" was concerned, no doubt harbored by Bonnet: the publication of a joint communiqué by the three parties announcing to the world that they "agreed on the main points of the political agreement." Bonnet prepared a simple and clear text.[151]

The British immediately proposed changes to tone down the language and Molotov rejected any communiqué. There would never be a communiqué at all!

On July 23 Molotov had at least accepted that the military negotiations should begin immediately. On the 24th Bonnet told Naggiar that the French delegation was basically ready. On the same day Corbin told him that the British would require ten days to set up their delegation.[152]

5.

THE FAILURE
OF THE MILITARY NEGOTIATIONS

On July 27, four days after Molotov agreed, the French government appointed General Doumenc, an eminent specialist of motorization, to head the military delegation. On the same day Gamelin gave him instructions that were rather vague.[153] The negotiations were to begin only on August 12.

Once more we find that the French were very much in a hurry and that the British were not at all. But there is a document proving that their slowness was by choice. On August 3 the British government's instructions to its negotiators reached the Quai d'Orsay,[154] which transmitted them to Gamelin. It states, *"The British delegation is to conduct negotiations very slowly,* keeping closely abreast of the political discussions." [Emphasis added.] It was to be driven by an extremely suspicious attitude toward the Soviets. "It is aware of the danger that the information it passes on may be leaked to Germany." Since everyone knew that military plans were dependent upon the Polish and Romanian attitude, this should "encourage the Russians to engage in direct talks with Poland and Romania." It must speak "in the most general terms possible."

Bonnet met with Doumenc as he was about to leave. "I drew his attention," he said, "on the need to reach the military agreement as quickly as possible." According to Beaufre, when Doumenc visited Daladier on July 31 the latter had said, "Get us an agreement at any price."[155]

Two crucial points explain the French attitude. First, there was the information coming from Germany, unrelated to what was taking place in Danzig,[156] that Germany was mobilizing. Production was increasing "the war machine keeps on being wound up and improved as if the decision to use it very soon had been made."[157] On July 25 the chargé d'affaires, Tarbé de Saint-Hardouin, noted "a mobilization of sorts" that he estimated at 1 million men, very different from that of September 1938, which was "ostentatious." A clear attempt at camouflage could be detected.[158] General Le Rond, who had played an important part at the Peace Conference and in Upper Silesia, met with Bonnet on July 27 after a trip of one month to Germany and spending eight days in Danzig. This "excellent observer of things German" was clearly pessimistic.[159] On August 1, Saint-Hardouin informed the government that there was a noticeable acceleration in preparations—movements to the "West Wall," call up of reservists of the classes 1902 to 1910, requisitions, etc. Regimental numbers, shoulder boards, and badges had all been carefully removed.[160] After a period when everyone felt safe, he noticed a return to the concept that a "lightning action" could be launched against Poland during the second fortnight of August.[161]

The other French motivation was the growing fear of a German-Soviet rapprochement. There is a well-known document by Robert Coulondre, who had been ambassador to both Moscow and then Berlin. As he paid his farewell visit to Litvinov on October 16, 1938, he wrote:

> We must expect…an imminent and undoubtedly unofficial and indirect initiative by the Kremlin to approach Berlin… It is obviously difficult to know what the offers and the response will be. Yet I can see only one proposal susceptible of awakening Germany's greed, and that is a division of Poland.[162]

Based on information gathered by the SR, the army's *Deuxième Bureau* was even more explicit: "The possibility of a secret German-Soviet agreement toward a division of Poland requires our attention."[163]

This message is only the first in a long series coming with increasing frequency from the embassies in Berlin and Moscow, as they got closer to August 1939. Of particular interest were the commercial negotiations between the Soviets and Germans that Dr. Schnurre was directing for Berlin. On January 27, 1939, Payart still believed that they would not extend beyond the economic area.[164] Naggiar mentioned the issue on February 22 following a conversation with Litvinov.[165] Vaux-Saint-Cyr, the chargé d'affaires in Berlin, reported on April 22 that "some Hitlerian officials" have said that "after all Germany could seek an understanding with Russia at Poland's expense and offer a share of that country to the Soviets."[166]

Litvinov's replacement with Molotov on May 4 immediately led Coulondre to face the issue of a reversal of alliances and the division of Poland. However, he felt that the Führer would be against it despite "the deep similarities between the two regimes."[167] According to information that Captain Stehlin obtained from German General Bodenschatz on May 7, he again mentioned "the fourth partition of Poland."[168] This time he felt the matter was so important, given the quality of the source, that he sent Stehlin to Paris to carry his dispatch. Stehlin said that he waited unsuccessfully for five days for a meeting with Bonnet and left without having seen him.[169] On May 10 from Moscow, Payart felt that a sudden Soviet reversal "appears unlikely *for the moment*. But we should not be lulled into not worrying about an about-face."[170] Bonnet was finally impressed and in a note following a visit by Soviet Ambassador Suritz on May 26 he wrote, "We must not overlook any possibility, such as the USSR remaining out of the conflict or even that it might reach an agreement with Germany."[171] Rochat, the deputy director of political affairs, in the course of the weekly liaison meeting of May 24 in discussing the Anglo-Franco-Russian negotiations, added, "We are informed of contacts between Moscow and Berlin that could change everything." That information came from the *Deuxième Bureau*. There was even a rumor that General von Fritsch was in Moscow with a German delegation. But the USSR denied it.[172] On May 17 Molotov had spoken to German Ambassador von der Schulenburg about "the political foundations" that should be given to the commercial negotiations and that Hitler had decided on May 29 and 30 to enter into negotiations.[173]

On July 8 Coulondre met Soviet chargé d'affaires Astakhov in Berlin, who "stated in the most categorical manner that there were no political talks taking place between Berlin and Moscow." Astakhov knew full well that he wasn't telling the truth because he was involved in it up to his neck. But Coulondre was not convinced. "If, as it is being said in some German circles, there are political contacts between Berlin and Moscow—these were not being handled through official channels."[174] From Moscow, Naggiar mentioned a possible partition of Poland and of the Baltic States.[175] The rumor became even more insistent by early July. The imminent arrival of von Papen in Moscow was being discussed.[176] The military attaché, General Palasse, stated that no German delegation had arrived; however, he underscored the possibility of a partition of Poland.[177]

We should linger no further. All these communications indicated that the thought of a possible reversal of alliances went beyond the dreams of diplomats seeking explanations and was viewed as a serious possibility by the Quai d'Orsay, which was the reason to want to reach a quick resolution. The objectives of the two delegations were not the same. General Doumenc's was to "*obtain the signing of a military agreement in the shortest time available in view of a war thought to be imminent.* [Emphasis added.]

The British delegation led by Admiral Drax-Plumkett was also looking for an agreement "difficult to secure rapidly" but if not, it "*planned for some lengthy negotiations, to keep Germany under the threat of an Anglo-Franco-Soviet military pact and therefore reach the fall on the winter thereby delaying the war.*"[178] [Emphasis added.]

Chamberlain had some strange ideas regarding the methods that were likely to intimidate Hitler. The French began traveling to London, then to Tilbury on August 4. The trip on the passenger liner *City of Exeter* took them through the Baltic and lasted a little more than four days at a speed of 13.5 knots per hour. The two delegations (twenty-six officers in all) held discussions among themselves in a perfectly cordial atmosphere. First, a very general draft of military agreement was prepared, it being decided that plans and operations would be discussed only after the draft was signed. All preparatory draft documents were incinerated before arrival in Leningrad on August 10. They were given a thoughtful welcome. The two delegations traveled to Moscow in special rail cars where they arrived on August 11 and were welcomed there by many officers. The meeting of August 11 was basically to introduce them to Marshal Shaposhnikov, the chief of staff, Admiral Drax and General Doumenc, accompanied by Naggiar and Sir William Seeds, then went to the Kremlin to meet with Molotov. Finally, there was a formal dinner at the Commissariat of Defense with toasts and a concert. Everything started off in a euphoric atmosphere. The meetings took place in a handsome building on Spiridonovka Street and everyone in attendance was in uniform.

As early as August 12, Marshal Voroshilov, who chaired the meetings, took over the proceedings. Drax and Doumenc proposed to begin with a discussion of general principles. Voroshilov refused, saying that they must work usefully and exchange definite plans. The two westerners were forced to give in. Thus the Franco-British project drafted aboard the *City of Exeter* was no longer operative.

On August 13 Doumenc attempted in any case to return to certain parts of the plan. As Beaufre said, "One had to seem sincere and give the impression of revealing secrets."[179] Voroshilov was savvy and tackled the difficult issue: "Will Poland accept the entrance of Soviet troops on its territory…in order to make contact with the enemy?" It was, as the author of one of the accounts we have, navy captain Willaume wrote, "The obstacle upon which all our discussions were to stumble." Voroshilov also noticed that his counterparts were not "plenipotentiaries" and were constantly obliged to refer back to Paris and London. It was therefore necessary for those two governments to reach an agreement with Poland and Romania. "Without answers to these questions the work that had begun would be destined to fail."[180]

The August 14 meeting was the most dramatic one.[181] Voroshilov immediately requested an answer to the question he had asked the day before. Doumenc proposed that Soviet troops be ready to help Poland and Romania should those countries request it; the USSR could in the meantime offer weapons. Voroshilov, turning red with anger, restated the question, "Will Poland accept the entrance of Soviet troops into its territory in the Vilno corridor to make contact with the enemy; can Poland also allow passage in Galicia; and the same for the passage of Soviet troops in Romania?" And, since his counterparts were using deceptive language, he went on mercilessly, "I have not mentioned concentrations" but rather "contact with the enemy in East Prussia." To wait idly by for the two countries to request Soviet help was unacceptable.

"I truly believe that our mission is over," said Admiral Drax during a pause in the proceedings. The discussion resumed in the same rough vein. "Without details, without clear answers, to continue our conversations would be useless," said Voroshilov.

The French and British then answered with a written text. "Poland and Romania are sovereign states… the authorization the Marshal is mentioning must therefore come from their governments. This becomes a political issue and we propose that the Soviet government ask the Polish and Romanian governments the question… it's the most simple and direct way. If desired…we are ready to communicate this to London and Paris…" And the idea of urgency resurfaced: "It is possible that the German army could enter Poland tomorrow—if we wish to avoid wasting precious time could we not continue our work under the assumption of a positive answer?"

The Soviets discussed the matter among themselves. Their answer was unequivocal. They would not ask Poland or Romania anything themselves. It was up to the western governments to take the initiative. "The Soviet military mission feels that without getting an answer to these questions all the work accomplished until now by the three delegations would be unsuccessful."

On the evening of the 16th the French government refused to send Doumenc's deputy, General Valin, to Poland "because of the reaction it might produce," and preferred to negotiate through General Musse, the military attaché in Warsaw.

On the 17th Voroshilov requested that the discussions be adjourned until August 21, which was agreed. On the same August 17 Doumenc, on his own initiative, decided to dispatch Captain Beaufre to Warsaw. Beaufre arrived by train on the evening of the 18th and immediately met with Ambassador Léon Noël and General Musse, who had just returned from Paris the day before. What could be done? Léon Noël felt that Franco-Polish friendship was rather fragile. Musse was very suspicious of Soviet good faith. In any case, they both agreed to take some initiatives; the ambassador would see Beck, while Musse would meet with General Stachiewicz, the Polish army chief of staff. Lukasziewicz, the Polish ambassador to Paris who had met with Georges Bonnet, had already informed Beck. The latter was totally negative and his attitude was confirmed by that of the commander in chief Marshal Rydz-Smigly.

Musse called very energetically for the creation of a "resistance front in the East of Europe" showing how the break in the Moscow negotiations would have immeasurable consequences. "Hitler is hesitating between peace and war, the break-up of negotiations could be a factor prompting him to undertake the boldest kind of gamble." He insisted on the limited nature of the corridors to be used to get through. Poland's agreement could remain totally secret. "I know that your idea is to wait for the fighting to begin before holding talks with the Russians, but by then it will be very late."

Stachiewicz refused. "I cannot believe that the Russians really want to fight the Germans... It's too obvious a bluff, it is blackmail... If we allowed them into our territory they would stay there." So there was no hope. A new initiative by Musse with his British colleague Colonel Sward on August 19 yielded the same results. "Yet we tried every possible language to reach a compromise," wrote Musse. The Poles were unmovable.

Léon Noël was given the same answer during a new visit to Beck. At least it was agreed that this would not be an "official" answer.

Beaufre left on the 20th and reached Moscow on the evening of the 21st. That morning the newspapers had published the German-Soviet economic agreement. Then the scheduled meeting took place. After a few acrimonious exchanges, Marshal Voroshilov put an end to the meeting. No date was set for a resumption of the discussions.[182]

A few hours after Beaufre's return, Doumenc received a cable from Daladier at 10:30 p.m. stating, "You are authorized to sign as best you can, in the common interest and with the ambassador's agreement, the military agreement pending approval by the French government." Did this mean that Paris had obtained an approval from Poland on its own? Obviously not.[183] It meant rather that in desperation Daladier intimated that the opinion of the Poles would not be considered as to the passage of Russian troops on their territory. Beaufre thought that had it been sent four days before such a cable would have been effective. This is highly improbable because four days before August 21, the Soviet position regarding Germany had already been decided.

On the morning of August 22 the Soviet press announced the imminent arrival in Moscow of the German Minister of Foreign Affairs, Joachim von Ribbentrop, to sign a German-Soviet non-aggression pact. Doumenc, through his insistence, was able to meet with Voroshilov at 7 p.m. while Naggiar was received by Molotov. When he was told about Daladier's attitude, Voroshilov immediately asked whether the Polish government agreed. Doumenc obviously was unable to give him a positive answer. The break-up of the military discussions was complete by August 25. It was a complete failure.

6.

On the Periphery—The Near East

French foreign policy's greatest effort took place in continental Europe and in the western Mediterranean. There were possessions elsewhere requiring protection but these were relatively secondary or so distant from France that they could not be defended. The possessions in the Americas could well be considered as being beyond the reach of the Rome-Berlin-Tokyo Axis. The same could be said of Madagascar, the Comoro

Islands and La Réunion in the Indian Ocean, and French Polynesia in the southeastern Pacific. What remained were the French mandates in the Levant and Indochina, which could not be defended at all.

The defense of Syria and Lebanon[184] relied mostly on the British fleet at Alexandria assuming that it was powerful enough, meaning that France played a key role in the western Mediterranean that was in any case a vital area for transporting troops from North Africa. But France's position would greatly improve if Turkey were to participate. The idea of convincing Turkey into joining an alliance was a common worry for both Britain and France.

The Turks, however, had a territorial ambition at the expense of the Syrian mandate. They wanted to reannex the Sandjak of Alexandrette or Hatay where they claimed, without it being really certain, that a majority of the population was Turkish.[185] The Franco-Syrian treaty of 1936 with Syria—that had never been ratified—was being used as a pretense to their demand for a special statute for the territory that the Council of the League of Nations had established on May 29, 1937. Syria—and therefore the mandated power—retained foreign affairs, customs and finance; internal affairs had an autonomous status. The Turks did not like this outcome and on July 4, 1938, wound up obtaining an agreement whereby a Turkish and a French battalion would each occupy the territory. The Turks, however, considered that state of affairs as temporary. Mustapha Kemal, the president of the Turkish Republic,[186] did not hesitate to refer to Hatay as an independent country, while stating that it constituted "the basis of the development and crystallization of Franco-Turkish friendship."[187]

Obviously, the Turks wanted to annex the territory, while the French and the British wanted an alliance with Turkey. The Turks cleverly used the idea of a political and military agreement in attempting to reach their objective.

On the French side negotiations were undertaken by two outstanding men who did not always agree, Gabriel Puaux, who had been appointed as High Commissioner to Syria where he arrived on January 7, 1939, and René Massigli, who was ambassador to Ankara since October 1938. Puaux, determined to enforce strongly the French mandate, was attempting to keep the Syrian nationalists at bay.[188] He was at pains to accept what they were refusing, namely the loss of a province on the periphery.[189] Massigli was much more sensitive about the necessary political imperatives. The Turks, on the other hand, were secretly satisfied with France's lack of vigor at Munich and were ready to give her a very hard time.[190]

On January 10 Massigli met with the Turkish minister of foreign affairs, Numan Menemencioglu, who, along with Prime Minister Saracoglu a few days later, did not hide the fact that they wanted to annex Hatay, at the most as an independent state under a Franco-Turkish guarantee. Massigli noted a "stiffening" and "impatience." He offered three solutions: to hold strictly to the terms of the statute and the mandate; to let ourselves be "nibbled away" which meant losing face; to face the issue openly and allow for annexation if it was accepted by Damascus. He also complained of not having received instructions. It must be pointed out in this regard that Bonnet and Massigli were not on good terms, and that the ambassador never missed an opportunity to remind his own minister of his duty.[191] What was actually happening was the nibbling. The Hatay government, located in Antioch, was taking instructions from Ankara. The "Turkization" of the Sanjak was continuing. "Our authority is withering away." Massigli, who returned to Paris at the beginning of February 1939, had strongly recommended ceding the territory on condition that there be compensations *for Syria* (who then made its peace with the outcome but was to blame France in the future); and its borders should be clearly determined, otherwise the Turks could pursue their claims all the way to Aleppo and beyond; *for France*, that its interests in the Sanjak should be recognized and that a Franco-Turkish mutual assistance pact be signed. As for the method, it could either be a series of compromises or a general settlement.[192]

Gabriel Puaux was opposed to Massigli's plan. "To agree to Turkey's annexation of Hatay at this time would be a gratuitous concession, bearing heavy consequences and dangerous to France's prestige." Puaux suggested that expressions of friendship toward Turkey be increased and wait until possible hostilities began in order to negotiate the alliance because he felt she would then be only too happy to sign it.[193]

What would Bonnet decide? He started by adopting Puaux's point of view and rejecting any new demand coming from Ankara.[194] The ambassador to Ankara, who had met with Saracoglu on February 17, answered him that to engage in the operation right away was less useful than to wait for the first emergency warning. The Turks, he said, "are convinced that time is on their side."[195] Things did not change for a few weeks.

Following the momentous events of March 1939, Bonnet began to change. He instructed Massigli to attempt a political type of negotiation.[196] Was it because of the increasing danger or the unrest that began in February and mostly in early March in Syria (six dead on March 19)?[197]

There was the lingering fear that the Hatay government might suddenly proclaim the annexation of the Sanjak to Turkey. France would not accept it, as the minister wrote on April 4.[198]

The issue sharpened when England was ready to guarantee Greece and the *status quo* in the eastern Mediterranean, while France was attempting to convince her to issue a guarantee to Romania. The French minister thought this implied the approval of the British government. In any case, he noted, we set forth our "close and deep agreement with Great Britain."[199] On April 14 France and England agreed to extend their guarantee to Turkey.[200] Massigli once again complained about not being properly informed. "From the point of view of our authority here it is...generally preferable that instructions agreed to between Paris and London reach me at the same time as my British colleague."[201] He did not know what the intentions of the French government were regarding the revision of the Franco-Turkish commercial agreement that he felt was very important because it would be a way to reduce German penetration.[202]

At the end of April Bonnet adopted Massigli's position. He asked him to begin negotiations, using border modifications and protection for the Armenians. "I authorize you to inform the Turkish government that France, as far as she is concerned, would agree to ceding the Sanjak" and would gradually reduce its garrison to make it happen.[203] Massigli immediately replied that he would begin talks with Saracoglu very shortly.[204]

The discussion dragged on. Saracoglu rejected the French conditions, saying that he was "deeply disappointed" that no date had been set for ceding the territory.[205] Bonnet was insisting on the independence of the "political agreement" and the accord on Hatay and reminded Massigli that if he was "resigned" to give away that area "it was only because of the general situation in Europe," stating the serious repercussions this would have in Damascus, the bitterness of the Armenian population and the resistance at the Chamber of Deputies, etc.[206] In order to unravel the matter, Massigli suggested the visit of a top military leader to Turkey.[207] It so happened that General Weygand, who had served as French High Commissioner to the Levant, was going to represent France at the wedding of the crown prince of Iran and the sister of Egypt's King Farouk (Herriot, who had wanted that mission of protocol, had finally withdrawn). On his way back he received a cable requesting that he go to Ankara.[208] He accepted because of his friendship toward Massigli. The objective was to develop relations with Ismet Inonu, whom Weygand already knew, Saracoglu and Marshal Czakmak, chief of the general staff, and the former army commander in the First World War. He was, wrote Weygand in his report, "simple, direct and very understanding." Weygand became convinced that it was urgently necessary "to put an end to the matter of the Sanjak of Alexandretta and…place what now appears to be essential ahead of what has become secondary,"[209] which he said did not please Daladier.[210] Weygand spoke of a war where they could be blocked on French and German fortifications and with large forces landing at Dedeagach or Salonika. (Clearly there was no escaping the First World War.) It was agreed that 100 to 200 officers or noncommissioned officers would be trained at French schools. Beyond that the band played the *Marseillaise*. For von Papen, the new German ambassador who had arrived the day before, it was an unpleasant start.

On May 12 Massigli was convinced he would sign the political agreement before the negotiations on Hatay ended and sent the text to Paris.[211] Alas! Menemencioglu injected a last minute maneuver. Nothing was signed.[212] The Turks were too cunning to forget their friendly blackmail weapon. On May 19 they signed with England alone, while announcing a similar agreement with France. This, wrote Massigli, "forces me to return to that sorry matter of the Sanjak that overshadows all our negotiations for so long, depriving us of any freedom of action." In the eyes of the Turks it was quite simply "blackmail." Massigli used the word. But "I don't think we have anything to gain by remaining in the somewhat ambiguous situation we are in right now."[213]

On June 23 the Sanjak agreement was finally signed. The government, wrote Massigli, decided to take the wise decision that was called for. But everything was given away. Nothing guaranteed French interests whether cultural or economic (the *Société d'électricité d'Antioche* and the *Société du port d'Alexandrette* requested to leave the territory).[214] The two countries were committed to mutual assistance[215] pending the signing of the Franco-Anglo-Turkish alliance treaty that was to take place only on October 19, 1939, and having no effect whatsoever. General Huntziger paid a formal visit to Turkey. It was agreed that the 2,500 French soldiers would leave the territory by July 23. The French flag would continue to fly…over the Alexandrette military cemetery.

Chapter XIV

FINAL PREPARATIONS

1.

ECONOMIC READINESS

Since war was possible and even probable, how could the economy be prepared for that event? It became obviously necessary to enhance armaments production and create large supplies of petroleum products and raw materials. The financing of the military and war budgets also had to be addressed. Therefore, the idea of preventing the expatriation of funds and even compelling the return of those that had fled became the obsession of the politicians of the time. The increase in the gold reserves of the Bank of France provided a test of sorts.

October and November 1938 were the crucially important months concerning all these issues. The main debate centered on the forty-hour week. Socially it had a symbolic value, but created two serious problems, one economic and the other tied to national defense. Between 1936 and 1938 unfilled employment applications were reduced from 468,000 to 424,000. Partial unemployment (under forty working hours) was 20.4% in April. An arithmetic calculation led to the belief that if the weekly working hours increased, then the number of unemployed workers would also increase.[1]

Alfred Sauvy was able to prove the uselessness of that kind of thinking. Most of industry was working fully within the rigorous limits of the forty hours. There was no other way to increase production than to allow greater flexibility and authorize overtime. By itself increased production would reduce unemployment.

Daladier faced the issue as soon as he came to power. In his government policy statement of April 12, 1938,[2] he declared, "All financial, economic, social and political issues are closely tied to that of our security." In the aftermath of a strike, aviation industry workers had agreed to work five hours more. The problem also involved metal workers who were also on strike. The Metals Federation agreed to five hours overtime but management opposed it because the agreement rested on a fundamental salary increase. On August 21 Daladier gave a speech on radio where he expressed his intent to "get France back to work." His conclusion was, "As long as the international situation is this sensitive we must be able to work more than forty hours and up to forty-eight hours in national defense-based industries. Faced with totalitarian states that are rearming without any regard for the work time involved, will France waste its time in disputes?"[3] The speech led to the resignation of two cabinet ministers, Ramadier, an independent socialist at Labor who was replaced with Pomaret, and Frossard at Public Works, replaced with de Monzie. A law decree dated August 31 gave the government the freedom to authorize overtime in defense-related industry.

On October 4, immediately following Munich, the Daladier government was granted full power until November 15 by a vote of 331 to 78 (basically the communists) and 203 abstentions (many socialists and part of the right).[4]

Full power was to last until November 15. It therefore seemed clear that it would not be renewed. It became necessary to take action prior to that date. Finance minister Marchandeau was an advocate of a planned economy. He agreed to suspend the forty hour law, but above all he wanted to set up foreign exchange controls to stop the exit of capital funds and the drop in the price of gold. Daladier showed no enthusiasm for this plan. In his October 28 speech to the Radical Party convention in Marseille he had violently severed relations with the communists who were strong backers of foreign exchange controls. During the entire month of October he received negative opinions regarding the Marchandeau plan. On

October 30 and 31 and on November 1 there were meetings of the Cabinet Council where Paul Reynaud vigorously attacked the program. On October 31 Daladier called Reynaud and Marchandeau to his office and asked that they switch positions as of November 1. Marchandeau agreed not to resign to avoid endangering the government. There was immediately "a complete change of atmosphere. The will to win replaced resignation and the desire for rapid and efficient reforms overcame passivity."[5]

Paul Reynaud assembled a brilliant team. Gaston Palewski was his cabinet director; D. Leca was the head of the cabinet, which also included Michel Debré. He benefited from the active collaboration of the general secretary of the finance ministry, Yves Bouthiller, the director of the *Mouvement général des fonds*, Jacques Rueff, and his deputy Maurice Couve de Murville. Finally, he consulted with Alfred Sauvy, a specialist in economic statistics. Everyone worked very hard at preparing the law decrees. It was what Alfred Sauvy called the "crazy week."

A heavy load of fifty-eight law decrees was published from November 12 to 15. Everyone found something to criticize. "The right was particularly aroused and upset,"[6] due to the tax increases. Exchange controls were rejected. The left was incensed at the "misery-making law decrees" and expressed itself through the strikes that peaked on November 30. The forty-hour law, "an unprecedented suicide" as Sauvy was telling Paul Reynaud,[7] was strongly amended. Working hours could be extended to fifty hours without administrative approval and were to be paid at higher wages by 10 to 25%. Beyond fifty hours a special authorization was required. The work week would be six days rather than five. Refusing to work overtime in the interest of national defense would be subject to imprisonment.

Jean Zay considered resigning because of this "patently reactionary and stock market-oriented plan." Léon Blum and Herriot encouraged him to stay.[8] De Monzie hated Paul Reynaud, "whose political assurance irritates me." But Reynaud had the support of Mandel, Champetier de Ribes, at times of Bonnet and Pomaret and, above all, of Daladier.[9]

We shall not analyze the social and financial aspects of this reversal of policy but will examine its results. Paul Reynaud modestly termed what took place during the eight months that followed as the "French miracle,"[10] as the London *Times* stated. It is best to follow his collaborator Alfred Sauvy, whose figures are at least more reliable.

First of all there was the seriousness of the situation prior to Paul Reynaud's arrival. On the basis of an index of 100 for 1928, by April

1936 industrial output had fallen from 88 to 82 in April 1938 and to 83 in October. By June 1939 it was at 100. The average workload went from 39.2 hours in October to 41.9 hours in July 1939. The trade deficit was reduced by 26%. The increases of monthly prices went from 1.1% (July to November 1938) to 0.25% (April to August 1939). Unemployment, which had increased by 9% from August 1937 to August 1938, declined by 10% from August 1938 to August 1939.[11] For the first time since 1931 France was coming out of the crisis (way behind Germany and England). Capital funds returned and the gold reserves of the Bank of France went from 56 to 92 billion. "The result was," wrote Paul Reynaud, "that I was able to find 55 billion for national defense in a country where tax collection during the preceding year had been a total of 47 billion..." "France has the largest gold reserve in the world after the United States."[12] This was a well-known idea at the time, that of the "war chest."

The most important issue for a country threatened by war was obviously that of production. "*The French economy,*" wrote Sauvy, "*experienced under very difficult circumstances the fastest rebound in its history.*" [Emphasis added.] In the course of eight months industrial production increased by 20%.[13] Some of the potential criticism was tied to a few demographically inspired measures—for example, the refusal to use the labor force represented by the 400,000 Spanish refugees in 1939. Sauvy, who had been informed by Claude Bourdet, failed to convince his minister. The man's unpopularity was also an issue. "Paul Reynaud, who was wise but dry and unpopular, made the technical decisions and Daladier, whom the Chamber accepted more easily, would push them through politically."[14] There was, in fact, a remarkable rebound but due to the absence of economic information the public by and large knew nothing about it; something was felt and diplomatic correspondence often refers to the "French rebound." But the country, disillusioned by eight years of crisis and fifty rescue plans, did not sense that this one was better than any of the others.[15]

France's military budget, which had been declining from 1932 to 1935, was improving steadily since then. In millions of present-value francs (of 1930) *the actual payments* for military expenditures, including the colonies, were as follows:[16]

1934	13,983	1937	21,299
1935	16,654	1938	25,552
1936	18,606	1939	78,072

Half of the financing was based roughly on tax revenue and half on loans. The law decrees of November 1938 increased taxes. The "confidence" of the capitalists, following the elimination of any threat of exchange controls, prompted the return of a lot of funds leading to the issue of Treasury bonds with a broad edge over redemptions and the launch of a successful large bond issue in May 1939. On March 19, 1939, on the other hand, full power was extended until November 30.[17]

Theoretically this placed France in the best position to face a war.

The feverish and enthusiastic activity at the ministry of finance continued. It allowed France to enter the Second World War on September 2, 1939, with healthier finances than had ever existed during the preceding decade.[18]

After Munich the problem of stockpiles was also examined. The minister of public works, de Monzie, was mainly in charge, with the cooperation of the three branches of the military. The controller, General Robert Jacomet,[19] named by Daladier on October 27, 1936, to be general secretary of national defense, played a key role in "industrial mobilization." Louis Pineau, the director of the office of fuel supply, did not get along with de Monzie who said of him that "he didn't encourage friendship" but was "an honest and powerful servant of the state."[20] A law passed on July 11, 1938, after some ten years of debate, could be used for "the organization of the nation in time of war." The absence of detailed historical studies will limit us to a few main points.

First of all, the differences compared with 1914–1918 were extremely clear in 1938, the main one being the relative weakening of British naval superiority. The French and British navies would certainly dominate the Atlantic, although Britain's merchant marine did not amount to more than 26.4% of the world's tonnage versus 41.6% in 1914. Discussions had been taking place in London since March 1938 between French and British representatives of supplies, services and transportation to examine the opportunities for cooperation. The issues examined dealt with food, coal, liquid fuels and raw materials. In order to avoid competition, it was decided to set up a "Franco-British coordinating committee" (actually created in September 1939 and headed by Jean Monnet). As far as tonnage went, however, the British did not hide the fact that they would not lend any to France, which represented less than 5% of world tonnage. A report by General Lelong reached the following conclusion:

Briefly, Great Britain is not a general store where we can go. It is even less of a freight forwarder. And, as far as we are concerned, we must draw the appropriate conclusions.[21]

The idea of economic cooperation was offered once again in the spring. On June 1, Paul Morand traveled to London, heading a delegation whose mission it was to "prepare for economic warfare." He discovered that rather than insulated administrative services, as was the case in France, the British had an Industrial Intelligence Center. He wanted France to create an economic action service. That project, however, was not acted upon before the war.[22]

De Monzie prepared a whole set of decrees to regulate hydrocarbons—"the production and protection of combustible liquids in the interest of national defense." Between September 1938 and April 1939, the date of the decrees, he ordered a number of very broad studies. He was hoping that the air force could use an "autonomous" source of gasoline which meant going in the direction of synthetic fuel. Louis Pineau, who worked at building French refineries, was not too favorable. A system similar to the German method—using hydrogenation—was shelved in December 1938. De Monzie then wrote to Eugène Houdry, a French engineer, "who had been disappointed by his industrial endeavors in France, and had been able to create his method called cracking with the help of a powerful company in the United States." Houdry came to see him and gave a few demonstrations. The decree of April 1 provided incentives to the industrialists who would use the method.[23] But this was a long-term project.

Along with the British, an attempt was made to find potential sources for oil supplies. On February 9, 1939, a meeting was held in London at the Petroleum Department attended by Pineau, the commercial attaché, and two other French experts. The French estimated their needs at 1 million tons for the air force and 1.4 million tons for the navy. A decision was reached to not rely on the oil supplied by the Dutch East Indies, nor on the Mediterranean route. Most of it could come from the United States and Iraq, and after that from Iran and Venezuela. However, oil tanker tonnage was insufficient, especially if the Mediterranean were closed. Pineau proposed the creation of a "transportation subcommittee." The British were against it, saying it was not urgent.[24]

At the Franco-British military conversations of the spring of 1939[25] the British were to reverse their position. The importance of economic preparation was no longer overlooked by anyone and the idea that only joint operations could solve problems took hold.[26] The effort at economic preparation was undeniable but fragmented. As Jacques Néré commented, Paul Reynaud had given himself three years to succeed. Was that compatible with a war that was imminent? On the other hand, the methods used were still very liberal. It was not at all an "industrial mobilization," and even less of a "war economy."[27]

2.

The Air Force from Munich to the War

Germany had started rearming at the air force level in May 1934. England began in May 1935. France had really not started until March 1938 when the V plan was determined by the Superior Air Council. Consequently, France was very much behind. It was, wrote Bonnet to Air Minister Guy La Chambre, a "key element of the political as well as military situation."[28]

The true results[29] (number of war planes to come out of the factories and accepted by the receiving center for planes built in series) were:

BEFORE PLAN V
(see Plan II known as "1,500 planes" plan 1936)

1935	Third quarter	163	}
			} 291
	Fourth quarter	128	}
1936	First quarter	177	}
	Second quarter	148	}
			} 569
	Third quarter	101	}
	Fourth quarter	143	}
1937	First quarter	79	}
	Second quarter	105	}
			} 369
	Third quarter	107	}
	Fourth quarter	78	}

PLAN V (SINCE MARCH)

1938	First quarter	114	}	
	Second quarter	112	}	
			}	432
	Third quarter	84	}	
	Fourth quarter	122	}	
1939	January to February	160	}	
(first eight months)	March-April	286	}	
			}	1261
	May-June	353	}	
	July-August	462	}	

The airplane deficit compared with Germany at Munich was sadly familiar. We have noted that General Vuillemin, air force chief of staff, had spent a week visiting the aircraft factories and Luftwaffe units beginning August 17, 1938.[30] It is therefore easy to understand his pessimistic note of September 26, 1938. The air forces that were currently available in metropolitan France were: 250 daytime fighter planes, 320 bombers, and 130 strategic reconnaissance planes. There was "a huge disproportion of forces that was very heavily tilted in Germany's favor." He estimated French air force losses would be 40% by the end of the first month and 64% by the end of the second month. And those losses would not be replenished. Moreover, the performance of those planes was clearly insufficient. For example, French bombers could only operate at night.[31]

In 1937 French factories delivered to the armed forces 146 fighter planes and 226 bombers; in 1938 131 fighters and 190 bombers; in 1939 (including the beginning of the war) 1,896 fighters and 215 bombers. Nevertheless, France had started very late and did not manufacture heavy bombers. The number of workers in the aeronautics industry increased from 38,495 in 1937 to 82,289 in 1939 (250,000 by June 1940; it would have been over 500,000 by 1941). We should note that in 1944 the British aeronautics industry employed 1,820,000 workers and that of the United States, 3 million.

A detailed study by Raymond Danel on "the French air force at the outbreak of war" provides the following numbers as of August 16, 1939.[32]

Both in metropolitan France and in the Empire the air force had 7,450 planes, including 3,959 war planes (the others were used for training, liaison and health related missions, etc.). There were 353 additional naval airplanes.

The number of war planes (3,959) was very good, but first the very old models that dated from before Plan I of April 1, 1933 or some *1,264 planes* had to be deducted. Then came the "transitional" models from Plans I and II that were completely outclassed by most German planes; these numbered 1,617. There remained 1,078 modern planes. Considering the last two categories, out of the total number (2,881) the planes actually *operating* were:

	Modern	Transitional	Total
Fighters	561	173	734
Bombers	—	440	440
Reconnaissance	53	349	402
Total	614	962	1,576

But not all of these were immediately available.

	Available planes		
	Modern	Transitional	Total
Fighters	416	144	560
Bombers	—	346	346
Reconnaissance	47	301	348
Total	463	791	1,254

These numbers are very interesting. They indicate that it took a long time from when new planes were received to the moment they were actually ready to be placed in service in the flight squadrons. In other words, the considerable progress made by French production in 1939 was only a beginning and the situation would really improve only in 1941. On the other hand they backed up the statement by the air force chief of staff that as of September 1, 1939, he could only count on 494 readied modern planes (as of August 16 they were 463) including 442 fighter planes (416 on August 16), 52 for reconnaissance (53 on August 16), and 0 bombers.[33]

However, 20 modern bombers had really already been completed, 704 single-seater fighters and 277 multiseater fighters for night and day missions or a total of 981 fighters to be held against the 463 available planes.

What was the estimated strength of the German air force at that time? A report by Colonel de Geffrier, air attaché in Berlin, dated November 9, 1938, gave a summary of production. He estimated at 150,000 the workers in the avionics area and at 58,000 the workers in engine factories. Adding in weapons systems, the total was three times the French personnel of 1939. Furthermore, he wrote that "all the foreign technicians visiting Berlin…are amazed at the size of the industrial achievements of the Reich where aeronautics are concerned." He estimated production at close to 600 military planes per month; production would soar to 1,000 in August and September. The pace was a ten-hour workday with two teams for twenty-four hours.[34]

A memo from Vuillemin to Guy La Chambre, dated August 26, 1939, gave the following estimate of the Luftwaffe's plane strength:

	First Line	Second Line
Fighters	900	—
Bombers	1,620	over 5,800
Reconnaissance	708	—
Total	3,228	5,800

He came up with the following chart as an estimate of the forces of both coalitions:

	France Great Britain Poland	Germany Italy
First line	3,800	6,500
Second line	1,900	6,000

In a confrontation with the Luftwaffe, what kind of help could France expect from the Royal Air Force? It had started rearming much earlier, and for one or two months in 1939 its production would be greater than Germany's. The British were producing many bombers and even heavy bombers. The *Deuxième Bureau* of the air force chief of staff estimated that in November 1938 in England proper there were 430 fighters, 820 bombers, 300 reconnaissance and support planes, or 1,550 planes with a general reserve of about 500. There were additionally 330 planes overseas and 250 on board navy ships.[35] But not all this equipment was up to date.

At Munich the (very pessimistic) assessments by the French military attaché reached the conclusion that the British would hold on to all their fighter planes to defend London and the cities but could send over a score of bomber squadrons or 120 planes.[36]

Since Chamberlain and Halifax were coming to France on November 24, 1938, the Air Force high command made some suggestions to Daladier as to what France should request as far as air force assistance was concerned. Unfortunately, their policy was becoming defensive. During his November 10 speech, Air Minister Sir Kingsley Wood announced the quadrupling of fighters in order to protect London, which was highly exposed. This was very dangerous for France.[37] Since the war would probably be fought against Germany and Italy, it was necessary that as soon as the fighting began Great Britain would: 1) Send fighter squadrons in Lorraine and Champagne to improve the air cover of French forces; and 2) Lead the attack on Germany with its bomber squadrons. France would cover the Italian sector. The British "advanced air force" based on French territory was to include at least twenty squadrons.[38]

Buoyed by this information, Daladier began a very suggestive conversation with the British prime minister on November 24. "Mr. Daladier freely admitted, since he was talking to friends, that there had been a crisis in the French air force." The industrial methods "had not been too felicitous" and remained those of small-scale shops: 800 million had been earmarked for the purchase of machinery. France could count on 2,600 planes in November (the number included many rickety old planes). It would have 4,000 in 1939. The pace of production was now 80 per month (the figure was totally false as we have mentioned; in October, November, and December France produced a total of 122 planes). "By the spring French factories will produce about 400 planes per month." At this point the notes show that "Mr. Chamberlain was very much impressed." In spite of enormous outlays, England was unable to reach that number. Nevertheless, Daladier went on. The appointment of an engineer, Caquot, to head all the aviation-manufacturing plants will allow improved coordination among the companies. If these numbers "prove to be too optimistic" he was ready to purchase 1,000 American planes by the spring. Chamberlain "wished to be forgiven if he still remained somewhat skeptical."

On the other hand, while Daladier was discussing bombing Germany—by the British—Chamberlain kept insisting on defending London with fighter planes and anti-aircraft artillery. It was finally agreed that fighter planes and anti-aircraft artillery were both very useful and they left it at that.[39]

Italy was another potential enemy with an aircraft production of 160 planes per month in 1938.[40] A memo from General Vuillemin to Guy La Chambre[41] concluded that France's fighter planes had the edge, while Italy was stronger in bombers whether they were heavy, midsize or light. France did have 48 heavy bombers and 588 (transitional) bombers with a speed under 400 km/hour. Italy, on the other hand, did have 360 midsize and 55 light bombers with a speed of over 400 km/hour. French bombers were slow and could attack the coastline at night less than 300 kilometers from the border, but could not venture into the Po Valley. By the spring of 1939, however, the French air force would cover the entire national territory and North Africa. He felt that by that date France would have some 530 with a speed over 400 km/hour and Italy would have 100.

One possible way to catch up was to purchase planes overseas. Daladier brought up the matter before becoming prime minister. He mentioned the United States and the USSR. There would even be an attempt at negotiation right after Munich to buy 300 engines from…Germany. Daladier discussed the issue with Charles Lindbergh, who was on his way to Germany. When he returned he met with Guy La Chambre who called deputy air attaché Captain Stehlin to Paris in January 1939. He asked him to hold a secret negotiation with General Udet to purchase Daimler-Benz 601 engines for the French Dewoitine 520. Göring, he said, was informed of the matter. Stehlin felt he should discuss the request with his boss General de Geffrier, the air attaché, who was amazed. A few aeronautics engineers went to Germany and some of Udet's people traveled to Paris. The negotiations went on for a few months without Stehlin knowing anything about it.[42]

A few German planes used by nationalist Spain (in January) and one that crashed in the Jura region at the end of May provided intelligence "giving us one year's advance in technical knowledge for our engine manufacturing."[43] It should be noted that Hitler approved the negotiations on the engines on condition that the deliveries would begin to be fulfilled at the end of 1939. The whole matter was kept strictly secret between Daladier and La Chambre since Daladier did not trust Bonnet's discretion. Guy La Chambre consulted the United States through Ambassador

William Bullitt. Roosevelt sent his answer only on March 23 and it was negative.[44] The March events put a stop to everything and also prevented France from receiving forty-five plane engines it had ordered from the Skoda works in Czechoslovakia.

French negotiations to purchase modern American planes were studied in depth and quite remarkably by an American historian, John McVicar Haight, first in a series of articles and then in a book.[45] We can only summarize his research here.[46]

It started in January 1938. Guy La Chambre sent Baron Amaury de La Grange, a senator, one of the authors of Plan V and an eminent aviation specialist, to study the possibility of purchasing 1,000 modern American planes. La Grange was a personal friend of President Roosevelt, who said he was very much in favor, but American industry was producing next to nothing. This came as an unpleasant surprise and, furthermore, there was opposition in France, namely within the Air Commission of the Chamber, which intended to "protect" French industry. He was only able to obtain an authorization, in spite of the American military, for the great pilot Michel Détroyat to secretly test the Curtiss P36, the only plane with a performance equal to the German Messerschmitt 109.

The matter was revisited right after Munich. At the beginning of October there was a luncheon given by American Ambassador Bullitt, with Daladier, Guy La Chambre and Jean Monnet. Daladier made the case for the purchase of American planes, proving how the weakness of France's air force explained "the huge defeat at Munich." Bullitt was so impressed that he traveled to the United States to study the issue. Charles Lindbergh, who had been in France in September, confirmed Daladier's conclusions. Daladier decided to send Jean Monnet who had very many American friends, to meet with President Roosevelt. In order to get around the embargo of the Neutrality Act, Monnet was also to examine building assembly lines in Canada that would use component parts made in the United States. Monnet arrived in the United States on October 18. He met with the president at his private home in Hyde Park along with Treasury Secretary Henry Morgenthau and William Bullitt. Roosevelt decided to increase American production to 15,000 planes per year, allowing the fulfillment of France's needs. Morgenthau suggested that France make the repatriation of capital funds that had fled the country compulsory and promised to help—which implied instituting exchange controls.

Monnet returned to France on November 4 and his recommendations were of the greatest interest to Daladier. However, the appointment of Paul Reynaud as Minister of Finance excluded the possibility of exchange controls. Monnet suggested ordering 100 planes for April 1939, followed by increasing quantities (700 bombers and 700 fighters by July) 2,500 at the beginning of 1940.

The meeting of the Permanent Committee of National Defense on December 5, 1938[47] was exceptionally important. Paul Reynaud the new minister of finance, was immediately opposed to financing 1,000 modern planes that would cost 2.5 billion francs. The budget of the branches of the military for 1939 was 15 billion with military spending at 25 billion, 8.5 billion of which was allocated to the air force that would probably insufficient. He could only spare 800 million—because he promised not to have any long-term borrowing for six months. Thus, 1.7 billion had to be saved from the agreed budget.

Guy La Chambre felt that the savings should not be made on investments for the air force that required 2,000 planes manufactured in France.

Gamelin agreed to equip the air force especially in fighter planes. But, according to him, "from the viewpoint of the supreme conduct of the war" the navy and, above all, the ground forces had priority. "We have lost the support of 30 Czechoslovak divisions."... "Our ground forces are smaller in numbers; they can only keep their value through equipment." As for tanks, "we must accelerate the delivery of standardized matériel."... "In a country with a very low birth rate you need very modern war equipment." Paul Reynaud agreed, but he said that "it's impossible to hold our borders and handle Italy without British help." The Germans were now working fifty-two hours per week.

The committee then began to cut some appropriations for propaganda, gas masks, some investments, uniforms, and stockpiles for the navy. By the end of the meeting they were short only by 340 million! As of December 9 Daladier felt he could issue the purchase order of 1,000 planes in July 1939. Roosevelt had already made sure that U.S. aircraft production reached 10,000 planes in 1939.

Jean Monnet was immediately sent to the United States on a second mission, arriving in Washington on December 16, 1938, accompanied by Roger Hoppenot, the head of Guy La Chambre's cabinet, and two officers. Roosevelt stated that he was very much in favor of the French plans and waved away all the objections offered by his advisors. The French, however, wanted planes that went faster than 500 km/hour which the

Americans did not manufacture. Monnet then asked whether they could test the very latest prototypes, namely the Curtiss P40. The air force and especially its commander General Arnold was against it. Besides, secrecy was suddenly lifted when on January 23, 1939, Colonel Jacquin and Captain Paul Chemdlin boarded a Douglas airplane for a demonstration flight. When the American pilot pushed the plane to the limits it crashed with the two Frenchmen miraculously escaping death. Since there was a large crowd, all the Americans found out that the United States, a neutral country, was allowing French air force officers on their most modern prototypes. Roosevelt had to publicly state that he approved the sale of planes to France. In the end Monnet ordered 555 planes in February for 60 million dollars without prejudice to what may follow and returned to Paris in March.

There would be no other French orders to the United States until the war began. The work done by Guy La Chambre and La Grange succeeded in obtaining the support of the Senate air committee. The show of Franco-American friendship satisfied a segment of public opinion that was worried about France's problems in developing its own production. Daladier went so far as to offer to resume payments of war debts up to 300 million dollars in gold (about one-tenth of the amount). Bullitt was delighted but Roosevelt did not want to send the proposal to Congress because he was hoping to get a revision of the Neutrality Act and was fearful of upsetting the atmosphere. He also rejected the building of a French aircraft factory of Amiot planes in the United States. At the beginning of May Jean Monnet returned to the United States for the third time to find that negotiations could not be carried any further but he attempted to offer a broad plan to resolve the debt issue. This was also to be rejected.

The negotiations with the United States prompted French diplomacy to constantly examine American rearmament plans[48] and the failed attempt by Senator Pittman with the administration's support to lift the embargo on weapons and munitions in time of war as the Neutrality Act of May 1, 1937, stipulated.[49]

When the war broke out in September, out of the 555 planes ordered, France had received 200—and only fighter planes. Since the embargo had not been lifted, any export of aircraft had to stop until a new law was passed in November 1939 canceling the embargo. A conclusion emerges from all the numbers and negotiations: Since the start of 1938 and especially following Munich, France made a remarkable effort to catch up on its air force lag compared to Germany. The large increase in military spending and the percentage allowed the air force out of that total (from 12.3% in 1934 to 23% in 1938),[50] the standardization, the studies, massive purchases of machine tools, assembly line manufacturing, the start of new investments in building new plants, the coordination, and purchasing overseas would have allowed France to become a great air power...in 1941. She could not catch up with Germany, but France and Great Britain together could outclass Germany.

The obvious conclusion is that the effort came several years too late. But why?

The two main air ministers of the time, Pierre Cot[51] and Guy La Chambre,[52] were critical of one another at the hearings of the parliamentary investigative commission in 1945. The former was more in favor of bombers, while the latter wanted more fighters. Yet their viewpoints were similar.

It is also not possible to point to the law of August 11, 1936, that nationalized war-related industries in a very flexible way. It actually had two great advantages, allowing to do away with a plethora of midsize and small companies that, due to their size, had to work in competition on a small scale and to group them into a few large national companies. After that a remarkable geographic decentralization, encouraged by Pierre Cot, was enacted.

The explanation by prototypes is far more convincing. Assembly line manufacturing was unknown prior to Pierre Cot. Until 1930 there were 332 different prototypes manufactured. On January 1, 1930, the ministry of air would order 115 planes...of 37 different models.[53] The perfectionism, the "absence of boldness" within the ministry and among the manufacturers did not reach assembly line production under the pretense that new prototypes were going to be ready. In launching Plan I Pierre Cot had planned for models to be built in series but the industry was not yet ready for it, which explains its lack of organization until 1936 and the need for the consolidation that Pierre Cot, who had returned to the ministry of air, brought about. "Guy La Chambre having a more favorable political position within the government and no doubt better advice, drew from the reports on foreign industry and the progress of the Luftwaffe a simple but excellent idea, to build in large series."[54] Pierre Cot prepared Plan V; Guy La Chambre would reinforce it and get it passed.

Both ministers had to overcome the resistance of both the administration and the high command, whose competence was overestimated.

Guy La Chambre would state later on, "Had the high command not indulged in its penchant for perfection and had been content with the equipment we offered it would certainly not have experienced in the area of attack planes and dive bombers the kind of acute deficiencies we suffered from during the battle."[55]

Basically France started too late and for a time did not plan big enough. The rebound was vigorous but it came so late that in 1938 it could not counter Hitler's bold moves, or in 1939 deter him from going to war and in 1940 hold out long enough to confirm the rigorously correct statement within the realm of possibilities. "We will win because we are the strongest."

3.

BATTLE PLANS

As of November 1938 the status of the "alliances" was not good. There no longer was a Czechoslovak army that could be relied on, depriving France of a committed ally, with a minimum of thirty divisions, the Skoda works, and potentially strategic locations for the air force. Poland, having taken part in the kill, felt only contempt toward France and still believed in an endless romance with Germany. Belgium was more riveted than ever to its policy of "independence;" had she not sent reinforcements to the French border during the September crisis? Great Britain was determined to limit any promised help to the specific event of a violation of French territory and was politely avoiding French offers to hold military discussions.

Everything changed in March 1939. True, with the disappearance of Czechoslovakia, France's net loss turned into a gain for Germany. Poland, on the other hand was now feeling threatened. Public opinion was way ahead of the pro-German Beck and Pilsudsky's disciple, Marshal Rydz-Smigly. As early as the end of February there were anti-German demonstrations, described in detail by Léon Noël. Poland needed France even more so as it rejected any help from the Russians. Since February, Great Britain, believing a threat existed against the Netherlands, was suddenly interested in holding staff talks with France. Chamberlain's "conversion," potentially allowing for a much closer collaboration was modeled on what had been achieved between the two countries, without a formal alliance thanks to the Entente Cordiale from 1904 to 1914.[56] It should be pointed out that in the spring of 1939 the immediate danger was so palpable that other friendly but further removed countries, such as Yugoslavia and even Romania, were ignored.

It was clear as early as April 1939 that Poland was the most threatened country if only because of its refusal to let Germany reannex Danzig. The March 31 guarantees, proclaimed by Chamberlain, held military implications. In a telegram dated April 7, Ambassador Léon Noël was asking insistently for the "immediate reinforcement of the Polish army." But Poland lacked the funds. It became necessary for Great Britain and France to provide the funding. Léon Noël was pessimistic about an army of brave men but with inadequate equipment. The air force required an almost total overhaul despite the dazzling impression it made (a brilliant presentation at the aeronautics show in Paris in January): 3 factories, soon to have 2 more, 6,000 workers, 500 planes, all of them obsolete.[57] Stockpiles were certainly insufficient even though "it is impossible to secure precise information." Poland lacked heavy artillery and tanks and wanted to order them from France. Léon Noël was hoping there would be a staff meeting in the short term.[58]

That report prompted the Quai d'Orsay to inform Daladier as early as April 10.[59] When consulted, Gamelin said he was against sending more arms because, he said, "our entire production is required by our ground and air forces." But he was ready to contact Rydz-Smigly and coordinate Franco-Polish military discussions. Daladier immediately accepted.[60]

Gamelin wrote to the Marchhal and got him to delegate his minister of military affairs,[61] General Kasprzycki to travel to France. He arrived in Paris on May 15. Earlier he had prepared a note, working on the assumption of a long war. Poland had to hold out, which meant building fortifications with expert French assistance, getting help with armaments, having stronger ties to Romania and Russia—it was well known that the Pilsudsky legacy precluded the Poles from accepting any help from the Red Army on their soil.[62]

Kasprzycki's arrival was closely followed by Hitler's April 28 cancellation of the German-Polish declaration of 1934 and Colonel Beck's May 5 answer to that initiative. Ambassador Léon Noël was attempting at that time to tone down the excitement of the Poles, his basic principle being to avoid underscoring the certainty of French military help. The minister of public works, Anatole de Monzie, traveled to Poland to inaugurate a railroad financed by French investments (April 21–27). Like

Léon Noël, he was very noncommittal regarding possible French intervention.[63]

But, without informing Noël, Daladier and Bonnet followed the opposite policy and were giving Poland increasing assurances.[64] Gamelin went even further and, with General Kasprzycki, initialed a very detailed document in the event of a German aggression against Poland or Danzig:

1. Immediate action in the air.

2. As of the third day "offensive actions on limited objectives" against Germany.

3. "As soon as the main German effort begins against Poland, *France would start an offensive action by engaging the bulk of its forces against Germany.*" [Emphasis added.] This could take place as of the fifteenth day.

Poland, for its part, would engage "with all its forces" in defensive actions and would take the offensive "as soon as circumstances allow it." Should Germany attack France through Belgium or Switzerland, "the Polish army would make every effort to engage a maximum of German forces."[65]

Such emphatic exaggeration of both French possibilities and of the Polish ability to resist is difficult to explain. It should also be pointed out that both generals had not at all discussed their respective military plans. Daladier gave the text to Bonnet on May 19.[66] Bonnet became frightened and was able to have Gamelin write an interpretive letter to General Kasprzycki on May 20: "According to instructions I have received from my government the protocol of the conversations we have just held will become a military agreement once the political agreement that is now being discussed is signed and naturally inasmuch as it fits in with the latter." The implementation will depend on the two governments. A handwritten note by Gamelin on the cover sheet of the letter states, "I have again met with General Kasprzycki and he told me that he agreed with this interpretation."[67]

There were to be no further military command talks.[68] On September 1 the French would still not have any information regarding Polish plans and vice versa. Léon Noël noticed the surprising degree of suspicion displayed by the Warsaw leadership.[69] They showed an extraordinary optimism that was truly surprising, reported very accurately by military attaché General Musse. He was in constant contact with General Stachiewicz, the chief of staff, and even with Marshal Rydz-Smigly. On August 9 General Stachiewicz, witnessing German troop movements near the borders, "feels that the intimidation ploy will be pushed very far by the leadership of the Reich and even going so far as to be concentrated on the Polish borders. But Poland will not bend and *if Hitler thinks that an attack on Poland would start a general war, he will stop in time.*" [Emphasis added.] He didn't think the discussions taking place between the west and the USSR were of any importance. "The main point is that the Reich cannot plan to consider the USSR as being on its side, *and that does not appear to be a likely possibility.*"[70] [Emphasis added.] And the Ribbentrop-Molotov agreement was only two weeks away!

The discussions did in fact continue. But they dealt exclusively with possible help with armaments and its financial aspects. Léon Noël insisted with Bonnet who did so with Daladier. On May 17 the Poles requested a 2 billion franc loan. Gamelin agreed (on June 23) on condition that it would not reduce French arms manufacturing in any way. The chiefs of staff reached the conclusion "on the need to give priority to Poland."[71] Paul Reynaud was favorable when approached but suggested that the Poles be asked for a specific list. General Faury was sent to Poland for this purpose at the end of June.[72] Polish General Kossakovsky arrived with the list at the beginning of August.[73] A few light tanks were shipped in time and that was all.

The Franco-British staff talks went much further as expected, and deserve to be examined closely. In order to follow the discussions we shall first examine the army and air force on one hand; and then the navy. The talks were held in three phases in London: March 29 to April 4; April 24 to May 5; and August 28 to 31. We shall only cover the first two phases here.

Regarding the army, Gamelin was completely confident. "We may consider quite dispassionately," he wrote to Daladier on January 7, 1939, "the possibility of a coming conflict that would pit France and England against the totalitarian states of the Axis."[74] And Weygand, despite the fact that he did not like his successor that much, added in July 1939, "The French army is now greater than at any time in history; it has first class equipment, top of the line fortifications, its morale is excellent and the commanders are excellent. No one here wants war but I can say that if we must win a new victory we shall win it."[75]

Gamelin led the discussions regarding the army. Regarding the air force, he was in the difficult role of being the one asking. The actual initiative for the talks—which France had proposed for a long time—came from Great Britain and was dated February 25, thereby preceding the Prague incident, that would delay them until March 29. However,

Daladier and Gamelin had prepared the directives for the French delegation as early as March 7 and 8.[76] Those directives are of great interest in
that they show the "general strategic conception of the war": "In a conflict opposing England and France on one side to Germany and Italy on
the other, Germany was to be sure "the biggest chunk," morally and
materially much stronger than its ally. Therefore, the French high command felt that continental, insular and colonial Italy would be the initial
target of the offensive effort." It would be necessary to cover ourselves
from Germany and consider "some offensive (at least on the local level)
to create a diversion" in case Poland and Romania enter the war. "Regarding an offensive on German soil, it should only begin after decisive
results are achieved…against Italy."

To reach this objective a reinforcement of the British expeditionary
force and the need to distribute the tasks accordingly became necessary,
should the Italians attack Corsica, Tunisia, or Egypt, in order to counter
them in Libya, or if they attacked Djibuti, then foment rebellion in Italian
East Africa through political action. Finally, "if Japan enters the conflict
it will be necessary to help China by all available means and reestablish as
quickly as possible its best supply route by clearing the Hong Kong-Can-
ton region. We should expel the Japanese from Hainan as soon as possible."[77] One has to marvel at how easily Gamelin uses terms such as "it's
necessary," and "we should" without stating which forces he intended to
use for those objectives.

We must also point out a first attempt at a unified command—something that was so hard to achieve in 1914–1918. From the start a "Franco-
British High Committee" worked discreetly and included government
leaders, defense ministers and commanders in chief. The head of the
British delegation was Captain Dankwerts, head of planning at the Admiralty. General Lelong, military attaché, or Vice-Admiral Odend'hal in
his absence, headed the French delegation. We shall rely mostly on the
brief summaries that were prepared for Daladier.

The first set of meetings (March 29 to April 4) was mainly explor-
atory. The French plan to contain Germany and knock Italy out first was
retained. The transport plans of the British expeditionary force to France
were no cause for optimism—a first group of two infantry divisions and
a few other elements would be ready within thirty days; a second group
(one infantry division) would be ready within three months! "The British
at first seemed obsessed with a defensive posture in every theater; it was
only little by little that they agreed to not systematically neglect the op-

portunity to take the offensive."... "They were mostly interested in the threat coming from the air, and above all where London was concerned."

Regarding the air force, the British *initially* refused to send fighter units to France. On the other hand, they accepted to engage units into battle, especially in the event Germany were to attack Belgium. They would bomb enemy convoys. The danger came from the fact that Germany's bombers were double the size of the Allies'. The bombing of Germany's industry was discussed at length but during the initial phase "the allied reaction as far as the air force is concerned will be mainly concentrating on security."[78]

The most interesting element is the joint French and British note regarding general strategy. It is indicative of what would be—rightly or wrongly—the war doctrine of the allies.[79] Would it be a short war or long war? Germany and Italy cannot hope to increase their resources appreciably during the course of the war; they therefore were counting, in order to achieve success, *on a short war.* [Emphasis added.] "France and England are, on the contrary, more likely to see their war potential increase month by month on condition that they successfully protect their war industries and maritime communications from air and naval attacks..." "Facing the initial German-Italian effort *they will first have to hold out, then last until such a time as the offensive becomes possible.*" [Emphasis added.] Shortly after the initial phase of the discussions the Italians took over Albania, leading the French to reconsider the issues.

On April 9, Daladier, Bonnet, Campinchi and Guy La Chambre; Generals Gamelin, Vuillemin, Bührer and Colson, a representative of Darlan, and Alexis Léger met to discuss Mediterranean issues. Tunisia was already protected as we have indicated previously. One-fourth of France's air defenses were located in Tunisia from where they could bomb Rome. For political reasons Bonnet recommended to not garrison too many troops at the Belgian and Spanish borders. He offered a broad diplomatic survey showing how Great Britain for the most part "was as involved as possible."[80]

Six days later the Army high command produced a study of the forces with related numbers[81] insisting on the Eastern alliances that could divert 25 to 30 German infantry divisions. Once Germany was denied resources from the East, "Germany would be engaged in a long war." The Axis could not fight such a war. Yet there were in Germany:

54 regular army divisions
35 to 40 reserve divisions
35 to 36 Landwehr divisions

About 17 *Grenzschutz* (border defense) divisions. Soon Germany would have 200 then 240 divisions. Italy had 85 divisions, 75 of which were in Italy proper. The Axis could count immediately on a total of 250 divisions.

The Allies facing them had only 120. One hundred French divisions (82 of them within metropolitan France) and 19 potential British divisions! How could the balance be tilted more evenly? By either using the Eastern allies (50 Polish divisions, 35 Romanian, and 25 Yugoslav divisions), or through a heavy bombing campaign...that could not be undertaken. Therefore "we must" hold out (once again "we must").

During the second phase of the Franco-British talks (April 24 to May 4) some issues were discussed in greater detail. First of all, the British promised that within eighteen months they would be able to send to France: 1. Four infantry divisions and two mobile divisions during the first six weeks; 2. Ten territorial divisions in months 4, 5, and 6; 3. The final 16 territorial divisions during the ninth to twelfth month or 32 divisions in one year! There were no specific decisions made regarding Poland; perhaps the expected alliance with the USSR would allow for the creation of a "continuous Eastern front."

In the Far East they adopted a defensive stance in the expectation of starting an offensive from Indochina.

A "plan for the deployment of the air force on the continent" was prepared and this time the British committed themselves in the event of an invasion of Belgium and Holland to use their "entire" bomber air force. In the event of an attack on Italy, the British would relieve the French air force against Germany—this was, as previously noted, an old French project.

The British stuck to their point of keeping *almost all their fighter planes in Great Britain* at least during the initial months.[82] Other meetings handled coordination in North Africa, in Rabat between General Noguès and General Ironside,[83] in the Middle East and in Singapore[84] from June 22 to 27.[85] The conclusion of that last meeting was very clear: "The conference wishes to state that the weakness of our naval and air forces in the Far East is a source of worry. Our weakness gives the Japanese such superiority by preventing us from keeping open our vital lines of communication and preventing the enemy from taking advanced operational bases from where he could directly threaten our vital interests."

England, naturally, was the leader where naval matters were concerned.[86] During the meetings we mentioned, the naval experts usually sat apart. The two allies to be were burdened with heavy duties:

Security in the Channel, mainly, for the passage of the British expeditionary corps;

Security in the Atlantic, mostly for commercial navigation if the Suez route was cut;

Security of communications in the western Mediterranean (transport between French North Africa and metropolitan France) and as a secondary task the eastern area (communications with Egypt and the Levant).

It was decided that the *North Sea* would be England's sole responsibility. Because of "autarky" its stockpiles and free access to Swedish iron ore, and Romanian oil, Germany could launch a naval offensive. However, in that area England enjoyed a 4 to 1 advantage in overall strength ("The Main Fleet"), but the British, going back to an old idea, asked that the French send their battleships *Strasbourg* and *Dunquerque* to the area since they were better equipped to prevail over the German "pocket battleships." The French admiralty refused.

In the *Channel* the system called for a very close Franco-British collaboration. The British would place mines in the waters of the Pas-de-Calais.

In the *North Atlantic* the fear of German submarines had not yet appeared. Hitler had not shown much interest and there were only 22 able to patrol the ocean. On the other hand, there could be destructive raids by surface ships. It was decided that France would watch the area— Ouessant-Azores—Cabo Verde Islands (based in Brest). The British would be based in Halifax, the Antilles, Plymouth, and possibly Dakar. The British would be escorting most of the convoys.

The western Mediterranean was set aside for the French navy (its advantage in strength over Italy was 1.25 to 1). But some kind of British collaboration was necessary. Gibraltar was almost depleted. The British fleet would be based at Malta and Alexandria. Admirals Connigham and Ollive met in Malta on July 27 and 28 and decided to "coordinate" their operations in a flexible manner.

Elsewhere a defensive posture would prevail. In the Red Sea or in the Far East, in case of war against Japan, the bulk of forces would fall back to Indochina and Malaysia, practically abandoning Hong Kong.

On August 8, 1939, Fleet Admiral Darlan and Admiral Dudley Pound met at Portsmouth on board the *Enchantress*.[87] They agreed to the final details. It should be pointed out that Darlan wanted a preventive operation against Spain through the conquest of Spanish Morocco, but Dudley

Pound was against it, just as he opposed a French proposal that had been discussed with the Turks to send a French division to Salonika in order to "be ahead of the Axis in the Balkans."

Finally, as Reussner[88] concluded, "the Mediterranean was a secondary theater within British strategy…And on the eve of war, while Franco-British naval discussions achieved complete success in dividing operational zones and naval responsibilities, an agreement on strategy was still far from being reached."

Finally we should mention relations with two neighboring countries that were potential passageways for Germany, namely Switzerland and Belgium.

Strangely enough, *Switzerland*, a country that was voluntarily and legally neutral, wanted to reach an understanding with the French.[89] Thanks to the military attaché Colonel de La Foirest-Divonne, there were ongoing conversations regarding international constraints preventing France from fortifying the region near Huningue and Basel. After that unofficial discussions on possible cooperation could take place. There were meetings among officers as early as 1937. The press was openly mentioning the issue. The high point came on July 31, 1939, when Colonel Petitpierre, representing Corps Commander Colonel Guisan met secretly with Gamelin in Paris. Petitpierre presented what the Swiss wanted: the immediate intervention by the French army, reinforcements in artillery, air force, and liaison between the two armies. Technical agreements were reached and the entire matter would remain completely secret.

However, where *Belgium* was concerned, due to internal politics and also the fear of "provoking" Germany, there were no staff talks, even in secret, from 1936 to September 1939. During the meeting of the chiefs of the general staff that took place on April 22, the Belgian issue was discussed:[90] "General Gamelin upheld his previous viewpoint. It would be absurd to engage the French army piecemeal in a type of battle amounting to a frontal clash." In other words, nothing would be done if the Belgians do not request it. If they do call, two possibilities should be considered: 1. They do it in time. Then we move behind the Belgian deployment "ready to shore it up should it threaten to break;" 2. They call us too late. In that case we occupy the Escaut with major forces because it is the only position after the Albert Canal.

It so happened that General Weygand enjoyed a good relationship with Belgian Minister Devèze. Was it through him that a liaison was established?[91] In any case, "the head of the Belgian general staff asked whether we were still thinking along the lines of the previous agreement." We answered yes but on condition that the Belgian call came before Belgium was attacked.

Clearly the ambiguity remained—on the defensive but with a planned movement into Belgium. Nothing was certain should the Belgians not call but in any case there would be no extension of the Maginot Line.

4.

TOWARD A UNIFIED COMMAND?

Gamelin's greatest dream was to establish in advance what took four years to achieve during the First World War, namely a commander in chief of the allied forces. But it would not have been in character for him to strongly request it.

The initial idea was of a permanent organization. At a meeting of the heads of the general staff on June 16, 1939, Gamelin brought up a recent conversation he had with Admiral Lord Chatfield. The British, he said, were not too far removed from wanting to revive the Versailles "High Military Committee" in other words, the body made up of political and military leaders to which Foch reported.[92]

Three weeks later, on July 13, General Gort, the British army chief of the general staff, met with Gamelin who explained the French organizational structure to him, his own role as coordinator of defense and commander in chief of the army and with General Georges, the commander of the armies in the northeast, reporting to him.[93]

Was it a follow-up to this meeting? In any case, on July 26 Chamberlain wrote to Daladier offering the immediate creation of an "Interallied General Staff." To discuss this he would send General Ismay to Paris on July 29. Later a "Supreme War Council" would be set up similar to that of 1917–1918. But it would not be created before the beginning of hostilities. It could be located either in France or England; but the General Staff would have a fixed location in England.[94]

Daladier forwarded that letter to the Army High Command, which offered its opinion that a single command of operations was required as of July 28. A "Supreme War Council" should be created; that was "a government matter"—Gamelin liked to clearly divide responsibilities. But a "commander in chief of interallied forces" with a staff was required.

The headquarters were to be in France. There was an *"obvious advantage that the Chief of Staff of the Interallied forces would be the general chief of staff of French national defense."* [Emphasis added.] Obviously, but let's not get ahead of ourselves! We should assemble staff officers in Paris; draw up in peacetime initial operational plans. Later on there would always be time.[95] On August 1 during a new meeting of chiefs of the general staff, Gamelin quoted the letter from Chamberlain, whom, he said, was confusing the "general direction of the war" and the "supreme conduct of operations." He rejected the Interallied High Command and proposed a simple committee of military studies to which "top level leaders" would purposefully not be appointed. We should note that Darlan was not for it. Regarding the "Supreme War Council" Darlan wanted it to include the commanders in chief because he said "in time of war, the ministers of national defense are only order carriers."[96]

Having received these opinions Daladier answered Chamberlain on August 3.[97] He retained the idea of a "Supreme War Council" meeting alternately in France and in England. On the other hand he rejected the immediate creation of a High Command. Without revealing Gamelin's ambitions regarding the *command*, he adopted his idea of a sort of "Interallied Military Studies Committee" that would meet in peacetime with the mission of creating the wartime organizations, to prepare external fronts, elaborate common plans, and—which was eloquent enough—to organize interallied theaters of operations. Gamelin had also discussed it with Ismay when he came to Paris.

Until the beginning of the war, matters would go no further. In any case, would we not force Germany into a long war? On this, as on other points, Gamelin thought that time was on his side.

Chapter XV

Toward the Inescapable Conclusion

August 22–September 3, 1939

"The bogeyman will deflate," as poet and diplomat Paul Claudel wrote in *Le Figaro* as late as August 18, proving to be neither much of a poet nor a diplomat on that occasion.

From August 22 onward even the most optimistic Frenchmen lost whatever high hopes they still had. The about-face by the USSR made even the thickest minds understand that this was giving Hitler license to attack Poland. It took a strong faith to say, like Aragon in *Ce soir* or *L'Humanité*, that this was a grand gesture toward peace. Many people suspected, and rightly so, that there was some kind of secret agreement, a promise for the partition of Poland.[1]

However, the idea of a Hitlerian "bluff" had not completely disappeared. France, which had paraded the most impressive army in the world on July 14, and England, the rich and all-powerful ruler of the sea, both displayed their cold resolve. Would anyone attempt to take action against such a coalition? On the other hand, it would take Hitler a long time to understand that the two decadent democracies were not about to agree to a new Munich.[2]

1.

France Remains Passive
(August 23–31, 1939)

During the eight days following the German-Soviet pact French diplomacy, interestingly enough, appears to be one of the most passive in Europe.

England was intensely active. Its position was absolutely firm and made sure that this was clearly understood. Sir Nevile Henderson in Berlin and Sir Percy Lorraine in Rome were in the limelight. They excluded the idea of a "conference" that was on everyone's mind since Munich. British policy was completely oriented toward what seemed to be the final opportunity for peace, namely, direct German-Polish negotiations.

Italy took a realistic position. Italian diplomatic documents[3] show, 1) During his conversations on August 12 in Salzburg and Berchtesgaden with Ribbentrop and Hitler, Ciano understood that the latter had decided on war;[4] 2) That Ciano—as opposed to Hitler until August 23—was absolutely convinced that England and France were not bluffing; 3) That Mussolini, knowing that Italy was not ready, was concentrating all his efforts at getting out of the Pact of Steel (his first letter to Hitler on that subject was dated August 21);[5] 4) That as of August 17 the Italians knew that Ribbentrop was going to sign an agreement in Moscow.[6]

Poland, despite warnings from England and France, continued to declare that it would make no concessions and would rather go to war. It was also known that Poland refused any change to Pilsudsky's doctrine, to never under any circumstances grant passage to the Red Army. But was that an absolute certainty?

In France, more than in England, there was a lingering doubt that could be used by the pacifists. Going to war to help Poland was fine. But to go to war because the Poles considered that the forced seizure of Danzig was a *casus belli* seemed to be too much, especially if the Poles deep down were ready to make some sacrifices[7] that they would only reveal at the very last minute.

This made Ambassador Léon Noël's position particularly uncomfortable. He had to assemble a huge amount of data relating to Polish military forces, the movements of German troops, the incidents in Danzig, and the alleged persecutions of the German minority created by Goebbels' propaganda. With the assistance of military attaché General Musse, he transmitted detailed information on a daily basis. He noted the admirable calm of the population, the gallantry of the soldiers but also the dramatic lack of modern equipment. Like the other ambassadors, he had little information concerning France's true strength, or potential military plans to bring help to the Poles. He could see the huge danger looming and the month of August went by for him in a kind of "breathless anxiety."[8]

The worse part was that he had to deal with the Polish government and Colonel Beck, whom he had never trusted. His instructions from Bonnet were to "moderate" the Poles, to tone down their uncompromising attitude, to encourage them not to take excessively provocative mobilization measures, but Beck's proud confidence was enough to drive him crazy. When he met with Beck on August 22, immediately following Ribbentrop's trip to Moscow, he found him to be "very calm." "For him materially, nothing had changed"—that prompted Daladier or one of his staff to note on Noël's cable: "Stupid tactics by Poland."[9] The French ambassador found Beck's display of confidence irritating. For example, Beck could not believe that the dangerous time would come at the end of August. Using the pattern of 1938 he felt it would be at the end of September.[10] He therefore tended to delay mobilization measures beyond the limit. But Léon Noël's instructions did not allow him to exert pressure.

An initial mobilization had taken place in the spring. It was only on August 23 that more reservists were called up;[11] then on the night between August 27–28 Poland was placed on war alert.[12] General mobilization would be seriously impaired by the start of the war.

There was, however, a point on which Beck gave in—but too timidly and too late. During the night of August 22–23 Léon Noël was instructed to make a final attempt to request that the Poles authorize the passage of the Red Army. He met with Beck on the morning of August 23. Shaken, Beck requested time think it over, then summoned Noël once again at half past noon. "During that second meeting," wrote General Musse, "*Mr. Beck gave in.*" [Emphasis added.] He agreed to send to General Doumenc a message worded as follows: "We are certain that in the event of a common action against German aggression, a collaboration between Poland and the USSR, within technical conditions to be determined is not to be excluded."[13] Would this vague statement be satisfactory to the gruff Voroshilov, allowing for the resumption of the Franco-Anglo-Soviet military talks? Could it prevent the signing of the Ribbentrop-Molotov agreement at the last minute? It was wishful thinking. Léon Noël quickly cabled it directly to Moscow, just in case, and informed the Quai d'Orsay accordingly.[14]

There were a few optimists. General Doumenc, as we have noted, took some time to understand the depth of the reversal that had taken place. On August 23 General Palasse, the military attaché in Moscow, still believed that "for the USSR the choice of an agreement with Germany was only a last resort and possibly a device to bring pressure for a faster conclusion to the desired coalition."[15] As for former Air Minister Pierre Cot he would tell his friend Jean Zay "one day we will go back to Russia, with whom negotiations had been carried out with incredible clumsiness, while this in no way is an excuse for its betrayal."[16]

Let us move back to France and examine what was taking place in Paris. Daladier and Léger were convinced that the understanding with the USSR could still be salvaged. On August 22 at 5 p.m. Daladier held a meeting of the Council of Ministers. That was when he proposed a final threatening initiative toward Warsaw, the one that Léon Noël undertook as we have mentioned. No decision was reached on anything else. A general mobilization as suggested by Paul Reynaud and Georges Mandel? Let's wait. What will Italy do? Couldn't we send the Italophile de Monzie to stop her on her drift toward intervention? Let's wait. Is England firmly committed this time to intervene if Poland is attacked? Yes, answered Jean Zay. "It's not that certain," replied Georges Bonnet.[17] How do we stand with our air force? Guy La Chambre made an exaggeratedly optimistic statement: "Our bomber planes will come out in the fall." Yet on August 1 Captain Stehlin had come to Paris to report on the Luftwaffe's mobilization measures and met with General Vuillemin, who admitted, "The government is well aware of it, I am no more encouraged than I was at the time of Munich."[18]

On August 23, at Bonnet's request, Daladier organized an unofficial meeting of the members of the "Permanent Committee of National Defense." According to de Monzie, at the time Daladier and Léger were still denying that a new partition of Poland was possible.[19] The prime minister asked three questions: 1) Could France watch Romania and Poland disappear without reacting? The answer was "no!"; 2) What means did France have to oppose this? Gamelin answered that France was ready. Darlan said the same thing. The only reservations concerned the air force;[20] 3) Which measures should be taken now? The military men were requesting partial mobilization. It was up to the Cabinet to decide.

Daladier called a meeting of the Council of Ministers on August 24 at 10 a.m. Partial mobilization was approved. Daladier announced that the Poles would agree to the passage of the Red Army and answering a question from the president of the republic, Albert Lebrun, declared that an agreement with the Soviets was still possible. The illusion had not yet vanished.

The real problem was that of France's commitments. Those in favor of "resistance"—Mandel, Reynaud, Sarraut, Campinchi, and Zay—said that intervention was required in any case if Poland was attacked even if the aggression was provoked by a Nazi revolt in Danzig. There were still a few "pacifists" like Bonnet, Marchandeau, and Guy La Chambre who were very reticent because they thought Polish concessions were possible. Zay mistakenly placed de Monzie among the "resisters." As for Daladier he "was wrapped in a gloomy kind of mystery."[21]

Actually, at the ministry of public wde Monzie met with the major French *appeasers*—Paul Baudoin; Maurice Petsche, a moderate deputy from Besançon; Socialist Deputy Lazurick; the Socialist Senator Felix Gouin; the syndicalist René Belin; university chancellor Roussy; these were reinforced by Paul Faure, Marcel Déat, Jean Mistler, president of the foreign affairs commission of the Chamber and Bérenger, president of the same commission in the Senate. Monzie was in constant contact with Bonnet, who that same day offered to send him to Italy but cancelled the idea once Daladier voiced his opinion. There was also the thought, but remained as a vague idea coming from Roger Genébrier, Daladier's cabinet director, of sending Pierre Cot on a mission to Moscow.[22]

On that same August 24, Bonnet instructed Léon Noël to "take a very insistent step with the Polish government for it to refrain from any immediate reaction in the event the Senate of the Free City announced that Danzig would become part of the Reich."

August 25 was the day France apparently stepped into the tunnel. The walls were covered with posters announcing "the call-up of certain categories of reservists." Once more the electric lights were dimmed, soon communist publications would be banned and censorship was instituted. Germany also cut telephone communications, making the exchange of letters between Hitler and Daladier that much more difficult. That exchange was to be, at least as far as France was concerned, the big event from August 25 to 27.

On August 25 at 5:30 p.m. Hitler summoned Ambassador Coulondre and gave him a message addressed to Daladier. He harbored, he said, no hostility toward France. He had renounced the Alsace-Lorraine. The idea of fighting France because of Poland was "extremely painful" to him.[23] It obviously was part of his tactics to break up the potential coalition. Coulondre answered, "If you attack Poland, France with all of its forces will fight on the side of the allies." He gave him his word as a soldier. Hitler rose for him to take his leave. Coulondre, while standing up, mentioned the world war where the winner could turn out to be...Trotsky. "He gave a start as if I had hit him in the stomach." But the pressure on Hitler was now complete.[24]

Before Daladier sent in his answer we should mention a brief attempt to find a solution that would also surprise Hitler. The idea was to offer Germany and Poland a population exchange. The British agreed. Léon Noël presented the idea to Deputy Undersecretary for Foreign Affairs Arciszewsky, who viewed the idea favorably. Beck agreed with the proposal but not to taking it to the Germans.[25] The British then dropped the project.[26] When Coulondre mentioned it, Hitler "only answered with an exclamation."[27]

The important part—Daladier's answer—was drafted on that same August 26 and transmitted at 2:50 p.m. It was a sentimental letter. "I owe it to our two peoples to say that the peace is still held in your hands alone." The national honor of the French people, as high as that of the German people, implied France's commitment to its Polish alliance. The crisis could be resolved "with honor and dignity." A final attempt for a peaceful arrangement between Germany and Poland was required. "Like myself you were a fighter in the last war...Should French blood and German blood flow again as they did twenty-five years ago, each of the two peoples will fight confident in its victory, but the most certain victory will be that of destruction and barbarism."[28]

Coulondre handed that letter to Hitler on the same day at 7 p.m. The Führer's expression had "hardened." He was acting the part, said Coulondre, who during forty minutes had "used up all the arguments, exhortations and pleas." Was he able to move him for an instant by mentioning the women and children who were going to die? In any case, he closed saying that the entire responsibility lay fully with Poland. That was what Coulondre cabled to Daladier immediately after.[29] Daladier no doubt had exaggerated expectations of the impact his letter would have. He was deeply disappointed.

The final episode of this correspondence came on August 27 at 4 p.m. Ribbentrop handed Hitler's reply to Coulondre. It was obviously a rejection written in the Führer's typically confused style. Hitler understood Daladier's thinking and recognized the Alsace-Lorraine borders. As usual, he offered the history of his efforts to revise the "Diktat of Versailles." Poland, encouraged by the French and the British, had unleashed an "intolerable terror" against the Germans living on its land. What would France do if Marseille, like Danzig, was taken away and its territory was cut in half by a corridor? It wasn't possible for an honorable nation to see two million of its sons be mistreated close to its territory. It would be painful to him to have to fight against France but that was France's choice. Hitler's letter included a very serious sentence proving that the bidding was going higher: "I have made a definite demand: *Danzig and the Corridor must be returned to Germany.*"[30] [Emphasis added.]

From August 27 to 30, inclusive, French diplomacy seems to fade. As Jean Zay put it, "The empty and anguished days of September 1938 were back."[31]

England would handle the major negotiations. It did so alone as usual, but requested France's support, which was given wholeheartedly but purely in a passive role. It must be said that rather than choosing the slippery context of sentimentality as Daladier did, Chamberlain, Halifax and their ambassador to Berlin, Sir Nevile Henderson, placed themselves squarely at the center of the problem: there had never been real negotiations between Germany and Poland and that thread had to begin.

Those negotiations have been studied in great detail and are beyond our subject matter. We shall recall that they started on August 25 and that Henderson traveled to London and returned to Berlin on the evening of the 28th. Hitler would accept the talks—he said—on condition that a Polish plenipotentiary would come to see him before the evening of the 30th. Mindful of the sad precedent of the Czechoslovak president, Hacha, on March 14, the Warsaw government refused to delegate Beck or Rydz-Smigly[32] and limited itself to instructing its ambassador, Joseph Lipski, to carry on the negotiations. Furthermore, Lipski could only take the initiative on August 31 allowing Ribbentrop to tell Nevile Henderson that it was too late. Hitler wished to artificially create a situation where it would appear that Poland rather than Germany was responsible for refusing.[33]

Captain Stehlin was a witness to those events in Berlin, and despite additional surveillance he was able to continue his flights over Germany until August 23 and was totally convinced that an attack was imminent, stating that he was "surprised to see that Coulondre was joining his British colleague in suggesting to the Polish ambassador to have his government agree to the German proposal of direct negotiations."[34]

It actually was a British proposal that Germany had reluctantly accepted, with the intention of not allowing it to come to pass. Stehlin could not believe that this time the British position remained firm. Around August 29 and 30 "a kind of euphoria spread through the embassies and the legations," and even among German circles. That euphoria— Coulondre used the same word—no doubt explains the decision made by Coulondre to write a personal letter to Daladier. He had met the "specialist" of France, the shady writer Friedrich Sieburg who, with tears in his eyes, told him that "the situation was worsening quickly in Germany. Hitler was hesitating, the party was adrift, the population was grumbling. Germany was supposed to attack Poland on the morning of the 26th. The Führer decided against it at the last moment." Why not consider a conference with Hitler to revise the Treaty of Versailles?[35]

The ambassador then wrote to Daladier, whom he knew personally, to report on this "drift." Hitler was backing up. "The brisk tone of the answer given to the British government was meant to cover up this weakening attitude."… "Mr. Hitler is wondering how he can get out of the dead-end in which he placed himself." In other words, here was Coulondre once again converted to the belief in a Hitlerian bluff. We should point to the fact that he did draw a positive conclusion: "We just must hold out, hold out, hold out." With Danzig and the extraterritorial highway Hitler would be satisfied. Let us, therefore, be firm "to convince him that he will get nothing more with the methods he has used until now." Coulondre gave that letter to Dayet, the consul in Frankfurt, who, like the other French consuls, was packing his bags on the ambassador's orders and traveling to Paris by car. "It is of prime importance," wrote Coulondre, "that these thoughts not be leaked out." It was up to Daladier to pass his message along to Bonnet and Léger.

Suddenly, on August 31, France would once more be in the limelight because of an Italian initiative. On that day François-Poncet met with Count Ciano late in the morning. The Italian minister was very "upset" because "war in his opinion was only a matter of hours away." The Italian people were satisfied with the nonbelligerent status adopted by their government. Mussolini, for his part, felt extremely humiliated. His armaments were inadequate. He was unable to honor the Pact of Steel and be at Germany's side. In his almost daily correspondence with Hitler at the time, the latter took a patronizing tone. "The Duce is nervous. He wants to do something," wrote Ciano on August 29.[36] "A new event" was required, he told François-Poncet. The ambassador sent a cable at 12:15 p.m. to report on this rather vague conservation.

Then Ciano suddenly summoned him once more. He had just seen Mussolini, who had thought up a "new event." He was offering a conference with Germany on September 5 to France and England to examine "the clauses of the Treaty of Versailles that were the cause of the current problems." Mussolini would only invite Hitler if the two democracies agreed to it. François-Poncet welcomed the offer with satisfaction and a bit of skepticism. He phoned Paris at 1:05 p.m.[37] At 1:30 p.m. Corbin phoned from London. Lord Halifax and Chamberlain accepted with little enthusiasm but with one precondition, that the armies be demobilized.

Everything indicates that Mussolini was the originator of the idea. In the cited volume of *Documenti Diplomatici Italiani*,[38] there are some 24 messages from Ambassador Sir Percy Lorraine to Ciano between August 24 to 31, but not once was the topic of a conference raised. Contrary to September 1938, England was not at all involved in the matter. But neither was France. François-Poncet did not discuss it during his August 24 meeting with Ciano nor in his dispatches to the department. On August 28 the Italian ambassador to Paris, Raffaele Guariglia, had long talks with Anatole de Monzie and Mistler. Both told him of the French will to resist and begged him to prevent Italy from entering the war. How could they keep the peace? They felt that a conference had become impossible and were only attempting to get a "mediation" by Mussolini.[39] On the following day, August 29, Bonnet transmitted the report of his discussion with Guariglia to François-Poncet, "a long and cordial" conversation. Italian neutrality was discussed but absolutely not a conference.[40] Guariglia liked Bonnet but not Daladier who was very close to his personal enemy, American Ambassador William Bullitt.[41]

The 31st therefore came as a complete surprise. Bonnet, delighted, consulted with Daladier, who called a Council of Ministers meeting the same day, August 31, at 6 p.m. Monzie, who had lunch with Guariglia, was alerted by Bonnet and met with Queuille, Pomaret and Jean Zay, who said he would agree to accept "if this is not a new Munich." Zay then went to see Léon Blum, who was "very worried" and in favor of accepting conditional to "remaining in complete agreement with England."[42]

The Council held a meeting. Bonnet said they had to accept. This would give France a few more days. But the unrealistic British condition on demobilization should be rejected, the presence of Poland should be required and the conference broadened to most of the problems regarding peace in the world.

Daladier began by stating his opposition. He "looked like a hedgehog with all his quills pricked up against someone or something that wasn't clear. He turned his back on Bonnet from the very beginning. He was pouting with disgust and contempt."[43] When he spoke it was to say that France must refuse: it would be a new Munich. "Do we agree to go and chop up Poland and dishonor ourselves...then wind up with war in any case? The lesson of Munich is that Hitler's signature isn't worth anything." As for demobilizing, Gamelin told him it would be "insanely imprudent." He knew through Corbin that Chamberlain was opposed to a conference regarding the fate of Poland. The results of the direct contact between Poland and Germany had to come in first. In other words, Bonnet felt that Chamberlain would favor the Italian proposal and Daladier thought he was against it.[44] Daladier knew that Alexis Léger viewed that initiative as a trap. During the cabinet meeting Daladier received a note from Corbin following a discussion with Halifax, stating that the Italian offer was a dangerous "maneuver." At that point the famous letter from Coulondre was brought in by an officer of the military mission. Far from limiting it to Bonnet and Léger, Daladier read it to the Cabinet. How comforting! "The object was to bluff," wrote de Monzie. "The one who bluffs last will have the upper hand... We must just be brazen. When the objective is to wait and be bold, enthusiasm and the easy way out go hand in hand. No more debates! Coulondre's opinion shut up those who were recalcitrant."[45]

After some statements with de Monzie, in favor of accepting, and Paul Reynaud, who was against it, the Council made no clear decision, to the point that two contradictory conclusions emerged. The minister of the interior, Albert Sarraut, gave the press a communiqué that appeared to reject all mediations. On the contrary, Bonnet and Monzie wrote a dispatch that seemed to imply acceptance. However, Bonnet did not send it on August 31.[46]

2.

The Last Three Days
(September 1–3, 1939)

The German attack on Poland on its northern, western and southern borders took place on September 1, 1939 at 4:45 a.m. The French government found out through two cables from Léon Noël received at 8:20 and 8:30 a.m.[47] France had been allied to Poland since 1921[48] and would go to war only on September 3 at 5 p.m., or six hours after Great Britain. That time lag, which surprised public opinion and brought about energetic protests by the Polish ambassador, Lukasziewicz, has been the object of a number of more or less serious explanations. Some people attributed it to the British leadership. As British historian A.J.P. Taylor supported the thesis that up to the end Chamberlain had attempted to avoid war and that he had been compelled to give in by pressure from of the members of Parliament at the House of Commons and in particular the "backbenchers"—the bulk of ordinary members of Parliament.[49] That view has been strongly criticized by another British historian, R.A.C. Parker,[50] who we believe clearly demonstrates that Chamberlain at that time did not attempt to return to the policy of *appeasement* and that the delay was due to French authorities. Parker had been unable to consult the archives at the Quai d'Orsay that confirm his views most emphatically.

Who wanted such a delay in France? The military leaders for one. Gamelin feared that the general mobilization operations, decided by the Council as of the morning of September 1, could be disrupted by bombing. But Gamelin's role appears to be secondary compared to that of Georges Bonnet. He was the one, contrary to the British, who continued the *appeasement* policy and wanted a new Munich; he was the one who was determined to delay the outbreak of the tragedy in the hope of preventing it even if it may mean breaking France's commitments once more. He did this so cleverly that Mandel said that he was working "for the *Livre Jaune*." Daladier, who was much more inclined than Bonnet to honor France's commitments, showed some hesitation. But between Bonnet's maneuvering and the haste of the British he practically severed his relations with his minister in the end.

What makes the negotiations of September 1 and 2 appear obscure up to the night of September 2–3 when everything becomes clear, was the existence of two attitudes and, therefore, of two diplomatic activities. On one hand the British, no longer feeling that it was possible to avoid war, were determined to serve Hitler with an ultimatum and were increasingly in a hurry to do so. Georges Bonnet, on the other, with the "objective" support of Daladier and Gamelin, wanted to delay such an ultimatum as long as possible. His leverage was the Italian conference project.

But in these two debates the British needed the French as much as the French needed the British. Each side was forced to make some concessions, at least until the final clarification. To understand all this the facts must be examined, at times on an hourly basis. There should, however, be no mistake; this was not a "superstructure" as some would call it. It was the clash between two deeply rooted ways of thinking. The British Tories, who remained blind and deaf for a long time, were still fortified by a solid principle: one must give one's word sparingly, but once it was given it must be kept. Munich was legitimate since the British had never promised the Czechs anything. *A new Munich would go against honor and therefore against Great Britain's interests.*

The French leaders facing them belonged to a different social class for the most part, and twenty years of "pact-making" had effectively adulterated their instincts. In the cunning of some radicals like Bonnet (not of all of them, obviously!) was the almost subconscious idea that a treaty was only worth its escape clauses. On that point he was like Léger and the entire Briand tradition. As a Polish diplomat told Hervé Alphand, Léger "introduced ambiguity into French policy. In the past alliance treaties were simple and clear...The treaties Briand made did not use that honest approach."[51]

The relationship between those two attitudes and the British and French regimes of the time deserves some thought. From September 1–3 the House of Commons met three times and held wide open debates. The French Parliament met only once in the afternoon of September 2. It was understood that no one would speak following the government's statement. The stability of the British system during those days of anguish allowed for broad consultations among the people's representatives. The unstable regime of the Third Republic during its final moments (no one knew that it was near death at the time) forced the executive branch to take multiple precautions and leading it to trickery toward the members of Parliament, just as it had done with foreign countries.

* * * *

On September 1, following Hitler's aggression, the Council of Ministers was summoned to a meeting at 10 a.m. The business at hand was dealt with quickly and only two important decisions were reached: the general mobilization orders were issued—September 2 being the first day of the mobilization—and Parliament was called to meet on the afternoon of the 2nd. The cabinet set additional military funding at 75 billion to be submitted for approval.[52]

At the close of the meeting Georges Bonnet began his maneuver. At 11:45 a.m. he sent his version of the decisions made by the cabinet on August 31 to Rome.

France would agree to the Italian conference proposal on condition that the Poles be invited and that its objective be a general discussion regarding peace. In other words, Bonnet on his own authority: 1. Felt that the cabinet meeting of August 31 had given him a free hand; 2. Totally ignored the condition set by the British on the 31st, namely to only accept if there were a prior demobilization; 3. *Failed to take into consideration that between the vague position taken on August 31 and his cable of September 1, Hitler had invaded Poland.*

It was necessary, however, that the slight incident during the night did not alter the views held by Italy and Great Britain and that an invaded Poland would accept. Bonnet spent part of his day on the matter.

On the Italian side, Ambassador Guariglia in Paris received a phone call around 9 a.m. from a French cousin of his, Count de Ronceray, who had probably been pressured by de Monzie or Piétri, announcing that the French Council of Ministers had accepted the Italian proposal the ambassador knew nothing about, and also insisted that the events which he called "a mishap" notwithstanding, Rome should stand by its proposals. He paid him a visit, then went to see Piétri. Bonnet phoned Guariglia just before 10 a.m. Guariglia went to the Quai d'Orsay where he had meetings with Mistler, Bérenger and Piétri, who also reiterated the same positions. Then he met with a newsman who was an emissary of Guy La Chambre and who gave him a statement from Daladier to "restore Franco-Italian friendship." Guariglia sent a cable to Ciano at 11 a.m.[53]

At the same time François-Poncet was getting ready to meet with Ciano at 12:15 p.m. and handed him the text of Bonnet's message.[54] Ciano was both satisfied and skeptical. "He…added that he was unable to tell me whether the Italian proposal still had any justification."[55] If, on the 31st, Mussolini could still hope to do Hitler a good turn by allowing him to obtain what he wanted without war, by the 1st his initiative could be taken as a scheme to break his thrust.[56] Nevertheless, after meeting with Daladier at 3 p.m., Bonnet phoned Corbin at 3:40 p.m. "He informed him about the phone call he received from Mr. François-Poncet. The Italian government believes it is possible if the agreement of France and England is secured, to offer the proposal made yesterday once more; it feels that Poland must be present at the conference." Bonnet demanded that Corbin find out the exact answer that the British had given to Mussolini.[57]

The English answer, coming as a verbal communication from Percy Lorraine, stated exactly the following: "It appears that, according to the information received, the action of the German government now makes it unfortunately impossible to follow this path."[58] While Corbin investigated, Bonnet called British Ambassador Sir Eric Phipps at 3:48 p.m. He gathered the impression that the British government "thought that it would not be useful to call for such a conference given the circumstances." Corbin's report given by phone at 4:10 p.m. was even more specifically negative. "Sir Percy Lorraine answered that England would have been favorable had Hitler not started the hostilities." It would be, said the British government "like throwing holy water to a man with a rope around his neck."[59]

Léon Noël could not be reached by phone even when attempting to place the call through Bucharest. It was only at 6:25 p.m. that Bonnet was able to ask the ambassador to probe the Poles regarding such a conference. Beck answered that—obviously—"the question at hand is not about a conference but rather about the joint action that must be taken by the allies."[60] The Polish ambassador to Paris, Lukasziewicz, was indignant to see no action being taken on the French side.[61]

All these setbacks did not stop Bonnet from phoning François-Poncet at 4:50 p.m., asking him to press Ciano. "It is agreed to hold a conference. If there are refusals we shall advise."[62] Had Daladier been kept informed after the 3 p.m. conversation? In any case he informed Ambassador Guariglia that he wished Mussolini would intervene with Hitler… to obtain a truce—which in itself was wishful thinking.[63]

While Bonnet's maneuver regarding a possible conference on September 5 was underway, the British felt that another initiative was required to notify the German government that England and France would stand by their commitments if German troops did not evacuate Polish territory. That decision had been taken late that morning by the British inner cabinet. Corbin was informed about the decision by phone on September 1 at 2:30 p.m. Then, following a meeting with Alexander Cadogan at 3:15 p.m., he said that the British government wanted the two ambassadors in Berlin to take identical steps.[64] Bonnet immediately discussed the matter with Daladier. They could only accept. He phoned Coulondre at 4:55 p.m., instructing him to take part in that operation,[65] and confirmed by cable at 5:55 p.m.[66] An amusing detail was that Bonnet was so deeply involved in his Italian business that he could only instruct Coulondre to say exactly the same thing as Sir Nevile Henderson. "Well that makes my task so much more simple!" the French ambassador wrote ironically.[67] The two diplomats went to the Wilhelmstrasse. At 10 p.m. Coulondre told Ribbentrop that unless the German government was "ready to promptly withdraw its forces from Polish territory the French government would unhesitatingly fulfill its obligations toward Poland."[68]

France was therefore involved in two negotiations. As of the evening of September 1, the conflict between Bonnet and the British regarding Mussolini's proposal was clear. We must quote the important telegram sent by Georges Bonnet to Corbin two hours later, at 6:15 p.m. "You have told me after chatting with the Foreign Office that the Secretary of State felt that at this time the project did not appear to be viable to him and that 'it was like throwing holy water on a man with a rope around his neck.' I would request that you say that I do not agree with that view. We certainly do have the firm intention of living up to our commitments. I have just given my approval to the draft of a note sent to me by the British government to order a joint initiative of our ambassadors in Berlin to so inform the government of the Reich. But I feel that the very firmness of our resolve compels us until the last minute not to neglect any effort in attempting to reestablish peace."[69]

It should be noted that on September 1 the House of Commons had voted war funding of 500 million pounds sterling.

September 2 was even more dramatic and was to prove the energy of Georges Bonnet in fighting for his "cause," which was to avoid or at least delay the reckoning.[70] The day before he had offered the idea that France could not, according to the constitution, decide anything before Parliament assembled as planned during the afternoon of the 2nd. On the morning of the 2nd he felt that there had to be a forty-eight hour delay. Where did that idea originate? From Gamelin, who was haunted by his general mobilization seeing that Polish mobilization, had been completely disrupted by the Luftwaffe? Or was it Italy? In any case, at 9 a.m. Ciano sent to Attolico, his ambassador to Berlin, a memorandum to inform Hitler that Italy "still could get France, England and Poland to accept a conference on the basis of the following:

1) Armistice holding the armies where they are at the moment;

2) Starting the conference in two to three days;

3) Resolving the Polish-German dispute in a manner that, given the situation, could only be to Germany's advantage."

And Ciano added: "The idea that had originated with the Duce was now being supported by France in particular."[71]

At the same time, at 9 a.m. in Paris, Bonnet received Polish Ambassador Lukasziewicz and told him about the forty-eight hour delay. This would indicate that there had been an unofficial understanding between France and Italy on that issue. The unhappy Pole was so incensed that he wrote a vengeful letter to Daladier as soon as he left—and sent Bonnet a copy.[72] He reminded the prime minister that assistance to Poland should be immediate and was extremely urgent from the strategic point of view. He demanded—unsuccessfully—that the delay be reduced from forty-eight to twenty-four hours.

On the same subject, Ambassador Phipps cabled his government at 9:55 a.m. that "every extra hour allowing the French mobilization to continue without hindrance was precious."[73] The Foreign Office got worried and asked that Phipps do everything he could to "inspire in Mr. Bonnet courage and determination."[74]

Shortly after noon Ciano summoned François-Poncet and Percy Lorraine to tell them—as he had done with Attolico early that morning and using the same words—that Mussolini was maintaining the project of a conference under the conditions mentioned above. Hitler had been informed of his message. He was not opposed to the idea of a conference. However, he had received the French and British notes the evening before. Should these be viewed as ultimatums? Henderson had reassured him that they were not ultimatums. Germany could then examine the issue.[75] After meeting with the two ambassadors, Ciano directly called first Bonnet and then Halifax. That chronological order is not unimportant. Bonnet was naturally delighted to see that Italy was taking his initiative and insisting on the forty-eight hour delay.[76] Halifax, on the other hand, stated that it was too late unless Germany withdrew its troops. He would inform the Cabinet, about to meet, and would then confirm that condition. "It seems to me that nothing else can be done," wrote Ciano. "It is not my business to give Hitler such advice since he would firmly reject it, perhaps with contempt."[77] During the night Guariglia informed him of the new French position: partial withdrawal of German troops. Ciano took it upon himself to reject it immediately without even consulting Mussolini.[78]

But in the course of the afternoon and evening Bonnet would act as if he still considered the Italian offer as valid. The important event was the meeting of the French Parliament at 3 p.m. The House of Commons was to meet at 6 p.m. Sessions took place simultaneously at the Chamber and the Senate.[79] At the Chamber, President Edouard Herriot spoke first.[80] All the deputies rose—including the Communists—and cheered him after he expressed "the disapproval of any honest person" of the German-Soviet Pact. A number of pacifist deputies, from the USR (Marcel Déat, Frot) to Gaston Bergery and on the right (Scapini and Tixier-Vignancour), requested a secret session which was rejected by a show of hands. Daladier read the government's message, inspired by that of Viviani in 1914. "But Viviani," wrote Rossi-Landi, "used the word peace six times and the word war sixteen times; Daladier spoke of war only three times and of peace eleven times."[81] In the bill to authorize funding of 70 billion in additional expenses in order to "face up to the requirements of the international situation," war was not mentioned. For some this was an issue. Did this vote allow the government to declare war since it implies tacitly that the Chamber accepted, or would a second specific vote be required?

It had been agreed that no one would speak. Yet Gaston Bergery, an irregular of radicalism, went to the rostrum intending to say that the French Parliament had been "forced." Herriot succeeded in talking him out of facing an "unruly" assembly. The entire text was approved with apparent unanimity; any opponents did not speak up. The session ended at 7:10 p.m.

In the Senate President Jeanneney did not speak. Chautemps read the government's message. There was no request for a secret session; however, like Bergery at the Chamber, Laval went up to the rostrum. He was only able to say a few words recalling the Rome agreements of January 1935. No one understood how they related to the current situation. Later he explained that he wanted to ask Parliament for a vote on going to war.[82] The Senate ended up voting unanimously in favor of the funding. The constitutional issue is not relevant for discussion here since it would mostly be used in future disputes.

Actually, if the word "war" had not been uttered in the text of the bill on military funding, it was probably because of the message from Ciano that Georges Bonnet continued to present as valid. It would be the same for the cabinet council meeting at 7:30 p.m. That council was rather interesting because Bonnet and Daladier agreed to use the Italian proposal and therefore wait at least until noon of the following day before taking action. Bonnet was hoping in that final delay to keep the peace. And what about Daladier? He said "he agreed. There was a military advantage in gaining twenty-four or forty-eight hours of mobilization time (which was what Gamelin said in the waiting-room to a few of us)," wrote Jean Zay.[83]

The entire Council agreed except for Mandel, Paul Reynaud and Campinchi. Reynaud asked the question, "What if Italy were only seeking to gain time for Germany? What if the latter, having reached its objectives tomorrow, offers to make peace? Will we not be in an awkward position to declare war?" The answer given to Reynaud was "in any event we will demand the evacuation of Poland."[84] De Monzie once again took the lead. France could not follow the British. "To require the withdrawal of German troops from Poland is an impossible demand." He suggested a compromise, "a symbolic retreat, a withdrawal of a few kilometers." That evening he had dinner at the residence of Ambassador Guariglia, along with Piétri and Mistler. The Italian ambassador was satisfied and de Monzie phoned Bonnet with advice to speak up to London.[85]

However, the British had to be taken into account. Already at the September 1 session the Commons had been surprised to hear that there was no decision to take action. "British public opinion was noticeably heating up."[86] On the evening of the 2nd Chamberlain and Halifax were terribly embarrassed. They did not dare act without France, which was delaying everything. Chamberlain's embarrassed speech was viewed by many members of Parliament as an attempt to shirk the imperative obligations of the nation. Hence, the famous words, "Speak for England," aimed at the liberal Arthur Greenwood. The result was "a feverish atmosphere that the prime minister's statements did not manage to quiet."[87] The mention of the Italian project "gave rise to vehement protests from laborites and from many conservatives." Chamberlain was compelled to promise a final declaration on the following day.

Sir Eric Phipps was instructed to tell the Quai d'Orsay that the decisive undertaking in Berlin must not be delayed beyond midnight.

However, the French Cabinet Council had decided to take no action before September 3 at noon on an ultimatum that would expire on the 4th at 5 a.m.[88]

Corbin went to 10 Downing Street where he met with Halifax and Chamberlain, who was worried. He "described the stormy meeting that had just ended at Westminster. The displeasure of the MPs was first directed against France, accused of shirking its duty. No one wanted to hear about the Italian offer—it was viewed as a trap to favor the German advance." There was a lot of uneasiness.

"The Admiralty is also complaining that these delays are preventing certain defensive measures. The Germans are taking advantage of it to send submarines into the Atlantic and lay mines in the North Sea." Corbin protested, expressing the opinion that French mobilization had to be pursued without enemy attacks—that was the position of Gamelin and Daladier.

Then for three-quarters of an hour Chamberlain and Halifax phoned Paris, the former speaking with Daladier and the latter with Bonnet. When Chamberlain suggested that he present the ultimatum the next morning, Daladier said he could not do it earlier "unless the British air force bombers can give us immediate assistance." He added that there was a possibility, according to Ciano, for Germany to agree to withdraw its forces. Since Ciano had said exactly the opposite, the interpretation advanced by Parker of an intentional distortion of his words by Georges Bonnet is plausible if not proven.[89] Halifax told Bonnet he saw only one solution which was that the ambassadors in Berlin act separately.[90]

The British cabinet then met from 10 p.m. to around midnight. Corbin has admirably described the split that existed at that juncture between the two governments. His report deserves to be quoted at length.

The British government, which had assembled its Parliament twenty-four hours ahead of us, was being accused in political circles of being slow, of hesitating, of being derelict of its duties in the face of aggression by the Reich. Many members of parliament, haunted by the memory of recent events, suspect that the Prime Minister, despite the firmness of his statements, to be involved in who knows what type of scheme. The Cabinet therefore felt compelled to reach a decision and let it become effective in the hours that followed. It should be noted that within its assessment of events the Italian offers carried very little weight...

The French government did not have the same haste in announcing its decision. Public opinion was very calm in the country and was satisfied for the moment with the statements made in Parliament. It had therefore complete discretion to choose its hour…

In France and Great Britain purely political considerations had the opposite effect; from the viewpoint of the navy it was best to immediately take security measures at sea that could include acts of war. On land it was obvious that operations could not start for some time and that the declaration of war, being rather platonic at first, it was therefore preferable to ensure the protection of convoys, communications junctions, the evacuation of women and children from any surprise from the air and allow our troop concentrations to progress.[91]

Corbin faced up to the anti-French wave that was developing and spoke with Sir John Simon and Churchill. He had to "be very aloof" with some journalists. Around fifteen minutes past midnight Corbin was summoned to number 10 Downing Street following the Cabinet meeting. He was told that on the 3rd, at 9 a.m., Henderson would be instructed to inform Ribbentrop that if England did not receive a satisfactory answer within two hours, it would be war. The timing was dictated by the session at the House of Commons. Halifax wished, should a simultaneous action not take place, that France undertake a similar initiative at noon.

Georges Bonnet, now reconciled, cabled Coulondre at midnight, asking him to take the steps with the Wilhelmstrasse on Thursday September 3 at noon (three hours after the British). Then at 10:20 a.m. on September 3 he explained that this step was intended to say that the French government, not having received an answer to its communication of September 1, was now compelled "to fulfill its commitments, as of today September 3 at 5 p.m., that France had with Poland, which are known to the German government."[92] Coulondre had phoned the Quai d'Orsay between those two cables to ask him to explain some points and had spoken with Léger. Bonnet explained his plan to him verbally at that time.

Coulondre had a lot of difficulties in securing an appointment. Ribbentrop could only see him after twelve noon; he demanded to meet with State Secretary von Weizsäcker. At 12:30 p.m. he was received by Ribbentrop himself at the Reich Chancellery. Judging that his answer was negative, the ambassador then made the prescribed declaration. "Well then!" answered Ribbentrop in a toneless voice, "France will be the aggressor." "History will judge," I told him, and withdrew. Mr. von Weizsäcker, who was present, shook my hand at length. I had not attempted to shake hands with Ribbentrop. We looked into each other's eyes. Even better than if he were speaking, I knew he was saying: I did not want this."[93]

The fact that France went to war at a bad time and in adverse conditions is a fact that subsequent events would prove. That, following Munich, there was still time to disengage from the Polish alliance was not at all certain. The fact that France at the time, as we have shown, followed the "British line" seems obvious as most politicians of the time accepted. That the British, after years of often blind *appeasement,* finally took a firm stance appeared to meet with the wishes of the French. The final attempt by Georges Bonnet at the beginning of September 1939, therefore, appears futile. On two occasions he tried to avoid war despite the German aggression against Poland: 1) By encouraging Ciano on September 1 to pursue his conference project in spite of the fact that on August 31 the French government had deliberated before the aggression; and 2) On September 2 by trying to delay the ultimatum by forty-eight hours. It was the firm attitude of the British cabinet, encouraged by the House of Commons, that during the night of the 2nd to the 3rd led Ciano to give up and Bonnet to end his initiatives.

At 5 p.m. France was at war. Notwithstanding what was said later the French people were sad, yes, but determined. A volume to follow will show what happened to the millions of men that Gamelin wished to keep disengaged. It should be said that for this peaceful people war itself was a first defeat.

* * * *

As an afterword to this volume I shall quote Montesquieu in Chapter XVIII of *Grandeur et décadence des Romains.*

There are general causes whether moral or physical at work in every monarchy, elevating, maintaining or knocking it down; all the accidents are subjected to those causes; and if the fate of a battle, meaning a particular cause, destroyed a State, there existed a more general cause to have that State perish in the course of a single battle.

ABBREVIATIONS

ADAP	Akten zur deutschen auswärtigen Politik
CEP	Commission d'enquête parlementaire. Les événements survenus en France de 1933 à 1945.
DBFP	Documents on British Foreign Policy.
DDF	Documents diplomatiques français.
DDI	Documenti diplomatici italiani.
DGFP	Documents on German Foreign Policy (translation of the *ADAP*. We generally quote the original German texVol.)
FRUS	Foreign Relations of the United States.
JODP	Journal officiel. Débats parlementaires.
LJ	Livre jaune (français).
MAE	Archives du ministère des Affaires étrangerès.
RHDGM	*Revue d'histoire de la deuxième guerre mondiale*
RHMC	*Revue d'histoire moderne et contemporaine.*
SHA	Service historique de l'armée.
SHAA	Service historique de l'armée de l'air
SHM	Service historique de la marine.

NOTES

Important note: The current status of the French archives that are being reconstituted and reorganized makes it impossible to have a separate presentation of the sources. As the collection nears completion, a special volume with sources and bibliography will be published. We therefore invite the reader to consult the notes below to trace the sources of the articles and books used. *The asterisk (*) indicates the first mention of a book or article.*

INTRODUCTION

1. His main publications are: *From Wilson to Roosevelt: Foreign Policy of the United States, 1913–1945* (translation of *De Wilson à Roosevelt: politique étrangère des États-Unis, 1913–1945)* trans. by Nancy Lynn Roelker (London: Chatto and Windus 1964); *France and the United States: From the Beginnings to the Present* (translation of *La France et les États-Unis des origines à nos jours,* Paris: Seuil 1976) Chicago: University of Chicago Press, 1978; *Le Conflit de Trieste 1943–1954* (Brussels 1966); *Itinéraires: Idées, Hommes et Nations d'Occident xix–xx siècles* (Paris 1991); *La Grande Guerre des Français 1914-1918* (Paris: Perrin 1994); *L'Europe, histoire de ses Peuples* (Paris: Perrin 1990); *Clemenceau* (Paris: Fayard 1988); *Histoire diplomatique de 1919 à nos jours* (Paris: Dalloz, 10ed 1990); *Introduction to the History of International Relations,* with Pierre Renouvin, trans. by Mary Ilford (London: Pall Hall 1968); *L'Europe de 1815 à nos jours: vie politique et relations internationales* (Paris: PUF 1964); *La France et les Français, 1914–1920,* 2 vols (Paris 1973); *Tout Empire périra :une vision théorique des relations internationales* (Paris 1981); *L'Abîme, 1939–1945* (Paris 1982).
2. Cited in G. M. Young, *Victorian England: Portrait of an Age* (New York 1954), 155.
3. J. B. Duroselle, "L'Histoire des relations internationales vue par un historien," *Relations internationales,* 83, automne 1995, 296.
4. *Histoire des relations internationales,* tome 1 (Paris 1953) Introduction générale, (Paris 1953) xv.

5. Two standard texts published in the 1980s showed no awareness either of Annales or Renouvin's *Histoire des relations internationales.* F.R. Bridge and Roger Bullen, *The Great Powers and the European State System, 1815–1914* (London: Longman 1980); Graham Ross, *The Great Powers and the Decline of the European States System 1914–1945* (London: Longman 1983)

6. *Introduction to the History of International Relations* (London, 1968, viii).

7. *Relations internationales*, 83, automne 1995, 278.

8. With two exceptions: Anthony Adamthwaite, *France and the Coming of the Second World War* (London: Frank Cass 1977) and Robert J.Young, *In Command of France: French Foreign Policy and Military Planning 1933–1939* (1978). For my own work Renouvin allowed me advance access to the documents selected for publication in the series *Documents diplomatiques français 1932–1939.*

9. *France and the Nazi Threat*, 20.

10. Marc Bloch, *Strange Defeat* (New York: Norton & Company 1968), ix.

11. *France and the Nazi Threat*, 358.

12. O. H. Bullitt (ed.), *For the President: Personal and Secret* (London 1973), 308–10.

13. *Documents diplomatiques français 1932-1939*, 2 série, t. xiv, no. 248.

14. For strategy, intelligence and the mesentente cordiale see Martin S. Alexander, *The Republic in Danger: General Maurice Gamelin and the Politics of French Defense 1933–1940* (1992); Peter Jackson, *France and the Nazi Menace. Intelligence and Policy Making 1933–1939* (Oxford 2000); Martin Thomas, *Britain, France and Appeasement* (Berg 1996); Elisabeth Du Réau, *Édouard Daladier 1984–1970* (1993).

15. Robert Young, 3, 150.

16. *France and the Nazi Threat*, 20.

17. For this approach see Anthony Adamthwaite, *Grandeur and Misery: France's Bid for Power in Europe 1914–1940* (London Arnold 1995).

18. Valentine Lawford, *Bound for Diplomacy* (London 1963), 267–8.

19. Georges Bonnet, *Dans La Tourmente* (Paris 1971), 66–7.

PREFACE

1. *Le Temps*, 22 septembre 1931, quoted by Sauvy (Alfred), *Histoire économique de la France entre les deux guerres*, 1965-1972, Vol. II, p. 17.

2. *Sauvy, op. cit., Vol. I. p. 119.

3. Ibid., Vol. II, p. 28.

4. *Sieburg, Heinz Otto, *Deutschland und Frankreich in der Geschichtsschreibung des neunzehnten Jahrhunderts*, 2 Vols., 1954 and 1958.

5. *De Gaulle, General Charles, *Mémoires de guerre*, 1954–1959, Vol. I, *L'Appel*, p. 1.

6. See for instance *Olle-Laprune, Jacques, *La stabilité des ministres sous la Troisième République*, 1962.

7. *Nicolson, Harold, *Journal des années tragiques* (1936–1942), French translation, p. 227: English edition, *The War Years: 1939–1945, vol. 2, Diaries and Letters* (New York: 1967), p. 79.

8. *Herriot, Édouard, *Jadis*, 1952, Vol. II, p. 440.

9. Ibid., pp. 465–467.

10. Blum, Léon, *A l'échelle humaine*, 1946, p. 95.

11. *Bariéty, Jacques, *Les relations franco-allemandes après la première guerre mondiale*, Paris, Publications de la Sorbonne, 1977.

12. *Bérard, Armand, *Au temps du danger allemand*, 1975, pp. 371–372. Jean Paul-Boncour was his nephew.

13. *Noël, Léon, *Les illusions de Stresa*, 1976, p. 40.

14. Ibid., p. 46.

15. Ibid., p. 47.

16. *Szembek, Jan, *Journal. 1933–1939*, French translation. 1952, 21 May 1935, p. 87.

17. *Pertinax, *Les Fossoyeurs*, 1943, Vol. II, p.169.

18. Op. cit., pp. 50–51.

19. For instance in 1932, *Les doctrines monétaires à l'épreuve des faits* (where the names of Piétri, Flandin, and Rueff appear) and 1934, *L'Économie dirigée* (with Siegfried, Paul Reynaud, Mönick, and Gignoux).

20. Except for the ageing Joseph Caillaux for four days in 1935.

21. Sauvy, op. cit., Vol. I, p. 432.

22. See *Germain-Martin, *Le problème financier, 1930–1936*, where according to Sauvy the statistics are obscure and messy. Op. cit. Vol. I, p. 34.

23. *Romains, Jules, *Cela depend de nous*, 1939, p. 103.

24. Blum, Léon, *À l'echelle humaine*. op. cit.

25. *Piobetta, J.-B., *Le baccalauréat de l'enseignement secondaire*, doctoral dissertation, 1937.

26. Words used by the Greek diplomat Politis. See Chapter V.

27. *De Monzie, Anatole, *Ci-devant*, 1941, pp. 116–120. He knew him from the Collège Stanislas.

28. See Nicolson, op. cit., p. 195 (Eng. edition p. 44).

29. Loustaunau-Lacau, *Mémoires d'un français rebelle*, 1948, p. 57.

30. Title of a booklet he published in April 1935.

31. I spell Léger rather than Leger, because during the seven years this man, known by many different names, was heading the Quai d'Orsay, the *Annuaire* kept the accent. There is no scientific non-hagiographic biography of the man. The one in La Pléiade, *Saint-John Perse, Œuvres complètes, Paris 1972, XLII-1417 p. is an incomplete and totally flattering one. His former secretary Etienne de Crouy-Chanel wrote a nuanced and favorable portrait in *Le Monde* on September 9, 1980. One may argue about the "great capacity for work" by Léger. Very extensive conversations with foreign diplomats and

journalists. Almost no notes, instructions, practically no comments on cables, nor any synopsis of meetings held.

32. See *Chambrun, Charles de, *L'esprit de la diplomatie*, 1946.
33. *Morand, Paul, *Souvenirs d'un attaché d'ambassade*, p. 22.
34. *Auffray, Bernard, *Pierre de Margerie*, 1976, p. 254.
35. Morand, op. cit., p. 12.
36. *Chauvel, Jean, *Commentaires*, Vol. I, 1971, p. 42. See also *Hoppenot, Henri, *De Saint-John Perse à Alexis Léger* and *Saillet, Maurice, *Saint-John Perse, poéte de gloire*, suivi de *Un essai biographique d'Alexis Léger*.
37. Op. cit., p.22.
38. Op. cit., Vol. I, p. 44.
39. *Fabre-Luce, Alfred, *Journal de la France (1939–1944)*, 1969, quoted by Guyot, op. cit., p. 4.
40. Statement in Guyot, op. cit., p.6.
41. *Bonnet, Georges, *Dans la tourmente, 1938–1948*, 1971, p. 20. See Guyot, ibid.
42. Chauvel, op. cit., p. 45.
43. Chauvel, op. cit., p. 58.
44. For instance *Weiss, Louise, *Mémoires d'une Européenne*, Vol. II, p. 223; *Tabouis, Geneviève, *Ils m'ont appelée Cassandre*, 1942; *Bois, Paul-Elie, *Le malheur de la France*, 1941; *Allard, Paul, *Le Quai d'Orsay*, 1938.
45. Perinax, *Les Fossoyeurs*, Vol. I, pp. 293–294.
46. Ibid., p. 293.
47. Saint-John Perse, op. cit., pp. 605–614.
48. *Eden, Anthony, *Facing the Dictators*, 1962, p. 232.
49. *Gamelin, General Maurice, *Servir*, 1946–1947, 3 volumes.
60. *Le Goyet, Pierre, *Le mystère Gamelin*, 1977.
51. Le Goyet, op. cit., p. 17.
52. Ibid., p. 21.
53. Ibid., p. 64.

Chapter I
THE RETURN OF EDOUARD HERRIOT

1. *Jadis*, II, p. 294.
2. Sauvy, *Histoire économique de la France*, Op. cit. Vol. II, pp. 37–38. Sauvy somewhat exaggerates this unawareness of the economic upswing. During his speech in Potiers (where he traveled on October 30, 1932), Herriot was pleased about the improved economy, the reduction in unemployment and the increase in exports. See *Soulié, Michel, *Le vie politique d'Édouard Herriot*, 1962, p. 307.
3. *Jadis*, Vol. II, p. 301.

4. *Weygand, General Maxime, *Mémoires,* 1950, Vol. II, *Mirages et réalités,* pp. 388–389. The best work on Weygand during this period is *Bankwitz, Philip C., *Maxime Weygand and civil-military relations in modern France,* Harvard, 1968.

5. Frankenstein, Robert, "À propos des aspects financiers du réarmement français (1935–1939)," RHDGM, no. 107, April 1976, pp. 1–20.

6. I have offered the thought that he was an "innovator" in the collection of essays *Édouard Herriot, Études et témoignages,* 1975. I must admit that since then the dissertation by Jacques Bariéty, *Les relations franco-allemandes après la première guerre mondiale,* op. cit., appears to prove rather decisively Herriot's lack of seriousness at least in 1924.

7. *Jadis,* Vol. II, pp.287–367.

8. *Jadis,* Vol. II, p. 357.

9. *Jeanneney, J.-N., *François de Wendel en République,* 1976, p. 194.

10. Faure, Paul, *Le Populaire,* 24 May 1932, quoted in Soulié, *La vie politique d'Édouard Herriot,* op. cit., p. 356.

11. *Lapie, Pierre-Olivier, *Herriot,* 1967, pp. 305–324.

12. *Jeanneney, Jules, *Journal politique,* edited by Jeanneney, Jean-Noël, Paris, 1972, p. 9.

13. *Jadis,* p. 317.

14. *Jadis,* p. 322.

15. It is difficult to agree with Soulié, op. cit., p. 369, that "the Lausanne conference was a diplomatic success for Herriot."

16. This was actually the impression gained by the French financial attaché to Washington, Mönick, see DDF, 1, I, no. 97, 11 August 1932.

17. DDF, 1, I, no. 1, 2 July 1932.

18. DDF, 1, I, no. 16, 13 July 1932.

19. DDF, 1, I, no. 17, 13 July 1932.

20. DDF, 1, I, no. 20, 14 July 1932.

21. DDF, 1, I, no. 23, Laroche, Warsaw, 15 July 1932. See also no. 75, Cambon, 28 July 1932.

22. DDF, 1, I, no. 24, Arnal, 15 July 1932.

23. DDF, 1, I, no. 28, Arnal, 16 July 1932. See also no. 49, 21 July.

24. DDF, 1, I, no. 30, Note for distribution by Herriot, 17 July 1932.

25. DDF, 1, I, no. 59, François-Poncet, 25 July 1932.

26. DDF, 1, I, no. 31, Claudel, 17 July 1932.

27. Maurice Vaïsse, "Continuité et discontinuité dans la politique française en matière de désarmement (February 1932–June 1933): the example of control." *Colloque franco-allemand* of March 1977; and mostly in Maurice Vaïsse, *Sécurité d'abord. La politique française en matière de désarmement* (December 9, 1930–April 17, 1934), Paris 1981, 653 pages (Doctoral dissertation).

28. Herriot would repeat it in his governmental statement of June 7 JODP, *Chambre,* 7 June 1932, p. 2234.

29. *Castellan, Georges, *Le réarmement clandestin du Reich*, 1954. This excellent dissertation is based upon the opening of the archives of the *Deuxième Bureau*. To be complemented by W. Sauer "Die Reichswehr," in *K.D. Bracher ed. *Die Auflösung der Weimarner Republik*. My intent here is not the study of Germany's rearmament as it actually took place, but rather the subjective idea the French had of it. Vol. See *Edward Bennett *German Rearmament and the West 1932–1933*. Princeton, 1970.

30. See *Bariéty, Jacques, "Les relations internationales en 1932–1933," *Revue historique*, October-December 1967, pp. 347–364. *Bariéty J. and Bloch, Charles, "Une tentative de réconciliation franco-allemande en 1932-1933 et son échec," RHMC, July-September 1968, pp. 433–465.

31. DDF, 1, I, no. 46, Herriot to François-Poncet, 20 July 1932.

32. DDF, 1, I, no. 68, Herriot to François-Poncet, 27 July 1932.

33. Ibid., see Bariéty and Bloch, quoted article, p. 453. DBFP, Series B, III, nos. 148–150, 172, 175, 184. Herriot, *Jadis*, Vol. II, p. 321 sq. (who doesn't discuss those conversations that much).

34. See Weygand op. cit., p. 384, he states that the French government having received from von Neurath the proposal for direct negotiations on equal rights, sent Lieutenant Colonel de Lattre de Tassigny to Brittany where Weygand was vacationing to give him the text and bring back his answer.

35. Bariéty, quoted article, p. 351.

36. DDF, 1, I, no. 244, 14 Oct. 1932. Final text in ibid., no 331, 14 November 1932.

37. DDF, 1, I, no. 268, 22 October 1932.

38. Soulié, op. cit., attributes the French plan to him. Bariéty in his quoted article p. 353, shows that if Paul-Boncour discussed it with De Gaulle (see *Paul-Boncour, *Entre-deux-guerres*, 1946, Vol. II, pp. 228–229), nothing leads us to believe that he played a major part as his ideas in any case do not appear (there is no mention of "armored divisions").

39. DDF, 1, I, nos. 272 and 273.

40. DDF, 1, I, no. 286.

41. Quoted article, p. 352.

42. *Entre-deux-guerres*, Vol. II, p 223.

43. As Bülow told François-Poncet, DDF, 1, II, no. 2, 15 November 1932.

44. DDF, 1, II, nos. 3 and 4, 16 November 1932.

45. DDF, 1, II, no. 5, Conversations between M. Massigli and Norman Davis, 16 November.

46. DDF, 1, II, no. 6.

47. DDF, 1, II, nos. 25, 33 (25 November) 39 (26 November).

48. DDF, 1, II, no. 59, Note from the French delegation, 2 December 1932.

49. DDF, 1, II, no. 60, 3 December 1932.

50. Paul-Boncour, *Entre-deux-guerres*, Vol. II, p. 231.

51. DDF, 1, II, no. 71, 6 December 1932.

52. *Humanité*, 2 Feb. 1932. See *Schumacher, Aloïs, *La politique de sécurité française face à l'Allemagne. Les controverses de l'opinion française entre 1932 et 1935*, 1972.

53. Ibid., 7 February 1932.

54. See. Speech by Gabriel Péri in the Chamber, JODP, *Chambre*, 28 October 1932, p. 2931.

55. All these figures come from *Bonnefous, Édouard, *Histoire politique de la III République*, 1959–1962, Vol. V, pp. 119–120.

56. Article by Pertinax, *Écho de Paris*, 19 July 1932.

57. See Pertinax, ibid., 15 November 1932.

58. 16 January 1933.

59. See DDF, 1, I, no. 125, 25 August 1932.

60. Schumacher, op. cit., p. 114.

61. Besides JODP, see comments by Bonnefous, op. cit., pp. 130–131. Schumacher, op. cit., p. 103–104. Soulié, op. cit., pp. 394–395.

62. For this study we were able to use an important unpublished work by *Schram, Stuart, *Les relations franco-soviétiques de 1924 à 1939* (Fondation nationale des Sciences politiques). This work is based on definitive research from published Russian and German documents and most of all a very detailed research of the archives of the Quai d'Orsay by Mrs. Anna Hogenhuis-Seliverstoff. We have personally also consulted those archives. See also *Scott, William E., *Alliance Against Hitler*, 1962 a work written without the benefit of the French archives but that actually sticks very close to the facts.

63. DDF, 1, I, no. 38, Dejean, 19 July 1932.

64. DDF, 1, I, no. 42, 20 July 1932. See also MAE, D. no. 103, Dejean.

65. DDF, 1, I, no. 3, Report by the French delegation at Geneva, 9 July 1932.

66. MAE, T. no. 352–355, de Martel, 8 July 1932.

67. On this issue see also specifically DDF, 1, I, no. 61 (25 July) 66 (27 July), 134 (1 September), 176 (14 September) 212 (24 September) 251 (19 October) 314 (9 November).

68. DDF, 1, I, no. 74, Note to the President of the Council, 28 July 1932.

69. On this issue see the work by de Castellan, G., "Reichswehr et Armée rouge," in *Duroselle, J.-B., ed., *Les relations germano-soviétiques*, 1954. See also, regarding Marshal Tukhachevsky's trip to Germany, end of September 1932, DDF, 1, I, no. 217, Chautemps Minister of the Interior to Herriot, 28 September 1932.

70. T. II, pp. 354–355.

71. DDF, 1, II, no. 29, Department Note for the President of the Council, 23 November 1932. See Scott, op. cit., p. 67.

72. DDF, 1, II, no. 48, 29 November 1932.

73. DDF, 1, II, no. 53, François-Poncet, 1 December 1932. See. Scott, op. cit, pp. 72–73.

74. The most complete dissertation by *Artaud, Denise, "Le problème de dettes de guerre de la France," 1976, stops in 1929 but is very useful to understand

the resolution of this problem. I have attempted to explain the American point of view in J. B. Duroselle, *De Wilson à Roosevelt*, 1961. See also for 1931, *Bennett, Edward W., *Germany and the Diplomacy of the Financial Crisis, 1931*, 1962.

75. DDF, 1, I, no. 297, Germain-Martin to Herriot, 4 November 1932. See also no. 302 (5 November).
76. DDF, 1, I, no. 316, Herriot to Claudel, 10 November 1932.
77. DDF, 1, II, no. 10, Claudel, 18 November 1932.
78. DDF, 1, II, no. 27, Note from the United States Government, 23 November 1932.
79. DDF, 1, II, no. 45, Note from the Service du mouvement général des fonds, 28 November 1932.
80. JODP, Chambre, 12 December 1932.
81. Soulié, op. cit., p. 413.
82. Op. cit., p. 324.

Chapter II
THE YEAR OF PAUL-BONCOUR

1. *Entre-deux-guerres*, Vol. II, p. 122.
2. Soulié, op. cit., p. 416.
3. Besides our own press clippings we also consulted for this work: *Grosser, Alfred, *Hitler, la presse et la naissance d'une dictature*, 1959 (Kiosque Collection); *d'Hoop, J.M., "Frankreichs Reaction auf Hitlers Aussenpolitik 1933–1939," *Geschichte in Wissenschaft und Unterricht* 1964, Vol. IV; *Micaud, Charles, *La droite française face à l'Allemagne*, English edition 1943; *Hörling, Hans, "L'opinion française face à l'avénement d'Hitler au pouvoir," Francia, 1975, Vol. III, p. 584–641, with a good bibliography; *Kimmel, A. *Der Aufsteig des Nazional-sozialsmus im Spiegel der französischen Presse 1930–1933*, Bonn, 1963; and the Master's thesis by Miss Geneviève Bureau *Les premières reactions françaises à l'avènement d'Hitler*, janvier à mars 1933.
4. DDF, 1, I, no. 216, De La Forest-Divonne to Paul-Boncour, Minister of War, 27 September 1932.
5. DDF, 1, I, no. 218.
6. DDF, 1, II, no. 111, François-Poncet, 15 December 1932.
7. DDF, 1, II, no. 144, François-Poncet, 29 December 1932.
8 . See Bureau, G., op. cit.
9. See Hörling, Hans, op. cit.
10. Rosenfeld, Oreste, *Populaire*, 5 February 1933.
11. *Humanité*, 30 January 1933.
12. *Temps*, 1 February 1933.
13. *Europe nouvelle*, "Triomphe du nationalisme en Allemagne," 11 March 1933.

14. *Populaire*, 1 February 1933.
15. See Micaud, op. cit.
16. *La Victoire*, 31 January. 1933.
17. *Quest-Éclair*, 10 February 1933.
18. Regarding this issue, which is not my concern, I recommend a very good work by *Hildebrand, Klaus "La politique française de Hitler jusqu'en 1936," *Colloque franco-allemand* of March 1977; to be completed by *Knipping, Franz, "Frankreich in Hitlers Aussenpolitik, 1933–1939," in *Funke, M., ed., Hitler, Deutschland und die Mächte, Düsseldorf 1976. See also *Jäckel, Eberhard *Frankreich in Hitlers Europa. Die deutsche Frankreich-politik in Zweiten Weltkrieg,* 1966.
19. Hildebrand, op. cit., p. 7.
20. Quoted by Hildebrand, op. cit., p. 1.
21. *Seydoux, François, *Mémoires d'Outre-Rhin*, 1975, p. 53.
22. Bérard, op. cit., p. 100.
23. See mainly DDF, 2nd series, Vol. II, no. 165 (T. of 6 May 1936).
24. *Stehlin, General Paul, *Témoignage pour l'histoire*, 1964, p 44 sq. Stehlin mistakenly places this event at the end of April. The meeting took place on May 28.
25. See DDF, ibid., no. 271 (Note from the political section, June 4, 1936: "Should the presence in Berlin of the head of operations of the Italian Air Ministry, encountered in Berlin on May 28 in the company of the head of the French and Italian section of the German Ministry of Aeronautics be considered a simple exchange of courtesies…?").
26. DDF, 2nd series, I, no. 351. Mr. Léon Noël says that *Mein Kampf* was rarely mentioned at the Quai d'Orsay. Mr. Degros, who was the curator of the library at the time, remembers that the book was very much in demand.
27. DDF, 2nd series, I, no. 457 (D. of 18 March 1936).
28. DDF, 2nd series, I, no. 457 (D. du 18 March 1936).
29. DDF, 2nd series, II, no. 387 (T. du 4 July 1936).
30. DDF, 2nd series, II, no. 455 (D. du 15 July 1936).
31. DDF, 2nd series, II, 21 December 1936.
32. DDF, 2nd series, I, 27 February 1936.
33. DDF, 2nd series, II, 21 December 1936.
34. CEP, Vol. I, p. 89. It appears to have been the same for the British according to *Rowse, *All Souls and Appeasement*, 1961, p. 31. He points to Vanisttart and the great historian Namier as the exceptions.
35 Kimmel, A., op. cit., p. 19-21 and Schumacher, A., op. cit., p. 178.
36. Herriot, Edouard, *Jadis*, Vol. II, p. 399 (March 1934).
37. *Gauché, General, *Le deuxième bureau au travail* (1935–1940), 1953, p. 32.
38. He only mentions it twice in his book written during the German occupation *Entre-deux-guerres*, Vol. II, p. 361: "That amazing *Mein Kampf* where never a head of state had warned his future victims so precisely." And Vol. III,

p. 116: "Then it was Poland's turn...It was written all over the map and in *Mein Kampf*."

39. All these movements were examined in detail by *Delbreil, Jean-Claude, *Les catholiques français et les tentatives de rapprochement franco-allemand (1920–1933)*, Metz, 1972.

40. 14 October 1930. Quoted in Delbreil, op. cit., p. 178.

41. *De Pange, Jean, *Journal*, 1964, Vol. II, p. 306.

42. L'Huillier, Fernand, *Dialogues franco-allemands, 1925–1933*, 1971.

43. See *Bariety, J., *Bulletin de la Société d'histoire moderne*, 1969, no. 2. *Schlumberger J., Meyer, Robert and Rieben, Henri, *Émile Mayrisch, précurseur de la construction de l'Europe*, Lausanne, 1967.

44. Bariéty and Bloch, quoted article, p. 444.

45. Bariéty and Bloch, quoted article, p. 456. Duchemin drafted a note, which he send to Bücher. See *ADAP*, C, I, 1, No. 2, January 30, 1933. Von Neurath was very much opposed. See *ADAP*, CI, 1, no. 18, Neurath to Vice-chancellor von Papen, February 9, 1933. Bülow informed him of his opposition to Köster, ambassador to Paris, ADAP, I, 1, no. 19, 10 February 1933.

46. DDF, 1, II, no. 212, François-Poncet, 19 January 1933.

47. DDF, 1, II, no. 358, Paul-Boncour to Massigli, 1 March 1933, and 364, Massigli, 2 March 1933.

48. DDF, 1, II, no. 290, Note by Massigli, 11 February 1933.

49. DDF, 1, II, no. 356, 28 February 1933.

50. DDF, 1, II, no. 381, Massigli, 8 March 1933.

51. DDF, 1, II, no.409. Note to the Minister of 14 March 1933. However, it is not mentioned when Macdonald and Simon met with Daladier and Paul-Boncour in Paris on their way back from Rome on 21 March 1933. See DBFP, 2,V, no. 46 21 March 1933. There is no French synopsis.

52. DDF, 1, II, no 378, François-Poncet to Paul-Boncour, 7 March 1933.

53. DDF, 1, III, François-Poncet, 22 March 1933.

54. Hildebrand, quoted article, p. 16, *Jacobsen, O.A., "Deutschland 1933-1945," in *Hauser, O., *Weltpolitik*, 1932–1939, p. 262.

55. DDF, 1, III, no. 105, François-Poncet to Paul-Boncour, 8 April 1933. See ADAP, C, I, 1, no. 163, note from Bülow, 12 April 1933.

56. DDF, 1, II, no. 418, Franco-British conversation of 11 March 1933 (between Daladier and Paul-Boncour, Macdonald and Sir John Simon).

57. *Temps*, 3 March 1933, quoted by Vaïsse, Maurice, "Continuité et discontinuité dans la politique française en matière de désarmement... l'exemple du contrôle," op. cit., *Colloque franco-allemand* of March 1977.

58. Vaïsse, T. quoted, DDF, 1, III, no 229. Instructions générales du Conseil des ministres, 2 May 1933. Daladier Papers (Fondation nationale des sciences politiques).

59. DDF, 1, III, 8 June 1933 (with Eden and Norman Davis. See DBFP, 2, V, no. 207, 9 June 1933).

60. See in Hildebrand, op. cit., for an interesting analysis of Hitler's "French policy." It may be that he believed a long-term Franco-German rapprochement could be possible at that time.

61. DDF, 1, III, no. 314, François-Poncet, 23 May 1933.

62. We should point out that on 16 March 1933 German chargé d'affaires Braun von Stumm had sent a message from de Brinon to whom Daladier had suggested he meet either von Neurath or von Papen for Easter on the Riviera or the Swiss lakes. François-Poncet had not been told of this. ADAP, C, I, 1, no. 92.

63. See Hildebrand, op. cit., and *Michilka, *Ribbentrop und die deutsche Englandpolitik*, p.68 sq. The idea actually came from Henderson who was president of the Disarmament conference on a "pilgrimage" around Europe in an attempt to revive it and promoting a conversation between Daladier and Hitler, see DDF, 1, IV, no. 16, François-Poncet to Paul-Boncour, 19 July 1933. The Germans were so full of praise of Daladier to the point that embassy councilor Forster recommended toning down the German press to avoid creating internal problems for himself. ADAP, C, II, 1, no. 27, 25 October 1933.

64. DDF, 1, IV, no. 215, François-Poncet, 15 September 1933. See ADAP, C, I, 2, no. 430, note by von Neurath, 15 September 1933.

65. G. Castellan, op. cit. See also *Diest, Wilhelm, "Le problème du réarmement allemand dans les années 1933–1936," *Colloque franco-allemand* of March 1977. See DBFP, 2V, no. 399. Conversations between Eden and Paul-Boncour in Paris on September 18, 1935, showing the increasing worry of the French and ibid., no. 406. Simon met with Daladier and Paul-Boncour in Paris on September 22, 1933, no. 407. With Norman Davis.

66. DDF, 1, IV, nos. 181, 5 September, and 182, 6 September 1933.

67. DDF, 1, V, no. 64, note by the French delegation, 30 November 1933.

68. DDF, 1, IV, no. 307, Arnal, 14 October 1933.

69. Paul-Boncour, *Entre-deux-guerres*, Vol. II, p. 338; Léon Noël, *Les illusions de Stresa*, p. 20.

70. *Entre-deux-guerres*, ibid.

71. *Entre-deux-guerres*, Vol. II, p. 141. See the book Jouvenel had just published in 1932: *Jouvenel, Henry de, *La paix française*, p. 203 sq. See the opinion of Sir R. Graham, the British ambassador to Rome. DBFP, 2, V, no. 37, 4 March 1933.

72. DDF, 1, II, no. 182, note from the Sub-Section of Africa-Levant, 10 January 1933, with 7 annexes.

73. DDF, 1, II, no. 288, 10 February 1933.

74. DDF, 1, II, no. 368, Jouvenel, 3 March 1933. See also no. 382, 8 March 1933.

75. DDF, 1, II, no. 427, Jouvenel, 17 March 1933, and III, no. 2, 18 March 1933. The plan originated with the British in pT. See *Jarausch, Konrad H., *The Four Power Pact 1933*, 1966, a book written with British and German but not French documents.

76. DDF, 1, III, no. 2, Jouvenel, 18 March 1933.

77. DDF, 1, III, no. 3, 18 March 1933.
78. Jarausch, op. cit., p. 83–89.
79. DDF, 1, III, no. 12, Jouvenel, 20 March 1933.
80. DDF, 1, III, no. 357, François-Poncet, 4 June 1933.
81. *Entre-deux-guerres*, Vol. II, p. 339. Léon Noël, for his part, believes in Léger's Italophobia. (op. cit., p. 41).
82. DDF, 1, III, no. 38, Massigli to Léger, 24 March 1933.
83. DDF, 1, III, no. 44, Jouvenel.
84. Poland and Czechoslovakia.
85. Yugoslavia and Romania.
86. DDF, 1, III, no. 48, Note by the French delegation at the disarmament conference of 25 March 1933. The final French text in no. 108, 10 April 1933.
87. DDF, 1, III, no. 62.
88. DDF, 1, III, no. 55.
89. DDF, 1, III, no. 84, Laroche to Paul-Boncour, 4 April 1933.
90. DDF, 1 III, no. 62, Paul-Boncour to Jouvenel, 29 March 1933.
91. DDF, 1, III, no. 354, Corbin, 3 June 1933.
92. DDF, 1, III, no. 362, Jouvenel, 6 June 1933.
93. MAE, T. no. 666, Jouvenel.
94. DDF, 1, IV, no. 1, 16 July 1933.
95. DDF, 1, III, no. 415, 22 June 1933.
96. MAE, Léger papers, letter dated 12 June 1933.
97. *Entre-deux-guerres*, Vol. II, p. 362–363.
98. We are using much of the unpublished work by Schram, quoted above.
99. *Monzie, Anatole de, *Du Kremlin au Luxembourg*, 1924.
100. *Monzie, Anatole de, *Petit manuel de la Russie nouvelle*, 1931.
101. Herriot says so already in the book he published at the start of 1933, *Herriot, Édouard, *La France dans le monde*, 1933, p. 9.
102. JODP, Chambre, 16 May 1933. See Duclos J., *Mémoires*, Vol. l.
103. DDF, 1, II, François-Poncet, 1 March 1933.
104. DDF, 1, III, no 235, 3 May 1933.
105. Schram, op. cit.
106. DDF, 1, III, no. 98, note from the political director (Coulondre), 4 April 1933.
107. DDF, 1, III, no. 404, 18 June 1933.
108. DDF, 1, III, no. 391, Alphand, 14 June 1933.
109. Schram, op. cit., who had access to the private papers of Mendras. See also Scott, op. cit., p. 106.
110. DDF, 1, III, no. 487, 14 July, and 488, 15 July 1933.
111. Herriot met with Litvinov. See DDF, I, IV, nos. 195, 10 September 1933, and 204, 12 September 1933.
112. DDF, 1, III, no. 358, Cot to Daladier, 4 June 1933.
113. DDF, 1, IV, no. 308, Cot to Paul-Boncour, 14 October 1933.

114. DDF, 1, IV, no. 136, Protocol by Raymond Patenôtre and M.G. Gourevitch, 23 August.

115. DDF, 1, IV, no. 395, Alphand, 5 November 1933.

116. DDF, 1, IV, no. 156, Colonel Mendras to Georges Leygues, Minister of Marine, 1 August 1933.

117. La "air mission," planned by Pierre Cot, was approved on 23 October par Paul-Boncour, DDF, 1, IV, no. 354, 23 October 1933.

118. DDF, 1, V, note from the subsection for commercial relations, 9 January 1934.

119. DDF, 1, IV, no. 251, 27 September 1933. See. Scott, op. cit., chap. VII, pp. 130–152.

120. DDF, 1, V, note from the Department, 4 January 1934.

121. Sauvy, op. cit., Vol. II, p. 564.

122. DDF, 1, II, no. 125, 20 December 1932.

123. DDF, 1, II, no. 161, 5 January 1933.

124. DDF, 1, II, no. 185, Claudel, 11 January 1933.

125. DDF, 1, II, no. 221, 21 January 1933. See also the visit paid by Mönick to Walter E. Edge U.S. ambassador to Paris, ibid., no. 232. Note of 24 January 1933 from the political directorate on the debt situation and comments by Jacques Rueff regarding the meager chances of success of those negotiations. Ibid., no. 271, Rueff to Georges Bonnet, Minister of Finance, 7 February 1933.

126. DDF, 1, II, no. 256, Paul-Boncour to Claudel, 3 February 1933.

127. DDF, 1, II, no. 315, Paul-Boncour to Claudel, 17 February 1933.

128. DDF, 1, II, nos. 317 and 318, Claudel, 18 February 1933.

129. DDF, 1, II, no. 326. Note from the deputy director of commercial affairs, 20 February 1933. See also no. 397. Note from Rist and Parmentier regarding the meetings of experts on 9 and 20 January, 1933 that mentions "the unanimous good will welcoming the project of establishing a common monetary fund."

130. See Herriot, Jadis, Vol. II, pp. 362, 364.

131. Jadis, Vol. II, p. 366. See also DDF, 1, III, no 195, Herriot to Paul-Boncour, 27 April 1933. Regarding the very good personal relationship between Roosevelt and Herriot, see *Mönick, Emmanuel, Pour mémoire, 1970, pp. 140–143.

132. DDF, 1, III, no. 180, Paul-Boncour (distribution memo), 25 April 1933.

133. DDF, 1, III, no. 341, Laboulaye, 1 June 1933.

134. DDF, 1, III, no. 417, Coulondre, London, 22 June 1933.

135. DDF, 1, III, no. 436, Bonnet to Paul-Boncour, 30 June 1933.

136. In a communication to the Académie des sciences morales et politiques of January 1935.

137. DDF, 1, IV, no. 169, Paul-Boncour to François-Poncet, 2 September 1933.

Chapter III
The Barthou Era

1. See the recollections of Lucien Lamoureux in Bonnefous, op. cit., Vol. V, p. 217. See also p. 214.
2. 10 February 1934.
3. Edited by his friend Georges Lamiraut.
4. There is no good biography of Barthou. Only *Bertaut, Jules, *Louis Barthou*, Paris, no date, 1918; *Aubert, D., *Louis Barthou*, Paris, 1935; *Herzog, Wilhelm, *Barthou*, Zurich, 1938.
5. *Barthou, Louis, *Le Politique*, Paris, 1933, see pp. 15–16. (See in the same series *Cambon, Jules, *Le Diplomate*.)
6. Recollection by Mrs. Gaston Doumergue, quoted by Bonnefous, Édouard, op. cit., Vol. V, pp. 214–215.
7. See the pamphlet by *Daudet, Léon, *Le garde des Sceaux Louis Barthou*, Paris, 1930.
8. See *Wormser, Georges, *La présidence de Poincaré*, 1976.
9. *Donnay, Maurice, *Discours prononcés...pour la réception de M. Louis Barthou* (at the Académie française, 6 February 1919), Paris 1919.
10. JODP, Chambre, 2 September 1933.
11. *Barthou, Louis, *Promenades autour de ma vie. Lettres de La Montagne*, Paris 1933, see p. 27.
12. Paul-Boncour, op. cit., Vol. II, p. 370.
13. *Hymans, Paul, *Mémoires*, 1958, Vol. II, p. 682.
14. DDF, 1 V, no. 463, 5 March 1934. See also Herzog, *Barthou*, pp. 94–95.
15. DDF, 1, VI, no. 283, 4 June 1934.
16. Op. cit., Vol. II, p. 357.
17. MAE. Communiqué from the Minister's Cabinet, 11 July 1934. Transcript of the Franco-British meeting in London, 9–10 July 1934.
18. JODP, Chambre, 25 March 1920, pp. 711–718.
19. Chap. VII.
20. DDF, 1, V, no. 34, 20 November 1933.
21. DDF, 1, V, no. 47, François-Poncet, 23 November 1933.
22. DDF, 1, V, no. 66, Paul-Boncour to Corbin.
23. DDF, 1, V, no. 73, Paul-Boncour to Corbin, 3 December 1933.
24. DDF, 1, V, no. 76, Viénot to Massigli, 3 December 1933.
25. DDF, 1, V, no. 201, 6 January 1934.
26. DDF, 1, V, no. 411, Pétain to Barthou, 20 February 1934. See also the important note from Army High Command.
27. See the collection *Négociations relatives à la reduction et à la limitation des armements*...14 October 1933–17 April 1934.
28. DDF, 1, III, no. 296, Distribution memo from Daladier, 30 January 1934.

29. DDF, 1, III, no. 303, Note from the French Service at the League of Nations.

30. DDF, 1, III, no. 367, Note from the French Service at the League of Nations, 31 January 1934.

31. DDF, 1 III, no. 376, Note from the French Service at the League of Nations, 12 February 1934, and DDF, 1, III, no. 391, 15 February 1934.

32. DDF, 1, V, no. 465, Notes concerning disarmament.

33. DDF, 1, V, ibid.

34. DDF, 1, V, no. 477, Note from the Vice-President of the Superior War Council, 8 March 1934.

35. Weygand explained his struggle against the compromise in *Mémoires*, Vol. II, *Mirages et réalités*, pp. 417–424. His account is confirmed in the archives.

36. François-Poncet, André, *Souvenirs d'une ambassade à Berlin*, 1946, pp. 175–176.

37. DDF, 1, VI, no. 93, Transcript of the meeting of 14 April 1934 (pp. 220–237).

38. *Souvenirs d'une ambassade à Berlin*, p. 162 sq.

39. DDF, 1, VI, no. 98, 16 April 1934.

40. DDF, 1, VI, no. 97, 16 April 1934.

41. DDF, 1, VI, no. 104, 17 April 1934. See also no. 105, Note by the Minister regarding his conversation with Sir Ronald Campbell, where the government's unanimity is mentioned "from Mr. Louis Marin to Messers. Marquet and Edouard Herriot."

42. François-Poncet, op. cit., p. 179.

43. Eden, op. cit., p. 89, says that Barthou led Campbell to believe that he would have been placed in the minority. This appears to be completely mistaken.

44. DDF, 1, VI, no. 254, Massigli to the ministry, Geneva, 30 May 1934.

45. Ibid., no. 268, François-Poncet, 1 June 1934.

46. Hymans, op. cit., p. 968 and 983.

47. DDF, 1, VI, no. 269, Massigli, Geneva, 1 June 1934.

48. DDF, 1, IV, no. 113, Chambrun.

49. Ibid.

50. Regarding Hungarian ambitions see *Zsigmond, L., "La politique extérieure de la Hongrie de 1933 to 1939", RHDGM, no. 62, April 1966, p. 7–18; *Adam, Magda, "Les pays danubiens et Hitler (1933–1936)", ibid. no.98, April 1975, pp. 1–26. Regarding Romanian policy *Giurescu, Dinu, "La diplomatie roumaine et le Pacte des Quatre," *Revue roumaine d'histoire*, 1969, 1, pp.77–102; *Deutsch, L., "The Foreign Policy of Romania and the dynamics of Peace (1932–1936)," ibid., 1966, 1, pp. 121–132; *Campus, Eliza, "Nicolae Titulescu et la politique pour le maintien de l'intégrité territoriale de la Roumanie," ibid., 1966, 3, pp. 441–469. All these articles are based on the archives of the countries concerned.

51. DDF, 1, IV, no. 180, Chambrun, 5 September 1933.

52. Adam, quoted above, p. 10.

53. Campus, quoted article, pp. 450–451.

54. See DDF, 1, V, no. 13, Chambrun, 15 November 1933.

55. See his book, *Laroche, Jules, *La Pologne de Pilsudski, Souvenirs d'une Ambassade, 1926–1935*, 1953. "Mr. Beck takes on some mysterious airs," as he mentions in his telegram of 17 July, DDF, 1, IV, no. 3.

56. *Noël, Léon, *L'agression allemande contre la Pologne*, 1946, p. 104, and his last book, *La Pologne entre deux mondes*, Sorbonne, 1984.

57. Charles Bloch was able to prove that those rumors were baseless. See his article *Bloch, Charles "La place de la France dans les différents stades de la politique extériuere du troisième Reich (1933–1940)," *Les relations franco-allemandes*, pp. 19–31. See p. 19.

58. See the conversation between Belgian Minister Hymans and Paul-Boncour and Léger on 25 September 1933. Hymans, Paul, *Mémoires*, Vol. II, pp. 943–944. And that of the American diplomat Norman Davis with Paul-Boncour on September 19, DDF, 1, IV, no. 229, 19 September 1933.

59. François-Poncet, op. cit., p. 165.

60. DDF, 1, IV, Laroche, 2 November 1933. See also no 417, 10 November.

61. DDF, 1, V, no. 19, François-Poncet, 16 November 1933.

62. DDF, 1, V, no. 44, 22 November 1933.

63. DDF, 1, V, no. 282, Noël, 28 January 1934.

64. DDF, 1, V, no. 278, 27 January 1934.

65. DDF, 1, V, no. 288, Laroche 29 January. 1934.

66. *Van Zuylen, Pierre, *Les Mains libres*, p. 262.

67. Pierre Renouvin summed up those sometimes Byzantine debates very clearly in his article "La Belgique vue par les diplomats français à l'avènement de Leopold III," *Les relations franco-belges de 1830 à 1934*, pp. 349–357.

68. Van Zuylen, op. cit., p. 276.

69. DDF, 1, VI, no. 41, summary, 27 March 1934. See *Documents diplomatiques belges, 1920–1940*, Vol. III, no. 121.

70. DDF, 1, VI, no. 90, 13 April 1934.

71. DDF, 1, VI, no. 133, Laroche to MAE, 24 April; no. 139, id., 26 April.

72. DDF, 1, VI, no. 151, Léon Noël to MAE, 28 April 1934.

73. DDF, 1, VI, no. 299, Barthou to Corbin.

74. DDF, 1, VI, no. 362, Puaux to MAE, 20 June 1934.

75. DDF, 1, VI, no. 366, Note for the political directorate.

76. DDF, 1, VI, no. 472, d'Ormesson, 16 July 1934.

77. DDF, 1, VI, no. 432, Naggiar, 5 July 1934.

78. DDF, 1, V, no. 458, 3 March 1934.

79. DDF, 1, VI, no. 54, 30 March 1934.

80. DDF, 1, VI, no. 54, 28 April 1934.

81. *Jadis*, Vol. II, p. 401.

82. Op. cit., p. 167. See also Cameron, E., quoted article, p. 385.

83. Transcript in DDF, 1, VI, no. 221.

84. DDF, 1, no. 431, Laroche, 5 July 1934.

85. MAE, communiqué from the Minister's Cabinet, summary of the Franco-British meeting in London on 9–10 July 1934, 17 July 1934.

86. MAE, T. from Monicault the chargé d'affaires in Prague, 10 August 1934.

87. MAE, T. from Naggiar, 25 August 1934.

88. DDF, 1, VI, no. 278, Note from the political directorate. Proposal for an oriental pact, 3 June 1934.

89. DDF, 1, VI, no. 309, Communication from the Department to the People's Commissar…Regional Assistance Treaty, 8 June 1934.

90. DDF, 1, VI, no. 368, Arnal, chargé d'affaires in Berlin, to Barthou, 21 June 1934.

91. DDF, 1, VI, no. 395, Arnal to Barthou, 27 June 1934.

92. MAE, T. from Bressy, chargé d'affaires in Warsaw, 3 October 1934.

93. MAE, T. from Payart to Barthou, 20 August 1934.

94. Eden, *Facing the Dictators*, p. 99.

95. DDF, 1, VI, no. 338, Corbin, 14 June 1934.

96. DDF, 1, VI, no. 457, Note from the French service at the League of Nations, 11 July 1934, and above all the MAE, communiqué from the Minister's Cabinet, 9–10 July 1934.

97. MAE communiqué from the Minister's Cabinet, 9–10 July 1934. We did not follow the exact order of the answers within a rather confused conversation nor did we distinguish between the debates of 9 and 10 July that are in any case very similar.

98. DDF, 1, VI, no. 488, 20 July 1934.

99. DDF, 1, VI, nos. 407, 408, 409, Arnal, chargé d'affaires, 30 June 1934; 418, Aimé Leroy, chargé of the legation in Munich, 3 July.

100. DDF, 1, VI, no. 417, François-Poncet, 3 July 1934. Bülow suggested to Röhm to take advantage of a reception at the embassy of Argentina to meet François-Poncet, ADAP, C, II, 1, no. 412, 26 January 1933.

101. DDF, 1, VI, no. 420, François-Poncet, 4 July 1934. He was informed by Major Réa, deputy military attaché

102. DDF, 1, VI, nos. 423, 4 July and 430, 5 July 1934. "Absurd, a fairy tale," said von Neurath. See ADAP, C, III, 1, no. 97. Léger to Köster, 18 July 1934. See also no. 64, Note from von Neurath, 5 July 1934.

103. DDF, 1, VI, no. 448, 8 July 1934.

104. DDF, 1, VI, no. 450, 9 July 1934.

105. DDF, 1, VI, no. 461, Corbin, 12 July 1934.

106. MAE, T. from Barthou in Rome, 31 July 1934.

107. Barthou used these words in August 1934, in speaking with the Swiss newsman Wilhelm Herzog. See Herzog, op. cit., pp. 93–95.

108. Scott, op. cit., p. 173.

109. DBFP, VI, 875–876, 893, 2 August 1934; VII, 717–718, 10 August 1934. Scott, op. cit., pp. 198–199.

110. Quoted in Scott, op. cit., p. 201.

111. Laroche, op. cit., p 171.
112. Article by Marcel Cachin, *Humanité*, 22 February 1934.
113. *Humanité*, 16 April 1934.
114. *Humanité*, Gabriel Péri, 25 May 1934.
115. *Humanité*, Gabriel Péri, 19 May 1934.
116. *Humanité*, Gabriel Péri, 27 May 1934.
117. *Humanité*, Gabriel Péri, 2 June 1934.
118. *Humanité*, Gabriel Péri, 8 June 1934.
119. *Humanité*, Gabriel Péri, 10 July 1934.
120. *Humanité*, Gabriel Péri, 18 July 1934.
121. See in particular the articles by M.M. (Monmousseau), *Humanité*, 4 September 1934; by André Marty, "Victoire éclatante," ibid., 8 September 1934; and Marcel Cachin, ibid., 9 September.
122. *Humanité*, 5 October 1934.
123. *Humanité*, 9 October 1934. See also his article of 10 September where one paragraph was captioned "Barthou 1922 and Barthou 1934."
124. *Humanité*, 14 October 1934.
125. *Populaire*, 13 July 1934.
126. *Populaire*, O.R. (Oreste Rosenfeld), 31 August 1934. See also a leaflet published on 17 August denouncing the "sabotage of peace" by the National Bloc and the "abandonment of the policy of enetente and international collaboration within the league of Nations."
127. *Figaro*, 10 September 1934.
128. *Figaro*, 14 September 1934.
129. *Homme Libre*, 24 May 1934. See also Pierre Dominique in *La République* on the same day.
130. *Œuvre*, 4 and 29 July 1934.
131. *Œuvre*, 21 July 1934.
132. *Œuvre*, 1 August 1934.
133. *Œuvre*, 4 September 1934. See also 22 September.
134. *Œuvre*, 16 September 1934.
135. *Figaro*, 24 April 1934.
136. See his book: *Le triomphe des bolcheviks et la paix de Brest-Litovsk. Souvenirs 1917–1918.*
137. *Figaro*, 8 August 1934.
138. *Petit Journal*, 16 September 1934.
139. *Figaro*, 11 August 1934.
140. See in particular *Figaro*, 27 March 1934: "Une grave menace pour la paix internationale."
141. See the editorial by d'Ormesson, "Le Pacte oriental," 12 July 1934.
142. Ibid., id., 4 September 1934.
143. Ibid., id., 12 September 1934.
144. *Écho de Paris*, 16 September 1934.

145. See in particular *Écho de Paris*, 10 July 1934 and 13 September 1934.
146. Ibid., 19 July 1934.
147. *Écho de Paris*, 16 September 1934.
148. *Écho de Paris*, 18 August and 7 September 1934.
149. *Écho de Paris*, 8 August 1934.
150*Matin*, Henry de Korab, 11 July 1934.
151. *Matin*, 20 July 1934.
152. See in particular 20 July and 2, 11, 13, 15 September 1934.
153. *Matin*, 5 September 1934.
154. *Action française*, 13 July 1934.
155. See in particular *Action française*, 6, 10, 12 August, and 8 September 1934.
156. 10 September 1934. Daudet never forgave Barthou for having ordered an inquiry against him while he was Minister of Justice. See his rather disgusting book quoted above.
157. 15 September 1934.
158. 14 September 1934.

Chapter IV
THE LAVAL ERA

1. His biographers, McGeorge Bundy and Elting Morison, told me that no other French statesman in the 1930s had so successfully seduced the American government and public opinion as Pierre Laval.
2. *Politique française*, p. 169.
3. Quoted by *Kupferman, Alfred, *Pierre Laval*, 1976, p. 37, where I draw all these reference to the press. The German ambassador to London von Hösch wrote a description of Laval on 17 October 1934 that was sent to Hitler see ADAP, C, III, 1, no. 254, 17 October 1934. "Unabashed opportunist," he said. Laval was a disciple of Caillaux and Briand.
4. *Mallet, Alfred, *Pierre Laval*, 1954, Vol. l, *Des années obscures à la disgrace du 13 décembre 1940*.
5. MAE, SDN. Avenol, Vol. 29. Note from Avenol on the Rome agreements, January 1935 (the date is uncertain).
6. Mallet, op. cit., Vol. I, pp. 62–63.
7. See his book *Les illusions de Stresa*.
8. *Rueff, Jacques, *Autobiographie*, 1977, p. 120.
9. *Shamir, Haim, "Le plébiscite de la Sarre et l'opinion publique en France," RHMC. January–March 1970, pp. 104–111.
10. See his diary, op. cit., Vol. III, and his book *De Pange, Jean, *Ce qu'il faut savoir de la Sarre*, Paris, 1934.
11. De Pange, Jean, op. cit., Vol. III, pp. 23–37. Quoted by Jeanneney J.-N., op. cit., pp. 543–544.

12. Jeanneney, op. cit., p. 544.

13. MAE, T. 972–975 from Laval to several embassies, 9 November 1934. A personal letter from Fouques-Duparc, head of a division of the French service at the League of Nations to Massigli. Confirmed in ADAP, C, III, 2, no. 307, Köster, 7 November 1934.

14. Jeanneney, op. cit., pp. 544–545.

15. MAE, T. 2012, François-Poncet, 1 November 1934, as well as T. 2023, 2 November, D. 1564, 3 November 1934.

16. MAE, T. 2119, François-Poncet, 16 November 1934, and T. 1768, Laval to François-Poncet, 18 November 1934.

17. MAE, T. 2267–2268, 6 December 1934.

18. MAE, D. 73, 17 January 1935.

19. MAE, T. 91, François-Poncet, 16 January 1935.

20. MAE, Laval to Germain-Martin, Minister of Finance, 22 November 1934.

21. Rueff, op. cit., p. 121–122.

22. MAE, T. 1263–1268, Chambrun, 23 November 1934.

23. MAE, T. 1627–1630, Laval to Chambrun, for Rueff.

24. Rueff, op. cit., pp. 119–121.

25. Most German writers believe that Hitler was seeking an agreement with France against the USSR in 1935. See Hildebrand, quoted report p. 37–40. The object was no doubt to prevent the signature and subsequent ratification of a Franco-Soviet pact. See also Bloch, Charles "La place de la France dans les différents stades de la politique extérieure du IIIe Reich," quoted article p. 22. On the other hand the Wilhelmstarsse was against it. See Knipping, quoted report pp. 17–18.

26. MAE, Massigli Papers, Note on the present condition of German rearmament.

27. MAE, T. 253–256, François-Poncet, 31 January 1935.

28. MAE, T. 267, 1 February 1935. See also T. 390, 14 February 1935.

29. See below, p. 144.

30. MAE, T. 287–196, François-Poncet, 4 February 1935.

31. MAE, D. A 42, François-Poncet, 6 February 1935, with an eight-page annex.

32. MAE, T. 577–579, François-Poncet, 11 March 1935.

33. MAE, T. 589–594, François-Poncet, 12 March, and T. 599–604, 12 March.

34. See Hildebrand, quoted report, especially p. 13. Regarding the continuing French initiatives for a Franco-German rapprochement, see those by Laval to Köster in ADAP, C, IV, 2, no. 415, Köster 18 November 1935, no. 419, report by Ministerialdirektor Köpke, 19 November 1935; and those by François-Poncet in Berlin, ADAP, C, IV, 2, no.425, note by Neurath, 22 November 1935 (Hitler met with François-Poncet). In no. 435, 30 November 1935, Köster reports citing Léger, that Laval disagreed with François-Poncet and could replace him with Léon Noël. Neurath commented: "Opponent of Germany."

35. Noël, *Les illusions de Stresa*, op. cit., p. 31.
36. General view in Herriot, *Jadis*, Vol. II, pp. 483–484.
37. MAE, R. 1131–1135, Dampierre, chargé d'affaires, Rome, 2 November 1934; T. 1234–1241, Chambrun, 20 November 1934.
38. MAE, Laval, T. 1049–1050, 5 November 1934.
39. MAE, no. 149/A-S, General Parisot, military attaché, Rome, 18 November 1934. See the Chambrun-Mussolini meeting of 20 November T. 1234–1241, Chambrun, 20 November 1934.
40. MAE, T. 1295, Chambrun, 28 November 1934.
41. MAE, T. 1310–1311, Chambrun, 1 December 1934.
42. See also MAE, T. 1274–1282, Naggiar, Belgarde, 29 December 1934, and T. 1284, 30 December 1934. Regarding the last negotiations there are many telegrams from Chambrun, precisely T. 3–6, 1 January 1935 where Chambrun states that the Italians demand "a clearer statement of disinterest in Ethiopia."
43. See below, p. 145.
44. MAE, Conversations dans T. 16–23, Chambrun, 7 January 1935; T. 24–29, 7 January 1935. See *Duroselle, J.-B. and Serra, Enrico, ed. *Italia e Francia dal 1919 al 1939*. Milano (ISPI), 1981.
45. On the other hand contrary to what Mallet, op. cit., Vol. I, p.71 states there was no secret military alliance. For the agreements on Tunisia and Africa see the very detailed analysis by *Watt, Donald, C., "The Secret Laval-Mussolini Agreement of 1935 on Ethiopia," Middle East Journal, Winter 1961, pp. 69–78. He attributes the desire for an alliance to France. The military documents below actually show its Italian origin. See also *Bessis, Juliette *La Méditerranée fasciste*, 1982.
46. MAE, see Note for the Minister by Léger, 30 December 1935: "One can search these documents in vain to find a clause whereby the Italian government may have found the slightest encouragement to undertake a policy of war against Ethiopia." There was during the evening of January 6 a Laval-Mussolini conversation in the presence of Léger and Suvich (was there also one between them alone?). During that conversation they discussed "free hands," Laval said laughing: "I see that you have strong hands. I sincerely hope you do not intend to misuse them." See MAE, Laval Papers, Laval to Mussolini 23 January 1936.
47. To such an extent that Léger, much later thought he could categorically deny Mussolini's statement. Mussolini told Eden in June 1935 that Laval had given him a free hand. See *Chambrun, Charles de, *Traditions et Souvenirs*, Paris 1952, pp. 192–197. The criticism by Watt in the cited article p. 73 confirms this: in June Mussolini only mentioned to Laval about annexing *a part of* Ethiopia. Hw could he obtain then Laval's agreement for the *entire* territory?
48. MAE, T. Chambrun, 12 January 1935, with T. no 7/A-S., Parisot, 20 January 1935.

49. MAE, T. Laval to Chambrun, 26 January 1935.

50. MAE, T. 13/A-S., Parisot, 29 January 1935. Conversation with Marshal Badoglio.

51. SHA, meeting of the High Military Committee, 20 February 1935.

52. SHA (copy MAE), T. 24/ A-S, Parisot, 25 February 1935.

53. MAE, T. Chambrun, 27 February 1935, with a letter from Badoglio to Parisot dated 23 February.

54. SHA (transmitted MAE), T. 40/A-S, Parisot, 19 March 1935.

55. SHA (transmitted MAE), T. 50/A-S., 28 March 1935.

56. SHA, Transcript.

57. SHA, Note regarding the relative status of the German and French forces and the consequences from the national and international standpoint, March 1935.

58. Le Goyet, op. cit., p. 104. Regarding naval operations, see SHM, Answer to the questions asked of the President of the Council of Ministers, 8 April 1935 (signed by Admiral Durand-Viel).

59. On the other hand there is no summary within the archives of the Quai d'Orsay.

60. Noël, op. cit., pp. 63–67.

61. *D'une guerre á l'autre*, p. 132. See Noël, op. cit., p. 67.

62. *Kirkpatrick, Sir Ivone, *Portrait d'un démagogue*, British edition 1959, p. 333. See Noël, op. cit., p. 72.

63. See *Parker, R.A.C., "Great Britain, France and the Ethiopian crisis," *English Historical Review*, April 1974, pp. 293–332, see p. 295.

64. Noël, op. cit., p. 77.

65. Op. cit., p. 333–335. See Noël, op. cit., p. 82.

66. *Flandin, Pierre-Étenne, *Politique française, 1919–1940*, 1947, p. 178.

67. *Renouvin, Pierre, "Les relations franco-anglaises (1935–1939). Esquisse proviso ire," *Les relations franco-britanniques de 1930 a 1939*, pp. 15–51, see p. 19. Parker, cited article, p. 297.

68. *Servir*, op. cit. Le Goyet, from the archives of the SHA, shows that Gamelin, in *Servir* fails to mention a part of what Mussolini told him.

69. Le Goyet, op. cit., p. 105–106.

70. MAE, T. 1204, Rome, 18 September 1935.

71. Mallet, op. cit., Vol. I, p. 82. Besides the archives, I am using here the unpublished work by Schram, op. cit., and the book by Scott, op. cit.

72. Herriot, *Jadis*, Vol. II, p. 488.

73. MAE, T. 493–497, Laval to Alphand, 10 November 1934.

74. JODP, Chambre. 1937, p. 2572.

75. MAE, T. 2165–2166, François-Poncet, 23 November T. 1139, Corbin, 23 November 1934; T. 545, Alphand, 23 November 1934.

76. MAE, Protocole dated 5 December 1934.

77. Herriot, *Jadis*, Vol. II, p. 499–500.

78. Herriot, *Jadis*, Vol. II, p. 523. See Scott, op. cit., p. 243.

79. Herriot, *Jadis*, Vol. II, p. 525.

80. Herriot, *Jadis*, Vol. II, pp. 529–530.

81. It is what Simon writes on 21 December 1934. Cited by *Parker, R.A.C., "Great Britain, France and the Ethiopian Crisis," *English Historical Review*, April 1974, pp. 293–332, see pp. 293–294.

82. MAE, D. 838, Laval to Piétri, 19 December 1934.

83. SHM (sent to MAE), Letter from Decoux to Latham, 17 December 1935; see also D. 760, Piétri to Laval, 10 December 1935.

84. *Les illusions de Stresa*, op. cit., pp. 45–53.

85. See a detailed account of this incident in MAE, SDN, Note of the Secretary General, 4 September 1935.

86. MAE, T. 180–182, Bodard, 12 December

87. MAE, T. 2, Laval to the French delegation at Geneva, 11 January 1935. Actually on 19 January, the Counsel decided to postpone the matter to a later date.

88. MAE, Laval to Rome, London-Geneva, 17 January 1935.

89. MAE, Note from the French delegation at Geneva, 11 January 1935.

90. Parker, quoted article, p. 300.

91. MAE, D. 203, Baelen, chargé d'affaires at Addis Ababa, 5 November 1934.

92. MAE, T. 196–200, Chambrun, 11 February 1935.

93. MAE, T. 238–240, Chambrun, 16 February 1935.

94. See what Parker writes regarding this British policy, quoted article, *passim*.

95. Regarding that meeting MAE, Note of 2 September 1935.

96. MAE, T. 180, Léger, Geneva, 19 September 1935, and MAE, T. 191–195, Laval, 19 September Sent to Rome with response from Chambrun, T. 1206–1212, 21 September following a two-and-one-half hour meeting with Mussolini.

97. MAE, T. 1204–1207, Corbin, 1 September 1935. See also T. 1212–1217, Corbin, 3 September following a visit to Hoare.

98. MAE, T. 1138–1143, Chambrun, 3 September 1935. See also regarding the meeting of the Council of the League of Nations, on 3 September T. 115–121, Massigli, Geneva 3 September 1935.

99. MAE, T. 1167–1172, Chambrun 11 September 1935.

100. MAE, T. 1298, Corbin, 18 September 1935.

101. MAE, T. 1206–1212, Chambrun, 21 September 1935.

102. See MAE, Notes taken during a conversation at the Hotel des Bergues on 11 and 12 September 1935. British historian Sir W. Deakin feels that at this meeting Laval had envisaged giving strong support to England in exchange for specific commitments by the British in central Europe and that the British government had refused the proposal on 24 September. See *Relations franco-britanniques de 1935 à 1939*. 1975. The French summary of the conversations of 10 and 11 September doesn't show Laval being so precise.

103. MAE, Note to the President of the Council of Ministers, n. d. (September 1935).

104. MAE, T. 240–244, Massigli, 5 October 1935.

105. MAE, T. 275, Massigli, 10 October 1935.

106. MAE, T. 279, Massigli, 12 October 1935.

107. MAE, T. 295, Massigli, 14 October 1935.

108. See MAE, T. 2390–2391, Laval to Corbin, 26 October 1935; T. 2195–2197, Léger to Chambrun, 26 October 1935.

109. MAE, T. 2210–2217, Laval to Chambrun, 29 October 1935.

110. SHA (sent to MAE), General Parisot.

111. See mostly *Reussner, M.A., *Les conversations franco-britanniques d'État-Major (1935–1939)*, 1969, pp. 33–77.

112. Parker, quoted article, p. 310.

113. MAE, Notes taken during a conversation at the Hotel des Bergues, 1 November 1935. *Hoare, Sir Samuel does not pipe a word about it in his book *Neuf années de crises*. (French translation.) Furthermore he states—mistakenly—that only the issue of League of Nations mandates was being considered before that date.

114. See an interesting article (written without French documents) by *Braddick, Henderson B., "The Hoare-Laval Plan. A Study in International Politics," *Review of Politics*, July 1962, pp. 342–364.

115. Hoare, op. cit., pp. 136–137, states that he went to Paris, "weakened" by overwork. He appears to forget that the two day negotiation was preceded by long preparation.

116. Hoare, op. cit., p. 142. according to Mallet A., *Laval*, op. cit., p. 111, a Quai d'Orsay secretary handed a copy to François Quilici, of the Havas agency, who in turn sent it to Geneviève Tabouis, and Pertinax as well as *The Daily Telegraph*.

117. Unproven allegation by Allard, Paul, *Le Quai d'Orsay*, op. cit., p. 57.

118. DGFP, III, 910–912, 5 February 1935, quoted in Scott, op. cit., p. 235.

Chapter V
THE RHINELAND TRAGEDY

1. See specifically DDF, 2, I, no 67, Chambrun, 16 January 1936, quoting various accounts, as for example that of novelist Henri de Monfreid.

2. DDF, 2, I, no. 145, Lieutenant Colonel de la Forest-Divonne, military attaché in Berne, 5 February 1936.

3. See specifically DDF, 2, I, no. 9, Laboulaye to Laval, 4 January 1936.

4. See specifically DDF, 2, I, no 55, François-Poncet to Laval, 14 January 1936.

5. DDF, 2, I, no. 108, Chambrun, 28 January 1936.

6. JODP, Chambre, 1936, p. 134.

7. DDF, 2, I, no. 142, Note from the political section, 6 February 1936.
8. *Politique française, 1919–1940*, op. cit., p. 188. See DDF, 2, I, no. 190, Bodard, 14 February 1936.
9. *Politique française, 1919–1940*, op. cit., p. 189.
10. DDF, 2, I, no. 283, Flandin to Corbin, 5 March 1936, with an aide-mémoire dated 3 March as attachment. See the very vivid account of the conversation between Flandin and Eden in Eden, A., *Facing the Dictators*, pp. 327–329.
11. DDF, 2, I, no. 46, Moscou, 14 January 1936.
12. *Action française*, 19 January 1936.
13. Ibid., Manchette du 23 February 1936.
14. See for example article of 10 February.
15. Texte dans *Populaire*, 11 January 1936.
16. *Populaire*, 8 February 1936.
17. François-Poncet, op. cit., pp. 245–246.
18. DDF, 1, IV, no. 175, Daladier to Paul-Boncour, 4 September 1933.
19. François-Poncet, op. cit., p. 245.
20. See DDF, 2, I, no. 37, Note from the European section, 11 January 1936.
21. DDF, 1, I, no. 30, François-Poncet, 10 January 1936.
22. DDF, 2, I, no. 37, Note from the European section.
23. DDF, no. 40, Corbin, 13 January 1936.
24. DDF, 2, I, no. 49, 14 January 1936.
25. See above all Dobler, DDF, 2, I, no. 75, 17 January 1936; no. 96, 22 January 1936; no. 126, 1 February 1936 (clearly more optimistic); no. 183, 14 February (even more optimistic).
26. DDF, 2, I, no. 122, Noël Henry, 31 January 1936; no. 188, 14 February 1936.
27. DDF, 2, I, no. 147, 7 February. 1936.
28. DDF, 2, I, no. 242.
29. DDF, 2, I, no. 286, 6 March 1936.
30. DDF, 2, I, no. 294.
31. DDF, 2, I, no. 294.
32. CEP, II, p. 469 sq.; see p. 503.
33. Ibid., p. 500.
34. Ibid., IX, p. 2669.
35. Bérard, op. cit., p. 154.
36. Stehlin, op. cit., p. 32.
37. *Blondel, Jules-François, *Au fil de la carrière, récit d'un diplomate, 1911–1938*, 1960, p. 366.
38. SHA, Renondeau to Fabry, D. 492.
39. Ibid., D. 937.
40. DDF, 2, I, no. 63, 15 January 1936.
41. DDF, 2, I, no. 277, 4 March 1936.
42. DDF, 2, I, no. 288, 25 February 1936.
43. *Humanité*, 12 January 1936, "L'Hitlérisme et Locarno."

44. *Humanité*, 2 February 1936.
45. *Œuvre*, 14 January 1936.
46. *Œuvre*, 17 January 1936.
47. *Œuvre*, 28 January 1936.
48. *Œuvre*, 23 January 1936.
49. *Œuvre*, 12 February 1936.
50. *Œuvre*, 15 February 1936.
51. *Œuvre*, 6 March 1936.
52. *Action française*, Delebecque J., 19 January 1936.
53. *Action française*, Maurras, 8 February 1936.
54. *Action française*, 26 February 1936.
55. *Jour*, 8 January 1936.
56. *Jour*, 14 February 1936.
57. DDF, 2, I, no. 255, François-Poncet, 29 February 1936.
58. DDF, 2, I, no. 265, 2 March (account written immediately following the meeting by François-Poncet) and no. 349, 8 March (account written after the coup).
59. Regarding this issue besides the archives at the Quai d'Orsay and the *Services historiques militaries*, and the parliamentary commission of inquiry we can rely on four recent and excellent works. That of *Defrasne, Colonel "L'évènement du 7 March 1936...," Les relations franco-allemandes, op. cit. p. 247-276. And three papers from the *Colloque franco-allemand* March 1977: *Michalon, Colonel Roger and Vernet, Jacques (battalion leader), "L'armée française et la crise de March 1936"; *Masson, Philippe, "La marine française et al crsie de March 1936"; *Christienne, General C., and Buffotot, P., "L' armée de l'air française et la crise du 7 March 1936."
60. DDF, 2, I, no. 125, 1 February 1936.
61. DDF, 2, I, no. 169, 12 February 1936.
62. DDF, 2, I, no. 1936 (summary from the navy archives).
63. DDF, 2, I, no. 170, Maurin to Flandin, 12 February 1936.
64. Michalon and Vernet, quoted article, p. 12.
65. Defrasne, quoted article, p. 262, and DDF, 2, I, Maurin to Flandin, 17 February 1936.
66. DDF, 2, I, no. 186, 14 February 1936.
67. DDF, 2, I, no. 196, Maurin to Flandin, 27 February 1936. See also a note from the Army High Command, drafted by General Colson and approved by General Georges, regarding Franco-British cooperation, ibid., no. 202, 16 February 1936.
68. DDF, 2, I, no. 223, Note from the Department, 24 February 1936.
69. DDF, 2, I, no. 241, Note from the Minister's Cabinet, 27 February 1936.
70. DDF, 2, I, no. 203, Transcript from the navy archives, written by Admiral Abrial.

71. DDF, 2, I, no. 325, note by General Gamelin, 28 March 1936.
72. Quoted article, p. 9.
73. JODP, Chambre, 1936, p. 140.
74. Quoted by Defrasne, quoted article, p. 259.
75. Ibid., p. 258.
76. Defrasne, op. cit., p. 259.
77. Michalon and Vernet, op. cit., p. 24.
78. Private recollections by General Jacques Humbert and Colonel Defrasne.
79. Withdrawal Hitler had planned according to interpreter P. Schmidt. Discussed by *Watt, Donald. *Journal of Contemporary History.*, October 1966
80. *Servir*, Vol. II, p. 215.
81. DDF, 2, I, no. 296, 7 March 1936.
82. DDF, 2, I, no. 298, 7 March 1936.
83. DDF, 2, I, no. 300, 7 March 1936.
84. Article quoted, p. 7.
85. *Humanité*, 8 March 1936.
86. *Populaire*, 8 March 1936.
87. *Populaire*, 12 March 1936.
88. *Œuvre*, 8 March 1936.
89. *Matin*, 8 March 1936.
90. *Jour*, 8 March 1936.
91. *Jour*, 9 March 1936.
92. See *Jour*, 9 March 1936.
93. See *Jour*, 12 March.
94. *Action française*, 10 March 1936.
95. See *Jour*, 10 March 1936.
96. *Humanité*, 11 March 1936.
97. Flandin, op. cit., p. 201, states that he had drawn Sarraut's attention to that sentence.
98. Letter from Prime Minister Van Zeeland to Ambassador Laroche. Texte in *Les relations militaires franco-belges, March 1936–10 May 1940*, 1968, pp. 46–47.
99. DDF, 2, I, no. 32, Corbin to Laval, 10 January 1933.
100. DDF, 2, I, no. 301, Corbin to Flandin, 7 March 1936 (received at 6:25 p.m.).
101. Flandin, op. cit., p. 199.
102. CEP, IV, p. 907 sq., V, pp. 1262–1268. See above all Maurin, Philippe *Figaro*, 8 March 1984.
103. DDF, 2, I, no. 303, Noël, 7 March 1936.
104. DDF, 2, I, no. 366, Corbin, 10 March 1936.
105. DDF, 2, I, no. 327, Noël, 8 March 1936, and ibid., no. 408, Noël, 12 March 1936.
106. DDF, 2, I, no. 394, François-Poncet, 11 March 1936.
107. Eden A., *Facing the Dictators*, pp. 343–378.

108. Eden, op. cit., p. 404.

109. Eden, op. cit., p. 359.

110. DDF, 2, I, no. 390, Instructions to Mr. Flandin before leaving for London, 11 March 1936.

111. DDF, 2, I, no. 391. Vice-Admiral Durand-Viel to Vice-Admiral Robert, 11 March 1936 (from the navy archives).

112. Masson, quoted article, p. 6, and DDF, 2, I, no. 406, Piétri to Sarraut, 12 March 1936.

113. Christienne and Buffotot, quoted article, p. 15.

114. Op. cit., II, pp. 197–198.

115. Le Goyet, op. cit., p. 119.

116. DDF, 2, I, no. 392, Note from Army High Command, 11 March 1936.

117. At the end of March, Gamelin buried the project. See DDF, 2, I, Note from General Gamelin, 28 March 1936.

118. DDF, 2, I, no. 407, Note for the Minister, 12 March 1936.

119. Eden, op. cit., p. 355.

120. Nicolson, *Journal des années tragiques*, pp. 25–26.

121. Conditions that were discussed on 13 March during a meeting with General Georges, held at Flandin's request while in London. DDF, 2, I, no. 425, 23 March 1936.

122. Eden, op. cit., pp. 357–358. DDF, 2, I, Massigli to MAE, 17 March 1936.

123. Eden, op. cit., p. 360 sq.

124. *Politique française*, pp. 208–209.

125. DDF, 2, I, no. 496, Corbin, 19 March 1936.

126. DDF, 2, II, no. 2, German government peace plan dated 31 March 1936, that von Ribbentrop handed to the British government, 1 April 1936.

127. DDF, 2, II, no. 6, Corbin, 2 April 1936.

128. DDF, 2, II, no. 17, Transcript of 3 April 1936.

129. With Belgium only, conferences of 15 May. Texts in *Les relations militaires franco-belges, mars 1936-10 mai 1940*, pp. 52–58, and DDF, 2, II, no. 217.

130. DDF, 2, II, no. 97. General Schweisguth to General Maurin, 20 April 1936 (with exhibits).

131. DDF, 2, I, no. 332, Puaux to Flandin, 8 March (conversation between Puaux and Schweisguth).

132. DDF, 2, I, no. 373, Monicault, chargé d'affaires, 10 March 1936. *Id.*, no. 424, 13 March 1936.

133. DDF, 2, II, no. 168, Dampierre, 6 May 1936.

134. DDF, 2, I, no. 494, D'Ormesson to Flandin, 23 March 1936.

135. DDF, 2, I, no. 457, 18 March 1936.

136. DDF, 2, I, no. 503, 25 March 1936.

137. CEP, passim.

138. Our emphasis.

139. DDF, 2, I, no. 270, Laroche, Bruxelles, 2 March 1936.
140. DDF, 2, II, no. 23, Transcript (from the navy archives, handwritten by Abrial), 5 April 1936.
141. DDF, 2, I, no. 447, Charles-Roux, 17 March 1936.

Chapter VI
THE ATMOSPHERE

1. For 1936 and 1939 there is a need for dissertations comparable to the excellent doctorate by *Becker, Jean-Jacques, *L'opinion française en 1914*, 1975. As a starting point one may use the "Barodet" publications for 1932 and 1936 (*Programmes, professions de foi et engagements électoraux des députés élus*) and after 1938 the public opinion polls, see within Chapter XI and following.
2. The is a whole range of published material on this subject. See the play by Donnay, Maurice, *La chasse à l'homme*, given in 1919; in Hamp, Pierre, *Une nouvelle fortune* (1926), chapter entitled: "Trop de femmes."
3. *Bodin, L. and Touchard, Jean, *Front populaire 1936*, 1961, pp. 24–26.
4. *Sanson, Rosemonde, *Les 14 juillet, fête et conscience nationale, 1789–1975*, 1976.
5. See on the issue a master's thesis which I supervised, by *Azria, Sylvain, *Le tour de France cycliste dans les années 1930*, 1974.
6. *Paoli, Colonel François-André, *L'Armée française de 1919 a 1939*, s. d., II, pp. 59–60. There were 117,000 career military men in 1935, 30 000 of them being officers.
7. *Missiones catholicae*, 1930.
8. *Cotte, Jules, *Un ingénieur français en URSS*, 1946, p. 271.
9. Ibid., p. 273. Cotte gave lectures in France with Barthou's support; only *L'Humanité* made mention of them.
10. Ibid., p. 275.
11. This information come from the master's dissertation which I directed by *Madame Laverrière, maiden name Boutet, Marie-Françoise, *Les relations culturelles franco-américaines de 1919 à 1939*. She used the reports written by the director of the national office of universities, Charles Petit-Dutaillis.
12. See the description by Bérard, Armand, op. cit, pp. 67–71.
13. Coulondre deplored this and wanted 10,000 Germans to come to France every year to "cement the links of a true rapprochement." See MAE, T. 4532, 20 December 1938. There is no important example of this "trip around the world" that some rich young people such as André Siegfried took at the end of their studies at the close of the nineteenth century.
14. *Combe, Paul, *Niveau de vie et progrès technique en France depuis 1860*, 1955, p. 58. *Bloch-Lainé, François, *Profession: Fonctionnaire*, Paris, 1976, p. 26, notes that he traveled at the ages of 16 to 18 as a "little pilot" to Africa and America but that this was exceptional.

15. Ginier, op. cit., p. 143. To be compared to 12 million arrivals in 1967 (ibid., p. 166).

16. Ibid., p. 182.

17. *Siegfried, André, *Aspects du XXie siècle*, Paris, 1955, Chap. V, "L'âge du tourisme," p. 109–148.

18. Two excellent dissertations increase our understanding of the international issues of immigration. Bonnet, Jean-Charles, *Les pouvoirs publics français et l'immigration dans l'entre-deux-guerres*, Lyon (Centre d'histoire économique et sociale de la region lyonnaise), 1976 and *Schor, Ralph, *L'opinion française et les étrangers en France, 1919–1939*, Aix, 1980 (to be published) with large bibliographies. Mrs. Ponty, Jeanine is preparing a dissertation with us regarding Polish immigration.

19. Bonnet, J.C., op. cit., p. 16 sq.

20. Bonnet, J.C., op. cit., p. 22.

21. Bonnet, J.C., op. cit., p. 378.

22. Bonnet, J.C., op. cit., p. 22 sq.

23. Bonnet, J.C., op. cit., p. 328 sq. See also Jeanneney, op. cit., pp. 481–482.

24. Bonnet, J.C., op. cit., p. 205–207.

25. Bonnet, J.C., op. cit., p. 220 sq.

26. Bonnet, J.C., op. cit., p. 228 sq.

27. Bonnet, J.C., op. cit., p. 232.

28. Bonnet, J.C., op. cit., p. 24.

29. *Armengaud, André, *La population française au XXe siècle*, 1973, p. 55.

30. Regarding most of these issues, see *Pike, David W., *Los republicanos españoles refugiados en Francia 1939-1944*, Paris, 1969. For the negotiations, see within, Chaps. XII and XIII.

31. Bonnet, J.C., op. cit., p. 367.

32. All this information in *DDF*, 2, XII, no. 348, Note from the deputy director-ate of administrative and international union affairs, 21 November 1938.

33. Perhaps in September 1938; see *Bonnet, Georges, *De Washington au Quai d'Orsay*, 1946, p. 212.

34. DDF, 2, XII, no. 390, Transcript of Franco-British conversations, 24 November 1938.

35. *Thibaudet, Albert, *Histoire de la littérature française de 1789 à nos jours, 1936*, p. 539.

36. See in, Chap. VII, § IV.

37. Thibaudet, op. cit., p. 539.

38. See the dissertation by *Gadoffre, Gilbert, *Claudel et l'Univers chinois*, 1969. See also *Cahiers Paul Claudel*, n. 4, 19: *Claudel diplomate*, that assembles for the period after 1919 writing on Germany, the United States and Belgium.

39. *Body, Jacques, *Giraudoux et l'Allemagne*, Paris, Publications de la Sorbonne, 1975.

40. The chart and information that precedes is from *Girou de Buzareingues, Claire, "La traduction en France," *Le livre français hier, aujourd'hui, demain*, 1972, pp. 267–268.

41. See from a literary point of view, *Pistorius, G., *L'image de l'Allemagne dans le roman français entre les deux guerres (1919–1939)*, 1964.

42. Body, op. cit., p. 386.

43. See *Robichez, Jacques, *Romain Rolland*, 1961.

44. *Europe*, 15 November 1934, "Je ne peux pas oublier," quoted by *Mysyrowicz, Ladislas, *Anatomie d'une défaite*, dissertation, Lausanne, 1973, p. 305.

45. *Europe*, 15 November 1934, quoted by Mysyrowicz, op. cit., p. 323.

46. See Micaud, *La droite française et l'Allemagne*, op. cit.

47. Mysyrowicz, op. cit., p. 302.

48. See *Reinhard, Marcel and Armengaud, André, *Histoire générale de la population mondiale*, p. 410 sq.; Armengaud, *La population française au XXe siecle*, op. cit.

49. *Sieburg, Friedrich, *Dieu est-il francais?*, 1940; see p. 243.

50. Juvisy, 1931, p. 147. See also Delbreil, Jean-Claude, *Les catholiques français et les tentatives de rapprochement franco-allemand (1920–1935)*, op. cit., p. 254.

51. *Vienot, Pierre, *Incertitudes allemandes*, 1931, p. 167, see pp. 117–118.

52. *Problèmes franco-allemands d'après-guerre*, Paris, 1932, p. 242. See also L'Huillier, Fernand. *Dialogues franco-allemands*. 1925–1933, op. cit., p. 175.

53. An excellent analysis of the issue in the recent dissertation by *Ostenc, Michel, *L'éducation en Italie pendant le fascisme*, Aix, 1977, see pp. 1214 et seq. Ostenc quotes among others *Preti, Luigi, *Giovinezza, Giovinezza*, 9th edition, Milan, 1972. Abridged edition of the dissertation; *Ostenc, M. *L'éducation en Italie pendant le fascisme*. Sorbonne, 1980. See also * Ostenc, M. *Intellectuels italiens et fascisme 1915–1919*, 1983.

54. Romains, Jules, *Cela dépend de nous*, op. cit., 135 p.; see pp. 97 and 103.

55. *Larès, Antoine, *T.E. Lawrence et la France*, 1976.

56. See the excellent dissertation by *Guyard, Marius-François, *L'image de la Grande-Bretagne dans le roman français*, 1954. On "Le Gentleman," see pp. 111–162.

57. *Gilbert and Gott, *The Appeasers*, 1963, passim, and Rowse, A. L., *All Souls and Appeasement*, op. cit. *Mommsen, W., and Kettensker, L., *The Fascist Challenge and the Policy of Appeasement*, 1983.

58. *Spears, Sir Edward, *Prelude to Dunkirk*, 1954, Vol. I, p.4, p. 11.

59. *Journal des années tragiques*, op. cit., passim.

60. MAE, Corbin to Bonnet, 21 December 1938.

61. Op. cit. p. 57. Daladier on the other hand enjoyed a close friendship with American Ambassador William Bullitt who exaggerated his own influence on Daladier. See *Bullitt, Orville, ed. *For the President. Correspondence between Franklin D. Roosevelt and William C. Bullitt*, Boston, 1972.

62. *Bonafé, Felix, *Jacques Bardoux*, 1977, p. 35.

63. Noël, Léon, *Les illusions de Stresa*, p. 47.

64. *Giraud, General Henri, *Un seul but, la victoire*, 1949.

65. Guyard, op. cit.; see pp. 275–277.

66. *Europe nouvelle*, 10 October 1938, quoted in *Ageron, Ch.-R., "L'opinion publique française pendant les crises internationales de septembre 1938 à juillet 1939," *Cahiers de l'Insitut d'histoire de la presse et de l'opinion*, no. 3, pp. 203–223.

67. See an excellent summary in *Ageron, Ch.-R., "La vénalité de la presse française dans la première moitié du XX e siècle. L'action des États étrangers," ibid., no 3, pp. 107–130.

68. See Ageron, second article quoted, p. 129.

69. *Gallo, Max, *Contribution à l'étude des méthodes et des résultats de la propagande et de l'information de l'Italie fasciste (1933–1939)*, dissertation of the 3rd cycle.

70. See Ageron, quoted article, p. 127.

71. See mostly *Bariety, Jacques, "L'appareil de presse de Joseph Caillaux et l'argent allemand, 1920–1932", *Revue historique*, no. 502, April–June 1972.

72. All these details are in Ageron, quoted article, pp. 121–125.

73. *Milza, Pierre, "Les problèmes financiers de *L'Humanité*, 1920–1939," *RHMC*, October–December 1973.

74. See Ageron, quoted article, p. 121.

75. Ageron, quoted article, p. 130.

76. The most important study is that by *Kupferman, Alfred, "Diplomatie parallèle et guerre psychologique: le role de la Ribbentrop-Dienststelle dans eles tenattives d'action sur l'opinion française: 1934–1939," *Relations internationales*, n. 3, 1974, pp. 72–95. Otto Abetz the main protagonist provided an embellished picture in *Abetz, Otto, *Histoire d'une politique franco-allemande 1930–1950*, 1953.

77. *Matin*, 22 November 1933. Dans *DDF*, 1, V, no. 44, 22 November, François-Poncet his unhappiness with de Brinon who had lied to him. He had already met with Hitler when he saw the ambassador. But he told him the opposite.

78. *France-Allemagne*, p. 264.

79. See Jeanneney, J.-N., op. cit., pp. 357–362.

80. Kupferman, quoted article, p. 93. Most of what follows comes from that writer.

81. Daladier sent him on a mission to Germany in February 1939, which once again irritated François-Poncet even though he was in Rome; see MAE T. 573, 15 February 1939 on the missions by Baudoin (Rome) and Brinon (Berlin).

82. On 6 December 1938 he met with German interpreter Paul Schmidt. Not only he but also the delegation that had come with von Ribbentrop had read his books. Jules Romains found such flattery irresistible. See *Schmidt, Paul, *Statist auf diplomatischer Bühne*, 1950.

83. MAE, D. 1319, de Montbas, chargé d'affaires, to Bonnet, Berlin, 8 December 1938.

84. MAE, T. 327, Coulondre to Bonnet, 31 January 1939.

85. At the liberation of France Albert Bayet the left wing Radical-Socialist, president of the Resistance press and professor at the Sorbonne even published

a successful pamphlet, *Pétain et la cinquième colonne* which cannot be said to follow the rules of historical research.

86. MAE, T. 4515–4517, Coulondre to Bonnet, 19 December 1938.
87. MAE, T. 3654–3657, Coulondre to Bonnet, 20 December 1938.
88. Weber, Eugen, *L'Action française*, 1962, p. 461.

Chapter VII
France's Worldwide Economic Interests

1. Sauvy, op. cit., II, p. 58. See also the important article by Vaïsse, Maurice, "Le mythe de l'or en France; les aspects monetaires du New Deal vus par les francais," RHMC, July–September 1969, pp. 462–479.
2. *Bonnet, Georges, *Vingt ans de vie politique*, 1969; see p. 175: I set up the western gold bloc." In July 1933 the governors of the six central banks chaired by the Belgian Jaspar had reached an agreement.
3. Sauvy, op. cit., II, pp. 58–61.
4. I have directed a solid master's thesis: *de La Tour du Pin, Hadelin, *La presse de droite contre la dévaluation; sa campagne contre Paul Reynaud*, 1972.
5. Reynaud, Paul, *Mémoires*, I, p. 363. *La France a sauvé l'Europe*, 1947, I, p. 250.
6. Bonnet, op. cit., p. 194. What la Tour du Pin, op. cit., was able to prove is very convincing.
7. See la Tour du Pin, the list of financial speeches, p. III-V (4 in 1934, 3 in 1935, 4 in 1936) and the list of his writings, articles and interviews. pp. V–VII.
8. See Sauvy, op. cit., II, p. 90.
9. Sauvy, op. cit., II, pp. 103–104.
10. *Figaro*, 29 June 1934, cité par La Tour du Pin, op. cit., p. 81.
11. *Temps*, 30 June 1934. Ibid., p.82.
12. *Temps*, 18 August 1934, Ibid., p. 85.
13. Recouly, Raymond, in *Gringoire*, 17 August 1934.
14. *Temps*, 30 June 1934. Ibid., p. 91.
15. See Jeanneney, J.-N., pp. 525-540.
16. Was there "a covert orchestra conductor?"—in this case the Bank of France as claimed by *Delaisi, Francis, *La Banque de France aux mains des 200 familles?*, Vaïsse, see quoted article, p. 475, thinks this is a rather deeper influence.
17. MAE, Series B, carton 57.
18. See ibid., Letter from Fougère, 19 October 1934: "Confédération générale de la production française," "Association de l'Industrie et de l'Agriculture," "Chambre de Commerce de Paris," "Comité d'action économique et douanier," "Comité national des conseillers du commerce extérieur," "Fédération des associations régionales," and finally "Association nationale d'expansion économique."

19. MAE, Boissieu, consul general in Dresden, 3 October 1934, quotes an important article in the *Allgemeine Zeitung* in Chemnitz.

20. Document provided by the Finance Ministry to MAE, signed by Boisanger, 27 September 1934.

21. MAE, note to the Belgian embassy, 13 October 1934.

22. MAE, Notes from the deputy director for the Minister, 20 October 1934.

23. See MAE, Series B, carton 57: important report by the deputy director of Commercial Affairs, 26 June 1935.

24. Ibid., Letter from Marchandeau to Laval, 29 January 1935.

25. Ibid., Note from the deputy directorate of Commercial Affairs, 26 January 1935. See also T. 1085, Roger Cambon, chargé d'affaires, 25 October 1934 who met with Sir Frederick Leith-Ross, T. 1143, Corbin, 10 November 1934. The financial attaché Mönick met with Leith-Ross on the 22nd and he confirmed his refusal to tie the pound sterling to gold since the dollar was at the time "strongly devalued," he said (MAE, D. 18946 sent to Foreign Affairs).

26. Ibid., commercial attaché to Ambassador Laboulaye, and T. 464, Laboulaye, 23 November 1934.

27. Ibid., D. 34, Raymond Brugère, 5 December 1934.

28. MAE, T. 1025-1026, Chambrun, 6 October 1934.

29. MAE, Bouchet to Lamoureux.

30. MAE, Claudel, 3 November 1934.

31. Rueff, op. cit., p. 124.

32. La Tour du Pin, op. cit., pp. 118–120.

33. See Jeanneney, op. cit., p. 522.

34. See below, chap. X.

35. Rueff, op. cit. pp. 122–127. See his paper regarding the "market" as the only regulatory entity of human choices given at the Academy of moral and political sciences. Only the "monetary regulator" remained. "The post war period by extending to the currency the doctrine of planned economy, also attempted to free itself from that kind of influence." 5 January 1935.

36. Sauvy, op. cit., II, p. 133.

37. "A billionaire" wrote *Coston, Henry, *Les financiers qui mènent le monde*, p. 187. He inherited a large newspaper fortune from his American mother's side. See *Broustra, J.-C., *Le combat de Raymond Patenôtre*, 1969, pp. 17–18; Jeanneney, J.-N., op. cit. p.360.

38. As we shall do soon. Below, chap. X.

39. *Girault, René, "La dévaluation de 1936 et la conduite de la politique extérieure de la France," *Colloque de Nanterre*, 1977.

40. Figures taken from Sauvy, op. cit., II, p. 563.

41. See chart in Sauvy, op. cit., II, p. 562.

42. Sauvy, op. cit., pp. 572–574.

43. See below, Chap. XII, the "Alphand mission."

44. MAE, T. 3257, Lacroix, Prague, 28 December 1938 (commentary by the *Prager Tageblatt* on the same day).

45. By Raymond Poidevin, Pierre Guillen, René Girault, Jacques Thobie, Jean-Claude Allain, Pierre Milza.

46. This number is offered by *Feis, Herbert, *Europe, the World Banker*, and *Cameron, Rondo, *La France et le développement économique de l'Europe*, p. 86. The authors mentioned in the preceding note confirm this order of magnitude.

47. *Pose, Alfred, "Structures et Méthodes bancaires," in Rist, Charles and Pirou, Gaétan, *De la France d'avant-guerre à la France d'aujourd'hui*, Paris 1939; *Dauphin-Meunier, Achille, *La banque, 1919–1935*, Paris, 1936.

48. *Soutou, Georges, "L'impérialisme du pauvre," *Relations internationales*, no. 7, 1976, pp. 219–239.

49. *Teichova, Alice, *An economic background to Munich*, Cambridge, 1974, Chap. 1, "The distribution of International Investments."

50. Sauvy, Alfred, op. cit., I, p. 30, gives a much higher number. France would have lost 20 billion and liquidated 3 and one half billion (in gold francs). There was, therefore, 21.5 billion left.

51. *Marseille, Jacques, "L'investissement français dans l'Empire colonial: l'enquête du gouvernement de Vichy (1943)," *Revue historique*, October–December 1974, pp. 409–432.

52. *Debeir, J.-C., "Le problème des exportations de capitaux français de 1919 a 1930. Substitutions et concurrences," *Relations internationales*, no 6, 1976, pp. 171–182.

53. Op. cit., pp. 5–6.

54. See MAE, Léger Papers, letter from Fleuriau, former ambassador to London, 15 June 1933; letter from Claudel, 23 September 1933: "If you can find me any kind of board of directors I can assure you I would gladly give up my job to someone else."

55. See Jeanneney, J.-N., op. cit., p. 503: Initiatives by François de Wendel to Léger to secure French government backing regarding the very high taxes he was obliged to pay for his business in the Ruhr.

56. Coston, Henry, *Les financiers qui mènent le monde*, op. cit.; *Aymé-Martin, Aymé, *Nos grands financiers contre la Nation*, 1931; *Beau de Loménie, Emmanuel, *Les responsabilités des dynasties bourgeoisies*, Vols. IV and V. Beau de Loménie mentions the ties between Charles-Roux and the business community, however this diplomat was posted at the Vatican; see *Charles-Roux, François *Huit ans au Vatican*, Paris, 1946.

57. Jeanneney, op. cit., pp. 554 and 590.

58. For example in conquering Manchuria the Japanese, took over two French companies operating there. See *DDF*, 1, II, no 139, Wilden, Peking, 2 September 1932.

59. Despite the attempts made by Paléologue in 1920–1921 that are well described by *Toscano, Mario, "L'accordo revisionista franco-ungherese del 1920," *Pagine di storia dei trattati*, pp. 303–438.

60. Dauphin-Meunier, op. cit., p. 216.

61. All the information that follows originates from *DDF*, 2, XII, no. 30, Note for the Minister from the deputy political director, 5 October 1938.

62. *DDF*, 1, XII, note already quoted. Regarding the Rambouillet agreement, see *Lukasziewicz, Juliusz, *Diplomat in Paris, 1933–1939*, New York, 1970, pp. 12–21.

63. See below, chap. XII.

64. *Marguerat, Philippe, *Le IIIe Reich et le pétrole roumain, 1938–1940*, Geneva, 1977.

65. Below, chap. XII.

66. Below, chap. XII.

67. *Ageron, Ch.-R., in *Cahiers de l'Inst. d'histoire de la presse et de l'opinion*, Tours, no. 1, 1973, p. 3.

68. For a longer list, see *Leblond, Marius-Ary, *Anthologie coloniale*, 1943, p. 323.

69. All of these details in Ageron, op. cit.

70. Ageron, op. cit., p. 21.

71. See Andrew, C. M. and Kanya-Farstner, A. S., "*The groupe colonial* in the French Chamber of Deputies 1892–1932," *Historical Journal*, 1974, 4.

72. Marseille, J., "Le commerce entre la France et son Empire colonial dans les années 30," *Colloque de Nanterre*, March 1977.

73. See above, §3.

74. Numbers quoted from Ageron, op. cit., pp. 23–24.

75. Ageron, op. cit., p. 24.

76. Below, chap. XII.

77. In another article: *Ageron, Ch.-R., "L'idée d'Eurafrique et le débat colonial franco-allemand dans l'entre-deux-guerres," *RHMC*, July-September 1975, pp. 446–475.

78. Delavignette, R., "Équipe eurafricaine: place pour l'Europe," *Esprit*, 1 November 1938, quoted by Ageron, quoted article, p. 473.

Chapter VIII
ELUSIVE SECURITY

1. *Beaufre, General André, *Le drame de 1940*, Paris, 1965, pp. 57–58.

2. Besides Mysyrowicz, op. cit., see the more recent *Young, Robert. *In command of France. French Foreign Policy and military training, 1933–1940*, Cambridge, 1978. Pertinax, *Les Fossoyeurs*, Vol. I, "Gamelin."

3. *Bloch, Marc, *L'étrange défaite*, Paris, 1946, p.166. *Martel, André, in an illuminating paper at the *Colloque Daladier* (December 1975), "Le poids de la stratégie. Controverses et données contestées," has justifiably underscored this excellent text.

4. *Ducasse, André, Meyer, Jacques and Perreux, Gabriel, *Vie et mort des Français*, 1962, p. 38.

5. *Tournoux, General Paul-Émile, *Haut-Commandement: gouvernement et défense des frontières du Nord et de l'Est, 1919–1939*, 1960.

6. *Debeney, General *Sur la securité militaire de la France*, 1930, pp. 58–65.

7. Regarding the origins of the law the most important book is by Tournoux, op. cit., to be completed with the short book by *Hughes, Judith, M., *To the Maginot Line. The Politics of French Military Preparation in the 1920s*, Cambridge, Mass. 1971.

8. See Tournoux, op. cit., Chapter VII, the technical and financial description by Paoli, Colonel François-André, *L'armée française de 1919 à 1939*, II. *La fin des illusions, 1930–1935*, SHA, n.d., p. 197. *Dutailly, Lt. Colonel, *Les problèmes de l'armée de terre française 1935–1939*, SHA, 1980.

9. Michalon and Vernet, quoted report, 1977, p. 20.

10. See above, Chapter II.

11. See the excellent comparative study *Vial, General, "Doctrine militaire française et allemande au lendemain de la première guerre," *Colloque de l'École de guerre*, 1976, p. 25.

12. Quoted article, p. 22.

13. Ibid., p. 22.

14. Quoted work, see above note 11.

15. I am referring to Michalon and Vernet, op. cit., p. 11.

16. The quotation is in Michalon and Vernet, op. cit., p. 13. The underlined part of the text is their excerpt of the actual text of the plan.

17. For all this I am closely following the excellent study by General Christienne and D. Bouffotot, "L'armée de l'air française et la crise du 7 mars 1936," *Colloque franco-allemand*, mars 1977. I am also using an excellent master's thesis, which I directed: *Boussard, Dominique, *Un problème de défense nationale. L'aéronautique militaire au Parlement, 1928–1940*, 1977, where all the transcripts of the parliamentary commissions have been checked.

18. Note from the inspector general of the Air Forces to Weygand, 19 May 1932. Quoted in Christienne and Buffotot, op. cit., p. 3.

19. SHA, D. 309. See *Vauthier, Colonel P., *La doctrine de guerre du general Douhet*, 1935. Preface by Marshal Pétain and writing opposing Douhet by the naval engineer Camille Rougeron quoted in *Le Goyet, Colonel, "Evolution de la doctrine d'emploi de l'aviation française entre 1919 et 1939," RHDGM January 1969, pp. 1–41.

20. Note of 26 November 1934 regarding initial cooperative air force needs, quoted by *id.*, p. 4.

21 See below, § III.

22. Dans *Debeney, General, *La guerre et les hommes*, pp. 87–88. Debeney stated that he was delighted with the BCR. See, Mysyrowicz, op. cit., p. 181.

23. Prepared by Air Minster Pierre Cot, and General Denain, chief of staff, passed a vote in Parliament on 6 July 1934.

24. "La marine française et la crise de mars 1936," *Colloque franco-allemand*, March 1977.

25. Masson, op. cit., pp. 1–2.

26. Numbers in Michalon and Vernet, op. cit., pp. 11–12.

27. Paoli, op. cit., p. 110.

28. Ibid., pp. 110–111.

29. Ibid., p. 181.

30. Beaufre, *Le drame de 1940*, op. cit., pp. 82–85.

31. Op. cit., p. 28. As of 1 January 1936, the *Deuxième Bureau* found that there were 750 German airplanes instead of 864.

32. In this case I have used the master's thesis which I dircted by *Belugou, Sylvie, *Les Français et l'aviation militaire 1936-1939*, 1973. Boussard, op. cit., p. 139, shows the optimism of Pierre Cot in July 1937. In December 1937 he was more optimistic when facing the full Chamber than within the commission, see pp. 140–141.

33. Mysyrowicz, op. cit., p. 177. Quoting *Cot, Pierre, *L'armée de l'air, 1936–1938*, 1939, p. 50, and *Hebrard, General H., *25 années d'aviation.*

34. *JODP*, Chambre, 12 December 1937, quoted in *Friedenson, Patrick and Lecuir, Jean, *La France et la Grande-Bretagne face aux problèmes aériens (1935–May 1940)*, 1976.

35. Interview of Déat in *Paris-Soir*, 6 March 1936.

36. *L'armée de l'air, 1936–1938*, op. cit.

37. Op. cit., p. 14.

38. No. 5, May 1938, "Pour une armée de l'air plus forte." Cité par Le Goyet, op. cit., p. 29. Boussard, op. cit., p. 140, montre bien l'extrême pessimisme de Vuillemin en janvier 1938.

39. Masson, T. as quoted.

40. André Martel, in a lecture at Montpellier in 1975, spoke of the "unchanged and heaviness of the French military system."

41. See Christienne and Buffotot, op. cit., p. 16.

42. Quoted in Paoli, op. cit., pp. 24–25.

43. On this issue I have a written note by Jean-Marie d'Hoop based upon the archives of the SHA and SHM regarding the High Military Committee and another on the Permanent Committee of National Defense.

44. Above chap. IV.

45. See d'Hoop, quoted note.

46. See below, chap. XI.

47. According to *Weygand (Jacques), *Weygand mon père*, p. 239. Quoted by Le Goyet, op. cit., p. 71.

48. Ibid., pp. 70–71.

49. Ibid., p. 70.

50. Ibid., p. 70.
51. Who owed his career to Weygand, and whose direct collaborator he was for a number of years.
52. See his biography, *Weygand, General, *Le général Frère, un chef, un héros, un martyr,* Paris, 1949.
53. Weygand, *Mirages et réalités,* p. 313.
54. Ibid., p. 311.
55. His 1976 centennial was the occasion of an important colloquium, which I am using. It was published in 1977 for the most part.
56. Loustaunau-Lacau, op. cit., pp. 54–59.
57. See in *Centenaire,* the study by General de Boissieu, son in law of General de Gaulle, on " à l' École de guerre."
58. In *Centenaire.*
59. In *Centenaire.*
60. Op. cit., p. 60.
61. Op. cit., p. 62.
62. Op. cit., p. 64.
63. Quoted by Mysyrowicz, op. cit., p. 224.
64. *Centenaire,* "La doctrine militaire francaise entre 1919 et 1939."
65. Mysyrowicz, op. cit., p. 220 *sq.*
66. See *Tournoux, J.-R., *Pétain et de Gaulle,* p. 102 *sq.*
67. A very lively debate was taking place for several years in France on a professional army. See the excellent analysis by Mysyrowicz, op. cit., pp. 201–278.
68. Mysyrowicz, op. cit., p. 213.
69. Paul Reynaud felt that the book's title lacked caution. See *La France a sauvé l'Europe,* I, p. 313.
70. Mysyrowicz, op. cit., p. 264.
71. Reynaud, op. cit., p. 319.
72. Reynaud, op. cit., p. 322.
73. *RDM,* 1 March 1935.
74. Tournoux, J.-R., *Pétain et de Gaulle,* pp.174–175; *Werth, Alexander, *De Gaulle* (British edition), 1965, p. 87.
75. Mysyrowicz, op. cit., pp. 258–264.
76. Pertinax, *Les Fossoyeurs,* I, p. 30.
77. In the first chapter of a small book published in 1955 *Weygand, General, *En lisant les mémoires de guerre du général de Gaulle,* Weygand denies having been against armored units.
78. *Castex, Admiral Raoul, *Mélanges stratégiques,* 1976. Preface by Rear Admiral Lepotier, p. II.
79. His main work, *Castex, Admiral Raoul, *Théories stratégiques,* was in five volumes, published from 1930 to 1935.
80. Chap. VIII, pp. 321–373.

Chapter IX
The Diplomatic Machine

1. *Baillou, Jean, ed., *Les Affaires étrangères et le corps diplomatique français.* Vol. II, 1870–1980, Paris, CNRS, 1984, a monumental work of diplomats, archivists and historians; *Dischler, Ludwig, *Der auswärtige Diesnt Frankreichs,* Hamburg, 1952, 2 vols., offset.

2. Regarding the *Annuaire* of 1935 one finds 3 Bérard, 3 Billecoq, 2 Bradier, 2 Cambon, 2 Caluzel, 2 Guermonprez, 2 Gueyraud, 2 Hauchecorne, 2 Maugras, 2 Pineton de Chambrun, 2 Puaux, 2 Vacher-Corbière. Many other such as Roland Jacquin de Margerie and François Seydoux de Calusonne, Jacques Fouques-Duparc were the sons of very high-level diplomats.

3. *Zay, J., *Souvenirs et solitude,* p. 75.

4. A careful reading of the index of the book by Eugen Weber on *l'Action française* is very revealing in this case.

5. See my article *"Les ambassadeurs français," *Relations internationales,* 7, 1976, pp. 283–292.

6. Chauvel, op. cit., p. 46.

7. Ibid., pp. 46–47.

8. Bérard, Armand, op. cit., p. 327.

9. The same problem always reappears. Who was responsible for a number of decisions during the war of 1914–1918? Was it Pierre de Margerie or Philippe Berthelot? See Auffray, Bernard, *Pierre de Margerie,* op. cit.

10. See Chauvel's reminiscence, quoted in this Introduction.

11. Léger Papers. Éthiopia.

12. Bérard, op. cit., p. 91.

13. See Spears, *Prelude to Dunkirk,* I, p. 25.

14. For example when he states that Sir John Simon's policies were "most disastrous." Léger Papers. Confidential Note from Corbin, 27 March 1935.

15. Papiers Léger, letter of 11 March 1938.

16. *Facing the Dictators,* p. 407.

17. Léger Papers letter from Naggiar, 14 May 1938.

18. *Commentaires,* I, p. 59.

19. Op. cit., p. 480 sq.

20. *Commentaires,* I, pp. 323 and 339.

21. Below, chap. XII.

22. *Témoignages pour l'Histoire,* op. cit., pp. 119–120.

23. *Coulondre, Robert, *De Staline à Hitler,* 1950, p. 186.

24. Stehlin, op. cit., p. 123.

25. Coulondre, *De Staline à Hitler,* op. cit., pp. 198–201.

26. Noël, *L'agression allemande,* op. cit., pp. 345–346.

27. Szembek, *Journal,* p. 100 (June 1935).

28. See below, chap. XII.

29. *Ci-devant*, p. 108.
30. He was a secretary general of the Presidency of the Council of Ministers under Flandin, from January to May 1935. Laval and Flandin spoke well of him. See *Les illusions de Stresa*, p. 45 and 61.
31. "A mediocre, well-intentioned man, but without any peronsality," said Noël referring to Delbos, ibid., p. 112.
32. Ibid., p. 119.
33. Noel, *Les illusions de Stresa*, op. cit., p. 48.
34. Rueff, J. *Autobiographie*, Chapter VIII ("Trois ans à l'ambassade de France à Londres. Mai 1930 à décembre 1933") and Chapter XI "La vie d'un attaché financier de France à Londres." See also Mönick, Emmanuel, op. cit. especially Chapters I and VI.
35. On this issue I used an excellent master's thesis which I directed by *Carré, Capitan Claude, *Les attachés militaries français 1920-1945. Rôle et influence.* 1976. There are few memoirs published by military attaches, for our period: *Albord, *Pouquoi cela est-il arrivé, 1949.* *Béthouard, General, *Des héctombes glorieuses au désastre, 1914–1940.;* *Mast, General, *Histoire d'une rebellion*, 1969, and most of all Stehlin, Paul, *Témoignage pour l'histore*, 1964. We have consulted an unpublished work: *Catoire, Colonel, *Journal de ma mission à Rome, 1934–1937*, which is very interesting, as well as hundreds of reports from military attaches in the SHA.
36. To which Captain Carré dedicates a long passage of his study.
37. We have seen that based on Swiss informants he was completely mistaken regarding 6 March 1936.
38. Below, chap. XIV.
39. See Spears, op. cit., Vol. I, p. 143.
40. Below, chap. XIV.
41. Carré, op. cit., p. 202.
42. Unpublished diary quoted by Carré, op. cit., p. 202.
43. Above, chapter V.
44. Op. cit., p. 97.
45. Stehlin, op. cit., p. 97.
46. Gauché, General, op. cit., p. 97.
47. SHA, D. 122/V, 10 March 1939.
48. SHA, D. 148/V, 31 March 1939; D. 275/V, 27 June; D. 294/V, 10 July; D. 329/V, 1 August.
49. SHA, D. 232/V, 24 May 1939.
50. SHA, dispatches by squad leader de Kerhué (Buenos Aires, Montivideo), of General de Chadebec de Lavalade (Rio de Janeiro).
51. SHM, Ministry of Marine to EMA, 5 January 1939.
52. SHA, many dispatches from Guillermaz. General Lelong, military attaché in London, received large quantities of information from the British regarding the Far East. See SHA, D. 140/S, 18 May 1939.

53. We are using below, chapter XIII, a number of his dispatches (SHA).
54. See below, chap. XIII and XV, dispatches (SHA).
55. SHA, D. 3/S, 11 January 1939.
56. SHA, D. 29/39, Moscow, 22 February 1939. These were the results of a conversation with American air force attaché.
57. SHA, D. 458/S, 16 April 1938 and Coulondre, D. 121, 15 April 1938.
58. SHA, D. 586/S, 13 June 1939.

Chapter X
THE POPULAR FRONT

1. Bonnefous, op. cit., V, p. 419.
2. Renouvin (Pierre), "La politique extérieure du premier gouvernement Léon Blum," in *Léon Blum chef de gouvernement*, 1967, pp. 329–353, see p. 329.
3. Renouvin, ibid., p. 329.
4. *Léon Blum*, quoted work, p. 37.
5. Ibid., p. 213.
6. Comments by Mendès–France (Pierre), ibid., p. 233.
7. Ibid., p. 240.
8. Ibid., p. 37.
9. Blumel, ibid., p. 37 sq.
10. Julien, ibid., p. 40.
11. Also contains the general report by German historian *Ziebura, Gilbert, author of the excellent book *Léon Blum et le parti socialiste, 1872–1934*, 1967.
12. See *Dreifort, John E., *Yvon Delbos at the Quai d'Orsay*, Chapter II, pp. 21–29.
13. Bérard, op. cit., p. 326.
14. Noël, *Les illusions de Stresa*, op. cit., p. 112.
15. *DDF*, 2, II, no. 244, Corbin, 26 May 1936.
16. See above, chap. II. See Stehlin, op. cit, pp. 42–45.
17. *DDF*, 2, II, no. 271, Note from the political directorate. Orientation of Italian policy, and no. 278, François-Poncet, 6 June.
18. *DDF*, 2, II, no. 234, Puaux, 23 May 1936.
19. DDF, 2, II, no. 275, Departmental note (Massigli), 5 June 1936. The Nazis viewed France as "sick and dangerous." See no 317, François-Poncet, 18 June 1936. Regarding French public opinion see a master's thesis which I directed: *Normand, Gilles, *L'opinion française et l'axe Rome-Berlin*, 1970.
20. *DDF*, 2, II, no. 282, Note from the Minister. Conversation with the English ambassador (Sir George Clerk), 8 June 1936.
21. *DDF*, 2, II, no. 312, Personal letter from Corbin to Léger. Actually Eden was speaking without having consulted France. See no. 328, Delbos to Corbin, 20 June 1936.
22. *DDF*, 2, II, no. 325, François-Poncet, 20 June 1936.

23. See Noël, *Les illusions de Stresa*, op. cit., p. 108–109.
24. *DDF*, 2, II, no. 357, Gamelin to Daladier, 25 June 1936.
25. *DDF*, 2, II, no. 217. Transcript of the Franco-Belgian meeting of 15 May 1936. See also no. 480, Transcript of the mission of General Schweisguth to Brussels, 18 July 1936. Schweisguth felt that "The High Command as it is now made up is totally in agreement with a very close collaboration with the French army."
26. *DDF*, 2, II, no. 369, Transcript of 26 June 1936.
27. Reprinted in *DDF*, 2, II, no. 375, meeting of 1 July 1936.
28. *DDF*, 2, II, 372, note from the director of Political Affairs, 30 June 1936. See also on this issue *DDF*, 2, II, no. 419. Note of the EMA, "Obligations d'assistance mutuelle pouvant incomber à la France," 9 July 1936.
29. *DDF*, 2, II, no. 453, François-Poncet, 15 July 1936.
30. I used two studies by students: the master's thesis by *Archambalt, Annick, *Aspects politiques des jeux olympiques de Berlin, 1936*, 1972, and mostly the doctoral dissertation of the 3rd Cycle by *Braun, Didier, *La politiique du sport de la France entre les deux guerres*, 1977. See also another thesis which I supervised *Destrebecq, Annette, *Le role du parti communiste au parlement sous le Front populaire*, 1968; see p.29, on communist opposition to funding.
31. *DDF*, 2, III, no. 61, François-Poncet, 2 August 1936.
32. *Candide*, 13 August 1936, quoted in Braun, op. cit, p. 244.
33. *Humanité*, 18 August 1936, ibid.
34. See above in Chapter V.
35. *DDF*, 2, II, no. 464, Corbin, 17 July, nos. 471, 472. French counter projects, *DDF*, 2, III, no. 2, Corbin, 20 July
36. *DDF*, 2, III, nos. 18 and 19 (transcript); no. 20, final communiqué 23 July 1936.
37. Actually it did accept on 31 July. But would never find a suitable date. *DDF*, 2, III, nos. 23 and 55, François-Poncet, 1 August 1936.
38. *DDF*, 2, III, no. 63, François-Poncet, 3 August 1936.
39. *DDF*, 2, III, no. 196, François-Poncet, 24 August 1936. See also, no. 211, Aris, financial attaché to Baumgartner, Berlin, 27 August 1936.
40. *DDF*, 2, III, no. 209, François-Poncet, 27 August 1936.
41. There was trace to be found of the Schacht conversations with Delbos on 26 August and Auriol on 27 August.
42. *DDF*, 2, III, no. 213, 28 August 1936. Blum noted that this summary is correct, but that comparatively Schacht spoke at greater length. See comments by François-Poncet, no. 229, 2 September 1936.
43. No trace could be found in the French archives. See DDF, 2, III, no. 276, Massigli to Léger, personal letter, Geneva, 23 September 1936 regarding a conversation between Bonnet and Spinasse on one side and Eden and Halifax on the other in the presence of Massigli.
44. *DDF*, 2, III, no. 302, Arnal, chargé d'affaires, 30 September 1936.

45. *DDF*, 2, III, no. 351, François-Poncet, 14 October 1936. François-Poncet had met with Hitler at Berchtesgaden on 2 September (see no. 334).

46. *DDF*, 2, III, no. 354, 14 October 1936.

47. *DDF*, 2, III, no. 393, Aris to Baumgartner regarding devaluation. See below, § IV.

48. *DDF*, 2, III, no. 417, François-Poncet, 28 October 1936.

49. *DDF*, 2, III, no. 462, 10 November 1936.

50. The most detailed study is by Renouvin, Pierre in *Léon Blum, chef de gouvernment*, pp. 329–353, to be read together with the statement by Robert Blum, son of the President of the Council, André Blumel, the head of his cabinet, and several ministers from the time, Georges Monnet, Paul Bastid, Pierre Cot, Jules Moch, the general secretary and diplomats such as René Massigli and Jacques Fouques-Duparc. The book by *Lefranc, Georges, *Histoire du Front Populaire*, 1965, with a note by André Blumel. Regarding public opinion see a thesis which I supervised: *Antignac, Anne-Marie, L'opinon publique française sur la IIᵉ République espagnole (avril-juillet 1936), 1971.

51. All details in Renouvin, T. op. cit.

52. *DDF*, 2, III, no. 28, 25 July 1936.

53. *DDF*, 2, III, no. 30, note from the political directorate, 25 July 1936.

54. *DDF*, 2, III, no. 34, Delbos to Herbette, 27 July 1936 and no. 36. All posts were informed.

55. *DDF*, 2, III, no. 46, Peyrouton, Resident general in Rabat, to Delbos, 30 July 1936.

56. *DDF*, 2, III, no. 56, Delbos to Rome and to London, 1 August; no. 59, to London, Rome, Brussels, 2 August; no. 65 to François-Poncet, 3 August; no. 66, Delbos to Auriol, 3 August; no. 69 Delbos to Roger Cambon, London; 4 August, asking for the support of the principle of non-intervention.

57. *DDF*, 2, III, no. 71, Roger Cambon, 4 August 1936.

58. *DDF*, 2, III, no. 76, Delbos, 4 August 1936.

59. *DDF*, 2, III, no. 87, Transcript of the conversations of 5 August 1936 at the British Admiralty.

60. *DDF*, 2, III, no. 89, Payart, 6 August 1936.

61. *DDF*, 2, III, no. 90, Chambrun, 6 August 1936.

62. During those days all of Delbos' activity was centered on non-intervention. See mostly DDF, 2, III, no. 110, Delbos to many diplomatic posts, 9 August, 2 a.m.; no. 111 id., 9 August 3:45 a.m. (speaks of "the encouraging welcome"); no. 112 Delbos to Auriol, 9 August, 6:40 p.m.

63. In the words of Léon Blum. See Renouvin, quoted article p. 338.

64. *Léon Blum...*, op. cit., p. 351.

65. Dreifort, *Delbos*, op. cit., p. 49.

66. CEP, I, pp. 121–132, 215–229, 251–262.

67. For this paragraph I worked with the studies by J.-N. Jeanneney, Wilfrid Baumgartner and Pierre Mendès-France in *Léon Blum chef de gouvernment*,

L'Histoire économique de la France by Alfred Sauvy, Vol. II, and most of all by Mönick, Emmanuel, *Pour mémoire, op. cit.*, Rueff, *Autobiographie,* op. cit., as well as two important articles by *Girault, René, "Léon Blum, devaluation de 1936 et la conduite de la politqiue extériuere de la France," *Colloque de Nanterre,* 1977; and "Les relations inetrnationales et l'exercice du pouvoir pendant le Front Populaire, Juin 1936–Juin 1937," *Cahiers Léon Blum,* no. 1, May 1977, pp. 15–46.

68. Sauvy, op. cit., pp. 215–221.

69. See F 30 1419 and AMF B12618 and 12619 (Mönick Papers), quoted in Girault "Léon Blum...", op. cit., p. 6.

70. Rueff, op. cit., p. 126.

71. Mönick, op. cit., p. 48.

72. Ibid. see Girault, op. cit., p. 9.

73. Baumgartner, in *Léon Blum chef de gouvernement,* op. cit., p. 281–282.

74. Ibid., p. 282.

75. Moch, ibid., p. 283. See Frank quoted below.

76. All this in Girault, op. cit., p. 12. (Letter by Labeyrie in F 30 1420.)

77. Girault, op. cit., p. 13; see F 30 1420.

78. Girault, op. cit., pp. 14–15.

79. Girault, op. cit., p. 16.

80. Jeanneney, in *Léon Blum chef de gouvernement,* pp. 219–220.

81. Sauvy, II, p. 231.

82. Sauvy, II, pp. 239–241.

83. Rueff, *Autobiographie,* pp. 129–130. See also his memos to Vincent Auriol of 23 and 27 February, pp. 131–133.

84. Jeanneney, in *Léon Blum chef de gouvernement,* p. 221.

85. Rueff, *Autobiographie,* pp. 135–139.

86. Quoted in Sauvy, II, p. 259.

87. Rueff, *Autobiographie,* p. 143.

88. Sauvy, II, p. 264.

89. *DDF,* 2, IX, no. 291, Corbin, 6 May 1938.

90. Quoted article, p. 17.

91. *DDF,* 2, IV, no. 193, Note from the financial attaché in London: "Une initiative anglo-franco-américaine dans l'ordre économique et financier peut-elle sauver la paix?"

92 *Bullitt, Orville, H., ed. *For the President. Personal and Secret,* 1973, pp. 184–189. The thought of reapying part of the debt to acquire American support appeared here and there especially in 1939 (see Chapter XIV, n. 18). The Americans concluded that a default was preferable because it would preserve their isolation.

93. Ibid. p. 200–202. Roosevelt expressed these exact thoughts during his conversation with Ambassador Laboulaye, 31 December. *DDF,* 2, IV, no. 232, Laboulaye, 31 December 1936.

94. *DDF*, 2, IV, no. 193, quoted document

95. *Hull, Cordell, *Memoirs*, 1948, I, Chap. 37, pp. 518–530.

96. On the subject see the interesting remarks by Dreifort, *Delbos*, op. cit., pp. 86–88.

97. Bullitt, op. cit., p. 206.

98. See *DDF*, 2, IV, no. 229, François-Poncet, 31 December 1936.

99. *DDF*, 2, IV, no. 230, François-Poncet, 31 December 1936.

100. *DDF*, 2, IV, note on p. 533.

101. *DDF*, 2, IV, no. 325, Geneva, 20 January 1937. It should be noted that this economic issue takes 6 lines out of 205 in Massigli's memo.

102. The study of French public opinion with respect to the Spanish civil war remains a favorite subject of historiography. Here I use most of all *Breen, Catherine, La droite française et la guerre d'Espagne (1936–1937), thesis, Geneva, 1973, and of *Pike, David Wingate, *Les français et la guerre d'Espagne 1936–1939*, Paris, 1975.

103. Pike, op. cit., pp. 138–139. See Destrebecq (Annette), quoted thesis pp. 30–32.

104. *Fauvet, Jacques, *Histoire du parti communiste français*, I, pp. 207–208. The government was against the "formation of elements" on French territory but it allowed persons to leave on an individual basis with passports. DDF, 2, IV, no. 76, Delbos to Corbin, 2 December 1936.

105. *DDF*, 2, III, no. 472, Coulondre, 12 November 1936; no. 497, Coulondre, 16 November 1936; *DDF*, 2, IV, no. 153, Coulondre, 15 December 1936.

106. Ibid. pp. 205–209. The German press wrote about a "Communist Republic" in the Pyrénées orientales; *DDF*, 2, IV, no. 294, Arnal, 14 January 1937.

107. On 15 January 1937 at the Chamber with the unanimous vote of 598, on the 21st in the Senate with the unanimous vote of 285 the draft of the law granting full power to the government to prevent the volunteers from leaving. See Bonnefous, VI, p. 94.

108. Breen, Catherine, op. cit., pp. 46–52.

109. Ibid. pp. 68–69.

110. Ibid. p. 76.

111. *Wormser (Georges), *Georges Mandel, l'homme politique*, pp. 204–205.

112. Breen, Catherine, op. cit., pp. 120–128. See an annex diploma by *Mollat du Jourdin, Chantal, *Le journal "L'Aube" et la guerre civile espagnole, 1965*.

113. See CEP, I, p. 219. *Moch, Jules, *Naissance et croissance du Front populaire*, 1966, p. 47. See Dreifort, op. cit., p. 56.

114. *DDF*, 2, II, no. 39, Delbos to Corbin, 26 November 1936.

115. *DDF*, 2, IV, no. 62, Corbin, 30 November 1936.

116. *DDF*, 2, IV, no. 69, Delbos to Corbin, 1 December 1936.

117. *DDF*, 2, IV, no. 99, François-Poncet, 5 December 1936, and no. 130, 11 December 1936. Answer in no. 136, 12 December 1936.

118. *DDF*, 2, IV, no. 101, Laboulaye, 5 December. 1936, and no. 127, 10 December 1936.

119. *DDF*, 2, IV, no. 134, Aimé Leroy, Lisbonne, 12 December 1936.

120. *DDF*, 2, IV, no. 142, Blondel, 13 December 1936.

121. This number was suggested by Ambassador Herbette on 19 February 1937 (*DDF*, 2, IV, no. 471).

122. *DDF*, 2, IV, no. 78, Corbin, 2 December 1936,. A memo from the political directorate (no. 95, 4 December 1936) admitted that the distribution memos of 21 August and 29 November were practically ineffectual. The border was breached by "organized groups." Furthermore the Italian press published a letter from de Los Rios stating that Léon Blum promised to help Spain on July 25.

123. *DDF*, 2, IV, no. 147, Delbos to Corbin, 14 December 1936.

124. *DDF*, 2, IV, no. 199, Corbin, 23 December 1936.

125. *DDF*, 2, IV, no. 205, Delbos, 24 December 1936.

126. *DDF*, 2, IV, no. 343, Note from the deputy chief of staff of the Marine, Admiral Godfroy, regarding a conversation with Corbin, 23 January 1937.

127. *DDF*, 2, IV, no. 449, Corbin, 16 February. 1937.

128. *DDF*, 2, IV, no. 465, François-Poncet, 18 February 1937.

129. *DDF*, 2, V, no. 283, Corbin, 15 April 1937.

130. *DDF*, 2, V, no. 476, François-Poncet, 31 May, and no. 478, Corbin, 31 May.

131. *DDF*, 2, V, no. 99, Delbos, 20 June 1937.

132. *DDF*, 2, V, no. 125, Note of the Minister's audience, 25 June 1937.

133. *DDF*, 2, V, no. 355, Delbos to Cambon, 26 August 1937, asking about the expected English position.

134. *DDF*, 2, II, no. 461, 16 July 1936.

135. *DDF*, 2, V, no. 361, Note from the deputy directorate at the League of Nations, 27 August 1937.

136. *DDF*, 2, V, no. 364, Delbos to Cambon, 29 August 1937. Id., no. 265.

137. *DDF*, 2, V, no. 369, Cambon, 30 August 1937.

138. The French summaries of the meeting in *DDF*, 2, V.

139. *DDF*, 2, IV, no. 9, Note from the political directorate Paris, 20 November 1936.

140. *DDF*, 2, IV, no. 81, Lacroix, Prague, 2 December 1936; no. 156, Dampierre. Belgrade, 16 December 1936.

141. *DDF*, 2, IV, no. 334, 21 January 1937.

142. *DDF*, 2, IV, no. 281, Delbos to Lacroix, 11 January 1937.

143. See Dreifort, *Delbos*, op. cit., p. 137.

144. See Noël, *L'agression allemande...*, op. cit., pp. 139–143. See Gamelin, *Servir*, II, pp. 232–233; Lukasziewicz, op. cit., p. 15.

145. See *Michel, Henri, "Le Front populaire et l'URSS," *Les relations franco-britanniques de 1935 à 1939*, pp. 215–221, and *Costantini, Colonel A., "L'armée rouge. Son évolution de 1918 à 1938," offset; Lukasziewicz, op. cit., pp. 17–21.

146. Bérard, op. cit., p. 345.

147. Dreifort, op. cit., p. 141. Armand Bérard, who accompanied Delbos, wrote a very lively account of that trip, op. cit., pp. 346–369. See also Noël, *L'agression allemande...*, op. cit., pp. 174–179.

148. Noël, *L'agression allemande....*, op. cit., p. 175. On that occasion Beck demanded colonies for Poland.

149. See above, Chap. XIII.

Chapter XI
THE YEAR OF MUNICH

1. The summary was the famous "Hossbach Protocol," well known following the Nuremberg Trials. See *ADAP*.

2. *DDF*, 2, VII, no. 196, François-Poncet, 6 November 1937.

3. *DDF*. 2, VII, no. 215, 10 November 1937.

4. *DDF*, 2, VII, no. 220, 11 November 1937.

5. *DDF*, 2, VII, no. 212, 10 November 1937.

6. *DDF*, 2, VIII, no. 34, 25 January 1938. Very many other dispatches. See *Puaux, Gabriel, *Mort et transfiguration de l'Autriche, 1933–1935*, Paris, 1966, pp. 81–130.

7. See among others *DDF*, 2, VIII, no. 10, 19 January 1938, and no. 67, 30 January 1937.

8. *DDF*, 2, VIII, no. 140, Puaux, 11 February 1936.

9. *DDF*, 2, VIII, no. 205, Note from the French service at the League of Nations written by Pierre Arnal, 18 February 1938.

10. See Dreifort, J., *Delbos*, op. cit., p. 185.

11. *Werth, Alexander, *Twilight of France*, p. 142, quoted in Dreifort, op. cit., p. 186.

12. *DDF*, 2, VIII, no. 169, Delbos, 16 February 1938; no. 180, Corbin, 16 February 1938, no. 185, François-Poncet, 17 February 1938. "My British colleague did not receive instructions to coordinate with me," he wrote and that "he handled his initiative in the most benign manner."

13. *DDF*, 2, VIII, no. 190, 12 February 1938.

14. *DDF*, 2, VIII, no. 225, 21 February 1938.

15. Dreifort, op. cit., p. 187. Delbos and Eden met in Geneva on 28 January, *DDF*, 2, VIII, no. 53. Note from deputy division at the League of Nations.

16. See Rowse, op. cit.

17. *DDF*, 2, VIII, no. 275, Corbin, 25 February 1938.

18. See Dreifort, op. cit., p. 188.

19. Bonnefous, op. cit., p. 279.

20. *DDF*, 2, VIII, no. 372, Delbos to Corbin, 7, 8 p.m., and most of all no 375, Delbos to François-Poncet, 10:15 p.m.

21. *DDF*, 2, VIII, no. 378, 11 March, 11:45 p.m., received 12 March, 1:45 a.m.

22. *DDF*, 2, VIII, no. 384, 12 March 1938.

23. *DDF*, 2, VIII, nos. 385 and 386, Puaux, 12 March. On the final days of Austria, Puaux, op. cit., can be completed with Chauvel, op. cit., Vol. 1, pp. 11–39.

24. *DDF*, 2, VIII, no. 403, 12 March 1938.

25. See the collection *Léon Blum chef de gouvernement* and in particular Jeanneney, Jean-Marcel, "La politique économique de Léon Blum" mostly p. 233 sq., and Mendès-France, Pierre, "La politique économique du gouvernment Léon Blum," p. 233. He insists on the fact that Boris converted Blum to some of Keynes' ideas.

26. He writes this in *Entre-deux-guerres*, op. cit., III, p. 87.

27. Transcript in *DDF*, 2, VIII, no. 446.

28. See the great extension of thirty-six divisions and the big increase in tanks as reported by General Renondeau, *DDF*, 2, VII, no. 186, Berlin, 3 November 1937 (from SHA, D.820/AM).

29. See *DDF*, 2, VIII, no. 447, Transcript of the Superior Army Council, chaired by Daladier.

30. *DDF*, 2, VIII, no. 462, Note from the general chief of staff of national Defense and of the Army 16 March 1938.

31. *DDF*, 2, VIII, no. 432, 14 March, and no. 445, 15 March (a less complete text in Gamelin, *Servir*, III, p. 8).

32. *DDF*, 2, IX, no. 30, Corbin, 23 March 1938.

33. *DDF*, 2, IX, no. 32, Communications from the British embassy, 23 March 1938.

34. Ibid. Regarding France's lowering image in Great Britain, that Corbin felt, see *DDF*, 2, VIII, no. 416, Corbin, 13 March, and no. 481, Personal letter from Roger Cambon to Massigli, 17 March 1938.

35. *DDF*, 2, VIII, no. 481, *La Croix*, 14 March 1938. See n. p. 786, Paul-Boncour, op. cit., III, p. 83.

36. See the hostile reaction from Roger Cambon, *DDF*, 2, VIII, no. 481, 17 March 1938.

37. *DDF*, 2, IX, no. 112, Department Note of 5 April 1938, Paul-Boncour, op. cit., III, p. 93.

38. Paul-Boncour, op. cit., III, p. 72.

39. Ibid., pp. 89–92. *DDF*, 2, IX, no. 64, François-Poncet, 28 March; no. 97, Blondel, 1 April 1938. Transcript by Paul-Boncour of a conversation with Phipps, VIII, no. 449, 16 March 1938.

40. Among very many documents see above all *DDF*, 2, IX.

41. *DDF*, 2, IX, no. 129, Personal letter from Massigli to Blondel, 7 April 1938.

42. *Entre-deux-guerres*, op. cit., III, pp. 101–103.

43. *Entre-deux-guerres*, op. cit., III, pp. 103–104.

44. *DDF*, 2, X, no. 238.

45. Czechoslovak historian Anton Snejdarek, associate professor at the Sorbonne, confirmed to me that it was in July that Beneš understood that he could no longer count on France.

46. On 25 June Beneš and Lacroix had a private lunch. Beneš was sad and tired. "He had reached the point of questioning whether France now viewed Czechoslovakia as a burden." *DDF*, 2, X, no. 96, 26 June 1939.

47. *DDF*, 2, X, no. 242, Lacroix, 21 July 1938.

48. Transcript in *DDF*, no. 258, Corbin, 29 April. Corbin had this very detailed summary written. See mostly pp. 576–586.

49. *DDF*, 2, IX, no. 256, Note from M. Léon Noël. Situation in Czecholsovakia, end of April 1938. See Noël, *L'agression allemande....*, op. cit., pp. 198–202.

50. *DDF*, 2, IX, no. 281, Bonnet to Lacroix, 5 May 1938.

51. DDF, 2, IX, no. 378, Lacroix, 20 May 1938, 12:12 p.m. The studies of this crisis—see in *Slavonic and East European Review*, articles by Wallace, W.V., June 1963; Watt, D.C., of July 1966 with a response by Wallace; the booklet by Braddick, Henderson, R., "Germany, Czechoslovakia and the Grand Alliance in the May crisis, 1938."

52. *DDF*, 2, IX, no. 380, Renondeau, 20 May 1938.

53. *DDF*, 2, IX, no. 381, François-Poncet, 20 May 1938, 7 p.m.

54. *DDF*, 2, IX, no. 382, François-Poncet, 20 May 1938, 7 p.m.

55. *DDF*, 2, IX, no. 386, 20 May 1938.

56. *DDF*, 2, IX, no. 392, 21 May 1938, 2:30 p.m.

57. *DDF*, 2, IX, no. 402, Bonnet to Lacroix, 21 May 1938, 10:30 p.m.

58. *DDF*, 2, IX, no. 407, Renondeau, and no. 410, François-Poncet, 22 May 1940. See also no. 426, François-Poncet, 23 May; no. 427, Rewnondeau, 23 May, etc.

59. Bonnet did not meet with German Ambassador von Welczeck between 30 April and 27 May. It appears he met with Daladier in between. See *DDF*, 2, X, no. 458, Note from the Minister, 27 May 1938.

60. *DDF*, 2, IX, no. 419, Communication from the embassy of Great Britain, 22 May 1938.

61. *Œuvre*, 22 May 1938, quoted by *Vallette, G. and Bouillon, J. *Munich 1938*, p. 59. See also *Œuvre* du 23 May, where Geneviève Tabouis got mixed up.

62. *DDF*, 2, IX, no. 419, 22 May 1938.

63. See mostly *DDF*, 2, IX, no. 495, Noël, 31 May 1938.

64. See mostly *DDF*, 2 IX, no. 228, Note from the Department, 24 April 1938. Bonnet met with Litvinov on 12 May in Geneva, and no. 492, Coulondre, 31 May 1938.

65. *DDF*, 2, IX, no. 183, Bonnet to Blondel, 15 April 1938.

66. *DDF*, 2, IX, no. 194, Blondel, 16 April 1938.

67. *DDF*, 2, IX, no. 217, Blondel, 22 April 1938.

68. *DDF*, 2, IX, 252, Mercier, Tirana, 28 April 1938.

69. *DDF*, 2, IX, no. 261, Blondel, 1 May 1938.

70. *DDF*, 2, IX, no. 339, Blondel, 14 May 1938.

71. *DDF*, 2, IX, no. 486, Bonnet to Lacroix, 31 May 1938; no. 505, Bonnet to London, Prague, 2 June 1938. See no. 535, Communication from the Department to the Czechoslovak legation, 9 June 1938.

72. *DDF*, 2, X, no. 237, 20 July 1938.
73. *DDF*, 2, X, no. 325, 3 August 1938.
74. *DDF*, 2, X, no. 413, Bonnet to Lacroix, 19 August 1938.
75. *DDF*, 2, X, no. 507, Communication from the embassy of Great Britain. Corbin complained on 6 September that Lacroix was not being kept regularly informed of the initiatives taken by his British colleague Newton. See *DDF*, 2, IX, no. 15, 6 September 1938.
76. *DDF*, 2, X, no. 331, Lacroix, 5 August 1938.
77. *DDF*, 2, X, no. 369, Lacroix, 12 August 1938.
78. *DDF*, 2, X, no. 421, 20 August 1938. In *DDF*, 2, X, Telegrams from Lacroix. See also no. 324, 3 August no. 405, 18 August, and no. 517, Note from the Minister, 31 August.
79. *DDF*, 2, X, no. 200, Montbas, chargé d'affaires, Berlin, 13 July 1977; see no. 2.
80. See the summary of 18 August in *DDF*, 2, X, no. 412.
81. See among others, *DDF*, 2, X, no. 445, 24 August 1938.
82. *DDF*, 2, X, no. 401, François-Poncet, 18 August.
83. *DDF*, 2, X, no. 444, Transcript by Vuillemin, 23 August 1938.
84. *DDF*, 2, X, no. 537, Transcript of General Vuillemin's mission, 2 September 1938.
85. Stehlin, op. cit., p. 92.
86. Regarding Czechoslovak internal policy that is not part of our subject, see the harsh article by *Hajek, M. and Novotan, J.J., "La politique et l'armée de la Tchecoslovaquie devant la crise de Munich," RHDGM, October 1963, pp. 1–20.
87. See the harsh opinion of François-Poncet regarding his British colleague Nevile Henderson, *DDF*, 2, X, no. 246, 21 July 1938. See also no. 336, Lacroix, 7 August and no. 338, Lacroix, 8 August 1938.
88. *DDF*, 2, X, no. 245, 21 July 1938.
89. *DDF*, 2, X, no. 195, 12 July 1938.
90. *DDF*, 2, XI, no. 18, 6 September 1938.
91. Bonnet, *De Washington au Quai d'Orsay*, p. 209, Bullitt, op. cit., pp. 284–285.
92. Bullitt, op. cit., p. 282.
93. Account by Scapini in *DDF*, 2, XI, no. 28, 6 September 1938.
94. *DDF*, 2, XI, no. 22, François-Poncet, 6 September 1938.
95. *DDF*, 2, XI, no. 33, Bonnet to Corbin.
96. *ADAP*, D. II, no. 431.
97. *CEP*, IX, pp. 2601–2602.
98. *DDF*, 2, XI, no. 34, telephone conversation, 7 September 1938, 8:20 p.m. (Bonnet Papers.)
99. *DDF*, 2, XI, no. 94, 11 September 1938.
100. *DBFP*, 3, II, no. 834. See also *DDF*, 2, XI, no. 124. Telegram from Halifax, 12 September 1938. Transcript from Corbin, *DDF*, 2, XI, nos. 66 and 67, 9 September 1938.

101. *DDF*, 2, XI, no. 88, Corbin, 11 September 1938.

102. *DDF*, 2, XI, no. 125, Note from the Minister, 13 September 1938.

103. *DBFP*, 3, II, no. 807.

104. *DDF*, 2, XI, no. 122, 13 September, transmitted at 9 p.m.

105. *DDF*, 2, XI, no. 130, telephone communication from the embassy of Great Britain, 14 September 1938.

106. *DDF*, 2, XI, no. 133, Corbin, 14 September 1938, 11:15 a.m.

107. *DDF*, 2, XI, no. 152, Bonnet to Corbin, 15 September 1938. See also no. 168, conversation between Charles Saint, deputy head of Bonnet's cabinet and British first secretary Michael Wright, 15 September 1938.

108. Note from Massigli (who met with Osusky), 15 September 1938. *DDF*, 2, XI, no. 150, Lacroix, 15 September, and no. 166.

109. *DDF*, 2, XI, no. 171, François-Poncet, 15 September 1938.

110. *DDF*, 2, XI, no. 180, Lacroix, 17 September 1938.

111. *DDF*, 2, XI, no. 192, instructions from Beneš to Neczas, 17 September (Daladier Papers FNSP).

112. *DDF*, 2, XI, no. 208, General Faucher to Daladier, 18 September, 5:30 p.m. and no. 209, Bonnet to Lacroix, 18 September, 8:10 p.m.

113. *DDF*, 2, XI, no. 186, François-Poncet, 17 September, 9:30 a.m.; no 188, Corbin, 17 September, received at midnight.

114. *DDF*, 2, XI, no. 212, summary of the Franco-British conversations. See also *DBFP*, 3, II, no. 928. The French summary is twenty-four pages long.

115. His text in *DDF*, 2, XI, no. 213, Bonnet to MAE, 19 September 1938, 3:15 a.m.

116. See for example, in July, Reynaud, Paul, *La France a sauvé l'Europe*, I, pp. 557–558.

117. Werth, op. cit., pp. 218–220.

118. Monzie, *Ci-devant*, p. 29.

119. Ibid., p. 14.

120. Ibid., p. 31. *Carnets secrets de Jean Zay*, pp. 3–7.

121. Ibid., p. 4.

122. *DDF*, 2, XI, no. 222, 19 September 1938. Transcript of an Osusky-Bonnet conversation (Bonnet Papers). Another summary by Bonnet (in the same number) from the Daladier papers and drafted by Bonnet is shorter; Bonnet offered Osusky the advice to accept the Franco-British plan.

123. *DDF*, 2, XI, no. 217, Lacroix, 19 September 1938 (by wire).

124. *DDF*, 2, XI, no. 223, Notes by the political director, 19 September 1938.

125. *DDF*, 2, XI, no. 225, Note from the Minister, 20 September 1938, 1:30 p.m. (see also *DBFP*, 3, II, no. 967).

126. Ibid., note. See Kral, "Das Abkommen von München, 1938," *Tschechoslowakische diplomatische Dokumente*, no. 200, pp. 237–238.

127. *DDF*, 2, XI, no. 229, Lacroix (received 9:15 p.m.). Text of the answer in *DDF*, 2, XI, no. 234, Lacroix, 20 September 1938.

128. *DDF*, 2, XI, no. 232, Lacroix, 20 September 1938, received at 9:45 p.m. This document is certainly authentic since it can be found not just in the files of Bonnet but also in the Daladier papers. (*Fondation nationale des sciences politiques.*)
129. Bonnet, *De Washington au Quai d'Orsay*, p. 247 sq.
130. *CEP*, VII, p. 2178.
131. 21 September at 1:20 a.m. (*DBFP*, 3, II, no 991) or at 3:30 am (*DDF*, 2, XI, no. 250, Note from the Department.
132. See *DDF*, 2, XI, no. 252, Note from the Minister, 21 September 1938, and note p. 397.
133. *DBFP*, 3, II, no. 998.
134. *DDF*, 2, XI, no. 257, Lacroix, 21 September 1938 (received at 6:30 p.m.) and an account by Lacroix in no. 260.
135. *DDF*, 2, XI, no. 277, Corbin, 22 September 1938, 1:18 a.m.
136. *DDF*, 2, XI, no. 287, Corbin, 22 September 1938, 11:30 p.m.
137. *DDF*, 2, XI, no. 311, Corbin, 23 September 1938, 8 p.m.
138. *DDF*, 2, XI, no. 308, Lacroix (following a telephone conversation with Léger), 23 September 1938. See ibid., p. 477, no. 3, and no. 314, Corbin, 23 September 1938, 8:50 p.m. See notes of the *Deuxième Bureau* of the EMA (no. 354, 25 September 1938, and no. 355, 23 September 1938).
139. *DDF*, 2, XI, no. 343, Note from the Army High Command, 24 September 1939.
140. Monzie, *Ci-devant*, pp. 36–37.
141. *Carnets secrets de Jean Zay*, pp. 8–9; *Churchill, *L'orage approche 1919–1939 [The Gathering Storm]*, p. 309; Monzie, op. cit., pp. 34–35.
142. Monzie, op. cit., p. 33.
143. Ibid., p. 34.
144. *DDF*, 2, XI, no. 341, Flandin to Bonnet. Annex: Flandin to Daladier, 24 September 1938.
145. *Carnets secrets de Jean Zay*, pp. 11–17.
146. *DDF*, 2, XI, no. 357, Franco-British conversations of 25 September.
147. *DDF*, 2, XI, no. 359, Telephone conversation between Massigli and Lacroix, 26 September, and no. 375, Franco-British conversations of 26 September 1938.
148. *DDF*, 2, XI, no. 376, Transcript of the technical conversations of General Gamelin at the Cabinet Office, 26 September 1938.
149. *DDF*, 2, XI, no. 378, Note from the Vice Admiral, chief of staff of the Marine, 26 September 1938.
150. *DDF*, 2, XI, no. 377, Vuillemin to Guy La Chambre, 26 September 1938.
151. *DDF*, 2, XI, no. 29, Note from the political directorate, 6 September 1938 (answer from Litvinov to Payart, 2 September).
152. *DDF*, 2, XI, no. 96, Note from the Minister, 11 September 1938.
153. *DDF*, 2, XI, no. 96, Note from the Minister, 11 September 1938.
154. *DDF*, 2, XI, no. 216, Coulondre, 21 September 1938.

155. *DDF*, 2, XI, no. 267, Coulondre, 21 September 1938.

156. *DDF*, 2, XI, no. 292, Coulondre, 22 September 1938.

157. *DDF*, 2, XI, no. 318, Coulondre, 23 September 1938.

158. *DDF*, 2, XI, no. 367, Coulondre, 26 September 1938.

159. *DDF*, 2, XI. See from François-Poncet, nos. 382, 383, 386, 397, 27 September 1938.

160. *DDF*, 2, XI, no. 400. Note from the Minister 27 September 1938. See what Chautemps tells Bullitt about that Council meeting, op. cit. 392, and most of all *Carnets secrets de Jean Zay*, pp. 18–21; Campinchi and Reynaud were those most opposed to Bonnet.

161. Bullitt, op. cit., p. 290.

162. *DDF*, 2, XI, no. 403, Note from the President of the Council, 27 September 1938.

163. *DDF*, 2, XI, no. 413, Bonnet to François-Poncet, 28 September 1938, 1 am. See no. 420, Communication from François-Poncet to the Führer, 28 September 1938.

164. *DDF*, 2, XI, no. 422, Corbin, 28 September 1938, 1:19 a.m. Regarding the negotiations in Rome see no. 443, Blondel, 28 September 1938.

165. *DDF*, 2, XI, no. 427, François-Poncet, 28 September 1938, and mostly no. 450, Note from François-Poncet concerning the day of 28 September 1938.

166. See François-Poncet's picturesque and magnificent account op. cit., pp. 314–338.

167. I am mostly using *Vallette, Geneviève and Bouillon, Jacques, *Munich 1938*, Collection Kiosque, 1964, and an excellent master's thesis by one of my students, *Prévost, François, *L'opinion française après la conference de Munich, October-December 1938*, 1967. See *Daridan, Jean, *Le chemin de la défaite, 1938–1940*, 1980, which focuses on the role played by Léger at Munich. In the Daladier-Quai d'Orsay papers there is a long anonymous study with press clippings: "Positions de la gauche – Positions de la droite." The reader will have to wait for the important thesis under my supervision by Mr. Yvon Lacaze on "La France et Munich."

168. *Stoetzel, Jean, *Théorie des opinions*, Paris, 1943.

169. Published by the new magazine *Sondages*. See *Ageron, Ch. R., "L'opinion publique française pendant les crises internationales de septembre 1938 à juillet 1939," *Cahiers de l'Institut d'histoire de la presse et de l'opinion;* Tours, B., and Peyrefitte, Christel, "Les premiers sondages d'opinion," *Edouard Daladier chef de gouvernment*, 1977, pp. 265–278.

170. Quoted article, p. 211.

171. *Nogueres, Henri, *Munich ou la drôle de paix*, pp. 310–311. See Prévost, op. cit., p. 15.

172. 200,000 attended the ceremony according to Aragon—who opposed it!— *Ce soir*, 3 October 1938, quoted by Prévost, op. cit.

173. This is what he told American Ambassador Bullitt on 2 October. See *Haight, J. Mc V., American Aid to France*, 1970, p. 13 (from the Bullitt papers).

174. *JODP*, Chambre, 2 October 1938. The Senate voted 280 to 2 communist votes and abstentions (the socialists, Paul-Boncour, Pierre Laval, among them).

175. *Esprit*, 1 October, p. 4, Montherlant, p. 833. See Prévost, op. cit., p. 29.

176. 1 October 1938.

177. Monzie, *Ci-devant*, pp. 40–41.

178. Monzie, op. cit., p. 33.

179. See the master's thesis that I supervised by *Bellanger, Catherine, *La Flèche de Paris, étude du Frontisme à travers son journal*, 1929, which traces the evolution of Bergery very well from August 1938 from the resistance to "appeasement." However, he remained very anti-Italian.

180. Monzie, op. cit., p. 37.

181. Ibid., p. 39.

182. Prévost, op. cit., p. 212.

183. *Populaire*, 6 and 7 November 1938, quoted by Prévost, op. cit., p. 180.

184. See *Populaire*, 29 September 1938.

185. See Prévost, op. cit., pp. 183–184.

186. I have used a master's thesis which I supervised, *Perriot, Jean-Pierre, *Le syndicat national des instituteurs et le Front Populaire*, and a very good article by *Cointete-Labrousse, Michèle, "Le syndicat national des instituteurs, le pacifisme et l'Allemagne (1937–1939)," in *Les relations franco-allemandes*, op. cit., pp. 137–150.

187. According to Perriot, op. cit., p. 71, out of 23 school teachers elected as deputies in 1936, there were 17 SFIO, 3 PC, 3 radicals; p. 109 sq., 81% of school teachers were unionized by the end of 1938.

188. Weber, E., op. cit., p. 455; *Action française*, 27 October 1938; on the decline of the Action française, see p. 457.

189. Weber, op. cit., p. 455.

190. *Action française*, 4 October 1938. See Prévost, op. cit., p. 32; Weber, op. cit, p. 468.

191. *Combat*, November 1938. see Micaud, op. cit., p. 119; Prévost, op. cit., p. 50.

192. Weber, op. cit., p. 468.

193. *Petit Journal*, 16 November 1938, quoted by Prévost, op. cit., p. 96.

194. *Petit Journal*, 1 December 1938, quoted by Prévost, op. cit., p. 128.

195. Regarding this party see *Wolf, Dieter, *Die Doriot-Bewegung*, Stuttgart, 1967, and an excellent master's thesis that I supervised, *Conrad, Philippe, *Le parti populaire français de Jacques Doriot*, 1969.

196. *Emancipation nationale*, 14, 16 September 1938, quoted by Conrad, op. cit., p. 312.

197. Conrad, op. cit., p. 317.

198. Quoted article, p. 211

199. Kupferman, Alfred, *Pierre Laval*, p. 65.

200. Mallet, Alfred, *Pierre Laval*, I, p. 129.

201. I am using a master's thesis that I supervised by *Bellec, Anne-Marie, *Le nationalisme et le pacifisme dans les milieux catholiques de 1933 à 1939*, 1967.

202. This was the reason why under Vichy, Philippe Henriot published his *Carnets secrets* seized during a search. The object was to show that Zay, who was in prison at the time, was a "warmonger." Because of this it is highly probable that the text was not doctored. The admirable book by *Zay, Jean *Souvenirs et solitude*, 1945, written in prison, confirms his position of resistance to Hitler. See *Ruby, Marcel, *La vie et l'oevre de Jean Zay*, 1969.

203. *Souvenirs et solitude*, p. 60.

204. Soulié, M., op. cit., p. 489.

205. Marc Sangnier, the founder of this movement that had supported the Popular Front was true pacifist. See his book of 1936, *Le pacifisme d'action*. But according to his biographer *Mrs. Bathelemy-Madaule, Madeleine, *Marc Sangnier, 1873–1950*, Paris, 1975, he took few political positions at the time; see pp. 274–275. Yet he did make a pacifist speech at the beginning of November; see *Aube*, 9 November 1938.

206. Paul-Boncour, op. cit., III, pp. 106–108.

207. Prévost, op. cit., p. 191.

208. *Époque*, 13 October 1938. See Prévost, op. cit., pp. 192–193.

209. Prévost, op. cit., pp. 195–196.

210. Bellec, A.M., op. cit., p. 128. Regarding the nuances of the attitude of Esprit seethe discussion between *Winock, Michel, *Histoire politique de la revue Esprit, 1930–1950*, specifically p.175 sq., and *Senarclens, P. de, "L'image de l'Allemagne dans la revue Esprit de 1932 à 1941," *Relations internationales*, 1974, no 2, pp.123–145.

211. Vallette, G. and Bouillon, J., op. cit., p. 288. Regarding *L'Aube*, see *Mayeur, Françoise, *L'Aube* (Cahiers Fondation Nationale des Sciences Politiques), 1966.

212. Maternal grandfather of former president Valéry Giscard d'Estaing.

213. See *Bonafé, Felix, *Jacques Bardoux*, 1977, and *Bardoux, Jacques, *Journal d'un témoin de la Troisième, 1er septembre 1939–15 juillet 1940*, 1957.

214. Noël, L, *L'agression allemande contre la Pologne*, p. 228.

215. *DDF*, 2, XII, no. 49, 6 October 1938.

216. *DDF*, 2, 1, XII, no. 34, Lacroix, 5 October 1938.

217. *DDF*, 2, XII, no. 20, Coulondre, 4 October 1938. See also no. 17, Coulondre, 4 October 1938.

218. *DDF*, 2, XII, no. 95, Colonel Merson to Daladier, Belgrade, 2 October 1938 (excerpted from SHA).

219. *DDF*, 2, XII, Thierry, 19 October 1938.

220. *DDF*, 2, XII, no. 8, Cosme, 3 October 1938.

221. *DDF*, 2, XII, no. 190, Corbin, 20 October 1938.
222. *DDF*, 2, XII, 262, Saint-Quentin, 2 November 1938.
223. *DDF*, 2, XII, Bonnet to Saint-Quentin, 22 November 1938.
224. *DDF*, 2, XII, no. 48, d'Aumale, 6 October 1938.
225. *DDF*, 2, XII, Naggiar to Bonnet, Shanghai, 25 November 1938.
226. *DDF*, 2, XII, Georges Picot to Knobel, chargé d'affaires in Shanghai, 28 November 1938.

Chapter XII
AFTER MUNICH: EXPECTATIONS AND UNCERTAINTIES

1. *Carnets secrets de Jean Zay*, p. 5. See two important articles from a collection edited by Remond, R., and Bourdin, Janine, *Edouard Daladier, chef de gouvernment*: Bedarida, François, "La gouvernante anglaise" pp. 228–255 and Girault, René, "La decision gouvernemantale en politique extérieure," pp. 209–227.
2. Girault, art. quoted p. 222.
3. Bedarida, art. quoted, p. 238.
4. Adamthwaite, op. cit.
5. Bedarida, art. quoted, p. 238.
6. Noël (L.), *Les illusions de Stresa*, p. 143.
7. Adamthwaite, op. cit., pp. 398–399 and pp. 400–401.
8. *Fabre-Luce, Alfred, *Histoire secrète de la conciliation de Munich*, 1938.
9. *Thomas, Louis, *Histoire d'un jour, Munich, 29 septembre 1938*, 1939.
10. *Dominique, Pierre, *Après Munich veux-tu vivre ou mourir?*, 1938.
11. For most documents a cross verification can be made to the archives of the major embassies. See the introductions to Vols. X (p. ix) and XI (p. x) of DDF, 2. We find in the "Bonnet Files" within the "Fouques-Duparc Reconstruction" and the "Bonnet Papers"—what has been found of the archives of the Minister's cabinet.
12. *Ci-devant*, pp. 53–55. Polish Ambassador Lukasziewicz had excellent relations with Bonnet (Lukasziewicz, op. cit. p. 68), meeting with him very often. But he viewed him as being "weak," "incapable of being firm on anything," and "ready to fall into the tendency of adapting o each one of his various interlocutors" (ibid., p.157).
13. *L'agression allemande contre la Pologne*, p. 197.
14. Reproduced in part in ibid., pp. 247–257; see the complete text in DDF, 2, XII, no. 216, Noël, 25 October 1938. We should note that Coulondre felt that Poland and the USSR would find themselves on opposite sides, the Franco-Soviet Pact "considered defunct by Moscow, who will keep it only to cover up its isolation [...], was meaningless and can only create problems

for us." DDF, 2, XII, no. 164, Coulondre, 18 October 1938. General Musse, military attaché in Poland, agreed with his chief's opinion; see DDF, 2, XII, Musse to Daladier, 31 October 1938.

15. Noël, op. cit., p. 259. Such was the case for Flandin; see *Politique française*, op. cit., pp. 282–289.

16. MAE. Note from Louis Aubert, 21 October 1938. "Politique extérieure de la France après Munich."

17. DDF, 2, XII, note from the Department, Franco-Polish relations, 19 November 1938 (Bonnet Files.)

18. ADAP, 7 November 1938. I am of a slightly different opinion from that of Adamthwaite, op. cit., p. 286.

19. DDF, 2, XII, no. 86, Note from the Vice-President of the Superior War Council (excerpt from the SHA), 12 October 1938.

20. DDF, 2, XII, no. 147, 17 October 1938.

21. Dans Edouard Daladier, Girault (René), op. cit., p. 223.

22. Information coming from Jeanneney, J.-N., *François de Wendel...*, op. cit., pp. 580–584.

23. Teichova, Alice, *An Economic Background to Munich*, pp. 35–36.

24. All this information in Teichova, op. cit., see especially p. 118.

25. Ibid., p. 198.

26. Regarding that sale—to Czechoslovak banks—see MAE, Note for the Minister. Concerning the Skoda matter, Financial Aid to Czechoslovakia, 24 December 1938, and MAE, weekly Liaison, 28 December 1938.

27. MAE, Note from the deputy director of Political Affairs for the Minister, 3 October 1938.

28. Numerous papers on this theme in MAE, Serices 6, carton 26, file 4. Much attention was given to a long trip by German Economics Minister Funk, to Hungary, Romania, Bulgaria, Yugoslavia, Greece, and Turkey.

29. MAE, London embassy, commercial relations, no. 1117 (Series C, carton 26).

30. DDF, 2, XII, no. 109, 13 October 1938.

31. MAE, D. 1344, Coulondre to Bonnet, 14 December 1938.

32. It should be pointed out that in his recently published book, Marguerat feels that the scope of the German economic push should not be overly exaggerated. Marguerat, op. cit., pp. 23–24.

33. Many more statistics on German progress are in MAE, Series C, carton 26.

34. MAE, Mönick, D. 68383 (Series C, carton 26).

35. MAE, Series C, carton 26, D. 623, Corbin (commercial relations), 7 July 1938.

36. MAE, Series C, carton 26, Note for the Minister from the deputy director, 9 July 1938 "Separate actions towards the same goal." According to another note dated November from the deputy director.

37. MAE, Series C, carton 26.

38. MAE, Serie C, carton 26, Note from the deputy director, 26 October 1938.

39. MAE, Serie C, carton 26, Reynaud to Bonnet, 8 November 1938. See also Note from Alphand to de La Baume, deputy director of Commercial Affairs, 8 November 1938.

40. Ibid., 9 November 1938.

41. Ibid., 10 November 1938 (EMG, 2e Bureau, no. 2257).

42. MAE, Economic mission to Eastern Europe, 19 December 1938 (C. 104.1).

43. MAE, Coche, chargé d'affaires in Sofia, T. 520 (mail), 2 December. 1938; D. 341, Ristelhueber, Sofia, 6 December 1938 (a long report covering in particular, Alphand's visit to the king).

44. MAE, Bonnet to Daladier, D. 318, December 1938. See also, regarding this incoherence, MAE, Lacroix to Bonnet, T. 3257, Prague, 28 December 1938.

45. MAE, D. 20, to Daladier, 24 January 1939.

46. MAE, Queuille to Daladier, 17 January 1939 (Series C. carton 26).

47. MAE, Transcript of the meeting of 30 January 1939 (Series C, carton 260).

48. See Girault, T. as quoted, p. 223, according to the Daladier Papers (Fondation...), files 7 and 8.

49. In particular Adamthwaite, op. cit., pp. 293–296.

50. Ibid.

51. Alphand, Lamoureux were sent to London...and recalled because of the 15 March crisis. Adamthwaite, op. cit., p. 297.

52. Nothing comparable to the conversations between Robert Hudson, the British Minister and the German Wohltat at the end of July 1939 without the knowledge of the French government. The news having been leaked, caused a stir in France and was worrisome to the government.

53. Contrary to Duff Cooper in Great Britain. See *Carnets secrets de Jean Zay*, p. 9 (22 September), p. 33 (17 November).

54. See Monzie, *Ci-devant*, pp. 15, 44.

55. *DDF*, 2, XII, no. 29, Note from the political directorate, 5 October 1938.

56. *DDF*, 2, XII, no. 41, Corbin (following a conversation with Cadogan), 6 October 1938. Regarding the lack of popularity of this Anglo-German declaration in Great Britain, see DDF, 2, XII, no. 106, Corbin, 13 October 1938.

57. DDF, 2, XII, no. 18, François-Poncet, 4 October 1938. See also MAE, T. 1039, 4 October 1938. Chamberlain warned Daladier publicly on 2 Octobre of his agreement, and Daladier's response on the 4th underlining Franco-British collaboration.

58. *DDF*, 2, XII, no. 29, Note from the directorate of Political Affairs, 5 October 1938.

59. *DDF*, 2, XII, no. 49, 6 October 1938.

60. *DDF*, 2, XII, no. 60, François-Poncet, 10 October 1938.

61. Bonnet, *De Munich à la guerre*, p. 208; see *DDF*, 2, XII, p. 270, note.

62. Reprinted in François-Poncet, op. cit., pp. 342–344. See *DDF*, 2, XII, no 197, 20 October 1938.

63. *DDF*, 2, XII, no. 199, Bonnet to François-Poncet, 21 October 1938.

64. *DDF*, 2, XII, no. 205, François-Poncet, 23 October 1938.

65. *DDF*, 2, XII, no. 279, Montbas, Berlin, 8 November 1938.

66. See the summary by chargé d'affaires de Montbas, *DDF*, 2, XII, no. 300, 13 November 1938 and no. 309, 15 November 1938.

67. *Toscano, Mario, *Le origini diplomatiche del Patto d'Accaio*, p. 80 cites a telegram dated 6 November from Ciano to Attolico, stating that Mussolini "is asking to delay the visit by Ribbentrop to Paris until after the trip by Chamberlain to that same city." Corbin had heard about the Italian pressures. DDF, 2, XII, no. 382, 24 November 1938.

68. This is what Ribbentrop told Coulondre in the course of the first meeting. *DDF*, 2, XII, no. 333, Coulondre, 19 November 1938.

69. Adamthwaite, op. cit., p. 288. The information drawn from ADAP, D, IV, nos. 346, 348, 349, 351, and not corroborated in the French archives, that are possibly incomplete.

70. *DDF*, 2, XII, no. 280, Corbin, 8 November 1938.

71. A program—geographic numeration—was sent from the Quai d'Orsay to London and Corbin had the assent of Halifax. *DDF*, 2, XII, 21 November 1938.

72. A 27-page summary in *DDF*, 2, XII, no. 390. On the social side, see the amusing account in Adamthwaite, op. cit., p. 249.

73. *DDF*, 2, XII, no. 352, Lamarle, chargé d'affaires in Prague, 22 November 1938.

74. Renouvin, art. cit.

75. Daladier Collection, FNSP. Note of 5 December 1938.

76. See the excellent critical discussion of this point in Adamthwaite, op. cit., p. 401. Bonnet denies the meeting of 7 December in *Défense de la paix*, II, p. 39, but then confirms it in *De Munich à la guerre*, p. 224.

77. MAE, 7 December 1938. Coulondre mentions the meeting of the 7th at the hotel Crillon. Bonnet was alone. Coulondre, op. cit., p. 285.

78. ADAP, D, IV, no. 370.

79. Schmidt, Paul, *Statist auf diplomatischer Bühne*, p. 423

80. Text in *Livre jaune français*, p. 33.

81. MAE, Léger Papers, Letter to Outrey, 21 April 1952.

82. MAE, D. 188, Coulondre, 23 February 1939.

83. MAE, T. 367–69, Bonnet to Coulondre, 19 March 1939.

84. MAE, letter from Ribbentrop to Bonnet, Fischl, 13 July 1939.

85. MAE, answer from Bonnet to Ribbentrop, 21 July 1939.

86. We should note that as early as 11 December a Franco-British "representation" was made to Germany regarding Memel. See MAE, T. 117–118, Bonnet to Coulondre, 11 December 1938, and T. 4454, Coulondre, 12 December 1938.

87. MAE, T. 3654–3657, Coulondre, 20 December 1938.

88. Regarding this and what follows the best guide is Renouvin, Pierre, "Les relations de la Grance-Bretagne et de la France avec l'Italie en 1938-1939," in *Les relations franco-britanniques de 1935 à 1939*, pp. 295–317. On public opinion I have used a good thesis which I directed by *Casset, Jean-Michel, *L'attitude française vis-à-vis de l'Italie (oct. 1938–mai 1939)*, 1967.

89. Noël, L., *Les illusions de Stresa*, p. 127.

90. Noël, L., *Les illusions de Stresa*, pp. 118–120.

91. See Toscano, op. cit., pp. 79, 82.

92. See *François-Poncet, André, *Au Palais Farnèse. Souvenirs d'une ambassade à Rome, 1938–1940*, 1961: a grand picture, less detailed than the book by the same author regarding his Berlin embassy.

93. Carnets secrets de Jean Zay, p. 93. See Noël, op. cit. p. 128. Confirmed by François-Poncet. See MAE, T. 2231-2240, 3 December 1938. It should be noted that François-Poncet was optimistic at first. He noticed that Ciano knew about the ongoing Franco-German rapprochement. DDF, 2, XII, no. 285, 9 November, 287, 9 November 1938, 288, 10 November 1938.

94. MAE, T. 2190–2193, François-Poncet, 1 December 1938, 11 p.m.

95. MAE, T. 1039–1041, Bonnet to François-Poncet, 1 December 1938.

96. MAE, T. 3545–3548, Bonnet to Corbin, 1 December 1938, 11:45 p.m.

97. MAE, T. 2231–2240, François-Poncet, 3 December 1938.

98. MAE, T. 2439, François-Poncet, 17 December 1938.

99. MAE, T. 4438–4439, Coulondre, 10 December 1938.

100. JODP, Chamber, 13 December 1938.

101. MAE, T. 2267-2272, 4 December 1938.

102. MAE, Personal letter, 30 December 1938. Regarding he role played by Lagardelle, a follower of Georges Sorel, and former labor leader who had become favorable to corporative and was brought to Rome by Jouvenel in 1933 was finally not very efficient nor active, see Bérard, op. cit., pp. 400–401.

103. MAE, Note regarding Franco-British solidarity in the Mediterranean, 12 December 1938. See also T. 3204–3205, Corbin to Bonnet, 13 December 1938.

104. MAE, T. 1293, Noël to Bonnet, 12 December 1938.

105. MAE, Note from the Minister, 13 December 1938.

106. MAE, T. 2376 (mail), François-Poncet, 14 December 1938.

107. MAE, T. 3298, Corbin, 23 December 1938.

108. For example, MAE, T. p. 20, Bonnet to Corbin, and T. 29–32, Corbin, 5 January 1939.

109. MAE, D. 20, 9 January 1939.

110. MAE, T. 131–135, 12 January; T. 144–150, 13 January; T. 151–153, 13 January 1939.

111. MAE, D. 46, 26 January 1939.

112. MAE, T. 165–168, Bonnet to Saint-Quentin, 29 January 1939. See also Toscano, op. cit., p. 126, conversation between Corbin and Cadogan (*DBFP*, 3, IV, no. 76).

113. MAE, Note drafted by Bonnet, February 1939.

114. MAE, T. 597, François-Poncet, 16 February 1939.

115. MAE, Baudoin, "Transcript of my conversations with Count Ciano, 2 February 1939." See Daladier Papers, Sc. Po., 2 DA 5.

116. MAE, Note drafted by Bonnet, February 1939.

117. MAE, T. 401 (mail), 3 February 1939.

118. MAE, T. 573, François-Poncet, 15 February and T. 593, 16 February 1939. See also T. 564, 14 February where he mentions the dissatisfaction of Coulondre about a trip taken by de Brinon.

119. MAE, T. 597, 16 February 1939.

120. MAE, T. 173–174, Bonnet to François-Poncet.

121. See Bedarida, quoted article, he quotes the later article by *Baudoin, "Un voyage à Rome: février 1939," Revue de deux Mondes, 1 May 1962, p. 28–38; Bonnet, op. cit. p.69; *Guariglia, Raffaele, *La diplomatie difficile. Mémoires 1912–1946*, French translation, Paris, 1955, pp. 385–386.

122. Toscano, op. cit., pp. 118 and 167; Ciano, *Journal...*, 19 March, p. 59, and 21 March, p. 51.

123. MAE, T. 519, Noguès, Rabat, 16 December. 1938.

124. MAE, Mandel to Bonnet, 21 December 1938.

125. MAE, D. 478, Daladier to Bonnet, 17 February 1939.

126. MAE, Permanent Committee of National Defense, 24 February 1939.

127. MAE, weekly liaison, 1 March 1939.

128. MAE, T. 780–782, 1 March 1939.

129. *DDF*, 2, XII, no. 326, 18 November, and no. 356, 22 November 1938.

130. MAE, T. 4351, 1 December. 1938. See also T. 4345 on the same day.

131. MAE, T. 4410, Montbas, 6 December 1938; MAE, T. 2372, François-Poncet to Bonnet, 13 December 1938.

132. MAE, D. 688, Noël, 7 December 1938.

133. MAE, T. 1342, Coulondre, 13 December 1938. See also from Rome, T. 2372 from François-Poncet, 13 December 1938 and T. 2524, 23 December. Ciano was not informed.

134. MAE, D. 59, Noël to Bonnet, 13 December 1938.

135. MAE, T. 4487 (mail), Coulondre, 15 December. See also *URSS, Documents*, op. cit., no. 50, p. 85, 15 December 1938. See also D. 1379, 22 December and D. 615, 29 December 1938.

136. MAE, D. 717, Noël, 21 December 1938.

137. *URSS, Documents*, op. cit., no. 45, p. 81, 8 December 1938. Senator Jacques Bardoux felt the need to write to Daladier on 16 January 1939 announcing a violent coup attempt in the Polish Ukraine in February, and a second in the Soviet Ukraine in May; see *Journal d'un témoin*, p. 18.

138. MAE, T. 1 to 5, Coulondre to Bonnet, 14 January 1939.

139. MAE, T. 191, François-Poncet, 16 January 1939.

140. MAE, T. 202–203, 21 January 1939 and D. 82, 26 January As well as the military attaché in Warsaw, General Musse, SHA, 4/S, 19 January 1939.

141. *Potemkin, *Histoire de la diplomatie*, III, pp. 671 and 675.

142. MAE (excerpt from the archives of the Marine), 22 January 1939.

143. MAE, T. 134 (mail), Naggiar to Bonnet, 24 February 1939.

144. *URSS, Documents*, op. cit., no. 56, p. 97, 27 December 1938.

145. MAE, "Étude générale du Cabinet du minister," January 1939.

146. *URSS, Documents*, no. 55, p. 93, 22 December 1938.

147. MAE, T. 1150, Corbin, 16 December 1938.

148. Adamthwaite, op. cit., p. 274; *Niedhart, *Gross-Britannien und die Sowiet-Union, 1934–1939*, p. 391.

149. MAE, T. 235–243, Corbin, 28 January 1939. see *DBFP*, 3, IV, no. 18, Halifax to Sir N. Bland, The Hague, 26 January 1939, and no 27 (answer from Bland, 27 January). The news came from Roosevelt.

150. MAE, Aide-mémoire from the embassy of Great Britain, 29 January 1939.

151. MAE, Note from the political director, 29 January 1939.

152. MAE, T. 165–168, Bonnet to Saint-Quentin, 29 January 1939.

153. MAE, Note from the directorate of political affairs, 1 February 1939.

154. MAE, T. 176–180, Bonnet to Corbin, 5 February 1939.

155. MAE, T. 331–336, 4 February 1939.

156. MAE, T. 329, Corbin, 6 February 1939.

157. MAE, British note of 13 February 1939. See *DBFP*, 3, IV, no. 81, Halifax to Phipps, 3 February 1939, and ibid., no. 104, Phipps, 14 February 1939.

158. MAE, D. 47, Vitrolles, 3 February 1939.

159. MAE, T. 557, Coulondre, 28 February 1939.

160. See for example MAE, T. 1138, 2 December 1938.

161. Gauché, op. cit., p.96–97. See article by *d'Hoop, J.M., "La politique militaire de la France dans les Balkans de l'accord de Munich au début de la seconde guerre mondiale," in *Studia Balcanica*, Sofia, 7, 1973 pp. 79–89.

162. SHA, D. 1103/AM, 12 December 1938.

163. SHA, D. 5705/S, 19 December 1938.

164. SHA, D. 28/AM 10 January 1939. See also D. 43/AM, 17 January. At this time Coulondre was impressed by his subordinate. In a cable of 17 January 1939 (MAE, T. 141), he felt that Romania was the most threatened country.

165. MAE, Copy of a dispatch from Didelet to Daladier, 23 March 1939.

166. Ibid., 11 April, when he now insisted on Yugoslavia.

167. We now know that Hitler's directive regarding Bohemia and Memel was dated 21 October 1938 (ADAP, D, IV, pp. 90–91). Regarding the Czechoslovak internal crisis which is not part of our subject, I refer back to the October 1963 issue of RHDGM, and in particular the article by *Fichelle, A., "La crise interne de la Tchécoslovaquie," pp. 21–38.

168. *ADAP*, D. IV, p. 413.

169. MAE, 7 December 1938.

170. MAE, T. 3080, Lacroix, 3 December 1938. See also T. 4472 (mail) Coulondre, 13 December 1938; MAE, Weekly liaison, 28 December 1938., T. 238–239, Lacroix, Prague, 3 February 1939.

171. MAE, T. 3087 a 3092, Lacroix, 5 December 1938. A departmental note dated 5 December (ibid.) mentions this issue among those to be handled.

172. MAE, T. 3267, Lacroix, 30 December 1938.

173. MAE, D. 68.350 from Mönick, financial attaché in London to Paul Reynaud, 31 December 1938.

174. MAE, D. 172, Bonnet to Reynaud, 22 January 1939.

175. MAE, D. 972, Reynaud to Bonnet, 19 January 1933.

176. MAE, T. 4487 (mail), Coulondre, 15 December 1938. Ibid., D. 82, 26 January 1939. Ibid., D. 30, 7 February 1939.

177. MAE, D. 130, Coulondre, 8 February 1939.

178. MAE, D. 164, Coulondre, 16 February 1939.

179. MAE, T. 368, Lacroix, 18 February 1939.

180. MAE, Coulondre, 26 February 1939. This information originated in a conversation between Captain Stehlin and General Bodenschatz. See Coulondre *De Staline à Hitler*, p. 270–271; Stehlin, *Témoignages pour l'Histoire*, pp. 375–379 and MAE, D. 392, Coulondre, 7 May 1939.

181. MAE, D. 204, Coulondre, 28 February 1939.

182. MAE, T. 682, Corbin, 10 March 1939.

183. MAE, T. 653–655, 11 March 1939.

184. MAE, T. 672-677, Montbas, 12 March 1938.

185. MAE, T. 415–419, Bonnet to Corbin, 12 March 1939.

186. MAE, See also T. 682-686, 13 March.

187. MAE, T. T. 713 (telephone) 14 March, 6:30 p.m.

188. MAE, D. 200, Corbin, 15 March 1939.

189. MAE, T. 769–775, Corbin, 15 March 1939.

Chapter XIII
THE FAILURE OF THE GRAND ALLIANCE

1. MAE, D. 255, Corbin to Bonnet, 4 April 1939. See also T. 1047, 4 April, that mentions a "resurrection of national unity."

2. MAE, D. 255, Corbin to Bonnet, 4 April 1939. See also T. 1047, 4 April, that mentions a "resurrection of national unity."

3. MAE, D. 9, Coulondre to Bonnet, 27 April 1939.

4. DDF, 2, XI, no. 389, Lasmartres, 27 September 1938. See also 438, Corbin, 28 September; 437 Lasmartres, 28 September, 445; Bonjean, Madrid, 28 September; 494; Lasmartres, 30 September, 511; Bojean, 1 October; 518; Bonjean, 2 October 1938: XII, no. 24; Lasmartres, 5 October 1938. See also DDF, 2, XII, no. 28, Labonne (who was soon to leave his assignment),

Barcelona, 5 October 1938. See also no. 112, Castéran. consul at Bilbao, 13 October 1938, who insisted on the opposition of the "requests" and of the Church to the Falange, which was pro-German. On the German position, which was very much opposed to mediation, see DDF, 2, XII, no. 212 François-Poncet, 25 October 1938. Corroborated by Lasmartres, DDF, 2, XII, no. 138, 15 October 1938.

5. DDF, 2, XII, quoted summary, p. 769–770. Regarding the displeasure of the Francoists see DDF, 2, XII, no. 421, Lasmartres, 20 November 1938. Hemming, general secretary of the Non-Intervention Committee went to Spain for a few days, October 1938. He appeared more favorable to recognition. DDF, 2, XII, no. 298, Corbin, 11 November.

6. Actually these were infantry troops, without weapons and not air force as Lasmartres writes; see DDF, 2, XII, no. 224. Weekly liaison, 26 October 1938. "We have not repatriated units only individuals." DDF, 2, XII, no. 281, Lieutenant Colonel Morel, military attaché, Barcelona, 8 November 1938.

7. *DDF*, 2, XII, no. 281, Morel, Barcelona, 8 November 1938.

8. *DDF*, 2, XII, no. 336, Note from the political directorate, Spain: the withdrawal of the volunteers and the status of belligerent, 19 November 11938, and no. 337, Fouques-Duparc, chargé d'affaires in Barcelona, 20 November 1938.

9. *DDF*, 2, XII, no. 357, Aide-mémoire from the French government, 22 November 1938.

10. MAE, T. 29, 13 January, and T. 32–39, 13 January 1939.

11. MAE, Telephone conversation, 24 January 1939.

12. MAE, Weekly liaison, 25 January 1939. SHA, Morel, Barcelona, 19 January 1939.

13. MAE, Note from Bonnet regarding his conversation with the Spanish ambassador, Alvarez del Vayo, 26 January 1939. See also the conversation of Captain Luizet, military attaché in Tangier with Colonel Beigbeder, high commissioner in Spanish Morocco, SHA, Tangier, 18 January 1939.

14. MAE, Note from Bonnet, ibid., 1 February 1939.

15. MAE, Note from the Minister, 20 January 1939.

16. See MAE, Note from the legal advisor, Jules Basdevant, for the Minister. Sending an agent to Burgos implied de facto recognition.

17. *Midi socialiste*, 11 February 1939, quoted by Pike, David W., *Les Français et la guerre d'Espagne*, 1975, p. 351.

18. MAE, Note from Léon Bérard regarding his trip to Burgos, 3–6 February 1939.

19. See the series of telegrams from Jules Henry working from Perpignan on 5 February and the summaries of his telephone conversations. See MAE, T. 145–154, as well as several memos from the political directorate on the same day.

20. MAE T. undated no doubt from Bérard. Bonnet mentions this event during the Council of Ministers of 14 February undoubtedly to show the disintegration of the republican side. See *Carnets secrets de Jean Zay*, p. 43.

21. MAE, Note from Léon Bérard, second meeting with Jordana, 6 February 1939.

22. *Temps*, 1 February 1939, quoted by Bonnet, J.-Ch., op. cit., p. 362.

23. See Monzie, op. cit., 10 February 1939, pp. 84–87 (de Monzie was Minister of Public Works).

24. MAE, Communication from the embassy of Great Britain 13 February 1939.

25. MAE, Note reading the visit by Alvarez del Vayo, 17 February 1939.

26. Monzie, op. cit., 16 February 1939, p. 89.

27. *JODP*, Chambre, 24 February 1939.

28. *Carnets secrets de Jean Zay*, p. 43.

29. MAE, Note on the Bérard-Jordana conversations of 18–19 February, 20 February 1939.

30. MAE, personal letter from Bérard to Bonnet, 20 February 1939.

31. MAE, Instructions from Bonnet to Bérard, Tuesday 21 February

32. MAE, Note from Léon Bérard regarding his meetings of 23, 24, 25 February resulting in complete agreement regarding the council "unanimous," see Monzie, op. cit., 27 February p. 90.

33. MAE, Note on a Phipps-Bonnet conversation, 22 February 1939.

34. MAE, Weekly liaison, 1 March 1939.

35. MAE, D. 19, Pétain, Saint-Sebastian, 27 March 1939. The Bérard-Jordana agreement was dated 25 February.

36. MAE, T. 61, Pétain, 20 April, and T. 67, 22 April 1939.

37. Bonnet, J.-Ch., op. cit., p. 364.

38. JODP, Chambre, 10 March 1939, p. 902. See Bonnet, J.-Ch., op. cit., p. 363.

39. 2 February 1939. See Bonnet J.-Ch, op. cit., p. 365.

40. MAE, T. 252, Pétain, 28 July 1939.

41. MAE, T. 299–301, Bonnet to Pétain, 21 July 1939.

42. MAE, D., 17 July 1939.

43. MAE, Personal letter, Gazel, 6 august1939.

44. See Renouvin, T. cited p. 308.

45. MAE, T. 1202–1208, François-Poncet, 26 March 1939.

46. Baudoin, quoted article.

47. Monzie, op. cit., p. 116.

48. Regarding the two councils see Carnets secrets of Jean Zay, p. 50–54. See Adamthwaite, op. cit., p. 307, regarding the initiatives by Halifax and Phipps and on a note from Oudinot (President of the Council), "Objections to negotiating with Italy," 26 March 1936, Daladier papers. The same for the relations of Caillaux and Bonnet with the king of Italy, according to DBFP, V, no. 85.

49. MAE, T. 961, Corbin, 30 March.

50. MAE, T. 1278, 30 March 1939.

51. MAE, D. 182, 30 March 1939. MAE, T. 1303-1307, 2 April 1939. See also T. 53–54, Mercier, minister to Tirana, 3 April; T. 55-57, Mercier, 3 April 1939.

52. MAE, D. 197, 6 April 1939, and D. 204, 11 April 1939.

53. MAE, T. 1458–1460, 10 April 1939.

54. MAE, 12 April 1939 (13 p. dispatch).

55. MAE, D. 210, 13 April 1939.

56. MAE, T. 1697–1698, 24 April 1939.

57. MAE, T. 1726–1730, 26 April. See Renouvin, T. quoted, p. 310.

58. Renouvin, T. quoted, p. 310.

59. Renouvin, T. quoted, p. 310, note.

60. MAE, Note from Bonnet following a visit by Baudoin, April 1939.

61. MAE, Note from Bonnet, 2 May 1939.

62. MAE, T. 1949–1957, François-Poncet, 11 May 1939. He met with Ciano and secured a lifting of the ban on *Le Temps* in Italy.

63. MAE, T. 1893–1895, François-Poncet.

64. MAE, Transcript of the meetings of 20 and 21 May 1939. See the excellent analysis by Renouvin, T. quoted, pp. 311–312.

65. MAE, T. 2108–2111, 21 May 1939.

66. MAE, T. 2124–2130, 22 May 1939.

67. MAE, T. 1427, 23 May 1939.

68. MAE, T. 2243–2245, François-Poncet, 30 May 1939.

69. MAE, T. 2254–2263, 31 May 1939.

70. MAE, T. 2493, François-Poncet, 16 June 1939.

71. MAE, letter from Chamberlain to Daladier, 13 July 1939.

72. MAE, Daladier to Baudoin, 17 July 1939 (draft).

73. See Renouvin, T. quoted, p. 313.

74. On the subject there has been an interesting debate between P. Renouvin and D.C. Watt at the Franco-British Colloquium of September 1972. According to Watt it was British policy that held Italy back. According to Renouvin, whom we follow here, the explanation was that Italy was not ready. Ciano went to Germany in August and was frightened to discover that Hitler was not bluffing and that war was imminent (see Ciano, *Diary*, I). We note that Coulondre was aware of Ciano's displeasure. MAE, T. 2179–2181, Coulondre, 13 August 1939.

75. See a very noteworthy unpublished study by *Laloy, Jean, "Remarques sur les Anglo-Franco-Soviet negotiations of 1939," 1972. See *Taylor, A.J.P., *The Origins of the Second World War*, 1963, in particular p. 231.

76. For example MAE, T. 53–58, Payart, chargé d'affaires, Moscow, 1 February 1939; T. 82–88, Naggiar, ambassador, 9 February 1939; T. 127, Naggiar, 21 February 1939 (after having met with Mikoyan and Molotov).

77. MAE, T. 66–67, Payart, 5 February 1939; T. 104–111, Naggiar, 14 February 1939.

78. MAE, T. 90–102, Naggiar, 11 February 1939.
79. See MAE, T. 82–88, 9 February T. 104–111, 14 February mostly T. 124 (pouch), 20 February 1939.
80. MAE, T. 134 (letter), Naggiar, 24 February 1939 (summary of a meeting with Litvinov, 22 February).
81. MAE, T. 355–357, Bonnet to Coulondre, 17 March.
82. MAE, T. 816–822, Corbin, 18 March.
83. MAE, Note from the Minister. Conversation with Souritz, 18 March (Bonnet Files) and Note from the British Embassy to the French government, 18 March. See also T. 842–846, Corbin, 20 March.
84. Coulondre wonders about this point and refers to parts of *Mein Kampf* regarding France. MAE, D.262, 19 March 1939.
85. MAE, Note from the Minister, 19 March 1939 (Hoppenot Files).
86. MAE, T. 125–127, Bonnet to Thierry (Bucharest), 19 March 1939. See Lukasziewicz, op. cit., p. 175 sq. on these conversations with Daladier and Léger whom he found "very badly inclined" toward Poland (p. 176).
87. MAE, T. 448, Noël, 23 March.
88. MAE, T. 838–841, Corbin, 20 March 1939.
89. MAE, Conversation of 20 March with Souritz (Bonnet Papers).
90. MAE, T. 919–923, Corbin, 28 March.
91. MAE, T. 494–498, Noël, 29 March. See an important note from the deputy directorate to the League of Nations, "Poland, Germany, and Danzig," offering the account of events regarding Danzig since Munich (MAE, 30 March 1939). It should also be noted that Léon Noël had reported at length in February about anti-German agitation in Poland especially among students.
92. MAE, Payart, T. 235–239, 2 April 1939 (Bonnet Papers).
93. MAE, Payart, T. 245–246, 4 April 1939. The negotiations were not held in Moscow but rather in Paris between Bonnet and Ambassador Souritz. Payart on three occasions in April and May will request being informed. See Bonnet to Payart, T. 110, 113, 5 April 1939.
94. MAE, Bonnet to the embassy in Moscow. T. 116–121, 9 April (conversation Bonnet-Souritz of 8 April). See also T. 122, 10 April.
95. Quoted article, p. 3.
96. MAE, Payart to Bonnet, T. 259–263, 11 April 1939.
97. MAE, Payart to Bonnet. T. 265–269, 14 April 1939. See also Daladier to Bonnet, D. 1154 Z/EMA-SAE, 22 April (Hoppenot Papers).
98. MAE, Bonnet to Naggiar, T. 129–136, 15 April.
99. There is a misunderstanding on this subject. See MAE, Payart to Bonnet, T. 282–287, 18 April 1939.
100. See communication made on 15 April to the Quai d'Orsay by the British embassy regarding conversations between Halifax and Maisky, the Soviet ambassador to London (Bonnet Papers) and Corbin to Bonnet, T. 1235–1237, 15 April.

101. MAE, Bonnet to Naggiar, T. 138–141, 16 April 1939.
102. MAE, Analysis of the Draft of Assistance. Russian counter-proposals (probably 20 April 1939).
103. MAE, Corbin to Bonnet, T. 1289–1291, 21 April 1939.
104. MAE, Corbin to Bonnet, T. 1328–1331, 25 April 1939.
105. MAE, T. 1289–1291, Corbin, 20 April.
106. MAE see Note from the Deputy directorate for Europe, British aide-mémoire of 22 April and most of all Note of 24 April, Communication from the political section at the embassy of Great Britain: T. 1328–1331, Corbin 25 April 11939; expression given from Bonnet to Souritz, 29 April; British aide-memoire to France, 29 April.
107. MAE, T. 1389–1390, Corbin, 1 May 1939.
108. MAE, D. 338, 3 May 1939.
109. MAE, T. 326–329, Payart, Moscow, 4 May 1939.
110. MAE, T. 1893–1895, François-Poncet, 7 May 1939.
111. MAE, T. 346–349, Payart, 9 May. See Chamberlain's speech, 10 May. MAE, T. 1487 (wire), Corbin, 10 May 1939.
112. MAE, T. 358, Payart, 11 May 1939.
113. MAE, T. 362–366, Payart, 12 May 1932.
114. MAE, Note from the Minister. Visit from Souritz, 15 May 1939.
115. MAE, T. 962–966, Bonnet to Corbin, 15 May 1939.
116. MAE, T. 1560–1565, Corbin, 18 May.
117. MAE, Note from the political affairs directorate on Franco-Anglo-Soviet negotiations, 5 July 1939 (Bonnet Papers). On 8 May and American press agency announced an imminent German-Soviet pact.
118. MAE, Notes taken during a Franco-British discussion on 20 May 1939 (Hoppenot Files) and MAE, continuation of the conversations between Daladier, Bonnet, and Halifax, 21 May 1939.
119. MAE, T. 1629–1831, Corbin, 24 May 1939. See T. 1637, Corbin, 25 May, and T. 186, Bonnet to Payart, 26 May 1939.
120. This was the opinion of Rochat, deputy director of political affairs. MAE, weekly liaison, 24 May 1939.
121. MAE, Note from the minister. Visit by Souritz, 26 May 1939.
122. MAE, T. 400–405, Payart, 28 May 1939.
123. MAE, D. 115, Payart, 29 May 1939.
124. MAE, T. 406–407, Payart, 29 May 1939.
125. MAE, T. 408–414, 30 May 1939.
126. MAE, Note quoted dated 9 July 1939; T. 429–431, and 432–437, Naggiar, 2 June 1939. MAE, T. 198–205, Bonnet to Naggiar, 2 June.
127. We should note that "non!" is written on the margin of this telegram. We do not know by whom. It is not in Léger's handwriting. Lukasziewicz (op. cit. pp. 233–239) and Beck were furious about the Soviet answer that they knew through Bonnet on 3 June.

128. Laloy, T. quoted.
129. MAE, T. 416, Naggiar, 31 May.
130. MAE, T. 1097–1099, Bonnet to Corbin, 7 June.
131. MAE, T. 1768–1774, Corbin 9 June.
132. MAE, T. 481–483, Naggiar, 14 June; T. 488–492, Naggiar, 15 June.
133. MAE, T. 495–501, Naggiar, 16 June.
134. MAE, T. 502–506, Naggiar, 16 June.
135. MAE, T. 484–487, 15 June.
136. MAE, T. 525–527, Naggiar, 21 June 1939.
137. MAE, T. 528–533, 21 June; T. 543–547, 22 June 1939.
138. MAE, Bonnet to Corbin, 22 June; T. 1246–1253, Instructions from Bonnet to Corbin, 23 June, etc.
139. MAE, T. 1260–1261, Bonnet to Corbin, 24 June; ibid., T. 252–259, to Naggiar, 24 June; ibid., T. 268–277, to Naggiar, 24 June; ibid., T. 279–281, Naggiar, 24 June.
140. MAE, T. 1301–1307, Bonnet to Corbin; T. 299–302, Bonnet to Naggiar, 29 June 1939.
141. MAE, T. 331–332, Bonnet to Naggiar.
142. MAE, T. 340–344, Bonnet to Naggiar, 5 July.
143. MAE, T. 2110, Corbin, 6 July 1939.
144. MAE, T. 642–644, Naggiar, 7 July 1939.
145. MAE, T. 648–654, Naggiar, 8 July 1939.
146. Ibid.
147. MAE, T. 410–413, Bonnet to Naggiar, 9 July 1939. See the pessimistic confidences made by Bonnet to Monzie, *Ci-devant*, op. cit., 8 July 1939, p. 126.
148. MAE, T. 1346–1440, Bonnet to Corbin, 10 July 1939.
149. Also T. 655–663, Naggiar, 10 July 1939.
150. MAE, Message from G. Bonnet to Lord Halifax, 19 July 1939.
151. MAE, T. 511–514, Bonnet to Naggiar, 26 July 1939.
152. MAE, T. 1556, Bonnet to Corbin, 24 July 1932.
153. SHA, D. 1522/DN3, Gamelin to Doumenc, 27 July 1939. The program had been approved by Daladier on 24 July.
154. MAE, Note from the deputy directorate for Europe 3 August 1939. These instructions were published in DBFP, 3, VI, pp. 762–789. See also T. 571, Bonnet to Naggiar, 12 August 1939.
155. Beaufre, *Le drame de 1940*, p. 124. Adamthwaite, op. cit. p. 3336, is critical of an interpretation by *Aster, Sydney, *The Coming of the Second World War*, 1975, p. 296, who views this text as giving "full powers" to Doumenc. Adamthwaite is entirely correct. The French expression "à tout prix" doesn't exactly mean "at all costs" as Aster believes, but is very general. Spare no effort in order to… We do have tangible proof that Doumenc did not have full powers but at the most of those of the ambassador; see MAE, T. 821-822, Naggiar, 3 August 1939.

156. On 4 July, General Didelet could find no clue regarding a coming offensive, MAE, D. 565, Coulondre, 4 July 1939.
157. MAE, D. 602, Coulondre, 13 July 1939.
158. MAE, D. 638, Tarbé de Saint-Hardouin, 25 July 1939. This observation is corroborated by the *Deuxième Bureau*. See Gauché, General, op. cit., p. 99.
159. MAE, T. 1583–1585, Bonnet to Corbin, 28 July 1939.
160. MAE, T. 2063, 1 August 1939.
161. MAE, T. 2064, 1 August 1939. See Coulondre, op. cit., p. 275. Coulondre, was away on vacation since mid-July, returned to Berlin on 12 August and found "a much more tense situation."
162. *DDF*, 2, XII, no. 164, Coulondre, 18 October 1938.
163. *DDF*, 2, XII, no. 183 (excerpt from SHA), 20 October 1938.
164. MAE, T. 34–37, Payart, 27 January.
165. MAE, T. 134, 22 February 1939.
166. MAE, T. 1070–1073, 22 April 1939.
167. MAE, T. 1203, 4 May, and T. 1207, 4 May 1939.
168. MAE, D. 392, 7 May. See also Coulondre, op. cit., pp. 270–271; Stehlin, op. cit., p. 147 sq., pp. 375–379.
169. Stehlin, op. cit., p. 151–152. *Bonnet, Georges, *Dans la tourmente*, 1971, pp. 134–135.
170. MAE, T. 351–356, Payart, 10 May 1939.
171. MAE, Note from the Minister, 26 May 1939.
172. MAE, weekly liaison, 24 May 1939.
173. ADAP, D. VI, no. 414 and 424. See also MAE, T. 1054, Monicault, chargé d'affaires in Ankara; MAE, T. 27, Garreau, consul general in Hamburg, 4 July 1939.
174. MAE, T. 1865–1866, 8 July 1939.
175. MAE, T. 699–703, 16 July 1939. See his T. 741, 22 July, on economic talks.
176. MAE, D. 165, 22 July 1939.
177. SHA, 599/5, 13 July 1939.
178. SHM. Report on the mission to Moscow by Captain Willaume, August 1939 (the operative date appears to be the beginning of September), p. 3, and Beaufre, op. cit., p. 128. See British account in *DBFP*, 3, VII, appendix II, pp. 558–614.
179. Beaufre, op. cit., p. 138.
180. See also Note EMA, transcript of the third meeting (13 August evening).
181. Detailed account in Beaufre, op. cit., pp. 140–145. See also SHM, Report Willaume.
182. We are using in what follows besides the general account by Léon Noël also the description by Beaufre, op. cit. pp. 155–165, and a long report by General Musse, SHA, 163, 24 August 1939. General Beaufre advances the possibility that the telegrams sent by Musse every day from Warsaw could have been decrypted by the Soviets, op. cit., pp. 161–162. There is actually no proof.

183. As confirmed by a new meeting between Musse and Stachiewicz on 20 August, see the quoted report.

184. On this subject see in particular, *Puaux, Gabriel, *Deux années au Levant. Souvenirs de Syrie et du Liban 1939–1940*, 1952; *Massigli, René, *La Turquie devant la guerre, I. Mission à Ankara, 1939-1940*, Paris, 1964; the dissertation by *Lipschits, Isaac, *La politique de la France au Levant 1939-1941*; the book by *Longrigg, S.H., *Syria and Lebanon under French mandate*, London, 1958.

185. See Longrigg, p. 238.

186. He was to die on 10 November 1938 and was replaced by Ismet.

187. *DDF*, 2, XII, p. 429, note, and no. 251, Ponsot, Ankara, 2 November 1938.

188. Ratification agreements regarding the treaty of 22 December 1936 were passed on 14 November with Syrian Minister Djemil Mardam Bey, accompanied with additional clauses (DDF, 2, XII, no. 302). But the foreign affairs commissions of the Chamber and the Senate rejected them which created tension in Syria. See DDF, 2, XII, no. 328, a very favorable note from the deputy directorate of Africa-Levant.

189. Already regarding the agreement of 4 July 1939, Lagarde, the deputy director of Africa-Levant, did not hesitate to write: "We have not hesitated to sacrifice our moral obligations toward our protégés"; DDF, 2, XII, no. 358, 22 November 1938.

190. *DDF*, 2, XII, no. 320, Ponsot, 16 November 1938.

191. MAE, T. 17–20, Massigli, 11 January; T. 61–67, 21 January; T. 88, 24 January 1939.

192. MAE, Note from Massigli, Paris, 6 February 1939.

193. MAE, T. 149–152, Beirut, 8 February 1939. On the rather polite conflict between Massigli and Puaux, see Massigli, op. cit. p. 54, 102–108. They were to meet in Tripoli on 8 March and Massigli managed to get Puaux to partially accept his views. Puaux, op. cit. pp. 53, 147, etc.

194. MAE, T. 88–90, Bonnet to Massigli, 18 February 1939.

195. MAE, T. 146–153, Massigli, 20 February 1939. See also T. 167–171, 23 February 1939.

196. MAE, T. 222 sq., Bonnet to Massigli; T. 300–302, Massigli to Bonnet, 23 March 1939. See Massigli, op. cit., p. 110–117.

197. Lipschits, op. cit., pp. 42–45. See MAE, T. 372–377, Puaux, Beirut, 30 March 1939.

198. MAE, T. 228–230 to Beirut; T. 279–281 to Ankara, Bonnet, 4 April 1932.

199. MAE, T. 337, Bonnet to Ankara, Rome, Londres, etc., 12 April 1939.

200. MAE, T. 354–357, Bonnet, 14 April 1939.

201. MAE, T. 406–407, Massigli, 14 April 1939.

202. MAE, D. 38, Massigli, 21 April 1939.

203. MAE, T. 418–421, Bonnet to Massigli, 27 April 1939.

204. MAE, T. 512–513, Massigli, 28 April 1939.

205. MAE, T. 535–539, Massigli, 2 May 1939.

206. MAE, T. 459–470, Bonnet to Massigli, 5 May 1939.
207. MAE, weekly liaison, 20 April 1939.
208. Weygand, *Mirages et réalités*, p. 484.
209. SHA, Report by General Weygand, May 1939. Weygand then traveled to Romania and also wrote a report.
210. Weygand, op. cit., p. 492.
211. MAE, T. 628–629, and 830–832, 12 May 1939.
212. MAE, T. 633–638, 12 May, and 633–638, 12 May 1939.
213. MAE, D. 129, 19 May 1939.
214. MAE, T. 1038, Massigli, 24 June 1939.
215. MAE, T. 1118–1120, Massigli, 17 July 1939.

Chapter XIV
FINAL PREPARATIONS

1. Sauvy (Alfred), "L'évolution économique," *Edouard Daladier*, op. cit., p. 88.
2. JODP, Chamber, 12 April 1938. Quoted by *Du Réau, Élisabeth, "L'aménagement de la loi instituant la semaine de quarante hueres," *Edouard Daladier*, op. cit., p. 133. In what follows I used that excellent article. Mrs. Du Réau is preparing an important dissertation under my supervision on "Daladier et la sécurité de la France."
3. Du Réau, É., ibid., p. 137.
4. See Bonnefous, op. cit., Vol. VI, p. 352. Regarding the "inaction" of Marchandeau, see the harsh letter written to him by Jacques Rueff, on 17 October; Rueff, op. cit., p. 157.
5. Rueff, J. op. cit., p. 159. See letter from Marchandeau to Édouard Bonnefous, in Bonnefous Vol. VI, pp. 420–423. The answer from Paul Reynaud, ibid., p. 424; Monzie, *Ci-devant*, pp. 50–52; *Carnets secrets de Jean Zay*, p. 29; *Sauvy, Alfred *De Paul Reynaud à Charles de Gaulle*, 1972, p. 70.
6. Sauvy, *De Paul Reynaud…*, op. cit.
7. Du Réau (E.), T. quoted., p. 141.
8. *Carnets secrets de Jean Zay*, pp. 31–33.
9. *Ci-devant*, pp. 57–59.
10. *La France a sauvé le monde*, I, pp. 506–539.
11. Sauvy, T. quoted op. cit., pp. 95–96.
12. Letter to Édouard Bonnefous, in Bonnefous, op. cit., Vol. VI, p. 424.
13. *De Paul Reynaud…*, op. cit., Vol. VI, p. 424.
14. Sauvy, T. quoted, p. 93. On the resistance of some ministers such as Pomaret, see Rueff, op. cit., pp. 159–161.
15. Sauvy, *De Paul Reynaud*, op. cit., p. 78.
16. The best book is *Frank, Robert. *Le prix du réarmement français (1935–1939)*. Paris (Sorbonne).

17. Ibid., pp. 13–14, and Rueff, op. cit., p. 161.

18. Rueff, op. cit., p. 161. It is interesting to note the similarity of the conclusions of Jacques Rueff and Alfred Sauvy regarding those events.

19. See his book *Jacomet, Robert, *L'armement de la France 1936–1939* (1945), and his testimony to the parliamentary commission.

20. *Ci-devant*, p. 103.

21. *DDF*, 2, XII, no. 292, annex, General Lelong, military attaché, London, 8 November 1938.

22. MAE, D. 22, Paul Morand, 8 June 1939.

23. Monzie, op. cit., pp. 104–105.

24. MAE, Summary of the meeting of 9 February at the Petroleum Department. See the assessment by François-Poncet on Italian supplies, MAE, D. 358, 20 June 1939. See the one by Colonel Delhomme on German, Italian, Hungarian requirements in wartime. SHA, no. 117/S, Colonel Delhomme, Bucharest, 6 June 1939.

25. Below, § III.

26. In SHAA, documents AFC (J), nos. 5 and 11, "Questions économiques" and "protection du commerce maritime des Alliés."

27. See The discussion of a report by Alfred Sauvy, committee of history of the Second World War, 15 December 1975. Regarding the insufficient supplies at the start of the war. See *Alphand, Hervé, *L'étonnement d'être. Journal 1939–1973*, Paris, 1977, p. 29 (11 December 1939). Alphand pointed out the difficulties to financing and the resistance coming from the ministry of agriculture.

28. MAE, D. 943, Bonnet to Guy La Chambre, 21 December 1938.

29. Numbers provided by *Truelle, General of Engineers, "La production aéronautique militaire française jusqu'en June 1940," *RHDGM*, January 1969, pp. 3–42.

30. Stehlin, op. cit., pp. 86–93, and DDF, 2, X, no. 537, transcript of the mission of General Vuillemin to Germany, 2 September 1938.

31. *DDF*, 2, XI, no. 377, Vuillemin to Guy La Chambre, 26 September 1938.

32. *RHDGM*, January 1969, pp. 111–116.

33. Truelle, T. quoted, p. 98.

34. *DDF*, 2, XII, no. 292, Colonel de Geffrier to Guy La Chambre, 9 November 1938. The numbers mentioned in the following paragraph are from note no 620 CM/2R of 26 August 1939. Guy La Chambre to Daladier.

35. *DDF*, 2, XII, no. 463, Note, November 1938.

36. *DDF*, 2, XII, no. 293, General Lelong, 8 November 1938.

37. *DDF*, 2, XII, no. 463, Note from the *Deuxième Bureau* of the Air Force, November 1938.

38. *DDF*, 2, XII, no. 360, 22 November 1938.

39. *DDF*, 2, XII, no. 390, Franco-British conversations of 24 November 1938.

40. Truelle, T. quoted, p. 79.

41. MAE, December 1938 (excerpt from SHAA).

42. Stehlin, op. cit., pp. 129–132.

43. See MAE, weekly liaison, 1 June 1939. It must be noted that in January a Jeinkel 111 of the Spanish Nationalists crashed into French territory. The specialists were interested in the information they could find. MAE, Weekly liaison, 25 January 1939. Planes that had fallen into Republican hands and arrived in France were also noted. The Air force was only interested in the Dornier 18. See MAE, Weekly liaison, 1 March 1939.

44. Bullitt who was very friendly with Guy La Chambre and hoped that he would become ambassador to the United States, received him on 20 February. The Air Minister told him the story and asked how Roosevelt would react. See Bullitt, op. cit. pp. 312–314.

45. *American Aid to France, 1938–1940*, New York, 1970.

46. Confirmed by very few documents in the ministry of foreign affairs and the conversations we had with Jean Monnet.

47. Transcript of the SHA, 5 December 1938. We found in the Daladier collection several letters from Jean Monnet (16 May, 19 May) addressed to Daladier and Reynaud and a report from the same dated 28 July. He was the one suggesting $300 million in cash. Roosevelt refused due to the embarrassment it might cause.

48. For example MAE, D. 281, a long dispatch from Saint-Quentin, 9 December 1938. Baruch asked for funding for 4,000 planes on 14 October. On Navy Day 27 October there was the announcement of a increase in the navy, 19 November building of 40 ships, etc., campaigns by Walter Lippman and Dorothy Thomson in favor of rearmament and "international responsibilities." Ambassador de Saint-Quentin felt the Gallup polls to be very important. See MAE, D. 23, 8 February 1939; D. 80, 30 march 1939; T. 617–618, 10 April 1939. See MAE, T. 339–340. Saint-Quentin, 7 March 1939 on the voting of a program for 6,000 planes by the Senate by 77 in favor to 8 opposed.

49. See MAE, T. 349–352, Saint-Quentin, 8 March 1939; T. 612–615, Bonnet to Saint-Quentin, 8 May 1939.

50. Friedson, P. and Lecuir, Jean, *La France et la Grande-Bretagne face aux problèmes aériens (1935–May 1940)*, op. cit., p. 31.

51. 31 January 1933–7 February 1934; then 6 June 1936–December 1937, or 29 months.

52. December 1937 to the war: 17 months.

53. Mysyrowicz, op. cit., pp. 190–191. Figures quoted in *JODP*, Chamber, 3 February 1930, p. 372. See Boussard, op. cit., p. 39. Added to this were 26 prototypes of civilian transport planes, 130 seaplanes, 371 engines.

54. Friedenson and Lecuir, op. cit., p. 42.

55. See Friedenson and Lecuir, op. cit., p. 44.

56. Excellently described in *Williamson, S., *The Diplomacy of Grand Strategy*, 1969.

57. MAE, D. 36, Noël, 11 January 1939.
58. MAE, T. 553, Noël, 7 April 1939.
59. Through a note signed by Léger, MAE, D. 1282 to Daladier, EMA, 10 April 1939.
60. SHA, Minister's Cabinet. Aid to Poland 18 April 1939.
61. SHAA, transcript of the meeting of 16 May 1939.
62. Le Goyet, *Gamelin*, op. cit., p. 188. SHA, D. 73/S, General Musse, Warsaw, 11 May 1939.
63. Noël, op. cit., p. 370; Monzie, op. cit., p. 108.
64. Noël, op. cit., p. 364.
65. SHA, Protocols of conversations 15–17 May 1939. See also Lukasziewicz, op. cit., pp. 210–223.
66. MAE, D. 545, DN, Daladier to Bonnet, 19 May 1939.
67. SHA, Letter from Gamelin, 20 may 1939. "Seen by the Minister." Regarding the political negotiations Bonnet began with Polish Ambassador Lukasziewicz without the knowledge of Léon Noël (Noël, op. cit. p. 330), these dragged on for weeks. See MAE, Weekly liaison, 31 May 1939, and Lukasziewicz, op. cit. pp. 223–233.
68. There were on the other hand Anglo-Polish conversations in Warsaw (22–30 may) and British General Ironside went to Warsaw from 17 to 21 July (See SHA, D. 112/S, General Musse, 19 July 1939 and 138/S, 26 July 1939).
69. Noël, op. cit., p. 319.
70. SHA, D. 147/S, Musse, 10 August 1939.
71. SHA, DN, S. 1318, Gamelin to Daladier, 23 June 1939. See Rueff, op. cit., pp. 161–162 regarding Franco-British financial negotiations on Poland in July 1939. The Poles demanded gold and the agreement failed.
72. Many documents in MAE, D. 2567, Bonnet to Daladier, 14 June; D. 2585, Bonnet to Daladier, 15 June; D. 2631 Bonnet to Daladier, 17 June 1939. SHA, Minister's Cabinet 19 June; SHA, D. 1318 DNS, Gamelin to Daladier, 23 June.
73. SHA, D. 147/S, Musse, 10 August 1939.
74. Le Goyet, op. cit., p. 1781.
75. See Noël, op. cit., p. 346; Monzie, op. cit., 4 July 1939, p. 125.
76. We have used a questionnaire with answers signed by Daladier coming from the general secretariat of National Defense. SHA, 443/DN 2, 7 March 1939 and an "analysis" by Gamelin dated 8 March: SHA "Analyse," 8 March 1939.
77. The Japanese not only occupied the Chinese island of Hainan, over which France had some vague demands but also the Spratly islands and demanded in a sense the Paracels islands.
78. Friedenson and Lecuir, op. cit., pp. 124–128.
79. SHA, AFC (J) 29.
80. SHA, transcript …, 9 April 1939.

81. SHA, study of the strategic problem dated 10 April 1939, 15 April 1939.
82. Friedenson and Lecuir, op. cit., pp.132–141. In the pages that follow these authors examine all the practical decisions: British bomb supplies near Reims, placing of airfields for use by the British, etc.
83. Ironside does not mention it in his memoirs.
84. SHA, Information from the president, 8 May 1939. See also D. 110, Lelong to Gamelin, 15 May 1939.
85. SHAA, D. 792/S, Colonel Devèze, Air commander in Indochina, Saigon, 1 July 1939.
86. A complete study exists: *Reussner, A., *Les conversations franco-britanniques d'État-Major (1935–1939), Service historique de la marine*, 1969.
87. SHM, Conference on 8 August on board the *Enchantress.*
88. Op. cit., p. 245.
89. See the interesting book by *Kreis, Georg, *Auf den Spuren von La Charité. Die schweizerische Armeeführung im Spannungsfeld des deutsch-französischen Gegensatzes 1936–1941*, 1976.
90. SHA, 22 April 1939.
91. The only official link the Belgians agreed to was Colonel Laurent, military attaché in Brussels. See Le Goyet, op. cit., pp. 223–224.
92. SHA, Transcript of the meeting of the chiefs of the general staff, 16 June 1939.
93. SHA, Transcript, Franco-British conversations of 13 July 1939. It should be noted that the British were then ready to accept Gamelin as commander in chief. Hore-Belisha told Ironside 7 July (*Ironside Diaries*, pp. 76–77).
94. SHA, Letter from Neville Chamberlain to Daladier, 26 July 1939.
95. SHA, Opinion of the EMA regarding Chamberlain's proposal, 28 July 1939.
96. SHA, Transcript of the meeting of the chiefs of the general staff, 1 August 1939.
97. SHA, Letter from Daladier to Chamberlain, 3 August 1939.

Chapter XV
TOWARD THE INESCAPABLE CONCLUSION

1. Molotov will vaguely deny it in the course of a speech on 31 August. Payart, was reporting this did not believe it.. On the other hand the Polish ambassador felt confident. See MAE, T. 992–995, Payart, 1 September 1939.
2. Anatole de Monzie entitled the chapter of *Ci-devant* regarding the period between 1 August and 17 October 1939: "Spéculation sur le bluff" [Speculation on the Bluff], pp. 133–177.
3. *DDI*, 8, XIII. The book was prepared by the great historian Mario Toscano.
4. MAE, T. 3317–3320, François-Poncet, 18 August 1939. Ciano was unable to see him immediately.

5. DDI, 8, XIII, no. 136. See also the previously quoted telegram from François-Poncet and T. 3374–3377, 22 August. We should point out that it would be same for Spain that gave assurances of its neutrality. See MAE, T. 376–378, Léger to Pétain, 2 September 1939.

6. DEI, 8, XIII, no. 69.

7. Michel, Henri, T. quoted.

8. Noël, *L'agression allemande contre la Pologne,* op. cit., p. 385–393.

9. MAE, T. 1223–1227 and 1230, Noël, 22 August 1939 (copy of the Daladier Papers) and Noël, op. cit., pp. 404–405.

10. Noël, op. cit., p. 410.

11. MAE, T. 1255, Noël, 24 August 1939, 6 p.m.

12. MAE, T. 1308, Noël, 28 August 1939, 1:50 a.m.

13. SHA, Rapport 163, General Musse to Daladier, 24 August 1939.

14. MAE, T. 1258–1259, Noël, 24 August 1939, 6 p.m.

15. SHA, T. 622/S, Palasse to Daladier, 23 August 1939.

16. *Carnets secrets de Jean Zay,* op. cit., p. 70, 27 August 1939.

17. *Carnets secrets de Jean Zay,* pp. 60–64, Mardi 22 August.

18. Stehlin, op. cit., p. 165.

19. Monzie, op. cit., p. 139.

20. On this point, Gamelin and Bonnet disagree. A few years later the disagreement will turn into a violent dispute about the past. Bonnet, *Défense de la paix,* II, op. cit., pp. 297–309; Gamelin, *Servir,* III, op. cit., p. 301.

21. *Carnets secrets de Jean Zay,* op. cit., p. 66-67; Monzie, op. cit., pp. 139–140.

22. *Carnets secrets de Jean Zay,* op. cit., p. 69; Monzie, op. cit., p. 141.

23. Coulondre, op. cit., p. 287.

24. Coulondre, op. cit., p. 288–289. See his phone telegram in LJ no 242, 25 August 1939.

25. MAE, T. 1288–1289, 1295, 1301, Noël, 26 August 1939.

26. MAE, T. 2767–2769, Corbin, 27 August 1939.

27. MAE, T. 2398–2399, Coulondre, 27 August 1939.

28. LJ no. 253.

29. Coulondre, op. cit., p. 290–291. His telegram on the issue LJ, no 261, 27 August 1939.

30. LJ, no. 267, 27 August 1939.

31. *Carnets secrets de Jean Zay,* op. cit., p. 70, 27 August. The offers of mediation coming either from the Pope, and the King of the Belgians with the "Oslo group" may be considered very secondary. The unofficial round trips by the Swede Birger Dahlerus from Berlin to London appear of doubtful importance and in any case do not involve France.

32. This was indeed Coulondre's view. See MAE, T. 2454, "Extrême Urgence," by telephone at 1:40 a.m. on 30 August.

33. Account by Coulondre in MAE, T. 2492, Coulondre, 1 September 1939.

34. Stehlin, op. cit., p. 176.

35. Coulondre, op. cit., p. 298.
36. Ciano, *Journal*, op. cit., pp. 141–143; MAE, T. 3508, François-Poncet, 31 August. 1939, 1:10 p.m. received at 2 p.m.
37. MAE, T. 3510, François-Poncet, 1 August. 1:05 p.m.
38. Series 8, XIII.
39. *DDI*, 8, XIII, no. 405 and most of all 425, Guariglia to Ciano, 29 August. 1939.
40. MAE, T. 739–742, Bonnet to François-Poncet, 29 August. 1939.
41. *DDI*, 8, XIII, no. 320, Guariglia to Ciano, 26 August. 1939.
42. Monzie, op. cit., pp. 145–146.
43. *Ci-devant*, p. 146.
44. *Carnets secrets...*, pp. 80–81. At that point there was said to be a sharp incident between Bonnet and Daladier. According to Monzie, the incident was not that sharp and was because of two different messages coming in from Corbin one after the other.
45. Monzie, op. cit., p. 147.
46. Monzie, op. cit., pp. 148–149.
47. *LJ*, nos. 322 and 323.
48. An additional protocol that was intended to reinforce the military agreement of May (see above Chapter XIV), was signed on 4 September 1939. See on this subject the study by *Batowski, Henryk, "Les traits d'alliance polono-britannique et polono-français de 1939," La Pologne et les affaires occidentals, 1973, no. 1, pp. 89–108.
49. Taylor (A.J.P.), *The Origins of the Second World War*, op. cit., and *Taylor, A.J.P., *English History, 1914–1945*, pp. 450–452.
50. *Parker, R.A.C., *"The British Government and the Coming of War with Germany, 1939,"* in Foot, M.R.D., ed., *Historical Essays in Honour and Memory of J.R.. Western*, London, 1973, p. 14.
51. See *Alphand, Hervé, *L'étonnement d'être. Journal, 1939–1973*, Paris, 1977, p. 65. We know that Daladier will get rid of Bonnet on 13 September 1939, becoming Foreign Minister himself.
52. Monzie, op. cit., pp. 148–150; Guariglia, Raffaele, *La diplomatie difficile. Mémoires. 1922–1946*, op. cit., pp. 123–125.
53. See *DDI*, 8, XIII, no. 534, Guariglia to Ciano, 1 September, 11:20 a.m. A series of other telegrams follows naturally. The account of those events "that quickly became retrospective" in a dispatch of 2 September no. 608 Guariglia to Ciano.
54. See *DDI*, 8, XIII, no. 537; *LJ*, no. 328.
55. MAE, T. 3529, François-Poncet, 1 September, 2:30 p.m., received at 4:30 p.m. (but by telephone before 3 p.m.) and *LJ*, no. 332.
56. Ciano, *Journal*, op. cit., p. 144–146.
57. *DDI*, 8, XIII, no. 548, Percy Lorraine to Ciano, 1 September 1939. The chronology used places this meeting at noon. The *DDI* mention the evening as the time the telegram was handed over (p. 338, note).

58. MAE, Hoppenot Papers, chronology undoubtedly kept by the Minister's Cabinet. Useful to find out about telephone calls that normally precede telegrams.

59. MAE, Hoppenot Papers, Chronologie. See MAE, T. 3557, François-Poncet, 2 September 1939, 7:25 p.m., received at 10 p.m.; see *LJ*, no. 346.

60. See *LJ*, no. 338, Bonnet to Noël; no. 343, Noël, 9:31 p.m. (received on the 2nd at 3 p.m.).

61. Monzie, op. cit., p. 153.

62. MAE, Hoppenot Papers, Chronology.

63. *DDI*, 8, XIII, no. 543, Guariglia to Ciano, 1 September 1939, 3:10 p.m.

64. MAE, Hoppenot Papers, Chronology.

65. MAE, Hoppenot Papers, Chronology.

66. *LJ*, no. 337.

67. Coulondre, op. cit., p. 308.

68. MAE, T. 2498, Coulondre, 1 September 1938, telephoned in at 11 p.m.; see *LJ*, no. 344.

69. MAE, T. 1945–1946, Bonnet to Corbin, 1 September 1939, 6:15 p.m.

70. We have a long 19-page report of this day written a few days later (on 7 September) by Ambassador Corbin. See also on the British side *Harvey, John, ed., *Diplomatic Diaries of Oliver Harvey 1937–1940*, pp. 312–316.

71. *DDI*, 8, XIII, no. 571.

72. MAE, Hoppenot Papers, Letter from Lukasziewicz to Daladier, 2 September 1939. See in MAE, Corbin report, the visit to Halifax by the Polish ambassador to London. Halifax, agreed on the emergency. See Lukasziewicz, op. cit., pp. 273–278.

73. *DBFP*, 3, VII, no. 696.

74. *DBFP*, 3, VII, no. 699. See Parker, T. quoted, p. 4.

75. *DDI*, 8, XIII, no. 581, Attolico to Ciano, 2 September 1939.

76. MAE, Corbin report, p. 5.

77. Ciano, *Diary*, I, op. cit., p. 145. Mostly MAE, T. 3565–3566, François-Poncet, 2 September, 11:10 p.m. Received 3 September, 3:10 a.m. See *LJ*, no. 363.

78. Ciano, *Diary*, I, op. cit., p. 146.

79. A study in *Rossi-Landi, Guy, *La drôle de guerre*, 1971, pp. 15–23. see *JODP*, Chamber, p. 1949–1953; Sénat, p. 640.

80. Although it was greed that the government's communication would be read first. See *Jeanneney, Jules, *Journal politique*, op. cit., 1 September 1939, p. 6.

81. Op. cit., p. 17.

82. *Laval parle...* p. 275. Laval got word to Ciano through the Italian consulate agent in Clermont-Ferrand whom he met on 14 July that, as in January 1935, he favored a Franco-Italian rapprochement. See DDI, 8, XIII, no. 78, Guariglia, 17 August 1939. Laval handed the complete text of what he meant to Guariglia on 14 September. See Guariglia, op. cit. p.127.

83. *Carnets secrets...*, p. 86. On 1 September, Gamelin wrote a letter to Daladier regretting that he could not invade Belgium. "We could have spoken roughly to a man like King Albert." (Archives Riom Trial.)

84. Ibid., p. 86.

85. *Ci-devant*, p. 158. Bonnet received a phone call from Cadogan at about 5 p.m. He told him that France "strongly" on a 48-hours delay before beginning hostilities. He rejected the idea of an ultimatum expiring at midnight.

86. MAE, Corbin Report, p. 2.

87. Ibid., p. 5. According to MAE, Hoppenot papers, Chronology, Sir Eric Phipps telephoned Bressy, Bonnet's cabinet director at 6:40 p.m. to communicate the text of the declaration to Daladier and Bonnet. On the many telephone calls between London and Paris on the afternoon of 2 September, see DBFP, 3, VII, no. 718 (Cadogan-Bonnet, 5 p.m.), no. 727 (Halifax-Phipps, 6 p.m.), no. 740 (Chamberlain-Daladier, 9:50 p.m.), no. 741 (Halifax-Bonnet).

88. This is what Gamelin wrote to Daladier. Daladier telephoned Bonnet on the issue at 7:45 p.m. See MAE, Hoppenot Papers, Chronology.

89. Parker, T. quoted, p. 13. See DBFP, 3, VII, nos. 740 and 741.

90. Ibid., pp. 8–9.

91. MAE, Corbin report, pp. 9–10.

92. *LJ*, no. 364, Bonnet to Coulondre, midnight; no. 365, Bonnet to Coulondre, 3 September, 10:30 a.m.

93. Coulondre, op. cit., p. 314. See *LJ*, no. 367, 3 September 1939.

INDEX

Abetz, Otto 160–62, 293, 296, *448*
Abrial, Jean 136, *442, 445*
Adam, Magda 431
Adamthwaite, Anthony iv, xi, xxiv–xxv, 304, *418, 473–76, 479, 482, 486*
Ageron, Charles-Robert 159, 184–87, 291, 296, *448, 452, 470*
Albert I, King of Belgium xxxvi, 67, *497*
Albord *457*
Alexander, King of Yugoslavia 69, 71, 75
Alexander, Martin S. *418*
Allain, Jean-Claude xxvi, *451*
Allard, Paul 215, *420, 440*
Allemane, Jean 294
Aloisi, Baron Pompeo 88, 97, 107, 109
Alphand, Charles 25, 44–7, 69, 102, 311, 313, *428–29, 438, 450, 475*
Alphand, Hervé 309, 311, 406, *490, 495*
Amery, Leo 156, 222
Andrew, C. M. *452*
Antignac, Anne-Maries *460*
Antonescu, Victor 261–62
Aosta, Duke of 227
Aragon 395, *470*
Arbonneau, Charles de 230
Archambalt, Annick *459*
Archambaud, Léon 158
Archimbaud, Léon 100, 125
Arciszewsky, Miroslav 400
Aris, Jean 242, *459–60*
Armengaud, André 200, *446–47*
Arnal, Pierre 38, 73, *421, 427, 433, 459, 462, 464*
Arnim, Achim von 161
Arnold, Henry H. 382
Aron, Raymond 154
Arrighi, Lieutenant 298
Artaud, Denise *423*
Astakhov, Georgi 359
Aster, Sydney *486*
Astier de la Vigerie, Henri 299
Astor, Lady Michael 138
Astor, Lord Michael 138, 155
Attolico, Bernardo 237, 410, *476, 496*

Aubert, D. *430*
Aubert, Louis 306, *474*
Auburtin, a doctor 211
Aumale, Jacques de 301, *473*
Auffray, Bernard *420, 456*
Auriol, Vincent xxxiii, 23, 128, 166, 241, 243, 245, 247–50, 258, *459–61*
Avenol, Joseph 86, *435*
Aymé-Martin, Albert 178, *451*
Azaña, Manuel 340
Azria, Sylvain *445*

Badoglio, Pietro 95–7, 99, 228, *438*
Baeyens, Jacques 215
Bailby, Léon 27, 115, 121, 129, 293
Baillet-Latour, Count de 239
Baillou, Jean *456*
Bainville, Jacques 83, 114
Baldwin, Stanley 104, 106, 110, 130, 155, 240, 248, 254
Bankwitz, Philip C. *421*
Baraduc, Pierre 341
Barbanson, Gaston 33
Bardoux, Jacques 156, 256, 298, *447, 472, 478*
Bargeton, Paul xxxii, 71, 178, 217–18, 239
Bariéty, Jacques xxvi, xxxii, 12, 33, 158, *419, 421–22, 426, 448*
Barra, Francisco de la 339
Barrère, Camille 221
Barrès, Philippe 45, 83
Bartali, Gino 140
Barthou, Louis vii, xx, xxxi, xxxiv, 54–64, 66–81, 83–9, 93, 100–03, 111, 147, 160, 170, 262, *430–35, 445*
Basdevant, Jules 217, 347, *481*
Bastid, Paul 241, 245, *460*
Bathelemy-Madaule, Madeleine *472*
Batowski, Henryk xxvi, *495*
Baudelaire, Charles 56
Baudoin, Paul 225, 250, 307, 314, 326–27, 343–44, 399, *448, 478, 482–83*
Baulig, Henri 150

Baumgartner, Wilfrid 47, 170, 226, 247–48, *459–61*
Baumont, Maurice xxv, 152
Bayet, Albert *448*
Beau de Loménie, Emmanuel 178, *451*
Beaufre, André 191, 198, 208–09, 231, 357, 361–63, *452, 454, 486–87*
Beaussang, Guy xxvi
Beck, Josef xxxii, 7, 42, 65–6, 68, 70–1, 131, 135, 148, 219, 224, 261–62, 305, 325, 330, 362–63, 384–85, 397, 400–01, 408, *432, 464, 485*
Becker, Jean-Jacques *445*
Becq de Fouquières, Pierre 217
Bedarida, François *473, 478*
Bedouce, Albert 245
Beigbeder, Colonel *481*
Belin, René 188, 294, 399
Bellanger, Catherine *471*
Bellec, Anne-Marie *472*
Belugou, Sylvie *454*
Benaërts, Pierre 152
Benedetti, Vincent 323
Benedict, Ruth xxxiv
Beneš, Eduard 40–42, 66, 68, 71, 135, 219, 224, 262, 272–75, 277–80, 282–87, 290–91, 293, 295, 300, 305, *465–66*
Bennett, Edward *422, 424*
Benoist-Méchin, Jacques 161
Benoit, Pierre 151
Bénouville, Guillain de 162
Béra, Armand *464*
Beran, Rudolf 334
Bérard, Armand xxvi, xxxii, 216, 219, 223, 236, *419, 445, 456*
Bérard, Léon 295, 339–41, *425, 441, 456, 458, 463, 477, 481–82*
Béraud, Henri 151
Bérenger, Henry 20, 39, 149, 399, 407
Bergery, Gaston 17, 185, 188, 288, 293, 411, *471*
Bergson, Henri xli
Bernanos, Georges 257
Bernard, Augustin 150
Bernard, Claude 55
Bernus, Pierre 27, 83
Bertaut, Jules *430*